Global Jurisprudential Apartheid in the Twenty-First Century

Global Jurisprudential Apartheid in the Twenty-First Century

Universalism and Particularism in International Law

Edited by
Artwell Nhemachena,
Howard Tafara Chitimira, and
Tapiwa Victor Warikandwa

LEXINGTON BOOKS/FORTRESS ACADEMIC
Lanham • Boulder • New York • London

Published by Lexington Books/Fortress Academic
Lexington Books is an imprint of The Rowman & Littlefield Publishing Group, Inc.
4501 Forbes Boulevard, Suite 200, Lanham, Maryland 20706
www.rowman.com

86-90 Paul Street, London EC2A 4NE

British Library Cataloguing in Publication Information Available

Library of Congress Cataloging-in-Publication Data

Names: Nhemachena, Artwell, editor, author. | Chitimira, Howard, editor, author. | Warikandwa, Tapiwa V. (Tapiwa Victor), editor, author.
Title: Global jurisprudential apartheid in the twenty-first century :universalism and particularism in international law / edited by Artwell Nhemachena, Howard Tafara Chitimira, and Tapiwa Victor Warikandwa.
Description: Lanham : Lexington Books, 2021. | Includes index. | Summary: "This book argues that the world is witnessing the formation of a global jurisprudential apartheid despite the promotion of democracy, equality, human rights, and humanitarianism. The contributors examine global organisations to analyse the ways in which globalization upholds and contributes to global inequities"— Provided by publisher.
Identifiers: LCCN 2021038942 (print) | LCCN 2021038943 (ebook) | ISBN 9781793643360 (hardcover) | ISBN 9781793643377 (epub)
Subjects: LCSH: Equality before the law—Africa, Sub-Saharan. | Law and globalization—Africa, Sub-Saharan.
Classification: LCC KQC575 .G56 2021 (print) | LCC KQC575 (ebook) | DDC 342.60873—dc23
LC record available at https://lccn.loc.gov/2021038942
LC ebook record available at https://lccn.loc.gov/2021038943

∞™ The paper used in this publication meets the minimum requirements of American National Standard for Information Sciences—Permanence of Paper for Printed Library Materials, ANSI/NISO Z39.48-1992.

This book is dedicated to victims of the unrelenting global apartheid regime which has created a false impression of positive political, legal and economic successes in developing countries yet in reality has caused severe poverty. The post-colonial global apartheid regime presents a legal, political and economic order that supposedly promotes the rule of law, democracy and human rights, on the face of it, but in essence is a hoax or an elaborate fraud which is the root cause for poverty and death among millions in today's world. This global apartheid regime has been generated by a ruling class whose sole interest is to preserve economic and social privileges through the use of brazen expropriation, plunder and brute force. The machinations of these global oligarchs, which now include the use of the corona virus "global pandemic" (COVID-19) to hijack fundamental structural changes aimed at improving the welfare of the impoverished majority in developing countries in order to guarantee just societies, characterises the contemporary global apartheid regime's primary agenda. Driven by the false consciousness or a "secular opiate of the masses" called human rights, which is selectively applied when it best suits these global oligarchs' interests, global apartheid has sent many unsuspecting and innocent people to absolute ruin and chronic impoverishment. Employing a façade of the law and legality itself, global jurisprudential apartheid has thus emerged as an instrument of coercive oppression that has an image of legality and legalism which is nothing more than an inept yet convenient mask for a quest for brute and naked power. Characterised by the existence of laws without a relationship to justice, global jurisprudential apartheid must be frowned upon for what it truly is, a contemporary specimen of colossal evil driven by wicked and depraved human beings. We trust that victims of this regime will find solace in knowing that their cries are not in vain. Justice shall prevail one day!

Contents

Preface

We are increasingly witnessing the crystallisation of what we have called global jurisprudential apartheid, paradoxically in a world that evangelises democracy, equality, rule of law, human rights and humanitarianism. From the international criminal courts to the World Trade Organisation, from the United Nations Security Council to the International Monetary Fund and World Bank, we are witnessing variants of apartheid congealing at a global level. In the United Nations Security Council, we witness the dominance of the United States of America which without any electoral mandates governs the world, often unilaterally declaring war on sovereign states of the Global South. This book addresses pertinent questions regarding variants of global apartheid in the twenty-first century. For instance, the book unpacks the challenges of global jurisprudential apartheid, especially, the ongoing inequalities in respect of applications of the rule of law, human rights and humanitarianism between the countries in the Global North and those in the Global South. In this regard, the biased operation and application of the law, policies and regulatory principles in the international criminal courts, the World Trade Organisation, the United Nations Security Council, the International Monetary Fund and World Bank is a case in point. The book provides that globalisation is a variant of the apartheid-era particularism and not universalism. Put differently, globalisation is less about universalism and inclusivity than it is about global apartheid. The book argues that globalisation is merely a proselytisation of a particular form of particularism that is consistent with the development and sustenance of global apartheid, cloaked in humanitarianism.

Chapter 1

Global Jurisprudential Apartheid in the Emergent One World Government

A Decolonial Introduction

Artwell Nhemachena, Tapiwa Victor Warikandwa, and Howard Tafara Chitimira

INTRODUCTION: JURISPRUDENCE IN GLOBAL CONTEXT

One problem with the old legal maxim that law is the command of the [African] sovereign (Eleftheriadis 2010) is that it did not take into cognisance the problematics of colonial/apartheid aliens who usurped the sovereignty of others in order not necessarily to further the ends of the law but to plunder and rob the colonial victims. Put differently, in colonial and apartheid Africa, the law was not necessarily the command of the sovereign but rather it was the command of the colonial/apartheid alien criminocrats bent on dispossessing, robbing and exploiting Africans. In the same vein, with international law still in the hands of the United Nations Security Council and other "international" institutions, which are in essence imperial institutions, it is erroneous to consider the law as the command of the sovereign. In a global context where African sovereignty has been usurped by Western institutions and states, law has become the command of the emperor, who unfortunately is criminocratic in the sense of dispossessing and exploiting the subjects (see Nhemachena & Warikandwa 2019). Because international institutions such as the United Nations and the International Criminal Court (ICC) are funded by transnational corporations which also thrive on dispossessing and exploiting Africans (Nhemachena & Warikandwa 2017), this book argues that even at the level of international law, the law is not necessarily the command of the [African] sovereign but it is the command of transnational criminocrats lording over Africa. In other words, in global apartheid, the law is effectively the command of neo-imperial criminocrats and not the command of the [African] sovereigns. We argue in this book that this is the reason why international law cannot abate the dispossession, exploitation, theft and neo-enslavement perpetrated on Africans for centuries since the era of enslavement and colonisation. Similarly, if the law is effectively the command of neo-imperial criminocrats, the net effect is that African victims of enslavement and colonisation will find it difficult to effectively get restitution and reparations for the crimes of enslavement and colonisation. If the law, including at the level of international law, was really the command of [African] sovereigns, then Africans would have been granted restitution and reparations for enslavement and colonisation a long time ago. In fact, if the law was really the command of [African] sovereigns, Africans would not have been enslaved and colonised. The colonial usurpation of the law in Africa entailed the command of colonial criminocrats and not necessarily the command of the [African] sovereigns. In short, the decolonial era makes it imperative to interrogate the fit of Western jurisprudence in Africa where Africans' own jurisprudence has been consistently subjected to epistemicide.

In the light of the above, it is necessary to note one of the greatest ironies of the post–World War II era. The United Nations and other "international" institutions and organisations "imposed sanctions" on apartheid/colonial governments, in South Africa (Klotz 1995; Aftab 1991), yet the very same "international" institutions, including the United Nations, operate on the principles of global apartheid designed to keep Africans at the bottom of the world system. Ironically choosing to impose sanctions against apartheid states in Africa, the United Nations has surprisingly decided not to impose sanctions on imperial states that are refusing to return what they stole from Africans. For this reason, Africans have not had restitution and reparations for enslavement and colonisation – and so there is retention of apartheid and colonial land ownership patterns in Africa. The million-dollar question is why the United Nations has not imposed sanctions on neo-imperial states that are refusing to ensure restitution and reparations to Africans? The question is also why the United Nations is not imposing sanctions on transnational corporations and other Western institutions that continue to dispossess and exploit Africans even in the ongoing twenty-first-century scramble for Africa? Instead of imposing sanctions on the imperial states and transnational corporations that continue to dispossess and exploit Africans (Warikandwa et al. 2017), the United Nations has recently entered into a Global Compact with the transnational corporations such that their power over United Nations policy-making has increased (Nhemachena & Warikandwa 2017).

As if restitution is not a human right, the United Nations only harps about every other kind of human right except restitution to African victims of enslavement and colonisation. Similarly, as if reparations are not a human right, the United Nations only harps about every other kind of human right except reparations to African victims of enslavement and colonisation. Of course, restitution and reparations to Africans would harm the transnational corporations that fund the United Nations Organisation but the million-dollar question is whether it does not constitute high-level corruption, at the United Nations level, to turn a blind eye to African rights for restitution and reparations simply because restitution and reparations would harm the criminocratic transnational corporations that continue dispossessing and exploiting Africans even in the twenty-first century? Instead of also exposing the apartheid, corruption, dictatorship and oppression taking place at the United Nations level and via transnational corporations, the media, Non-governmental Organisations (NGOs) and civil society organisations (CSOs) simply focus on exposing the supposed corruption, oppression, human rights abuses, bad governance and dictatorship by African states which are then depicted as candidates par excellence for indictment at the ICC (Nhemachena & Bankie 2017). Of course, it is necessary to note that the global media, the NGOs and CSOs are also funded by the same transnational corporations that are dispossessing and exploiting Africans – and some of the CSOs and NGOs are also affiliated to the United Nations Organisation. In other words, the United Nations and other international institutions and states that purport to have helped dismantle apartheid are themselves ironically constitutive of global apartheid. Put differently, although some scholars and thinkers write in terms of post-apartheid eras in Africa, in reality the world system did not change its global apartheid order which still impinges on Africans. With the Western countries still dominant in the United Nations Security Council that excludes African states, it is erroneous to write and think in terms of post-apartheid era in the world. With Western states and the United Nations Security Council monopolising the powers to impose sanctions in the world, it is also erroneous to write or think in terms of post-apartheid eras in the world. Sanctions are largely imposed by Western countries on states of the Global South. In other words, much as the apartheid state, in South Africa, for example, monopolised the power to impose sanctions on African chiefs [with responsibility to govern homelands], in the contemporary era, the United Nations Security Council is playing the role of the apartheid state exercising power over African presidents who have been reduced to the level of chiefs running de facto African homelands.

GLOBAL JURISPRUDENTIAL APARTHEID IN CONTEXT

In the same way African chiefs were forced to function as homeland tax collectors and recruiters of forced cheap labour on behalf of the apartheid state and colonial corporations, in the contemporary era, African presidents have been effectively reduced to tax collectors on behalf of owners of the neo-colonial economy desirous of appropriate infrastructures. Similarly, African presidents have been reduced to ensure that there is availability of cheap labour in African states that attract transnational corporation investors by availing cheap labour on the continent of Africa. The point here is that African states have effectively become homelands in the context of resilient global apartheid (Butler et al. 1978; Mukonoweshuro 1991; Blausten 1976). To ensure that post-independence African states became mere tax collectors and ensurers of cheap labour, the World Bank and the International Monetary Fund designed economic structural adjustment programmes wherein they stipulated conditionalities and austerity measures for Africans. As part of the conditionalities of the economic structural adjustment programmes, post-independence African states were ordered to stop interfering with the economy and to cede the economic matters to private companies – in effect, to transnational corporations (see Mlambo 1997). In this sense, African state leaders, like homeland chiefs, were and are supposed to focus on homeland politics while the economic matters were managed by the [global] apartheid government.

Post-independence African states were forced to privatise parastatals so that the state would not be involved directly in the economy; nevertheless, the state was supposed to continue to collect taxes and to ensure that the transnational corporations' economies were supplied with necessary infrastructure and cheap labour. In other words, the African states were supposed to play the role of maids in relation to owners of the neo-colonial economies on the continent – providing services but not owning the economy, including material resources. Much like the work of chiefs in the apartheid homelands, African presidents are expected not to prioritise their own citizens/kith and kin but they are expected to prioritise the transnational institutions and corporations even where these are callously dispossessing and exploiting African citizens. Thus, much like in the case of African chiefs in the apartheid homelands, African presidents have been globally constituted as shock absorbers for global capital and transnational criminocrats. Although African resources are not necessarily owned and controlled by African presidents, who have instead become vassals of global criminocrats, African frustrations about poverty, absence of service delivery, lack of jobs, and pain of taxation and so on are vented on African presidents instead of on transnational corporations (Nhemachena & Warikandwa 2019). The point here is that much as African homeland chiefs were hated for collecting taxes and ensuring the supply of African cheap labour for the colonial economy, African presidents have been constituted as underwriters of global capital and criminocrats running the contemporary global apartheid. Global criminocrats in global apartheid benefit in two ways from this arrangement. First, because they are not the ones directly collecting taxes and managing the cheap labour reserve, they do not get blamed for African suffering. Second, because it is African presidents that are more visible on the African terrain marked by dispossession and suffering born of global apartheid, the global criminocrats benefit when African citizens begin to hate and fight their own presidents and states – much as when Africans fought their own apartheid homeland chiefs that were more visible in the collection of taxes and ensuring of cheap labour supplies for the apartheid state.

Implied in the foregoing is the fact that much as the apartheid era creation of homelands was meant to create the illusion of African independence, the contemporary global apartheid has constituted African states as homelands with illusive independence. Much as Africans had attrition with their apartheid homeland chiefs who were constituted as vassals and conduits for the apartheid state, contemporary global apartheid has set up African presidents for attrition with their citizens who continue to suffer dispossession and exploitation arising from global apartheid. Of course, African presidents that please the elites of global apartheid are given kudos and support at that level. However, in so far as they facilitate the dispossession, oppression and exploitation on Africans, the presidents risk attrition with their subjects. Much as during the earlier apartheid era, global criminocrats want freedom to dispossess and exploit without responsibility and accountability. Thus, in the contemporary era, responsibility and accountability have been shifted to African states and presidents even though the crimes of dispossession and exploitation are actually being committed by transnational corporations and global criminocrats operating on the African continent. Global criminocrats' quest for freedom to dispossess and exploit without responsibility is also evident in their refusal to be responsible and accountable for the crimes of enslavement and colonisation: the refusal to ensure restitution and reparations to African victims of enslavement and colonisation is symptomatic of the global criminocrats' quest for freedom to dispossess and exploit without responsibility and accountability (Nhemachena & Warikandwa 2019). In other words, the problem as viewed from an Afrocentric point of view is that the law is not necessarily the command of the African sovereigns but it is the command of the global criminocrats that use some African leaders as their vassals and conduits. In such a scenario, the law becomes the command of the [African] conduits and not necessarily the command of the [African] sovereigns. The point here is that when African sovereignty is eroded, as is the case, African leaders become mere conduits and the law becomes the command of [African] conduits of global elites that have usurped African sovereignty.

Much as during the apartheid era in South Africa, where some places or areas were off-bounds to Africans, contemporary Africans do not have the freedom of movement to travel to Western countries. Apart from the fact that dispossessed and exploited Africans no longer have the material resources to travel to the West, Westerners are currently securitising migration and refugees, building walls and fortressing their borders to prevent African migrants from "invading" and flooding Europe and America (Nhemachena & Mawere 2020). The irony here is that Westerners expect African borders to remain open to admit Western migrants even as the Westerners are building walls and securitising migration in ways that debar Africans from entering Europe and America. These logics of apartheid at a global level speak to the resilience of apartheid. Much like during the apartheid era in South Africa, Westerners dispossess and exploit Africans, they steal and siphon African resources to Europe and America yet when Africans migrate to Europe and America in pursuit of their stolen resources, the Africans are debarred and have walls built to prevent them from entering Europe and America (Nyamnjoh 2015; Nhemachena & Mawere 2020). The question here is why the United Nations Organisation, that professes to have fought apartheid, does not fight this global apartheid that continues to harm Africans even in the twenty-first century. The question is why it should not be a human right for Africans to migrate in pursuit of their resources that are being siphoned to Europe and America. Why can't there be amendments of international laws to make it a human right for Africans to enter Europe and America in pursuit of their stolen resources? Why should parties looting African resources be allowed, at the United Nations level, to build walls and prevent the entry of the victims of the theft? What human right is more meaningful than pursuing and recovering one's stolen resources? The point here is that during the apartheid era in South Africa, African resources were stolen and siphoned yet Africans were not allowed to enter the areas or zones, deemed to be European zones, where their stolen resources were subsequently lodged. Similarly, at a world systems level, African resources are stolen and siphoned to the West yet Africans are not allowed to freely enter the Western countries where their resources are currently lodged. Such looting of African resources is well captured in Patrick Bond's (2006) book entitled *Looting Africa: The Economics of Exploitation.*

One of the greatest misrepresentations by the global media, in the context of global apartheid, is that Africans migrate from Africa simply because Africa is poor, or simply because African leaders have failed, are dictatorial, authoritarian, undemocratic, bad governors or abusive of human rights (Nhemachena & Mawere 2020; Nhemachena & Warikandwa 2019). When Africans migrated from their homelands, it was not simply because African leaders had failed, were dictatorial or abusive of humans rights – rather, it was because colonialists had stolen African resources including land and livestock such that the Africans were forced to migrate and seek employment in the mines and factories owned by the colonialists. At a global level, in the contemporary era, the same logics apply – African resources that have been stolen for centuries have not been returned and Africans who have been exploited for centuries have not been compensated yet African resources are still being stolen and siphoned by transnational corporations. It should therefore not be surprising that Africans are migrating and seeking to enter Europe and America in large numbers. The migration is not explicable simply in terms of failure on the African continent – rather the migration is explicable in terms of the ongoing and resilient dispossession and theft of African resources which are being siphoned to Europe and America. In fact, during the colonial era, colonialists even kidnapped African women and children as a way to force African husbands and fathers to yield and [physically and psychologically] migrate into colonial exploitation as cheap labour. Paradoxically, Western or Eurocentric scholarship focuses on condemning African marriages and families as having failed when in fact the marriages and families were failed or destroyed by colonialists who tore family members including spouses apart. Typical of apartheid that blames its victims; global apartheid condemns its African victims as having failed.

Forced to become cheap labour in towns and cities and in mines far away from their spouses, African men had their marriages destroyed by colonialism and apartheid. Forced to become cheap labourers away from their families including their children, African fathers had their relations with their children destroyed by colonialism and apartheid. With their livestock, including cattle raided and stolen by colonialists, African young men could no longer afford marriage payment and so African young men and young women have since faced mammoth difficulties in getting married because the material means of getting married had been stolen by colonialists (Nhemachena et al. 2018; Van Onselen 1980). Today, young African men and women roam the streets unmarried, jobless and landless – some even famililess. To cover up for their theft of material means of African marriage, colonialists taught African students that their African marriages were worthless, oppressive, harmful and patriarchal – this was meant to prevent young African men and women from fighting the colonialists to recover their stolen livestock and other material means of marriage payments. African wives were also taught that their husbands were oppressive, patriarchal, harmful and hence worthless – by this means, colonialists succeeded in preventing revolts by African women who would have fought to recover the livestock and other material means of marriage payments that colonialists had stolen (Nhemachena et al. 2018). The point here is that if Africans continued to value their African marriages, by extension, they would have continued to value the cattle, goats, sheep, land

and minerals that acted as marriage payments; but had been stolen by colonialists. It is much like the case of a thief who steals a house or a cow and then to prevent the owner-victim of theft from claiming it back or fighting for its return, the thief tells the victim that the house or cow is worthless, harmful, oppressive and patriarchal. If colonialists had not convinced African women that their marriages were worthless, patriarchal, harmful and oppressive, then African women would have resisted the exploitation of their husbands as colonial cheap labour. If colonialists had not convinced young African men and women that their marriages were harmful, patriarchal and oppressive, the young Africans would have resisted working, as migrant labourers, away from their spouses and families – in fact, they would have resiliently fought colonialists for the return of stolen cows, goats, sheep and land. Condemning African marriages and families as patriarchal, oppressive, harmful and worthless was a colonial ploy to ensure that Africans would not forcefully resist colonial dispossession and exploitation. It was a ploy to ensure that Africans, instead, fought their own parents and grandparents who were depicted by the loot-wise colonialists as oppressive, authoritarian, harmful, worthless and patriarchal. The point here is that there is need for an African jurisprudence that takes these realities into account. The jurisprudence that currently holds sway in Africa is a colonial form of jurisprudence that is not designed to help Africans. The current jurisprudence is an apartheid-era homeland type of jurisprudence – it is a jurisprudence that legitimises the sacrifice of Africans at the altar of global jurisprudential apartheid.

The problem is that Western-sponsored CSOs have not focused on civilising the Westerners, choosing as they do to focus on civilising the centuries-old African victims of enslavement and colonisation (Nhemachena & Bankie 2017). Western-sponsored CSOs continue the colonial missionary work of trying to civilise the victims of colonisation. For this reason, the CSOs which proliferated soon after African independence should have focused on advocacy to decolonise jurisprudence but on the contrary they chose to deepen neo-colonial jurisprudence on Africa. Western-sponsored CSOs have focused on condemning African states for corruption, dictatorship, human right abuses, bad governance and so on – the CSOs ignored addressing the corrupting effects of neo-colonial jurisprudence on Africa; they ignored addressing the dictatorship by global elites on Africa; they ignored addressing the dictatorship of the United Nations Security Council on Africans; they ignored the human rights abuses and bad governance by global elites and criminocrats that continue to dispossess and exploit Africans. The CSOs ignored the abuses that Africans are suffering in the hands of transnational corporations that continue to dispossess and exploit the Africans. Put differently, CSOs ignore the fact that Western refusal to ensure restitution and reparations to Africans constitute human rights abuse, corruption, bad global governance and dictatorship at a global level. Dictatorship, bad governance, human rights abuses and corruption know no scale – they are experienced and perpetrated even at the global level as a function of the resilient global apartheid.

BUILDING A TWENTY-FIRST CENTURY ONE WORLD GOVERNMENT BASED ON GLOBAL APARTHEID

In the contemporary era, some Western-sponsored media, academics, NGOs and CSOs push for the constitution of a One World Government, led by the Westerners, as if the primary problem for Africans is absence of One World Government (Nhemachena 2021). They ignore the fact that the primary problem for Africans is the Western refusal to ensure restitution and reparations for enslaving and colonising Africans for centuries. The CSOs, NGOs and so on ignore the fact that when Africans fought for independence, they were not necessarily fighting for the constitution of a One World Government led by the West but they were fighting for restitution and reparations for enslavement and colonisation. Put differently, the Western-sponsored academics, thinkers, NGOs, CSOs and media are not pushing an African agenda – their agenda is not to liberate Africans but to fasten Africans even more tightly to neo-imperialism. So, when Africans fight to repossess their stolen land, Western-sponsored CSOs, NGOs, media, thinkers and academics offer them the proposal of a One World Government, that is, in fact effectively a proposal for tighter integration into the neo-imperial world order marked by global apartheid. In other words, the CSOs, NGOs, academics thinkers and media are not necessarily minded on the liberation of Africans from global apartheid but they are bent on liberating empire from African claims and demands for restitution and reparations. The Western-sponsored CSOs, NGOs, thinkers, academics and media have nudged Africans and their states to accept assimilation into the neo-imperial system marked by global apartheid. It may not be surprising that some Africans believe that the ICC has been set up to help them – they ignore the fact that the ICC does not help them in repossessing their land and other resources stolen by imperialists/colonialists; the ICC does not help them to get reparations for enslavement and colonisation; and also that the ICC does not help Africans pushback neo-imperialism; it does not even help them pushback the ongoing dispossession and exploitation by transnational corporations that are currently grabbing land from African peasants. The ICC simply "helps" Africans to arrest their own kith and kin – it does not help Africans by arresting and indicting global criminocrats that have dispossessed, exploited, enslaved and colonised Africans for centuries. Just like during the old apartheid, global apartheid helps Africans to arrest, kill or assassinate their own leaders be they chiefs, kings, prime ministers or

is that when elected African presidents assume more authority over Africa, Westerners condemn the African leaders as authoritarian and dictatorial. The point here is that, surprisingly, when Western institution and corporations including the United Nations, the International Monetary Fund, the World Bank, transnational corporations and even Western states assume authority on Africa, they are not condemned as authoritarian but when elected African leaders assume more authority in Africa they are summarily demonised as authoritarian (Nhemachena & Warikandwa 2019; Gostin April 30, 2020; Rinke & Nebehay August 19, 2020; Gostin et al. 2015). When Western transnational corporations abuse the human rights of Africans, they are not described as human rights abusive organisations worth trial at the ICC; when Western institutions, individuals and organisations including the World Health Organisation suppress freedom of information over COVID-19, for instance, it is surprisingly tolerated but when elected African leaders control the media through pieces of legislation, they are demonised by global media as draconian, as oppressive and as insensitive to media or press freedom or freedom of information.

The point in the above is that even in the ongoing COVID-19 context, Western individuals and organisations and corporations retain the liberty to describe other people and institutions' communication as mis-informative and worth banning or condemnation yet when elected African leaders do the same by curtailing pro-Western media, they are summarily demonised as oppressive, authoritarian and dictatorial to the media, freedom of information and communication (Nhemachena & Warikandwa 2019). One may note the example of the late Robert Mugabe whose media control laws were summarily condemned by global media, academics, NGOs, CSOs among others, as oppressive, draconian and insensitive and so on. Yet, in the contemporary era, the World Health Organisation and other Western corporations have suppressed the freedoms of other people whose efforts to communicate have been described as infodemic and misinformation (Nhemachena et al. this volume). Put differently, Western institutions and individuals do not notice their hypocrisy. They do not even notice that by suppressing and oppressing other people who wish to share information, which they call infodemic, they have, as Nhemachena et al. (ibid) argue, become suppredemics and oppredemics – suppressing and oppressing freedom of information. Western oppredemics and suppredemics are fortunately viewed more favourably than when Africans similarly seek to control the flow of information. To make matters worse, the World Health Organisation and other Western institutions dismissed African herbal cure for COVID-19 and so the Madagascan president has been annoyed, as are many Africans who are sensitive to the resilience of global apartheid. The point here is that there is need to craft international laws and policies that destroy global apartheid including in matters of drug patenting and intellectual property rights. Africans deserve their intellectual property rights, if the global apartheid is to discontinue. To deconstruct global apartheid, it is imperative to undo the ghostly hold of Western epistemologies on the minds of Africans and the entire world. Decolonising jurisprudence is the name we give to undoing the ghostly hold of Eurocentric epistemologies on African minds.

DECOLONISING JURISPRUDENCE AND EPISTEMOLOGIES: JURISPRUDENTIAL ISSUES ON COVID-19 AND NANOVACCINES

The contemporary era has seen proliferation of discourses on decoloniality and decolonisation yet we are also witnessing the intensification of mental colonisation by a neo-empire that is anxious to retain the ill-gotten privileges that it acquired as a result of enslaving and colonising Africans. Even as some Africans are writing and advocating for decolonising the mind and the curricula, we witness the scientific production of cerebral internet and nanobots or nanorobots and brain microchips to be inserted or implanted into the minds and bodies of indigenous Africans in the emergent transhumanist era (Nhemachena et al. 2020). Once the microchips and brain nanobots are inserted or implanted into the minds, Africans will be subjected to remote control by the transnational corporations that own and control the technologies of global surveillance, sousveillance and control. Such invasive technologies are not necessarily designed to liberate African minds but to control them remotely from the neo-imperial centres. Marketed as human enhancements or augmentation, the technologies of control are made to appear as beneficial yet they assist neo-imperialists to remotely control the minds of Africans and other subjects of neo-empire. Put differently, the enhancement or augmentation devices/technologies are meant to enhance and augment the imperialists or global elites rather than enhance the imperial subjects of global apartheid. In this sense, we argue that although the technologies are described as human enhancement devices, they are actually empire enhancement devices, in the sense that they enhance the empire by enabling it to remotely control the imperial subjects of global apartheid.

It is the awareness of such nefarious plans by the global elites that some human beings are resisting COVID-19 vaccinations. They are aware that the nanobots or nanorobots will be injected into their bodies in the guise of nanomedicine or nanovaccines that are already being produced by some leading global pharmaceutical corporations that are engaged in the race to produce COVID-19 vaccines. Nanovaccines and nanomedicines are by their nature concerned with nanorobots that make it possible for the human bodies and brains to be wirelessly connected, through the Internet of Things, to other devices and, thus, to be remotely controlled. To be remotely controlled does not entail freedom or liberation yet global elites market such projects as liberating and as enhancing freedoms. The question is who do they ultimately enhance and free? Connecting African minds to the Internet of Things and to the Battlefield Internet connected to global military establishments, the technologies do not entail freedom or liberation for Africans. In fact, once connected via nanobots/nanorobots to the global elites who then remotely control African minds, the Africans will be subjected to direct brain shocks, to hacking of the minds and to breaches of privacy because they will be subjected to constant surveillance, sousveillance and uberveillance by the global elites who become all-seeing, all-knowing and omnipresent gods watching everyone else and controlling everyone else in the world. Decolonising jurisprudence must of necessity involve resistance to these machinations by the nefarious global elites who, like the colonialists before them, pretend to be driving or ushering civilisation when in fact they are colonising other people. In a world where Africans are successfully turned into transhumans embodying nanorobots, it will be pointless to hope for African human rights. Discourses about human rights are set to disappear with the emergence of the transhumanist era into which everyone is being pushed by the nanomafia of global elites who are anxious to insert nanobots, nanorobots, nanomedicinnes and nanovaccinesinto human bodies (Flores 2018). Of course nanobots can be injected into bodies; they can be put in the water that human beings drink; they can be put in the food that human beings eat and they can be put in the air that human beings breathe. The net effect of embodying nanobots is that the human body and brains become open to manipulation by global elites – the human bodies begin to speak to the Western advocacy for open societies in Africa. Put differently, global elites do not only want to establish open societies in Africa but they also want to establish open bodies and open minds that can be remotely controlled and read by the same global elites.

Of course, slave owners and colonialists assumed that the enslaved and colonised people were open and so this legitimised invasions of the spaces and minds of the enslaved and colonised. In this regard, to be regarded as open is not necessarily a compliment – rather to become open is to be amenable to colonisation and enslavement (Nhemachena et al. 2020). Empire likes everyone else to become open and amenable to its control. African men and women are thus urged to become sexually open and ready for penetrations of different kinds. Empire does not like Africans who maintain their virginity because to be a virgin implies thorough gatekeeping. Empire does not want Africans to do serious gatekeeping of their bodies, resources, territories, homes, cultures, religions, land, minerals and so on. Rather, global elites like Africans to be loose, open and sexually indiscriminate – including engaging in homosexuality with open anuses (Nhemachena & Warikandwa 2019). No wonder that Eurocentric thinkers demonise African virginity rituals while at the same time they encourage liberalisation of prostitution, homosexuality and divorce in the guise of human rights. As noted above, Eurocentric thinkers argue that virginity tests and marriages objectify and dehumanise women/men and therefore that they must be granted liberal rights to be open, prostitute and divorce. Yet, African jurists have not managed to grasp the underlying motivations in such advocacy which is to create recklessly open Africans who cannot keep guard over their resources, bodies, properties, homes, cultures, religions, territories and land. Some are even encouraged to be so recklessly open as to engage in homosexuality and queer sex. The point we are making here is that African jurists and legal scholar need to construe the deep meaning of imperial exhortations for Africans to be open. There are fundamental connections to property law and jurisprudence here – when the Eurocentrists encourage Africans to be open, they are in essence encouraging them to be recklessly open and hence training them to see all sorts of penetration, and failures to gate-keep, as normal. The point is that jurists need to cognise this intersection between personhood and property jurisprudence. Openness of personhood implies openness to indiscriminate penetration and robbery at a material level.

Because of the Eurocentric advocacy of openness and hence failure to gate-keep, some Africans have given away their marriages, families, religions, cultures, material resources and epistemologies. Imperial elites are desirous to monopolise gatekeeping even over African bodies and brains. It is also necessary to note in African jurisprudence that to be open, as advocated for by Eurocentrists, is to become other-than-human. If one is open, as such, this entails that one can be anything and may not necessarily be human. To be human entails possessing boundaries that define one as human. By extension, to be human means to do gatekeeping such that the boundaries of humanity are kept and maintained. It is invasive bacteria and viruses that celebrate openness of human bodies, yet some Westerners even fund NGOs and CSOs to advocate for African openness, including in the guise of ideologies about inclusivity, diversity and plurality. At a more philosophical level, the question is who would want to be as open and inclusive as to embody viruses and bacteria of imperialism? Besides, the point is that prostitution, adultery, fornication and lack of gatekeeping are generally underwritten by logics or rather illogics of indiscriminate inclusivity, diversity and plurality. In a jurisprudence that celebrates indiscriminate inclusivity, plurality, multiplicity, diversity and openness – prostitution, fornication, homosexuality, adultery and lack of gatekeeping all become normal because all these are premised on openness. African jurisprudence should critically question these Eurocentric ideologies that appear innocent yet they are actually toxic at a jurisprudential and cognitive level, more broadly.

If, at a jurisprudential level, the current Western efforts to produce nanovaccines or nanomedicines for Africans are understood in terms of Western celebrations of indiscriminate inclusivity, diversity, plurality, multiplicity, openness, transhumanism, posthumanism, post-anthropocentrism and anti-humanism, it becomes possible to see how even infections with viruses are celebrated. If the apparent humanistic and ostensibly philanthropic moves by Westerners seeking to produce nanovaccines for Africans are understood in terms of contemporary Western celebrations of anti-humanism and transhumanism, it becomes possible to see that humanitarianism and philanthropy cannot be the motivation is a context marked by paradoxical Western celebrations of anti-humanism and transhumanism and posthumanism. The apparent concern for humanity and for human welfare has been used for centuries since the colonial era to hide nefarious imperial projects. The point is that Africans need to be on guard and to be thorough at gatekeeping so that they do not get imperially penetrated again. A jurisprudence for Africans is one that trains law students to be perceptive and deep thinking. It is a jurisprudence that enhances African students to use their history to interpret the present and anticipate the future. A jurisprudence for Africa is one that enables students and jurists to evade capture.

While South Africa has recently been seized with discourses and court cases on state capture, we hold that an even more virulent form of capture is lurking – neo-empire seeks to technologically capture African brains and to turn Africans into transhumans embodying technologies of surveillance, sousveillance and uberveillance to enable the global elites and their corporations to remotely control the world (Flores 2018; Nhemachena et al. 2020). The current neo-imperial efforts to technologically capture and remote-control African minds underscore the fact that empire does not only capture or arrest only those that have committed crimes. Empire arrests Africans simply because it desires to own and control them. Similarly, the ICC, as an imperial court has not been set up to arrest and capture only those that have committed crimes. It has been set up to control Africans via lawfare or via the use of international lawfare. The ICC is part of the imperial technologies of penetration, capture and control. Of course to be able to capture, penetrate and control, one has to be dazzlingly and deceptively philanthropic/humanitarian.

GLOBAL APARTHEID'S APPARATUSES OF CAPTURE AND CONTROL

The Westerners have set up organisations and institutions like the United Nations Organisation, World Health Organisation, International Monetary

Fund, World Bank, World Trade Organisation, World Economic Forum and the ICC but the role of African jurists and lawmakers should be to critically question how these institutions and organisations speak to African freedom and liberation including restitution and reparations that are long overdue from the Westerners. The question is how these institutions and organisations can be made relevant to African liberation including restitution and reparations for enslavement and colonisation. At the international level, Africans are still dictated to by the United Nations, the World Health Organisations, International Monetary Fund, World Bank, World Trade Organisation, The ICC, World Economic Forum and even by Euro-American states that have not been voted for by the Africans. Even Euro-American NGOs and CSOs, which have not been voted for by Africans, meddle in African affairs *ad libertum.* The United Nations Security Council which is not voted for by Africans, takes liberty to determine security issues in the whole world; also, the International Monetary Fund and the World Bank which have not been voted for by Africans take liberty to indulge in African economic and political affairs to the extent that they even impose austerity measures on Africans, who have already suffered centuries of enslavement and colonisation by Westerners some of whom own and control the International Monetary Fund and the World Bank. The ICC, which sadly selectively indicts Africans, is not even located on the African continent. It is in fact reminiscent of the colonial Privy Councils and other colonial courts that were biased against Africans and other people of colour. Indeed, even today, African Americans are disproportionately represented in the jails because of selective indictments and stereotyping of people of colour (Roberts 2004; Pawasarat & Quinn 2013). The point here is that the selective indictment of Africans in the ICC parallels the stereotyping and disproportionate representation of people of colour in American jails. This, we call global jurisprudential apartheid.

Although Eurocentric scholars and thinkers address Africans as post-apartheid, this book argues that Africans are still suffering global apartheid in a world that is still owned and controlled by Westerners running the United Nations, World Trade Organisation, International Monetary Fund, the World Bank, the ICC, World Economic Forum and the panoply of CSOs and NGOs that have arrogated the role of policing contemporary African states. Heavily and disproportionately policed by the ICC; by the United Nations Security Council; by the CSOs; NGOs; by the World Trade Organisation and so on, Africans are still suffering virulent global apartheid. In global apartheid, Africans and their states are denied their autonomy and sovereignty. African states and governments are stereotyped as violent, oppressive, authoritarian, dictatorial and so on. Eurocentric academies and media persuade Africans that it is only their own states and governments that are exploitative, oppressive, violent, authoritarian and dictatorial and undemocratic yet Western transnational corporations and Euro-American states also oppress and suppress Africans particularly those that threaten imperial interests by seeking to redistribute land and other resources that were stolen during the colonial era. Africans that seek restitution and reparations for enslavement and colonisation are suppressed by the Western institutions that seek to retain ownership and control over stolen African resources. However, Eurocentric academies and media hardly describe this as suppression or oppression occasioned on Africans by Western institutions and states that sanction and prevent Africans from restitution and reparations. The point we are making here is that apartheid is still alive and is in fact more virulent at national levels where descendants of colonialists still own and control stolen land, minerals and other resources; at the global level where the Westerners still monopolise ownership and control of global institutions which are ironically funded from proceeds of exploiting Africans.

While Westerners would want to justify their ownership and control of global institutions on the pretext that they are funding those organisations, we argue here that the global organisations and institutions are in fact funded by Africans who are dispossessed and exploited by transnational corporations and whose land and other resources are still in the hands of descendants of colonialists. In this regard, it is not Westerners who fund global peace institutions, rather global peace comes at the expense of Africans whose resources and labour are exploited so as to fund the global peace initiative and organisations. The United Nations itself is not necessarily funded by Westerners but it is funded by hapless Africans whose resources and labour are exploited to fund the United Nations and other institutions. Africans are hoodwinked to believe that it is Westerners who are supposedly generously funding the United Nations, and other institutions when in fact a close analysis of the world shows that these institutions are funded from proceeds realised by dispossessing and exploiting Africans and other colonised peoples in the world. Whereas Westerners would want the world to believe that they are generously funding the ICC, a close analysis of the world system indicates that the ICC is in fact funded by Africans whose labour and resources are exploited by Westerners to fund the ICC. Whereas Westerners would want the world to believe that Africans are indebted to Western institutions such as the International Monetary Fund and the World Bank, a close analysis of the issues shows that it is in fact the Westerners and their institutions that are indebted to Africans whom they have dispossessed and exploited for centuries since the enslavement era (Warikandwa et al. 2019). The point here is that jurisprudential issues and discourses around debts, indebtedness, funding, ownership and control over international institutions need to be rethought and corrected so that they reflect the reality of what is going on in the world.

One of the major problems is that Western education and media ideologies have clouded African thought systems such that those that owe African restitutions and reparations are erroneously descried as creditors. Africans who are owned debts by Westerners are erroneously described as indebted to the Westerners. Africans who have been dispossessed and exploited for centuries are erroneously described as simply poor - there are jurisprudential matters here because describing the dispossessed and exploited as simply poor conceals the crimes of dispossession and exploitation. Erroneously describing the Africans, who are owed debts by Westerners, as indebted to Westerners has the effect of reversing the roles of the debtor and the indebted. Similarly, the Westerners who have stolen land, minerals and other resources from Africans are erroneously described simply as rich and industrialised. This too has jurisprudential import because it cancels out the crimes of theft of African resources. The point here is that those that have stolen resources and exploited other people cannot and should not be simply described as rich, creditors and industrialised because to do so disables international jurisprudential lucidity. In fact, this warps international law and ossifies global jurisprudential apartheid. At the level of logic, to simply describe a robber or thief as rich, industrialised, developed, first-world and so on would be to err: those that have robbed and stolen from Africans need to be described as such for the sake of jurisprudential lucidity. If they continue to be simply described as rich, industrialised, developed, first-world and so on, future African generations will lose touch with the reality of enslavement and colonial robbery and plunder perpetrated on Africans by the so-called rich and developed countries. The jurisprudential record must be set straight and correct.

Because literature on jurisprudence and social sciences is predominantly Western, international law and jurisprudence have been twisted such that they conceal the criminality of the West while stereotyping the Africans and people of colour as the international criminals par excellence. The West that has historically stolen land, minerals and labour power from Africans is erroneously described as first world, as advanced world, as developed world, as industrialised world and as civilised nations – all these epithets conceal the historical theft and robbery that the West has perpetrated on Africans. In fact, Western transnational corporations are still dispossessing and exploiting Africans particularly in the light of the ongoing transnational corporations' land grabs from African peasants. Concealed as land deals, the ongoing theft of land from African peasants is denied jurisprudential lucidity. Similarly, Western corporations that come to Africa to dispossess and exploit Africans are erroneously described as investors (Nhemachena et al. 2019): this effectively conceals the ongoing crimes of dispossessing and exploiting Africans many of whom remain without remedies. Dispossessed and exploited by transnational corporations, Africans are also subjected to medical and technological experimentations by global pharmaceutical corporations that test their drugs on the hapless and desperate Africans. There are jurisprudential issues around these issues; major among them is the question of how to protect Africans from these Western transnational corporations that dispossess, exploit and experiment on Africans with impunity. They are not even subject to the ICC for human rights abuses on Africans yet the same transnational corporations provide funds to Western states, NGOs and CSOs that stereotype, police and bully African states while hiding behind human rights discourses.

International human rights are peddled in a context where Eurocentric thinkers and scholars are also pushing for post-human security and for post-anthropocentrism, both of which seek to decentre African humanity and human rights (Nhemachena & Mawere 2020). Human rights are peddled by the NGOs and CSO in a context where African security and human rights are ironically threatened and effaced by the transnational corporations that fund the NGOs and CSOs. Similarly, the NGOs and CSOs peddle human rights in a context where some of the NGOs and CSOs are also advocating for biocentrism, earthcentrism and ecocentrism rather than anthropocentrism and humancentrism. In fact, the so-called Anthropocence era is supposed to be marked by voluntary extinction and the disposal of what are regarded as surplus humans in the margins of empire (Nhemachena & Mawere 2019). Instead of prioritising African human rights, the Western transnational corporations are dispossessing and exploiting Africans while at the same time advocating for ecocentrism, biocentrism, earthcentrism and the decentring of African human rights and anthropocentrism. The surprising thing is that Westerners have never in history advocated from Afrocentricity yet they are advocating for ecocentricity, biocentrism, earthcentrism and so on.

The question is why such Western transnational corporations and states that are loathe to Afrocentricity pretend to offer humanitarianism to Africans. There is a paradox here that needs critical juristic attention. As noted above in respect of COVID-19 nanovaccines that are being produced for Africans by the Western transnational corporations and global elites, our question is about how safe such vaccines will be for Africans. If nanovaccines are produced by the same transnational corporations that are currently involved in transnational corporations land grabs from African peasants [who are suffering the new scramble for Africa], then how safe are the African peasants? To get nanovaccines produced by the same people and corporations and states that are currently dispossessing and exploiting Africans is itself a big risk. Similarly, for Africans to be injected with nanovaccines produced by Western corporations, states and individuals who have refused to return stolen land, minerals and to pay reparations is itself a risk. The safety of vaccines is not a monopoly of scientists to test – rather African jurists and lawmakers need to be physically and cognitively on guard if Africans are to be safe. African jurists and lawmakers need to notice that the safety of Africans is not guaranteed in the scientific labs which are owned and controlled by the same Westerners that are dispossessing and exploiting the Africans. Besides, the million-dollar question is, why the Westerners and their institutions who oppose the fast tracking of restitution and reparations for Africans would want to fast track their vaccines for Africans?

International institutions themselves are not accountable, transparent and responsibly acting in Africa. Whereas Africans can utilise administrative law to seek recourse against their own states when they wrongfully act, there is no international mechanism to ensure that there is administrative fairness and accountability on the part of international institutions and states that have arrogated administrative action from African states. The United Nations Security Council for instance often acts on the African continent yet there is no administrative law recourse by Africans who become aggrieved by the actions of the United Nations Security Council, the International Monetary Fund, the World Bank, the World Trade Organisation and so on. Even the ICC is not open to administrative review, accountability and transparency on the part of Africans who are aggrieved by its administrative actions. Arguably, the bias by the ICC could have been addressed or challenged in terms of administrative action if there was an administrative law remedy available for Africans who have raised concerns about such bias. The question is also about why there should not be an administrative remedy against the action of the IMF and World Bank and WTO and so on all of which are meddling in African administrative and political affairs.

CHAPTER OUTLINES

In chapter 2, Samuel Kwesi Amoo and Clever Mapaure argue that jurisprudence as a law module in law schools should not be merely presented as a restatement of theories. There is ample evidence in case law from various jurisdictions demonstrating the relevance of jurisprudence in the judicial process. The chapter highlights this primary fact and it establishes that jurisprudence is an integral part of both the legislative and judicial processes of the legal systems of many countries. It further attempts to establish that pretences of value-neutral principles of legality, which have been used as the justification for the totalitarian abuses of the supposedly positive law, are capable of being explained in jurisprudential theories. Furthermore, it also attempts to explain that not all principles of legality emanating from the courts are value neutral. For instance, a great deal of case law is based on value judgments. This goes to establish the relationships between these principles and jurisprudential theories. Specific references to some pre- and post-independence Namibian and South African cases are made in the attempt to explain judicial behaviour in jurisprudential theories as a consequence of the prevailing political and legal regimes. Amoo and Mapaure's chapter is primarily devoted to the question of the relevance of jurisprudence in both judicial and legislative processes. It also seeks to address the issue of the apparent dearth of legal theories propounded by jurists of African pedigree in contemporary jurisprudence.

In chapter 3, Pilisano Harris Masake and Lizazi Eugene Libebe contend that Africa and the African states bore witness to the legal paradigm shift from the pre-colonial, colonial and post-colonial African legal systems. Colonialism disrupted and obliterated the pre-colonial African legal system. This chapter critically addresses the issue of decoloniality from a distinct normative imperative of the Afro-legal centricity. The theoretical standpoints in this chapter are premised on a working assumption that there is a need to trace the pre-colonial African legal philosophies and to understand how these philosophies informed the political, social and economic cohesion. Further, there is a need to decolonise law to include organically created laws and the relevant legal education. The decolonised legal education should inform the legal curriculum. Derived from the normative imperatives and theoretical assumptions, it is this chapter's argument that for decoloniality of legal education to be evocative, it is necessary to trace, revive and, where necessary, modify the pre-colonial African legal philosophies and incorporate same in the current legal education.

In chapter 4, Dunia Prince Zongwe critically argues that lawyers in Namibia should have cold shoulders and cold feet when considering transformative constitutionalism and the dangers it poses. Among other dangers, transformative constitutionalism will likely confuse those who use it because it means different things to different people. It will further confuse its users about what transformation should consist of. It will provide no detailed guidance as to how lawyers should teach, research, practice and interpret the law. And, because it tends to exclude or marginalise other theories, principles and legal methodologies, such as doctrinal methodologies, it does not fit the Namibian context. Zongwe further contends that transformative constitutionalism tries to besiege legal education and interpretation as a supreme principle, and it oversells politics in constitutional adjudication. Given these tendencies, it is argued that lawyers should prevent it from dominating the Namibian legal scene. When or if lawyers in Namibia or elsewhere in Africa adopt transformative constitutionalism, then they should only treat it as one possibility among a varied and rich menu of possible techniques to teach, research, practice and read the law. For Zongwe, transformative constitutionalism has much to offer to develop Namibia's constitutional jurisprudence, but that potential and promise can only materialise if Namibian lawyers, judges and educators use it alongside other constitutional approaches, say liberal positivism and Dworkin's theory, and provided lawyers leave the door open for new and hopefully better methods of reading legal texts.

Julius Cosmas's chapter (chapter 5) notes that *Clausula rebus sic stantibus* is a Latin expression literary referring to inapplicability of treaties because of standing situations. He notes that the principle of *clausula rebus sic stantibus* originates from treaty laws. The application of the principle of *clausula rebus sic stantibus* has extended to investment agreements, which generally regulate investment relationships between states and investors. Cosmas further contends that the principle of *clausula rebus sic stantibus* contradicts or at least conflicts with the principle of *pacta sunt servanda*, which compels parties to remain bound by their concluded obligations, and to carry out such obligations in good faith. The principle *of clausula rebus sic stantibus* would open an alternative chance to parties, of renegotiation upon substantial change of business environment or simply fundamental change of circumstances. It is further argued that when a government wants to renegotiate the investment contract, it will invoke the principle of *clausula rebus sic stantibus* the investor will invoke the doctrine of *pacta sunt servanda*. Thus, the question of application of the principle of *pact sunt servanda* to investment agreements between states and private investors is not a disputable fact in developed countries, but the displacement of the principle of *clausula rebus sic stantibus* in such agreements is not controversial. Developed countries would wish not to see developing host states applying the principle of *clausula rebus sic stantibus* in their investment relations, simply because application of the principle of *clausula rebus sic stantibus* would open these agreements to renegotiation which is the last thing investing companies would desire. As a matter of fact, many countries have now incorporated the principle of *clausula rebus sic stantibus* in their domestic laws. Whether the principle of *clausula rebus sic stantibus* is acceptable to developed countries and to international courts or not, it is argued that this development which essentially covers renegotiation of investment contracts is of importance, provided the proof for fundamental change of circumstances can be provided. It is unfortunate that the principle of *clausula rebus sic stantibus* is not embedded in many of the investment agreements which Tanzania is a state party to.

Chapter 6, which is authored by Eric Omo Enakireru and Anya Kingsley Anya, contends that the importance of law in promoting effective environmental governance cannot be underestimated. The legislative arm of government can be a useful tool and a powerful agent of change in sustainable environmental governance. Therefore, there is a need for a principal statute for the management of the Nigeria environment. For the authors, Nigeria is in need of an integrated and coherent framework for its environmental management.

Nigeria needs a strong legislative system if it is to achieve its environmental commitment and goals. The authors further argue that Nigeria needs a robust all-encompassing and well-focused environmental regime to serve as a core principal legislation on the management of the Nigeria environment. Thus, the capacity of the Nigerian legislature needs to be strengthened not only to enable it to legislates for sustainable environmental governance, but also to enable it to promote institutional reforms that will bring about sustainable environmental governance. Enakireru and Anya argue that environmental sustainability should be made an integral part of economic planning at all levels of governance and integrated into all policies in Nigeria. For this reason, economic policies which aim at balancing sustainability initiative backed by conscious efforts to safeguard and protect the environment should also be made use of. It is also important to have adequate institutional machinery for supervising implementation of environmental obligations/commitments. The legal and political framework for environmental governance requires effective enforcement mechanism. Therefore, there is the need for the full utilisation of the law as an instrument of social changes or social engineering to achieve a balance between environmental protection and development activities. The chapter notes that the need for environmental protection rights should be balanced as against the need for development of immediate host communities. The two factors should not be compromised in favour of the other. The authors argue that sustaining a balance between environmental protection laws and development of communities is a desideratum for a stable socio-economic and politico-cultural society devoid of any form of rancour.

Oyesola Animashaun and Howard Tafara Chitimira's chapter (chapter 7) argues that many African states have been weakened by colonialism, apartheid, trans-Atlantic slavery, Arab slave trade, structural adjusted programmes and human trafficking. Some of these African states are further weakened by double standards perpetrated by international organisations like the ICC. This is usually perpetrated through the Rome Statute 1998, which the unsuspecting African leaders subscribed to in large numbers. The chapter addresses the geopolitical imbalance in the indictment, investigation and prosecution at the ICC. The authors argue that the court's main focus seems to be only on Africans and espouses the indictment of a serving African head of state whose country is not a party to the Rome Statute, contrary to customary international law is of particular concern. It also interrogates the contentions in the referral and deferral powers of the permanent members of the United Nations Security Council, majority of whom are not party to the Rome Statute. The chapter further examines the flaws in the Rome Statute, the cases instituted and similar cases that were ignored by the ICC prosecutor which suggests that there may be some justification for the allegation of global apartheid levied against the body by some authors, politicians and the AU. There are also indications that the independence of the ICC is compromised because it focused mainly on African states while ignoring similar violations of the Rome Statute by the "powerful nations" such as United States of America (US), Russia and China and their allies. The chapter concludes that African countries need strong national and regional mechanisms to promote transparency in governance, and should be circumspect in adopting treaties without weighing the implications.

In chapter 8, Clemence Rusenga contends that among its objectives, the South African land reform programme that was introduced in 1994 sought to correct the historical injustices caused by apartheid in relation to ownership, control and use of natural resources which disadvantaged the black majority. While the post-apartheid government committed itself to redistribute natural resources to the formerly disadvantaged black majority, where beneficiaries acquire land the government force them to produce on a large scale without subdividing the land. A combination of factors, among them the imposition of large-scale farming, have contributed to the failure of many beneficiaries to neither sustain production nor benefit from their land. That failure to sustain large-scale production is used by the government as the pretext to introduce strategic partnerships and mentorships, effectively allowing agribusiness and white commercial farmers to have influence and control in the land reform projects. Consequently, agribusiness and white commercial farmers have become the 'real beneficiaries' of land reform at the expense of their black partners. They gain control over land reform projects, use them for secure supplies to their downstream processing and marketing facilities while, at the same time, receiving state subsidies and cheap labour of the land beneficiaries. The chapter argues that strategic partnerships in the context of the Proactive Land Acquisition Strategy facilitate the dispossession and disempowerment of land beneficiaries and deepens an already acute land and agrarian question in the country. Instead of being a solution, strategic partnerships facilitate agribusiness' accumulation of natural and financial resources earmarked for black Africans in the context of land reform itself are a reincarnation of apartheid in the democratic dispensation.

In chapter 9, Tapiwa Victor Warikandwa contends that customary law has been in operation in Namibia for over twenty-eight years, since this legal system was recognised in the constitution as an equal part of the legal order collectively with common law. This chapter examines policy and legislative frameworks that have had an impact on the recognition of customary land rights emanating from pre-colonial Namibia and related cases of communal land claims in post-apartheid Namibia, against the background of the protections that the constitution gives to cultural property rights. The chapter concludes that the cause of incorporation has not been well-served by the legislature which has shied away from protecting the deep values embedded in customary law by deferring too readily to Western notions that have found their way into the Namibia's Constitution. The chapter concludes by advocating for a different approach that is more considerate to the values underpinning customary law even where, as sometimes happens, these have been obscured by practices that appear adverse to Namibia's Constitution. Land tenure reform remains a key policy issue in Africa, given the large proportion of the population that relies on land and natural resources for their livelihoods. It is not enough to recognise the socially and politically embedded character of land rights, or the unequal outcomes of contemporary forms of "enclosure." Privatisation and complete individualisation of land are uneven and contested, and in many places the nature and content of land rights remain quite distinct from "Western-legal" forms of property. In these situations, individual titling is not a feasible solution, and adapted and democratised versions of communal tenure should be promoted by law and policy. Viewed from within a "rights without illusions" perspective, legal recognition of these distinctive forms of land rights can form part of a broader strategy to secure rights through political mobilisation and pressure for democratic systems of land governance, and must involve external support for rights holders within local institutional and political processes. Customary norms must be at the centre of this approach.

Liina Kalili's chapter (chapter 10) argues that there are people who are more privileged because they have adequate access to national resources than others. Some people may lack opportunities and become disadvantaged due to large societal conditions, which must be attended to. The theory of distributive justice means that those who have must give to those who have not, to realise a fair society. It is possible to decide whether people are treated fairly in the society by examining their access to primary social goods. Thus, for Kalili, the main question is who owns mineral resources in Namibia? The chapter examines available pieces of legislation and the current status quo of mass exports of rough diamonds and other mineral resources sold for the purposes of beneficiation.

In chapter 11, Ndatega Victoria Asheela-Shikalepo and Tapiwa Victor Warikandwa argue that public interest demands the protection of aggrieved bidders, particularly where such interest inevitably protects the public interest. Thus, it is imperative that clear remedies are spelt out for the bidders to ensure the rule of law in public procurement. All bidders must therefore be treated fairly, reasonably and lawfully to achieve a transparent and competitive procurement process. Where a decision is made by the administrative body to terminate the offer to award procurement to a bidder, such constitutes an administrative action which had to be exercised in compliance with the provisions of the Namibian Constitution and Act. The authors further contend that at minimum, the administrative body is required to notify the bidder of its decision to withdraw the offer, provide reasons for such withdrawal after having afforded the bidder an opportunity to make representations before it. This is so because withdrawing an offer which has granted benefits to the successful bidders creates a legitimate expectation on the part of the successful bidder, which can be used as a basis to render the subsequent award procedurally unfair. If the principles of natural justice and provisions of the Act are upheld at all stages of the public procurement process, administrative justice will be achieved and at the same time assist in the upholding of the principles of transparency and accountability.

Lekunze Joseph Nembo and Luvhengo Usapfa's chapter (chapter 12) critically interrogates the premise that failures of land reform programme in South Africa from 1994 are solely due to weaknesses in section 25 of the 1996 Constitution of the Republic of South Africa. The chapter is premised on the idea that, if section 25 of the constitution is amended, "new nonracial minority land owners" may emerge, leading to a future land reform debate on equity in redistribution not based along racial lines. The authors review both colonial and post-colonial pieces of legislation and policies including some recent articles on the discourse surrounding the amendment of section 25 of the South African Constitution in 2018. Furthermore, the authors develop a conceptual process based on the social facilitation theory to explore the ideological and equity strands around the amendment of section 25. The chapter concludes that an amendment of section 25 of the South Africa Constitution is justifiable as long as equity in redistribution of land to all South Africans is achieved.

In chapter 13, Job Shipululo Amupanda focuses on corruption. He argues that to a developing society, corruption is what cancer is to a human body as billions of dollars that could build hospitals, educate the learners, build public infrastructures and feed the hungry in Africa are diverted to few individuals whose main concern is crass materialism. To avoid this scourge, international, continental, regional and national legal institutions have been put in place to counter the tide of corruption. Amupanda argues that harmonisation of scattered corruption mandates in Namibia is necessary and prudent. The chapter provides evidence of a public trust deficit in the Anti-Corruption Act (ACC) and finds that section 21 and section 31 of the Anti-Corruption Act 8 of 2003 is the foundation of current problems at the ACC. This chapter argues that these sections need to be amended and democratised as is the case with Mauritius's Prevention of Corruption Act 5 of 2002. For Namibia, given the current state of affairs, the chapter argues that an effective strategy of ensuring meaningful participation of the civil society in the fight against corruption is the creation of a buffer zone between whistle-blowers and corruption fighting bodies. This buffer zone will serve as a safe space for whistle-blowers. The work of the affirmative repositioning movement in fighting corruption over the years is presented as a possible model for consideration.

Howard Tafara Chitimira's chapter (chapter 14) notes that Zimbabwe has made numerous efforts to enhance its financial markets, foreign direct investment, gross domestic product and economy. Various legislative and socio-economic policies have been introduced by the policy makers and the Zimbabwe African National Union – Patriotic Front government from time to time since 1980 to date. Chitimira argues that most of the statutes and policies such as Economic Structural Adjustment Programme, Zimbabwe Programme of Economic and Social Transformation, Short-term Emergency Recovery Plan, Medium Term Plan and Zimbabwe Agenda for Sustainable Socio-Economic Transformation were largely and wrongly premised on Eurocentric and Global North policies. Furthermore, most statutes and policies that were adopted in Zimbabwe were wrongly influenced by Rhodesian socio-economic policies which were unlawfully employed by Ian Smith's regime to promote colonialism and white supremacy. Consequently, Zimbabwe has encountered numerous investment and socio-economic challenges owing to its blind reliance on incompatible Rhodesian, Eurocentric and Global North policies since 1980 to date. These policies and statutory regulatory measures have been inconsistently enforced in Zimbabwe since 1980 to date. Accordingly, it is submitted that Zimbabwe should carefully review its laws and policies to remove provisions and policies that unfairly advance Eurocentric and colonial interests of the Global North. It is further submitted that Zimbabwe should decolonise its legislation, investment and economic policies to introduce indigenous policy measures so as to attract more Foreign Direct Investment. This approach could enable more indigenous people to actively participate and invest in the Zimbabwean economy.

In chapter 15, Fritz Nghiishililwa examines the problems of poverty and other related political and social challenges in developing countries, particularly, in Africa with a view to determine whether the failure of the continent to effectively address the social and political problems stems from poor leadership or the use of inappropriate political institutions which the former colonial authorities left behind. Could it be said that poverty, political instability and the claim of corrupt African leaders is attributed to incompetency of the leadership or is caused by the nonexistence of suitable institutions. Furthermore, the chapter investigates the root cause of the lack of food needed to feed many starving African population and how to deal with the issue of corrupt public officials and corrupt transnational corporations operating in and on Africa.

Brighton Nyagadza, Itai Kabonga and Promise Machingo Hlungwani's chapter (chapter 16) examines the importance of financial inclusion basing on empirical review of agency banking in Zimbabwe. Nyagadza, Kabonga and Hlungwani argue that it is necessary to appreciate the value behind financial inclusivity as a means to level the field and allow all value contributions towards reduction of the adverse effects of global apartheid. The chapter contends that financial inclusion needs to be aligned to the general populace's needs and it has to help deliver services expected by the majority. The argument is that global apartheid is not just a metaphor: it is a reality marked by the operation of undemocratic institutions that systematically generate economic inequality. Therefore, financial inclusion through agency banking can help to counter the related problems. The chapter examines policies that govern financial inclusion in agency banking through effective use of a wide range of products and services, quality, accessibility, fairness and transparency, formal regulation of entities as well as sustainability. Nyagadza, Kabonga and Hlungwani contend that all these aspects challenge the phenomenon of global apartheid.

Pilisano Harris Masake and Lizazi Eugene Libebe's chapter (chapter 17) discusses human trafficking in the context of globalisation and human security. It touches on issues of inequality, poverty, vulnerability, security, policing systems and technological forces among others. To address the question of human trafficking, this chapter identifies and analyses several practical strategies that may be adopted and applied in combating human trafficking or modern slavery. The strategies that they discuss include education and awareness among the victims and potential victims, curbing demand, allowing citizens to participate in the fight against the scourge, criminalising, prosecution and punishment of offenders, support the victims. In pursuit of these other strategies, the authors argue that there is a need to reconsider and integrate indigenous community policing practices and *Ubuntu* philosophy in combating human trafficking in Africa.

In chapter 18, Artwell Nhemachena, Clifford Kendrick Hlatywayo and Tapiwa Victor Warikandwa examine the current Coronavirus disease (COVID-19) "global pandemic" using the conceptual framework of what they call the coloniality of nudging. Noting ways in which colonialists and slave-drivers similarly nudged Africans by limiting their choice architectures, the chapter connects COVID-19 to colonial pandemics and epidemics through which the choice architectures (environments within which choices are made) of the colonised were limited by the colonialists. It is argued that limiting choice architectures is a way of channelling the behaviour of the enslaved and colonised towards directions desired by the slave-drivers and colonisers. Nhemachena, Hlatywayo and Warikandwa further argue that COVID-19 is also coterminous with the emergence of a world wherein some humans are deemed to be "dispensable" and to constitute "surplus" people. Thus, the chapter argues that COVID-19 effectively constitutes an apparatus with which to nudge the world into the anti-humanist and transhumanist New World Order marked, on the one hand, by the disappearance of humanism and human rights (in particular Ubuntu-based human rights in the African context) and, on the other hand, the emergence of posthumanism, cyborgs, post-liberalism, post-freedom, post-politics, post-democracy and post-identitarianism. In this sense, COVID-19 can be understood as constituting a mask for the anti-humanist and transhumanist New World Order.

BIBLIOGRAPHY

Adebayo, B. (16 October 2019). AU faces backlash after terminating ambassador's appointment. *CNN*. https://edition.cnn.com/2019/10/16/africa/petition-over-sacking-of.

Aftab, M. M. (1991). "UN efforts: Removal of apartheid in South Africa and liberation of Namibia." *Pakistan Horizon*, Volume 44(3), 55–66.

Belay, M., and Nyambura, R. (24 June 2013). GM crops won't help African farmers. *The Guardian*. https://www.theguardian.com/global-development/poverty.

Blausten, R. (1976). "Foreign investment in the Black Homelands of South Africa." *Foreign Affairs*, Volume 75(299), 208–223.

Bond, P. (2006). *Looting Africa: The Economics of Exploitation*. London: Zed Books.

Butler, J., Rotberg, R. I., and Adams, J. (1978). *The Black Homelands of South Africa: The Political and Economic Development of Boputhatwana and KwaZulu*. Berkeley: University of California Press.

Eleftheriadis, P. (2010). "Law and sovereignty." *Law and Philosophy*, Volume 29(5), 535–569.

Flores, D. S. (2018). "Transhumanism: The big fraud-towards digital slavery." *International Physical Medicine & Rehabilitation Journal*, Volume 3(5), 381–392.

Gostin, L. O. (30 April 2020). COVID-19 reviews urgent need to strengthen the World Health Organisation. https://jamanetwork.com/channels/health-forum/full article.

Gostin, L. O., Sridhar, D., and Hougendobler, D. (2015). "The normative authority of the World Health Organisation." *Public Health*, Volume 30, 1–10.

Klotz, A. (1995). "Norms reconstituting interests: Global racial equality and U.S. sanctions against South Africa." *International Organization*, Volume 49(3), 451–471.

Mlambo, A. S. (1997). *The Economic Structural Adjustment Programme: The Case of Zimbabwe; 1990–1995*. Harare: University of Zimbabwe Publications.

Mukonoweshuro, E. (1991). "Between Verwoerd and the ANC: Profiles of contemporary repression, deprivation, and poverty in South Africa's 'Bantustans'." *Social Justice*, Volume 18(1/2), 170–185.

Nhemachena, A. (2018). Beyond Eurocentric human rights jurisprudence and towards animality? Humanoid robots and the decomposition of African humanism and personhood. In Nhemachena, A., Warikandwa, T. V., and Amoo, S. K. (eds.). *Social and Legal Theory in the Age of Decoloniality: (Re-)Envisioning Pan-African Jurisprudence in the 21st Century*. Bamenda: Langaa RPCIG.

Nhemachena, A. (2019a). Anticipating African economic futures – Or is it time to look in the rear view mirrors? Land restitution, unemployment and the figure of the post-human. In Warikandwa, T. V., Nhemachena, A., Mpofu, N., and Chitimira, H. (eds.). *Grid-Locked African Economic Sovereignty: Decolonising the Neo-Imperial Socio-Economic and Legal Force-Fields in the 21st Century*. Bamenda: Langaa RPCIG.

Nhemachena, A. (2019b). Enjoying queer sex but forgetting to repossess African land? Between land and orifices in Zimbabwe. In Nhemachena, A., and Warikandwa, T. V. (eds.). *From African Peer Review Mechanisms to African Queer Review Mechanisms? Robert Gabriel Mugabe, Empire and the Decolonisation of African Orifices*. Bamenda: Langaa RPCIG.

Nhemachena, A. (2021). *Kusina amai hakuendwe*: Diasporan Zimbabweans, COVID-19 and nomadic global citizenship. In Endo, M. (ed.). *Africa Potentials for Convivial World-Making*. Bamenda: Langaa RPCIG.

Nhemachena, A., and Bankie, B. F. (2017). Footsoldiers of the new empire or horizontal saviours? Interrogating civil society organisations and fundamentalism in twenty-first century Africa. In Nhemachena, A., and Mawere, M. (eds.). *Africa at the Crossroads: Theorising Fundamentalism in the 21st Century*. Bamenda: Langaa RPCIG.

Nhemachena, A., Hlabangane, N., and Kaundjua, M. (2020). "Relationality or hospitality in twenty-first century research? Big Data, Internet of Things, and the resilience of coloniality on Africa." *Modern Africa: Politics, History and Society*, Volume 8(1), 105–139.

Nhemachena, A., Hlabangane, N., and Matowanyika, J. Z. Z. (eds.). (2020). *Decolonising Science, Technology, Engineering and Mathematics (STEM) in an Age of Technocolonialism: Recentring African Indigenous Knowledge and Belief Systems*. Bamenda: Langaa RPCIG.

Nhemachena, A., and Mawere, M. (2019). *Necroclimatism in a Spectral World (Dis) Order? Rain Petitioning, Climate and Weather Engineering in 21st Century Africa*. Bamenda: Langaa RPCIG.

Nhemachena, A., and Mawere, M. (eds.). (2020). *Securitising Monstrous Bottoms in the Age of Posthuman Carnivalesque? Decolonising the Environment, Human Beings and African Heritages*. Bamenda: Langaa RPCIG.

Nhemachena, A., and Warikandwa, T. V. (eds.). (2017). *Mining Africa: Law, Environment, Society and Politics in Historical and Multidisciplinary Perspectives*. Bamenda: Langaa RPCIG.

Nhemachena, A., and Warikandwa, T. V. (eds.). (2019). *From African Peer Review Mechanisms to African Queer Review Mechanisms? Robert Gabriel Mugabe, Empire and the Decolonisation of African Orifices*. Bamenda: Langaa RPCIG.

Nhemachena, A., Warikandwa, T. V., Mpofu, N., and Chitimira, H. (2019). "Explosive economic minefields in invisible neo-imperial force-fields: An introduction to decolonising economies in Africa." In Warikandwa, T. V., Nhemachena, A., Mpofu, N., and Chitimira, H. (eds.). *Grid-Locked African Economic Sovereignty: Decolonising the Neo-Imperial Socio-Economic and Legal Force-Fields in the 21st Century*. Bamenda: Langaa RPCIG.

Nhemachena, A., Warikandwa, T. V., and Mtapuri, O. (2017). "Transnational corporations' land grabs and the on-going second mad scramble for Africa: An introduction." In Warikandwa, T. V., Nhemachena, A., and Mtapuri, O. (eds.). *Transnational Land Grabs and Restitution in an Age of the (De-)Militarised New Scramble for Africa: A Pan-African Socio-Legal Perspective*. Bamenda: Langaa RPCIG.

Nyamnjoh, F. B. (2015). *C'est L'homme Qui Fait L'homme: Cul-de-sac-Ubuntuism in Cote d'Ivoire*. Bamenda: Langaa RPCIG.

Pawasarat, J., and Quinn, L. M. (2013). Wisconsin's mass incarceration of African American males: Workforce challenges for 2013. *ETI Publications*, 9. https://dc.uwn.edu/eti_pub/9.

Rinke, A., and Nebehay, S. (19 August 2020). Exclusive: Germany, France want more funding, power for WHO as part of sweeping reforms. *Reuters*. https://www.reuters.com/article/us-health-coronavirus.

Roberts, D. E. (2004). The social and moral cost of mass incarceration in African American communities. *Faculty Scholarship at Penn Law*, 583. https://scholarship.law.upenn.edu/faculty_scholarship/583.

Shiva, V., and Shiva, K. (2019). *One Earth, One Humanity vs. the 1%*. Los Angeles: PM Press.

Thomson, J. A. (17 July 2015). Why is Africa reluctant to use GMO crops. *World Economic Forum*. https://www.weforum.org/agenda/2015/07/why-is-africa-reluctant.

Van Onselen, C. (1980). *Chibaro: African Mine Labour in Southern Rhodesia, 1900–1933*. London: Pluto Press.

Chapter 2

The Relevance of Jurisprudence as a Course of Study

Samuel Kwesi Amoo and Clever Mapaure

INTRODUCTION

Jurisprudence as a law module in law schools should not be merely presented as a restatement of theories. There is ample evidence in case law from various jurisdictions demonstrating the relevance of jurisprudence in the judicial process. This chapter seeks to highlight this primary fact and establish that jurisprudence is an integral part of both the legislative and judicial processes of the legal systems of many countries. It further attempts to establish that value-neutral principles of legality, which have been used as the justification for the totalitarian abuses of positive law are capable of being explained in jurisprudential theories. Furthermore, it also attempts to explain that not all principles of legality emanating from the courts are value neutral. For instance, a great deal of case law is based on value judgements. This goes to establish the relationships between these principles and jurisprudential theories. Specific references to some pre- and post-independence Namibian and South African cases are made in the attempt to explain judicial behaviour in jurisprudential theories as a consequence of the prevailing political and legal regimes. This chapter is primarily devoted to the question of the relevance of jurisprudence in both judicial and legislative processes. It also seeks to address the issue of the apparent dearth of legal theories propounded by jurists of African pedigree in contemporary jurisprudence.

Jurisprudence as a module is taught at almost all the Anglophone universities in Africa. Our encounter with jurisprudence as a law module has been at two levels, namely, at undergraduate and graduate tuition levels, as students and lecturers of the module. Notably, in whatever capacity, either as a student or lecturer at universities in Africa, there have been pervasive issues associated with the teaching of jurisprudence as a law module; namely, the relevance of jurisprudence as a course of study; the reliance on theories of jurists of ancient repute and the status of jurisprudence of African pedigree. This chapter explores the question of the relevance of jurisprudence as a law module by looking at how jurisprudential theories can be utilised in the courts.

THE RELEVANCE OF JURISPRUDENCE IN THE LEGAL PROCESS

The genesis of this subliminal attention to the relevance of legal theories in the legal process may be traced to the methodology and the anticipated learning outcomes of jurisprudence as a course of study in the curricular of law faculties. Conclusions drawn from experience tend to indicate that the teaching of jurisprudence, especially, at the undergraduate level, has to a large extent, been a restatement of theories that students are expected to agree or disagree with in lectures and tutorials. A similar approach has been taken by the earlier writers of publications on *jurisprudence.* However, one must concede that this trend has changed. William and Miers (Twining and Miers 1986) depart from this traditional approach. MDA Freeman, in his advocacy of the holistic approach to the study of jurisprudence under the title "The Relevance of Jurisprudence," states that:

> Jurisprudence involves the study of general theoretical questions about the nature of laws and legal systems, about the relationship of law to justice and morality and about the social nature of law. A proper discussion of questions such as these involves understanding and use of philosophical and sociological theories and findings in their application to law. A study of jurisprudence should encourage the student to question assumptions and to develop a wider understanding of the nature and working of law. Questions of theory constantly spring up in legal practice, though they may not be given very sophisticated answers. (Freeman 2001, 2–5)

Jurisprudential theories on the nature and function of law almost invariably deal with the relationship between theories of law and the legal process. In other words, hypotheses on law are meant to be utilised as tools to analyse law towards better understanding of the legal systems. The task of unravelling and understanding the nature of law is an enterprise that encompasses the application of legal theories to the entire legal process, including the promulgation of the law. To achieve this objective, the teaching of jurisprudence must be purposively oriented. It is not a difficult enterprise for one to identify theories of law as the underlying principles of both court decisions and legislation.

Let us start with natural law for example. There is ample evidence in both the legislative and judicial processes of the application of the principle advanced by the proponents of natural law that the validity of law must be measured against some moral ethical and formal requirements and/or imperatives. Not all judgements on principles of legality are value neutral. This is manifested in judgements of superior courts in cases on, for example, inheritance, the defence of necessity and sexual orientation. The question of the relationship between law and principles of morality or ethics and the moral criteria for the evaluation of positive law and the implications of their application constitute the core postulates of naturalists. It can certainly be argued that Lord Devlin (Devlin 1965) was an exponent of value judgements and advanced the position that law, especially the criminal law, can be used to enforce principles of morality because the state has a claim to legislate on matters of morals. In the famous English case of *Shaw v DPP* (1962) AC 220; (1961) 2 WLR 897 HL, the concept of the courts of law their inherent jurisdiction over the community's morals was discussed at length by the House of Lords. Shaw was convicted on several charges, including publishing an obscene libel (a booklet in which prostitutes advertised their services) and conspiring to corrupt public morals. On appeal to the House of Lords, the question arose as to whether the courts possessed moral jurisdiction. Lord Simonds argued that:

> When Lord Mansfield . . . said (R *v Delaval* (1763) 3 Burr 1434) that the Court of King's Bench was the *custos morum* (guardian of morals) of the people and had the superintendence of offences *contra bonos mores)* against good behaviour, he was asserting, as I now assert, that there is in that court a residual power, where no statute has yet intervened to supersede the common law, to superintend those offences which are prejudicial to the public welfare. Such occasions will be rare, for Parliament has not been slow to legislate when attention has been thoroughly aroused. But gaps remain and always will remain, since no man can foresee every way in which the wickedness of man may disrupt the order of society.

In *Re Sigsworth: Bedford v Bedford* (1934) All ER Rep.113, the court pronounced itself on the propriety/validity of the claim of an adjudged murderer to inherit the property of his victim. The reasoning of the court was grounded on the well-established principles of morality that public policy precludes a sane murderer from taking a benefit under his victim's will. In coming up with this decision, the court held that the principle was to be extended in its application to the construction of Acts of Parliament so that general words which might include cases obnoxious to the principle must be read and construed as subject to it. Thus, it was held that the principle of public policy which precludes a murderer from claiming a benefit conferred on him by his victim precludes him also from claiming a benefit conferred on him, in case of his victim's intestacy, by a statute.

In *Riggs v Palmer* 115 NY 506, the facts of which are similar to those in *Re Sigsworth,* the court approached the issue on moral grounds and used the rationality principle to deny the claim to the property. The law principle applied by the court in interpreting the statutes that regulate the making, proof and effect of wills and devolution of property was that if any absurd consequences arise that are manifestly contradictory to common reason, such statutes are void. Therefore, judges are at liberty to expound the relevant statutes by equity and only *quoad hoc* disregard it. The court held that all laws as well as all contracts may be controlled in their operation and effect by general fundamental maxims of the law based on principles of morality. One such maxim is that no one shall be permitted to profit by his own fraud, or to take advantage of his own wrong, or to found any claim upon his own iniquity, or to acquire property by his own crime. It was held that one cannot vest oneself with title by crime. Consequently, one ought to be deprived of any interest in an estate deemed to have been acquired under such circumstances.

In *Dudley v Stephens* (1881–1885) All ER Rep.61, two prisoners who had wilfully murdered a young boy on the high seas upon the chance of preserving their own lives by feeding upon his flesh and blood after he was killed. In their defence, they sought to rely on the defence of necessity. The court rejected the plea of necessity. The principle applied was that there is no absolute and unqualified necessity to preserve one's life by killing an innocent, unoffending and unresisting boy unless the killing can be justified by some well-recognised excuse by law. In view of that principle, the court opined that:

> Though law and morality are not the same, and though many things may be immoral which are not necessarily illegal, yet the absolute divorce of law from morality would be of fatal consequence, and such divorce would follow if the temptation to murder in this case were to be held by law an absolute defence of it. It is not so.

Consequently, the court found that there was no legal justification of the homicide and prisoners were declared guilty of murder.

In *Port Elizabeth Municipality v Peoples Dialogue on Land and Shelter and Others* (2000) 2 SA 1074 (SE), the respondents had unlawfully occupied land owned by the applicant and earmarked by it for housing. Upon refusal by the respondents to vacate the land so that the applicant could proceed with its development, the applicant applied for their eviction. In dealing with this matter, the court was forced to balance two diametrically opposed fundamental principles emanating from the implementation of the Prevention of Illegal Eviction from and Unlawful Occupation of Land Act 19 of 1998, to bring about a "just and equitable" decision. On the one hand, there was the traditional real right inherent in ownership reserving exclusive use and protection of his property to the land owner. On the other hand, there was the genuine despair of people in dire need of adequate accommodation. The court took the position that the interpretation and application of what constitutes "just and equitable" in relation to both competing interests obliged the court to "break away from a purely legalistic approach and have regard to extraneous factors such as morality, fairness, social values and implications and circumstances which would necessitate bringing out an equitably principled judgment", that is, rationality had to be employed to temper the rigours of analytical positivism.

Common law principles are grounded on rationality and reasonableness. Students of jurisprudence are well aware of the central position of rationality in natural law. Lord Simonds in the quotation cited above alludes to the residual power of the courts and/or judicial activism. In the context of interpretation of statutes, this may arise in the interpretation of the penumbral, grey, or nondescript areas of the law. Courts have often times used the concept of reasonableness, public policy and what Justice Holmes terms the "inarticulate major premise" as the basis of their decisions. Are these variables not related to theories of law such as natural law, Roscoe Pound's jural postulates and the assertion by the realists that the law is what the judges declare to be the law? What is the role of jurisprudence in all this? Teachers of jurisprudence must be able to provoke students through appropriate pedagogic methodology to be able to trace the relationship between legal theories and the exercise of this jurisdiction by the courts. There are several reasons advanced for the courts to exercise this residual jurisdiction.

The tyrannical use of positive law by a variety of political regimes has its jurisprudential dimensions. It is not farfetched for law students in Namibia and South Africa to discuss the constitutional developments of the two countries in the context and perspectives of legal theories.

In the context of the Namibian constitutional development, one can discuss the jurisprudence evolving from the decisions of the Namibian courts, during the pre- and post-apartheid era within the context and perspectives of natural law and analytical positivism.

In the context of legal theories, analytical positivism can certainly be discussed as the underlying principle of the literal rule of interpretation where the courts treat fidelity to legislative enactment as the overriding value. It has also been pointed out that the South African legal system was constrained before the promulgation of that country's new Constitution by the jurisprudence and principles of legislative supremacy and analytical positivism (Dugard 1971, 181–200, 1981, 372–387). John Dugard asserts that an empirical study of the legal process in South Africa leads to the conclusion that "judges adopt(ed) a neutral, non-activist position in their approach to human rights issues and that a form of positivism may account for this phenomenon" (Dugard 1981, 373–387). This position has been confirmed by MM Corbett, the then Chief Justice of South Africa, in his presentation to the Truth and Reconciliation Commission in these words:

> There are, and in the past always have been, constraints upon the exercise of judicial power. A judge is not always at liberty to do what he thinks is the best or most fair or expedient. He is required to dispense justice in accordance with the law. In the ideal situation law and justice coincide, but this need not necessarily be so, especially where the law consists of legislation. These truths are reflected in the oath which a judge is required to take upon assuming office. Prior to the coming into effect of the Interim Constitution, Act 200 of 1993, the oath prescribed was by section 10(2)(a) of the Supreme Court Act 59 of 1959 and it required the judge to swear to . . . administer justice to all persons alike without fear, favour or prejudice, and . . . in accordance with the law and customs of the Republic of South Africa. (Corbett 1998, 18)

This apologia was re-echoed in the submission of Justice G. Friedman as follows:

> By virtue of the oath which the judges were required to take, they had no option but to apply the laws of apartheid whether that was anathema to them or not. The only latitude they had was to ameliorate the harshness of these laws if they found them to be ambiguous. (Friedman 1998, 59)

It has been argued that the decisions of the superior courts of South Africa created a particular type of jurisprudence with an epistemological paradigm towards denial of civil liberties and a departure from liberal principles and presumptions of common law that constitute the cornerstone of Roman-Dutch law, especially, when interpreting legislation dealing with state security, interracial marriages and legislation *sui generis* (Dugard 1981, 372–387). Dugard asserts that:

> Positivism has not served South Africa well as a guide to legal thinking. It has prevented judges from fully perceiving that the judicial function is essentially an exercise in choice in the penumbral area of legal uncertainty, and it has discouraged lawyers from playing a more active role in the protection of those principles which make up the country's legal heritage. (Dugard 1978, 397)

The courts of South West Africa/Namibia were bound to be influenced by this jurisprudence and the related epistemological paradigm by the application of the doctrine of judicial precedent and stare *decisis*. As pointed out by Justice Bryan O'Linn:

> The (Namibian) Courts functioned in a legal system where Parliament was supreme, not the Constitution and that notwithstanding the considerable constraints of security legislation and the effects of racist indoctrination of society, the courts generally allowed considerable freedom of expression and the opportunity to place both sides on the table in accordance with long established legal procedures. (O'Linn 2003, 179)

Prior to the coming into effect of the Namibian Independence Constitution and also for reasons stated above, the Namibian judiciary comprised South African-appointed judges applying South African law with the constraints imposed by reliance on the jurisprudence of legislative supremacy and analytical positivism. However, after the enactment of Proclamation R. 101 of 1985 by the South African government, the Namibian legal system assumed a dimension that engendered an important differentiation and digression, both in principle and practice, from the South African legal system. The Proclamation provided for a Bill of Rights against which the Namibian courts could test and review the validity of certain laws and administrative decisions and actions. These rights included protection against execution without due process (article 1); liberty, security of person and privacy (article 2); equality before the law (article 3); fair trial (article 4); freedom of expression (article 5) peaceful assembly (article 6); freedom of association (article 7); participation in political activity (article 8); freedom of culture, language, tradition and religion (article 9); freedom of movement and residence (article 10); and ownership of property (article 11)). In this regard, reference should be made to the observations of Bjornlund when he wrote:

> Cases in South West Africa Supreme Court between 1985 and 1990 seem especially significant because of the vigour with which the South African appointed Namibian judges expressed civil liberties principles regardless of whether the holdings were explicitly based on the constitutional text . . . To the extent that the South African Appellate Division prevented the Namibian judges from giving effect to the Bill of Rights through judicial review, those judges often used grounds other than the Bill of Rights to emasculate repressive legislation and in the process created a bully pulpit to take the place of genuine judicial review. These cases suggest that Namibian judges believed that courts are empowered to promote the rule of law, and the Bill of Rights only strengthened their resolve. (Bjornlund 1990, 429)

The South West Africa/Namibian Courts had to apply South African laws in their judicial functions in the area of civil law where the application of the generality of Roman-Dutch common law was an issue. The courts were always at liberty to be guided by the liberal presumptions and principles of

Roman-Dutch common law on the principles relating to practices and behaviour *contra bones mores*. Their mettle and resolve to maintain these liberal ideals were put to the test in cases where the application of relevant South African legislation was potentially inconsistent with the rule of law and civil liberties of the individual (O'Linn 2003,179). As mentioned earlier, these were cases involving the security laws and emergency regulations including detention without trial, the presumptions of fair trial in criminal proceedings, the review of administrative discretion, restrictions on freedom of expression and apartheid laws regulating residence.

In *State v Heita & Others* 1987 (1) SWA 311, the defence succeeded in their argument that the Bill of Rights constituted higher imperatives which executive/legislative enactments should comply with for the achievement of the rule of law. This was a ruling based on principles of constitutional supremacy and the moral principles against retroactivity. In this case, Judge Levy's views on constitutional interpretation were a clear testimony of the shift from analytical positivism to reliance on the Bill of Rights as higher imperatives to promote the rule of law (O'Linn 2003, 24).

As indicated earlier, after the attainment of independence and sovereignty Namibia adopted a Constitution with an entrenched Bill of Rights and a provision that elevates the Constitution as the Supreme Law of Namibia (Article 1(6) of the Constitution of Namibia, provides that this Constitution shall be the Supreme Law of Namibia). This effectively replaced the doctrine of legislative sovereignty which came from the history of the legal systems of both South Africa and Namibia. Constitutional supremacy has provided the Namibian judiciary with a constitutional leverage to promote the principles of the rule of law, constitutionalism and to protect and advance the fundamental rights of all persons. This exercise has involved the interpretation of the Constitution and the Namibian Courts adopted a values-oriented approach to the interpretation of the Constitution since independence. The Namibian courts have developed a jurisprudence based on value judgements and an epistemological paradigm rooted in the values and norms of the Namibian people. Justice Strydom, the Chief Justice of the Republic of Namibia (at the time), in his address to the judicial officers at the first retreat of the Office of the Attorney-General at Swakopmund November 20–22, 2002, stated:

> It is trite that ordinary presumptions of interpretation will not independently suffice in interpreting such a document (constitution) and that our Courts must develop guidelines to give full effect to the purport and aim of our Constitution. The Constitution remains the Supreme Law of Namibia from which all laws flow and against which all laws can be tested . . . in interpreting the Constitution, particularly Chapter 3, the Courts are often called upon to exercise a value judgment. It was this exercise that led the Court in the Corporal Punishment by

Organs of State (1991 (3) SA 76 (NmS) decision to encompass both aspects of constitutional interpretation and judicial independence" (The address was entitled, *Namibia's Constitutional Jurisprudence-The First Twelve Years).* Chapter 3 of the Namibian Constitution entrenches fundamental human rights and freedoms. The Constitution, however, draws a distinction between rights and freedoms. Article 21(2) for example, provides that they "shall be exercised subject to the law of Namibia, in so far as such law imposes reasonable restrictions on the exercise of the rights and freedoms conferred by the said sub-article, which are necessary in a democratic society and are required in the interests of the sovereignty and integrity of Namibia, national security, public order, decency or morality, or in relation to contempt of court, defamation or incitement to an offence".

These limitations together with the general nature of the provisions of a constitution, *prima facie,* require the exercise of the constitutional jurisdiction of the courts in interpreting the grey or penumbral areas of the Constitution as to, for example, what constitutes decency or morality. The Namibian courts have since independence been called upon to interpret similar provisions of the Constitution and as mentioned earlier, they have adopted what may be termed, to borrow John Duggard's expression, a natural law-cum-realist or a purposive approach and have developed a particular jurisprudence based on the values of the Namibian people. These cases include the interpretation of the constitutionality of legislative provisions or practices relating to corporal punishment (*Ex Parte Attorney-General, Namibia: in re Corporal Punishment* 1991(3) SA 76 (NmS)) the restraining of prisoners by chaining them to each other by means of metal chains *(Namunjepo & Others v Commanding Officer, Windhoek Prison & Another,* 2000 (6) BCLR 671 (NmS)), homosexual relationships. (*The Chairperson of the Immigration Selection Board v Erna Elizabeth Frank & Another* 2001 NR 107 (SC)). In the address mentioned above, Justice Strydom stated:

> in the two *Mwandinghi* cases the High and Supreme Courts of Namibia accepted the principle that a Constitution, and more particularly one containing a Bill of Rights, calls for an interpretation different from that which courts traditionally apply to ordinary legislation. Dealing with instances where the courts were required to make value judgments the corporal punishment case authoritatively laid down that a court, in coming to its conclusion, should objectively articulate and identify the contemporary norms, aspirations and expectations of the Namibian people and should have regard to the merging consensus of values in the civilized international community. These cases set the tone for Namibian courts and the way it was required of them to interpret the constitution.

In the case of *Minister of Defence v Mwandinghi* 1992 (2) SA 355 (NmSC), the Namibian Supreme Court approved the *dictum* in *S v Acheson* 1991 NR 1 (HC) at 10 AB that:

> (t)he Constitution of a nation is not simply a statute which mechanically defines the structures of government and the relations between the government and the governed. It is a mirror reflecting the national soul, the identification of the ideals and aspirations of a nation; the articulation of the values bonding its people and disciplining its government. The spirit and tenor of the Constitution must therefore preside over and permeate the processes of judicial interpretation and judicial discretion.

In the case of *Government of the Republic of Namibia & Another v Cultura 2000* (I993 NR 328 (SC) at 340 B-D; 1994 (1) SA 407 NmSC, at 418 F-G), the Late Mahommed CJ, reiterated this approach to the interpretation of the Constitution as follows:

> A Constitution is an organic instrument. Although it is enacted in the form of a statute, it is *sui generis.* It must broadly, liberally and purposively be interpreted so as to avoid the "austerity of tabulated legalism" and so as to enable it to continue to play a creative and dynamic role in the expression and the achievement of the ideals and aspirations of the nation, in the articulation of the values bonding its people and in disciplining its Government (See also *Minister of Defence, Namibia v Mwandinghi* 1993 NR 63 (SC) at 68-71 (1992 (2) SA 355 (NmS) at 361-3); *S v Acheson* 1991 NR 1 (HC) at 10A-C at 10 A-C (1991 (2) SA 805 (Nm)) at 813 A-C)).

As mentioned above, this approach requires judicial decisions to be oriented to value judgements and it has been followed in Namibian decisions. However, the value-judgement approach raises questions regarding:

i. the identification of not only the values but also the authoritative source that has the mandate to do so;
ii. the inherent elements of the subjectivity of this approach;
iii. the nature of the mechanism to be employed to ascertain the values and norms and
iv. the binding effects of the values.

These issues will be addressed in the analysis of the cases in which this approach has been used to interpret relevant provisions of the Constitution. One could perhaps refer to the views of Justice Strydom on the question of the ascertainment of the norms and aspirations of the people of Namibia as an initial point of reference. In the same address, he stated that:

to determine the contemporary norms, aspirations and expectations of the Namibian people is a most important requirement when it comes to the interpretation of the Constitution and how it should be applied. What those norms and aspirations are is not always easy to determine and the parameters thereof is always not limitless. When the Constitution says that there shall be no discrimination on the grounds of sex, even if there is a majority who may be in favour of such discrimination it cannot change the express prohibition against discrimination, set out in the Constitution. Many of the norms and aspirations of the people are contained in the Constitution itself. Discrimination on the basis of certain stereotypes is rooted out. The dignity of all persons is guaranteed by the Constitution. The theme against the violation of a person's dignity starts with the preamble of the Constitution and can be traced to many of the provisions of Chapter 3 and other provisions of the Constitution. These and other provisions should constantly be in the mind of the judge called upon to interpret the Constitution.

The matter relating to the identification and ascertainment of the norms and values of the Namibian people, unfortunately, does not rest there. It is trite that constitutional provisions and legislation *sui generis* are couched in a language that is often broad and vague and therefore, will require judicial interpretation. The Constitution may be the reference point to identify these norms and values but as Justice Strydom correctly pointed out the parameters of determining them are limitless.

Inhuman or degrading conduct is inconsistent with article 8 of the Constitution. In *Ex Parte Attorney General Namibia: in re Corporal Punishment,* 1991 (3) SA 76 (NmS) at 91 DF national institutions were used as sources of identification of norms and values of the society and therefore, added another dimension to the jurisprudence. The court held that:

> The question as to whether a particular form of punishment authorized by the law can be said to be inhuman or degrading, involves the exercise of value judgment by the court. It is however a value judgment which requires objectively to be articulated and identified, regard being had to the contemporary norms, aspirations, expectations and sensitivities of the Namibian people as expressed in its national institutions and its Constitution, and further having regard to the emerging consensus of values in a civilized international community (of which Namibia is a part) which Namibians share. This is not a static exercise. It is a continually evolving dynamic. What may have been acceptable as a just form of punishment some decades ago, may appear to be manifestly inhuman or degrading today. Yesterday's orthodoxy might appear to be today's heresy.

It will be observed from the *Cultura 2000* case that even though the court laid down the value-oriented or purposive approach to the interpretation of the Constitution as one to be used by the Namibian Courts in interpreting the Constitution, the *Corporal Punishment* case identified some institutions and the values that should be protected under the Constitution.

In *the Chairperson of the Immigration Selection Board v Erna Elizabeth Frank and Elizabeth Khaxas* 2001 NR 107 (SC), the court identified some of these institutions and gave some guidelines regarding how the norms and values are to be identified. In the words of Justice AJA O'Linn the institutions referred to were also described in the decision of the High Court in *State v Tcoeib* 1993 (1) SACR 274 Nm at 284 D-E. The *Shorter Oxford English Dictionary* was referred to wherein the following definition appears:

> an established law, custom, usage, practice, organization or other element in the political and social life of the people; a well-established or familiar practice or object; an establishment, organization or association, instituted for the promotion of some object, especially one of public utility, religion, charitable, education.

The Namibian parliament, courts, tribal authorities, common law, statute law and tribal law, political parties, news media, trade unions, established Namibian churches and other relevant community-based organisations can be regarded as institutions for the purposes hereof.

In this court's judgement in *S v Namunjepo* 2000 (6) BCLR, 671 NmS, at 678 H, it was also accepted that the parliament, is one of the most important institutions to express the current day values of the people of Namibia. This attracts a few comments and observations. First of all, parliament's legislative function is exercised by way of debates to ascertain the weight of authority to be placed on an opinion and in most cases a decision is taken by the requisite majority vote followed by the enactment of the relevant legislation. In this case, the guideline being offered here is not adequate as it does not indicate whether the contemporary values of the Namibian people are those that have been articulated and enacted in the form of legislation, or whether they are those that constitute mere expressions of opinions of members of parliament in the form of debates. To do justice to the decision of Justice O'Linn, however, it must be added that with reference to the recognition of homosexual relationships in Namibia, certain specific reasons and yardsticks, including public opinion, were provided for the reliance on parliament as one the sources of the identification of the values and norms of the Namibian people. He stated that:

> The relevance and importance of public opinion in establishing the current or contemporary values of Namibians when the court makes its value judgment, has been discussed in various decisions, including the decision in *State v Vries*.

> To avoid any misunderstanding, I reiterate what I said in *State v Vries* in this regard; "In my respectful view the value of public opinion will differ from case to case, from fundamental right to fundamental right and from issue to issue. In some cases, public opinion should receive very little weight; in others it should receive considerable weight. It is not a question of substituting public opinion for that of the court. It is the courts that will always evaluate the public opinion. The court will decide whether the purported public opinion is an informed opinion based on reason and true facts; whether it is artificially induced or instigated by agitators seeking a political power base; whether it constitutes a mere 'amorphous ebb and flow of public opinion' or whether it points to a permanent trend, a change in the structure and culture of society . . . The court therefore is not deprived of its role to take the final decision whether or not public opinion, as in the case of other sources, constitutes objective evidence of community values."

The issue of public opinion raises questions relating the doctrine of separation of powers and the very nature of public opinion as a legitimate source of law because of, *inter alia,* the vicissitudes inherent in the nature of public opinion. It would appear from the position taken by the court in this case that the integration of public opinion as a legal norm by the courts is a balancing act between what could be called the "utopian" and "Rawlsian" approaches to the issue of public opinion.

The other element involved in the issue of public opinion is one relating to separation of powers. It is recognised that it is within the purview of the mandate of the legislative branch of government to legislate for matters raised to the level of national awareness by public opinion. It is also an acceptable principle that in the interpretive jurisdiction of the courts, the courts have a creative role that may involve the interpretation of the Constitution or an ordinary legislative enactment. The courts will be called upon to make authoritative pronouncements on grey or penumbral areas of the law, sometimes involving areas of public policy and values of the society, without first referring the matter to the legislature to be settled in a legislative enactment in certain circumstances. The courts will therefore have to play a balancing act to avoid what might constitute usurpation of the functions of the legislature. The degree of reliance on public opinion has to be determined by whether the issue involves the interpretation of a constitutional provision or a mere legislative enactment. In this regard, the courts will have to be mindful of the fact that values may not be equated with public opinion and that it is the function of the courts to protect the rights of minorities in the face of the vicissitudes of the public opinion of the majority.

With regard to the binding effect of values, the general principles of the judicial process (cognizance being taken of the principles of separation of powers, judicial precedent and *stare decisis*) are that these values become binding if they are incorporated in legislation that is not inconsistent with the higher imperatives of a constitution or where they are given the status of legal principles through judicial interpretation. The source of the binding effect of values elevated to principles of law through judicial interpretation is located and inherent in the constitutional jurisdiction of the courts and therefore, these values get the authoritative stamp of legal principles and the force of law through the decisions of the court and in this regard, through decisions involving interpretation of the Constitution.

Legal theories have also been used by the courts to determine the legitimacy of certain regimes the resolution of which has involved the analysis and application of the Kelsynian theory of the Grundnorm. Here, one has in mind such cases as *EK Sallah v The Attorney-General for and on behalf of the Government of Ghana* Const. SC 8/70 and *Madzimbamuto v Lardner-Burke, NO and Another NO* 1968 (2) SA 284 (See also Palley 1967, 263).

One may argue that the above exposition only represents the application of legal theories to the substantive law and may seek to ascertain the relevance of jurisprudence in the area of the procedural law. Lon Fuller's principles of the inner morality of the law and Hart's rule of recognition are jurisprudential theories meant as yardsticks to measure the validity of the positive law.

HOME-GROWN AFRICAN LEGAL THEORIES

During colonial times African laws existed as a hodgepodge of colonial compromises acceded to by expansionist figures consolidating their conquests. Central to this, was the perception that Africa lacked a theory of jurisprudence. The belief in the nonexistence of what qualifies as law was split into two schools of thought being the absence thesis and the sceptical argument. The absence thesis posits that there is no African jurisprudence (Idowu 2006, 9–24). The nonexistence of African philosophy of law is premised on the nonexistence of written records about the law. Is this tenable? In all societies, a people's philosophy constitutes their system of thought and has always served as the basis for their attitudes towards life. In this light, to deny the existence of African law is to deny the premise of African life and the values that underpin it. Philosophy does not exist only in written form but also in substance. A system of thought does not have to be written in order for a philosophy to exist. It is thus superfluous to suggest that because there are no written records in Africa regarding any jurisprudence there is no African jurisprudence. In fact, the problem of written ness is a defect common to almost all legal philosophy whether in the West, Africa or the Far East (Durant 1954, 556–561). The Africans saw no need to write as they viewed the verbal word as more effective than the written mode.

Face-to-face storytelling is captivating and personal. Literacy was rare. The written word was hard to come by and cool, distant, and impersonal by comparison. Elders in oral societies passed along their wisdom in poetry and song. When those cultures disappeared, however, their ideas and whole civilisations, in effect were lost to us (Solomon and Higgins 1996, 6).

Closely aligned to the absence theses is the sceptical argument. The sceptical argument also rests on the premise that is nothing called African jurisprudence. The reason is not that it is not written but that there is simply no philosophy of law with the tag "African." There is acceptance of some ordered political systems in African communities but they do not have a philosophy of law. This is basically scepticism. The scepticism has different variations among the authors. Driberg denies that Africans have a clear conception of law thus "symbols of legal authority . . . are completely absent, and in the circumstances would be otiose" (Driberg 1934, 237–238). Holleman contends that an African jurisprudential frame is missing and lacking in the African system of rules thus there is nothing like an African jurisprudence (Holleman 1974, 12). M'Baye similarly argues that the rules governing social behaviour in traditional African societies are the very negation of law (M'Baye 1975, 56). In the same vein, Smith postulated that African peoples only know of customs instead of law (Smith 1965, 32). The thrust of the theory thus is that even if Africans had indigenous systems of social control, such systems lacked substantially, any trace of legality, legal concepts and legal elements.

The attack on the idea of African jurisprudence has been reduced to the idea that African rules of societal control and norms could not be distinguished from rules of polite behaviour. The basis for this assertion and the denial of African jurisprudence, perceptively, can be explained in the light of three reasons: first, the absence of a legislative system, with the existence of a formal court system and legal officials; second, due to the absence of a recognised system of sanctions; and thirdly, the presence on a large scale of authoritarianism which is not subject and controlled by law. Interestingly, the import of these attacks consists in the view that African jurisprudence is at best queasy (Idowu 2006, 6).

To appreciate African jurisprudential claims, it is important to put on the Afrocentric goggles. Sustainable African peace and educational development should be informed by flexible Afrocentricity. Afrocentricity is a world view that considers African people, their cultures, histories, collective struggles, needs and aspirations, to be central to the interpretation and utilisation of data. Afrocentrists commonly contend that approaching knowledge from a Eurocentrist perspective, as well as certain mainstream assumptions in the application of information in the West, has led to injustices and inadequacies in meeting the needs of African peoples, meaning indigenous, black Africans and the peoples of the African diaspora. As a result, the Afrocentrist paradigm is one that seeks to discover and also reinterpret information through African eyes, utilising it in ways that inure to the benefit of Africans.

Contrary to Western scepticism about the existence of African jurisprudence, some of the first generation of African leaders, such as Kwame Nkrumah (*Nkrumaism and Consciencism*); Leopold Senghor (*Negritude);* Julius Nyerere (*Ujamaa*); Kenneth Kaunda (*Humanism)* and of late, Thabo Mbeki *(African Renaissance)* have attempted to articulate philosophies relating to the nature and soul of the African personality. These theories were regarded with a great deal of scepticism by academics who regarded these as political ideologies rather than philosophical principles worthwhile the analysis and support of the academia to the extent that these theories or philosophies have virtually vanished with the demise of these leaders from political offices. The aforementioned ideas on African jurisprudence will now be dealt with in more detail below.

UBUNTU AND *UBUNTUISM*: AFRICAN HUMAN RIGHTS?

If we take the celebrated concept of *unhu* (Shona) or *ubuntu* (Zulu) for example we see that there we have a typical African human rights jurisprudential concept. *Ubuntu* is in itself a revitalisation of African values and moral principles. It owes so much to African traditional law. This concept was born bred and is developing in Africa. The book *African philosophy through Ubuntu* which Ramose published in Zimbabwe in 1999 (Ramose 1999, 1–200) is in several respects a remarkable and refreshing contribution to African legal philosophy. It is clear in this book that African societies have suffered greatly in the process or law making and trying to legally identify themselves, but their lasting value orientation in terms of *Hunhu/Ubuntu* holds up an alternative in the sense that it advocates a renewed concern for the human person.

Ubuntu as a form of African philosophy blends in with other potential, imagined or actual gifts of Africa to the wider world: African music and dance, orality and orature, kingship, healing rituals in which trance and divination play major roles, a specific appreciation of time, being and personhood. All these aspects are cultural achievements from which especially the North Atlantic could learn a lot and (to judge by the latter's dominant forms of popular music and dance throughout the twentieth century) is increasingly prepared to learn, in a bid to compensate such spiritual and corporeal limitations and frustrations as may be suspected to hide underneath the North Atlantic's economic, technological, political and military complacency (Van Binsbergen 2001, 6).

Viewed as a moral and political exhortation and an expression of hope for a better future, *ubuntu* just like *humanism* to be discussed below, creates a moral community, admission to which is not necessarily limited by biological ancestry, nationality, or actual place of residence. To participate in this moral community, therefore, is not a matter of birthright in the narrower, parochial sense. If birthright comes in at all, it is the birthright of any member of the human species to express concern vis-a-vis the conditions under which her or his fellow humans must live, and to act on that basis. This moral community consists of people sharing a concern for the present and future of a particular local or regional society, seeking to add to the latter's resources, redressing its ills, and searching its conceptual and spiritual repertoire for inspiration, blueprints, models, encouragement in the process. Thus, *Ubuntu* cannot exist in a society driven by purely positivistic principles. The success of *Ubuntu* in Africa will only be had if principles of African natural law are maintained. In fact, the concept in itself embodies African traditional law principles which have to be enforced from an Afrocentric perspective for the integration of societies divided by colonialism and apartheid. In South Africa, this is referred to as the programme of the African renaissance (Van Binsbergen 2001, 8; Mbeki 1999; Diop 1948, 57–65; Diop 1996, 33–45).

Ubuntu has to be aided by the central concept of Afrocentricity, a concept which seeks to protect African values. It creates moral community for the revitalisation of African morals and values. A cultivation of concepts such as *Ubuntu*, focusing not on a particular locality or region, but on the African continent as a whole is needed (Van Binsbergen 2001, 10). The people thus implicated may be expected to identify with each other and to be solidary in the pursuit of their concern (Asante 1987, 24). Whoever sets out to publicly deconstruct and even debunk the available conceptual and spiritual repertoire, dissociates from this moral community, rents its fabric, and jeopardises its project and the project of African integration.

HUMANISM: AFRICAN CHRISTIANITY?

During his presidency of Zambia, Kenneth David Kaunda promoted what he called "Christian Humanism." This was a philosophy with an African flavour heavily laden with natural law principles. In this philosophical concept, he stressed the importance of the centrality of humanity while embracing a progressive conception of Christianity in an African context incorporating principles of African culture. Kaunda believed that education that respects African values and cultural norms is the vehicle in the upliftment of an African people and in broadcasting the humanist thought. On the humanitarian front, Kaunda believed that with humanism as amoral and truly African concept, Zambia would become a leader in the fight against apartheid (Van Binsbergen 2001, 11).

In 1986, Kaunda lost a son to AIDS and influenced by his humanism he discussed the ordeal publicly. Driven by the same philosophy he became and has since become an outspoken activist in opposition to the disease, promoting the use of condoms in preventing its expansion. Bill Jones makes the point that Black Humanists reflect upon their own circumstances when developing their world view:

> black Humanism emerges as part of a debate that is internal to black life and thought. It is not a spin-off of the enlightenment, the scientific revolution or, as Deotis Roberts has suggested a borrowing from Comte. Rather, as Benjamin Mays, an eminent representative of black Christian theism, has correctly perceived, black incredulity about the divine, as well as agnosticism and atheism "do not develop as the results of modem science, nor from the observations that nature is cruel and indifferent; but primarily because in the social situation, [the black American] finds himself hampered and restricted . . . Heretical ideas of God develop because in the social situation the 'breaks' seem to be against the Negro and the black thinkers are unable to harmonize this fact with the God pictured by Christianity." (Van Binsbergen 2001, 41)

From the foregoing, it is easy to see that Zambian humanism and *Ubuntu* are not in the first place factual descriptions. Van Binsbergen comments that these concepts primarily express the speaker's dreams about norms and practices that allegedly once prevailed in what are now to be considered peripheral places, while the speaker herself or himself is situated at or near the national or global centre. Van Binsbergen goes on to postulate that such dreams about the past and the periphery are articulated, not because the speaker proposes to retire there personally or wishes to exhort other people to take up effective residence there, but because of their inspiring modelling power with regard to central national and even global issues – in other words, because of these dreams' alleged persuasive/perlocutionary nature outside the peripheral domain in which they are claimed to originate and to which they refer back. Thus, one commentator said:

> If, thirty years later, I have much less difficulty in identifying, in my capacity as a social actor in a concrete Southern African setting, with Zambian humanism, and with ubuntu, it is because I have enjoyed, for these many years, the (part-time) membership of the kind of local communities by distant reference to these two ideologies have been constructed in the first place. (Van Binsbergen 2001, 10)

Throughout the 1970s and 1980s Africa learnt Zambian *humanism*, was not so much as a value system spelled out explicitly but especially more implicitly as a diffuse value orientation informing the lives of the people. It was in terms of this very value orientation that African people were allowed to share their lives, and despite frequent transgressions both on the part of colonisers and the colonised and apartheid enforcers and the oppressed. This admission on both sides of the communities has been one of the greatest sources of pride and joy that underline *humanism* just like *Ubuntu*.

Some philosophers have asked questions regarding whether large numbers of Africans accept a humanist life stance? That remains to be seen. However, there is no good reason why humanism cannot have great influence in Africa. We have already seen some of the precedents. With enough aid from the West, humanist organisations in Africa could make numerous positive contributions to the continent. Why should the twenty-first century not be the century of Humanism if African traditional law principles as embodied in humanism itself are not eroded or diluted? In the words of Humanist philosopher Kurtz:

> Is it not the turn of the Eupraxophers [i.e., Humanists] to set forth-to draw wisdom, not based upon philosophy alone, but upon the sciences, and concerned not simply with the love, but the practice, of wisdom? We need men and women of good intentions and moral empathy and compassion, who drink deeply at the well of Sofia, and attempt to apply with reason and understanding the best knowledge of the day. They are unwilling to abandon ethical means to achieve ideal ends (as the Utopian purveyors of ideals of past generations did with tragic results), but will attempt to help develop the highest potentialities, for the fullness of life.

From this, there is no doubt that the success of humanism can only be realised if principles of traditional law in an African context have been revitalised and embraced.

NEGRITUDE: THE FLAVOUR OF BLACKNESS AND AFRICANNESS

In 1990, Leopold Sadar Senghor, the former Senegalese president, was elected to the International Academy of Humanism. The academy is composed of Humanists that are committed to free inquiry, the scientific methods of investigation, and the furthering of "Humanist ethical values and principles." Senghor was largely responsible for popularising the term "negritude" a way of identifying with "Blackness" without having to draw upon culture, language, or nationality (Wilder 2005). Senghor is thus best known for championing negritude on a grand scale. Hence negritude, as interpreted by Senghor, encompasses "the whole of the values of civilization-cultural, economic, social, and political-which characterize the . . . Negro African World"

(Colvin 1981, 229). Senghor admitted that negritude was spirit centred and marked by a characteristic rhythm and symbolism when he said "[t]there is a certain flavour, a certain odour, a certain accent, a certain black tone inexpressible in European . . . [languages]" (Vaillant 1976, 158).

Inspired by African values elements of African traditional law in a world of competing perspectives on law, Senghor's particular brand of negritude was largely a neo-African cultural challenge in which he equated cultural by-products such as art as a marker of civility (Sidney and Kelly 1994, 87). This connects clearly to Okafor's assertion that African jurisprudence can only be understood in the context of African ontology. Once this happens we are apt to have labels that *ubuntu*, humanism or negritude is racism. This is what happened to Senghor. Because negritude surfaced partly from French colonial rejection, critic Mphahleles claimed that, "Negritude is an inferiority complex," though Senghor retorted that negritude is neither self-hate nor racialism. Yet, considering Senghor's negritude against the Western notion of a universal civilisation, it becomes clear that Senghor's quest "to assimilate, not be assimilated" indicates a more inclusive civilisation rather than sheer mimicry of Western concepts (Bunnin and James 1996, 575).

Senghor's cultural policies in Senegal reflect negritude schemata fully aware of the potential power of African people creating and defining their own images (Campbell 2006, 33). For example, implementing the *Ecole de Dakar*, a school of art in Senegal, it was clear that he wanted Africa to have "a certain active presence in the world, or better, in the universe" (Senghor 1995, 46). This indicates the spiritual and cosmological link between African values and African identity and culture. In this light, Senghor called African art a constructive "spiritual food" parallel with the aim of being while Skurnik argued that Senghor's artistic vision propelled African people from mere consumers/recipients to creators/producers of a civilised world (Skurnik 1965, 365). Showing the foundation of negritude as African Natural law, Senghor illustrates that African art held the possibilities of dignity, necessity and sustenance for the future via negritude (Campbell 2006, 34), with his stance on African culture catalysing a national Senegalese identity within African nationalism and African socialism (Skurnik 1965, 367). Therefore, African Socialism can be regarded as an off-shoot of African traditional law – an interesting relationship which needs another deeper analysis.

CONSCIENCISM: THE PRINCIPLE OF AFRICAN LIBERTY

The book *Consciencism: Philosophy and Ideology for De-Colonization with Particular Reference to the African Revolution* (Nkrumah 1970) is pre-eminently a work in socio-political philosophy but remains helpful in exhuming some important concepts of African traditional legal thought in a world of competing perspectives. In this book, Nkrumah's conception of African particularity does not warrant the presumption that African and European cultural differences are mutually exclusive but as Oruka insightfully observes, "one remarkable characteristic of this [African professional] philosophy is that it employs techniques commonly associated with European or Western philosophy. Yet, contrary to the general claim, such techniques are not unique to the West" (Oruka 2003, 48). *Consciencism* formed the foundation of African nationalism hence the underlying principle is that of human liberty.

Oruka (2003, 48) is clear, although African professional philosophy shares certain commonalities, definitive techniques, with European/Western philosophy, yet these techniques are not unique to Western legal or political philosophy. Nkrumah's philosophical practice, from an ethnophilosophical assessment, more approximates the Western prototype albeit it assumes the character of an African Marxist philosophical text, and hence stands in opposition to bourgeois academic philosophy (McClendon 2003, 3). His professional philosophical outlook has a dialectical relation to ethnophilosophy. Indicating the influence of African natural law principles, McClendon comments correctly that "Nkrumah's adoption of the Marxist philosophical problematic over and against African metaphysical exclusivism was the *tour de force* that sustained his particular professional mode of discourse" (McClendon 2003, 4). McClendon comments further:

> Nonetheless, when particularity is conflated with African exclusivism, we discern that texts in African philosophy assume the determinate character of ethnophilosophy. For instance, W.E. Abraham's The Mind of Africa and/or Julius Nyerere's Ujamaa are closer to ethnophilosophy. Nkrumah departed from this philosophical tradition and its idealist ontological foundation. Those readers who identify a philosophy of particularity with ethnophilosophy are bound to be lost when approaching his text. For in Consciencism, rather than describe how the Akan conceptualizes the nature of being as pivotal to philosophical practice, Nkrumah instead scrutinized and inquired into such philosophical problems as the contradiction between materialism and idealism and the dialectical process of categorical conversion. (McClendon 2003, 4)

CONCLUSION

It is clear from here that for the African possessed of the colonial syndrome we find that the intrinsic value of African moral and value systems is uppermost. Their clarion call, "Philosophy for the sake of philosophy" means African philosophical and legal thought should not be lowered from the cultural clouds of speculation into the contaminated terrain of material practice (McClendon 2003, 3). Nkrumah himself writes and repeats that philosophy is a purely cultural product not to be used as a means to any other ends; moreover, it is a product of a specific cultural heritage (McClendon 2003, 5, 55 and 63). Given that some philosophers argue about African philosophy from outside, Nkrumah says that such philosophies are bereft of African social and political conditions, such conceptions of philosophy can only assume an alienated form as well as an exclusivist approach which will not aid in the revitalisation of African values and moral systems in a world of competing perspectives (McClendon 2003, 5, 55 and 63).

Consciencism, for Nkrumah, is a Marxist text in an African context inspired by African values and black identity. *Consciencism* is thus employed in the interest of the ideological struggle against African metaphysical exclusivism and African socialism. It is a text that affirms scientific socialism (Marxism) in the particular circumstances of African reality by the accentuation of the need to affirm materialism as the ontological foundation for scientific socialism. Furthermore, these perspectives on philosophy are short of the humanist values that are so vital and foundational to African traditional society and which constitute what Nkrumah defined as "the African personality" (McClendon 2003, 79). Thus, Nkrumah and Kaunda as the fathers of Africa get their theories and ideologies married here, a clear reflection of the value of African ontology and principles of African value systems and traditional law in contemporary African jurisprudence.

Cultural and national identity underpin the; concept of *ubuntu*, humanism, negritude and consciencism. These four concepts have a lot in common. They are typical African ideologies which identify themselves with the values of the African race. They are underpinned by dignity, liberty and unity among the people. They advocate an African that is founded on humanity, humanness, liberty and conscience as African- identity. These concepts cannot be divorced from African ontology and value systems thus they were and are still generally acceptable across the continent. General acceptability shows the universality of the principles of law that underpin them. This is a typical characteristic of African traditional law in a globalised world of competing perspectives on law. If universally acceptable and appreciable principles which underpin these broad ideologies are normative and derived from African cultural and moral precepts which can be revitalised for sustainable continental development.

BIBLIOGRAPHY

Asante, M. K. (1987). *The Afrocentric Idea*. Philadelphia: Temple University Press.

Bjornlund, C. E. (1990). "The Devil's Work? Judicial Review Under a Bill of Rights in South Africa and Namibia." *Stanford Journal of International Law*, Volume 26, 391–433.

Campbell, C. Z. (2006). "Sculpting a Pan-African Culture in the Art of Negritude: A Model for African Artist." *The Journal of Pan African Studies*, Volume 1(6), 28–42.

Colvin, L. G. (1981). *Historical Dictionary of Senegal*. Metuchen, NJ: The Scarecrow Press, Inc.

Corbett, M. M. (1998). "Presentation to the Truth and Reconciliation Commission." *South African Law Journal*, Volume 115, 17–20.

Devlin, P. (1965). *The Enforcement of Morals*. London: Oxford University Press.

Dugard, J. (1971). "The Judicial Process, Positivism and Civil Liberty." *South African Law Journal*, Volume 88, 181–200.

Dugard, J. (1978). *Human Rights and the South African Legal Order*. Princeton, NJ: Princeton University Press.

Dugard, J. (1981). "Some Realism about the Judicial Process and Positivism – A Reply." *South African Law Journal*, Volume 98, 372–387.

Durant, W. (1954).*Our Oriental Heritage*. New York: Simon and Schuster, 556–561.

Ex Parte Attorney-Genera, Namibia: In re Corporal Punishment 1991(3) SA 76 (NmS).

Freeman, M. D. A. (2001). *Introduction to Jurisprudence*. London: Sweet & Maxwell.

Friedman, G. (1998). "Submission to the Truth and Reconciliation Commission on the Role of the Judiciary." *South African Law Journal*, Volume 115, 56–63.

Idowu, W. (2006a). "African Jurisprudence and the Reconciliatory Theory of Law." *The Cambrian Law Review*, Volume 37, 5–10.

Idowu, W. (2006b). "Against the Skeptical Argument and the Absence Thesis: African Jurisprudence and the Challenge of Positivist Historiography." *The Journal of Philosophy, Science & Law*, Volume 6(2), 9–24.

McClendon, J. H. (2003a). "Nkrumah's Consciencism as Philosophical Text: Matters of Confusion." *Journal of African Philosophy*, Volume 3, 48.

McClendon, J. H. (2003b). "Nkrumah's Consciencism as Philosophical Text: Matters of Confusion." *African Philosophy*, Issue 3, 3.

Minister of Defence, Namibia v. Mwandinghi, 1993 NR 63 (SC) at 68-71 (1992 (2) SA 355 (NmS), 361–363.

Namunjepo & Others v Commanding Officer, Windhoek Prison & Another, 2000 (6) BCLR, 671 NmS, 678 H.

Nkrumah, K. (1970). *Consciencism: Philosophy and Ideology for De-Colonization with Particular Reference to the African Revolution*. London: Heinemann.

O'Linn, B. (2003). *Namibia: The Sacred Trust of Civilization Ideal and Reality*. Windhoek: Gamsberg Macmillan.

Oruka, H. O. (2003). "Sagacity in African Philosophy." *International Philosophical Quarterly*, Volume 22(4), 383–393.

Palley, C. (1967). "The Judicial Process: UDI and the Southern Rhodesian Judiciary." *Modern Law Review*, Volume 30, 263–275.

Ramose, M. B. (1999). *African Philosophy Through Ubuntu*. Harare: Mond Books.

Sedar, S. L. (1995). *Negritude: A Humanism of the Twentieth Century*. Berlin: DeGrutyer.

S v. Acheson, 1991 NR 1 (HC) at 10A-C at 10 A-C (1991 (2) SA 805 (Nm)) at 813 A-C).

Sidney, L., and Kelly, R. D. G. (eds.). (1994). *Imagining Home: Class, Culture, and Nationalism in the African Diaspora*. New York: Verso.

Skurnik, W. A. E. (1965). "Leopold Sedar Senghor and African Socialism." *The Journal of Modern African Studies*, Volume 3(3), 349–369.

Smith, M. G. (1965). "The Sociological Framework of Law." In H. Kuper and L. Kuper (eds.). *African Law: Adaptation and Development*. Berkeley, CA: University of California Press.

State v Heita & Others 1987 (1) SWA 311.

The Chairperson of the Immigration Selection Board v Erna Elizabeth Frank & Another, 2001 NR 107 (SC).

Twining, W., and Miers, D. (1986). *How to Do Things with Rule*. London: Weidenfeld & Nicolson.

Vaillant, J. G. (1976). Perspectives on Leopold Senghor and Changing the Face of Negritude. *Anthropology Southern Africa Review of Books*, Volume 2, 154–162.

Van Binsbergen, W. M. J. (2001). "Ubuntu and the Globalisation of Southern African Thought and Society." In van Binsbergen, W. M. J. (ed.). *Intercultural Encounters: African and Anthropological Lessons Towards a Philosophy of Interculturality*. Berlin/Muenster: LIT Verlag.

Wilder, G. (2005). *The French Imperial Nation-State: Negritude & Colonial Humanism Between the Two World Wars*. Chicago, IL: University of Chicago Press.

Chapter 3

Decolonisation of Legal Education (Miseducation and Ignorance)

Excerpts from Afrocentric Perspectives in Southern Africa

Pilisano Harris Masake and Lizazi Eugene Libebe

INTRODUCTION

Africa and the African states bore witness to the legal paradigm shift from the pre-colonial and colonial to post-colonial African legal system. Colonialism disrupted and obliterated the pre-colonial African legal system. This chapter critically addresses the issue of decoloniality from a distinct normative imperative of the Afro-legal centricity. The theoretical standpoints in this chapter are premised on a working assumption that there is a need to trace the pre-colonial African legal philosophies and to understand how these philosophies informed the political, social and economic cohesion. Further, there is a need to decolonise law to include organically created laws and the relevant legal education. The decolonised legal education should inform the legal curriculum. Derived from the normative imperatives and theoretical assumptions above, it is this chapter's argument that for decoloniality of legal education to be evocative, it is necessary to trace, revive and, where necessary, modify the pre-colonial African legal philosophies and incorporate same in the current legal education.

The chapter departs with a primer note on education and legal education that subsisted during the pre-colonial era. The object is to discount the ahistorical discourse levelled against the African philosophies. The assumption is clear. There was, there is and there will always be an African legal philosophy that needs to be taught in our current universities. The primer note further serves to place the discussion in its proper context. That is to say, decoloniality of colonial knowledge or legal education is justified since there was a disruption of African philosophies at the behest of colonial laws and (mis)education. It is important to note here, an argument that colonialism, particularly colonial education, inculcated negative knowledge or by extension ignorance into the African scholars. The essence of this postulation is to underscore the effects of colonialism, namely: colonialism did not bring positive knowledge and power, rather, it massively brought ignorance and powerlessness, which in turn requires to be decolonised. The second part provides an exposition on how the African legal philosophies were obliterated by colonialism and how coloniality of knowledge continues unabated to perversely place the legal education into disarray. Third, the chapter provides a working definition of what decolonising legal education is. This definition articulates into addressing the importance and justification of decolonising the legal education. Further, the chapter outlines how teaching and curriculum may be applied to advance the decolonisation agenda. Finally, challenges that underpin the decolonisation agenda are identified and recommendations on how to counter such challenges are postulated.

A PRIMER ON LEGAL EDUCATION IN PRE-COLONIAL AFRICA

The modern perceptions on education retained much resemblance and share overwhelming similarities, notwithstanding the current geo-environment and enhanced technological revolution to the classical perceptions on education. This argument is supported by the fact that both the modern and classical philosophy on education, conceive education to entail the process imbued with the art of facilitating learning, transfer or acquisition of knowledge, values, skills, habits and beliefs (Bartlett and Burton 2016, 11). The classical (pristine *cum* pre-colonial era) pedagogical methodologies in Africa and worldwide, among others, included narration or telling of stories, discussions, teaching, to mention a few (Assmann 2002, 27). The process of learning, in the pristine period in Africa, was effected or could take place, both, through informal (important to note here that the concepts of formal or informal are used in their relative context. For instance, what may be perceived as formal in one situation may equally be construed as informal in another. Notably, the practice of unwritten cultural and customary rules by a given society may easily be construed and labelled as "informal" in the eyes of a society that have caused its customary rules to be ascertained and written) and in formal settings, legal education was not an exception. Interestingly, Africa is recorded to have hosted the first university (University of Timbuktu) in the world that taught a variety of programmes, including, legal education. This buttresses the proposition that the African legal philosophies were taught beyond storytelling, through a legal curriculum (Nhemachena et al. 2018). These classical pedagogical methods still find relevance nowadays. Legal education, which is this chapter's area of focus, is a *subletora* branch of education which is perceived as conglomerate of specialised form of pedagogical field of study that focuses on the law. Likhovski described legal education with reference to "the process in which law students are taught what law is and what is not, the description of law relates to society and the role of lawyers in society" (Likhovski 2002, 75).

There is a plethora of legal literature (especially, literature produced during the African renaissance agenda) that has unearthed, grounded and confirmed the existence of pre-colonial African legal pedagogics and philosophies. This includes written and unwritten or oral traditions, practices of *Ubuntu*, culture and customs (Hellen 2002, 3; Graness 2016). This literature, in the defence of the existence of African legal pedagogics and philosophies during the pre-colonial era, discounts the ahistorical characterisation of the African legal pedagogics. At this juncture, Graness observes that:

> [T]he characterization of Africa's precolonial indigenous cultures as significantly ahistorical in character has been dismissed as patently false. The significance of the word "primitive," as originally used by non-Africans to type Africa's cultures – *legal education* – was that those cultures could serve as contemporary exemplars of how human beings had lived in primeval and pristine times, before recorded history. (Graness 2016, 132)

The essence of these African cultural and customary practices was to inform the political, social and economic cohesion among the African people and states. Simply put, these cultural practices formed the regulatory framework for social and political cohesion. In relation to political cohesion, these practices informed the substantive and procedural aspects of laws that governed a range of activities. For example, rules and laws on coronation, succession in Kingship and Queenship, protocols on intra-relationships, international relations with other Kingdoms or communities or groups of people – which was practised in most of the African societies in the pre-colonial era. Equally, in terms of social cohesion, the pre-colonial laws regulated the administration of marriages; property rights; estates; how criminal suspects and convicts were dealt with; dispute settlements; how the breach of cultural norms were dealt with and punishment, to mention a few. By explication, these African cultural practices informed the prescriptive, adjudicative and enforcement mechanisms for social control of societies. These practices partly put to rest several questions on whether there were any legal philosophies or laws that existed prior to colonisation of Africa. If so, how did these African legal philosophies and laws inform the political, social and economic cohesion?

Therefore, it is undeniable that prior to colonialism in Africa, there existed legal pedagogics. Having confirmed the existence of legal pedagogics in pre-colonial Africa, the questions that follow are: What happened to the African legal pedagogics which existed prior to colonialism? Why is the African legal pedagogy not developed and taught at universities within Southern African Development Community (SADC) member states with the exactitude comparable to the coloniser's (northern and western) legal education. Why is the latter occupying the large chunk of the universities' legal education curriculum? These above questions are unpacked in the succeeding discussion. A prevue, from the Afrocentric perspective need to be highlighted here: that is, colonial legal education is perceived to have propagated miseducation. It is labelled as miseducation premised on fact that it failed to incorporate African legal philosophies, discounted the African values and sciences. There are various theoretical assumptions or arguments that underlie the extinction of the African legal philosophies in universities, *inter alia*, the claim of lack of great figures whose philosophy could be studied; the perception that African philosophy is not logical and it is not identified with scientific or empirical science (Omotosho 2014, 62) and colonialism. This chapter recognises, with the exactitude that they deserve, all other factors that may directly or indirectly have had impact on the extinction of the African legal philosophies in universities within SADC member states. However, the scope of this chapter is limited to colonialism and decoloniality. The succeeding section unpacks the impact of colonialism and coloniality on legal education.

IMPACT OF COLONIALISM AND COLONIALITY ON LEGAL EDUCATION

To place the discussion on decolonising legal education in its proper context, it is vital to concisely examine the impact of colonialism and subsequent coloniality on legal education. Equally, to comprehend the impact of colonialism and coloniality on legal education and the necessity of decoloniality, this chapter argues that one needs to have a fair grasp of the conceptual meaning of the terms: colonialism and coloniality. The description of these terms helps in a myriad of ways, including, delineating and weaving among the various forms (classification) of colonialism. The effort, here, is not to achieve some form of individualisation of the types of colonialism but to afford the distillation of ideas around the nature and impact of colonialism. There are several forms of colonialism as there are differentiated levels of power and domination at various domains such as social relations, wealth and economic status, and it may stretch further to include the family and clan, intragroup (homogeneity) and intergroup (heterogeneity) levels (Horvath 1972, 46).

The differentiated power and domination noted above, renders it difficult to, with precision, of course from a *Eurocentric-cum-Postmodernist* perspectives, to define the concept of colonialism. On this score, the intellectual meaning of the concept of colonialism is perceived by *Eurocentric-cum-Postmodernist* subscribers to be contentious. Otherwise stated, the Eurocentric infused literature suggests that there is no universal definition of what colonialism is. In instances where colonialism is defined, such definition disassociates colonialism from the criminogenic scheme that underlay it. A survey of literature on what constitutes colonialism reveals this definitional deficit. Oxford Dictionary defines colonialism with reference to, "The policy or practice of acquiring full or partial political control over another country, occupying it with settlers, and exploiting it economically" (Oxford Online Dictionary 2019). Horvath defines colonialism with reference to, "A form of domination – the control by individuals or groups over the territory and/or behaviour of other individuals or groups" (Horvath 1972, 46). Further, Grosfoguel defines colonialism with reference to:

> Colonial situations enforced by the presence of a colonial administration such as the period of classical colonialism. Colonial situation is explained with reference to the cultural, political, sexual, spiritual, epistemic and economic oppression or exploitation of subordinate racialised/ethnic groups by dominant racialised/ethnic groups with or without the existence of colonial administrations. (Grosfoguel 2007, 213)

It is observed, from a cluster of these definitions that the core attributes that accompanied colonialism are concealed, namely: theft, dispossession of land and properties, murders, exterminations, displacement, looting and plunder, to mention a few. In this context, colonialism is seen as a form of a negative domination and adverse exercise of power of one (the coloniser) over the other (the colonised). On this score, this chapter adopts, subject to amendments noted below, the formulation and characterisation of colonialism devised by Horvath, without considering these classifications as hard and fast forms of colonialism. Horvath identifies three categories (situations) of colonialism, namely:

A) Colonialism in which the relationship between the coloniser and colonised is the extermination (*genocide, killings, dispossession, theft, exploitation*) of the latter.
B) Colonialism with object of assimilative relationship, where the coloniser stands as the "cultural donner" and colonised as "cultural host."
C) Colonialism without wholesale acculturation but does not exclude cultural exchange (Horvath 1972, 46–47).

Properly understood, from an Afrocentric enunciation, empowerment and mastery over own (African affairs by Africans) affairs are necessary. Of course, this justifies the call for decolonisation. However, as is demonstrated below, in the context of colonialism, arbitrary power and domination, implies subjecting the colonised (African states and peoples) to the rule and administration of the colonisers. Beyond the implantation and imposition of the colonial rule and ill-administration is the abuse of such power and dominion by the coloniser. The assumption is that power and dominion were abused by the coloniser/settler, in that, such abused power was used or it facilitated the commission of heinous crimes, such genocide, rapes, displacement of indigenous people, theft of indigenous people's land, and plunder of resources to mention but a few (Nhemachena et al. 2018).

It is important to note here that scholars, to a great extent, perceive colonialism to be related to imperialism and vice versa. The conceptual meaning of imperialism entails a, "political and economic control and *exploitation* over a dependent territory" (Grosfoguel 2017, 212). In this chapter, these concepts are used conveniently in as far as they relate to decolonising legal education. In this context, colonialism is understood to entail a practice, whereas, imperialism is construed as the ideology (plundering of resources for the unjust enrichment of the empire) that underpins the practice (colonialism), the identical malevolent doppelgangers. The categories of colonialism identified by Horvath above, to a great extent, present an enormous impact on legal education and education in general. For instance, colonialism with object to exterminate the colonised (genocide, forced removal, plunder), indirectly impacts or decimates the laws and cultural practices of the exterminated population. This could procure direct decimation of the laws of the exterminated community. However, the indirect impact resonates from adverse argument that the object of extermination could be to annihilate or wipe out a given community but not its practices. Wherefore, the unintended consequences of extermination could include extinction of such community's laws and cultural practices.

That is, if a population is exterminated such a population's laws and cultural practices cease or risk being dowsed. Cultural practices are directly linked to education, and by extension, to legal education. The link between cultural practices and legal education is uncontested because it is supported by legal theories which presuppose that law is an organic creation of the national community (Likhovski 2002, 76). The theory postulates that the law must be derived, in a didactic manner, from the customs and cultural practices of the community itself, rather than imposition of the laws imported from the cultural practices of other communities. The Afrocentric perspective subscribes to this postulation, and it does not turn a blind eye on the merits of comparative study in the field of law, or the application and enforcement of international law, but rather, it seeks the African enunciation on African philosophies. The theory on organically created law, has been recognised by various countries' high statements such as national constitutions, through which, indigenous people's customs and traditions are recognised and elevated to a law status (article 66 of the Namibian Constitution; sections 211 and 212 of the 1996 South African Constitution; section 46(1)) of the 2013 Constitution of Zimbabwe). Contrasted from the form of colonialism with object to exterminate the colonised, colonialism with object of assimilative relationship through which the coloniser is perceived as "cultural donner" and the colonised as "cultural host" attracts much debate when discussing decoloniality of legal education. The latter was the pinnacle of what transpired in most SADC member states in as far as imposition of legal education by the coloniser was concerned.

It was identified above that in pre-colonial era, African legal pedagogy subsisted both in an informal and formalised manner. Formalised, in the sense that the African universities, such as University of Timbuktu that taught legal education. In as far as the informal setting is concerned, the facilitation of African legal philosophies occasioned through storytelling and imitation, where adults taught the youth, *inter alia*: the customs, cultural practices and history. It is important to note that the formalisation of legal education, on account of University of Timbuktu, was achieved in Africa, though not at larger scale, prior to colonialism. At the advent of colonialism, the English legal education was introduced in the colonies. For example, aspirant lawyers in the British colonies such as Kenya, Tanganyika (Tanzania) and Northern Rhodesia (Zambia), to mention a few were trained in Britain where they joined the Inns of Court (Likhovski 2002, 75). Through these arrangements, these aspirant legal practitioners were exposed to the English legal education to the exclusion of the African legal education (Ndulo 1985, 446). Likhovski argued that the object of training the "colonial law scholars in Britain was to imbibe them with the glorious traditions of the English Bar" (Likhovski 2002, 78). The significance of this strategy was to extend colonisation to go beyond the sphere of political domination and to include the art of indoctrinating and colonising minds and knowledge production. Thereby, teaching the colonial law scholars English law at the expense of the African indigenous laws (Seroto 2018, 4). The colonial legal education lacked the African cultural flavour or African organic linkage (Ocheni and Nwankwo 2012). Ocheni and Nwankwo (2012, 51) argue that "the colonial education was not rooted in African culture and therefore could not foster any meaningful development within the African environment because it had no organic linkage." On this score, it is important to point out the adverse nature of the colonial education. There is scholarly agreement that the colonial masters introduced poor education to the colonised. Writing on the relationship between the colonial master's schools and those of the colonised, Kelly postulated that:

> Colonial school systems, while established by Europeans for persons in their overseas African and Asian possessions, were rarely organised along the lines of metropolitan schools. Not only were these schools organisationally different from metropolitan schools; they held little or no promise of evolving into the comprehensive systems of education that could be found, for example, in Britain and France. (Kelly 1971, 209)

It is an uncontested fact that there was a distinction (both in structure and curriculum) between the standard of education that was taught to the colonised when compared to the standards of education that were taught to the children of the colonial masters. The substandard nature of education to which the colonised were exposed to, led to the production of miseducation and ignorance among the colonised. Derived from the Afrocentric perspective, the assertion is clear: colonial education, of which legal education is not an exception. It is squarely the source of the present experienced powerlessness, ignorance and inequality among the African people. These uncontested theoretical assertions buttress the assumption that not only did the colonisers impose their administration and thus subjecting the colonised to such imposed administration, but colonialism included imposition of the colonisers' legal education on the colonised. Postulating the experience and impact of colonialism in Zimbabwe Sibanda argued that:

> Soon after colonisation in 1890, the colonial government dismantled, and in some places replaced, traditional governance structures with "modern" state institutions. It embarked on a number of measures that corrupted and eroded the institution of traditional leadership. Some of the powers of traditional leaders, such as the power to allocate land, were usurped by the European moguls. Thereafter, the role of the institution was under constant redefinition by the successive governments in the colonial period. (Sibanda 2016, 53)

Deduced from Sibanda's exposition above, it is agreeable that the impact of dismantling traditional governance did not only or just alter the structure of the traditional leadership, rather it negatively affected the cultural practices and customs of the communities. For instance, prior to colonialism traditional leaders applied their customs and cultural practices that governed the allocation or distribution of land parcels to community members. It obviously follows that there were certain traditional rules that guided traditional leaders in allocating the land. The fact that the traditional leaders' powers of allocating land were, at the onset of colonialism, usurped by the moguls inks the decimation of the traditional rules which were applied by the traditional leaders. By explication, these traditional rules were not carried over by the moguls. Rather, the moguls applied the coloniser's law to orchestrate or facilitate theft of land. Ocheni et al. (2012, 51) postulates that "colonial education brought about distortion and disarticulation in African indigenous pattern of education which was rooted in African technology. The introduction of colonial education made Africans to abandon their indigenous technological skills and education in preference to one which mainly emphasizes reading and writing." To underscore the above argument, from the Namibian context, Melber elucidates how the German settlers in Namibia unlawfully acquired land from the Namibian indigenous people. Melber postulates that:

> German colonialism created the infamous structures of an apartheid society, in which the forced removal of the colonised people from their land in substantial parts of the country and its subsequent occupation by white settlers became an enduring and essential component of a past that remains alive in the present. The primary resistance against the foreign invasion triggered the first genocide of the twentieth century among the Ovaherero, Nama, and other groups as the main occupants of the eastern, central, and southern regions of the country, where they were forced from their land into so-called native reserves. (Melber 2019, 73–74)

Subsequent to these land dispositions, the settlers introduced laws that protected their criminal acts. These laws are still enforced, in many of the present African countries, of which Namibia is not an exception. An example is the compromise of article 16(2) of the Namibian Constitution which requires payment of compensation in the event where government expropriate land from the owner (colonisers and their descendants). There are questions that may be asked here. Is it legal or lawful to compensate a person who stole the land for the land which he stole? What should be done to restore the ancestral land to the rightful heirs? Revolution? Restitution? These burning questions ignites the decoloniality agenda – the need to decolonise law and legal education and by extension, legal minds. The impact of imposing the coloniser's legal system and education on the colonised is self-evident in the present legal system and education among the formerly colonised states. The legal philosophies that have dominated the legal education within the universities in SADC are those wrought by the colonisers at the expense of the African legal philosophies. For instance, predominantly, the common law of the respective SADC member states is the common law as derived from the cultural practices of their colonial masters. A cavernous inquiry on these issues appears to be addressed by understanding one of the philosophical objects of colonialism. At this juncture, there is scholarly agreement, and as it is well articulated by Grosfoguel that, "the success of colonial world system consists in making subjects that are socially located in the oppressed side of this colonial difference, to think epistemically like the ones on the dominant positions" (Grosfoguel 2007, 213).

To effectuate the above object of colonialism, the colonisers, such as Britain, instead of advocating for legal philosophies that conceive law as an organic creation of the national community and therefore teaching law in its social and historical context, Britain advocated for an adaptive or transferable nature of law. The teaching of law was much concerned with legal philosophies which advanced a theory that law needs not to be created by the society it served, rather, the law could be created by one community and applied by and against another community (Likhovski 2002, 76). The advocated "ease transplant" nature of English law facilitated its acceptance and ordination within the colonised states – of which SADC member states were not an exception. It is demonstrated above that colonialism, indeed had to a great extent impacted the legal education in most of the colonised states. This confirms the claim that the colonisers as *cultural donner* imposed their legal education on the colonised who are the *cultural host*. It is factual that the colonised states, in SADC, all achieved their political independence. However, the consequences of colonialism are still so graphic in many fields of the independent African states and legal education is not an exception. That is, as was stated above, the law and legal education which was wrought by the colonisers still dominate the universities' legal education curriculum in post-colonial era. These post-colonial era effects bring to the fore, the theory of coloniality. Grosfoguel postulates that, "Coloniality allows us to understand the continuity of colonial forms of domination after the end of colonial administrations, produced by colonial cultures and structures in the modern/colonial capitalist/patriarchal world system" (Grosfoguel 2007, 219).

Understood in this context, coloniality refers to the continuity of the colonial exploitation which is evident through the retention and adaptation, *inter alia,* of the colonial hierarchy of systems, politics, manner and methods of administration (*being*) that produced disorder and ignorance. Labour and economic structures which are based on global capitalism (*power*), which produced inequality; and enforcement of Eurocentric forms of miseducation and knowledge production (*knowledge*) of which legal education is not an exception, by the formerly colonised states. Therefore, it suffices to state that the model of coloniality encapsulate various strands, namely, coloniality of *knowledge*, *power* and *being*. The underlying scheme of the theory of coloniality of knowledge is to presuppose that the art of colonialism extended beyond the obvious dialectics of politics and economies (*power*), and liberation of being (*being*) to include coloniality of knowledge or legal mind. Legal theories from the cultural donners continue to shape the legal education within the cultural host states. For instance, the legal positivism theory which sacrifices substance over form formalistic, and it is used to distinguish between norms (law) and anything that does not constitute law. This theory is an affront to the indigenous customary law. Himonga and Diallo argue that "the rules of living customary law cannot be abstracted from their social contexts. They are embedded in the social realities within which people live" (Himonga and Diallo 2017). In this sense, customary law is an organic creation of the national community and it possesses enough linkage to the cultural practices of the national community.

There is scholarly agreement that the object of coloniality of knowledge or ignorance was/is to Westernise different areas of knowledge or ignorance production. The art of Eurocentric form of knowledge accounts for the reluctance and lack of appropriate appreciation of the African legal philosophies within the universities (Seroto 2018, 4). Seroto (2018, 4) further identifies that "the purpose of promoting Western and Eurocentric thought, imagination and knowledge in Africa was to erase the colonised from mainstream existence and place them as "things" in the realm of otherness." The proponents (uncut conservative) of Westernised legal education perceive that the capacity to produce scientific knowledge, theories and philosophies belongs to an exclusive club of the few (*Western men*) to the exclusion of the "others." The effort is to discount and discredit any form of knowledge that is procured or that resides outside the Western realm of knowledge and ignorance as *particularistic* and lacking universal consciousness. These efforts effectuated the subsistence and practice of colonial legal miseducation in the former colonies. Ndima summarises the Westernised point-zero perennial syndrome as follows:

> Western anthropologists conceptualised and defined philosophy in the image of the dominant Euro-American thought systems, which they considered benchmarks for measuring the propriety of all philosophical thought. Consequently, late comers to mainstream philosophical reasoning such as African philosophy had already been excluded as *other* thought systems, when they entered the scene, as an indication of their "unphilosophical" nature. (Ndima 2015, 359)

Ndima explains that the classification of the "other" is the consequence of the West's perceived domination over education or ego politics of knowledge. This domination endeavours to control what knowledge/ignorance is produced, by whom is the knowledge/ignorance produced and the purpose of such knowledge/ignorance production. The *other* philosophies "were so regarded because Euro-American philosophy had already taken centre stage as the norm when the former systems started being considered as thought systems in their own right" (Ndima 2015, 359). The effect is that it renders it difficult for the new philosophies emanating from the realms of the "other" to be recognised and accepted as possessing the requisite requirements of logic and linguistic. The theory of coloniality of knowledge allows academics and politicians to transcend beyond the liberation of the *power* and *being*. Rather, to engage in meaningful conversations with the object of decolonising knowledge or ignorance. The section below deliberates on decolonisation of colonial knowledge with the undertone of legal education.

DECOLONISING LEGAL EDUCATION: WHAT IT IS?

There are burning questions that still lingers long after most African countries attained their political independence. To exemplify some of these burning questions, Mukoma wa Ngugi asked conundrums in his opening remarks at the launch of the Writers Unlimited International Literature Festival in the Hague: "What happened to the villages and towns in Africa after slave traders started disappearing their population?" "What happened to those communities that were raided for their mothers, fathers, sisters and brothers, aunts and uncles?" "How does renaming the streets of Bristol speak, in real terms to towns like Keta still reeling from slavery?" "Can what we in the West are calling decolonisation in philosophical and material terms really address historical inequalities?"(Mukoma wa Ngugi 2020). These questions underscore the understanding of the concept of decolonisation from an Afrocentric perspective. As it is demonstrated above, colonialism was not just the imposition of the colonial master's administration rather, it transcended to include a criminocratic dispensation. Equally, the efforts of decolonisation require more than the symbolic attributes such as political independence, renaming of streets in a bid to restore the breach that was caused by colonialism. The meaning of the concept of decolonisation is dependent on the form or type of colonialism in question, such as coloniality of *power*, *being*, or *knowledge*. Scholars argue that the question of what constitutes decolonisation requires an outlook of various perspectives – as such, it does not admit a one-dimensional answer (Motshabi n.d, 9). In relation to colonisation of being, decolonisation refers to acts or process of elimination or removal of any form of domination of one person or group over the other (Betts 2012, 28–38) and to redesign appropriate sphere of influence where both actors are placed on equal footing (Joseph 2017, 8). Mignolo (2007, 459) defines decolonisation and decoloniality with reference to, "[a]n act or process of working towards a vision of human life that is not . . . structured by the forced imposition of one ideal of society over those that differ, which is what coloniality does and hence, where decolonisation of the mind should begin."

There is a distinction between decolonisation of law and legal education. This distinction is necessary for reasons, *inter alia*, that primarily the law informs legal education. In this regard, Himonga and Diallo (2017, 5) postulate that decolonisation of law, "is defining of law from a non-colonial position and from alternative legal epistemologies. *They further argue that – in this context*, decolonisation draws from different sources of law and normative agencies to promote the transformative potential of law in achieving more social and economic justice."

Decolonising law is a necessary step in the quest of decolonising legal education and subsequent decoloniality of knowledge. As was stated above, the law informs what type of the legal education calculation/curriculum is to be taught, whereas, the latter constitute the legal education. Inevitably, legal education informs knowledge. Scholars argue that there is a link between education of any form and knowledge. On this score, Lakshminath (2008, 607) postulates that:

> [L]egal education is a means by which legal knowledge is transmitted and skills developed . . . a complex matrix of pedagogic and cultural practices that inform, shape and give effect to what information is chosen and how it is understood, transmitted and received.

In this chapter, the link between knowledge and education can be construed as follows: education is a process of gaining knowledge for some useful application, whereas, legal knowledge is facts acquired from legal education. Thus, in the context of this discussion, decoloniality of knowledge and ignorance requires, in the *first* place, to decolonise the legal education system. Decolonising legal education which we linked with decoloniality of knowledge refers to the open-mindedness of the colonial laws and legal education, and simultaneously, to be attentive to the re-definition of the laws with object to formulate laws in the context of a national community, and thereby, recalculate the legal education curriculum to include the re-defined laws, as well as re-mandating the universities from a distinctive non-colonial perspective.

In terms of this definition, the primary object is to embrace the law as an organic creation of the indigenous community and teach the law in its social and historical context without losing grasp of the need of the laws that are created outside the community. This is done, notwithstanding the fact that such laws lack the perceived organic linkage to an indigenous community. A balancing act is required between the competing laws, namely, the organically created laws and legal education as a result of decolonisation on one end, and on the other end, the colonially imposed laws and legal education. There are good reasons for balancing these competing interests, *inter alia*, to encourage pluriverse/pluralism which is key in search of the truth (Motshabi n.d, 10). Further, is to refrain from advancing biased forms of centrism; and, to be attentive to the call for not reducing decolonisation to "some naïve desire of returning to a pristine Africa" (Himonga and Diallo 2017, 5). It is important to note here that decolonisation agenda does not necessarily require the re-adoption, indiscriminately, of the harmful cultural practices i.e. female genital mutilation, corporal punishment. Rather, to ascertain helpful practices that advance humanity. In this context, decolonisation should be with an object to achieve positive outcomes, re-calculate our legal education curriculum to incorporate the African enunciations. As explained above, of course from an Afrocentric perspective, if colonialism is perceived to encapsulate the disdain of the African people underscored by theft, dispossession of land, displacement of people, cause for disorder, extermination, proliferation of slave trade, just to mention a few, then, decolonisation should achieve good objects. In this vein, decolonisation is construed to include restitution or to restore the breach that was committed by the colonial masters, recovery of the ancestral lands, to compensate the indigenous people for the damages caused by colonial masters, and to effectively empower the formally colonised. The intellectual meaning of decolonising education aside, what follows is a discussion on the motivation for decolonising legal education.

MOTIVATION FOR DECOLONISING LEGAL EDUCATION

There are several reasons as to why it is important to decolonise legal education. This chapter demonstrated that through colonialism, education was used as an *input strategy* responsible for the infestation of the pre-colonial era African legal philosophies by the colonial legal education, thereby miseducating the African scholars. Therefore, the motivation for decolonising legal education, *inter alia*, to state a few, include *first*, is the recognition that the consequence of colonial legal education, as repetition (Ocheni and Nwunkwo 2012, 51). The effort here is to distil the legal education so that it centres an African context with prime focus on African legal pedagogy. The Westernised legal education was found to lack the organic linkage to African cultural practices rendering it to be skew and irrelevant for Africa. In other words, the colonial legal education that was designed for African scholars was of such substandard to an extent that it produced ignorance and powerlessness.

The *second* motivation is construed from an epistemic point of view. It is necessary to decolonise legal education "to make it possible and move toward a true intellectual communication" (Motshabi n.d, 9). Suffices to argue that this has potential to move towards the pluriversality of knowledge, and it counter the point-zero or God eye perception on knowledge production held by the West. The assumption is simple, currently, any form of education which is external to the West (not produced by the West), is perceived as inferior. The implication being that for an education to be acceptable, from Eurocentric perspective, that education needs to be measured against the Western form of education or Western set criteria. *Third*, it helps Africa and the African scholars to tell their story, produce and interpret the body of knowledge in the African social and historical context. By explication – this has a potential to trace and develop, the once lost, African legal philosophies (Chikaonda 2019). Chikaonda (2019) identifies the need to decolonise as follows:

> One wonders how the well-being of the African can be pursued in future when the LLB curriculum fails to trace for students how the law on the continent was used and perceived as a tool for social, economic and political cohesion since the past and until now. Making the links between how those perceptions have developed from pre-colonial times is necessary for students to understand their legal history.

It is important to point out that the colonial form of legal education advocated for non-organic creation of law. Further, they imposed their laws and legal education on the colonised which caused the pre-colonial African legal philosophies to be obliterated.

Fourth, the motivation for decolonisation, it is submitted in this chapter, should be broadened to include issues that are often not addressed by the decoloniality agenda, namely: the criminogenic nature of colonialism. Here, the discourse should provide an African enunciation in as far as addressing the theft, murders, exterminations, dispossessions of lands, plunder of African resources. In so doing, the conundrum that arises such as ignorant legal minds that decide to compensate settlers who stole the lands from indigenous people, for purposes of recovering the stolen lands. Legal minds that device strategies such as *willing buyer willing seller* scheme as a mechanism to lure the dens of thieves to sale the stolen ancestral lands to the rightful owners and heirs of such lands. Legal minds that continue to make laws that perpetuate coloniality and ignorance. Legal minds that advocate for compensating settlers for the rightfully repossessed lands but dissuades the recognition and compensation for heroes and heroines. All these illustrations point and confirm the Afrocentric proposition that there is a need to decolonise the ignorant legal minds.

In a nutshell, it is undeniable that there is a need to decolonise the law and the legal education as it has potential to remove the current hegemony experienced in knowledge or ignorance production. Once the hegemonic perception is removed, decolonisation may function as an instrument to advance equality, diversity and restoration of the African legal philosophies. On this score, it is argued that decolonising legal education is one of the strategies aimed at the restoration of the African legal philosophy with the exactitude it deserves. In this vein, decolonising the law and legal education serves as an indictment on simplistic political independence and uncritical advocacy for transformative constitutionalism. Regarding political independence of states, prior to the colonised states gaining the political independence, the anticipation was that the absence of the colonial administration and governance would put an effective end to colonialism and its consequences. This perception presents a checkered past. It is, in post-colonial era, vividly clear that the removal of the colonial administration and governance failed to achieve decoloniality of adverse *power* and that of *knowledge or ignorance*. Most of the formerly colonised, now notionally independent states, are still economically yoked to their former colonisers. Equally, these formerly colonised states are still highly dependent on the colonial laws and legal education which were imposed onto them by their colonial masters. For example, in the Namibian context, section 17(6) of the *Administration Proclamation* 15 of 1928 that continue to torment the Namibian matrimonial regime. It is discriminative, yet it is still applicable. There are several other legislations that stem from the colonial era not only in Namibia but in most of formerly colonised states. This is a clear indication that political independence failed to achieve decolonisation. Suffice to advance a theoretical assumption that the nominal political independence of SADC member states from their colonial powers at best succeeded in achieving decoloniality of *being* and self-governance of states. This raises further questions regarding what ordinary Africans want? What does it mean to decolonise being without getting back what was stolen, looted and plundered by colonialists? Would this be meaningful and relevant decolonisation? In the face of these questions – it is prudent to argue that the decolonisation agenda should transcend beyond decoloniality of *being* and should include all facets that afford the effective decoloniality of *being*, namely, to include reparations, restoration stolen lands and African resources. It is recognised here that to achieve the decoloniality aspirations, Africa and the African people need to be freed from the bounds of colonial ignorance or knowledge. Decoloniality of knowledge as Motshabi proffers is largely not addressed and is yet to be attained (Motshabi n.d, 104).

The other strategy that failed to advance the decoloniality agenda, is transformative constitutionalism. Transformative constitutionalism is a purpose-driven strategy that is understood as a commitment to substantive equality and improving socio-economic conditions. It is accredited to the South African democracy which witnessed a transitional constitutional order; however, its application has permeated the legal order in most of the formerly colonised states (Kibet and Fombad 2017, 349). The constitutions of the formerly colonised states provide for the right to education and the powers of governments in ensuring that the rights are protected. However, these constitutional provisions fail to provide for decolonisation of education. For instance, as it was argued above, the current legal education is still based on the legal system of the former colonisers and there is little attention paid to the African legal philosophies. From a South African perspective, Madlingozi (2018) argue that transformative constitutionalism failed to provide for living the philosophy of *Ubuntu* and summarises that:

> A constitution cannot be regarded as decolonising if it does not reflect the living philosophy and mores of the majority of its citizens; if instead of being a "mirror of society," it continues to be experienced by most of its subjects as a petrifying and alienating deity. (Madlingozi 2018)

Madlingozi (2018) further opines that the concept and the living philosophy of *Ubuntu/Botho* (African Humanness) is missing from the South African constitution. Again, South Africa's constitution can be compared with those of Bolivia and Ecuador. The latter constitutions seek to valorise indigenous cosmologies in the form of Pacha-Mama (Mother Earth) and sumak kawsay (Good Living). The enduring marginalisation of *Ubuntu/Botho* and African jurisprudences is symptomatic of the fact that African lifeways, their epistemologies and systems of social ordering (misnamed "customary law") are still deemed inferior in the "new South Africa." Considering the above discussion, it may be argued that the absence of the colonial administration and governance (independence of states) and presence of transformative constitutionalism have failed to provide strategies to thwart the consequences of coloniality. Thus, the meaningful proposal is to engage in decolonisation agenda, specifically, the decoloniality of ignorance or knowledge and legal education to realign the miseducation.

DECOLONISATION OF THE LEGAL EDUCATION CURRICULUM

The curriculum is the centre of the academic project and much thought needs to go into designing new curricula and reviewing existing curricula. Broadly, a curricula refers to all learning experiences that a student goes through at a university, while narrowly, it's a formal academic plan (programme of studies) for the learning experiences of students in pursuit of a qualification (Luckett 1995). It includes outcomes of student learning; content; sequence; teaching and learning methods and activities; teaching and learning resources; methods used to assess student learning, and evaluation of courses (Luckett 1995). Barnett et al. (2001) indicate that modern curricula can be viewed as an educational project that forms identities founded on three domains:

knowledge, action, and self. A responsive curriculum is essential for meeting the needs of a transforming society (Moll 2004) and by extension a decolonising society. More so, design of curricula at all levels should be responsive to the discipline, students' learning needs, and social context, taking into account our position as a university in Africa (Moll 2004; Pade-Khene 2015). Curricula should be relevant, up-to-date, and demonstrate awareness of apartheid and negative colonial influences on the disciplinary canon and teaching and assessment approaches in the discipline (Rhodes University 2018). A number of lecturers at Rhodes University in South Africa have grappled with how to transform and or decolonise their curricula. However, some of their ideas are documented in a set of case studies (Rhodes University 2018).

There is a consensus among social scientists and other practitioners about the importance of decolonising the education system particularly in Africa. Decolonising the education system is viewed as a catalyst to create human capital that will promote meaningful economic development to end the scourge of poverty (Musitha and Mafukata 2018). The colonial curricula in southern Africa seem to have promoted white supremacy and dominance, as well as stereotyping of Africa (Heleta 2016). The current higher education curriculum and landscape still largely reflects the colonial worldviews and is disconnected from African realities, including the lived experiences of the majority of Black Africans. It can be arguable that such a curriculum does not develop students' critical and analytical skills to understand and move the African continent forwards (Heleta 2016). Scholars in decoloniality are spreading the good gospel according to the total decolonisation of tertiary education and advocating for an era in which African universities will use curricula that are free from the vices or evils of colonialism, apartheid and imperialism (Kangira 2019). For example, South Africans and Namibians have had a long history of colonial education dictated by the monstrous Bantu Education Act 47 of 1953 which was later called the Black Education Act of 1953. Professor Kangira asserts that this atrocious piece of apartheid legislation legalised the racist and supremacist ideals of the white colonialists over the indigenous majority Black people in education, politics, and socio-economic sectors of society (Kangira 2019, 2).

In East Africa, the movement to decolonise education started in Kenya at the end of the 1960s, after the country won independence from Britain. Author and academic Harry Garuba (2015) said that a "fundamental question of place, perspective and orientation needed to be addressed in any reconceptualization of the curriculum" (The Conversation 2016). Garuba points out that one of the decolonisation movement's main desires was that "Kenya, East Africa and Africa needed to be placed at the centre of teaching, learning and research at Kenyan universities" (The Conversation 2016). According to Garuba, the work that began more than four decades ago has led to "major curriculum transformation" not only in Kenya but across East Africa. Still, while Kenya is far ahead of South Africa, the decolonisation process there isn't over yet (The Conversation 2016). Furthermore, a more detailed account of the quest for decolonisation of the curriculum in post-colonial Kenya is in Ngugi wa Thiong'o's *Decolonising the Mind: The Politics of Language in African Literature* (Ngugi 1981). Ngugi opines that the transformation required looking at the curriculum in terms of the "[r]elevance to our situation [*and the*] contribution towards understanding ourselves, and that, the ultimate goal was to establish the centrality of Africain the curriculum" (Ngugi 1981, 94).

In South Africa, the Supreme Court of Appeal in *Hotz v University of Cape Town* 2017 2 SA 485 (SCA) pronounced itself on the legal status of protest action within the constitutional framework that protest action is not itself unlawful and that the right to protest against injustice is protected by the Constitution. This was an appeal from the High Court decision granting an interdict to the University of Cape Town barring five participants in one of the protest actions on the campus from entering the premises of the University because they had allegedly committed unlawful acts in the course of their protest (the "*Rhodes Must Fall*" and "*Fees Must Fall*"). The student protests which started in 2015 to 2016, demanded the decolonisation of certain aspects of higher education (Himonga 2017, 11). In the protests, issues of the decolonisation of the curriculum connected with the country's history of colonialism and apartheid also emerged. In law schools, the demands for curriculum change are accompanied by the broad issue of the decolonisation of law, translating into questions of legal history, the concept of law, the role of law in African societies, the status of indigenous systems of law in the post-independent/apartheid legal system, and how law is taught in law schools (Himonga 2017, 11). The university curricula remain largely Eurocentric, dominated by what some academics have called "white, male, Western, capitalist, heterosexual, European worldviews" (Himonga 2017, 11). However, students are railing against this dominance at the expense of theories, thinkers and ideas from Africa and the global South (The Conversation 2016). While these protests have had a profound impact in southern Africa and globally, many universities in southern Africa have not embarked on similar protests.

Himonga and Diallo (2017) examine the idea of the decolonisation of law in relation to the teaching of law in African states previously under the influence of English or Roman-Dutch colonial/apartheid legal history. They examine the design of legal education with reference to three elements that are essential to the decolonisation of law and legal education. The elements in their review are the inclusion of living customary law in legal education, a shift in the legal theoretical paradigm within which law is taught, and the interdisciplinary study of law (Himonga and Diallo 2017). According to them, these three elements are essential for decolonising law and legal education. They assert and show that the overall shift in the paradigm of teaching law will increase the potential of law to transform African societies and enhance social justice in a manner that is consistent with decolonisation (Himonga and Diallo 2017). Motshabi (n.d, 107) points out that "the principal success of colonialism is to make the colonised think epistemically like the coloniser." According to Grosfoguel (2007, 218), "the success of the modern/colonial world-system consists in making subjects that are socially located in the oppressed side of the colonial difference, to think epistemically like the ones on the dominant positions." This postulation is challenged by the Afrocentric that is if the coloniser thought that ownership and control of resources was central to the development and modernisation in Africa, then it was not conceivable that the colonisers would have exposed the colonies to proper education that would allow their realisation. The point here is that whereas colonisers know that ownership and control of resources is central to development, Africans think that they can only develop by getting aid and donations from the colonisers. This is why there is a need to decolonise ignorance by restructuring the legal education to provide for African enunciation. Self-reflection is then thus a critical first step to assess and change our situation (Motshabi, 105). Black students, in particular, justifiably object to being "confronted by texts and theories that negate their own history, lived experiences" and "dreams" (Heleta 2016, 3). Thus, colonial curricula malign student image and self-concept and causes students to despise themselves (Mamdani 2016). Unsurprisingly, students feel estranged and cannot relate (Mamdani 2016). This cannot be conducive to learning and teaching. Epistemic decolonisation, through the curriculum, is "necessary to make possible and move toward a truly intercultural communication; to an exchange of experiences and significations as the foundation of an-other rationality" (Motshabi n.d, 105).

The decolonisation project needs to encompass more than just changing the curriculum, how things are taught and academics' attitudes to this process matter just as much (Motshabi n.d, 105). A more Africanised diverse curriculum, student body and academic body, to mention a few, would guarantee that the diverse ways of being, and diverse knowledge that international students bring are accommodated and represented among other dominant ways of being, and that these universities can continue to claim their role as global centres of learning (Wamai 2016). Decolonising the curriculum promotes a relativism about knowledge that presents the works of different thinkers or different schools of thought as all being of equal worth (Williams 2017). According to a leading scholar in decoloniality, Artwell Nhemachena of the University of Namibia, the decolonisation of the curricula cannot possibly take place without attending specifically to decolonising languages that constitute the media of instruction in the universities. It follows that "at the core of decolonising languages and the broader university curricula is the issue of decolonising materialities of which the languages constitute the symbols" (Kangira 2019, 2). Critically, this infers that the language issue is at the centre of decolonising university curricula in South Africa, Namibia and elsewhere in Africa. If the Chinese, Japanese, German, and Finnish, for instance, use their languages in their education systems and can also use their languages to understand the phenomena around them, why do universities in Africa still rely on foreign languages in their university curricula? (Kangira 2019, 2).

While it is true that the decolonisation of universities' curricula will not occur overnight, it is important to support the efforts that student movements are making in the long journey of totally decolonising tertiary education in Africa (Kangira 2019). It is arguable that the current Eurocentric curricula, coupled with epistemic theft and violence, do not contribute to a much-needed reimagining of the past and shaping of the present and future on the African continent (Heleta 2016, 7). For example, indigenisation of education measures in Canada, Australia and the Philippines are followed by an increase in student representation from marginal groups, a new understanding of citizenship and a more robust curriculum (Gumbo 2016, 46–48). Freire's ideas about "situationality" have therefore proven merit (Freire 2000). African governments and institutions of higher learning must continue to decolonise their curricula, conceptually and contextually, to live up to African realities, aspirations and challenges. Coherence and alignment of curriculum to the decolonisation discourse in law and other disciplines is essential to Africanisation of the higher education landscape in Africa.

DECOLONIALITY AND TEACHING LEGAL EDUCATION

Teaching and learning are essential activities for any university. According to Devlin and Samarawickrema (2010), effective teaching and learning in higher education are understood to comprise particular skills and practices applied in particular contexts. They further argue that context is critical and that it is subject to continuous and multiple changes imposed by forces from within and outside the universities (Devlin and Samarawickrema 2010). Effective teaching and learning must continually evolve in an order that reflects and responds to the context of learning and teaching (Devlin and Samarawickrema 2010). The decolonial turn, like sustainable development and the fourth industrial revolution, are recently shaping thinking about teaching and learning in higher education. There is a call to integrate these aspects in university curricula in order for graduates to remain relevant to African socio-cultural precepts in the twenty-first century. Some universities in Namibia and South Africa are integrating these frameworks in their institutional and departmental policies, assessment policies, teaching and learning approaches.

The University of Cape Town experienced a raw and appalling but gripping conflict over the teaching of African Studies (Motshabi n.d, 7). In South Africa, the idea of decolonisation frightened many academics. Since students launched the movement to decolonise higher education in early 2015, they have asked questions like "What do 'they' mean by decolonisation? Going back to the Stone Age? Teaching only about South Africa and Africa? Isolation from the rest of the world?" (The Conversation 2016). Decolonisation, for them, involves fundamental rethinking and reframing of the curriculum and bringing South Africa and Africa to the centre of teaching, learning and research (The Conversation 2016). They believe that the world views expressed through colonial knowledge systems were designed to degrade, exploit and subjugate people in Africa and other parts of the formerly colonised world (The Conversation 2016). These views persist today at South African universities. Black students are confronted by texts and theories that negate their own history, lived experiences and their dreams. They get little exposure to their own continent and all its complexity (The Conversation 2016). Mbembe points out, decolonisation, "is not about closing the door to European or other traditions. It is about defining clearly what the centre is" (Mbembe 2015, 4–5; The Conversation 2016).

African overreliance on Western scholarship is due to colonial history and the history of African colonial universities (Mamdani 2016, 69). Heleta (2016, 9) asserts that the curricula remain largely Eurocentric and continues to reinforce white and Western dominance and privilege. The author traces the roots of Eurocentrism and epistemic violence at universities. The author argues that South Africa must tackle and dismantle the epistemic violence and hegemony of Eurocentrism, completely rethink, reframe and reconstruct the curriculum and place South Africa, Southern Africa and Africa at the centre of teaching, learning and research (Heleta 2016, 9). However, like many scholars, she concludes that decolonisation will not be easy as opposition to change is entrenched in the university structures. Maldonado-Torres (2011, 4) postulates that:

> what intellectuals seeking to advance the discourse of decolonization make clear, is that beyond the dialectics of identity and liberation, recognition and distribution, we have to add the imperative of epistemic decolonization, and in fact, of a consistent decolonization of human reality. For that one must build new concepts and being willing to revise critically all received theories and ideas.

Furthermore, universities should be anxious about their inability to teach in indigenous or local languages as Kiswahili, Oshiwambo, Lozi, chiTotela, IsiXhosa and Sesotho. Kenyan author Ngũgĩ wa Thiong'o writes that decolonisation of knowledge "calls for more than choice of materials." While adding the literature from the African continent and the Global South is crucial in the decolonisation project, it is not enough. The attitude to the materials used in the curriculum is as critical. This presents a massive challenge (The Conversation 2016). Universities can easily prescribe new readings and other materials for teaching and learning but what about the academics' attitudes to these and to new ways of thinking especially about decolonisation? Paulo Freire was a Brazilian educator whose ideas on pedagogy are encapsulated succinctly in his book The Pedagogy of the Oppressed in 1968 (Adebisi 2016). Freire contended that knowledge is formed and reformed through persistent human inquiry about the world (Freire 2000, 72). He asserted that education should transcend understanding the world to encompass changing the world; education should transform and empower participants, not make them conform to prototypical representation (Freire 2000, 72). He was a firm believer that education should reflect the lived experiences of participants in education, especially their "situationality" (Freire 2000, 54). To achieve these aims, Freire argued that the "oppressed" have to "unveil the world of oppression" themselves. This can be done through an equal relationship of dialogue so that education "expresses the consciousness" of the teachers and students (Freire 2000, 89). Freire recognised that anti-colonial leaders may step into the shoes of the colonisers and use education to silence, in a similar fashion to their predecessors (Freire 2000, 89). Silence and freedom, he stressed, are a contradiction (Freire 2000, 89). Freire understood that education had revolutionary capacities and could be used to change the course of history – in this he mirrors post-colonial deconstruction's thesis of possibility through education (Freire 2000, 89). His work has had particular significance for pedagogical reform in the African countries of Guinea-Bissau, Egypt and Kenya, and his pedagogy is especially relevant for rural Africa where illiteracy is high (Nyirenda 1996, 19).

Teaching and learning practices and strategies must embrace the decolonial turn and align well with their decolonised curricula. Teaching and learning methods, and not only the curriculum, are critical to advance the decolonisation project in African universities. In decolonising legal education, critical questions need to be asked: Do we have a decolonial discourse in the SADC universities' higher education curricula or landscape? What issues are we raising and striving to transform to decolonise our legal education? In recent years, the decolonial project has been one of the most critical aspects of African universities to decolonise and transform their teaching and learning. Therefore, in redefining higher education in the twenty-first century, SADC universities in particular, must strive to integrate and align the appropriate decolonial legal discourses to their contexts.

CHALLENGES OF DECOLONIALITY

Decolonial theory is criticised for being too general, for not emancipating and for having been surpassed by events (Motshabi n.d, 107). However, it is arguable that the objective of decolonial theory goes beyond emancipation to a struggle for revolution and liberation (Motshabi n.d, 107). Contrary to what some academics fear, decolonisation is not about moving backwards nor is it about isolating Africa's universities from the rest of the world. In South Africa, the country's Higher Education and Training Minister Blade Nzimande has made this clear, saying at a 2015 summit that "Building African universities does not mean creating universities that are globally disengaged. They should be globally engaged, but not only by being consumers of global knowledge. They should be producers of knowledge as well, knowledge that is of relevance locally, continentally, in the South and globally" (The Conversation 2016). In addition, the majority of academics in Africa are cut from the cloth of Western knowledge and are often reluctant to repudiate their very make-up through dismantling colonial knowledge systems (The Conversation 2016). Research findings indicate that "staff is underprepared to champion a decoloniality transformation project because they themselves are products of coloniality (educated by a colonial education system), evident in their ignorance of and resistance to decoloniality" (Joseph 2017, 4).

CONCLUSIONS AND SOME RECOMMENDATIONS

The Western theories we use are inadequate to local problems and the European lens does not perceive our complexity (Motshabi n.d, 109). Thus, southern Africa and African law schools or universities must develop theories and practices based on key features of African law and society. As was, pointed out above, this may be achieved by advancing theories that encourage organic creation of laws by Africans. The theories so developed must be included in the curriculum, teaching and learning strategies. It is submitted that appropriate African perspectives, content and context can better teach the functioning of the law. In as much as the object is to avoid centric approach, it is agreeable that there is a need to lock the primary focus on Africa and its jurisprudence. This has potential to direct the attention to the issues, concerns, problems and debates of the continent, which in turn may be a conduit to place the indigenous law and African values in modern continental legal systems

(Motshabi n.d, 112). The other aspect, worthy of noting, is the African universities' contribution to epistemic perspectives. Here, the universities' must *incorporate* epistemic perspectives, knowledge and thinking from the African continent and the Global South into their curricula, teaching, learning and research methodologies. It was pointed out that the absence of colonial administration and the presence of the theory of transformative constitutionalism have failed to forestall coloniality. To bolster the decoloniality agenda, institutions should consider revision of the decolonisation policies and frameworks in primary, secondary and tertiary education. Another approach to advancing the decoloniality agenda is the proposal that African philosophy can be used as a tool in the decolonisation movement through engaging with questions of what it means to humanise pedagogy in our context (Oelofsen 2015). Finally, it is recommended that decolonisation of legal education in Africa in general has to take into account decolonised pedagogy, research-intensive, interdisciplinary, cross-cultural, egalitarian, overt, persistent, capacity-sharing and competence-building (Higgs 2012). Therefore, the main emphasis in decolonising education in Africa should involve a process of continuous and persistent critical engagement with, and selective incorporation of, African knowledge (pre-colonial or post-colonial), while simultaneously resisting the lure of the instinctive ascription of inferiority to different systems of knowledge.

BIBLIOGRAPHY

Adebisi, F. (2016). "Decolonising education in Africa: Implementing the right to education by re-appropriating culture and indigeneity." *Northern Ireland Legal Quarterly*, Volume 67(4), 433–452.

Assmann, J. (2002). *The Mind of Egypt: History and Meaning in the Time of the Pharaohs*. New York: Metropolitan Books.

Barnett, R., Parry, G., and Coate, K. (2001). "Conceptualising curriculum change." *Teaching in Higher Education*, Volume 6(4), 435–449.

Bartlett, S., and Burton, D. (2016). *Introduction to Education Studies* (4th ed.). London: SAGE.

Betts, R. F. (2012). "Decolonisation: A brief history of the word." In E. Bogaerts and R. Raben (Eds.), *Beyond Empire and Nation – The Decolonisation of African and Asian Societies 1930–1970s*. Leiden: Brill.

Chikaonda, G. P. (2019). "To decolonize our LLB degree we have to understand and incorporate the roots of African Law." https://www.dailymaverick.co.za/opinionista/2019-07-09- to-decolonise-our-llb- degrees-we-have-to-understand-and-incorporate-the-roots-of-african-law/.

Devlin, M., and Samarawickrema, G. (2010). "The criteria of effective teaching in a changing higher education context." *Higher Education Research & Development*, Volume 29(2), 111–124.

Freire, P. (2000). *Pedagogy of the Oppressed*, Myra Bergman Ramos (trans). Continuum.
Garuba, H. (2015). "What is an African curriculum?" *Mail & Guardian*, 17 April. http://mg.co.za/article/2015-04-17-what-is-an-african-curriculum/.
Graness, A. (2016). "Writing the history of philosophy in Africa: Where to begin?" *Journal of African Cultural Studies*, Volume 28(2), 132–146.
Grosfoguel, R. (2007). "The epistemic decolonial turn: Beyond the political-economy paradigms." *Cultural Studies*, Volume 21(2), 211–223.
Gumbo, M. T. (2016). "A model for indigenising the university curriculum: A quest for educational relevance." In V. Msila and M. T. Gumbo (Eds.), *Africanising the Curriculum: Indigenous Perspectives and Theories* (pp. 39, 46–48). Sun Media Metro.
Hallen, B. (2002). *A Short History of African Philosophy*. Bloomington: Indiana University Press.
Heleta, S. (2016). "Decolonisation of higher education: Dismantling epistemic violence and Eurocentrism in South Africa." *Transformation in Higher Education*, Volume 1(1). http://dx. doi.org/10.4102/the.v1i1.9.
Higgs, P. (2012). "African philosophy and the decolonisation of education in Africa: Some critical reflections." *Educational Philosophy and Theory*, Volume 44(2), 37–55.
Himonga, C., and Diallo, F. (2017). "Decolonization and teaching law in Africa with special reference to living customary law." *Potchefstroom Electronic Law Journal*, Volume 20, 1–19.
Horvath, R. J. (1972). "A definition of colonialism." *Current Anthropology*, Volume 13(1), 45–57.
Hotz v University of Cape Town 2017 2 SA 485 (SCA).
Joseph, T. R. (2017). "Decolonising the curriculum; transforming the university: A discursive perspective." https://www.dut.ac.za.
Kangira, J. (2019). "Decolonisation of tertiary education a must." *New Era Newspaper, Thought Leaders*. https://neweralive.na/posts/decolonisation-of-tertiary-education-a-must.
Kelly, G. P. (1979). "The relation between colonial and metropolitan schools: A structural analysis." *Comparative Education*, Volume 15(2), 209–215.
Kibet, E., and Fombad, C. (2017). "Transformative constitutionalism and the adjudication of constitutional rights in Africa." *African Human Rights Law Journal*, Volume 17(2), 340–366.
Lakshminath, A. (2008). "Legal education, research and pedagogy-Ideological perceptions." *Journal of the Indian Law Institute*, Volume 50(4), 606–628.
Likhovski, A. (2002). "Colonialism, nationalism and legal education: The case of mandatory palestine." https://www.researchgate.net/publication/45579276.
Luckett, K. (1995). "Towards a model of curriculum development for the University of Natol's Curriculum Reform Programme." *Academic Development*, Volume 1(2), 127–138.
Madlingozi, T. (2018). "The proposed Amendment to the South African Constitution: Finishing the unfinished Business of Decolonisation?" *Critical Legal Thinking*.

http://criticallegalthinking.com/2018/04/06/the-proposed-amendment-to-the-south-african-constitution/.

Maldonado-Torres, N. (2011). "Thinking through the decolonial turn: Post-continental interventions in theory, philosophy, and critique – An introduction." *Transmodernity*, Volume 1(2), 1–15.

Mamdani, M. (2016). "Between the public intellectual and the scholar: Decolonization and some post- independence initiatives in African higher education." *Inter-Asia Cultural Studies*, Volume 17(1), 68–83.

Mbembe, A. (2015). "Decolonising knowledge and the question of the archive." http://wiser.wits.ac.za/system/files/Achille.pdf.

Melber, H. (2019). "Colonialism, land, ethnicity, and class: Namibia after the second national land conference." *Africa Spectrum*, Volume 54(1), 73–86.

Mignolo, W. D. (2007). "De-linking: The rhetoric of modernity, the logic of coloniality and the grammar of decoloniality." *Cultural Studies*, Volume 21(3), 449–513.

Moll, I. (2004). "Curriculum responsiveness: The anatomy of a concept." In H. Griesel (Ed.), *Curriculum Responsiveness: Case Studies in Higher Education*. Pretoria: South African Universities Vice-Chancellors Association.

Motshabi, K. B. (n.d). "Decolonising the university: A law perspective." *Strategic Review for Southern Africa*, Volume 40(1), 104–115.

Musitha, M. E., and Mafukata, M. A. (2018). "Crisis of decolonising education: Curriculum implementation in Limpopo Province of South Africa." *Africa's Public Service Delivery and Performance Review*, Volume 6(1), 179.

Ndima, D. D. (2015). "Reconceiving African jurisprudence in a post-imperial society: The role of Ubuntu in constitutional adjudication." *The Comparative and International Law Journal of Southern Africa*, Volume 48(3), 359–380.

Ndulo, M. (1985). "Legal education in Zambia: Pedagogical issues." *Journal of Legal Education*, Volume 35(3), 445–454.

Ngugi, W. T. O. (1981). *Decolonising the Mind: The Politics of Language in African Literature*. Nairobi: East African Educational Publishers Ltd.

Nhemachena, A., Warikandwa, T. V., and Amoo, S. K. (2018). *Social and Legal Theory in the Age of Decoloniality: (Re-)Envisioning Pan-African Jurisprudence in the 21st Century*. African Book Collective. Project MUSE. muse.jhu.edu/book/60159.

Nyirenda, J. E. (1996). "The relevance of Paulo Freire's contributions to education and development in present day Africa." *Africa Media Review*, Volume 10(1), 19.

Ocheni, S., and Nwankwo, B. C. (2012). "Analysis of colonialism and its impact in Africa." *Cross- Cultural Communication*, Volume 8(3), 46–54.

Oelofsen, D. (2015). *Decolonisation of the African Mind and Intellectual Landscape*. University of South Africa. http://www.scielo.org.za/pdf/phronimon/v16n2/08.pdf.

Omotosho, I. F. (2014). "A critique of the question of African philosophy." *IOSR Journal of Humanities and Social Science*, Volume 19(7), 61–66.

Oxford Online Dictionary Definition of Colonialism. https://www.google.com/search?q=colonialism+definition&rlz=1C1GCEU_enNA82 0NA820&oq=col&aqs=chrome.0.69i59j69i57j0l4.3368j0j8&sourceid=chrome&ie=UTF-8.

Pade-Khene, C. (2015). "Curriculum development of an ICT4D module in the South African context." *Issues in Informing Science and Information Technology*, Volume 12, 111–140. http://iisit.org/Vol12/IISITv12p111-139Pade-Khene1788.pdf.

Rhodes University. (2018). "Brief guide for designing a curriculum and constructing a course document." *Centre for Higher Education Research, Teaching and Learning, Rhodes University*. https://www.ru.ac.za/media/rhodesuniversity/content/chertl/document/2018_Brief_ guide_for_d>esigning_a_curriculum_and_constructing_a_course_document.pdf.

Seroto, J. (2018). "Dynamics of decoloniality in South Africa: A critique of the history of Swiss Mission education for Indigenous People." *Studia Historiae Ecclessiasticae*, Volume 44(3), 114.

Sibanda, S. (2016). "An analysis of traditional leadership, customary law and access to justice in Zimbabwe's constitutional framework." A paper presented at the *2016 National Symposium on the Promise of Declaration of Rights under the Constitution of Zimbabwe- Final Papers.* https://zimlii.org/content/analysis-traditional-leadership- customary-law- and-access-justice-zimbabwe%E2%80%99s-constitutional.

The 1990 Namibia Constitution.

The 1996 South African Constitution.

The 2013 Constitution of Zimbabwe.

The Conversation. (2016). "Decolonisation: Academics must change what they teach, and how." http://theconversation.com/decolonisation-academics-must-change- what-they-teach-and-how-68080.

Wamai, N. (2016). Decolonising the academy – Towards a global movement? *University World News.* https://www.universityworldnews.com/post.php?story=20160524135416842.

Wa Ngugi, M. (2020). "The pitfalls of symbolic decolonization opening remarks at the launch of the 2020 Writers Unlimited International Literature Festival in the Hague." https://africasacountry.com/2020/01/the-pitfalls-of-symbolic-decolonisation.

Williams, J. (2017). The 'decolonise the curriculum' movement re-racialises knowledge. *Open Democracy*. https://www.opendemocracy.net/en/decolonise- curriculum-movement-re-racialises-knowledge/.

Chapter 4

The Dangers of Transplanting Transformative Constitutionalism into Namibia

Dunia Prince Zongwe

INTRODUCTION

One good reason why Namibian lawyers should cold-shoulder "transformative constitutionalism" as a distinct strategy for interpreting the Constitution to bring about transformation in society by openly embracing the politics involved in reading the Constitution is that the lawyers who use that phrase seldom know what they talk about. As I show in this chapter, although those lawyers employ one and the same phrase, they actually have different ideas in mind. They think that they are engaging one another in an intelligent and deep conversation when, in reality, they simply talk past one another.

But, regardless of whether lawyers know what transformative constitutionalism truly means, talk about it they must. Transformative constitutionalism should not form the subject of conversations in small academic and judicial circles. It concerns everyone living in southern Africa, given their relatively recent history with apartheid and minority-ruled colonisation.

In the seminal article in which he coined the phrase "transformative constitutionalism," Karl Klare did not merely ask whether transformative constitutionalism would be a viable project for South African lawyers only; he also wondered whether transformative constitutionalism would work "within other legal regimes" (Klare 1998, 150), such as Namibian law.

Regrettably, questions of constitutionalism remain confined to research by very few academics and judges. Horn lamented that:

> [t]here is no public legal debate in Namibia on issues like majoritarianism and constitutionalism, positivism, natural law and post-modernism. . . and other constitutional issues. Whenever these debates take place, it is often populist

> politicians attacking the judiciary for not taking the will of the people into account, for being unpatriotic, for taking sides with oppressors, racists and enemies of the state. (Horn 2016, 9)

In 2016, Horn sparked off the much-needed debate on transformative constitutionalism in Namibia by publishing a book on that topic (Horn 2016, 9). Twenty years earlier in South Africa, the then-chief justice Pius Langa asserted that transformative constitutionalism "places the Constitutional dream at the very heart of legal education" (Langa 2006, 356). Today, the Council on Higher Education (CHE) requires all law faculties in South Africa to have a component on transformative constitutionalism (Council on Higher Education 2018, 18–19, 52, 54, 59 and 65). In practical terms, this implies that, if a law faculty does not include transformative constitutionalism throughout its curriculum, the CHE may withdraw the accreditation of that law faculty's bachelor of laws (LLB) programme.

While the CHE probably meant well when it made transformative constitutionalism compulsory, the reality is that this move impoverishes legal education in South Africa because transformative constitutionalism works like a trojan horse designed to introduce into South Africa an ideological project driven by a group of influential theorists in the United States. Namibia must not make the same mistake.

In this chapter, I urge Namibian educators to avoid the short-sightedness of the CHE and to refrain from transplanting an ideological project that endangers the quality of legal education into the country. Through the four substantive sections of this chapter, I support this urgent plea by showing that great dangers await Namibia if it buys that ideological project. In the first section, I discuss how transformative constitutionalism would trap Namibia's idea of "transformation" into a particular American style of left-wing politics. In the second section, I move on to demonstrate how talk of transformative Constitution will confuse lawyers, judges and law students about what this general principle exactly covers. In the next section, I explain that confusion reigns precisely because many lawyers and stakeholders in South Africa, chiefly the CHE, do not really understand transformative constitutionalism. More specifically, the fourth part backs up my main thesis by focusing on the Namibian legal context and explaining why that context should discourage lawyers in Namibia from emulating the South African obsession with transformative constitutionalism. Finally, in the conclusion, I reveal the greatest danger that legal education in Namibia faces if it embraces transformative constitutionalism.

Lawyers, judges, law students, learners and experts in other disciplines and the general public in Namibia must enter this debate about transformative constitutionalism. This "transformation-oriented" (Pieterse 2005, 155, who notes that the scholarship in much of contemporary South African human rights and constitutional law designates the constitutional project as "transformative" or "transformation-oriented") constitutional project deals with identifying, interpreting and articulating the core values that define Namibia as a nation. Ironically, failing to grapple with this project may lead to a situation whereby educators in Namibia adopt the project without fully comprehending what it means and what it implies.

I must stress that I have no misgivings about transformative constitutionalism as such. Rather, I rail against allowing transformative constitutionalism to *dominate* legal education and constitutional interpretation. At the symbolic level, the fact that the CHE in South Africa endorsed transformative constitutionalism makes it a state-sanctioned legal philosophy. It sends a powerful message that transformative constitutionalism is more legitimate than other constitutional theories.

TRANSFORMATION AND CONSTITUTIONALISM

Constraining the State

One severe difficulty with transformative constitutionalism lies in the risk that it creates that lawyers and judges may expand the meanings of legal texts without expressly agreeing as to how far they can stretch such meanings. This poses a problem because, at the core of constitutionalism, sits the idea of "constraint." While lawyers typically apply it to the executive branch, this idea of constraint definitely applies to the judiciary as it forms part of the state.

The Traditional Conception

To understand the point, I have just made about transformative constitutionalism, I must first explain what constitutionalism involves. Nonetheless, the two have in common that they do not easily lend themselves to commonly accepted definitions. Gordon wrote that "constitutionalism" denotes that the coercive power of the state is constrained (Gordon 1999, 5; Fombad 2014, 415–416, who argue that constitutionalism combines the idea of a government limited its acts and accountable to its citizens for its actions). He explains that, although the expression "constitutionalism" emerged recently, the idea actually dates back to classical antiquity (Gordon 1999, 5, indicating that the word "constitutionalism" was first used in 1832). An-Na'im warns against efforts to give a single, universally accepted meaning of this general principle because he believes that constitutionalism necessarily results from each society's experiences in their many settings (An-Na'im 2006, 3). However, a common thread seems to have emerged over time. Thus, McIlwain observed that:

> [i]n all its successive phases, constitutionalism has one essential quality: [I]t is a legal limitation on government . . . The most persistent and the most lasting of the essentials of true constitutionalism still remains what it has been almost from the beginning, the limitation of government by law. (McIlwain 1940, 24)

Thus understood, constitutionalism refers to constraining the power of the state (to use force) by dint of legal rules. This understanding subsumes a system of checks and balances, and a rule-based social order.

Gordon disputes McIlwain's view of constitutionalism, not because it focuses on "the limitation of government," but because it focuses on "limitation by law" (Gordon 1999, 5). He rightly remarks that, if a body in the state makes law, then "the only legal constraints under which it operates consist of laws that it itself makes; that is, there are no constraints at all." Indeed, McIlwain's perspective on constitutionalism as "limitation of government by law" would not have prevented a judge during the apartheid days from applying an arbitrary and cruel law. For that reason, I prefer Gordon's concept of constitutionalism as "*controlling* the coercive power of the state."

Elements of Constitutionalism

Constitutionalism also relates to the rule of law and to the slogan "a government of laws and not of men." However, the elements of constitutionalism tend to change as societies find or devise better ways of limiting governments and protecting citizens (Fombad 2014, 416). With regard to the rule of law doctrine, constitutionalism connotes that laws passed by authorised lawmakers apply to everyone, including judges, soldiers, and executive officers from the highest rank to the lowest (Gordon 1999, 7). In addition, the celebrated doctrine also means that only courts of law can restrict the rights and freedoms of individuals. As Fombad explains, the rule of law safeguards constitutionalism because "without the rule of law there can be no constitutionalism" (Fombad 2014, 418).

The political theorists who developed the slogan "a government of laws, and not of men" thought that all legitimate governmental power derives from the people, but they equally believed that even a government that passed this test of legitimacy should be constrained (Gordon 1999, 7). History teaches that democratically elected rulers in a "republic" can abuse power (Levitsky and Ziblatt 2018, describing how democracies can gradually descend into dictatorships, such as Germany in the 1930s, Peru in the 1990s and Venezuela from the 1990s onwards). Hence, the necessity to constrain state power in both monarchies and republics. In that sense, constitutionalism heeds call for a government of laws, and not of men.

Liberal Constitutionalism

Liberal constitutionalism insists on separating law from politics (transformation; Le Roux 2013, 32). It concerns itself with protecting the rights of individuals, especially vested property rights and the economic distribution of the private sphere (Le Roux 2013, 32). Its proponents have designed it to limit policy makers from interfering with the market (Le Roux 2013, 32). Liberal constitutionalism's discourse focuses on the negative obligations of the state, the justness of the market, and a largely unregulated society (Le Roux 2013, 32).

This point on liberal constitutionalism speaks to transformative constitutionalism because it raises the question of the political or ideological orientation of the South African Constitution. Klare argues that the South African Constitution is postliberal (Klare 1998, 150–156), suggesting that the Constitution departs from or objects to liberal constitutionalism. Klare's argument may accurately portray most of the Constitution, but not the whole of it. For instance, the provisions on the South African Reserve Bank (SARB) (Constitution of the Republic of South Africa 1996, "South African Constitution," s 224) embody a neoliberal philosophy of central banking as it emphasises price stability, central-bank independence and inflation targeting.

Closing Notes

Given that modern constitutions like the ones that Namibia and South Africa adopted constrain the coercive power of the state, can we conclude that constitutionalism merely consists in strictly enforcing the Constitution? Understanding constitutionalism as merely enforcing the rights and clauses in the Constitution is misguided because constitutionalism, just like transformative constitutionalism, denotes more than having a written constitution. Constitutionalism has little to do with a written constitution (Gordon 1999, 5). Indeed, constitutionalism applies to countries like the United Kingdom (UK) and Israel, which do not have written constitutions.

Last but not least, constitutionalism relates to human rights. An-Na'im adds that, whether based on a written constitution or not, constitutionalism always aims to uphold the rule of law, enforce effective limitations on government powers, and protect fundamental human rights (An-Na'im 2006, 3).

In short, constitutionalism means controlling the power of the state to coerce and protecting human rights. It thus manifests in *negative obligations* stopping the state from abusing its power to coerce individuals and in *positive obligations* to protect their rights. Seen like this, transformative constitutionalism radically departs from constitutionalism insofar as it imposes *specific positive obligations* on the state to fundamentally change the society in which those individuals live.

TRANSFORMATION AND TRANSFORMATIVE CONSTITUTIONS

Transformation

If lawyers and law teachers in Namibia subscribe to transformative constitutionalism, they will struggle hard to achieve a consensus on what transformation exactly entails. As Bilchitz correctly remarked, the notion of "transformation" tells very little about what to do (Bilchitz 2010, 267). Pieterse also feared that using "transformation" readily in variety of overlapping contexts runs the risks of "deflating" or over-generalising the meaning of that term in those contexts (Pieterse 2005, 155). He noted that the "many-nuanced" word "transformation" has become a popular buzzword that covers a broad array of processes and programmes, ranging very widely from affirmative action and black economic empowerment to the rebuilding of South Africa's legal culture (Pieterse 2005, 155). To avoid diluting the meaning of that word, he submitted that the transformation required by the South African Constitution must comprise these four elements, namely substantive equality, social justice, the extension of human rights to the private sphere and a culture of justification in public law (Pieterse 2005, 161 and 165).

However, Pieterse admits that his rendition of "constitutional transformation" does not rule out the possibility that it may prove incorrect, neither does it exclude other (conflicting) vistas (Pieterse 2005, 156). Below I expose the differences between Klare, Langa and le Roux in conceiving transformation differences that also contradict certain aspects of Pieterse's concept. Those differences persist to this day, and the issue of unifying the content of "transformation" remains whole.

Klare himself does not say precisely what transformation entails. He explains the "transformation" he envisages, not in terms of its contents, but in terms of its scale. He considers his notion of transformation too vast for the word "reform" to capture it but not vast enough to qualify as a "revolution" (Klare 1998, 150).

To compound matters, Klare and Langa do not agree on the scale of the change envisioned by transformation. For Klare, as I have just mentioned, that transformation falls short of a revolution (Karl 1998, 150) whereas, for Langa, it amounts to "a social and an economic revolution" (Langa 2006, 352).

Transformation resonates in the South African and Namibian contexts because, upon democratisation and independence, respectively, these nations had inherited a highly unequal society produced by decades of institutionalised discrimination and racism. In 1948, the National Party (NP) won the general elections and formally introduced apartheid. With this policy, the NP aimed at racial, cultural and political purity (Khunou 2009, 81). Today, like Namibia, South Africa has a "society of extreme imbalances and socio-economic inequalities" (Rapatsa 2014) and still ranks among the world's most unequal society in terms of income disparities (The World Bank, February 21, 2020; Beaubien, April 2, 2018). This state of affairs calls for the "transformation" of this "racially-based, class-based, and resource-biased" society to an egalitarian one (Rosa 2011, 542; Rapatsa 2015, 18; Klare 1998, 150–151 and Langa 2006, 352, for an explanation on the new South African society is one based on substantive equality). In *Makwanyane,* Mahomed DP echoes this transformation towards an egalitarian society as a decisive break from, and a ringing rejection of, that part of the past which is disgracefully racist, authoritarian, insular, and repressive and a vigorous identification of and commitment to a democratic, universalistic, caring and aspirationally egalitarian ethos (*S v Makwanyane* 1995 3 SA 391 (CC) para 262).

Similarly, Albertyn & Goldblatt (Albertyn and Beth Goldblatt 1998, 249–250) and Pieterse (2005, 155–156 and 159) insist that transformation in South Africa consists in redistributing power, resources and social capital along egalitarian lines.

Unsurprisingly, in both nations, the governments have embraced policies aimed at "transforming" society. When Klare underlined "transformation," it directly appealed to South Africans given their historical, socio-economic and political circumstances. The Klarean "transformation" would also seduce many because it evokes a "highly egalitarian, caring, multicultural community, governed through participatory, democratic processes" in both the polity and large sections of the private sphere (Klare 1998, 150).

However, Klare's use or understanding of "transformation" is not a theoretically neutral one. Transformation, as used by Klare, and the transformative constitutionalism that branches off from it both flow from the ideals of emancipation championed by the Critical Legal Studies (CLS) movement. In CLS, the notion and the idea of "emancipation" stand as one of its central tenets. For lawyers, judges and law teachers in Namibia this aspect of Klarean transformation must worry them because, if they accept it uncritically, they will commit themselves to pushing an American leftist political agenda. I do not insinuate that the United States has exerted pressure, or imposed any sanctions for that matter, on people in Namibia so that they welcome transformative constitutionalism with open arms, if only because the United States does not put this sort of left-wing constitutional principle into the liberal policies that it usually champions worldwide.

While Namibia and South Africa both need to restructure their societies to make them fairer and more just, the Klarean notion of "transformation" is neither the only way nor the better way of changing the foundations of a historically unequal society. Other ways to transform society, other than transformative constitutionalism, do exist.

Transformative Constitutions

If the language of transformation filters through a constitution, the most conservative or positivist judge would nonetheless issue judgements that produce social transformation. Nonetheless, would such a judge qualify as a transformative constitutionalist? I think that question does not really arise because the words "transform," "transformative" or "transformation" do not appear, not even once in the South African and Namibian constitutions. Nonetheless, assuming that those constitutions featured the language of transformation expressly, Klare does not answer that question satisfactorily as he suggests that positivists may produce transformative constitutionalism (Klare 1998, 170). By contrast, Roux says that, if the language of the Constitution compels a transformative reading, then liberal legalists and mainstream liberals (and positivists, I would add) can read the Constitution in a transformative manner (Roux 2009, 266). Such transformative reading would then be legally compelled, and not merely plausible.

Like the South African Constitution, the Constitution of Namibia brought about major changes. Among others, it replaced a parliamentary democracy characterised by legislative supremacy with a constitutional democracy in which the Constitution reigns supreme (Constitution of the Republic of Namibia, "Namibian Constitution," article 1(6). In the preamble, the Constitution recalls that the equal and inalienable rights of all members of the human family, including the right to life, liberty and the pursuit of happiness, have long been denied to the Namibian people by "colonialism, racism and apartheid." The Constitution translates the wish of Namibians to break from that ugly past and expresses "for ourselves and our children our resolve to cherish and to protect the gains of our long struggle" (Namibian Constitution preamble).

The Constitution provides for affirmative action (Namibian Constitution, article 23). It also promotes socio-economic rights as policies of the state (Namibian Constitution, chapter 11), even if the courts cannot enforce them (Namibian Constitution, chapter 11). Fombad considers these directive principles of state policies as "sham" elements of a constitution (Fombad 2014, 415). Thus, unlike its South African counterpart, the Namibian Constitution does not provide for justiciable socio-economic rights. In other words, although they no longer resorted to the formalistic positivism of the old constitutional dispensation, judges seem to stick to the traditional notion of constitutionalism.

After Independence in 1990, judges in Namibia extended the transformative character of the Constitution to the manner they interpreted it.

They abandoned the legal positivism they used to rely on in the erstwhile oppressive system to interpret the law (Horn 2016, 8). Judges shifted from positivism and "the austerity of tabulated legalism" (*Mwandingi v Minister of Defense* 1992 (2) SA 355 NmSC at 362), to a method of interpreting the Constitution that jurists can fairly describe as value based. Horn regards this method based on value judgements as "transformative interpretation" (Horn 2016, 12).

In light of the transformative content of the Namibian Constitution, one can logically and plausibly infer here that, if the Constitution already contains transformative language, interpretation no longer needs to become transformative to transform society. Rapatsa seemingly concurs. He says that transformative constitutionalism entails that challenges in society can best be addressed by using the supreme law, the Constitution, as the basis for transforming the society (Rapatsa 2015, 887).

The protagonists divide into two different camps. On the one hand, persons such as the CHE assert that law faculties, academics and students must distinguish what the transformative Constitution commands from what transformative constitutionalism demands (Council on Higher Education 2018, 18, 52).

On the other hand, Roux notes that no South African lawyer, reading the text of the Constitution conscientiously according to accepted conventions of legal reasoning, could arrive at a different outcome regarding the transformation that text expressly provides for (Roux 2009, 262). Unlike the situation in the United States, the transformative reading of the Constitution has a solid footing in the constitutional text, which will make it hard for any conservative judge to reverse the progressive ideals of the Constitution (Roux 2009, 284–285). In fact, the main argument of Klare that transformative constitutionalism represents the best way of interpreting the Constitution is belied by his observation that a positivist reading of the Constitution can bring about transformation just like a transformative reading of the Constitution.

Transformation in Transformative Constitutionalism

Still, the idea of transformation contributes to the fog surrounding transformative constitutionalism, not only because lawyers do not agree on what transformation means but also because they seem to regard a judge who interprets the Constitution so as to advance "transformation" as espousing transformative constitutionalism. For example, in evaluating Namibia's constitutional jurisprudence in the light of transformative constitutionalism, Horn sought to determine the extent to which a given judgement transformed society (Horn 2016, 12). His attention to the extent of transformation suggests that he associated (or confused) transformation with transformative constitutionalism (Horn 2016, 12).

Is a positivist judge who applies the Constitution with the goal of transforming society or who uses the language of transformation a transformative constitutionalist? Or does a conservative judge who renders a decision that has the effect of changing society a transformative constitutionalist? Or does transformative constitutionalism convey more than transformation?

DISAGREEMENTS OVER "TRANSFORMATIVE CONSTITUTIONALISM"

Lawyers in Namibia should stay clear of transformative constitutionalism because those who use it cannot actually say or agree on what that phrase relates to. Former Deputy Chief Justice Moseneke admits that "the meaning of transformation in juridical terms is as highly contested as it is difficult to formulate" (Moseneke 2002, 315). Similarly, the CHE accepts that scholars have not defined transformative constitutionalism consistently (Council on Higher Education 2018, 18). Yet, the CHE went on to demand that law faculties or law schools in South Africa comply with something that it knows means different things to different people.

KLARE: INTERPRETING THE CONSTITUTION POLITICALLY FOR A FAIRER SOCIETY

Klare's Influential Definition

Probably the most cited (at the time of writing, Klare's article had accumulated 456 citations on Google Scholar) and arguably the most influential research piece in South African constitutional law, Klare's seminal article has convinced many South African lawyers and academics to reconsider the nature of law and legal method (Roux 2009, 271). Klare defines "transformative constitutionalism" as (Klare 1998, 150):

> a long-term project of constitutional enactment, interpretation, and enforcement committed (not in isolation, of course, but in a historical context of conducive political developments) to transforming a country's political and social institutions and power relationships in a democratic, participatory, and egalitarian direction.

He adds that transformative constitutionalism connotes "an enterprise of inducing large-scale social change through nonviolent political processes grounded in law" (Klare 1998, 150).

Constitutional Interpretation

Klare's transformative constitutionalism zoomed in on constitutional interpretation. Philosophically, Klarean transformative constitutionalism rejects textualism. It mandates judges to interpret the Constitution liberally, to "press legal materials toward the limits of their pliability" (Klare 1998, 171). Horn concurs when he affirms that "a transformative constitutionalism, or a value judgment, leans more towards a broader interpretation to uphold the spirit of constitutional values" (Horn 2016, 12).

Like many other South African scholars, Botha echoed Klare's theory of constitutional interpretation. According to him, the new South African Constitution requires that lawyers abandon the formalism, objectivism and reductionism which defined law under apartheid (Botha 2003, 20). It requires them to rethink basic notions such as individual rights, democracy, intergovernmental relations, the separation of powers, and the rule of law in less essentialist terms (Botha 2003, 20).

LANGA: CHANGE FROM THE WOUNDS OF THE PAST TO A BETTER FUTURE

For his part, Langa based transformative constitutionalism on the Epilogue to the interim South African Constitution, which reads as follows:

> This Constitution provides a historic bridge between the past of a deeply divided society characterised by strife, conflict, untold suffering and injustice, and a future founded on the recognition of human rights, democracy and peaceful co-existence and development opportunities for all South Africans, irrespective of colour, race, class, belief or sex. (The provision on "national unity and reconciliation," following section 251 of the interim Constitution of the Republic of South Africa, Act 200 of 1993)

Based on that provision, he goes on to say that the "magnificent goal" of the Constitution to "heal the wounds of the past and guide us to a better future" constitutes "the core idea of transformative constitutionalism" (Langa 2006, 352). He imagines a better, future South Africa premised on substantive equality and socio-economic rights (Langa 2006, 352–354).

LE ROUX: SOCIAL CHANGE THROUGH CONSTITUTIONAL RIGHTS

Le Roux writes that "transformative constitutionalism" signifies "social change (transformation) through law (constitutional rights)" (Le Roux 2013,

31; Roux 2009, 260). This constitutionalism promises that South Africa can achieve fundamental social change (transformation) through legal reforms, supported by popular mobilisation, and enforced through the courts (Le Roux 2013, 31).

The position that le Roux reflects appears to close the distance between what a transformative Constitution provides for and what transformative constitutionalism calls for. And, even though the CHE expressly endorses Klare's rendering of transformative constitutionalism, it also embodies explicitly the position that transformative constitutionalism consists in changing society by enforcing constitutional rights (Council on Higher Education 2018, 18).

Do we even know what we are talking about? Though Langa insisted on the necessity to agree at any rate on some basis for understanding it (Langa 2006, 352), transformative constitutionalism has no single meaning accepted by most people. Horn, for example, conceives of transformative constitutionalism more broadly than Klare's CLS-informed and politicised version of transformative constitutionalism. Horn sees transformative constitutionalism as transformation. He argues that:

> [t]he usefulness of a transformative interpretation of a liberal constitution lies in the fact that it treats a constitution with an entrenched bill of rights as a *sui generis* that needs to be interpreted in a manner that appreciates the necessity of an interpretation that will lead to a transformed society. (Horn 2016, 13)

Because of his broader conception of transformative constitutionalism, Horn traces the first steps to formulate this constitutional theory to the apartheid days when Dugard sought to move away from the rigidity of the positivism then obtaining in South Africa (Horn 2016, 14). By contrast, Klare and Langa find the first written signs of transformative constitutionalism in the 1994 interim Constitution.

So when people brandish the term "transformative constitutionalism," do they even know what they are talking about? Disagreements concerning the core content of transformative constitutionalism should discourage lawyers in Namibia from accepting it blindly. First of all, because of these disagreements, Namibian lawyers will struggle to separate transformative constitutionalism from the more traditional sorts of constitutionalism, like that they already practice in Namibia. Nor would they be able to tell transformative constitutionalism from other strands of constitutionalism, such as the "transformative" constitutionalism found in Latin America (Von Bogdandy 2015, 109).

More worrying, the absence of consensus on transformative constitutionalism may explain why it remains unfinished business. Some scholars such as le Roux regard the promise of "transformative constitutionalism" as "unfulfilled" (Le Roux 2013, 32). As Le Roux alluded to, transformative constitutionalism may have so far failed to deliver on its promise of radical social transformation because of a "normative failure built into it," as opposed to failed implementation (Le Roux 2013, 33). For this reason, le Roux urges scholars, policy makers and other stakeholders to clarify what they mean by transformative constitutionalism (Le Roux 2013, 33).

Perhaps more importantly, lawyers in Namibia would not know for sure what transformative constitutionalism expects of them in terms of methodology. How should they teach, practice and research the law? Or how should they read a transformative constitution?

NO CLEAR METHODOLOGY FOR TRANSFORMATIVE CONSTITUTIONALISM

Following Klare equals following the CLS movement. Namibian lawyers should also think twice before they embrace transformative constitutionalism because it would require them to commit to a certain sort of politics and morality. Klare knew that many people would not agree with the political and moral commitments that his transformative constitutionalism entails (Klare 1998, 150). He nonetheless believed that they do not need to endorse his commitments to engage with his argument (Klare 1998, 150). I beg to disagree.

Granted, people will not need to share Klare's commitments to critically engage with his argument, but they will not be able to accept his argument without sharing the politics and morality that shaped it. Since Roux does not believe in the premises of the CLS movement, he discounts Klarean transformative constitutionalism as flawed (Roux 2009, 259) and ideologically driven.

By contrast, Horn prescribes transformative constitutionalism in Namibia (Horn 2016, 313) because, like he himself acknowledges, he has "sympathy for both the American Realists and the critical legal studies movement" (Horn 2016, 14, 312) and for "the work of Karl Klare in South Africa" (Horn 2016, 16). Likewise, Botha sounds like Klare because he too espoused Klare's ideas and the main themes of the CLS movement. Like Klare, Botha says the new South African Constitution requires lawyers to rethink relationships, between law and politics, the individual and society, private and public law, and common law and legislation, in ways that transcend the classifications and hierarchies that typified law under apartheid. For Botha, the Constitution seeks to uphold the rule of law without assuming a rigid division between law and politics (Botha 2003, 20).

In the same way, if lawyers and judges in Namibia sign up for Klarean transformative constitutionalism, they would be adhering consciously or unwittingly to the principles of the CLS movement.

THE CRITICAL LEGAL STUDIES (CLS) MOVEMENT

Overview

Klare forms part of the most notable professors associated with the CLS movement, alongside Duncan Kennedy, Roberto Unger and Mark Tushnet. The Conference on Critical Legal Studies ("CCLS," "CLS" or "the Crits") emerged in American law schools in the 1970s and 1980s, around the same time both postmodernism and post-structuralism rose to prominence (i.e., in the 1960s). The CLS movement was profoundly influenced by the Frankfurt School, which featured thinkers such as Jürgen Habermas, Theodor Adorno and Herbert Marcuse (Presser 2017, 279).

A number of elements characterise the CLS movement. Overall, CLS reinvigorates American Legal Realism; it borrowed from Europe; it boasts a wide, ecumenical scope; and it has passion for social change (Presser 2017, 288). CLS perfected and completed what American Legal Realism had begun (Presser 2017, 280). Legal Realism dominated legal thought for most of the 1920s and 1930s (Note 1982, 1671, "hereinafter 'Bramble bush'"). Three tenets characterise realist methodology: an emphasis on the study of how legal doctrine evolved, criticism of formalistic reasoning, and a firm commitment to progressive law reform grounded in social scientific reform (Note 1982, 1671).

Connection to Transformative Constitutionalism

Some features of CLS directly speak to transformative constitutionalism. First, following postmodernism and post-structuralism, CLS aims to refute claims to objectivity (Presser 2017, 288–289). Incidentally, Davis rebuffed legal postmodernists whom he called academics "with bare souls and full pockets" for playing an "indeterminate game around language" and wasting time on the latest fashionable philosophical "fads" (Davis 1999, 178–179 and 711).

Moreover, some CLS scholars, especially Horwitz, underscore the contingent nature of law and argue that lawyers and judges can always change what looks like immutable laws or even immutable constitutional rights (Davis 1999, 292). In particular, emphasising that lawyers can even change constitutional principles, Horwitz wrote that they should recognise that "constitutional principles, like all legal principles, are inevitably created by judges in accordance with their conceptions of moral values and social needs" (Horwitz 1998, 28–29).

The CLS movement also concerns itself with issues of radical change and transformation. Presser notes that some CLS scholars, if not most of them, seek to "generate radical political alternatives to existing institutions" (Note

1982, 1684). These alternatives would encompass anarchism and chaos theory. CLS does not seek reformist policy programmes, but a radical political agenda (Note 1982, 1677).

CLS scholars dismiss liberal legalists. Specifically, Klare dismissed Hart, Ely, Dworkin and Wechsler as liberal legalists who aim to maintain the law-politics boundary by describing rational decision procedures (e.g., deduction, balancing, purposive reasoning) with which to arrive at legal outcomes from neutral, consensus-based general principles expressed in the legal order (Klare 1998, 158). For Roux, Klare accuses these liberal legalists as incapable of getting over the fact that legal interpretation, especially constitutional adjudication, is inevitably political (Roux 2009, 267).

Much of the criticisms levelled against postmodernism applies to CLS too because of CLS's close affinity with postmodernism. Accordingly, lawyers in Namibia could fault CLS for believing that, in law, the worth of all values depends on the morality and the politics of the judges or the society who interpret the law in question. Granted, the Supreme Court of Namibia in the leading case of *Corporal Punishment* held that the interpretation of the Constitution must identify and rely on the values of the Namibian people (*Ex Parte Attorney-General: In Re Corporal Punishment by Organs of State* 1991 NR 178 (SC) at 188, hereinafter "*Corporal Punishment*"), but it does not follow from this holding that those values are easily changeable, elastic, or as "plastic" as Klare contends. For one thing, the majority of Namibians may not think it worthwhile to spend the amounts of money that people in Western countries pay for the care of animals and pets.

Postmodernism resembles CLS in throwing off appeals to truth and objectivity, and there lies CLS's biggest flaw. In rejecting any pretention to truth and objectivity, CLS basically defeat its own purposes of presenting itself as a true or objectively real theory.

A METHODOLOGY OF TRANSFORMATIVE CONSTITUTIONALISM?

Just like constitutionalism in general, transformative constitutionalism has no methodology of its own. One could infer from its origins in the CLS movement that the methodology of transformative constitutionalism corresponds to the one used by CLS scholars. Roux also associated Klare's argument with the "methodology" of the CLS (*Corporal Punishment* at 259). But that inference assumes that CLS has a methodology in the first place, which is inaccurate. CLS does not have any single methodology. In fact, CLS does not even amount to a theory; it better qualifies as a movement – a movement that brings together different ideas, different methodologies, often conflicting. As Minkkinen said:

> [b]ut one could also well claim that the CLS movement was never really a proper "movement." It was, rather, a community of loosely affiliated individuals who worked mainly in North American law schools from the late 1970s to the mid-1980s representing various non-doctrinal approaches. Although CLS researchers were politically all clearly left-of-centre, their political kinship was never enough to consolidate the various approaches into a method. (Minkkinen 2018, 148)

Klare himself, in a bibliography he wrote with Duncan Kennedy, recognised that the CLS has no clear methodology:

> CLS scholarship has been influenced by a variety of currents in contemporary radical social theory, but does not reflect any agreed upon set of political tenets or methodological approaches. Quite the contrary, there is sharp division within the CLS movement on such matters. CLS has sought to encourage the widest possible range of approaches and debate within a broad commitment to democratic and egalitarian values and a belief that scholars, students, and lawyers alike have some contribution to make in the creation of a more just society. (Kennedy and Klare 1984, 461–462)

No jurist or lawyer can derive the methodology of transformative constitutionalism through the methodology of CLS movement for the simple reason that the movement has no single methodology. This state of affairs should concern Namibian lawyers and law teachers because, given the absence of any clear methodology for transformative constitutionalism, they would not know how to teach it, let alone how their students should carry out research, in a fashion that they can confidently describe as "transformative constitutionalist."

UNFIT FOR THE NAMIBIAN CONTEXT

Namibian lawyers should not wish to emulate transformative constitutionalism as practised and variously understood in South Africa. Transformative constitutionalism has become dominant, if not hegemonic, in legal education and constitutional interpretation in Namibia's southern neighbour. In fact, the way South African lawyers apply transformative constitutionalism contravenes the emancipatory ideals of the CLS movement that inspired it. Nor does it sit comfortably with ongoing efforts to decolonise the law in South Africa.

NAMIBIA'S BOND WITH SOUTH AFRICA

A Common History

Like its South African counterpart, the Constitution of Namibia has a transformative character. However, unlike their South African colleagues (Langa 2006, 351; Moseneke 2002, 315), Namibian judges have not fashioned any theory of transformative constitutionalism. Namibia shares a lot in common with South Africa such that the transformative constitutionalism evolved in its neighbour persuade or otherwise appeal to lawyers in Namibia, who will find it hard to resist the allure of transformative constitutionalism.

Both countries suffered from colonisation, slavery, racism and legislated discrimination. In 1915, South Africa invaded Namibia/South West Africa during World War I (Zongwe 2019, 133–134). In 1919, South Africa then administered Namibia on behalf of the British Crown for the League of Nations (and later the United Nations) (Zongwe 2019, 44–45). South Africa administered Namibia/South West Africa as one of its provinces. In 1948, the South African government introduced apartheid in Namibia. In 1966, that legitimate administration of Namibia became an occupation (Zongwe 2019, 133–134). Namibia gained independence from apartheid South Africa in 1990 whereas South Africa achieved majority rule and democratisation in 1994.

Through this common history, both countries feel the strong moral and democratic pressure to transform their respective societies. Understandably, South African judges and lawyers got seduced by the language and vocabulary of transformative constitutionalism. Namibia could follow suit, but Namibian judges and lawyers should refrain from the almost irresistible temptation to underwrite transformative constitutionalism. They should weigh up carefully how this project will affect Namibian adjudication and jurisprudence.

The Namibian Legal System

Because of its closely related histories, Namibia has largely inherited the legal system of South Africa. The Mandate for South West Africa specifically mandated South Africa to extend its legal system to Namibia, which South Africa did (Mandate for South West Africa, 1919, article 2. mandating South Africa on behalf of the League of Nations and later the United Nations to apply its legal system in Namibia). See Zongwe 2019, 135 and 416. Proclamation 20 of 1919, applying the law of South Africa); and Administration of Justice Proclamation 21 of 1919, section 1(1) introducing Roman-Dutch law "as existing and applied in the Province of the Cape of Good Hope" into South

West Africa/Namibia. See Amoo 2008, 55–77). As a result, the main features of the Namibian legal system resemble those of South Africa.

Constitutional Adjudication

And, even after independence, Namibia relied, in many constitutional law cases, on jurisprudence from South Africa. One notable exception is transformative constitutionalism.

Generally speaking, Namibian courts do not approach the interpretation of the Constitution in any consistent or dogmatic fashion. Horn discerns no clear constitutional model for interpreting the Constitution by superior courts in Namibia (Horn 2016, 309). He perceives some traits of a battle, waged during the early years after Independence in 1990, between positivism (O'Linn) and transformative constitutionalism (Mahomed) (Horn 2016, 307). However, none of them were consistent or dogmatic in their different approaches (Horn 2016, 307).

Horn observed that Namibian courts prefer formalistic arguments (Horn 2016, 306). According to him, they prefer to solve constitutional issues by referring to formalistic law rather than substantive argument (Horn 2016, 310). As a rule, Namibian superior courts still approach the law as sacrosanct principles and seldom mention the idea that a constitutional problem may have more than one "correct" answer (Horn 2016, 306). They present every judgement as the only possible interpretation (Horn 2016, 306).

Judges in Namibia have read the Constitution by drawing on value judgements. Mahomed first formulated this way of interpreting the Constitution in the leading case of *Corporal Punishment* at 188. The question as to whether a particular form of punishment authorised by the law can properly be said to be inhuman or degrading involves the exercise of a value judgement by the Court. It is however a value judgement which requires objectively to be articulated and identified, regards being had to the contemporary norms, aspirations, expectations and sensitivities of the Namibian people as expressed in its national institutions and its Constitution, and further having regards to the emerging consensus of values in the civilised international community (of which Namibia is a part) which Namibians share.

While this method has enabled the judiciary to look cleaner in the eyes of the majority given Namibia's colonial and apartheid past, it risks falling victim to judicial populism. In democratising the judiciary in that manner, it may end up tyrannising minorities, as shown in *Frank* (*Chairperson of the Immigration Selection Board v Frank and Another* 2001 NR 107 (SC)" (hereinafter, *Frank*). (See Horn 2016, 311, claiming that O'Linn, the judge who the majority opinion, relied on populist political statements to determine that the reference to sex in the equality clause of the Constitution excluded sexual orientation). In that case, O'Linn AJA wrote in the majority judgement that, based on the values of the Namibian people (Frank 2001, 135–137, 141, 142, and 150), "sex" in Article 10 of the Constitution (dealing with equality and freedom from discrimination) does not include "sexual orientation" Frank 2001, 149–150). He further held that parliament, "one of the most important institutions to express the present day values of the Namibian people" (Frank 2001, 141), stands in a better position than the Supreme Court to insert sexual orientation into the ambit of "sex" under Article 10 (Frank 2001, 157). Judicial populism, which Mudde deems "a form of extreme majoritarianism," advances democracy, but it would contravene constitutionalism by failing to constrain both popular sovereignty and majority rule (CasMudde 2013).

Even though Namibia should not buy transformative constitutionalism, judges would enhance the quality of their decisions in constitutional cases if they could circumscribe their value-laden method with the traditional concepts of constitutionalism or with other strategies for interpreting the Constitution.

NAMIBIAN LEGAL CULTURE AND EDUCATION

A Conservative Culture

Just like its legal system, Namibia's legal education fell heir to the culture that South Africa left behind after Namibia became independent in 1990. Today still, many of the textbooks recommended in Namibia, just like many of the laws used, originate from South Africa. In addition, many of the lecturers and legal practitioners obtained degrees from South Africa.

In 1998, Klare described the legal culture underpinning legal education in South Africa as conservative (Klare 1998, 168). This description would apply to Namibia as well. By "legal culture," Klare did not refer to political ideology; rather, he meant the "professional sensibilities, habits of mind, and intellectual reflexes" (Klare 1998, 166). He viewed this legal culture as "conservative" in the sense that lawyers schooled in that culture have a "relatively strong faith in the precision, determinacy and self-revealingness of words and texts" (Klare 1998, 168). More specifically, he depicted legal culture in South Africa (and thereby, to a large extent, Namibia) in the following words:

> Legal interpretation in South Africa tends to be more highly structured, technicist, literal and rule-bound than in the States, whereas U.S. legal culture is much more policy-oriented and consequentialist. South African lawyers appear more prepared than their U.S. counterparts to deduce relatively specific conclusions from general and abstract premises, with fewer intermediate steps than the Americans would look for. There is a bit more reverence for law among

> South African lawyers and, I might add, South African politicians. (Klare 1998, 168–169)

While this portrayal of legal cultures in the United States and South Africa appears fairly accurate, Karl left out of his account the jurists, lawyers and judges in the United States who also profess a strong textualism, a "relatively strong faith" in legal texts like Scalia (Scalia and Garner 2012, in the introduction of their book, the authors defend textualism as a sound theory of constitutional and statutory interpretation).

Langa did not fully agree with Klare on legal culture, which further underscores the rifts among those who propound transformative constitutionalism. In tune with Klare, Langa described legal education in South Africa as mainly focusing on private and commercial law and as rewarding "the rational deduction of inevitable conclusions from unquestionable principles" (Langa 2006, 355). That "tradition of analytical argument," as he called it, actually refers to the doctrinal legal method (Hutchinson 2018, 14, explaining that what characterises doctrinal work the most is that "arguments are derived from authoritative sources, such as existing rules, principles, precedents, and scholarly publications"). Langa claimed that such tradition no longer suffices, but he differs from Klare because, unlike Klare, he recognises that this tradition still forms "a vital part of any lawyer's arsenal" and that educators would fail in their duties if they did not pass on that tradition to students (Langa 2006, 355–356; Hutchinson 2018, 39, who argues that lawyers may use other methods after conducting doctrinal research method, but that they must commence any legal discussion by using the doctrinal method). For reasons I provide later in this chapter, I also think that doctrinal legal methodologies should retain their place in the legal curriculum.

The Legal Curriculum under the Transformative Constitutional Dispensation

The CHE in Namibia has not (yet) elevated transformative constitutionalism to the status it enjoys in South Africa. It does not require the University of Namibia (UNAM) to expressly incorporate transformative constitutionalism in its legal curriculum. Nor did any judge in Namibia invite lawyers and law teachers to make transformative constitutionalism the heart of legal education in Namibia. However, this situation rather advantages Namibia as it affords Namibian law teachers an opportunity and distance to learn from South Africa's (mis)take and ponder whether they should espouse Klarean transformative constitutionalism.

Langa recognised that law faculties in South Africa have done a lot to bring legal education in line with the ideals of transformative constitutionalism

(Langa 2006, 356). In particular, he says that constitutional law and human rights law occupy a far greater space on the curriculum and that sections of most courses and textbooks on private and commercial areas now deal with how the Constitution has impacted those fields of law (Langa 2006, 356).

In Namibia, the University Senate-approved prospectus of the UNAM Faculty of Law indicates that the Constitutional Law module does not compel lecturers to teach transformative constitutionalism (University of Namibia 2019, 12). The module expressly comprises constitutionalism only (University of Namibia 2019, 12). However, for a long time in recent years, the module was taught by Nico Horn, a noted constitutional expert in Namibia. Interestingly, Horn wrote his doctoral dissertation on the subject of transformative constitutionalism in Namibia, which he subsequently published as a book (Horn 2016). Presumably, he discussed transformative constitutionalism in his Constitutional Law classes.

On final analysis, whether a constitutional law lecturer teaches transformative constitutionalism or not, does not matter that much. What does, the lecturer must ensure that he or she teaches transformative constitutionalism as one of several other possible methods of interpreting the Constitution. The constitutional law lecturer should not allow transformative constitutionalism to swamp legal thinking.

THE HEGEMONY OF TRANSFORMATIVE CONSTITUTIONALISM IN SOUTH AFRICA

Lawyers and educators in Namibia should refuse to entrench transformative constitutionalism as deeply as their colleagues in South Africa embedded it in the South African legal educational landscape because, deployed in that fashion, it tends to rule out or marginalise other useful strategies for reading the Constitution. Transformative constitutionalism does not constitute the only angle from which to approach the Constitution, and it certainly does not represent the only tool to transform a society, away from its brutal, unequal and racist past.

Transforming Legal Education

Klare sought to align South Africa's "conservative" legal culture with the values and aspirations enshrined in the Constitution (Klare 1998, 151, 168, 170, 171). He believes that, though not sufficient, a "progressive" legal culture and judicial method are a necessary condition for transformative constitutionalism to succeed in the long run (Klare 1998, 170, 188). However, neither Klare nor Langa precisely showed how South African universities should re-align the way they teach law. Quinot did, and in doing so he offered a theoretical framework within which South African universities must teach law (Quinot 1992, 412).

Quinot's theoretical framework, which he calls "transformative legal education," advocates shifting from a formalistic legal reasoning to substantive reasoning under a transformative constitution (Quinot 1992, 412, 417). This reasoning corresponds to what Mureinik (Mureinik 1994, 32) referred to as shifting from a "culture of authority" to a "culture of justification" (Quinot 1992, 413). This shift means understanding that an authoritative source, for instance a statute or a court decision, does not validate a legal position; only the norms explicitly considered by that position can validate it (Quinot 1992, 417).

Transformative legal education aims to shift legal education towards a "constructivist student-centred teaching model" and "non-linear, relational or complex" (Quinot 1992, 412, 412). Constructivism views the process of learning as one of constructing knowledge; it rejects a single "correct" construction of knowledge, thereby enhancing the possibility of imagining new ways of doing things (Quinot 1992, 423, 424). And student centredness in Quinot's framework puts learning, the learner and her context at the centre, and moves from a system where printed word dominates to a system where the student immerses herself in a digital world that fundamentally changes the notion of knowledge (Quinot 1992, 432). It embraces transformative constitutionalism as guiding the discipline of law and constructivist pedagogies as directing strategies to teach law (Quinot 1992, 432).

Quinot's theoretical framework fails in two crucial respects. First, despite the absence of any consensus on what transformative constitutionalism means, Quinot does not define the term that underlie his framework. Instead, he adopts Klare's politicised account (Quinot 1992, 414). This poses a problem because the Klarean rendering of transformative constitutionalism derives from the CLS movement, which does not have one single methodology. Consequently, Quinot's theory fails to show that his transformative legal education conforms to the Klarean version of transformative constitutionalism.

In fact, with a few exceptions as seen in some strands of positivism, Quinot's framework would work with any progressive jurisprudential school of thought, including natural law, Dworkin's theory (Roux 2009, 259, who argue that lawyers and judges may interpret the Constitution as a transformative constitution, and to engage in transformative constitutionalism, through Dworkin's interpretive method), Marxism and the economic analysis of law. Let me rephrase it: Quinot's framework aligns with transformative constitutionalism in an arbitrary manner. The Constitution itself does not prescribe the interpretive theory to follow when reading it.

Quinot fails to show that his framework inescapably flows from transformative constitutionalism. For example, the shift from the printed word to the digital word can be encouraged by virtually all philosophy of law. Even positivists can embrace teaching that heavily relies on digital technologies.

Surely, law faculties in South Africa, Namibia and elsewhere in Africa should seriously consider switching to student-centred pedagogies, but Quinot gives no evidence that this upgrading of legal teaching can only be justified by transformative constitutionalism. Quinot's framework does not even reflect Klare's emphasis on politics as a virtue or on adjudication, which further disconnects his framework from Klarean transformative constitutionalism.

One reason why transformative constitutionalism may not serve legal education well lies in its scope. While hardly anyone will dispute the important place of transformative constitutionalism in public law, primarily human rights and constitutional law, many will doubt that transformative constitutionalism can enjoy the same pride of place in commercial law and private law. Van der Walt described the question as to whether the bill of rights "can and should permeate (or affect the development of) private law" as "[o]ne of the most complicated and controversial questions in contemporary South African legal theory" (Van Der Walt 2005, 655).

Indeed, lawyers, judges, academics and the general public have used transformative constitutionalism to a wide array of situations in South Africa, including the effective implementation of domestic workers' rights (Le Roux 2013, 31–63), corrective rape against lesbians (Koraan and Geduld 2015, 1931), equality (Rapatsa 2015, 18), animal rights (Bilchitz 2010, 267), and the role of a developmental state approach to socio-economic transformation (Rosa 2011, 543, arguing that shifting to a democratic developmental state best guarantees that the state will achieve socio-economic transformation in South Africa). But they have drawn on transformative constitutionalism in private law and commercial law only rarely (For instance, Moseneke 2009, 3; Pieterse 2005, 155, 156 and 160–162, arguing that addressing imbalances in private power forms part of constitutional transformation).

How Transformative Constitutionalism Impoverishes Legal Education

Transformative constitutionalism deploys a very sophisticated reasoning and language, just like the CLS movement that spun it off. And, like the Legal Realism from which it stems, transformative constitutionalism can prove especially insightful when assessing adjudication and court judgements. However, when educators make it the centre of legal education (Council on Higher Education 2018, 52, stating that transformative constitutionalism "underpins" LLB programmes in South Africa), it no longer serves the same emancipatory ideals that ignited it in the first place; it becomes indoctrination. Habermas affirmed that what motivates all critical research aims to emancipate (Habermas 1966, 294, affirming that the motivation of all critical research is self-reflection with the objective to emancipate). In that sense, the way lawyers and law teachers practice transformative constitutionalism in South Africa impoverishes legal education.

The South African CHE now expects law faculties or schools to "demonstrate that transformative constitutionalism is a *dominant* principle embedded in their LLB programmes" (Council on Higher Education 2018, 18). It also expects them to fully internalise the notion of transformative constitutionalism both in their curricula and in "the attitudes and mind-set of staff and students" (Council on Higher Education 2018, 52, 59). Inexorably, these expectations suggest that a lecturer who spurns transformative constitutionalism may today be dismissed as unfit to teach law in South Africa. In the same manner, a bar or law society may treat a student who rejects transformative constitutionalism as not fit and proper to practice law.

In a perfect world, legal education and education in general should empower students, not indoctrinate them. Law faculties could empower students most effectively by presenting them with a palette of solutions to social problems and with alternative approaches, including devising their own. However, when the government takes a political decision that one particular theoretical model should dominate legal education and act as a precondition for accreditation, education becomes indoctrination. Such decision may even impinge on academic freedom (Van Staden 2019, arguing that the CHE threatens academic freedom with transformative constitutionalism). Quinot also acknowledges that what threatens transformative legal education the most is a pedagogy that privileges certain skills and forms of knowledge that may exclude alternatives – the very thing that pedagogies aim to avoid (Quinot 1992, 423). He also recognises that this threat – excluding alternatives – could destroy the project of transformative constitutionalism (Quinot 1992, 423).

Transformative constitutionalism has morphed into such a paramount principle in South African legal education that even the CLS scholars who inspired it and who intended to emancipate rather than dominate, would no longer condone.

An Unnecessary Dominance in Constitutional Interpretation

Namibian lawyers may wish to pause before buying the transformative-constitutionalism idea because its South African apologists sell it as the best interpretation of the Constitution. Klare makes it clear that transformative constitutionalism is the best way to interpret the South African Constitution (Klare 1998, 151).

Ideally, transformative constitutionalism should remain but one mode of interpreting the Constitution. Roux contends that Klare's interpretive method does not represent the only way to read the South African Constitution, and thinks that Dworkin's adjudication theory offers a method easier to defend and better apt to realise the progressive values of the South African Constitution than Klare's (Roux 2009, 259). By the same token, with specific reference to Namibia, Mundia prescribes Dworkin's theory of "constructive interpretation" and "law as integrity" to read the Constitution (Mundia 2016, 73).

Judges and lawmakers should not make transformative constitutionalism the sole and unique tool to read the Constitution, for they may come up with more innovative and more adapted interpretive approaches going forward. Policymakers should not close out other avenues for taking constitutional interpretation in alternative directions; they should always leave the door open for future improvements, refinements and adjustments.

Judges should keep open the range of interpretive approaches, progressive and conservative. Klare himself acknowledged that legal formalism, though widely discredited by jurists, could produce politically and morally progressive results in human rights, criminal proceedings and labour law (Klare 1998, 170). Similarly, Macedo remarks that (neo)liberal constitutionalism can have a "radically transformative dimension" (Macedo 1998, 56, 57). And, as a matter of fact, the so-called "conservative" legal cultures in South Africa and Namibia did produce progressive judgements, judgements in line with the values and the aspirations of the Constitution, implying that they can contribute to transforming society even if they do not embrace the philosophy of transformative constitutionalism.

Horn does not see positivism as the enemy of Namibian transformative jurisprudence either (Horn 2016, 314). O'Linn's positivism and literal interpretation yielded several good, transformative judgements such as the *Mushwena* case (*S v Mushwena and Others* 2004 NR 276 (SC); Horn 2016, 305). Horn noticed that some judgements came to the wrong conclusion mainly because the judges did not motivate them well enough, not because they adhered to positivism (for example, in *Frank*), while judges with known positivist leanings gave good transformative judgements (e.g., in *Mwilima (Government of the Republic of Namibia and Others v Mwilima and All Other Accused in the Caprivi Treason Trial* 2002 NR 235 (SC); Horn 2016, 314)). Though O'Linn (positivism) and Mahomed (transformative constitutionalism) obviously operated from different jurisprudential models, their judgements seldom produced different outcomes (Horn 2016, 307).

Transformative Politics

The big danger in allowing Klarean transformative constitutionalism to pervade the interpretation of the Constitution is that, apart from being unnecessarily dominant, it will over-politicise constitutional adjudication. Roux sees Klarean transformative constitutionalism as nothing more than an ideological project (Roux 2009, 271). The CLS that shaped transformative constitutionalism wears a mantra that says that all law is essentially politics (Presser 2017, 291).

In the eyes of Klare, South African and Namibian lawyers show "caution," they downplay the "plasticity" of legal materials, and they hesitate to press those materials "toward the limits of their pliability" (Klare 1998, 171). Warnings against the risks of unbridled judicial activism and of reading a constitution too liberally form the backdrop of Klare's perspective. Kentridge reminds people of the necessity to constrain constitutional interpretation: "[It] cannot be too strongly stressed that the Constitution does not mean whatever we might wish it to mean" (*S v Zuma* 1995 (4) BCLR 401 (CC) para 17).

Horn stresses the point that transformative constitutionalism gives credence to both text and political context, which he considers important in a new democracy with an undemocratic oppressive past like Namibia (Horn 2016, 13). However, Klare does not sound concerned about text, preferring instead to highlight the indeterminacy of legal texts (Klare 1998, 151 and 159–166).

Perhaps, the most controversial aspect of Klare's theory of adjudication relates to his attitude towards politics as a "virtue." Klare says that discussing transformative constitutionalism implies that judges and other adjudicators ought to acknowledge the political character of adjudication (Klare 1998, 151 and 187, 188). In short, Klare thinks that transformation requires that judicial method and legal interpretation match the substantively progressive aspirations of the Constitution (Klare 1998, 188). But, here, Klare appears to contradict himself. Earlier in his same seminal article, he observed that no correlation exists between judicial style and interpretive method, on the one hand, and political ideology, on the other (Klare 1998, 169, 170). Yet, he concludes that transformation (politics) calls for a progressive judicial method and legal interpretation (Klare 1998, 188).

While Klare claims that transformative constitutionalism urges a "politicized account of the rule of law" (Klare 1998, 188), he himself does not disclose that his transformative constitutionalism mirrors the political commitments of the CLS movement he belongs to. As Roux remarks, calling on lawyers to read the Constitution in a Klarean-transformative manner is to read it in an "ideologically loaded way" (Roux 2009, 267).

Roux does not deem Klare's proposal (that the South African Constitutional Court's frankly admits its political role) as wise (Roux 2009, 284). He thinks that, if it heeded Klare's advice, the Constitutional Court would expose itself to more charges that it comprises unelected judges who oppose the people's revolution (Roux 2009, 284). I would add that, if the apex court publicly and routinely declares that it hands down judgements based on (its) political or moral choices, it should expect litigants and people to reject their judgements more often and lose confidence in the impartiality of that court.

An-Na'im observes that a stronger judiciary may tackle more politically sensitive controversies and, in doing so, it may be supported by a well-informed and active citizenry but, from the perspective of constitutionalism, that may prove in fact unwise and imprudent for the judiciary (An-Na'im 2006, 7). What may at first look like a victory for one side of the controversy can create greater constitutional or political problems and prompt the government to defeat such victory by, for example, appointing ideologically driven judges who can shift the policies of the country in the opposite direction (An-Na'im 2006, 7). If the Supreme Court in *Frank* had interpreted "sex" to include "sexual orientation," the Namibian parliament could have easily defeated such interpretation by amending the Constitution to exclude sexual orientation from provision prohibiting discrimination on the basis of "sex." The Court's interpretation would have certainly been progressive, and even transformative in the Klarean sense, but what would have first appeared as a victory one day would end in defeat the next day. Hence An-Na'im's advice that constitutionalism should generally include the principle of separation of powers (An-Na'im 2006, 7), unlike Klare who dismisses such principle as "traditional" (Klare 1998, 159).

If Namibians wish to have judges play an overtly political role, then they should as a nation and through a political process, decide that judges should be either appointed through a partisan political process for their ideology or that people should elect judges like they do in some states of the United States. Unless they decide democratically to have political judges, they should resist such suggestion. After all, if any nation wants political judges, it can simply have its parliament decide court cases. Actually, this would go against constitutionalism as a political culture, which essentially constrains the power of the state even in a democracy, including a democracy that freely elected its judges or decided that they should primarily engage in making laws.

The liberal legalists (for instance, Hart and Dworkin) that Klare dismisses as failing to recognise the political character of adjudication actually acknowledge the importance of value judgements or value choices. Roux gets it right when he says that liberal legalists try to explain why recognising judicial value choice does not unavoidably conflict with the proposition that legal reasoning differs from political reasoning (Roux 2009, 267). Roux believes that Klare's dismissal of liberal legalists like Dworkin and Wechsler is unwise and unnecessary because it makes transformative constitutionalism depend on lawyers' readiness to also dismiss all these theorists as fundamentally misguided (Roux 2009, 267).

In sum, similar to most legal realists, Klare has exaggerated the role of politics in interpreting the Constitution. Specifically, Posner remarked that CLS scholars like Klare "exaggerated when they generalized their criticisms to all courts exaggerated to a point at which they were seen as a residue of 1960's-style infantile leftism" (Posner 2016, 263–264).

CONCLUSION: WHERE DID *UBUNTU* GO?

Lawyers in Namibia should have cold shoulders and cold feet when considering transformative constitutionalism and the dangers it poses. Among other dangers, transformative constitutionalism will likely confuse those who use it because it means different things to different people. It will further confuse its users about what transformation should consist of. It will provide no detailed guidance as to how lawyers should teach, research, practice and interpret the law. And, because it tends to exclude or marginalise other theories, principles and legal methodologies, such as doctrinal methodologies, it does not fit the Namibian context. It tries to besiege legal education and interpretation as a supreme principle, and it oversells politics in constitutional adjudication. Given these tendencies, lawyers should prevent it from dominating the Namibian legal scene. *When or if lawyers in Namibia or elsewhere in Africa adopt transformative constitutionalism, then they should only treat it as one possibility among a varied and rich menu of possible techniques to teach, research, practice and read the law.* Transformative constitutionalism has much to offer to develop Namibia's constitutional jurisprudence, but that potential and promise can only materialise if Namibian lawyers, judges and educators use it alongside other constitutional approaches, say liberal positivism and Dworkin's theory, and provided lawyers leave the door open for new and hopefully better methods of reading legal texts. Roux rightly says that Klarean transformative constitutionalism has no special claim to constitutional endorsement (Roux 2009, 271).

The fact that the practice of transformative constitutionalism takes on some dominant, if not hegemonic, overtones signals that it has become a good candidate for decolonisation. The CHE recognises, on the one hand, the national imperative to decolonise and "Africanise" higher education curricula (Council on Higher Education 2018, 18, 52), yet it demands, on the other hand, that an American left-wing ideological project "dominate" legal education (Council on Higher Education 2018, 18). In other words, it attempts to decolonise the legal curricula so that another, more sophisticated foreign legal ideology can colonise legal education in South Africa.

The CHE claimed that legal education cannot be divorced from transformative constitutionalism and it expressly endorsed Klare's understanding of transformative constitutionalism (Council on Higher Education 2018, 65). One part of the problem is that very few scholars engaged Klare's argument (Roux 2009, 258). The other part is that, except for a handful of scholars like Roux, almost no one addressed the theory that informs that argument. I therefore humbly submit that the CHE does not deeply understand the ideological foundations of Klare's argument and that, as a consequence, it does not really know what it did.

Since CLS heavily weighs in Klarean transformative constitutionalism, lawyers in Africa should not regard it as an indigenous theory. Roux seems to agree with this position when he maintains that Klare should not use the South African Constitution to settle old scores in Anglo-American legal theory (Roux 2009, 267).

Probably, the greatest danger of transplanting transformative constitutionalism resides in the manner it ostracises *Ubuntu*, an admittedly African philosophy and worldview. Lawyers and policy makers could have grounded the entire transformation agenda on *Ubuntu*. For instance, Langa's insistence on socio-economic rights and equality could draw from the values enshrined in *Ubuntu*. Elsewhere, I have already explained that South African constitutional law largely articulated a truly African philosophy of equality, but that early scholars have not based though they could and should have built that philosophy on Ubuntu (Zongwe 2016, 32).

Lawyers and judges in South Africa have wasted a great deal of resources on transformative constitutionalism that they could have used to flesh out a political theory based on *Ubuntu* to give content to the Constitution. Transformative constitutionalism has thus worked as a wasteful distraction from the necessity to decolonise law and evolve a richer and more indigenous jurisprudence. Nowhere in its 2018 report on the status of the LLB qualification in South Africa, did CHE mention *Ubuntu*, yet it imposes transformative constitutionalism on all law faculties and schools. The greatest danger of transplanting transformative constitutionalism is to distract Africans from themselves, their inner self, their *Ubuntu*.

BIBLIOGRAPHY

Albertyn, C., and Goldblatt, B. (1998). "Facing the challenge of transformation: Difficulties in the development of an indigenous jurisprudence of equality." *South African Journal on Human Rights*, Volume 14, 248–250.

An-Na'im, A. A. (2006). *African Constitutionalism and the Role of Islam*. Philadelphia: University of Pennsylvania Press.

Beaubien, J. (2018). "The country with the world's worst inequality is. . ." *NPR*, 2 April 2018. https://www.npr.org/sections/goatsandsoda/2018/04/02/598864666/the-country-with-the-worlds-worst-inequality-is.

Bilchitz, D. (2010). "Does transformative constitutionalism require the recognition of animal rights?" *Southern African Public Law*, Volume 25(2), 267–300.

Botha, H. (2003). "Metaphoric reasoning and transformative constitutionalism (part 2)." *Journal of South African Law*, Volume 2003(1), 20–36.

Constitution of the Republic of South Africa. (1996).

Council on Higher Education. (2018). *The State of the Provision of the Bachelor of Laws (LLB) Qualification in South Africa: Report on the National Review of LLB Programmes in South Africa.*

Davis, D. (1999). *Democracy and Deliberation: Transformation and the South African Legal Order*. Kenwyn: Juta.

Ex Parte Attorney-General: In Re Corporal Punishment by Organs of State 1991 NR 178 (SC).

Fombad, C. M. (2014). "Strengthening constitutional order and upholding the rule of law in Central Africa: Reversing the descent towards symbolic constitutionalism." *African Human Rights Law Journal*, Volume 14(2), 412–448.

Government of the Republic of Namibia and Others v Mwilima and All Other Accused in the Caprivi Treason Trial 2002 NR 235 (SC).

Habermas, J. (1966). "Knowledge and interest." *Inquiry: An Interdisciplinary Journal of Philosophy*, Volume 9, 285.

Horn, N. (2016). *Interpreting the Interpreters: A Critical Analysis of the Interaction Between Formalism and Transformative Adjudication in Namibian Constitutional Jurisprudence 1990–2004*. Windhoek, Namibia: Konrad Adenauer Stiftung.

Horwitz, M. J. (1998). *The Warrant Court and Pursuit of Justice*. New York : Hill and Wang.

Hutchinson, T. (2018). "Doctrinal research: Researching the jury." In D. Watkins and B. Mandy (Eds.), *Research Methods in Law* (2nd ed.). Oxford: Routledge.

Kennedy, D., and Klare, K. E. (1984). "A bibliography of Critical Legal Studies." *Yale Law Journal*, Volume 94(2), 461–490.

Khunou, S. F. (2009). "Traditional leadership and independent bantustans of South Africa: Some milestones of transformative constitutionalism beyond apartheid." *Potchefstroom Electronic Law Journal*, Volume 12(4), 81–122.

Klare, K. E. (1998). "Legal culture and transformative constitutionalism." *South African Journal on Human Rights*, Volume 14(1), 146–188.

Koraan, R., and Geduld, A. (2015). "'Corrective rape' of lesbians in an era of transformative constitutionalism in South Africa." *Potchefstroom Electronic Law Journal*, Volume 18, 1931.

Langa, P. (2006). "Transformative constitutionalism." *Stellenbosch Law Review*, Volume 17(3), 351–360.

Le Roux, W. (2013). "Advancing domestic workers' rights in a context of transformative constitutionalism." In D. Du Toit (Ed.), *Exploited, Undervalued – and Essential: Domestic Workers and the Realisation of Their Rights*. Pretoria: Pretoria University Press.

Levitsky, S., and Ziblatt, D. (2018). *How Democracies Die*. New York: Crown Publishing Group.

Macedo, S. (1998). "Transformative constitutionalism and the case of religion: Defending the moderate hegemony of liberalism." *Political Theory*, Volume 26, 56–80.

McIlwain, C. H. (1940). *Constitutionalism: Ancient and Modern*. Ithaca, NY: Cornell University Press.

Minkkinen, P. (2018). "Critical legal 'method' as attitude." In D. Watkins and M. Burton (Eds.), *Research Methods in Law* (2nd ed.). London: Routledge.

Moseneke, D. (2002). "The Fourth Bram Fischer Memorial Lecture: Transformative adjudication." *South African Journal on Human Rights*, Volume 18(3), 309–319.

Moseneke, D. (2009). "Transformative constitutionalism: Its implications for the law of contract." *Stellenbosch Law Review*, Volume 20, 3–13.

Mudde, C. (2013). "Are populists friends or foes of constitutionalism?" *The Foundation for Law, Justice and Society Policy Brief.*

Mundia, K. F. (2016). "A constructive interpretation of the Namibian Constitution: Transposing Dworkin to Namibia's constitutional jurisprudence." *Southern African Public Law*, Volume 31(1), 73–90.

Mureinik, E. (1994). "A bridge to where? Introducing the Bill of Rights." *South African Journal on Human Rights*, Volume 10, 31.

Mwandingi v Minister of Defense 1992 (2) SA 355 NmSCat 362.

Pieterse, M. (2005). "What do we mean when we talk about transformative constitutionalism?" *Southern African Public Law*, Volume 20(1), 155–166.

Posner, R. A. (2016). *Divergent Paths: The Alchemy and the Judiciary*. Cambridge: Harvard University Press.

Presser, S. B. (2017). *Law Professors: Three Centuries of Shaping American Law*. St. Paul, Minnesota: West Academic Publishing.

Quinot, G. (1992). "Transformative legal education." *South African Law Journal*, Volume 129(3), 411–443.

Rapatsa, M. (2014). "Transformative constitutionalism in South Africa: 20 years of democracy." *Mediterranean Journal of Social Sciences*, Volume 5(27), 887–895.

Rapatsa, M. (2015). "The right to equality under South Africa's transformative constitutionalism: A myth or reality?" *Acta Universitatis Danubius*, Volume 11(2), 18–35.

Rosa, S. (2011). "Transformative constitutionalism in a democratic developmental state." *Stellenbosch Law Review*, Volume 22(3), 542–565.

Roux, T. (2009). "Transformative constitutionalism and the best interpretation of the South African Constitution: Distinction without a difference?" *Stellenbosch Law Review*, Volume 20(2), 258–285.

S v Makwanyane 1995 3 SA 391 (CC) para 262.

S v Mushwena and Others 2004 NR 276 (SC).

S v Zuma 1995 (4) BCLR 401 (CC) para 17.

Scalia, A., and Garner, B. A. (2012). *Reading Law: The Interpretation of Legal Texts*. Minnesota: West Publishing Company.

Scott Gordon, S. (1999). *Controlling the State: Constitutionalism from Ancient Athens to Today*. Cambridge: Harvard University Press.

The World Bank. (2020). GINI index (World Bank estimate). https://data.worldbank.org/indicator/SI.POV.GINI.

University of Namibia Faculty of Law: Prospectus 2019. (2019).

Van Der Walt, A. J. (2005). "Transformative constitutionalism and the development of South African property law (part 1)." *Journal of South African Law/Tydskrifvir die Suid-Afrikaanse Reg*, Volume 2005(4), 655–689.

Van Staden, M. (1029). "The dangers of 'transformative constitutionalism'" *Politicsweb*, 19 June 2019.

Von Bogdandy, A. (2015). "*Ius constitutionale en América Latina:* Observations on transformative constitutionalism." *American Journal of International Law Unbound*, Volume 109, 109–114.

Zongwe, D. P. (2016). "The articulation of an African philosophy of equality as legacy of the South African Constitution." *Southern African Public Law*, Volume 31, 32.

Zongwe, D. P. (2019). *International Law in Namibia*. Bameda: Langaa RPCIG.

Chapter 5

African States' Quest for Reclaiming Sovereignty over Natural Resources through Revamping the Legal Framework

A Useful Lesson from Tanzania's Mining Sector

Julius Cosmas

INTRODUCTION

At different phases before and after independence, the legal and regulatory framework for investment in the mining sector in Tanzania has been influenced by a number of internal and external factors. These factors include the internal policy changes and the global dynamics that were largely dictated and subsequently transformed in style and shape by the global economic changes as well as the deeply harboured economic interest of the former colonial powers that dominated Tanganyika (Peter and Mwakaje 2005, 9). Prior to the attainment of independence in 1961, Tanganyika was colonised by two European colonialists: the Germans and the British. The approach and operating legal regime on investment and business adopted different approaches during the reign of those two colonialists, mainly because of their diverse views of Tanganyika as their colony, which consequently determined the nature of investments that were then prioritised (Peter and Mwakaje 2005, 9). During German era, the major thrust was to exploit raw materials and natural resources which were abundant in Tanganyika so as to feed the growing needs of the manufacturing industries in Europe (Peter and Mwakaje 2005, 9). To facilitate this mission, the Germans embarked into one of the major infrastructural investment, mainly for their own benefits, in early 1900s by constructing the Tanganyika central railway from Dar es Salaam to Kigoma covering a total distance of about 1237 kilometres. This massive exportation oriented investment paved the way for an order transportation of raw materials from interior parts of Tanganyika to the coast ready for transportation outside Tanzania. In addition, the broader context of the scheme was to turn the Tanganyika into a market for the finished products from the industries in Europe (Peter and Mwakaje 2005, 9).

The British colonial period (1918–1961) was predominantly associated with exploitation-based investments in mineral prospecting following the disruptions caused by World War I. This was propelled by, among others, the dramatic increase in gold prices between 1920 and 1925, leading to gold rushes in many colonies (Ngowi 2005, 4–5). During this era, the mining industry was regulated by the Mining Ordinance of 1920 which had more or less the same terms as those of the German colonial period. However, in 1929, the British colonial government came up with a new legislation (the 1929 Mining Ordinance) which aimed at encouraging large-scale mining sector exploitation (The Law Reform Commission 2001).

In 1979, eighteen years after attaining its independence, the Tanzanian government made a fundamental change by enacting the Mining Act (17 of 1979) which nationalised the sector by placing all the undertakings and operations under the control of two executive agencies, namely, National Development Corporation and the State Mining Corporation. However, due to pressure from the World Bank and IMF, Tanzania, just like other developing countries, was forced to enter into privatisation of its key economic activities through the so-called structural adjustment programme (SAP) in the early 1980s.

To implement the SAP, the government undertook rigorous restructuring of the economic activities, including the mining sector, so as to encourage and promote the sector by attracting private sector to run the industry in a move to comply with the World Bank (SAP; Peter and Mwakaje 2005, 13). This move was followed by the creation of the Tanzania Investment Promotion Policy in 1990 followed by the enactment of the Investment (Promotion and Protection) Act (10 of 1990). These two instruments facilitated the expansion of the mining sector and attraction of foreign investors. The government's intention in formulating the policy was to ensure that investment would be promoted in a manner that would: (i) foster utilisation of the nation's natural and other resources, (ii) maximise foreign resource inflows through export-oriented activities.

During this period, the government undertook rigorous restructuring of the mining sector so as to encourage and promote the sector by attracting private sector to run the industry. These efforts helped the government in collaboration with the private sector in prospecting for mineral resources throughout the country and managed to come up with a geo-data revealing Tanzania's diverse mineral resources base. It was during this period that Tanzania and other developing countries engaged themselves into signing Bilateral Investment Treaties (BITs) with western capitalist countries. The purpose of the BITs was, alleged, to promote and protect investment flowing in the developing countries (Guzman 1998, 642). Tanzania is among states which signed the BITs which are normally referred to as first-generation BITs (Spear 2010, 1038). The so-called first-generation BITs were concluded before and during 1990s. They widely provide for foreign investment protection without imposing any obligations to foreign investors (Spear 2010, 1040). These BITs do not acknowledge that host states have the right and the duty to regulate in pursuit of policy objectives other than investment promotion and protection. In as far as BITs are concerned, Tanzania has concluded 17 BITs with Canada, Denmark, Egypt, Finland, Germany, Italy, Jordan, Korea, Republic of Mauritius, Oman, South Africa, Sweden, Switzerland, Turkey, United Kingdom and Zimbabwe (UNCTAD Treaty Database 2019). As pointed out in the introduction, these BITs have provisions that ensure that foreign investments are protected to the maximum level. The Tanzanian BIT provides, among other things, for the obligation to compensate in case the investment is expropriated (article 4 of An Agreement between the Government of UK and Northern Ireland and the Government of the United Republic of Tanzania for the Promotion and Protection of Investment of 07/01/1994, "hereinafter, Tanzania–UK BIT"; see also article 5 of An Agreement between the Government of Republic of Korea and the Government of the United Republic of Tanzania for the Promotion and Protection of Investment, "Tanzania–Korea BIT"; see also article 6 of An Agreement between the Kingdom of Netherlands and the Government of the United Republic of Tanzania for Encouragement and Reciprocal Protection of Investments of 31/07/2001 "Tanzania–Netherlands BIT" and article 5 of the Agreement between the Government of the Republic of South Africa and the Government of the Republic of Zimbabwe for the Promotion and Reciprocal Protection of Investments of 27/11/2009 "South Africa–Zimbabwe BIT"), obligation to treat all foreign investment fairly and equitably (article 2 of Tanzania–Korea BIT; article 2 Tanzania–UK BIT; article 3 Tanzania–Netherlands BIT; article 1 of the Treaty between the Federal Republic of Germany and the United Republic of Tanzania concerning the Encouragement and Reciprocal Protection of Investment of 30/01/1965 "Tanzania–Germany BIT" and article 3 of South Africa–Zimbabwe BIT), obligation to ensure that all foreign investments are accorded protection and security (article 2 Tanzania–UK BIT) and the obligation to allow foreign investors to move capital and currency from one country to another (article 6 of Tanzania–Korea BIT; article 5 of Tanzania–Netherlands BIT; article 4 Tanzania–Germany BIT; article 5 of the Agreement on encouragement and reciprocal protection of investments between the Republic of South Africa and the Kingdom of the Netherlands of 09/05/1995 "hereinafter South Africa–Netherland BIT"). Since 1992, Tanzania has acceded to the Convention Establishing the International Centre for the Settlement of Investment Disputes between states and nationals of other states (ICSID Convention) of 1965. Tanzania has been a party to the Convention Establishing the Multilateral Investment Guarantee Agency of 1985 since 1992. Tanzania has acceded to the New York Convention on the Recognition and Enforcement of Foreign Arbitral Awards of 1958, which came into force in 1965. All these commitments entered in the 1990s come with several issues with regard to country sovereignty over its natural resources, mining sector included.

INTERNATIONAL INVESTMENT LAW PRINCIPLES AND ITS CONSEQUENCES TO TANZANIA'S SOVEREIGNTY IN THE MINING SECTOR

As stated before, Tanzania has signed and ratified several treaties with regard to attraction, admission and protection of foreign investments. These Treaties have a number of common features/principles which in one way or the other affects the host state power to regulate investors in its territory. As a member of the Vienna Convention of law of Treaties, Tanzania is obliged to honour its international commitments, including investment commitment. Following hereunder is a discussion on these international law principles, which in one way or the other hinders developing countries from benefiting from their own natural resources, including mining sector.

The first principle is known as the National Treatment (Brownlie 2003, 502). This principle requires host states to accord to foreign investors' similar treatment as given to national or local investors in like situations or circumstances. According to this principle, nationals or local inventors are not supposed to be accorded with favourable treatment than could be to foreigners. Sornarajah observes that the grant of National Treatment standard to foreign investors and their products has implications (Sornarajah 2010, 343). It denies state ability to protect local business; as providing priority to local investors or subsidising small minors so as to boost their capital will ultimately be considered as breaching the NT principle by the foreign investors. This principle feature in a number of BITs that Tanzania has signed (see article 3 of the Tanzania–Finland BIT; article 3 of the Tanzania–UK BIT; article 3 Tanzania–Netherlands BIT; article 2 of the Treaty between the Federal Republic of Germany and the United Republic of Tanzania concerning the Encouragement and Reciprocal Protection of Investment of 30/01/1965, "Tanzania–Germany BIT"). Essentially, NT requirement is not encouraging development of domestic investors. This is due to the fact that domestic investors require special incentive or privileges to enable them to grow economically before competing with big multinational foreign investment.

The second common principle found in BITs that Tanzania has signed is that of fair and equitable treatment (FET). The principle of FET asserts a bundle of rights to investors, which contain the following terms of demand: stability, predictability, consistency; protection of confidence and legitimate expectations; administrative due process; transparency and reasonableness and proportionality in the administration of investment (Bering et al. 2009, 14–23). The UK-Tanzania BIT demands that investments of national or companies of each Contracting Party shall at all time be accorded FET (article 2(2) of the UK–Tanzania BIT). The same requirement is found in the German-Tanzania BIT (article 1 of the German–Tanzania BIT), the Tanzania–Netherlands BIT (article 3 of the Tanzania–Netherlands BIT), The Tanzania–Denmark BIT (article 3(2), of Tanzania–Denmark BIT), and the Tanzania–Korea BIT (article 3(2) of Tanzania–Korea BIT).

The main challenge about the principle of FET is that the main scope of this principle has not been agreed either in treaty law or in practice. So in case of dispute on the content of this principle, it remains the work of individual *ad hoc* tribunals to determine the scope. Strict observance of FET is not good for developing countries. It affects special arrangements which aim to offering special technical assistance, technological transfer and training to nationals as means to help to build their capacity to compete in the mining sector with multilateral companies. In addition, full application of FET normally jeopardise governmental plans of securing employment opportunities and building capable small minors who can later be integrated into the sector as main players.

The third equally thorny principle is *Pacta Sunt Servanda* (Sqrensen 1968, 148). *Pacta sunt servanda* is a Latin expression which means that agreements must be kept and are binding upon the parties. Under international agreements, specifically the law of treaties, the principle of *pacta sunt servanda* obliges states or other subjects of international law to remain bound by their concluded obligations and are obliged to carry out such obligations in good faith (article 26 of the Vienna Convention on the Law of Treaties of 1966; Sqrensen 1968, 127). In the context of mining sector, *Pacta sunt servanda* means that Mineral Development Agreements (MDAs) must be honoured and kept (Shaw 2008, 829).

In developing countries like Tanzania, the rule *pacta sunt servanda* causes the negative impact to achieving investment benefits. For example, it has been observed from mining investments that most entered MDAs between the government of Tanzania and mining companies do not cause any positive impact to country's economy and its people. Years back before the new laws were enacted, the government of Tanzania tried to initiate some negotiations with investors in its mining sector to remedy the situation with futile results. With the rule *Pacta Sunt Servanda*, it remains the wishes of the investor either to agree on the proposed changes or to proceed in honouring and keeping concluded terms of MDAs.

Another problematic principle is stabilisation clause principle. Under this principle, the government party undertakes the commitment neither to annul the investment contract nor to modify its terms, either by legislation or by administrative measures in the whole life of the contract (Brown 2003, 526). The impact of stabilisation clause in investment is noticeable and creates a tension between the investor and the state party as they preclude the government from unilateral change of the terms set under the contract for the whole duration of the project. In Tanzania Stabilisation clause subsists in all mining development agreements (MDAs) since 1997 in the form of freezing clauses and economic equilibrium clauses (articles 4(1)(c); 4(3)(c) and 13(1) of the Third Schedule to the Mining (Mining Rights) Regulations, 2010 GNNO 405 of 2010).

The fifth principle is on dispute settlement famously known as forum shopping. Foreign investors, instead of channelling disputes accruing from investment to local court, they decide to go for international arbitration provided by global arbitral bodies. The international forum clauses are normally inserted in the BITs (article 8 of the Tanzania–Korea BIT; article 9 of the Tanzania–Netherlands BIT; article 8 of the Tanzania–UK BIT and article of the South Africa–Netherland BIT) or a local statute (section 23 of the Tanzania Investment Act 1997). Currently, the most used dispute settlement system for investor–state dispute is the International Centre for Settlement of Investment Disputes (ICSID) (established by the Convention on Settlement of Investment Disputes between Contracting States and National of Other Contracting States, 1965, "The Washington Convention"). Literatures suggest that these international forums are akin to "state capture" institutions (Krzysztof 2017, 559–583; Srividya et al. 2011, 1047–1073). Tanzania ratified the Convention in 1992. The problem with the current arbitration system is that it allows forum shopping which may lead to parallel proceedings which in turn may results into conflicting decisions. Treaty and contractual claims may be brought simultaneously by the investor under the current settings (Cremades and Madalena 2008, 509). A contractual claim may be filed in accordance to UNCITRAL Arbitration Rules while a BIT claim may be filed at ICSID or under Additional Facility (Kreindler 2010, 128–150).

In addition, the international community has witnessed a number of cases challenging the host state's basic regulatory functions and sometimes the state's duty to provide public services to its citizens (*Aguas del Tunari S A v Bolivia* ICSID ARB/02/3 (2005); Azurix *Corp v Argentina* ICSID ARB/1/12 (2006), on measures to protect water services). In some cases, the main function of the state, viz., security and peace, is put in jeopardy but still the standard of review applied by the tribunals does not take these factors into consideration (*CMS Gas Transmission Company v The Argentine Republic* ICSID ARB/01/8(2005); *Sempra Energy International v The ArgentineRepublic* ICSID ARB/02/16 (2005) and *Enron Corporation and Ponderosa Assets L P v Argentine Republic* ICSID ARB/01/3 (2007)). Furthermore, state regulatory measures on environmental issues, health and other service delivery to the citizens have been declared illegal in favour of foreign investors' interests (*Philip Morris Asia Limited v The Commonwealth of Australia*, UNCITRAL, PCA Case No. 2012-12; *Vattenfall v Federal Republic of Germany,* ICSID Case No. ARB/12/12 (2012)).

All these challenges and issues accruing from BITs and other obligations were being noticed and some measures were undertaken. However, one may conclude that serious measures to address these challenges came after the coming into force of the fifth government as will be revealed later in this work (Curtis and Lissu 2008, 22). Almost all these issues have been addressed by the newly enacted laws.

PRELUDE TO RECLAIMING SOVEREIGNTY IN THE MINING SECTOR

Tanzania has undergone several stages in its quest to have sovereignty over its natural resources. Some of the stages have been discussed in the introductory part of this work. The following section is going to discuss the era that followed after the SAP.

Pro-foreign Direct Investment Era 1997–2010

This period witnessed a notable reform of taxation of mining companies in the country. It is at this era where the Mining Policy 1997 was formulated. The Policy imposed significant modification in tax laws. The changes resulted into a distinctive mining tax system separate from the general one applicable to other sectors. The Finance Act, 1997 and the Financial Laws (Miscellaneous) Amendment Act, 1997 provided the instruments for the enforcement of a distinct tax regime for the mining sector (Tonodeus 2012, 12). The new tax structure was aligned with the government attempts to motivate local and foreign investors to invest in the mining sector and bring capital, technology and expertise to the industry which was, at the time, missing (Tonodeus 2012, 12). The formulation of the policy resulted to the enactment of the Mining Act 143 of 1998 which repealed and replaced the Mining Act of 1979. The new law provided for more incentives to investor when compared to its predecessor. In particular, the new law empowered the minister responsible for mining activities to enter into MDAs with the holders of mining rights for the purposes of developing mining potential (section 10(1) and (2)). Through this power, the minister was empowered to sign agreements guaranteeing the fiscal stability of long-term mining projects (section 10(1) and (2)).

Apart from the Mining Act, there were other laws that also guaranteed incentives to investors in the sector. The respective laws are the Investment Act 38 of 1997, the Income Tax Act 33 of 1973, the Customs (Management and Tariffs) Act 148 of 1997, the Road and Fuel Tolls Act Cap 403, the Excise (Management and Tariff) Act Cap 220 and the Stamp Duty Act Cap 147.

The Investment Act provided for different forms of incentives. Transferability of net profit or dividends attributable to the investment and allowing offshore accounts, benefits in the provisions of the Income Tax Act, 1973, the Customs Tariff Act, 1976, the Sales Tax, 1976 or any other law in force during the time within which the benefits accrues were among the incentives provided.

In addition, section 19(2) when read together with section 22(1), (2) and (3) were of the effect that the incentives once guaranteed cannot be modified or changed to the detriment of the investor enjoying those benefits. This practice is in accordance to the stabilisation clauses which are found in different treaties to which Tanzania is a party. The Act further shielded foreign investors from nationalisation of their investment.

These incentives were provided in both, the Income Tax Act 1973 and its successor the Income Tax Act 2004. The repealed law, the Income Tax Act 33 of 1973 (section 34(1)) provided preferential treatment on withholding of taxes (section 16(1) of the second schedule to the Income Tax Act 33 of 1973).

The current Income Tax Act Cap 332, 2004 removed special treatment previously provided to holders of licences to the mining industry on the aspect of withholding taxes for new miners. However, the law continued to recognise other benefits provided in the repealed Act (Suleiman 2018, 23). The Act allowed mining companies to redeem funds devoted to environmental protection in implementing written conditions set out by the income tax commissioner, the tax depreciation rate for exploration and mining equipment's followed wear and treat deductions allowance, the mining assets were expensed at 100 per cent capital expensing (paragraphs 1(1) and 3(6) of the Third Schedule to the Income Tax Act Cap 332, 2004).

Under the Valued Added Tax Cap 148 of 1997 (section 9), export of minerals was zero-rated due to the fact that the country exports practically all the minerals that are mined and that being the case, the mining companies were eligible for refund of the value-added tax (VAT) paid in the mining processes. The Road and Fuel Act Cap 220, 2002exempted gold Mining Corporation with MDA's to pay fuel duty exceeding USD 200,000 Revenue per annum in their first year of production.

It is during this period where there was a public outcry that only the investors are benefiting from the vast natural resources of the country leaving the country in shambles (Suleiman 2018, 23). The investment policy was said to be very generous to foreigners, the institutions vested with the authority to control the sector were not performing well, there were a lot of claims of aggressive tax avoidance and smuggling of minerals, the mining companies were not adhering to their corporate responsibility which as a result ignited conflicts between investors and the members of the communities where mining exploration activities were conducted (Suleiman 2018, 23).

2010–2015 ERA

Following the public "outcry" that the tax regime from 1997 has provided more incentive to foreign investors, the new Mineral Policy of 2009 was adopted leading to new Mining Act Cap 123 of 2010. The Mining Act (section 10(1)(3)), retained the power of the minister to enter into MDA's under the conditions that the capital expenditure of establishing a mining operation is not below one hundred million dollars and that after the conduct of due diligence over the holder it is confirmed that the holder of the mining right have financial and technical capacity to be efficiently able to undertake a large-scale investment (section 10(1) and (3) of the Mining Act).

The Mining Act (sections 10(4), 11 and 12) provided that the MDAs entered shall be in a prescribed form containing provisions binding the government and the holder of the mining right for the lifetime of the mine or for the period which may be requested by the applicant subject to periodic review after every five years (sections 10(4); 11 and 12).

The Mining Act (section 10(1) and (2)) introduced government equity participation in mining operations, the government equity participation involves grant of free carried interest to the government through the signed MDA, which need to be negotiated among the government and the holder of mining right dependent of the kind of minerals involved and the level of investment injected in the project (section 10(1) and (2)).

The Mining Act (section 87(a–c) retained the provisional assessment of mineral royalties accompanied with reforms, the reforms included were the rate of royalty and the base for calculating royalty (Suleiman 2018, 23).The Mining Act provided that the legitimate miners shall pay a royalty on the gross value of mineral provided at the rate of 4 per cent for metallic mineral such as copper, gold, silver and platinum, 5 per cent for uranium, gemstone and diamond and 3 per cent for other minerals (Suleiman 2018, 23).

The base for calculations was changed from net-base value provided by the earlier Mining Act to gross value base which was defined to mean the market value of the minerals at the point of refining or sale or, at the point of delivery if the consumption is within the country (section 87(6)). The new Mining Act abandoned the power of the minister to defer payment of royalty upon applications by the authorised manner under the preceding Act.

During this period, the Income Tax Act 33 of 1973 provides rates for withholding tax on technical services at 5 per cent for residents and fifteen per cent for non-residents, 5 per cent management fees for residents and 15 per cent for non-residents replacing a 3 per cent rate across the board for fees not exceeding 2 per cent of operating costs and 20 per cent for fees above 2 per cent of operating cost provided by the earlier Income Tax Act (section 83(1)(a) and (b); Institute of Development Studies 2012, 22).

Under the Income Tax Act (section 83(1)(a) and (b)) withholding tax on interest was set at 10 per cent equally for residents and non-residents irrespective of the source of the loan and dividend withholding rate was set at 10 per cent (Adam 2008, 4). The Income Tax Act (section 12(2) as amended by section 14 of the Finance Act 15 of 2010) introduced 70:30 debt-equity ratio for deduction of interest expense for the year of income for the loan which has not been given by a connected company (Suleiman 2018, 34). The deduction under the scheme can be carried forward indefinitely (Suleiman 2018, 34).

The Value Added Act 1997 was repealed and replaced by the Value Added Tax, 2014. The new Act retained the application of VAT reliefs provided for under the repealed Act for the agreements conducted by the government relating to exploration and prospecting of minerals, gas or oil (section 95(2) of Value Added Act, Chapter 148 of 2014 and item 10 of part II of the 1st schedule).

Despite these changes, the sector did not improve much in terms of generating revenue to the government in terms of royalty, duties and levies. As discussed earlier, the same was contributed much with the existence of stability clauses in the mining contracts which hindered the applicability of new laws to the existing contracts (George 2015, 2).

THE FIFTH GOVERNMENT ERA: REASSERTING PERMANENT SOVEREIGNTY OVER NATURAL RESOURCES

The fifth phase government which came into power in 2015 under President John Pombe Magufuli has made several changes to the sector by amending the Mining Act in 2017 and enacting new legislations with a view of ensuring that the sector contributes sufficiently to the economy of the country. The laws to be thoroughly analysed includes the Written Laws (Miscellaneous Amendments) Act 7 of 2017, the Natural Wealth and Resources (Permanent Sovereignty) Act 5 of 2017 and the Natural Wealth and Resources Contracts (Review and Re-Negotiation of Unconscionable Terms Act 6 of 2017 and the Non-Citizen (Employment Regulations) Act 1 of 2015. The subsidiary regulations which will be scrutinised include Mining Local Content Regulations, GN 3/2018; Mining Local Content Regulations Amendments, GN 139/2019. In addition, two policies that were reviewed are the Mining Policy, 2009, and the Local Content Policy.

REASONS FOR THE CHANGES IN THE LAW REGULATING MINING SECTOR IN TANZANIA

The underlying factor for the changes in the extractive industry could be the change of government regime which seeks to make sure that, the national wealth and natural resources are being used for the beneficiation of the country and its people. This is substantiated by the requirements of article 9(c) and (i) and article 27 of the Constitution (the United Republic of Tanzania Constitution, 1977 as amended) which provides, *inter alia*, that the government under the president, shall protect the country's wealth and natural resources for the beneficiation of the nation and its people. This is what the fifth regime government is dedicated to do. As once H.E president, Dr. John Pombe Maguful was quoted saying "Even the devil must be mocking us . . . Enough is enough we need investors but not this kind of exploitation. We are supposed to share profits in a win-win situation" (Mwangonde 2017, 1).

Apart from that, there are other reasons which include the recommendations by the two mineral's probe committees appointed by the President Dr. John Pombe Magufuli which are commonly known as Professor Mruma and Professor Osoro's reports, respectively. Delivering his speech in the National Assembly, Honourable Professor Palamagamba J.A.M. Kabudi (Minister of Constitutional and Legal Affairs) mentioned the following reasons as driving factors for the changes in the extractive industry:

(a) Lack of recognition of the ownership and control over all minerals to the peoples of the United Republic of Tanzania;
(b) Lack of recognition of the government lien over all minerals and other related products extracted from mining operations and activities;
(c) To enable the president of the United Republic of Tanzania to declare minerals controlled areas for purposes of enhancing control and security;

(d) To establish a Mining commission responsible for the regulation and supervision of the mining sector;
(e) To eliminate all provisions in the Mining Act 14 of 2010 which empowers the Minister responsible for minerals to enter into Mining Development Agreements (MDAs);
(f) Lack of compliance of the Mining Act 14 of 2010;
(g) Poor management on export of mineral concentrates;
(h) Tax evasion by mining companies;
(i) Unsatisfactory collections of royalties;
(j) Misuse of tax exemptions;
(k) Poor management and control of mining areas; and
(l) Illegal repatriation of earnings generated from mining operations.

THE CURRENT LEGAL FRAMEWORK REGULATING MINING SECTOR IN TANZANIA

The new government of Tanzania which assumed power in November 2015 put the management of natural resources at the forefront of public policy. Following the recommendations made by the two Presidential Commissions on June 29, 2017, the National Assembly passed three laws. New legislation has been passed to ensure that minerals and other natural wealth benefit the people of Tanzania. The new laws include the Mining Act 14 of 2010 as amended by the Written Laws (Miscellaneous Amendments) Act 7 of 2017; the Natural Wealth and Resources (Permanent Sovereignty) Act 5 of 2017; and the Natural Wealth and Resources Contracts (Review and Re-Negotiation of Unconscionable Terms) Act 6 of 2017. The new laws are aimed at reasserting the state's permanent sovereignty over all natural resources to ensure that natural resources are exploited for the greatest benefit and welfare of the people of Tanzania by establishing a tight institutional control over such exploitation. Prior to the enactment of the new laws, in October 2016, the government published the Mining and (Minimum Shareholding and Public Offerings) Regulations 2016, which require special mining licence holders to issue a minimum of thirty per cent shares to the public to be listed on the Dar-Es-Salaam Stock Exchange (DSE) within one year of receiving a new licence and within two years for existing licence (Tanzania Extractive Industries 2018, 18).

In another move, in March 2017, the government banned the export of mineral concentrates and later on formed two Presidential Commissions, which among other things, noted that Acacia Mining Company which operates Bulyankulu, Buzwagi and North Mara gold mines understated the value of mineral concentrates for export in respect of tax disputes.

Collectively, the laws, which mainly focus on mining introduced substantive changes in the extractive sector in Tanzania. The new laws provide for establishment of a Mining Commission and reviewing of the existing natural resources contracts, advancing local beneficiation and procurement, limiting the use of offshore bank accounts, giving to the government a non-dilutable interest not less than 16 per cent on mining schemes in mining licence or a special mining licences (Tanzania Extractive Industries 2018, 18). The laws increased royalty rates for gemstones and diamonds from 5 per cent to 6 per cent and for gold and other metals from 4 per cent to 6 per cent, required adjudication of investment disputes to be conducted in domestic courts and gave the right for the government to acquire up to 50 per cent of any mining asset commensurate with the total tax expenditure incurred by the government in favour of the mining company (Tanzania Extractive Industries 2018, 18–19).

The Natural Wealth and Resources (Permanent Sovereignty) Act 5 of 2017 (sections 4(1)–(2) and 5(1)) declared people's permanent sovereignty over natural resources (PSNR), and vest the ownership and control over the natural resources to the people through the government. The Natural Wealth and Resources (Permanent Sovereignty) Act provided that any agreement or arrangement for natural resources extraction, exploitation, acquisition or use must ensure that beneficiation of won raw resources is done within the country and the earnings derived from the natural resources are retained in the banks and financial institutions within the country (sections 9(1) and 10(1)).

To safeguard sovereignty over natural resources, the Natural Wealth and Resources (Permanent Sovereignty) Act prohibits proceedings in foreign courts of all disputes arising from extraction, exploitation or acquisition and use of natural resources (sections 11(1) and (2); 12).

AMENDMENT OF THE MINING ACT

The Mining Act was amended by repealing and replacing the provisions giving power to the minister to enter into MDAs, with the provision providing for state participation in mining operation through acquiring not less than 16 per cent non-dilutable free carried interest shares in the capital of a mining company and up to 50 per cent of the shares of the company commensurate with the total tax expenditures incurred by the government in favour of the mining company (section 10 of the Mining Act as amended by section 9 of the Natural Wealth and Resources (Permanent Sovereignty) Act). The Mining Act was amended by repealing and replacing the provisions of sections 11 and 12 which provided for the validity of MDA's and power of periodic reviews of MDA's with a provision recognising the MDA's entered prior but subjecting them to review under the provisions of

Act 6 of 2017 (section 11 of the Mining Act as amended by section 11 of the Natural Wealth and Resources (Permanent Sovereignty) Act; Suleiman 2018, 36).

The amendment of the Mining Act changed the rates of royalty payable and the bases for determining the royalty (section 87(1)(b) and (c) as amended by section 23 of the Natural Wealth and Resources (Permanent Sovereignty) Act). Under the amendments the rate of royalty for gemstone and diamond is 6 per cent and metallic minerals such as copper, silver and platinum group minerals at 6 per cent compared to 5 per cent and 4 per cent, respectively, prior to the amendment (section 87(1)(b) and (c) as amended by section 23 of the Natural Wealth and Resources (Permanent Sovereignty) Act).

The definition of the term "gross value" was re-defined to mean the market value of minerals as determined through valuation to be done in the attendance of mines resident officer, an officer from TRA and other relevant institutions of state organ. The royalty will be determined after the benefaction of the minerals within Tanzania this being different from earlier provision which provided that the gross value means the market value of minerals at the point of refinery or sale, or in case of consumptions within Tanzania, at the point of delivery within Tanzania (section 87(6) of the Mining Act).

The amendment introduced a new subsection under section 88(1) of the Mining Act which provides that one-third of the royalty to be paid through depositing minerals equivalent to the ascertained royalty (section 88(2) of the Mining Act as amended). The amendment of the Mining Act introduced a new provision in relating to regulation over use of stabilisation clauses (section 100E(1) of the Mining Act as amended). The provision prohibited stability clauses that freezes the law, take away the sovereign of the country and that which is not bound by time or guaranteed to last for the life time of the mining project (section 100E(2) of the Mining Act as amended). The amendments requires the stabilisation arrangements to make provisions for renegotiation based on the economic equilibrium principle and providing for quantification of value of tax if such a clause involves tax expenditure (section 100E(3)–(5) as amended the Natural Wealth and Resources (Permanent Sovereignty) Act).

The period saw a clear shift of the public policy towards the administration and management of natural resources different committees have been formed to inquire on operation of mining companies on different mineral resources such as gold, diamond and tanzanite. New laws on mining have been enacted by the parliament that have raised a debate on their implementation and viability taking into regard international nature of contracts relating to exploitation of natural resources (Curtis 2012, 43).

KEY FEATURES OF THE NEW LAWS WHICH HAVE DIRECT IMPACT ON MINING SECTOR INVESTMENT

The new mining law features were not included in the MDAs and BITs that Tanzania has signed with investors and/or investors with investors' home states. As earlier discussed, the MDAs and BITs terms tends to provide for investors with a bundle of rights while placing no obligations to them. The new laws are trying to ensure that investors assume responsibilities and whatever is acquired in the mining activities benefits the people of Tanzania.

Inalienability of Natural Worth and Resources

Section 5 of the Natural Wealth and Resources (Permanent Sovereignty) Act 5 of 2017 provides for inalienability of the natural wealth and resources to the people of Tanzania. This means that investors may come and invest in the sectors but they will be only investors and not owners of the natural wealthy. In other words, investors only acquire usufruct rights while real ownership is vested to the people of Tanzania.

Exploitation of Natural Wealth and Resources for the Benefit of the People

Section 6 of the Natural Wealth and Resources (Permanent Sovereignty) Act provides that all agreements for the extraction, exploitation or acquisition and use of natural wealth and resources shall ensure the interests of the people and the state are fully secured.

In addition, the Natural Wealth and Resources (Permanent Sovereignty) Act requires that all arrangements or agreements for international cooperation for the economic and social development involving natural wealth and resources, whether in the form of public or private capital investments, exchange of goods and services, technical assistance or exchange of scientific information, shall be based upon respect for permanent sovereignty over natural wealth and resources.

State Equity in Natural Resource Operations

Section 8 of the Natural Wealth and Resources (Permanent Sovereignty) Act provides for the requirement of state participation (equity) in the extraction, exploitation or acquisition and use of natural wealth and resources. This means that all arrangements concerning mineral operations shall ensure that the government obtains an equitable stake in the venture. In addition, section 9 of the Written Laws (Miscellaneous Amendments) Act 7 of 2017 which amends section 10 of the Mining Act guarantees government participation by acquiring not less than 16 per cent non-dilutable free carried interest shares in the capital of a mining company in all mining operations under a mining licence or a special mining licence. Apart from that, the government shall also be entitled to acquire up to 50 per cent of the shares in the mining company.

Tax Expenditure Shall Not Exceed the Cost of Investment

The new law has changed the tax expenditure requirements by increasing it to 20 per cent straight line (instead of 100 per cent deductions), and depreciable cost not to exceed the cost of investment as determined by the Mining Commission (sections 33–36 of Written Laws (Miscellaneous Amendments) Act amending sections 8, 65E, 65M and 65N of the Income Tax Act, CAP 332). These changes seek to strengthen transfer of pricing regulations and combat tax avoidance.

Retention of Earnings

It is a new requirement that any earnings from the mineral developments must be retained in the banks and financial institution established in Tanzania. Section 10(1) of the Natural Wealth and Resources (Permanent Sovereignty) Act 5 of 2017 provides to the effect that any arrangement or agreement for extraction, exploitation or acquisition and use of natural wealth and resources shall include a provision requiring earnings from the disposal or dealings be retained in the banks and financial institutions established in Tanzania and that, it shall be unlawful to keep such earnings in banks or institutions outside Tanzania (section 10(2)). Thus, operational bank accounts should be held in Tanzanian banks rather than offshore. However, the provision does not restrict repatriation of profits in accordance with the laws of Tanzania (section 10(2)).

Beneficiation Requirements

Section 9(1) of the Natural Wealth and Resources (Permanent Sovereignty) Act, imposes a condition for forthcoming arrangements or agreements for extraction, exploitation or acquisition and use of natural wealth and resources to include a commitment for investors to establish beneficiation facilities within the United Republic of Tanzania (section 9(2)).

Dispute Settlement Mechanism

The new law requires all disputes relating to extraction, exploitation, acquisition or use of natural wealth and resources to be adjudicated in Tanzania in accordance with the laws of Tanzania. These changes r extinguish the chances of the investor company from taking investment disputes to international arbitration tribunals such as ICSID.

This would appear to rule out many of the arbitration clauses commonly seen in Tanzanian BITs. It is submitted that this move protects Tanzania's sovereignty and it is a very ripe opportunity to Tanzania to empower her local courts to resolve investment disputes which have high economic and national interest (Cosmas 2014, 35). To substantiate this, the world has witnessed a number of countries resorting to this mode. For example, Australia has issued a trade policy statement that sought to stop including investor-state dispute settlement mechanism in its future international investment agreements (IIAs) (Cosmas 2014, 35). However, for the changes to be valid and effective, reconciliation of these new requirements with the obligations under the existing BITs is required so as to accommodate these new changes. On the other hand, the new law appears to be inconsistent with the Tanzania Investment Act 26 of 1997 with regard to dispute settlement mechanism (section 23 which provides for settlement of disputes at ICSID Centre). Thus, it is urged that the government should revisit its investment laws and policy to avoid this conflict of laws.

INVESTOR'S PARTICIPATION IN THE GROWTH OF THE TANZANIA'S ECONOMY

Mineral rights owner must participate in the growth of the Tanzania's economy by investing a portion of the returns from mining and satisfy further provisions on local content and corporate social responsibility (CSR). This requirement is provided for under section 7 of the Natural Wealth and Resources (Permanent Sovereignty) Act which states that:

> In any arrangement or agreement for extraction, exploitation or acquisition and use of natural wealth and resources, there shall be guaranteed returns into the Tanzanian economy from the earnings accrued or derived from such extraction, exploitation or acquisition and use.

This requirement is also reflected under sections 102 and 105 of the Mining Act 14 of 2010 as amended, where it is insisted that a mineral right holder should give preference to goods produced in Tanzania or available in Tanzania.

Indeed, this is another problem to investors because the requirements increase financial liability on them. It should be borne in mind that the language used in that section compels investors to contribute part of their earnings into Tanzanian economy.

INCREASE OF ROYALTY RATES

Section 23 of Act 7 of 2017 which amends section 87 of the Mining Act 14 of 2010 increases the royalty from 5 per cent to 6 per cent of gross value for diamonds and gemstones and 4 per cent to 6 per cent for metallic minerals. It should be noted that previously the royalty base was defined as the market value at the point of refining or sale or at the point of delivery within Tanzania. The procedures of assessment of the market value are also provided. All these changes can bring negative impact on the part of investors as it reduces their profit margins as compared to previous regime. Thus, while the change is beneficial to the nation it is a disincentive on the part of the investors.

REVIEW OF CONTRACTS BY THE NATIONAL ASSEMBLY

Under the new law, the National Assembly has been given mandate to review and scrutinise all agreements concerning natural wealth and resources including mining investment agreements. The aim of this new requirement is to enable the National Assembly to advise the government on the respective agreements. Those powers are provided for under sections 4 and 5 of the Natural Wealth and Resources Contracts (Review and Re-Negotiation of Unconscionable Terms) Act reading together with section 12 of the Natural Wealth and Resources (Permanent Sovereignty) Act. In connection to that, the National Assembly has been given powers to advise the government to renegotiate unconscionable terms with a view of rectifying the terms.

It is further provided that, the terms of the arrangement or agreements shall be deemed to be unconscionable and treated as such, if they contain any provision or requirement stipulated for under section 6(2)(a) to (k) if includes any clause which subjects the contract to the jurisdiction of an international arbitration body (section 5(2) of Act 6 of 2017). This means that all future agreements concerning natural wealth and resources shall not be subjected to international tribunal in case of any disputes arising from natural wealth and resources agreements. This raises a need for Tanzania to renegotiate her BITs with investor states so as to either withdraw itself from being a member to ICSID Convention or to remove the requirement of investor-state dispute settlement mechanism.

All in all, it can be concluded that the reforms that Tanzania has made were necessary and they are in conformity with the objectives of the Mineral Policy of Tanzania of 2009 as they aim at benefiting both the country and investors. Indeed, what Tanzania has done is justifiable even by international instruments such as the United Nations Declaration to which Tanzania is a part.

For instance, article XXV of the Declaration on Principles of International Law Concerning Friendly Relations and Corporation among states (General Assembly Resolution A/RES/25/2625 of 24 October 1970), which provides to the effect that each state has the right freely to choose and develop its political, social, economic and cultural systems. The measures that Tanzania has taken are also justifiable under article 1 of the Charter of Economic Rights and Duties of States (General Assembly Resolution A/RES/29/3281 of 12 December 1974), which recognises the state's sovereignty and inalienable right to choose its economic system as well as its political, social and cultural systems in accordance with the will of its people, without outside interference, coercion or threat in any form whatsoever.

FORMATION OF A JOINT VENTURE BETWEEN THE GOVERNMENT OF UNITED REPUBLIC OF TANZANIA AND BARRICK GOLD TANZANIA

On January 24, 2020, Barrick Gold Corporation formalised the establishment of a joint venture between Barrick and the government of Tanzania (Barrick Press Release 2020). At a signing ceremony with the president of the United Republic of Tanzania, Dr John Pombe Magufuli, Bristow, Barrick president said the joint venture will give the government full visibility of and participation in operating decisions made for and by the North Mara, Bulyanhulu and Buzwagi mines, a partnership which changes the landscape of mining in Africa. The agreement also ratifies the creation of Twiga Minerals Corporation, the management company jointly owned by the government and Barrick, which will oversee the management of Barrick's local operations, which are now owned 84 per cent by Barrick and 16 per cent by the government (Barrick Press Release 2020). The deal provides for a 50/50 sharing in the economic benefits generated by the mining operations after the recoupment of capital investments. There are a number of matters which Barrick and the government will work together to implement. In particular, Barrick will partner with the University of Dar es Salaam and commit up to $10 million in funding over a ten-year period for training and skills development in the mining industry. It will also commit up to $40 million to upgrade the road between Bulyanhulu and Mwanza as well as constructing a housing compound and related infrastructure. In line with Barrick's commitment to employing and advancing locals at its mines, Tanzanian nationals are being recruited and trained to replace expatriate employees as has been successfully done at Barrick's other African operations (Barrick Press Release 2020).

One can note that this is a positive move towards Tanzania having control of what happens in the mining sector but also to be active participant in the operations. It is important to note that the arrangement will ensure that Tanzania benefits more from its endowed natural resources. It is a sincere hope that this progressive spirit will be spilled over to other natural resources sector in the country and other strategic economic activities.

LOCAL CONTENT REQUIREMENT

Mineral extraction and revenues in Tanzania have made very little positive impact on the lives of most Tanzanians. The government has taken a bold initiative through the enactment of the Local Content Regulations GN 3 of 2018. The Regulations reflects a strong will to foster diversification and linkages to the local economy, create jobs through the use of Tanzanian expertise, goods and services, businesses and financing in the mining value chain. It maximises on value addition. Not only does it force licensees and contractors to use indigenous Tanzanian companies for the procurement of goods and services, but also requires a physical presence in Tanzania (SUDI 2020). The regulations are aimed at ensuring that the investors in the mining sector participate fully to develop local employment and the domestic labour market; to transfer skills, technology and know-how and create local value, increase local linkages and develop domestic industry. The regulations help locals to diversify economically; promote innovation, technology, research and development, enhancement of technology transfer and creation of local technological capabilities; ensure local ownership of the mining industry; increase revenue streams from minerals and to develop local community projects (Regulation 4 of the Local Content Regulations GN 3 of 2018).

With regard, to local content plan, the regulations require that a contractor must submit a local content plan for approval by the Mining Commission prior to commencing the mining project (Regulations 4 and 10 of the Local Content Regulations GN 3 of 2018). The local content plan must ensure the following: first consideration is given to services provided within the country and goods manufactured in the country and guarantee to use locally manufactured goods. It is also stated that a local content plan must also contain 5 sub plans on (a) employment and training, (b) research and development, (c) technology transfer, (d) legal services and (e) financial services (Regulations 12; 24; 26 and 32 of the Local Content Regulations GN 3 of 2018).

The regulations also address the importance of local contents on employment. The regulations demand that employment priority be given to qualified Tanzanian nationals and on-the-job training must be given by employers. Junior and Management Level employment should be reserved for Tanzanians (Regulations 20-22 of the Local Content Regulations GN 3 of 2018). With regard to procurement, it is mandatory for the contractor or/licensee to establish and implement a bidding process for the acquisition of goods works and services. The Mining Commission must set up the bidding rules. In terms of awarding contracts, the principle of lowest bidder will apply and the regulations require that Tanzanians companies should be prioritised and awarded the contracts (Regulations 15; 20-22 of the Local Content Regulations GN 3 of 2018). On insurance, all insurable risks relating to mining activity in Tanzania must be insured through an indigenous brokerage firm or an indigenous a reinsurance broker and any offshore insurance service relating to Mining activities in Tanzania may be obtained only upon written approval of the Commissioner of Insurance (Regulations 30-31 of the Local Content Regulations GN 3 of 2018).

The same rule is set with regard to legal services. All entities engaged in mining activities that require legal services in the country are now required to only retain the services of a Tanzanian legal practitioner or a firm of Tanzanian legal practitioners whose principal office is located in Tanzania (Regulations 30-32 of the Local Content Regulations GN 3 of 2018).

Similarly, the rule is extended to services on financial matters. The contractor is obliged to retain the services of a Tanzanian financial institution or organisation. If it happens that the contractor wishes to engage the services of a foreign financial institution, it must seek approval from the Mining Commission (Regulation 34 of the Local Content Regulations GN 3 of 2018). A contractor is required to maintain a bank account with an indigenous Tanzanian bank and transact business through banks in the country. An indigenous Tanzanian bank means a bank that has 100 per cent Tanzanian or a majority Tanzanian shareholding (Regulation 34 of the Local Content Regulations GN 3 of 2018). In addition, foreign as well as domestic investors must source a certain percentage of intermediate goods or inputs from local producers.

In conclusion, one can say that reading the local content regulations in wholesome one can see that the Regulations aims at supporting local manufacturing and service provision through backward, forward and sideways linkages along the value chain.

INTERNATIONAL LAW JUSTIFICATION FOR RECLAIMING SOVEREIGNTY OVER NATURAL RESOURCES

Principle of Permanent Sovereignty over Natural Resources

Principle of PSNR articulates the right and duties of states and investors in natural resources investments. The principle of PSNR has been developed from the UN General Assembly Resolutions. The first Resolution that had featured the principle of PSNR is that of January 12, 1952 (UN General Assembly Resolution 523 (VI), January 12, 1952: Integrated Economic Development and Commercial Agreements; Schrijver 1997, 372). Since 1952 several UN General Assembly Resolutions on the principle of PSNR have been passed, the most famous is that of 1962. The principle of PSNR is applied and emphasised in various areas of economic law such as investment. It has expanded its application to include other areas of law such as the law of the sea, human rights and environmental law. Essentially, the principle of PSNR is the principle of rights and duties. This may be observed in the wide-ranging legal resources that contain the principle of PSNR. If these resources were construed in the context of investment, they would have suggested several rights and duties. These rights and duties which are the architecture of the principle of PSNR are related to country's enjoyment of its wealth and resources vis-à-vis the investor. In other words, the rights and duties which envisage the principle of PSNR are the shaping factors when it comes to investment and business facilitation in the country.

Varied rights which form the principle of PSNR are acknowledged as of state. These include the right: to possess, use and freely dispose of its natural resources; to determine freely and control the prospecting, exploration, development and exploitation, use and marketing of natural resources; to manage and conserve natural resources pursuant to national developmental and environment policies; to regulate foreign investment, including the right to admit or refuse admission of foreign investment; and the right to nationalise or expropriate investments of both, nationals or foreigners (Schrijver 1997, 372). Other rights include the right to share in the administration and management of local subsidies of foreign investment companies; the right to withdraw from unequal investment treaties and contracts, especially, when the other party is suspected to enrich itself unreasonably. The right to review unilaterally the terms of an agreed agreement in the exercise of its legislative competence, the right to determine unilaterally the amount, moment and mode of payment of damages for expropriation, nationalisation or requisition and the right to settle investment disputes exclusively upon the basis of national laws and by national remedies are also provided (Schrijver 1997, 373).

Duties which embody the principle of PSNR are as follows: the duty to practise the right of PSNR in the interest of national development to ensure that the population benefits from their natural resources, which includes the duty to respect peoples interests and the duty not to compromise the rights of the future generations in the exploitation of natural resources; and the duty to refrain from actions that would likely jeopardise the rights and interest of the people in the exploitation of natural resources, including the duty to observe sovereignty of state over its natural resources. Other duties include the duty to pay promptly a fair compensation in case of nationalisation, expropriation or requisition when so done in accordance with the rules in force in the state taking such measures, and in accordance with international law; the duty to observe international agreements, and to accomplish international obligations in good faith in the practice of PSNR; and the duty to ensure capacity building and assistance to nationals of developing countries at all levels and in all fields of exploitation, including capital goods and know-how for the exploitation and marketing of their natural resources to accelerate their development; and the duty to have due care of the environment.

Currently, the principle of PSNR is an international norm that has acquired a special status of *jus cogens* (Brownlie 2003, 488–489). It is being practised in international law, namely: international economic law, international environmental law, human rights law and the law of the Sea (Schrijver 1997, 357). As a *jus cogens* principle of international law, PSNR fall within the rules of customary international law which cannot be set aside by treaty or acquiescence but only by the formation of a subsequent customary rule of contrary effect (Brownlie 2003, 488–489).

The declaration is a good reference in as far dispute settlement is concerned as it encourages settlement of dispute in host state courts. In addition, since it is a jus cogens, it affirms Tanzania decision on settling investment disputes in local courts.

Clausula rebus sic stantibus is a Latin expression which literally means inapplicability of treaties because of the standing situation. The principle of *clausula rebus sic stantibus* originates from treaty laws. The application of the principle of *clausula rebus sic stantibus* has extended to investment agreements, which generally regulate investment relationships between states and investors. In essence, the principle of *clausula rebus sic stantibus* contradicts or at least conflicts with the principle of *pacta sunt servanda*, which compel parties to remain bound by their concluded obligations, and to carry out such obligations in good faith. The principle of *clausula rebus sic stantibus* would open an alternative chance to parties, of renegotiation upon substantial change of business environment or simply fundamental change of circumstances.

Therefore, when a government wants to renegotiate the investment contract, it will invoke the principle of *clausula rebus sic stantibus* the investor will invoke the doctrine of *pacta sunt servanda*. The question of application of the principle of *pact sunt servanda* to investment agreements between states and private investors is not a disputable fact in developed countries, but the displacement of the principle of *clausula rebus sic stantibus* in such agreements is not controversial. Developed countries would wish not to see developing host states applying the principle of *clausula rebus sic stantibus* in their investment relations, simply because application of the principle of *clausula rebus sic stantibus* would open these agreements to renegotiation which is the last thing investing companies would desire. As a matter of fact, many countries have now incorporated the principle of *clausula rebus sic stantibus* in their domestic laws. Whether the principle of *clausula rebus sic stantibus* is acceptable to developed countries and to international courts or not, it is argued that this development which essentially covers renegotiation of investment contracts is of importance, provided the proof for fundamental change of circumstances can be provided. It is unfortunate that the principle of *clausula rebus sic stantibus* it not embedded in many of the investment agreements which Tanzania is a state party to.

It should be noted that investors have not been happy with this development, because it is understandable that some of the things that could come under the ambit of review include consideration of fundamental change of circumstances in the fiscal framework. This could lead into change of terms in investment contracts. Developed countries and their investors have been reluctant to agree to the principle of *clausula rebus sic stantibus* to be embedded in investment agreements in order to rule out the possibility of reviewing the investment agreement, which could render into reviewing the fiscal framework and other terms of investment agreements in situations of windfall gains or windfall profits. Windfall gains or windfall profits are gains or profits that come about due to unforeseen circumstances in a product's market, such as unexpected demand or government regulation. Since the profits were unforeseen, some jurists believe that taxing them at a higher rate, or confiscating them outright, should not hurt the company.

However, the principle of *clausula rebus sic stantibus* is now evident in the substantive laws including the Mining Act 14 of 2010 and the Natural Wealth and Resources Contracts (Review and Renegotiation of Uncontainable Terms) Act 6 of 2017. Provisions of these laws have opened doors for invoking the principle of *clausula rebus sic stantibus* through imposing the requirement of subjecting MDAs to review (section 12 of the Mining Act 14 of 2010).

CONCLUSION

To make these changes valid and effective, Tanzania has to take further steps, including renegotiation of the current BITs and MDAs especially on mode of settlement of disputes and on the inception of investor's obligations to the host states such as importation of capital, local content, CSR, protection of public health and environment. The changes also raise the need for Tanzania to revisit her investment laws and policy so as to align them with these changes. However, all these changes could be regarded as risks and disincentives to the foreign investors, thus Tanzania is urged to undertake its reforms while considering this threat. Again, Tanzania should undertake these measures in observance of its obligation to protect foreign investments under both national laws (article 24 of the Constitution of the United Republic of Tanzania, 1977 and section 22 of the Tanzania Investment Act 26 of 1997, on payment of adequate, fair and prompt compensation in case of nationalisation or expropriation by the government) and international agreements in case of nationalisation or expropriation measures of foreign investments. One can confidently say that at least there is a sign of light at the end of the tunnel.

BIBLIOGRAPHY

Adam, S. (2008). "Stabilization Clauses and Human Rights: A Research Project Conducted for IFC and the United Nations Special Representative to the Secretary General on Business and Human Rights."

Afilalo, A. (2004). "Towards a Common Law of International Investment: How NAFTA Chapter 11 Panels Should Solve Their Legitimacy Crisis." *Georgia International Environmental Law Review*, Volume 17(51), 272.

Afilalo, A. (2005). "Meaning, Ambiguity and Legitimacy: Judicial (Re-) Construction of NAFTA Chapter 11." *North Western Journal of International Law & Business*, Volume 25(2), 279–314.

Aguas del Tunari S A v Bolivia ICSID ARB/02/3 (2005) (Decision on Jurisdiction).

Alvarez, J. (2008). "A Review on Investment Treaty Arbitration and Public Law by Gus Van Harten." *The American Journal of International Law*, Volume 102, 909–915.

Alvarez, J., and Sauvant, K. P. (Eds.). (2011). *The Evolving International Investment.* London: Oxford University Press.

Amerasinghe, C. F. (2009). *Jurisdiction of International Tribunals.* Boston: Martinus Nijhof.

Azurix *Corp v Argentina* ICSID ARB/1/12 (2006) (final award) (all cases concerned governed measures to protect water services).

Barrick Press Release. "Barrick Back in Business in Tanzania." https://barrick.q4cdn.com/788666289/files/doc_news/2020/01/Barrick-Back-in-Business-in-Tanzania.pdf. Accessed 19 February 2020.

Behring, J., Braun, T. R., Lorz, R. A., Tams, C., Schill, S., and Tietje, C. (2009). General Public International Law and International Investment Law: A Research Sketch on Selected Issues, Institute of Economic Law, Transnational Economic Law Centre. In A. Kilangi (Ed.), *Introduction to International Investment Law.* Halle: Beiträge zum Transnationalen Wirtschaftsrecht, International Law Association German Branch – Sub-Committee on Investment Law.

Borchard, E. (1915). *The Diplomatic Protection of Citizens Abroad.* New York: Banks Law Publishing Company.

Bossche, P. (2005). *The Law and Policy of the WTO: Text, Cases and Materials*. London: Cambridge University Press.

Brownlie, I. (2008). *Principles of Public International Law* (7th ed.). London: Oxford University Press.

CMS Gas Transmission Company v The Argentine Republic ICSID ARB/01/8 (2005) (final award).

Constitution of the United Republic of Tanzania. (1977).

Cosmas, J. (2014). "Investor-State International Arbitration System: Is ICSID the Appropriate Forum for Developing Countries Like Tanzania?" *Open University Law Journal*, Volume 5(1), 25–36.

Curtis, M. (2012). *The One Billion Dollar Question: How Can Tanzania Stop Loosing So Much Revenue*. Tanzania Christian Council (CCT), National Council of Muslims in Tanzania (BAKWATA) and Tanzania Episcopal Conference (TEC).

Curtis, M., and Tundu Lissu, A. (2008). *A Golden Opportunity? How Tanzania is Failing to Benefit from Gold Mining*. The Christian Council of Tanzania (CCT), National Council of Muslims in Tanzania (Bakwata) and Tanzania Episcopal Conference (TEC).

Dolzer, R., and Chreuer, C. (2008). *Principles of International Investment Law*. New York: Oxford University Press.

Electronic Official Proceedings of the National Assembly (Hansard), 59th Session, 4 July 2017.

Enron Corporation and Ponderosa Assets L P v Argentine Republic ICSID ARB/01/3. (2007). (final award).

George, C. (2015). Mineral Extraction for Socio-Economic Transformation of Tanzania: The Need to Move from Papers to Implementation of Mining Policy and Law. *Journal of Social Science Studies*, Volume 2(2), 160.

Gottward, E. (2008). "Leveling the Playing Field: Is It Time for a Legal Assistance Centre for Developing Nations in Investment Treaty Arbitration?" *American University International Law Review*, Volume 22(2), 237–275.

Grossman, N. (2009). "Legitimacy and International Adjudicative Bodies." *George Washington International Law Review*, Volume 41(1), 107–180.

Guzman, A. (1998). "Why LDCs Sign Treaties that Hurt Them: Explaining the Popularity of Bilateral Investment Treaties." *Vanderbilt Journal of Transnational Law*, Volume 38, 639–688.

Hiscock, M. E. (2009). "The Emerging Legal Concept of Investment." *Pennsylvania State International Law Review*, Volume 27, 765–782.

Hudec, R. E. (1999). "The New WTO Dispute Settlement Procedure: An Overview of the First Three Years." *Minnesota Journal of Global Trade*, Volume 8, 1–53.

Hurst, J. W. (1971). "Problems of Legitimacy in the Contemporary Legal Order." *Oklahoma Law Review*, Volume 24, 224–238.

Jackson, J. H. (1978). "The Jurisprudence of International Trade: The Disc Case in GATT." *American Journal of International Law*, Volume 72, 747–781.

Kairys, D. (2003). "Searching for the Rule of Law." *Suffolk University Law Review*, Volume 36(2), 307–330.

Karl, J. (2002). "On the Way to Multilateral Investment Rules – Some Recent Policy Issues." *ICSID Review – Foreign Investment Law Journal*, Volume 17, 293–319.

Kaufmann-Kohler, G. (2007). "Arbitral Precedent: Dream, Necessity of Excuse? – The 2006 Freshfield Lecture." *Arbitration International*, Volume 23(3), 357–374.

Kreindler, R. (2010). "Parallel Proceedings: A Practitioner's Perspective." In M. Waibel, A. Kaushal, K. Chung, and C. Balchin (Eds.), *The Backlash Against Investment Arbitration: Perception and Reality*. London: Kluwer Law International.

Kronfol, Z. A. (1972). *Protection of Foreign Investment: A Study in International Law*. Leiden: A.W Sijthoff.

Krzysztof, J. P. (2017). "What Explains the Low Success Rate of Investor-State Disputes?" *International Organisations Summer*, 559–583.

Mann, H. (2003). "The Right of State to Regulate and International Investment Law: A Comment." In *UNCTAD The Development Dimensions of FDI: Policy and Rule Making Perspective*.

Mining Act No. 14 of 2010.

Mwangonde, H. (2017). "JPM: Even the Devil Must Be Mocking Us." *The Guardian*.

Peter, C. M., and Mwakaje, S. J. (2005). *Investment in Tanzania: Some Comments – Some Issues*. Dar es Salaam: Friedrich Ebert Stiftung.

Philip Morris Asia Limited v The Commonwealth of Australia, UNCITRAL, PCA Case No. 2012–2012.

Potts, J. B. (2011). "Stabilizing the Role of Umbrella Clauses in BITs: Intent, Reliance and Internationalization." *Vanderbilt Journal of Transnational Law*, Volume 51(4), 1005–1046.

Regulation 4 of the Local Content Regulations GN 3 of 2018.

Sempra Energy International v The Argentine Republic ICSID ARB/02/16 (2005) (final award).

Sornarajah, M. (2010). *The International Law on Foreign Investment* (3rd ed.). Cambridge: Cambridge University Press.

Spear, S. (2010). "The Quest for Policy Space in a New Generation of International Investment Law." *Journal of International Economic Law*, Volume 13(4), 1037–1075.

Srividya, J., Henisz, W. J., and Mansfield, E. D. (2011). "Three Waves of BITs: The Global Diffusion of Foreign Investment Policy." *The Journal of Conflict Resolution*, Volume 55(6), 1047–1073.

Sudi, A. The Local Content Regulations in Tanzania and Its Compatibility and Compliance with the World Trade Organisation Laws. https://amnesuedi.com/category/the-local-content-regulations-in-tanzania-and-its-compatibility-to-the-world-trade-organisation-laws/.

Suleiman, N. H. T. (2018). *Critical Analysis on the Legal Implications of Mining Development Agreements in Taxation of Mining Companies in Tanzania*. Master of Laws in Taxation of the University of Dar es Salaam.

Tanzania Extractive Industries Transparency Initiatives: Final Report.

Tanzania Investment Act, No. 26 of 1997.

Tienhaara, K. (2009). *The Expropriation of Environmental Governance: Protecting Foreign Investors at the Expense of Public Policy*. Cambridge: Cambridge University Press.

Tonodeus, K. M. (2012). *Mining Sector Taxation in Tanzania: International Centre for Tax and Development*. Research Report 1, Institute of Development Studies, Brighton, BN 19 RE UK.

United Nations General Assembly Resolution 523(VI), 12 January 1952, Integrated Development and Commercial Agreements.

United Nations General Assembly Resolution A/RES/25/2625 of 24 October, 1970.

United Nations General Assembly Resolution A/RES/29/3281 of 12 December, 1974.

Van Harten, G. (2007). *Investment Treaty Arbitration and Public Law*. London: Oxford University Press.

Vattenfall v Federal Republic of Germany, ICSID Case No. ARB/12/12 (2012).

Written Laws (Miscellaneous Amendments) Act No. 7 of 2017.

Chapter 6

Crude Oil Exploitation and Environmental Laws as Mechanisms for Protecting Human Rights in African Societies

A Nigerian Perspective

Eric Omo Enakireru and Anya Kingsley Anya

INTRODUCTION

Environmental degradation implicates many human rights issues bordering on right to life, privacy, right to healthy environment, and right of self–determination (Human Rights Watch 1999; United Nations Environment Programme [UNEP] 2011). A worrisome dimension to the plethora of complications associated with the environment is the issue of environmental abuses inflicted by many multinational companies engaged in exploitation of oil, mineral, timber or other natural resources in the African continent, particularly Nigeria. The level of human rights abuse arising from oil production in Nigeria was graphically summarised by the Human Rights Watch in its 1999 report as follows:

> Oil production has had damaging effect on the environment of the oil-producing region, though the extent of the damage is subject to dispute . . . Despite decades of oil production, there is surprisingly little good quality independent scientific data on the overall or long-term effects of hydrocarbon pollution on the delta, yet oil led development has clearly seriously damaged the environment and livelihood of many of those living in the oil producing communities. The oil companies operating in Nigeria maintain that their activities are conducted to the highest environmental standards; but Nigeria environmental laws, in most respect comparable to their international equivalents, are poorly enforced. (Human Rights Watch 1999; UNEP 2011)

Occasionally, large oil spills pollute water, kill aquatic animals and damage agricultural crops. The spillage also has serious effects on the communities and families affected, especially on dry land or in freshwater swamp zones where spills are contained in a small area. The cumulative long-term effect of major pollutions and/or incidents of regular small spills and effluents deliberately or accidentally discharged to the environment is large and unevaluated. Poorly designed causeways and canals used by the oil industry affect the hydrology of the seasonally flooded freshwater swamp and the brackish water of the mangrove forest, destruction of crops, pollution of fishing grounds as well as sources of portable and drinking water supplies. Significantly, compensation for such damages is inadequate, and in the absence of a properly functioning court system, there is no effective recourse to an independent arbiter to determine the value of the damaged properties. It should be noted that the overall picture of the environment and means of sustenance are basically despicable and below average.

On the other hand, the oil companies also allege that many of such spills were caused by acts of sabotage. As a result, they surreptitiously evade compensation in such determination of the trial with the professional assistance of the best brains in the legal profession. The fact of sabotage having not been proved cumulatively furthers the injustice the affected community suffers.

Furthermore, at the community level, the companies are faced with ever-increasing protests and youth agitations directed at their activities which invariably stultify and continue to slow down the lack of infrastructural development of amenities in the Delta region. Notwithstanding the above, there are such incidents ranging from taking of hostages, wilful and aggressive closures of flow stations, sabotage and intimidation of staff.

The Niger delta has for some years been the enclave and hotspots of major confrontation between the host communities and regiments of the Nigerian government security operatives, an ugly trend that has resulted in extra-judicial executions, arbitrary detentions and draconian restriction on the rights to freedom of expression, association and assembly. These violations of civil and political rights have been committed principally in response to protest on the activities of the multinational companies that explore and produce oil in Nigeria.

Drawing attention to human rights and environmental abuses, it has been observed that one of the most disturbing aspects of public environmental litigation is the absence of a constitutionally guaranteed "environmental right" under Nigerian law to remedy these environmental abuses. This is because the right to a safe and healthy environment is as controversial as other debates concerning new or emerging rights (i.e., right to development, right of the people, indigenous rights). The existence of such a legally recognised right will in no small measure serves many purposes. Environmental right refers to the right of the citizen to have a clean, safe and decent environment and to enforce it in case of violation by the government or private citizens. We must warn that the terminology used in articulating the content of this right is diverse, vague, controversial and ever-changing. For example, many adjectives have been applied to the term "environment" in describing the particular environmental quality to which humans have a right to under international and national laws. The adjective most frequently found in legal literature for such a purpose include secure, safe, satisfactory, healthy, healthful, decent, adequate, clean, pure, natural, viable, ecologically sound and ecologically balanced. Moreover, the term environment has itself been the object of debate. First, it will provide the necessary substantive rights, in this case an obligation on individuals and government to protect the environment which can be enforced when violated. Second, it will obliterate the legal hurdle of locus-standi that is currently standing in the way of many environmental litigants.

Although at present, there is no specific constitutional provision directly proclaiming a right of environmental protection under the 1999 Constitution of Nigeria, there is, however, a mixture of ideas associated traditionally with the concept of environmental rights.

THE CONCEPT OF ENVIRONMENTAL RIGHTS AND LITIGATION

The proponents of this right have expanded and re-interpreted the Civil and Social Rights in the Universal Declaration of Human Rights (United Nations Declaration On Human Rights, hereafter UDHR, GA Resolution 217A (III)), the International Covenant on Economic, Social and Cultural Rights (United Nations Declaration On Human Rights, hereafter UDHR, GA Resolution 217A (III)) and other human rights instrument to suggest that the right to a clean environment is an integral part of the fundamental human rights of every citizen (Inter-American Convention on Human Rights Act; European Convention for the Protection of Human Rights and Fundamental Freedom, 1950, 312 UNTS.143, article 3; African Charter on Human and People's Rights, 1988, article 4; additional Protocol to the American Convention on the Right of the Child, 28 I.L.M.1448, (1989), article 24(2)(c)). Article 17 of the Covenant on Economic Social and Cultural Rights (ICESCR), for example, guarantees respect for private and family life and home. Again, article 25(1) of the UDHR asserts that: "everyone has the right to standard of living adequate for the health and well-being of himself and of his family." Article 3 of the UDHR asserts that "everyone has the right to life, liberty, and the security of person" (see other similar human rights treaties). Using this derivative right principle, human rights scholars argue that the civil and social rights to life, health and personal liberty guaranteed by many international treaties and municipal legislations would be meaningless if the environment was continually degraded to the detriment of the people (see generally, Boyle 1996, 43; Design 1995, 263; Okonmah 1977, 43; Fitzmaurice 1999, 611; Lee 2000, 283; Rodriguez-Rivera 2001, 12; Schoenbaum and Young 2017, 65–737). The state has a positive obligation to take steps to promote life expectancy of the citizens. Therefore, any person whose environment is wrongly degraded can rely on these civil and social rights to enforce his environmental right (on rights regarding the environment, see principle 1 of the Stockholm Declaration; article 24 of the African Charter on Human and Peoples' Rights, 21 I.L.M. 58 1982; Alston 1982, 307).

Critics of this right have argued that the concept is vague and non-justiciable. Core human rights scholars regarded environmental right as a third-generation right which cannot be enforced individually but by the collective effort of the people (Kiss and Shelton 1991, 23; Palmer 1992, 259, 266; Shelton 1991, 135). While the right is to be generally available, the content of the right is ultimately contingent upon the social and cultural context of those who are active participant in their own development. If the potential imperialism of the language of law, particularly, the language of rights as well as the language of needs is accepted, then what some would see as the failure to give more concrete expression to the content of the right to development, comes instead to be seen as its greatest virtue. It is submitted that the imprecise nature of the rights would make it difficult to enforce if environmental right is given a legal recognition. Again, since the scope of the right cannot be clearly defined, the determination of its scope and judicial enforcement of the right would depend solely on the court definition of "environment" and this may pitch the court against the legislature in a never-ending battle (see also the dictum of the lord Goff in *Cambridge Water Works v Eastern Leather Countries Plc* [1994] 1 ALL E.R. 53-57, which stipulates that there is less need for the courts to develop a common law principle to achieve the same end. Indeed, it may be well undesirable that they should do so . . . the parliament is the most competent authority to impose strict liability in respect of a polluter whose activities are risky and dangerous to the public).

Another problem is the resulting liability for environmental harms. Characteristically, human rights obligation imposes a duty on the state to enforce the right and to compensate or remedy the harm, if any, sustained by the citizen, in case of violation of such a right. Generally, states are unwilling to accept that the right to environment imposes an absolute legal obligation on them to protect the environment rather they are more contended with soft law and declaration which lack force and imposes no legal obligation on the state as illustrated by many UN declarations (Principle 1, Declaration on the Human Environment, Report of the UN Conference on the Human Environment (New York, 1973), UN Doc. 48/A/CONF14/Rev. 1; Principle 1, Declaration on Environment and Development, (New York, 1992) UN Doc.A/CONF.151/26/Rev. 1). Again, since environmental right is also a second-generation social, economic and cultural right whose full implementation cannot be fully ensured without economic and technical resources, education and planning the gradual reordering of social priorities and, in many cases, international cooperation (Marcus 2003, 250, arguing that the violation of the citizens right to food being a second-generation right is more tolerated by state and that deliberate promotion of famine through inaction, corruption, authoritarian governance should be criminalised internationally), state will be unwilling to assume such obligation because of the financial commitments involved. Thus, in practice, the enforcement of these rights is more observed in its breach, comparing the enforcement of political right vis-à-vis that of social and economic rights, David Marcus believes that "the violation of economic and social right is more tolerated by states. This tolerance reflects states weak or at least ambiguous acceptance of the social and economic rights" (Marcus 2003, 250). A fact corroborated by the United Nations committee on economic, social and cultural rights when it observes that:

> The shocking reality . . . is that states and the international community as whole continue to tolerate all too often breaches of economic, social and cultural rights which, if they occurred in relation to civil and political rights, would provoke expressions of horror and outrage and would lead to concrete call for immediate remedial action. In effect, despite the rhetoric, violation of civil and political rights continues to be treated as though they were far more serious and more patently intolerable, than massive and direct denial of economic, social and cultural rights. (World Conference on Human Rights, Preparatory Committee Contribution Submitted by the Committee on Economic, Social and Cultural Rights UN Doc. A/CONF.157/PC/62/Add.5, Para. %, 1993)

In addition, environmental right is often rebuffed because it implicates national development, for example, the states have to build dams, road, encourage the construction of factories, new settlement, explore mineral resources (including oil and gas), promote large-scale farming and provide basic infrastructure for human development – all these will have an adverse impact on the environment. A strict adherence to the promotion of environmental right will undoubtedly and ultimately hinder development, inconvenience the government encourage political resistance and engender political instability (World Conference on Human Rights, Preparatory Committee Contribution Submitted by the Committee on Economic, Social and Cultural Rights UN Doc. A/CONF.157/PC/62/Add.5, Para. %, 1993).

Significantly, an analysis on environmental right using the 1999 Constitution of the Federal Republic of Nigeria is appropriate here. Chapter II of the Constitution in its Fundamental Objectives and Directive Principle of the State Policy (FODPSP) directs the state to protect and improve the environment and safeguard the water, air and land, forest and wildlife of Nigeria (section 20). Similarly, the Constitution guarantees the right of every person to life (section 33(1)). The effect of these provisions ordinarily suggests that the right to a clean environment is guaranteed by the Constitution and that any individual or group of individuals whose environment is degraded can trigger an action to protest the degraded environment, if the government refuses, or neglects to enforce any environmental legislation (*Uzochukwu&ors v Ezeonu II* [1991] 6 NWLR (pt. 200) para 708). In practice, this is not necessarily so. Firstly, enforcement of fundamental human rights pursuant to special procedure made under section 42 of the 1979 Constitution does not admit of any right not enshrined in chapter IV of the 1999 Constitution. Second, the ability of Nigeria citizen to invoke the provision of section 20 of the Constitution has been whittled down by the provision of section 6(60)(c) of the Constitution, which clearly exclude judicial powers to decide on "issue or question as to whether any act or omission by any authority or person or as to whether any law or any judicial decision is in conformity with the fundamental objectives and directive principles section set out in chapter II of the Constitution."

Third-judicial attitude towards the interpretation of the FODPSP provision has typically been patronising cautious and restrictive. Nigerian courts have, by their rigid adherence to the "self-execution" cannon of statutory construction, refused to give full effect to the FODPSP provision engraved in the constitution. The provision of the FODPSP were construed as non-justiciable right but mere directives and lofty objectives of the state that cannot be elevated to the status of substantive rights except through legislative intervention (a provision constitute sufficient rule by means of which the right that it grants may be enjoyed and protected without the aid of a legislative enactment before it will be judicially enforced; *State ex Rel. City of Fulton v Smith* 194 SW 3d paras 302; 304, MO 146).

In *Okogie v Lagos State Government* (1981 2 NCLR 337), where the plaintiff brought an application challenging a circular issued by the Lagos State Government purporting to abolish private schools in the state on the ground that the circular infringed on the constitutional rights to receive and impart education guaranteed under section 36 of the 1979 Constitution. The defendant argued that the implementation of the circular was in conformity with the provision of FODPSP on educational matters as contained in section 18 of the 1979 Constitution. That the proviso requires the state to direct its policy towards ensuring that there are equal and adequate educational opportunities at all levels to the citizens (1981 2 NCLR 337). The issue before the court was how to reconcile the constitutional provision in section 36 that guarantees right to disseminate and impart education with that of fundamental objectives provision on education. The court of appeal, however, decided that the directive principle of state policy in chapter II of the 1979 Constitution is non-justiciable and must conform to and run subsidiary to the fundamental rights. The court held, in effect that an individual could not rely on FODPSP to assert any legal right.

It is pertinent to note that the decision in Okogie's case (1981 2 NCLR 337) was greatly influenced by an earlier Indian case of *State of Madras v Champakam* (1951 SCR 252). Incidentally, the Indian court appeared to have set a new standard in the field of environmental litigation. When the new standard in the field of environmental hazard became increasingly perceptible, in the field of environmental legislation, by invoking the power under articles 32 and 48 of the Indian Constitution (article 32 empowers the Supreme Court to enforce the rights conferred under the constitution and issue directions or writs in the nature of habeas corpus, mandamus, prohibition, *quo warranto* and *certiorari* for the enforcement of any rights conferred under the constitution). The concept of *locus-standi* is used to entertain a new genre of litigation and it allows a private attorney to institute actions to protect the fundamental deterioration (article 48 provides that the state shall endeavour to protect and improve the environment and safeguard the forest and wildlife of the country), proceeded on the premise that a clean and wholesome environment is prerequisite to enjoying the right to life enshrined in the Indian Constitution as fundamental right of all personate decision in rural litigation and entitlement was discussed in *Kendra v State of UP* 1966 AIR SC 1057, this was followed by the decision in *MC Mehta v Union of India* 1987 AIR 965 a case concerning the closure of a chlorine plant at Oleum due to leakage of hazardous gas. The Supreme Court, consisting of five constitutional judges having regard to the gravity of the environmental and legal questions under consideration, granted locus-standi to the petitioner to enforce the rights of the people affected by the leakage. In that case, the petitioner, the Indian council for enviro-legal action brought this action to stop and remedy the pollution caused by several chemical industrial plants in Bichri Village, Udaipur District, Rajasthan. The respondent operated heavy industry plants without permits producing chemicals such as oleum, single super phosphate and the highly toxic "H" acid which polluted the water and soil of the village and its environs. The Supreme Court ordered a major part of the quarrying activities to be closed down in public interest of the Kendra people. In few subsequent public interest litigation cases, the court recognised the right to environment and invoked the power under article 32 of the constitution to issue appropriate orders and direction. Thus, in *MC Mehta v Union of Indian* 1987 AIR 1086, the practitioner filed a writ at the Supreme Court ordered its office to serve notice of the suit on all industries concerned and, after hearing both tanneries not having pre-treatment plants approved by the pollution control board to stop their discharge of trade effluents. In *Indian Counsel for Environ Legal Action v Union of India* 1987 AIR 1086, where the sludge, a lethal waste, left out in a village for years after the chemicals industries were closed, caused heavy damage to the environment, the Supreme Court ordered the remedial action be taken and compensation be given for the silent tragedies in line with the "Mehta absolute liability" principle.

In a related environmental pollution case in the Philippines, the Philippines Supreme Court reached a similar decision in *Minor Oposa v Secretary of the Department of Natural Resource* 1994 33 I.L.M. 173, a case based on a substantive procedural right to a clean environment contained in article II of the Philippine constitution (article II provides that "the state shall protect and advance the right of the people to a balanced and healthful ecology in accord with the rhythm and harmony of nature"). The plaintiff in the case were a number of minors, together with the Philippines Ecological Network Inc., a non-profit organisation challenging the powers of the defendant to issue licence to a timber company to engage in logging business within the Philippines forest. The petitioners based their claim, *inter alia*, on section 16 of article II of the 1987 Constitution of Philippines, which recognises the right of people to a balance and healthful ecology the concept of generational genocide in criminal law, and the concept of man's inalienable right to self-preservation and self-perpetuation embodied in natural law. The respondent argument was grounded on two natural laws. The respondent argument was grounded on two points. First, the respondent argued that the petitioner failed to demonstrate in their complaint the violation of any specific legal right for which relief was guaranteed by law. Second the respondent argued that logging is a political not a legal question and should be dealt with by the executive or legislative branches, not by court law. The court upheld the argument submitted by the petitioners and held further that timber-licensing agreement were not contract that fell within the non-impairment clause of the Philippines Constitution. The court further replied on executive order 192 (1987), the administrative code and the Philippines environmental policy, which introduce the general policy of environmental protection. It made ground-breaking pronouncement concerning the right to clean environment as funding possible causes of action. In regard to these claims the court held that: "while the right to a balanced and healthful ecology is to be found under the declaration of principle and state policies and not under the bill of rights. It does not follow that it is less important than any of the civil and political rights enumerated in the latter. Such a right belongs to a different category of right altogether for it concerns nothing less than self-preservation and self-perpetuation aptly and fittingly stressed by the petitioners the advancement of which may even be said to predate all government and constitutions. As a matter of fact, these basic rights need not even be written in the constitution for they are assumed to exist from the inception of humankind. If they are now explicitly mentioned in the fundamental charter, it is because of the well-founded fear of its framers that unless right to a balanced and healthful ecology and to health are mandated as state policies by the constitution itself." (*Minor Oposa v Secretary of the Department of Natural Resource* 1994 33 I.L.M 173)

From the above analysis, it is obvious that the decision in Okogie's case should no longer be good law, particularly as it relates to environmental protection and sustainable use of resources. Unfortunately, the Supreme Court remains unyielding when in *Attorney-General of Ondo State v Attorney General Federation* 2002 9 NWLR Pt. 7720 para 222. It held that the provision of FODSP in chapter II of the constitution remain non-justiciable. The court further held that FODSP are mere declaration that lack the force of law and cannot be enforced by legal process except translated or elevated to the status of law by legislation. It is submitted that a liberal interpretation of the provisions of chapter II by the Supreme Court in future, particularly as it relates to environmental protection will undoubtedly promote sustainable development goals, public participation and access to environmental justice. This is because in most environmental-related litigation and policy implementation, what is expected of the court is to hold the balance between environmental consideration and developmental consideration. Such approach if and when adopted by the court, will be consistent with current national and international sustainable development policy which requires governments to consider development holistically by taking into consideration significant environmental factor in the development process.

Furthermore, since Okogie case, there has been positive development in the field of human rights protection culminating in the enactment of the African Charter on Human and People Rights Act and the Fundamental Rights (Enforcement Procedures) Rules 2009. This Charter represents the most progressive law in human right protection and contained far-reaching provision relating to the attainment of environmental rights in Nigeria. Article 24 of the African Charter on Human and People Rights I.L.M. 58 (1982). The Ratification and Enforcement Act (Chapter A 9, laws of the federation of Nigeria, 2010, expressly ratified the African Charter on Human and People Rights and made its provision applicable and enforceable at the national level) recognise the people's right to "a general satisfactory environment favourable to their development." People in this context includes individual or group of individuals sharing similar distinctive cultural and spiritual identity and should be broad enough to permit either individual or group of individuals to enforce any infraction of the environmental right. Although the interpretation of article 24 of the African charter has not been called into question by Nigerian courts, if and when the situation arise, the courts may be called upon to resolve one or more questions to wit: (1) whether the provision of article 24 imposes any duty on the state to improve the environment or mere directions to the state in the formulation of state policy on environment; or (2) whether the provision of article 24 is self-executor justifying private action to compel the government to promote environmentally sound policies and by extension enforce public violation of environment law in cases of state inaction/in the event of such a case arising the court may take one of the two possible options. The first option is to hold that the environmental rights envisioned under article 24 like those contained in the state directives are non-justiciable right and therefore, individuals cannot compel the state to act or institute actions to challenge infraction of public environmental wrongs. The second option is to hold that the provision of article 24 is self-executory as it establishes and guarantee environmental rights that are enforceable by the courts without any executive or legislative interventions.

In the *Social and Economic Rights Action Centre and the Centre for Economic and Social Rights v Nigeria*, where the applicant non-governmental organisations (NGOs), filed a complaint against the government of Nigeria for violating the rights of Ogoni people at the African Commission on Human and People Rights. In this regard, the interpretation of section 24 of the Charter became imperative. In the case the applicant alleged that Shell Petroleum Development Company and Nigeria National Petroleum Company (hereafter called "consortium"), exploited oil reserves in Ogoniland with no regards for the health or environment of the local communities disposing toxic wastes into the environment and local waterways in violation of applicable international environmental standards (Fifteenth annual report of the African Commission on human and people's rights 2001–2002).

The consortium also neglected and/or failed to maintain its facilities causing numerous avoidable spills in the proximity of the villages. The resulting contamination of waters, soil and air has had serious short and long-term health impact including skin infections, gastrointestinal and respiratory ailments, and increased risk of applicant further alleged that the Nigeria government has condoned and facilitated these violations by placing the legal and military powers of the state at the disposal of the oil companies and the government has neither monitored operations of the oil companies nor required safety measures that are standards procedures within the industry. The government has also withheld from Ogoni Communities information on the dangers created by the oil activities and has been denied access to vital environmental information.

In interpreting article 24 of the charter, the African Commission on human and people right took cognizance of Nigeria domestication of the provision of the African Charter on that all the right contained therein can be invoked in Nigeria courts by the citizens and held that article 24 clearly imposes obligations upon a government to take reasonable and other measures to prevent pollution and ecologically sustainable development and use of natural resources (Amokaye 2007). The commission observed that the Niger delta had suffered from degradation as a result of oil pollution and therefore, citing kiss, concluded that "an environment degraded by pollution and defaced by the destruction of all beauty and variety is as contrary to satisfactory living conditions and development as the breakdown of the fundamental ecologic equilibrium is harmful to physical and moral health" (Amokaye 2007).

The right to enjoy the best attainable state of physical and mental health enunciated in article 16(1) of the African Charter and the rights to a general satisfactory environment favourable to development in article 24 also oblige governments to desist from directly threatening the health and environment of their citizens (article 16 provides that: "(1) every individual shall have the right to enjoy the best attainable state of physical and mental health. (2) State parties to the present charter shall take the necessary measure to protect the health of their people and to ensure that they receive medical attention when they are sick." The state is also under an obligation to respect these rights and this entails largely non-interventionist conduct from the state, for example not from carrying out, sponsoring or tolerating any practice, policy or legal measures violating the integrity of the individual (article 16 of the African Charter). According to the commission, government compliance with the spirit of articles 16 and 24 of the African Charter must also include ordering or at least permitting independent scientific monitoring of threatened environment, requiring and publicising environmental and social impact studies prior to any major industrial development. These articles also provide for the undertaking of appropriate monitoring and providing information to those communities exposed to hazardous materials and activities and providing meaningful opportunities for individual to be heard and to participate in the development decisions affecting their communities (articles 16 and 24 of the African Charter).

Again, in *Sani Abacha v Gani fawehinmi* 2000 4 SC (pt. 11) para 22, the Supreme Court considered the status of African Charter vis-à-vis the constitutional rights of the citizens. In the case, the respondent, a legal practitioner and human right activist was unlawfully arrested and detained in a prison by the State Security Service without any formal charge. The respondent brought an application challenging his arrest and detention and contended that the arrest and detention was a gross violation of his fundamental rights guarantee under the constitution and articles 4, 5, 6 and 12 of the African Charter. One of the issues for consideration was whether the provision of the charter runs subsidiary to the provision of the human and people right though not superior to the constitution, are integral to laws the court must uphold them and in case of inconsistency between them and other statutes the provision contained in the charter will prevail for the reason that it is presumed that the legislature does not intend to breach some international obligations. The court further ruled that the charter gave to every Nigeria citizens' rights and obligations, which are enforceable by the court. Consequently, it is arguable that the individual rights contained in the charter are justiciable and our court can seek to protect them from violation and be ready to provide appropriate remedies in favour of the victims.

Going by these decisions, two theses could readily be formulated, particularly as related to access to environmental justice. First, the right of the people to clean environment and general satisfactory environment favourable to their development engraved in article 24 of the African Charter is judicially legalised (Churchill 1996, 174). A fortiori, the people can invoke the provision of article 24 of the African Charter to trigger state action in the formulation and implementation of sounds national environmental policies that will promote and encourage economic growth and sustainable development. Therefore, in cases of state inaction private individuals and NGOs can initiate action to remedy public stimulate and catalyse individuals and class actions to challenge the age-long degradation of the environment by the historic polluter should the state refuse to do so. Articles 5(3) and 34(6) of the protocol establishing African Court of Human and People Rights (African Court) further strengthen this position (see protocol to the African Charter on Human and People Rights on the establishment of an African court, 9 June 1998, OAU Doc. OAU/LEGL.EXP/AFCHPR/PROT(III); Udombana 2000, 101–165). The African Court of Human and People Rights guarantee directs access to individual and NGO litigants to bring applications for enforcement of their rights where the municipals courts fail to effectively apply the provision of the charter. Article 5(3) and 34(6) of the protocol confer direct access to individual and relevant NGOs with observer status to institute an action for violation of the right in the charter; a fact openly acknowledges by the commission in the *Social and Economic Rights Action Center and the Centre for Economic and Social Rights v Nigeria.* The major defect of the protocol is that access to court is subjected to the discretion of the court and state party to submit to adjudication. In most African countries where governments are unresponsive to their citizens, bringing such a state party to the African court may prove difficult and futile. Even in case where such state party submits to the jurisdiction of the court, the implementation of the court's decision is yet another tug of war, particularly in countries governed by military and unresponsive governments. That is why despite the establishment of the court though commendable the test of its existence and effectiveness on African people will take some time to appreciate. The second conclusion is that though these cases specifically recognised environmental rights the requirement of locus-standi to enforce the public violation of the environmental law must establish the violation of his civil right and pecuniary interest protected by law. This argument is premised on the courts failure to elevate the provision of the African Charter to constitutional status. In the words of the court, the African Charter is not superior to and does not override the constitution, although it is a legislation in a class of its own to the extent that it invests the citizens with civil rights and obligations. Consequently, an attempt to unduly broaden and elevate article 24 to a justiciable right might be defeated by the argument that it is inconsistent with section 1(1) of the constitution which renders such law null and no-effect. Similarly, the interpretation by the African Human Rights Commission of Article 24 is silent on the issue of *locus-standi* although recognition is given to the issue of access to environmental information and public participation in environmental management. Therefore, it will be presumptuous to assert that the article dispenses with the requirement of standing to sue, and that a fortiori it invest private individuals and NGOs with the power to enforce public environmental law. When the situation arises, the court might choose between the two option highlighted above. While the Nigerian law readily recognises environmental right, the question of enforcement of such right will ultimately depends on the judicial application of the locus-standi rule to accommodate or restrict the broad spectrum of environmental litigants that are likely to come before it.

ENFORCEMENT OF ENVIRONMENTAL PROTECTION RIGHTS

Generally, an Environmental Protection Agency (EPA) official or police officer has no power to search any premises without a search warrant issued by a Magistrate or High Court Judge unless expressly authorised by a statute (NESREA, sections 9 and 30 on endangered species). However, one of the main attributes of many environmental, public health and drug control statute is the power by the regulatory agencies to search, detain and confiscate items recovered from environmental polluters without any warrant of arrest (Harmful Waste (Species Criminal Provisions, etc.) Act, Section 10; National Agency for Food and Drug Administration and Control Decree 15 of 1993 as amended by decree 19 of 1999, section 24; National Parks Service Decree 46 of 1999; control of the importation regulations, regulation 6; Animals Diseases (Control) Act, Chapter 18, Laws of the Federation of Nigeria 1990, section 5).The exercise of this power will necessitate the officials of the EPAs and drug enforcement agencies or relevant government department to access the premises of the polluter without notification. In most cases, key evidence will include the analysis of a sample taken by the agency from the discharge point into the controlled waters, land or air or downstream into a water house or warehouse where the hazardous waste is kept. The public law aspect arising from this is how the exercise of this power will be undertaken without infringing on the constitution (the 1999 constitution preserves and guarantees the privacy of citizen, their homes correspondence, telephone conversation and telegraphic communication, see section 37). The right of privacy is "a generic term encompassing various rights recognized to be inherent in the concept of ordered liberty and such right prevents governmental interference in intimate personal relationship or activities; freedom of individual to make fundamental choice involving himself, his family and his relationship with others" (Black Law Dictionary 1990; Warren and Brandies 193; Knees and Lannelli 1986, 705). This will necessarily involve the recognition of the citizen's right to be secure in their person, houses, papers and effects, against unreasonable and unlawful searches and seizures. The limits and contour of the right to privacy have not received any judicial interpretation in Nigeria as in other jurisdiction like the United State and Canada. The slow development of privacy tight in Nigeria is largely attributed to the legacy of English Common Law system, which gave restrictive and cautious recognition to privacy right? English law though recognised the right of every person to enjoy his private property and his reputation such right are protected by the common law of reluctant to recognise privacy more than this. Nevertheless, the power of administrative search and seizure without warrant contained in this environment public health and drug control law has constitutional implications, which require that constitutional standards be met when this power is invoked. First, it is arguable that the provisions of these statutes are inconsistent with the constitutional right to privacy and therefore unconstitutional, null and void. The result is that a polluter may resist an attempt to search or detain any of his properties without lawful warrant on the pretext that his privacy is infringed. Second, even where it is conceded that national environmental standards and regulations enforcement act and harmful waste are species of public welfare laws, of the agency to search and seize environmental substance considered to be harmful or hazardous is not absolute. To constitute a lawful search under these laws, it must be shown that there is a reasonable ground for believing that an offence has been committed and that such search is necessary to prevent the polluter from destroying material evidence to prosecute the polluter. Reasonable ground for believing is not defined in any of these statutes. Whether a reasonable ground to believe exists will depend on the circumstance in each case, but there must be objective basis for it. The test to be applied is both in the absence of such circumstance or where such search is a device to serve other purposes beyond the authority scope of regulation in the public interest; such search is unlawful and an infringement of the right to privacy of the polluter. As a matter of judicial practice, courts, in the interest of the privacy of the citizens, have constructed narrowly the police power of entry, search and seizure. Through the power of the courts to hold search and seizure unlawful, the right to privacy prevents abuses of statutory powers of search by government officers. As Lord Denning remarked in *Ghani v Jones* 1970 1 QB 693, 708 have invoked the privacy interest to forbid any official search whatever under statutes not explicitly allowing entry into hoes. This is because, parliament should not be presumed to have authorised any greater invasion of privacy than what was expressly sanctioned (*Clowser v Chaplin* 1981 72 Crim App R. 342, 353, *R v Inland Commissioner, Ex Parle Ross minister* 1980) AC 952).

Nonetheless, the right to privacy is not absolute. It remains in conflict with other rights, value and interest. One countervailing consideration is the interest, which the public has in protecting public health, public safety and welfare. The right to privacy will therefore be conditioned by the provision of our constitution which validate any law that is reasonably justifiable in a democratic society in the interest of defence public safety, public order, public morality or public health (1999 Constitution of Federal Republic of Nigeria, section 47(1)). Section 45(1) of the 1999 Constitution provides that nothing in sections 37, 38, 39, 40 and 41 of this constitution shall invalidate any law that is reasonably justifiable in a democratic society–(a) in the interest of defence, public safety, public order, public morality or public health (section 1 of the Charter provides that the charter rights are subjected to such reasonable limits prescribed by law as can be demonstrably justified in a free and democratic society).

The Nigerian courts have not made any pronouncement on the scope and meaning of this section. Thus, whether the provision of environmental, public health and drug control statutes that permits searches and invasion of privacy of t citizen is a law that is reasonably justifiable in a democratic society is a matter of conjecture. If the practice in other jurisdiction such as Canada is any guide for a law to be reasonable justifiable in a democratic society, the law must meet the minimum requirement of section 1 of the Canadian Charter, the Canadian Supreme Court in *R v Oakes* 1986 1 SCR 103 laid down the broad criteria to satisfy the requirement of reasonable and justification. In this case, the issue was the validity of a provision of the federal narcotic control act, which provided that proof that the accused was in possessions of an illegal drug raised a presumption that the accused was in possessions for the purpose of trafficking. The effects of this provision were to cast on the accused the burden of trafficking. The Supreme Court held that this "reverse onus" clause was an infringement of section 11(d) of the Canadian Charter of rights and freedom, which guarantee the presumption of innocence. The court though accepted that the objective of the "reverse onus" clause was to protect the society from drug trafficking, and as such it was sufficiently important to justify limiting a Charter rights, the act failed the rationality test because "a rational connection between the basic fact of possession and the presumed fact of possessions for the purpose of trafficking" was non-existing. In the words of Dickson CJ, to establish that a limit is reasonable and demonstrably justified in a free and democratic society, two central criteria must be satisfied. First, the objectives, which the measure responsible for a limit on a charter right or freedom are designed to serve, must be "of sufficient importance to warrant overriding a constitutionally protected right or freedom." The standard must be high to ensure that objectives which are trivial or discordant with the principles integral to a free and democratic society do not gain protection. It is necessary, at a minimum, that an objectives relate to concern which are pressing and substantial in a free and democratic society before it can be characterised as sufficiently important.

Second, once sufficiently objective is recognised, then the party invoking section 1 must show that the means chosen are reasonable and demonstrably justified. This involves "a form of proportionality test." Although the nature of the proportionality test will vary depending on the circumstances, in each case court will be required to balance the interest of society with those of individual and groups. Although the consent of the occupier is not required to conduct a search, since the exercised of the power is in accordance with statutory enforcement provision as opposed to a judicial act (*Walker Snack Foods Ltd v Coventry City Council* [1998] 3 ALL ER 163, contrast with the restricted police powers of search, seizure and arrest under the Criminal Procedures Act, sections 107 and 109 and Police Act, section 24 (police power to issue a search warrant for the purpose of recovering stolen property; *R v Quinn* 1994 10 WACA, held that police officers have no absolute right to enter premises without a search warrant for the purpose of investigating a crime; *Kuku v Olusoga* 1962 ALL NLR 618, held that the issuance of the search warrant being a judicial act is unquestionable; *COP v Micheal David* 1963 NNLR 29). There are, in my view, three important components of a proportionality tests. First the measure adopted must be carefully designed to achieve the objective in question, they must not be arbitrary, unfair or based on irrational consideration. In short, they must be rationally connected to be the objective on the first sense, should impair "as little as possible" the right or freedom in question . . . third, there must be a proportionality between the effects of the measures which are responsible for limiting the charter right or freedom, and the objective which has been identified as of "sufficient importance." The four broad criteria formulated by the Supreme Court in the case are:

A. The law must pursue an objective that is sufficiently important to justifying limiting a constitutional right.
B. The law must be rationally connected to be objective.

C. The law must impair the right no more than is necessary to accomplish the objective.
D. The law must not have a disproportionate severe effect on the person to whom it applies.

The requirement in (a) above is not difficult to establish. The objective could be deducted from the content, preamble and explanatory note to the act parliamentary documents, hence, the court are generally hesitant in challenging the objectives of an act with a view of striking down the act based on the presumed objectives of the parliament. However, the law must further demonstrate that the objective is sufficiently important to justify overriding a constitutional right. To satisfy this, the legislative objectives must meet the standards implied in the words, "free and democratic society." It must also relate to the concerns that are pressing and substantial as opposed to mere triviality. Finally, it must be directed to the realisation of collective goals of fundamental importance. The rationality test will be satisfied if the law is "carefully designed to achieve the objectives in questions; it should not be arbitrary, unfair, or based on irrational consideration. The law should import the right no more than is necessary to accomplish the desired objectives, or, in other words, that the law should pursue the objective by the least drastic means.

A power to search without warrant could also be justified under this principle in that it allows the prosecution to obtain the material incriminating evidence to facilitate prosecution. However, searches without warrant of commercial property would be constitutionally objectionable if their occurrence was "so random, infrequent, or unpredictable that the owner has no real expectation that his property will from time be inspected by government officials". In *New York v Burger*, the court established three tests that must be met for pervasively regulated industry to be searched without a warrant: (a) there must be a substantial government interest involved; (b) the inspection without warrant must be necessary to further the regulatory scheme and (c) there must be certainty and regulatory of its application. In addition, searches and seizures prevent the destruction of incriminating evidence, discover more about possible evidence about the Act complained of, and make possible evidence which based upon initial search of the specified area may be in a different location. Take the position in the United States of America, for example, the courts formulated a theory of diminution in privacy right of "pervasively regulated business" whereby people participating in a closely regulated business may reasonably have only a diminished expectation of privacy interest theory is founded on the assumption that persons undertaking such a business impliedly content to search based upon their knowledge of the extent of government control over the business (*Marshall v Barlow's Inc.*

1978 436 US 307; Ringel 1990, chapter 14). The legal premises of pervasive regulations are that the statutes that regulate the industry are the fictional equivalent of search warrant.

In *Donovan v Dewey* 1981 452 US 594, the U.S. Supreme Court established a new standard permitting extensive government inspection of commercial property without a warrant. This case concerned the Federal Mine Safety and Health Act, which directs federal officials to inspect underground mines at least four times a year and surface mines at least twice a year to enforce safety standards. These statutes specifically provide for inspections without advance notice and require the secretary of labour to institute court actions in case where inspectors are denied admission. In declaring the act constitutional, the US Supreme Court found that the government had "greater latitude" to conduct search without warrant in commercial property than private homes (*Donovan v Dewey 1981* 452 US 594 paras 598–599). The court ruled that search without warrant of the safety inspections of mines was justified because of the notorious history of serious accidents and unhealthy working conditions in the mining industry, along with congress's determination that unannounced inspections were necessary if the safety laws were to be effectively enforced (*Gbemre* case Unreported 2005 FHC/B/CS/53/05, 28).

A RIGHTS APPROACH TO DETERRENCE

The point has to be made that even where a company has been adjudged guilty or liable, there has to be sanction that would sufficiently deter. This is so because if the only sanction is for the payment of some nominal fine, rather than deter, it would encourage the corporation to pollute and pay the assured meagre fines.

The emerging trend the world over is to impose strict liability on companies for pollution caused by them. This is in recognition of the fact that if a polluter can be found there is no guarantee that any compensation paid out will be spent on clean up, and that clean-up is likely to fall upon the public purse in any event.

Legislative, and more importantly enforcement measure, are put in place to encourage companies to limit their environmentally damaging activities, not because to do otherwise would be a crime, but rather because to do otherwise would be economically unwise. It was for this reason that the Niger delta technical committee that I headed, recommended the establishment by this year of regulations that would compel oil companies to have insurance bonds against environmental pollution, strength independent regulation of oil pollution and make enforcement of critical environment laws and prosecution of polluters and fraudulent cases of national priority.

More seriously, to complement such measures (Fontaine, Van Vliet and Pasquis 2007, 223–254), in the face of the obvious consequences of oil pollution on health which in some cases result in death the time has come for oil companies to be charged with murder of the innocent citizens of the Niger delta region who die daily as a result of contaminations from oil exploitation activities.

COMMON LAW REGIME

The torts relevant to the activities of the petroleum industry are negligence, nuisance and the rule in *Rylands v Fletcher*, except the statute and regulations empowering or granting right for petroleum exploration, prospecting and mining specifically exclude the application of these torts, communities or individual have the legal rights to sue the offending companies for any adverse consequences of their activities.

It should be noted that the provisions of the Mineral Act have not derogated from the rights enjoyed by dwellers of land in Nigeria including the respondent (*Adeshina v Lemonu* 1965, 233; *Braide v Adoki* 10 NLR para 15). It must be mentioned also that the common rights of fishery in Idal waters is not affected by the Mineral Act (*ELF (Nig) Ltd v Operesillo & Anor* 1994 6 NWLR (pt. 358) 258 paras 269–270). On application of the rule in Rylands v Fletcher, it is clear therefore that a person who is in possession or in control of land (such as appellant herein) and keeps on such land petroleum products exist under the rule in "*Rylands v Fletcher.*" It must be said also that the establishment of crude oil pipeline on land with the potential of escape or spill of its contents is clearly non-natural user of the land (*ELF (Nig) Ltd v Operesillo & Anor* 1994 6 NWLR (pt. 358) 258 paras 269–270). The rule laid down in *Rylands v Fletcher* is, on the other hand, to the effect that the occupier of land who brings and keep upon it anything likely to do damage if it escapes, is bound at his peril its escape, even if they have not been guilty of negligence (*Hale v Jennings Bros* (1938) 1 ALL ER 579 paras 582; 584; Akintan JCA paras 20–25).

Therefore, the proper recipient of an award of damages when an oil spillage occurs, "the award of damages for temporary loss of fishing made in the judgment ought not be seen as an award to the individual fisherman per se." Rather it is a compensation payment made to the respondent community for loss of income suffered by the community members who have a common interest or right to fish as member of respondent community to the exclusion of every other person who is not a member of the community. The right is communal not individual. It is enjoyed communally because it derives from a common and joint ownership and or possession of right to fish in Ofougbene ponds, creeks, and so on. As borne by the record, the respondent and appellant have always known this and in the past conducted affairs on that basis. It cannot therefore come from the mouth of the appellant to contend otherwise (section 151 of the Evidence Act; Rowland JCA paras 10–20).

NEGLIGENCE

The tort of negligence "connotes" the complex concept of duty, breach and damage thereby suffered by the person to whom the duty is owed. Negligence may consist of an action or omission. The main difficulties for the plaintiff remain the proof of sense of reasonable care on the part of the operator (Lord Wright in *Lochgelly v Iron Coal Co v M Mullan* 1934 AC pl para 25). The plaintiff also has the burden of showing causal link between his damage and the defendant's action (Uzodike 1987, para 237).

In a highly technical industry such as the petroleum industry, proof of negligence requires expert's scientific evidence, unavailable and unaffordable to the largely unschooled and poor victims who suffer from the ravages of exploratory activities of the oil companies. *In Chinda & 5 Others v Shell Petroleum Development Company of Nigeria Ltd* 1974 6.S.C. pl 19, the plaintiff alleged that owing to the defendant's company negligence in the control and management of their flares' site which was within a short distance of the plaintiff villages, a lot of damage was done to the plaintiff trees lands and houses. Holden CJ held that the plaintiff did not produce any evidence of negligence in the defendant operation of their flares sites and therefore would fail. In *Atubin v Shell BP Petroleum Development Company of Nigeria Ltd* UHC/48/73, the plaintiff claimed that the defendant caused crude oil, gas and chemicals to escape from pipelines under their control thereby destroying fishes in the lake and their farmland, the court held that the plaintiff did not prove that the defendant was negligent. In *Seismograph Service Ltd v Benedict Etedjere Onokpasa* (Kodilinye 1982, 47), the main question before the court was whether the shooting operations carried out by the defendant company caused extensive damage to some buildings owned by the plaintiff. Thus, the plaintiff had the burden to establish the negligence of the defendant company in its operation. He was, however, unable to do this because the negligence was not within his knowledge.

Although a plaintiff may successfully plead the doctrine of *res ipsa loquitur* to relieve him of the burden of establishing defendant negligence the defendant can rebut this presumption by mere explanation of the cause of spillage. The oil companies are well positioned, considering the enormous resources at their disposal to afford and supply expert evidence in rebuttal and if unchallenged, must be accepted and acted upon by the court. In *Seismograph Service*

Ltd v Akpornovu, the respondent case against the appellant was that the appellant had caused damage to his building during seismic operations.

The respondent failed to call expert evidence in support of the casual link between the damage and the appellant seismic operations as alleged. The appellant called a seismologist who gave unchallenged evidence. The learned trial judge nevertheless held the appellant liable. Dissatisfied, the appellant appealed and the Supreme Court reversed the decision of the lower court on the grounds that the learned trial judge ought to have acted upon the unchallenged evidence.

NUISANCE

Nuisance may be defined as an unjustified or unlawful interference with the plaintiff's use or enjoyment of his land (Kodilinye 1982, 90). A nuisance may be public or private. Whereas public nuisance which affects the public as a whole can rise to both civil and criminal proceedings, a private nuisance consists of an act or omission which materially affects the reasonable comfort and convenience of the general public or a section of the general public. Where the interference is with his land, then it is a private nuisance. Furthermore, it must be observed that an actionable nuisance is incapable of exact definition. It is an act or omission which is an interference with, disturbance of, or annoyance to a person in the exercise or enjoyment of (a) a right belonging to him as a member of the public, when it is a public nuisance or (b) his ownership or occupation of land or some easement, profit or other rights used or enjoyed in connection with land, when it is private.

Public nuisance is basically a crime, actionable by the attorney General. It is a tort actionable by an individual plaintiff only where he can show that the defendant's conduct has caused him particular damage over and above that suffered by the general public (Criminal Code Chapter C38 LFN 2004, section 23). In *Amos & Others v Shell BP Nigeria Limited* 1997 4 ECSLR 86, the plaintiff had claimed that the defendant by constructing a dam across their creek should be held liable in negligence. This is because the construction of the dam had resulted in flooding upstream causing severe damage to farmland and crops while downstream was experiencing a drought. The court held that since the creek was a public waterway the action by the defendant amounted to a public nuisance. Therefore, since only the attorney general can bring an action for a public nuisance, the action of the plaintiff must show that the he has suffered damage which is different in kind, not merely in degree, from that suffered by the general public (*Attorney General v PYA Quarries Ltd* (1975) All ER para. 894 & 908). But a better view is that it is sufficient for the plaintiff to show that he suffered damage which is appreciably greater in degree than any suffered by the general public. It seems most acts of nuisance committed by oil companies are public nuisance. The scope of remedy is highly limited and it is difficult to succeed in an action in nuisance in oil pollution cases. In Nigeria where the same person doubles as the attorney general and minister of justice, it is difficult for that person to bring an action against the national oil company or the subsidiaries of the multinational oil companies because the federal government of Nigeria has majority equity shares in the subsidiaries of most of the multinational oil companies operating in Nigeria.

THE RULE IN *RYLANDS V FLETCHER* 1866 LR, EX P265

The rule in *Rylands v Fletcher* 1866 LR, EX P265 is one of the common law remedies which have been widely acclaimed as a rule of strict liability and providing new remedies where none would otherwise have existed. Liability in the law of tort usually arises as a result of some wrongful or negligent act on the part of the defendant. Strict liability on the other hand connotes a situation where the defendant would be liable whether or not he was at fault and the fact that he exercised due in the circumstance will not exonerate him. The rule which evolved from the case of *Rylands v Fletcher* itself was stated by Blackburn J as follows, "A person who for his own purpose brings on his land and collect and keeps there, anything likely to do mischief of it escape must keep it in at his own peril and if he fails to do so, he is *prima facie* liable for all the damage which is the natural consequences of its escape."

Oil was held to be capable of constituting such a dangerous matter in *Machine Umudje v Shell BP Petroleum Development Company of Nigeria limited* 1975 9–11 SC para 155. In this case, the plaintiff who owned land adjacent to the area of exploration complained (a) that, in the course of road building the defendants had blocked and diverted a natural stream, thus interfering seriously with the plaintiff fishing rights and (b) that the defendant had accumulated oil waste on land under their control and that this oil had escaped onto the plaintiff land and caused damage there.

As regards the first complaint, the Supreme Court that under the rule in *Rylands v Fletcher* it is now generally accepted that a person who diverts a natural stream or cause same to become blocked and in this way diverts its natural course does so at his peril, and is liable for any damage caused by the failure of his works to contain the diverted stream although there was no negligence on his part. The court, however, held that in the present case the defendant was not liable because their blocking of the stream had not caused flooding of plaintiff's land but merely starvation of water and fish; there was, in other words, no escape of water from the defendant land to that of the plaintiff. With regard to the other complaint, the defendant was held liable under the rule, since there was clear proof that crude oil waste, which they had accumulated in a pit on land under their control, had escaped onto the plaintiffs' land where it had polluted certain ponds and killed the fishes therein. An essential requirement of the rule is that there must be a non-natural user of the land by the occupier. In *Edhemowe v Shell B.P Petroleum Development Company of Nigeria Limited* UHC/12/70, the court held the defendant liable for damage caused to the plaintiff fish ponds by the oil which escaped from the defendant waste pit holding that the accumulation of crude oil in a waste pit was non-natural user of land. Other cases where the rule was accepted by the court as the basis for their decisions include *Otuku v shell BP Petroleum Development Company of Nigeria Ltd* 1985 BHC/2/83; *Okoro v Shell BP Petroleum Development Company of Nigeria Ltd* 1972 W/2/21/77.

However, the court has accepted statutory authority as a complete defence to claim brought under the rule (*Ikpede v Shell BP Petroleum Development Company of Nigeria* Ltd (1973) MWSJ 6. Some doubt has been expressed in some quarter on the appropriateness of applying the rule in *Rylands v Fletcher* to oil operations in Nigeria in view of the fact that oil production being the bedrock of the country revenue could not be regarded as non-natural user of land (Omorogbe 1991, 155).

It has been submitted and rightly one thinks, that the utilisation of the rule might be defended as an effort by the Nigerian court to regulate oil pollution and provide relief to victims in the absence of any other basis for relief. Environmental injuries are often of long-lasting effect. In recent times, there has been a remarkable shift from the long-established common law concept of liability founded on the fault of the defendant, especially in ultra-hazardous activities like petroleum exploration and production, to that founded on absolute liability principle. This is the approach of the Indian Supreme Court in the case of *MC Mehte v. Union of India.* In this case, on an application for compensation following a leak of hazardous gas from a factory in Delhi owned by the Siram food and fertiliser company, the court moved from the strict liability principle as propounded in *Rylands v Fletcher* into absolute liability which is stated was not subjected to any exceptions which operate in the area of the principle of strict liability. In a potentially hazardous industry like the petroleum industry where the standard of operation in Nigeria is not comparable to international best practices, it is necessary that the court in Nigeria continue to make use of the rule in *Rylands v Fletcher* and gradually move to the absolute liability principle.

CONCLUSION

A healthy environment is vital to the quality of life of human being. This has made it imperative to safeguard the human environment for human interest.

Environmental right is one of the tools used to address environmental problems at the global, regional and national levels. It has been posited that environmental rights could be employed to restore the balance between man's activities and the preservation of the environment for future generations (Du Plessis 2008, 43). Environmental harm and the abuse of human rights often go together. An unhealthy and unfavourable environment is a violation of the right to life and human dignity every human being is entitled to a healthy and productive life in harmony with nature. A healthy and ecologically balanced environment is a fundamental right so as to enhance environmental governance in Nigeria. By so doing, the importance of the issues of environmental governance will be elevated in Nigeria and Nigerians will be assured of a healthy and ecologically balanced environment.

Procedural rights are indispensable to the implementation of environmental rights for the attainment of sustainable environmental governance. These procedural rights should be given effect to under the Nigerian laws to enhance the enforcement of environmental tights in Nigeria. Provision should be made for an environmental rights act which has incorporated in it "procedural rights" and such an act should be given effect to under the Nigerian constitution. Such procedural rights provide civil society with the mechanism for learning about actions that may affect them, participate in governmental decision-making processes and holding the government accountable for its action inactions. They also serve to enable civil society to be bond together to protect the environment through the exercise of those procedural rights

The importance of law in promoting effective environmental governance cannot be underestimated. The legislative arm of government can be a useful tool and a powerful agent of change in sustainable environmental governance. Therefore, there is a need for a principal statute for the management of the Nigeria environment. Nigeria is in need of an integrated and coherent framework for her environmental management. Nigeria needs a strong legislative system if she is to achieve her environmental commitment and goals.

Consideration for a reformed regime, taking into account both the economic and social benefits of preserving the environment needs to be looked into. Nigeria therefore needs a more robust all-encompassing and well-focused environmental regime to serve as a core principal legislation on the management of the Nigeria environment. The capacity of the Nigeria legislature needs to be strengthened not only to enable it legislates for sustainable environmental governance but also to enable it promote institutional reforms that will bring about sustainable environmental governance. Environmental sustainability should be made an integral part of economic planning at all levels of governance and integrated into all policies in Nigeria. Economic policies which aim at balancing sustainability initiative backed by conscious efforts to safeguard and protect the environment should also be made use of. It is also important to have adequate institutional machinery for supervising implementation of environmental obligations/commitments. The legal and political framework for environmental governance requires effective enforcement mechanism. Therefore, there is the need for the full utilisation of the law as an instrument of social changes or social engineering to achieve a balance between environmental protection and development activities. The type of balance recommended is and ought to be a delicate balance. Significantly, the need for environmental protection rights should be balanced as against the need for development of immediate host communities. The two factors should not be compromised in favour of the other. Sustaining a balance between environmental protection laws and development of communities is a desideratum for a stable socio-economic and politico-cultural society devoid of any form of rancour.

The type of balance recommended is and ought to be a delicate balance. Significantly, the need for environmental protection rights should be balanced as against the need for development of immediate host communities. The two factors should not be compromised in favour of the other. Sustaining a balance between environmental protection laws and development of communities is a desideratum for a stable socio-economic and politico-cultural society devoid of any form of rancour.

BIBLIOGRAPHY

Additional protocol to the American Convention on the Right of the Child I.L.M.1448 (1989).

Adeshina v Lemonu (1965) 1 All N.L.R. (pt. 1).

African Charter on Human and People's Rights 1988.

African Court on Human and Peoples Right, June 9, 1998, OAU Doc. OAU/LEGL. EXP/AFCHPR/PROT(III).

Amokaye, O. G. (2007). "Environmental Protection and Human Rights Nexus." *Human Rights Journal*, Volume 30, 231–265.

Attorney General v PYA Quarries Ltd (1975).

Barron, J. H. (1979). "Warren and Brandies, the Right to Privacy, Volume 4 Harvard Law Review 193 (1890): Demystifying a Landmark Citation." *Suffolk University Law Review*, Volume 13, 875.

Black Law Dictionary 6ed. (1990).

Boyle, A. (1996). "The Role of International Human Right Law." In A. E. Boyles and M. Anderson (Eds.), *Protection of the Rights Approaches to Environmental Protection*. London: Oxford University Press.

Braide v Adoki (1930) 10 NLR 15.

Churchill, R. R. (1996). "Environmental Right in Treaties." In A. Boyle and M. R. Anderson (Eds.), *Human Rights Approach to the Environmental Protection*. London: Oxford University Press.

Clowser v Chaplin (1981) 72 Crim App R 342.
Constitution of Federal Republic of Nigeria, 1999.
COP v Micheal David (1963) NNLR 29.
Criminal Code Chapter C38 L.F.N. 2004.
Declaration on Environment and Development, (New York, 1992) UN Doc.A/CONF.151/26/Rev. 1.
Declaration on the Human Environment, Report of the UN Conference on the Human Environment (New York, 1973), UN Doc. 48/A/CONF14/Rev. 1.
Design, R. (1995). "Integrating Environmental Values into the European Convention on Human Rights." *American Journal of International Law*, Volume 80, 263.
Donovan v Dewey. (1981). 452 U.S. 594.
Du Plessis, A. (2008). "Public Participation, Good Environmental Governance and Fulfilment of Environmental Rights." *Potchefstroom Electronic Law Journal*, Volume 11(2), 1–34.
ELF (Nig) ltd v Operesillo & Another (1994) 6 NWLR (pt. 358).
Endangered Species (Control of International Trade and Traffic) Act.
European Convention for the Protection of Human Rights and Fundamental Freedom, 4 November 1950, 312 UNTS.143.
Fifteenth Annual Report of the African Commission on Human and People's Rights 2001–2002. http://www.achpr.org/15thannual report AHG.pdf.
Fitzmaurice, M. (1999). "The Right of the Child to a Clean Environment." *Southern Illinois University Law Journal*, Volume 23, 611–656.
Gbemre case. (2005). FHC/B/CS/53/05.
Guillaum, F. (2007). "Green and Black: Environmentalism and Oil Conflicts in Ecuador." In G. Fontaine, G. Van Vliet, and R. Pasquis (Eds.), *Environmental Policies and Governance in Latin America*. FLACSO-IDDRI-CIRAD.
Hale v Jennings Brothers. (1938). 1 ALL ER 579.
Harmful Waste (Species Criminal Provisions) Act.
Human Rights Watch. (1999). *The Price of Oil*. New York: Human Rights Watch.
Ikpede v Shell B.P Petroleum Development Company of Nigeria Ltd (1973) MWSJ 6.
Indian Counsel for Environ Legal Action v Union of India (1987) AIR 1086.
Inter-American Convention on Human Rights.
International Covenant on Economic Social and Cultural Rights.
International Covenant on Economic, Social and Cultural Rights, December 16, 1966, 193 UNTS 3(1966).
John Frederic Clerk, J. F., and Lindsell, W. H. B. (2014). *Clerk & Lindsell on Torts*. London: Sweet and Maxwell.
Kodilinye, G. (1982). *Nigeria Law of Torts*. London: Sweet & Maxwell.
Kress, J. M., and Iannelli, C. D. (1986). "Administrative Search and Seizure Whither the Warrant." *Villanova Law Review*, Volume 31(3), 705.
Kuku v Olusoga. (1962). ALL NLR.
Leckie, S. "Violation of Economic, Social and Cultural Rights." http://www.law.uu.n/content/20-03.pdf.
Lee, J. (2000). "The Underlying Legal Theory to Support a Well-Defined Human Rights to a Healthy Environment as a Principle of Customary International Law." *Columbia Journal of Environmental Law*, Volume 25, 283.

Marcus, D. (2003). "Famines Crimes in International Law." *American Journal of International Law*, Volume 97(2), 245–281.

Marshall v Barlow's Inc (1978) 436 US 307.

MC Mehta v Union of India (1987) AIR 965.

National Agency for Food and Drug Administration and Control Decree No. 15 of 1993 as amended by decree No. 19 of 1999.

National Parks Service Decree No. 46 of 1999 Repealing National Parks Decree No. 36 of 1991.

Okonmah, P. (1977). "Right to a Clean Environment: The Case for the People of Oil Producing Communities in the Nigeria Delta." *Journal of African Law,* Volume 43(1), 43–67.

Okoro v Shell B.P Petroleum Development Company of Nigeria Ltd 1972 W/2/21/77.

Omorogbe Y. (1991). "Regulation of the Oil Industry Pollution in Nigeria." In E. Azinge (Ed.), *New Frontiers in Law*. Benin City, Nigeria: Oliz Publishers.

Otuku v Shell B.P Petroleum Development Company of Nigeria Ltd (1985) BHC/2/83.

Palmer, G. (1992). "New Ways to Make International Environmental Law." *American Journal of International Law*, Volume 86, 259–283.

Per Lord Wright in Lochgelly v Iron Coal Co. v M. Mullan (1934) AC pl 25.

R v Inland Commissioner, Ex Parte Ross Minister (1980) AC 952.

R v Quinn (1994) 10 WACA.

Ringel, W. E. (1990). *Searches & Seizures, Arrest and Confessions* (2nd ed.). Callaghan: Clark, Boardman.

Shelton, D. (1991). "Human Rights, Environmental Rights, and the Right to Environment." *Stanford Journal of International Law*, Volume 28, 103–138.

State ex Rel. City of Fulton v Smith 194 SW 3d 302, 304 (MO 146).

Turack, D. (1995). "Essays in Honour of Judge Taslim Olawale Elias Volume I: Contemporary International Law and Human Rights. Volume II. African Law and Comparative Public Law." ***Case*** *Western Reserve Journal of International Law*, Volume 27, 195–201.

Udombana, N. J. (2000). "Towards the African Court on Human and Peoples Right: Better Late than Never." *Yale Human Rights and Development Law Journal*, Volume 3, 101–165.

UNEP. (2011). *UNEP: Environmental Assessment of Ogoni Land.* Nairobi, Kenya: UNEP.

United Nations Declaration On Human Rights. http://www.unchr.ch/html/menu3/b/69.html.

Uzochukwu & Others v Ezeonu II [1991] 6 NWLR (pt. 200) 708.

Walker Snack Foods Ltd v Coventry City Council [1998] 3 ALL ER 163.

World Conference on Human Rights, Preparatory Committee Contribution Submitted by the Committee on Economic, Social and Cultural Rights UN Doc.A/CONF.157/PC/62/Add.5, Para. % (1993).

Chapter 7

The International Criminal Court and Its Targeting of African Leaders

A Case of Legitimising Another Global Apartheid Regime?

Oyesola Animashaun and Howard Tafara Chitimira

INTRODUCTION

Most African states have been weakened by colonialism, apartheid, trans-Atlantic slavery, Arab slave trade, structural adjustment programmes and human trafficking. Some of these African states are further weakened by double standards perpetrated by international organisations like the International Criminal Court (ICC). This is usually perpetrated through the Rome Statute 1998, which the unsuspecting African leaders subscribed to in large numbers. The chapter addresses the geopolitical imbalance in the indictment, investigation and prosecution at the ICC. The authors argue that the ICC's main focus seems to be only on Africans and they also submit that the indictment of a serving African head of state whose country is not a party to the Rome Statute, contrary to customary international law, is both unfair and unlawful. It also interrogates the contentions in the referral and deferral powers of the permanent members of the United Nations Security Council, majority of whom are not party to the Rome Statute. The chapter further examines the flaws in the Rome Statute, the cases instituted and similar cases that were ignored by the ICC prosecutor which suggests that there may be some justification for the allegation of global apartheid levied against the body by some authors, politicians and the African Union (AU). There are also indications that the independence of the ICC is compromised because it focused mainly on African states while ignoring similar violations of the Rome Statute by the "powerful nations" such as the United States of America (US), Russia and China and their allies. The chapter concludes that African countries need strong national and regional mechanisms to promote transparency in governance, and should be circumspect in adopting treaties without weighing the implications. Furthermore, the ICC must reinvent itself to escape the accusation of global apartheid due to its near-exclusive focus on Africans.

The term "global apartheid" simply refers to minority rule in international decision-making (Köhler 1995, 404). The term is derived from apartheid, the system which was officially used to rule South Africa from 1948 till 1994. Global apartheid describes the political and socio-economic disparities that exist between the rich countries of the Global North and the poor countries of the global South, caused by the deliberate policy of the Global North (Besteman 2019, 26–27; Adebajo 2009, 3). Global apartheid is therefore defined as "a structure of world society . . . a structure of extreme inequality in cultural, racial, political, economic and legal terms, as is South African apartheid" (Köhler 1995, 404). According to Mazrui (2007, 96, 98), global apartheid is driven by "pan-Europeanism" and Western-controlled transnational capitalism, two processes that have intensified since the end of the Cold War. Global apartheid is grounded in Global North–South relationship which is defined to be a political, economic and cultural system in which the Global North overwhelmingly controls power and material resources; global apartheid also comprises of Global North dominance and Global South subordination, which is daily reenacted across a broad array of institutions and social settings (Ansley 1997, 592).

Nour and Connell (2012, 13) argued that Global South serves as another metaphor for underdevelopment and it refers broadly to the regions of Latin America, most of Asia, Africa and Oceania (Nour and Connell 2012, 12–13). In the Global North–South configuration, it is not the geographical location that matters but the level of development and economic system adopted by each country (Müller 2018, 2; Nour and Connell 2012, 12–14). The Global North/South and Global East/West concepts are controversial and subject to criticism because of its inexactitude (Müller 2018, 2–3; Berger 1997, 260–261). In this chapter, Global North refers to North America (except Mexico), Western Europe, Israel, Australia, New Zealand, Russia and East Asia. The Global North is further sub-classified into the West (comprising United States, Canada, and Western Europe) and the East (comprising Russia and China). The other countries not included in the list above are classified as Global South. Thus, all countries on the African continent, which is of special concern in this chapter, are in the Global South.

Mutua (2017, 48) maintained that the African continent was inflicted with grave injustices and trauma such as colonialism, trans-Atlantic slavery and apartheid. All these unpleasant events as well as the cauldron of the cold war and the scandalous international order combined to ravage the emergent African states at and after independence from their erstwhile colonial masters (Mutua 2017, 48). Most African states attained independence between 1950 and 1970 and joined the United Nations (UN) afterwards, however, before the arrival of the newly independent Africa states, the rules of the UN had already been set by the original signatories to the UN charter (Birmingham 1995, 15; Adebajo 2009, 6; the UN Department of Public Information 2008, 5). These rules were meant to favour the Global North and these inequalities were deeply embedded in later international institutions (Adebajo 2009, 3–15). For instance, the official languages of the UN were Chinese, English, French, Russian and Spanish; and Arabic was later added later by the General Assembly. UN adopts no indigenous African language for conducting its business. Further, Alexander (1996, 40–46) and Huntington (2011, 81) enumerated some important mainstays of global apartheid employed by the Global North to include controlling powers at International Monetary Fund (IMF), World Bank and World Trade Organisation (WTO). Alexander (1996, 46) and Huntington (2011, 81) stated that global apartheid is perfected by the Global North through the following: the introduction and protection of some Western currencies – "hard currency" through the Bank of International Settlement, the use of aid and investment to control the Global South and support for military intervention in countries which defy Western dominance. Institutions such as the ICC, IMF, WTO, North Atlantic Treaty Organisation (NATO) and others are termed neo-colonial bodies because they are used to make Global South amenable to domination by the more affluent states from the Global North (Chipaike and Matarutse 2018, 2). These international institutions were created to shift and maintain the balance of power in favour of the West (Warikandwa and Amoo 2018, 301).

According to Mutasa (2005, 1), global apartheid is "hidden in global economic processes, political institutions and cultural assumptions," which fabricate programmes and policies detrimental to Africans (Steinberg 2016, 306; Bassiouni and Hansen 2016, 315, 318; Clarke 2016, 331; Odero 2011, 154–155; Mamdani 2008). The detrimental manifestation of the some of the programmes created by these international organisations to the African states include economic policies known as structural adjusted programmes, which led African countries that adopted it to higher debt profile, brain drain and unfavourable trade terms. Other unfavourable manifestation of some of these international organisations' programmes are selective prosecution and human trafficking (Odero 2011, 154–155).

Dersso (2017, 62–64, 72) and Seymour (2017, 107–108) argue that the ICC is one of the international organisations fostering global apartheid on the Global South. The ICC was conceived as an institution to investigate and prosecute international criminal cases and was widely embraced by Africans states with enthusiasm initially (Mutua 2017, 52; Seymour 2017, 107; Nyawo 2017, 36; Monageng 2014, 14–16; Murithi 2014, 179–180). African states were positively disposed towards ICC and embraced the court with enthusiasm initially (Mutua 2017, 52; Seymour 2017, 107; Nyawo 2017, 36;

Monageng 2014, 14–16; Murithi 2014, 179–180). African states' initial support for the ICC was based on many reasons. First, Nyawo (2017, 38) opined that the Lockerbie bombing case which pitted the West against Libya would not have occurred if there were a court like ICC. He reasoned that it would have been easier for the erstwhile Libyan head of state, Muamar Gadhafi to send the Libyan nationals accused of being involved in the Lockerbie's bombing to an ICC than the jurisdiction of another sovereign state. The insistence of the US and her allies that Libya, transfer her nationals, who were alleged to have committed international crimes to the jurisdiction of the Western courts was seen as a form of global apartheid (Nyawo 2017, 37). Further, the United States (US), United Kingdom (UK) and France rejected Libya's willingness to invite international observers to the trial of the suspects in the Lockerbie's bombing case (Nyawo 2017, 37). Thereafter, the United Nations Security Council (UNSC) imposed a crippling economic sanction on Libya (at the behest of the US and the UK) despite a subsisting application at the International Court of Justice (*Libya Arab Jamahiriya v UK, Order,* provisional measures, ICJ GL No 88, [1992] ICJ Rep 3, ICGJ 75 (ICJ 1992), 14th April 1992). The authors submit that this action was a manifestation of global apartheid, whereby UK and the US use their political and economic clout to control Libya, a sovereign state from the Global South. It is ironical that the West that is enamoured with democracy and the rule of law refused to abide with the dispute resolution mechanism outlined under international law for such cases (article 8, paragraph 2, Montreal Convention). UK and the US insistence that Libya extradite her citizen to either the US or UK when there was no extradition treaty between these countries and Libya was oppressive to the latter (Zubel 1999, 263–267). The fallout from the Lockerbie's case made the Ghanaian representative at the UN, George Lamptey to argue that if there was an international tribunal like the ICC, the Lockerbie debacle which pitted Libya against the West would not have occurred (Nyawo 2017, 38). Thus, the bid to avoid this form of global apartheid by powerful countries from the Global North, the African countries probably felt that the constitution of the ICC would be the solution.

African states attributed the international indifference to the Rwandan genocide in 1994 to global apartheid. Scholars such as Melvern and Williams (2004, 12) and Goldstone (2002, 78) observed that the response of the international community to similar incidents in the Balkans and other areas differs from the Rwandan episode. The interest of the Western countries such as the US, UK and France in Rwanda was initially limited to the evacuation of their nationals; and the indifference of the East too worsened the status quo (Berdal 2005, 118–130; Melvern 2009; Hintjens 1999, 273–274). Thus, Africa states submit that the creation of the ICC would curb the repetition of the Rwandan genocidal episode, and serves as an impetus for mass subscription to the

Rome Statute by these states (Nyawo 2017, 41; Mbizvo 2016, 41). The involvement and participation of the African states in the development of the Rome Statute was another cogent reason for the mass subscription to the Rome Statute (Mbizvo 2016, 41; Nmehielle 2012, 5).

Nyawo (2017, 35) submits that African states were active participants in the formation and drafting of the Rome Statute, in contrast to the other international organisations where there the rules had been set before their entry as members of the organisation by the original signatories. The fact that African states were instrumental to the setting of the rules in Rome Statute accounts for the mass appeal of the ICC to African states. Further, the initial support that the African states had for ICC, however, plunged when it was evident that all the cases on trial by the ICC involved only Africans (Dersso 2017, 62–64, 72; Seymour 2017, 107–108). Thus, this selective indictment and prosecution of only African was resented by African political leaders and regarded as global apartheid; moreso, the lack of support by African leaders became an open defiance with the arrest warrant issued against the then president of Sudan Al-Bashir and the indictment of President Uhuru Kenyatta of Kenya and his deputy (Mutua 2017, 49). The indictment and trial of only Africans from the Global South by the ICC, and such other discrimination by other international bodies is termed global apartheid (Nhemachena et al. 2018, 10).

A growing body of Third World Approach to International Law (TWAIL) scholars, like Anghie and Chimni (2003) and Mamdani (2008) have led evidence on how international law and international order was used and continue to be used to justify the suppression of the third world peoples (Mutua 2017, 49; Nwoko 2015, 3–5; Odero 2011, 155; Mamdani 2008). Mamdani (2008, 2) affirmed that "the language of the law is often subverted by powerful states with the effect of establishing a new humanitarian order in which the principle of state sovereignty obtains in the larger parts of the world but is suspended in many countries in Africa" (Odero 2011, 155). Taku (2016, 339, 343–347) submits that it seems as if only African political leaders and African problems were targeted by ICC, which gave rise to an outcry of global apartheid. Mills and Bloomfield (2018, 125–127), argued that the outcry against this specific targeting of African situations resulted in efforts to appease the African leaders by the ICC and other stakeholders such as UNSC, as all referrals were halted after the row.

It is against the background of the issues and contentions highlighted above that this chapter analyses the relationship between Africa states and the ICC. The chapter examines the indictment of the ex-Sudanese President Omar Al-Bashir by ICC, as an incumbent head of state; and the implication of the conflict between customary international law and the Rome Statute. It also interrogates the referral and deferral powers of the permanent members of the UNSC, majority of whom, are not party to the Rome Statute. Besides, the chapter examines the flaws in the Rome Statute, the cases instituted and similar cases that were ignored by the ICC prosecutor, which gave rise to outcry of global apartheid by African politicians and some scholars. Seymour (2017, 108), stated that till date only Africans have been indicted and tried by ICC. This inappropriate focus on African problems in the exercise prosecutorial discretion by ICC, while overlooking similar situations in other continents gave rise to allegations of global apartheid (Seymour 2017, 117; Taku 2016, 338).

PHASES IN AFRICAN STATES' RELATIONSHIP WITH THE GLOBAL COMMUNITY

The reaction of African leaders to the exclusive indictment and prosecution of Africans by ICC could not be separated from African history, as the subjugation and subordination of Africans by the West is still vivid in people's memory (Mutua 2017, 48; Imoedemhe 2015, 74). No "continent has suffered more trauma than Africa in the past 500 years" (Mutua 2017, 48; Monageng 2014, 13). The devastating effect of colonialism, trans-Atlantic slave trade and Arab slave trade on Africa is topical; ironically, international law played a significant role in the colonisation and subjugation of Africa (Mutua 2017, 48; Nwoko 2015, 11; Nyawo 2012, 149; Odero 2011, 155). Similarly, genocide, such as the Herero's genocide and brutality, and the colonial Belgium's mistreatment of the natives in Congo were not uncommon. Others include apartheid, forced removals, racial discrimination and other inhuman or degrading treatment on the African populace (Nyawo 2012, 149–159; Sarkin 2004, 67–68). These painful experiences are bound to have a far-reaching effect on the continent of Africa as most of the conflicts in which the continent was or is currently enmeshed in, was a carry-over of this episode.

Nyawo (2012, 149–157) argued that the double standard and selective application of the law to Africans is apparent because the reaction of the perpetrators to these traumatic experiences in Africa and similar harrowing experience elsewhere differ (Nyawo 2012, 149–157). The West is usually indifferent and unconcerned whenever the issue of revisiting the wrong done to Africans in the past was mentioned. For instance, Germany refused to pay reparations to the survivors of the Herero's genocide despite persistent demand, but voluntarily offered to pay compensation to the Jews for the holocaust (Nhemachena et al. 2018, 2; Nyawo 2012, 155; Howard-Hassmann 2007, 428–420; Sarkin 2004, 75; Spitzer 2002, 1319).

In addition, most modern African states are products of colonialism where the major European powers negotiated and formalise claims to territories in

Africa at the Berlin Conference of 1884–1885 and international law was used to freeze the territory under the principle of Uti possidetis juris (a principle of international law which provides that newly formed sovereign states should retain the internal borders) (Mutua 2017, 49; Schmitt 2017, 128; Nyawo 2012, 147; Shillington 2012, 318; Ofuho 2000). Some of these African states are patently dysfunctional (Mutua 2017, 49; Aluede 2017, 17; Schuerch 2017, 23; Bayeh 2015; Sarkin 2004, 68; Mbazira 2011, 197). The issue of global apartheid mentioned above are further complicated by the dominance of the West in the international economic and political arena. Hence, it is evident that the international legal order and institutions are manipulated against Africans (Harrison 2002, 52–54).

African political leaders who were initially warm, later became ambivalent and eventually hostile to ICC, when they observed that all those indicted and tried before the court were all Africans (Mutua 2017, 50). This gave the erroneous impression to any reasonable observer that the crimes that fall under the jurisdiction of ICC were committed only on the African continent. In the light of the above, it could be questioned whether the ICC is not the legitimisation of a subtle form of global apartheid?

THE ROME STATUTE: LEGAL AND MORAL FLAWS

The Rome Statute, which entered into force on 1 July 2002, and it provides for the role of the ICC in exercising criminal jurisdiction over perpetrators of specified crimes, such as genocide, aggression, crimes against humanity and war crimes (articles 5–8 bis of the UN General Assembly, Rome Statute of the ICC (last amended 2010, July 17, 1998; Brendon et al. 2016, 6).

African countries were actively involved in the establishment of the ICC and played a crucial role at the Rome conference when the ICC's Statute was drafted and adopted (Nyawo 2017, 36–45; Monageng 2014, 14). The Rome Statute allows accessibility to the ICC in three ways, that is, referral by states party to the Rome Statute, by the prosecutor or by the UNSC, and all these three mechanisms of accessing the ICC have been used on Africans only (Monageng 2014, 15–16). This selective investigation, indictment and trial of only Africans by the ICC seem like a form of global apartheid because similar violations elsewhere were ignored by the ICC.

Further, the ICC's mandate to investigate and prosecute under the Rome Statute may only be exercised over crimes committed on the territory of a state party to the Rome Statute (article 5 of the Rome Statute). The only exception can be made by the UNSC, if it uses its powers under Chapter VII of the UN Charter to refer a situation to the prosecutor of the ICC. Under articles 13(b) and 16 of the Rome Statute, the UNSC has the powers of referral and deferral of cases and has exercised these powers only on African leaders such as those of Libya and Sudan. This is a contentious issue. Besides, the referral of cases from the African continent only, is a form of global apartheid because similar infractions by some permanent members of UNSC and their allies are not referred to the ICC. In the same vein, it is important to reiterate that three out of the five (the US, Russia and China) permanent members of the UNSC are not party to the Rome Statute and not subject to the rule they are enforcing.

Ironically, the US, Russia and China are permanent members of the UNSC, who have referral and deferral powers not only on states parties to the Rome Statute but on states that are not parties to the Rome Statute like themselves. Unfortunately, these three veto-holding powers would not submit themselves or their allies to the jurisdiction of the ICC. Similarly, the US has signed several bilateral treaties with many states including a great supporter of the ICC on the African continent, Botswana, prohibiting the transfer of any US nationals to the court (Nyawo 2017, 45). The US has taken another step to shield her citizens from the ICC's reach, by enacting the American Service-Member Protection Act "ASPA 2002" 22 USC Public Law 107–206, August 2, 2002, as amended through P.L. 110–181). Sections 2007–2008 of the ASPA 2002 protects the US military, elected and appointed officials from arrest and trial in any ICC to which the US is not a party. It also provides that the US may use force to free her citizens from the authority of another state, to prevent ICC or any international court from exercising jurisdiction over them (Section 2008 of ASPA 2002; Odero 2011, 158; Akande 2003, 618–650; Faulhaber 2003, 537). Faulhaber (2003, 536) affirmed that the American Service Members Protection Act "was designed to prevent United States participation in the ICC and to discourage other members of the international community from participating in the Court or assisting it in any way."

Notwithstanding all these, the probability of investigating and trial of citizens and allies of US and China is seriously in doubt, even if they were signatories to the Rome Statute by virtue of their veto vote, military and economic might (Cannon et al. 2016, 12). The United States thus shielded itself and her allies from ICC's reach but was part of those enforcing the Rome statute especially on the Africans.

The issue on the immunity of serving heads of state and senior officials who have not waived their immunity by becoming signatories to the Rome Statute is also contentious. It is trite that the court of a sovereign state cannot issue summons to another head of state or foreign officials vested with immunity to appear before her courts, except with the consent of the state concerned (AU, 2008, paragraph 79, 17; *Tachiona v Mugabe*, 169 F. Supp. 2d 259 (SDNY, 2001). Customary international law, unlike conventional law, is binding on all states and cannot be derogated from, but there is disagreement on the human rights that are protected under customary international law (article 98(1) of the Rome Statute; Obura 2011, 24–26). The unanimous acceptability of immunity of heads of sovereign state and senior state officials under customary international law is well documented and incontrovertible (Schabas 2016, 119; Obura 2011, 24–26; Murungu 2011, 36–42; Arrest Warrant of April 11, 2000 (*Democratic Republic of Congo v Belgium* [2002] ICJ Rep 3; Joint Separate Opinion of Judges Higgins, Kooijmans and Buergenthal, at paragraph 75; *Tachiona v Mugabe*, 2001). However, an exception has been created under article 27 of the Rome Statute which removes immunity based on status or official capacity. This exception, as stated earlier, is only applicable to state officials from weak and relatively powerless countries of the Global South, but if the exception is equally applicable to officials from all states, the author will undoubtedly classify it as good law.

Schabas (2016, 120) and Gaeta (2016, 97) submit that when articles 98(1) and 27 of the Rome Statute are read together; it suggests that officials of states parties to the Rome Statute have waived their immunity while non-party states have not abandoned their immunity. The above position is at variance with the decision of ICC Pre-trial Chamber I in Prosecutor v Omar Hassan Ahmad Al Bashir No: ICC-02/05-01/09OA2 paragraph 41, "*Al Bashir case*"). In this case, the court stated erroneously in my opinion that the position of the accused as the head of state "has no effect on the court's jurisdiction." The position of the ICC seems erroneous due to the following reasons. It is an established rule that a treaty does not create any obligation or a right for a third state without its consent (Article 34 United Nations, Vienna Convention on the Law of Treaties, May 23, 1969, United Nations, Treaty Series, volume 1155, 331 Entry into force: January 27, 1980). If the reasoning of the court was correct in *Al Bashir case*, is it probable for the UNSC to strip the immunity of presidents of states like North Korea or Iran before the ICC and order their arrest? Chinese atrocities and genocide in its Uighur and Tibet provinces are well documented but ICC has not deemed it fit to attempt to investigate this crime (Byler 2019, 11; Cronin-Furman 2018, 4). China is a state not party to the Rome Statute like Sudan. Can the UNSC remove Chinese president's immunity even if China is not a member of the UNSC? Was the Al Bashir's case not the execution of global apartheid on the weak countries of the African continent?

A situation whereby any official with diplomatic immunity, particularly, an incumbent head of state could be picked up like a common bum and turned over to the ICC, irrespective of being a party to the Rome Statute is likely to create anarchy and a breakdown of the international relations. The power granted the UNSC to remove the immunity of sitting heads of state and senior state officials of sovereign states may impact adversely on the effective performance of their official functions and limit the conduct of foreign relations. This is likely to exacerbate conflict in international relations and jeopardise peaceful process initiated by well-wishers in the affected country. For instance, AU argued that the ICC's indictment of Sudanese head of state and other opponents had hindered the peace processes that were being negotiated by AU (Imoedemhe 2015, 74). The indictment of sitting presidents from the African continent only by ICC seems like a form of global apartheid and selective to an unbiased observer.

ICC AND AFRICA: FROM SUPPORT TO ACCUSATION OF GLOBAL APARTHEID

Africa was an enthusiastic and a devoted supporter of the ICC (Dersso 2017, 62; Nyawo 2017, 36; Monageng 2014, 14–16; Murithi 2014, 179–180). According to Mutua (2018, 49), the support was overwhelming to the extent that "there was a stampede in Africa to ratify the Rome Statute." The same African political leaders who ratified the Rome Statute in great numbers subsequently became its critics and threatened to withdraw their membership en masse (Nyawo 2017, 204–219; Knottnerus 2017, 152; Cannon et al. 2016, 24). Why and when did the AU and the African political leaders become ICC's most vociferous critics? This question would be answered in this section.

All the ICC's three activating mechanisms for investigation and institution of cases were used on African political leaders alone (Dyani 2012, 185). There were four situations that were self-referred by states parties – these were Uganda, Congo, Central African Republic and Mali. The second category was the two situations referred to the ICC Prosecutor by the UNSC – Darfur (Sudan) and Libya cases. The last category was investigations opened by the prosecutor proprio motu or on his initiative, in Kenya and Cote d'Ivoire (Monageng 2014, 15–16). All the above cases are in Africa and this in part turned African leaders and the AU, from passionate support to antagonists of the ICC (Nyawo 2017, 204–219; Okoth 2016, 195). The erroneous conclusion that a reasonable observer reaches from ICC's investigations, indictments and prosecution is that it is only Africa political leaders who commit international crimes. This exclusive focus on African situations made the AU, scholars and African political elites to attack the ICC of specifically targeting African leaders and warned that this could complicate reconciliation efforts in Africa (Brendon Pkalya and Maragia, 2016, 7; Imoedemhe 2015, 74; Clark 2011, 521). Nhemachena et al. (2018, 2) and Dyani (2012, 185) argue that the ICC is ignoring atrocities committed by the great world powers such as the US, Russia, UK, China and their allies. They also argue that the ICC is used to as an agent of neo-colonialism or global apartheid (African Union 2013, 2).

A serious sign of conflict between the AU and ICC occurred after the ICC indicted and issued a warrant for the arrest of the then Sudanese President Ahmad Al-Bashir, the Libya's case and the indictment of Uhuru Kenyatta and his deputy (Mutua 2017, 53–54). AU construed the refusal of the UNSC to allow mediation in these conflicts as unfortunate because AU is of the opinion that it was mediation and not litigation that could ensure lasting peace. The AU views the ICC as a neo-colonial court because of its near exclusive focus on African leaders (Nyawo 2012, 126–127; Chutter 2012, 179–180). It is on record that Al-Bashir had since his indictment by ICC visited China, Nigeria, Saudi Arabia, the United Arab Emirates, Egypt, Ethiopia, Kenya, Qatar, South Africa and other countries, all of which refused to surrender him to the ICC for prosecution (Cluskey 2019). South Africa went further by refusing to obey an interim order of a Gauteng High Court to detain Al-Bashir as an ICC fugitive (*Southern Africa Litigation Centre v Minister of Justice and Constitutional Development & 9 Others* (27740/2015) [2015] ZAGPPHC 402; 2016 (1) SACR 161 (GP) para 5). The refusal of certain countries to cooperate with ICC on the arrest of Al-Bashir is a protest against exercise of global apartheid and double standards by ICC on Africans (Nyawo 2017, 205). It is surprising that China, a permanent member of the UNSC hosted an ICC fugitive (Al Bashir), showed that even the UNSC is not impenetrable.

The opinion of African political leaders is better mirrored in the chairman of AU, Ethiopian Premier, Desalegn's speech where he likened ICC to an international hound "hunting Africans" (Mutua 2017, 48; Desalegn 2013, 1). When the ICC failed in the bid to oust Libya's former leader Gaddafi with his indictment before it, the West then resorted to the use of NATO to achieve their aim (Benyera 2018, 129). However, Libya is worse off after NATO's induced "liberation" than under Gaddafi's alleged dictatorial rule (Benyera 2018, 129). After the demise of Gaddafi, law and order broke down in Libya, the militia is in charge of a large part of the country; infrastructure is in a state of disrepair and all indices of development are in the negative (Imam et al. 2014, 1155–1166). The allegation of legitimisation of global apartheid through the ICC against the African leaders as highlighted above became a serious matter of concern and certain measures were put in place to appease the African leaders and the AU (Odero 2011, 155–158). Murithi (2014, 186) affirmed that "the appointment of Bensoudaas the Chief Prosecutor was a move calculated to appease the African members of the Assembly of States Parties. By appointing an African and former Minister of Justice of Gambia, the Assembly of States Parties is communicating the notion that it does not view the ICC as advancing an anti-African agenda." Similarly, Mutua (2017, 55), stated that the ICC was compelled to try Uhuru Kenyatta through video link and this "trial by skype" was mocked by some commentators such as James Mbaka.

Although the conduct of the African political leaders is not beyond reproach, the undue focus of the ICC on African leaders to the near exclusion of others amounts to global apartheid and double standards. ICC must be impartial and not run like a court specially created to try Africans alone (Cannon et al. 2016, 13–15). The African countries that are party to the Rome Statute are partially responsible for the harm they claim the ICC is inflicting on them. This is due to the failure of most of the African states to create credible and independent judiciaries that could adjudicate crimes under ICC's jurisdiction, thereby diminishing the relevance of the ICC (Cannon et al. 2016, 15). Most of the African leaders lacked the grit and the discipline to properly scrutinise international treaties before signing; thereby signing treaties or international agreements against their national or personal interests (Cannon et al. 2016, 15). However, one must not overlook the vulnerability of most African states that depend on aids from the more affluent countries from the Global North which makes them subscribe to international treaties without reservations, due to external influence from their Global North "benefactors" and the subsequent bemoaning of their fate (Harrison 2002, 52–54).

In addition, some of the African heads of state party to the Rome Statute were interested in using the ICC as a tool to deal with political opponents and were astonished when the ICC decided to investigate their crimes as well (Baroncelli 2014, 7–8). Some of these African leaders like Ugandan president, Yoweri Museveni, did not cry foul when marginal political leaders and "rebellious" elements, like the leaders and members of Uganda's Lord's Resistance Army and others were being indicted and prosecuted by the ICC (Nyawo 2012, 135). Similarly, the arrest of pro-Tutsi Rwandan Patriotic Front's Rose Kabuye for alleged genocide was condemned but the trial and conviction of pro-Hutu, Onesphore Rwabukombe was applauded by the same Rwandan authority (Jeßberger 2014, 155–156). However, the allegation that the ICC is being used to perpetrate apartheid against African leaders has been debunked by some authors like Monengeng and Trendafilova. Monengeng, a judge at the ICC, disagrees that ICC is being used to haunt African leaders.

Monengeng stated, citing article 27 of the Rome Statute, that the proceedings before the ICC are fully in conformity with the Rome Statute, including the cases against sitting heads of state (Monengeng 2014, 17). Similarly, another judge at ICC, Trendafilova (2014, 30), contended that the Assembly of States Party to the Rome Statute have waived the immunities of their senior officials under article 27(2) of the Rome Statute. Trendafilova further stated that the immunity of Al-Bashir was waived because the Sudanese president is sought by the ICC as a result of a UNSC referral in the exercise of its powers under Chapter VII of the Charter of the United Nations. Besides, he contended that the UNSC has "implicitly lifted the immunities accruing to President Al-Bashir" (Trendafilova 2014, 30). The question to ask here is, how can the UNSC, majority of whom, as permanent members are not states party to the Rome Statute, lift the immunity of the head of a sovereign state who is not a state party to the Rome Statute like themselves? Why did the UNSC not issue a warrant to arrest and "lift the immunity" of the North Korean president for various acts of aggression and gross violation of human rights committed by him? North Korea, for instance, is known to have violated many multilateral treaties and committed international crimes (Cho 2019, 78; Baum 2018, 1; Klinger 2010, 4). The exclusive focus on the weak nations only is one of the reasons for Africans to maintain that specifically targeting them alone constitutes global apartheid. The Gambia's former Information Minister, Bojang refers to ICC as "the international Caucasian court for the persecution and humiliation of people of colour, especially Africans" because only Africans had ever been tried at the ICC (Rukooko and Silverman 2019, 89).

It is ironic that the West, a part of the group that launched the manhunt against the ex-Sudanese president, Al-Bashir, as a sitting president, failed to apologise or pay compensation when the US on August 20, 1998, launched an airstrike against the Al-Shiffa pharmaceutical plant in Sudan. The US's claim that Al-Shiffa plant was a chemical weapons facility operated by the extremists was subsequently discovered to be false by international observers including US top officials (Robinson 2016, 2; Marc 2005, 5; Scharf 2001, 21). The suit filed against the US government in the US Court of Appeal on the El Shifa's matter was dismissed not on merit but on issues bordering on jurisdiction (*El-Shifa Pharmaceutical Industries Company and Salah El Din Ahmed Mohammed Idris v United States* Case No. 03-5098, Appeals Judgment, August 11, 2004).

The Sudanese president's calls for the international prosecution of the US officials responsible for the airstrike for war crimes as a result of killing civilians in the medical facility, went unheeded. Had the Rome Statute been in existence in 1998, was the UNSC going to attempt to charge US citizens with war crimes or crimes against humanity under article 12 of the Rome Statute? Was the UNSC going to withdraw the immunity of the US president even if the US was not a member of UNSC?

Similarly, despite evidence of international crime violations by the UK in Iraq, the ICC prosecutor decided that the human rights violation did not meet the threshold for investigation and prosecution (Nyawo 2017, 86). This issue of unequal treatment by ICC made the author to question the notion of equality of sovereign states under international law because of the different yardsticks used for different states under the Rome Statute (Dunoff 2013, 127; Paulsson 2010, 15–37). As enumerated above, persons from a particular geopolitical zone seemed to be earmarked for trial and investigation by ICC while similar infractions by Global North countries are ignored raises some questions on whether the ICC is not legitimising another global apartheid regime on the Global South, particularly, Africa.

ICC AND AFRICA: THE LEGITIMISATION OF ANOTHER APARTHEID REGIME?

There is no doubt that Africa has a long history of civil conflicts and atrocities (Mutua 2016, 102). Besides, the human rights abuses in Sudan (Darfur) and some African states are inexcusable, but, it is convenient for ICC to ignore international crimes and atrocities committed in Iraq, Yemen, Palestine-Israel, Mexico, Sri Lanka, Myanmar, Georgia and other states. As earlier stated, the crimes committed by Russia, the US, the UK, France and China, such as the alleged genocide in China's Uighur province or UK's conduct in Iraq were not investigated. It took the protest from Africa before investigations into these atrocities were commenced.

It was only in Africa that a warrant was issued by ICC against a sitting head of state. It is submitted that it would have been better to freeze the assets and impose sanctions on states not party to the Rome Statute, whose leaders are customarily entitled to immunity against trial and prosecution at the ICC. The assets freeze and imposition of sanctions could bring pressure on such regimes and force them to respect human rights of all persons in their respective countries.

Rukooko and Silverman (2019, 98) maintained that "by trying Uhuru Kenyatta and Laurent Gbagbo and indicting Bashir of Sudan, the ICC has demonstrated that, in international law, presidential impunity is dead." In line with Rukooko and Silverman submission, it would be an interesting phenomenon for the presidential immunity of the sitting president of a country from the Global North to be waived and a warrant issued for the arrest of such persons by the ICC. The ICC's Prosecutor's Office was criticised for its low record of conviction against the indicted African leaders. The quashing of ex-Congolese vice president, Jean-Pierre Bemba's conviction, the discharge of the ex-Ivory Coast president, Laurent Gbagbo, and his co-accused Charles Blé Goudé and the withdrawal of the case against Kenyatta and his deputy has further weakened the credibility of the ICC in Africa (Rukooko and Silverman 2019, 86). It is submitted that the ICC is employing a form of global apartheid by targeting the vulnerable and weak African political leaders. The ICC criticised the prosecutor in *The Prosecutor v Thomas Lubanga Dyilo* (ICC601/04601/06, Pre-Trial Chamber I, decision on confirmation of charges, January 29, 2007). This trial lasted for six years and it was marred by controversies. The ICC chastised the prosecutor for the manner in which the case was investigated and how the charges were drafted.

Taku (2016, 338) stated that regrettably, many African states and their leaders are puppets of the neo-colonial interests they are criticising because most of these states are economically weak and dependent on aids from the West, Russia or China which made them amenable to neo-colonial bondage. The office of the ICC prosecutor did not even deny that it "focused exclusively on Africa," but it denied that the focus was not inappropriate (Taku 2016, 339).

The arms used to foment trouble in Africa are not manufactured in Africa, but in the Global South countries. It is not clear whether the ICC may proprio motu go after those who violate international arms embargo and the Arms Trade Treaty of 2013, in facilitating genocide and gross human rights abuses in Africa (Kendall and Da-Silva 2017, 407–436; Taku 2016, 349). The issue of arms trade may be related to the functions of the office of the ICC prosecutor and it should seize the initiative and deal with individual culpability within the scope of the Rome Statute while the Arms Trade Treaty deals with state culpability.

THE WAY OUT FOR AFRICA

It is incontrovertible that there are many atrocities committed in brutal conflicts in some African states which may require interventions by the ICC. It is also incontestable that other continents in the world are not devoid of conflicts.

The ancient and recent oppressive history of Africans may not be unconnected to their sensitivity to the issue of separate treatment under the Rome Statute. For Africa to combat global apartheid, there is a need to, first, create credible, independent and viable judiciaries in the respective jurisdiction. The independent judiciary at the national level should effectively adjudicate gross violations of human rights and diminish the relevance of international courts like the ICC. Second, African political leaders should be wary of just signing any treaty without adequate consideration of the implication. The charge of selective justice raised by many African leaders may partly seem puerile because the subscription to the Rome statute was not done under compulsion.

Third, there is a need to strengthen the regional and AU judicial mechanisms to create courts at regional and continental levels to adjudicate on issues of gross violation of human rights. This mechanism would have dealt with cases that fall within ICC's jurisdiction under the principle of complementarity and render the issue of selectivity and global apartheid irrelevant. The unprecedented move to establish the African Criminal Court was not unconnected with the objection of African leaders to the ICC's exclusive focus on Africa (Manirakiza 2012, 380). Manirakiza (2012, 381–382) canvassed for the revival of the indigenous judicial systems of dispute resolution at both regional and continental courts to promote justice and peace. This idea of establishing regional and continental courts is laudable because it will help fight impunity at the highest level and effectively prosecute the majority of the perpetrators of crimes rather than a handful cases that are prosecuted by the ICC. The idea of establishing regional and continental courts in Africa, however, comes with a caveat. African countries must be willing to pay the requisite financial contributions to make these courts viable and must be willing to abide by the courts' decisions. It must be recalled that the refusal of Zimbabwe to abide with the decision of the regional tribunal in Mike Campbell (Pvt) Ltd and Others v Republic of Zimbabwe (2/2007) [2008] SADCT 2 (November 28, 2008), led to the demise of the Southern African Development Community Tribunal (SADCT).

Fourth, the AU must address the issue of sit-tight executives and ostracise African presidents who have stayed in office for longer than the terms initially allowed by their constitution such as Kagame of Rwanda and Museveni of Uganda. The limitation of terms of office could enable such heads of state to be liable for trial if they commit any crime punishable under the Rome Statute.

Fifth, the referral and deferral powers of the UNSC should be whittled down and the Rome Statute should be amended to exclude states not party to it from having rights and liabilities under the statute. Lastly, there is a need to give Africa a permanent seat with veto power in the UNSC in the light of the global apartheid challenges.

CONCLUSION

This chapter has shown that Africa has experienced economic, social and political problems than any other continent for the past four decades (Mbazira 2011, 197). The chapter underscores the importance of ICC in checking gross abuse of human rights in Africa and elsewhere. However, it is submitted that the biased indictment and trial of only Africans by ICC is giving the ICC a credibility challenge. According to Mutua (2017, 55), the ICC faces a challenge of "legitimacy if all its cases continue to be Africans. The appearance of selective, race-based justice will be difficult to avoid if the ICC does not . . . pursue egregious offenders elsewhere"). It is submitted that for ICC to be free of its current legitimacy challenge of global apartheid against Africans it must be seen to investigate and pursue cases in jurisdictions other than Africa with the same vigour it did on the African political leaders' cases. According to Mutua (2017, 55), the credibility challenge and criticism of ICC practices by scholars, AU and others led to the opening of preliminary investigations into situations outside Africa, but none has matured to full-fledged cases. The charge by African political leaders and AU that the ICC is being used as a tool of global apartheid to haunt Africans may be persuasive, but it did not exculpate some of the indicted African leaders from complicity and wrongdoing in the alleged crimes. The African political leaders and AU are as involved in the double standards as the ICC, in certain instances, because there were no complaint from these African political leaders when marginal political leaders and rebels like the leadership of the "Ugandan Lord's Army" were being indicted and prosecuted by the ICC. It appears that African political leaders and the AU submit that their heads of state and the ruling elites should not be prosecuted by the ICC.

The AU and African leaders need to operate under the rule of law, overhaul their relevant laws and judicial system to effectively deal with gross human rights abuses to render institutions like the ICC, irrelevant. The institutionalisation of credible national, regional and continental mechanisms for prosecuting gross human rights abuses by the Global South countries would obliterate the illicit global apartheid activities perpetrated against Africans under ICC's jurisdiction. Finally, the ICC must fairly and impartially apply the law equally to all the constituents of the global community to combat global apartheid, especially against Africa and its people.

BIBLIOGRAPHY

Adebajo, A. (2009). Ending global apartheid Africa and the United Nations. In Adebajo, A. (Ed.), *From global apartheid to global village: Africa and the United Nations*. Cape Town, South Africa: University of KwaZulu-Natal Press.

African Union. (2008). The executive council thirteenth ordinary session, report of the commission on the use of the principle of universal jurisdiction by some non-African states as recommended by the Conference of Ministers of Justice/ Attorneys General (Publication No. 9634). https://au.int/sites/default/files/decisions/9634council_en_24_28_june_2008_executive_council_thirteenth_ordinary_session.pdf.

African Union. (2013, October). Extraordinary session of the assembly of the African Union Addis Ababa, in decisions and declarations (Publication No. 9655). www.au.int/ en/ sites/ default/ files/ decisions/ 9655 -ext_ assembly_ au_ dec_ decl_ e_ 0. pdf.

Akande, D. (2003). The jurisdiction of International Criminal Court over nationals of non-parties: Legal basis and limits. *Journal of International Criminal Justice*, Volume 1(3), 618–650.

Alexander, T. (1996). *Unravelling global apartheid: An overview of world politics*. New York: Polity Press.

Aluede, J. A. (2017). Border relations in Africa and the impact on nation-building: A study of Nigeria and her limitrophe neighbours since the 1960s. *African Journal of Governance and Development*, Volume 6(1), 10–25.

Anghie, A., and Chimni, B. (2003). Third world approach to international law and individual responsibility in conflicts. *Chinese Journal of International Law*, Volume 2, 77–103.

Ansley, F. (1997). White supremacy (and what we should do about it). In Delgado, R., and Stefancic, J. (Ed.), *Critical white studies: Looking behind the mirror*. Philadelphia: Temple University Press.

Arms Trade Treaty. (2013) 52 ILM 988. https://www.cambridge.org/core/services/aopcambridgecore/content/view/FA29089F7174855B3E9C4B0E567EB218/S0020782900001509a.pdf/arms_trade_treaty.pdf.

Banyera, E. (2018). Colonialism, the theft of history and the quest for justice for Africa. In Nhemachena, A., Warikandwa, T. V., and Amoo, S. K. (Eds.), *Social and legal theory in the age of decoloniality: Towards an African jurisprudence in the 21st century*. Bameda, Cameroon: Langaa Research & Publishing Common Initiative Group.

Baroncelli, L. (2014). The fight against impunity in the Democratic Republic of Congo between justice and reconciliation. *ISPI*. https://www.ispi online.it/sites / default/files/pubblicazioni/analysis_248_2014.pdf.

Bassiouni, M. C., and Hansen, D. (2016). The inevitable practice of the office of the prosecutor. In Steinberg, R. H. (Ed.), *Contemporary issues facing the International Criminal Court*. Leiden, the Netherlands: Koninklijke Brill NV.

Baum, A. C. (2018). *South Korean efforts to counter North Korean aggression*. United States Air Force Centre for Strategic Deterrence Service Trinity Site Papers Publication. https://www.airuniversity.af.edu/Portals/10/CSDS/assets/trinity _site _paper11.pdf.

Bayeh, E. (2015). The legacy of colonialism in the contemporary Africa: A cause for intrastate and interstate conflicts. *International Journal of Innovative and Applied Research*, Volume 3(2), 23–29.

Benyera, E. (2018). Colonialism, the theft of history and the quest for justice for Africa. In Nhemachena, A., Warikandwa, T. V., and Amoo, S. K. (Eds.), *Social and legal theory in the age of decoloniality: (Re-)envisioning African jurisprudence in the 21st Century*. Bamenda, Cameroon: Langaa.

Berdal, M. (2005). The United Nations, peacebuilding, and the genocide in Rwanda. *Global Governance*, Volume 11(1), 115–130.

Berger, M. T. (1997). The triumph of the East? The East-Asian miracle and post-cold war capitalism. In Borer, D. A. (Ed.), *The rise of East Asia: Critical visions of the Pacific Century*. New York, USA: Routledge.

Besteman, C. (2019). Militarized global apartheid. *Current Anthropology*, Volume 60(19), 26–38.

Birmingham, D. (1995). *The decolonization of Africa*. London, England: UCL Press.

Byler, D. (2019, April 11). Hi-tech war on its Muslim minority. *The Guardian*. https://www.theguardian.com/news/2019/apr/11/china-hi-tech-war-on-muslim-minority-xinjiang-uighurs-surveillance-face-recognition.

Cannon, B. J., Pkalya, D. R., and Maragia, B. (2016). The International Criminal Court and Africa: Contextualizing the anti-ICC narrative. *African Journal of International Criminal Justice*, Volume 2, 6–28.

Chipaike, R., and Matarutse, H. K. (2018). *Cogent Social Sciences*, Volume 4, 1–16.

Cho, I. H. (2019). Aligning autonomy and alliance: Variation in South Korea's policy towards North Korea and the Moon Jae-in presidency. *Journal of Peace and War Studies*, Volume 1(1), 65–88.

Chuter, D. (2012). The ICC: A place for Africans and Africans in their place? In Nmehielle, V. O. (Ed.), *Africa and the future of international criminal justice*. The Hague, the Netherlands: Eleven International Publishing.

Clark, N. J. (2011). Peace, justice and the International Criminal Court: Possibilities and limitations. *Journal of International Criminal Justice*, Volume 9(3), 521–545.

Clarke, K. M. (2016). Why Africa? In Steinberg, R. H. (Ed.), *Contemporary issues facing the International Criminal Court*. Leiden, the Netherlands: Koninklijke Brill NV.

Cluskey, P. (2019, April 11). Ousted in Sudan, Omar al-Bashir is still "at large" at the ICC: Unclear if coup will lead to Bashir finally facing justice in The Hague. *The Irish Times*. https://www.irishtimes.com/news/world/africa/ousted-in-sudan-omar-al-bashir-is-still-at-large-at-the-icc-1.3857290.

Cronin-Furman, K. (2018, September 19). *FP News*. https://foreign policy.com/2018/09/19/china-has-chosen-cultural-genocide-in-xinjiang-for-now/.

Democratic Republic of Congo v Belgium, 2002 (Arrest warrant of 11 April, 2000), Judgement [2002] ICJ Report 3, at paragraph 58.

Dersso, S. A. (2017). The ICC's African problem: A spotlight on the politics and limits of international criminal justice. In Clarke, K. M., Knottnerus, A. S., and De-Volde, E. (Eds.), *Africa and the ICC: Perceptions of justice*. Cambridge, United Kingdom: Cambridge University Press.

Desalegn, H. (2013, May 27). AU accuses ICC of "hunting" Africans. *BBC News*. https://www.bbc.com/news/world-africa-22681894.

Dunoff, J. L. (2013). Is sovereign equality obsolete? Understanding twenty-first century international organizations. In Nijman, J. E., Wouter, W. G., and Werner, G. (Eds.), *Netherlands yearbook of international law 2012-legal equality and the international rule of law: Essays in honour of P. H. Kooijmans*. The Hague, the Netherlands: T. M. C. Asser Press.

El-Shifa Pharmaceutical Industries Company and Salah El Din Ahmed Mohammed Idris v United States Case No. 03-5098, Appeals Judgment, 11 August 2004.

Faulhaber, L. V. (2003). American Service Members' Protection Act of 2002. *Harvard Journal on Legislation*, Volume 40, 537–557.

Gaeta, P. (2016). Head of state immunity as a bar to arrest. In Steinberg, R. H. (Ed.), *Contemporary issues facing the International Criminal Court*. Leiden, the Netherlands: Koninklijke Brill NV.

Goldstone, R. (2002). *For humanity: Reflections of a war crimes investigator*. New Haven, USA: Yale University Press.

Harrison, F. V. (2002). Global apartheid, foreign policy, and human rights. *Souls*, Volume 4(3), 48–68.

Hintjens, H. M. (1999). Explaining the 1994 genocide in Rwanda. *The Journal of Modern African Studies*, Volume 37(2), 241–286.

Howard-Hassmann, R. E. (2007). Reparations for the slave trade: Rhetoric, law, history and political realities. *Canadian Journal of African Studies*, Volume 41(3), 427–454.

Huntington, S. P. (2011). *The clash of civilizations and the remaking of world order*. New York, NY. Simon & Schuster.

Imam, M., Abba, S., and Wader, M. M. (2014). Libya in the post Ghadaffi era. *Valley International Journal*, Volume 2(2), 1150–1166.

Imoedemhe, O. C. (2015). Unpacking the tension between the African Union and the ICC: The way forward. *African Journal of International and Comparative Law*, Volume 23(1), 74–105.

Jeßberger, F. (2014). 'On behalf of Africa': Towards the regionalization of universal jurisdiction? In Werle, G., Fernandez, L., and Vormbaum, M. (Eds.), *Africa and International Criminal Court: International criminal justice series volume 1*. The Hague, the Netherlands: T. M. C. Asser Press.

Kendall, S., and da-Silva, C. (2017). Beyond the ICC: State responsibility for arms trade in Africa. In Clarke, K. M., Knottnerus, A. S., and De-Volde, E. (Eds.), *Africa and the ICC: Perceptions of justice*. Cambridge, United Kingdom: Cambridge University Press.

Klinger, B. (2010). Another feeble response to North Korean aggression. *The Heritage Foundation*. https://www.heritage.org/asia/report/another-feeble-response-north-korean-aggression.

Köhler, G. (1995). The three meanings of global apartheid: Empirical, normative, existential. *Alternatives: Global, Local, Political*, Volume 20(3), 403–413.

Libya Arab Jamahiriya v UK (1992) Question of interpretation and application of the 1971 Montreal Convention arising from the aerial incident at Lockerbie (instituting proceedings) ICJ Application Instituting Proceedings filed in the registry of the court on 3 March, 1992.

Mamdani, M. (2008, September 10). Darfur, ICC and the new humanitarian order – How the ICC's "responsibility to protect" is being turned into an assertion of neo-colonial domination. *The Nation*. https://www.thenation.com/article/new-humanitarian-order/.

Manirakiza, P. (2012). The case of an African criminal court to prosecute international crimes committed in Africa. In Nmehielle, V. O. (Ed.), *Africa and the future of international criminal justice*. The Hague, the Netherlands: Eleven International Publishing.

Marc, L. (2005, October 20). Look at the place! *The New York Times*. https://www.nytimes.com/2005/10/20/world/africa/look-at-the-place-sudan-says-say-sorry-but-us-wont.html.

Mazrui, A. (2007). Global apartheid: Race and religion in the new world order. In das Gupta, T. (Ed.), *Race and racialization: Essential readings*. Toronto: Canadian Scholars Press.

Mbazira, C. (2011). Duty to prosecute international crimes under international law. In Murungu, C., and Biegon, J. (Ed.), *Prosecuting international crimes in Africa*. Pretoria, South Africa: Pretoria University Law Press.

Mbizvo, S. (2016). The ICC in Africa: The fight against impunity. In Clarke, K. M., Knottnerus, A. S., and De-Volde, E. (Ed.), *Africa and the ICC: Perceptions of justice*. Cambridge, United Kingdom: Cambridge University Press.

Meisler, S. (2007). *Kofi Annan: A man of peace in a world of war*. Hoboken, USA: John Wiley & Sons, Inc.

Melvern, L. (2009). *A people betrayed: The role of the west in Rwanda's genocide* (2nd ed.). Chicago, USA: University of Chicago Press.

Melvern, L., and Williams, P. (2004). Britannia waived the rules: The Major's government and the 1994. *Rwandan genocide. African Affairs*, Volume 103, 1–22.

Menon, B. (1998). Rough ride for S-G in Rwanda as UN inaction on 1994 genocide continues to raise unanswered questions. *International Documents Review*, Volume 9, 1–5.

Mike Campbell (Pvt) Ltd and Others v Republic of Zimbabwe (2/2007) [2008] SADCT 2 (28 November 2008).

Mills, K., and Bloomfield, A. (2018). African resistance to the International Criminal Court: Halting the advance of the anti-impunity norm. *Review of International Studies*, Volume 44(1), 101–127.

Monageng, S. M. (2014). Africa and the International Criminal Court: Then and now. In Werle, G., Fernandez, L., and Vormbaum, M. (Eds.), *Africa and International Criminal Court: International criminal justice series volume 1*. The Hague, the Netherlands: T. M. C. Asser Press.

Montreal Convention for the Suppression of Unlawful Acts against the Safety of Civil Aviation (1973). 974 U.N.T.S,178.

Müller M. (2018). In search of the global east: Thinking between north and south. *Geopolitics*. https://doi.org/10.1080/14650045.2018.147775.

Murithi, T. (2014). Between political justice and judicial politics: Charting a way forward for the African Union and the International Criminal Court. In Werle, G., Fernandez, L., and Vormbaum, M. (Eds.), *Africa and International Criminal Court: International criminal justice series volume 1*. The Hague, the Netherlands: T.M.C. Asser Press.

Murungu, C. (2011). Immunity of state officials and the prosecution of international crimes. In Murungu, C., and Biegon, J. (Eds.), *Prosecuting international crimes in Africa*. Pretoria, South Africa: Pretoria University Law Press.

Mutasa, C. (2005). *Global apartheid and African debt crisis*. Discussion Paper Series. http://www.quiendebeaquien.org/kitbcn/ppi-documents/d-africa-immigraci on/ingle /Global-Apartheid-African-Debt-Crisis.pdf.

Mutua, M. W. (2016). Closing the impunity gap and the role of state support of ICC. In Steinberg, R. H. (Ed.), *Contemporary issues facing the International Criminal Court*. Leiden, the Netherlands: Koninklijke Brill NV.

Mutua, M. W. (2017). Africans and the ICC: Hypocrisy, impunity and perversion. In Clarke, K. M., Knottnerus, A. S., and De-Volde, E. (Eds.), *Africa and the ICC: Perceptions of justice*. Cambridge, United Kingdom: Cambridge University Press.

Nhemachena, A., Warikandwa, T. V., and Amoo, S. K. (2018). Identity, originality and hybridity in jurisprudence and social theory: An introduction. In Nhemachena, A., Warikandwa, T. V., and Amoo, S. K. (Eds.), *Social and legal theory in the age of decoloniality: Towards an African jurisprudence in the 21st century*. Bameda, Cameroon: Langaa.

Nmehielle, V. O. (2012). Introduction: Africa and international criminal justice: Issues and contentions. In Nmehielle, V. O. (Ed.), *Africa and the future of international criminal justice*. The Hague, the Netherlands: Eleven International Publishing.

Nour D., and Connell R. (2012). The Global South. *Contexts*, Volume 11(1), 12–13. http://contexts.sagepub.com. DOI 10.1177/153650421243647.

Nwoko, S. N. (2015). *Right to self-determination of a people: A TWAILian analysis of ICJ decisions in Cameroon v. Nigeria, East Timor, and Western Sahara Cases* (LLM thesis). https://pdfs.semanticscholar.org/0a72/1c3806c7ca7f6b880dfa06 2c016ab3e61c6b.pdf.

Nyawo, J. (2012). Historical narratives of mass atrocities and injustice in Africa. In Nmehielle, V. O. (Ed.), *Africa and the future of international criminal justice*. The Hague, the Netherlands: Eleven International Publishing.

Obura, K. (2011). Prosecuting international crimes committed by the Lord's Resistant Army in Uganda. In Murungu, C., and Biegon, J. (Eds.), *Prosecuting international crimes in Africa*. Pretoria, South Africa: Pretoria University Law Press.

Odero, S. (2011). The politics of international criminal justice, the ICC's arrest warrant for Al Bahir and the African Union's neo-colonial conspirator thesis. In Murungu, C., and Biegon, J. (Eds.), *Prosecuting international crimes in Africa*. Pretoria, South Africa: Pretoria University Law Press.

Ofuho, C. H. (2000). The legitimacy and sovereignty dilemma of African states and governments: Problems of the colonial legacy. In Bakut, B. T., and Dutt, S. (Eds.), *Africa at the millennium*. London, England: Palgrave Macmillan.

Okoth, J. (2016). Africa, the United Nations Security Council and the International Criminal Court: The question of deferrals. In Werle, G., Fernandez, L., and Vormbaum, M. (Eds.), *Africa and International Criminal Court: International criminal justice series volume 1*. The Hague, the Netherlands: T. M. C. Asser Press.

Paulsson, J. (2010). *Denial of justice in international law*. Cambridge, England: Cambridge University Press.

Prosecutor v Omar Hassan Ahmad Al Bashir, Pre-Trial Chamber II, Decision on the noncompliance of the Republic of Chad with the cooperation requests issued by the court regarding the arrest and surrender of Omar Hassan Ahmad Al-Bashir, 26 March 2013.

Rome Statute of the International Criminal Court (1998). In force on 1 July 2002. United Nations, Treaty Series, vol. 2187, No. 38544, Publication No. 92-9227-227-6. Available at https://www.refworld.org/docid/3ae6b3a84.html.

Rukooko, A. B., and Silverman, J. (2019). The International Criminal Court and Africa: A fractious relationship assessed. *African Human Rights Law Journal*, Volume 19(1), 85–104.

Sarkin, J. (2004). The coming of age of claims for reparations for human rights abuses committed in the south. *International Journal on Human Rights*, Volume 1(1), 67–125.

Schabas, W. (2016). State obligations in implementing arrest warrants. In Steinberg, R. H. (Ed.), *Contemporary issues facing the International Criminal Court*. Leiden, the Netherlands: Koninklijke Brill NV.

Scharf, M. P. (2011). The ICC's jurisdiction over the nationals of non-party states: A critique of the U.S. position. *Law and Contemporary Problems*, Volume 64(1), 67–118.

Schmitt, P. D. (2017). France, Africa and the ICC: The neocolonialist critique and the crisis of institutional legitimacy. In Clarke, K. M., Knottnerus, A. S., and De-Volde, E. (Eds.), *Africa and the ICC: Perceptions of justice*. Cambridge, United Kingdom: Cambridge University Press.

Schuerch, R. (2017). *The International Criminal Court at the mercy of powerful states: An assessment of the neo-colonialism claim made by African stakeholders-international criminal justice series volume 13*. The Hague, the Netherlands: T. M. C. Asser Press.

Seymour, L. J. M. (2017). The ICC and Africa: Rhetorics, hypocrisy management and legitimacy. In Clarke, K. M., Knottnerus, A. S., and De-Volde, E. (Eds.), *Africa and the ICC: Perceptions of justice*. Cambridge, United Kingdom: Cambridge University Press.

Shillington, K. (2012). *History of Africa* (3rd ed.). London, England: Palgrave Macmillan.

Southern Africa Litigation Centre v Minister of Justice and Constitutional Development & 9 Others 2016 (1) SACR 161 (GP).

Spitzer, R. M. (2002). Holocaust: Should Europe pay reparations to Africa for colonialism and slavery? *Vanderbilt Journal of Transnational Law*, Volume 35(4), 1313–1347.

Steinberg, R. H. (2016). Introduction to part 7. In Steinberg, R. H. (Ed.), *Contemporary issues facing the International Criminal Court*. Leiden, the Netherlands: Koninklijke Brill NV.

Tachiona v Mugabe 169 F Supp. 2d 259, 309 (SDNY 2001).

Taku, C. C. A. (2016). International politics and policy considerations for the inappropriate targeting by the ICC OTP. In Steinberg, R. H. (Ed.), *Contemporary issues facing the International Criminal Court*. Leiden, the Netherlands: Koninklijke Brill NV.

Trendafilova, E. (2014). Africa and the International Criminal Court: A judge's perspective. In Werle, G., Fernandez, L., and Vormbaum, M. (Eds.), *Africa and International Criminal Court: International criminal justice series volume 1*. The Hague, the Netherlands: T. M. C. Asser Press.

Tyler, H. (1985, April 9). South Africa's black police: Focus of black civilian hostility. *The Christian Science Monitor*. https://www.csmonitor.com/1985/0409/oblac.html.

United Nations (UN) Department of Public Information. (2008). United Nations today. (Publication No. E.08. I.6). https://www.un.org/ar/geninfo/pdf/UN.today.pdf.

United Nations, Vienna Convention on the Law of Treaties, 23 May 1969, United Nations, Treaty Series, volume 1155, 331. https://www.refworld. org/docid/3ae6b3a10. html.

Warikandwa, T. V., and Amoo, S. K. (2018). African law in comparative law: A case of undermining African jurisprudence and promoting a new world order agenda? In Nhemachena, A., Warikandwa, T. V., and Amoo, S. K. (Eds.), *Social and legal theory in the age of decoloniality: Towards an African jurisprudence in the 21st century*. Bameda, Cameroon: Langaa.

Zubel, E. (1999). The Lockerbie controversy: Tension between the International Court of Justice and the Security Council. *Annual Survey of International & Comparative Law*, Volume 5(1), 259–285.

Chapter 8

The Reincarnation of Apartheid

Strategic Partnerships and Land Reform in South Africa

Clemence Rusenga

INTRODUCTION

Among its objectives, the South African land reform programme that was introduced in 1994 sought to correct the historical injustices caused by apartheid in relation to ownership, control and use of natural resources which disadvantaged the black majority. While the post-apartheid government committed itself to redistribute natural resources to the formerly disadvantaged black majority, where beneficiaries acquire land the government force them to produce on a large scale without subdividing the land. A combination of factors, among them the imposition of large-scale farming, have contributed to the failure of many beneficiaries to neither sustain production nor benefit from their land. That failure to sustain large-scale production is used by the government as the pretext to introduce strategic partnerships and mentorships, effectively allowing agribusiness and white commercial farmers to have influence and control in the land reform projects. Consequently, agribusiness and white commercial farmers have become the "real beneficiaries" of land reform at the expense of their black partners. They gain control over land reform projects, use them for secure supplies to their downstream processing and marketing facilities while, at the same time, receiving state subsidies and cheap labour of the land beneficiaries. The chapter argues that strategic partnerships in the context of the Proactive Land Acquisition Strategy (PLAS) facilitate the dispossession and disempowerment of land beneficiaries and deepens an already acute land and agrarian question in the country. Instead of being a solution, strategic partnerships facilitate agribusiness' accumulation of natural and financial resources earmarked for black Africans in the context of land reform itself are a reincarnation of apartheid in the democratic dispensation.

Since the advent of democracy in 1994, South Africa has implemented a land reform programme which sought, among other objectives, to correct the historical injustices of apartheid in relation to ownership, control and use of natural resources. The democratic government aimed to reform the agrarian sector while empowering the formerly disadvantaged black Africans through availing productive land and support. However, the government does not subdivide the land and pressure the beneficiaries of land reform to utilise land for large-scale production purposes regardless of the mismatch with their capabilities. Their inevitable failure to sustain large-scale production is used as pretext to introduce strategic partnerships and mentorships which effectively allow agribusiness and white farmers to take control and benefit from land reform projects, more often at the expense of the land beneficiaries.

The chapter argues that strategic partnerships, in the context of PLAS, facilitate the dispossession and disempowerment of land beneficiaries while effectively making agribusiness and white farmers (mentors) the "real beneficiaries" of the economic value of the land and agricultural businesses. Further, the manner in which land reform is conceptualised and practised in South Africa deepens an already acute land and agrarian question in the country, marginalising black farmers in favour of agribusiness. Thus, the contemporary agrarian question in South Africa is a product of the unequal accumulation processes under neoliberal capitalism (Samir Amin 2012).

The first section conceptually locates the strategic partnerships in the context of the contemporary agrarian question which is a product of the manner capital accumulation is achieved under neoliberal capitalism. The chapter then presents, and review case studies of projects where strategic partnerships have been implemented. In the conclusion an analysis is provided focusing on: (i) who really benefits from the strategic partnerships in land reform projects; (ii) what are the implications of strategic partnerships for the agrarian question in South Africa; (iii) what are the explanations for the manner in which land reform is conceptualised and practised in the context of strategic partnerships and PLAS; and (iv) last, the chapter suggests that most-black farmers may succeed in the small-scale model of production.

THE REINCARNATION OF (GLOBAL) APARTHEID

Apartheid was a policy introduced in South Africa by the National Party in 1948. It gained notoriety for its devastating effects on the lives of the black majority. The policy disempowered blacks through various means while simultaneously empowering white South Africans to dominate and prosper. With regards to access, ownership and use of natural resources such as land and minerals, the apartheid policy deepened the inequalities entrenched by colonialism and the Natives Land Act of 1913, in particular. The Natives Land Act had formalised, and continued the historical land dispossession black South Africans had experienced since the second half of the seventeenth century (Worden 2006). It allocated 7 per cent of the land to blacks with the rest reserved for whites' use (Ncapayi 2013). One cannot understand the current land and agrarian question in South Africa without looking at the legacy of apartheid.

Although other parts of colonial Africa did not call their policies apartheid, race was a significant factor in how development was planned and implemented (Arrighi 1970). What in South Africa was called apartheid represented that continent-wide (with evident localised variations) experience characterised by discrimination, disempowerment and inequality. Thus, the democratic project which started post–World War II (independence and liberation struggles for self-determination; Shivji 2004) sought to address the effects of colonialism and its variants such as apartheid.

The expectation was that independence in Africa would democratise access and ownership of natural resources such as land. In countries such as Zimbabwe, the restoration of land to the black majority was a powerful political narrative used by liberation movements and the post-independence The Zimbabwe African National Union – Patriotic Front (Zanu PF) government to galvanise support from the people (Moyo 2001). Even the Zimbabwean fast-track land reform programme of the early 2000s was justified against the slow pace of transformation in relation to the land and agrarian question. However, contrary to popular expectations the land and agrarian questions in Africa are worsening in most countries post-independence (Moyo 2004). We are actually witnessing what could be called "global apartheid" where agribusinesses and international capital are at the forefront of dispossessing many rural people in the global south in the name of investments and development, a phenomenon others described as land grabbing (Cotula and Vermeulen 2009).

Today's struggles for land in Africa need to be located within the context of contemporary capitalism and how it reproduces the agrarian question in the global south. According to Mafeje (1988, 2004), the agrarian question has to do with how to create conditions for the improvement of productivity of people who already have access to land whereas the land question is a problem of inequitable distribution of land. Sam Moyo (2004) argues that except for South Africa the entire "sub-Saharan Africa . . . where agriculture has suffered a steep output decline since 1979" has an acute agrarian question. In that Moyo agrees with Mafeje that the agrarian question affects the whole of sub-Saharan Africa. However, Mafeje (1988) argues that the former settler societies of southern Africa (Namibia, Zimbabwe and South Africa and to an extent Kenya) exhibit both the land and agrarian question. His view is that while sub-Saharan Africa, outside the former settler societies, never experienced permanent alienation of indigenous land by imperialists the latter experienced extensive alienation of land leaving the black majority with limited access to land.

The land and agrarian questions in Africa were shaped by the differential experiences of the colonial project in the continent's regions. Samir Amin (1972) divides Africa into three macro-regions: (1) traditional West Africa which constitutes Africa of the colonial economy; (2) the traditional Congo River Basin which he called Africa of the concession-owning companies; and (3) the eastern and southern parts of the continent, the Africa of the labour reserves.

In the Africa of the labour reserves, Amin argued that "capital in the centre needed to have a large proletariat immediately available" (Amin 1972, 114). There was great mineral wealth to be exploited as well as an untypical settler agriculture in tropical Africa. Violence was used to dispossess the African rural communities of their land to facilitate the availability of cheap labour. Black Africans were kept in the small regions without any means to modernise or intensify their farming. The expropriated land was allocated to white farmers who produced on a large scale for export. This created an acute land question that still defines post-independence politics in the settler societies. The African communities became "suppliers of temporary or permanent migrants providing cheap proletariat for the European mines and farms, and later for the manufacturing industries of South Africa, Rhodesia and Kenya" (Arrighi et al. 2010). According to Arrighi et al. (2010), the land appropriations were driven by the belief among the colonists that the dispossession of agricultural producers from the land was a precondition for successful capitalist development.

The extensive expropriations in southern Africa were not experienced in the other two regions identified by Samir Amin. In West Africa, the colonial project focused much on reorienting peasants towards producing what monopolists offered to buy. The traditional society produced for the world market without any prospect of radical modernisation (Amin 1972). The key features of the colonial-type trade, which characterised West Africa, included the constitution of a class of indigenous planters of rural origin who exclusively appropriated land and employed paid labour (Amin 1972, 116). In the savanna Amin argued that the Muslim brotherhoods permitted the "organisation of production and export in the context of vast areas subject to a theocratic political power . . . which kept the form of a tribute-paying social formation, but was integrated into the international system because the surplus appropriated in the form of tribute levied on the village communities was itself marketed" (Amin 1972, 116). Africans dominated the trade and where the main producers. In Central Africa, "[T]he low population density and the lack of sufficient hierarchisation made the colonial-type trade model non-viable" (Amin 1972, 117). Consequently, the colonial authorities allowed companies to establish industrial plantations, but this did not result is landlessness for the black majority. This is the context in which Mafeje (1988) argued that Africa outside the settler societies did not have a land question but an agrarian one.

However, Sam Moyo (2004) argues that "[T]he land question in Africa highlights the neglect of social justice and equity issues during the era of neoliberal economic reforms as witnessed by growing trends of unequal control of land and natural resources." For him, the land question has become internationalised as it "mirrors the incomplete decolonisation processes in ex-settler colonies, but also because global finance capital is increasingly entangled in conflicts over land, minerals and natural resources in Africa's rich enclaves." The emerging trends of rural land concentration alongside the marginalisation of various rural populations from "land by a growing number of agrarian capitalists, elites and state agents" (Moyo 2004, 2) is reproducing the land question throughout the African continent. According to Moyo, this growing trend of landlessness is building on existing problems over land rights, inheritance, selective exclusion, unequal gender relations and class differentiated access to the means of production thereby generating a relatively unique land question in Africa. Thus, the whole African continent has a land question rather than the settler societies only as argued by Mafeje (1988, 2004).

The relationship between the agrarian question and capitalism is an important link which Sam Moyo provides in his analysis. Samir Amin (2012) finds this relationship important in his understanding of the agrarian question in the global south. Amin locates the agrarian question in the quest by "[M]odern capitalist agriculture, represented by both rich family farming and/or by agribusiness corporations" to attack peasant agriculture in the global south (Amin 2012, 12). While capitalism solved the agrarian question in the developed centres, it did so by "creating a gigantic agrarian question in the peripheries, which it cannot solve but through the genocide of half of humankind" (Amin 2012, 14). The argument is that "[C]apitalist modernization has now reached a stage where its continued expansion requires the implementation of enclosure policies on a world scale similar to those at the beginning of capitalist development in England" (Amin 2012, 19). Amin is alerting us to how conditions are created to allow agribusinesses to "take possession of the land they need in order to expand." This is achieved, on a global scale, through promotion of the discourse of private property and private land ownership.

Harvey's (2004) concept of accumulation by dispossession is useful in explaining the manner in which international capital is at the forefront of land dispossession in the global south thereby creating the land questions, as pointed out by Moyo (2004) and Samir Amin (2012). Harvey's view is that when capital fails to accumulate through expanded production attempts are made to accumulate by dispossession. It is in this context that globalisation and neoliberalism are promoted to open new markets for capital and financial flows. These processes promote the commodification of nature in its all forms (land, water, air) leading to their concentration in the hands of multinational corporations and agribusiness. The result is multi-layered and multi-dimensional forms of dispossession of many rural dwellers in the name of development and investment.

Various reasons have been provided for the expropriation of land, often used for large-scale production purposes. For some investors, especially food-insecure countries, the lack of confidence in international markets as sources of food supply motivates outsourcing of food production by buying farmland in the global south (De Schutter 2011). Some investment funds also hedge "their assets against inflation, particularly in a context in which the stock markets remained unreliable and were providing at best low returns on investment" (De Schutter 2011). Like Harvey, McMichael (2011) locates the current commercial land deals in the context of the general capitalist accumulation crisis expressed through the conjunction of food, energy and financial crises which make agriculture a relatively safe investment haven for the relatively long term.

Ruth Hall (2011), writing in the context of southern Africa identified various dimensions of the mega land deals. The acquired land was used, among other things, for biofuel production, extractive industries (mining and forestry), with the state in certain instances grabbing land from the poor for "development purposes" or for the benefit of the politically connected. Thus, it is understood that what scholars consider land grabbing generally affect the poor (Cotula and Vermeulen 2009; De Schutter 2011).

But why is the current development-induced dispossession of the rural poor allowed by the states of the global south? Many reasons can be proffered to explain this. However, Boaventura de Sousa Santos (2006) offers a compelling explanation that helps us understand not only the development dilemma in the global south but also the emergent agrarian question in the context of contemporary capitalist accumulation. Santos bring to our attention how techno-scientific knowledge which presides over neoliberal globalisation, and is its source of hegemony, discredits all other rival knowledges by "suggesting that they are not comparable, in terms of efficiency and coherence, to the scientificity of the market laws" (Santos 2006, 13). Modern science claims to be the exclusive canon of production of knowledge while claiming as non-existent that which is not legitimated by it. As such other approaches to development, which are viewed as inferior as they do not conform to western modernity, are not regarded as credible alternatives to the "superior" approaches to development from the west.

The claim for universality exhibited in the western model of development has been challenged by Dani Nabudere who argued that the model has "certain inbuilt Euro-centric cultural and power biases which have been imposed on other cultures and peoples without their consent, thus inhibiting the emergence of different models to development based on these different cultural heritages" (Nabudere 1997, 203). The mainstream development model enjoys global hegemony with many rural people dispossessed in the name of development. This hegemony is sustained by a powerful neoliberal ideology resting on two main planks. First, increased competition, "achieved through deregulation and the opening up of domestic markets, including financial markets, to foreign competition," is viewed as important (Ostry et al. 2016, 38). Second, the state is given a smaller role in the economy achieved through "privatisation and limits on the ability of governments to run fiscal deficits and accumulate debt." The hegemony of neoliberalism, despite its negative effects, reflects the power of ideology in sustaining development models that do not benefit the majority (Ekeh 1975).

Therefore, the present global conditions exhibit what can be called global apartheid. It is global apartheid in as far as it imposes a development model that fosters inequalities, including in the ownership of natural resources such as land. Like apartheid, the current development model operates on the premises that the dispossession of the poor is a precondition for capitalist accumulation – accumulation by dispossession (Arrighi et al. 2010; Harvey 2004). As argued by Samir Amin (2012), the new agrarian question is a result of unequal development, where the poor are increasingly marginalised in favour of agribusiness and corporate investors. Thus, we are witnessing the enforcement of an agribusiness model globally (Movement of Rural Landless Workers 2013; Rusenga 2017). Agribusiness and corporate finance consolidate land ownership, production and distribution of agricultural products on a global scale. The accumulated land is often used on a large scale utilising a lot of labour-saving technology. The outcome is increased productivity on farms controlled by agribusiness alongside millions of poor rural producers on limited land with low productivity (Amin 2012).

AGRIBUSINESS AND LAND REFORM IN SOUTH AFRICA

In 1994, the democratic South African state inherited an acute land and agrarian question following more than 300 years of colonialism and apartheid. The new African National Congress (ANC) government moved with speed to introduce a land reform programme "to address effectively the injustices of forced removals and the historical denial of access to land" for the black majority (ANC 1994). Another key objective of the land reform programme is the need to build "the economy by generating large-scale employment, increasing rural incomes and eliminating overcrowding" (DLA 1997). That objective targets the poor, especially, the rural poor, as the intended major beneficiaries of land reform. In line with that focus, the Settlement and Land Acquisition Grants (SLAG; R16,000 per household) targeted poor households.

However, because the grants were too small to purchase the land in the market many beneficiaries bought land as groups (Hall and Ntsebeza 2007). Group projects were a product of higher land prices and the failure by government to subdivide the land before distribution to beneficiaries. A plethora of problems affected the land reform projects resulting in many failing to contribute to livelihoods (Anseeuw and Mathebula 2008).

SLAG was replaced by the land redistribution for agricultural development (LRAD) in 2001. LRAD required beneficiaries to make own contributions to qualify for grants on a sliding scale. It is this element of LRAD that made some scholars (Hall 2004) argue that it discriminated against the poor in favour of those with resources. LRAD has been viewed as focusing on creating a class of black commercial farmers (Hall and Ntsebeza 2007). However, the current PLAS (introduced in 2006) seems to have gone beyond the creation of black commercial farmers to create space for an agricultural sector dominated by agribusiness and large-scale commercial farmers. This is achieved in the context of a state leasehold model which replaced the original private ownership model. According to Hall and Kepe, the model "empowers state officials to buy farms on the open market and allocate them to selected beneficiaries" (Hall and Kepe 2017, 123). The initial three years' test period was amended in 2013 through the State Land Lease and Disposal Policy. The policy states that "[T]he lease period for all leases shall be 30 years, which may be renewable for another 20 years" (DRDLR 2013c). This means that it takes fifty years for the state to transfer the title to the beneficiary.

With the state owning the title to land, it makes the key decisions regarding how land should be used. Using its RADP policy, beneficiaries are pressured into accepting strategic partners in mentorship or joint venture arrangements. In fact, accepting the strategic partners is part of the preconditions for receiving assistance through RADP. The strategic partner "is required to mentor the emerging farmers, provide a business plan and assist with skills training in marketing and export" (Friedman 2019). The government's attempts to create a class of black commercial farmers are opening up land reform for control and dominance by agribusiness and large-scale farmers. The experiences of Nirwanda, a table grape farm in De Doorns, Western Cape province, clearly illustrate how agribusiness and the state elite have "captured" land reform. The 39-hectarefarm was bought by a company called Quickvest 427 in 2007, for R7.3 million. Quickvest is a "special purpose vehicle" or shelf company for a multinational Dutch agribusiness called South African Fruit Exporters (Safe) and its black economic empowerment partner, Bono Holdings. The farm was then sold to the government in 2012 for R19million (Friedman 2019). The farm was sold for a huge profit that was almost triple its 2007 purchase price. Safe, through Bono its partner, applied to the government to become a strategic partner for the new beneficiaries, the "Big Five, a registered farming co-operative" (Friedman 2019).

The Big Five were formally approved as the lessees for Nirwanda in July 2013 by the Department of Rural Development and Land Reform (DRDLR). However, six years later they still have not signed any lease agreement with the DRDLR. They also have not received government funding which affected their vineyards. Friedman reported that the Big Five were threatened with eviction in 2019 the main reason seeming to be their opposition to the imposition of Safe and Bono as their strategic partner.

Safe and Bono accrued some benefits from their involvement at Nirwanda while beneficiaries and farm workers had nothing to show for their involvement at the farm. The agribusiness invested little capital at the farm while reaping the benefits of the fruit exports. According to Hall and Kepe (2017), the agribusiness' strategy also involve selling to themselves without investing the dividends into the farms they control. They also utilise their pack houses for the packaging of the fruit with their logistics companies responsible for transporting the exported fruits. Thus, the agribusiness are able to "control the value chain and are able to manipulate pricing and profits" (Friedman 2019). At Nirwanda, when Safe and Bono left in June 2017, there was no electricity and water with some workers getting jobs on other farms to survive. Additionally, no dividends have been declared while the vineyards were left in ruins.

This practice where beneficiaries are relegated to the margins in favour of agribusiness has been observed by Hall and Kepe (2017) in their study in the Eastern Cape Province. Their study focused on eleven farms acquired under PLAS, where the state held the title to the land. First, the scholars observed that none of the beneficiaries in their study had signed any lease with the government. Although two projects had valid leases, they were signed between the government and strategic partners – agribusiness. Four of the projects had strategic partners. Hall and Kepe argued that beneficiaries "neither own the land nor lease it, but remain workers on state farms, working for strategic partners" (Hall and Kepe 2017, 128). The beneficiaries "lack control over land, capital and production" (Hall and Kepe 2017, 128). As in the case of Nirvana, Hall and Kepe observed that the strategic partners benefited from the farms while beneficiaries received nothing. For their role, the mentors received monthly cash payments from the DRDLR. On their part, the strategic partners held shares in the joint ventures while benefiting from state subsidies and state land. Further, they benefited from transfer pricing as they sold the produce to their downstream processing and packing factories. In one instance, an agribusiness operated the PLAS farm as its own, supplying the produce to its own processing facility while employing beneficiaries as its employees paying them below the minimum wage (and no dividends) on a farm they state claimed to have bought for them.

Corruption by DRDLR officials, ANC politicians and corporate executives has been noted as one of the reasons for this sombre state of affairs in land reform (Friedman 2019). However, equal attention should be given to the state's stubborn belief in the efficacy of large-scale production. The enforced large-scale model is not suited to the needs and capabilities of land beneficiaries, thereby deliberately setting them up for failure. Such policy "engineered" failure is the one being used to justify the imposition of agribusiness as strategic partners in joint ventures that provide little benefits, in any at all, for the land beneficiaries. This is more evident in the land restitution projects were many beneficiaries, often communities, are given very large farms.

The Levubu case study by Lahiff et al. (2012) demonstrates the point above. The authors noted that the push for strategic partnerships in Limpopo originated from the office of the Regional Land Claims Commissioner in Limpopo. The claimant communities, noticing the daunting task of managing complex agricultural businesses, also demanded for strategic partners. However, the white agribusinesses have also a special interest in entering into strategic partnerships for their benefit. Fraser (2007) describes the motives behind the involvement of an agribusiness called Mavu in the land restitution farms in Levebu, Limpopo province. The agribusiness is owned by white farmers from Levubu and the surrounding area. The same farmers own "upstream agricultural suppliers, downstream processing facilities (nut drying and hulling, juice processing) and have marketing channels to domestic and foreign buyers" (Fraser 2007, 307). The owners of Mavu viewed the direct transfer of farms to the beneficiaries as a risk to their up- and downstream investments. They believed that the beneficiaries would not be able to adequately farm the land, a view shared by the government also. Thus, the agribusinesses participation in strategic partnerships is driven primarily by the need to have secure supplies of raw material. Fraser quoted a member of Mavu saying "the best way to [secure your raw material base] is to farm it yourself" (Fraser 2007, 307). The same farmer went on to argue that without his investment in the factories he would not have been a strategic partner. For him, he needed to secure a stable supply of the raw materials he needed (Fraser 2007, 307). Furthermore, the same farmer went on to outline why he is of the view that strategic partnerships are beneficial to the agribusinesses. He said:

> Where in the whole wide world will somebody come and buy your assets from you and then give it back to you at no cost plus 50% of the share back to you? Where will that happen? And that's what's happening in Levubu. And they're not only buying my assets, they're giving me three times more, four, five times more assets. They're going to spend R231m and basically give 50% of R150m to MMS. Where in the world will you get that asset base for basically nothing? What's your investment? Your working capital? Where's your exposure? (Fraser 2007, 308)

The narratives above highlight the extent to which joint ventures in land reform reincarnate white control over land at the expense of the intended beneficiaries and their communities. For instance, the DRDLR brought in Mavu as a partner for the Ratombo (1,330 hectares) and Shigalo (715 hectares) farms in 2006. The farms produced high-value subtropical fruits. Mavu used its resources to invest in wages, new machinery and other inputs with the expectation of recovering costs from income from farm produce. The expected development grants from the Commission on Restitution of Land Rights had not materialised when Mavu exited the arrangement in 2007. Consequently, the two communities had to pay Mavu for the machinery and other assets it had invested on the farms. Although Mavu used crop revenues to cover some of the costs, "no financial benefit accrued to the communities in the form of either rent or profit share" ((Fraser 2007, 307). Lahiff *et al* have stated that even when South African Farm Management (SAFM) replaced Mavu as a strategic partner, revenues from the farms continued to go to strategic partners with no benefits for the communities. Where strategic partnerships failed, the communities were left owing substantial amounts of money to the banks.

In the case of the Moletele community, also in Limpopo province, some strategic partnerships collapsed with some struggling partly due to the delays in the transfer of state grants promised to the communities (39). Lahiff et al. (2012) observed that five years after the return of the community's first lands most households had "yet to see any positive impact on their livelihood" (Lahiff et al. 2012, 52). The Moletele Community Property Associations (CPAs) received intermittent land rentals below the expected rates with no dividends materialising due to losses by strategic partnerships.

However, the study by Bitzer and Bijman (2014), in the Eastern Cape Province, shows that the realities around strategic partnerships in the land reform sector should be seen as nuanced. They studied six strategic partnerships in the citrus sector, which is one of the key agricultural sectors in South Africa. Four projects had co-management partnerships while the other two had co-ownership partnerships. Under co-management partnerships agribusinesses and land beneficiaries/emerging farmers jointly manage the farm owned by the latter. The agreement focuses on mentorship and service provision. In this kind of partnership profit goes to the farmer with the agribusiness receiving a management fee for the services. In the co-ownership partnership a new operating company is established (with the agribusiness and the farmer(s) holding shares) to manage the business (Bitzer and Bijman 2014).

The aim of the study was to analyse the extent to which the strategic partnerships promoted the commercialisation of the black farmers, a key objective of the partnerships. Commercialisation entailed the "provision of access to mainstream agricultural markets – export markets. . ." and the "building of farmers' capacity to deal with and adapt to a continuously evolving market environment" (Bitzer and Bijman 2014, 170).

The authors found that the agribusinesses determined the terms and conditions of partnerships. They prepared the business plans, determined the objectives, scope of cooperation and roles and responsibilities of the actors. The agribusinesses provided training for the farm workers and potential farm managers. The training focused on production technology and business management. Mentors were also sent to the farms to allow the land beneficiaries/emerging farmers to learn practically.

Consequently, strategic partnerships were credited for closing the gap between the farming knowledge of the black farmers and the international quality standards. Thus, the authors concluded that strategic partnerships enhanced the black farmers' opportunities in the global markets. Based on this, one can say that there are some positives that can be achieved through strategic partnerships.

However, Bitzer and Bijman (2014) observed that while farmers were formally key decision-makers they had little say in the strategic direction of the partnerships. They observed that the black farmers were passive recipients of operational information with strategic decisions monopolised by the agribusiness partners. The farmers had no capacity to market on their own. They were obliged to market through the agribusiness partners in return for training and assistance. As such, the goal of achieving independent black commercial farmers was not met. Against that backdrop, the authors argued that strategic partnerships seemed to serve the objectives of the agribusinesses more than they benefited the black farmers. The partnerships facilitated agribusiness' access to secure supplies of products for their downstream processing facilities, in addition to the land and grants provided by the government (Hall and Kepe 2017).

Thus, while noting the positives that strategic partnerships contribute Bitzer and Bijman (2014) questions whether they can contribute to addressing the unequal agrarian structures in the country? Further, they argue that strategic partnerships enforce continuity in the agricultural sector through the preference for the export-oriented large-scale farming.

CONCLUSION: WHO ARE THE REAL BENEFICIARIES OF LAND REFORM?

The current configuration of land reform in South Africa, especially its implementation under PLAS, raises more questions than answers. Who are the real beneficiaries of land reform in South Africa? In fact, what does it mean to be a beneficiary of land reform in South Africa? These questions call for us to search for the deep-seated meanings of land reform and what it means to benefit from it.

The current state approach to land reform utilises a very narrow definition of beneficiary. Emphasis is placed on officially allocating land to black people (in name only) with limited attention given to whether they truly benefit from the economic value of the land and/or agricultural project. Land reform should be about empowerment, creating livelihoods and redress of the colonial legacy of inequalities in access and ownership of land. However, the experiences of the land beneficiaries in the current context of strategic partnerships question their status as beneficiaries.

It is conceivable to argue that in certain situations the real beneficiaries are the agribusiness partners, not land beneficiaries. Under PLAS the beneficiaries are not given the title to the land. Even if they received title deeds, as in the case of restitution projects (Lahiff et al. 2012), the configured joint ventures benefit the agribusinesses more than the beneficiaries. The state leases the land to blacks which they then deliver to the strategic partners who are mainly large-scale white farmers and agribusinesses (Hall and Kepe 2017). In most cases the beneficiaries lack control of the land and decision-making to the strategic partners (Bitzer and Bijman 2014). They also endure government interference in their agricultural activities – made possible by the latter's position as title holder (Rusenga 2017). Further, the promised dividends (in strategic partnerships) and/or income from agricultural projects are not being realised (Binswanger-Mkhize 2014; Lahiff et al. 2012).

On what basis, then, can we say that blacks are benefiting from land reform in the context of strategic partnerships? It is possible that there could be isolated "successes" but the overwhelming evidence point to the reversal of the purpose of land reform through strategic partnerships. PLAS and the strategic partnerships are enforcing coloniality in the land reform sector (Kepe and Hall 2018).

The poor expect the government to facilitate, through land reform, the rebalancing of the economic configuration to ensure that many blacks benefit from land reform and agriculture. Instead, the post-apartheid democratic state is championing the empowerment of former large-scale farmers and agribusiness through strategic partnerships. For the poor this has all indications of déjà vu. They are living the past in the present. The very same beneficiaries of colonial and apartheid agricultural policies are the same beneficiaries on the land blacks call theirs. It is a reincarnation of apartheid in the democratic era.

It is worth repeating the quotation from a farmer in Levubu commenting on strategic partnerships as shown earlier by Fraser:

> Where in the whole wide world will somebody come and buy your assets from you and then give it back to you at no cost plus 50% of the share back to you? Where will that happen? And that's what's happening in Levubu. And they're not only buying my assets, they're giving me three times more, four, five times more assets. They're going to spend R231m and basically give 50% of R150m to MMS. Where in the world will you get that asset base for basically nothing? What's your investment? Your working capital? Where's your exposure? (Fraser 2007, 308).

The above statement sums up the extent to which strategic partnerships empower those not meant to be the beneficiaries. Indeed, the agribusinesses are the true beneficiaries of land reform in the context of some strategic partnerships. They are empowered through state grants, access to land (which they sold to the state for higher prices in the first place) and access to cheap labour of the beneficiaries (Friedman 2019).

Are we arguing that former white farmers and agribusinesses should never assist black farmers? Certainly not! The government need to address the power relations in the land reform sector between the beneficiaries (on one hand) and the strategic partners and government (on the other) to make the collaborations beneficial to all. Currently, the government treat black farmers with suspicion and mistrust. It does not have confidence that black farmers can use land successfully.

The government needs a shift from its entrapment in the global "Euro-modernist" model of development and its claim for universal relevance (Ndhlovu 2017). Strategic partnerships are promoting an agribusiness model, which is the current and dominant model of agrarian capitalism which emerged towards the end of the twentieth century (Abbey et al. 2006). That model organises agricultural production in the form of monoculture on an ever-increasing scale with the intense use of agricultural machinery, toxic chemicals and genetically modified seeds (Stedile and Leon 2014) while consolidating land ownership, farm production and upstream and downstream agricultural activities in the hands of agribusiness (Movement of Rural Landless Workers 2013).

The continuity with large-scale models of farming on land reform projects is a futile project. Trying to duplicate such models on most black farmers without adaptation to accommodate the African endogenous forms of knowledge, creativity and innovation will not create the required conditions for growth and development.

In fact, there is no evidence of successful large-scale black farmers in Africa. On the contrary, there is evidence that historically successful black farmers who utilised land on a small scale existed. Bundy (1972), in the context of South Africa, detailed the rise and fall of the successful black peasantry that produced for both household consumption and the markets in the late nineteenth century and early twentieth century. In Southern Rhodesia (now Zimbabwe), Palmer (1973) also shows that between 1890 and 1908 a successful class of black commercial farmers (especially the Shona) emerged supplying foodstuffs to the Europeans who numbered around 11,100 in 1901, and the African labourers in the new mines. Although their land had been expropriated by the whites, the latter had no capacity to utilise it leaving the land literally under the control and use of black Africans until when the British South Africa Company decided to support established white agriculture. Empirical evidence also show that in the 1980s some black peasants in Zimbabwe were successful on the background of improved state support (Ncube 2018). Indeed, even in the era of the fast-track land reform programme Scoones et al. (2011) have shown that the smallholders in the A1 model farms were more successful (in comparison) than the relatively large farmers on A2 model farms.

In all the cases above, black farmers adapted the modern methods of production and inputs into their context and culture and successfully produced for household consumption and the markets. Such adaptation, especially in the context of South Africa, included the use of off-farm income as capital for investment in agricultural production (Mabandla 2015). These achievements were attained not in the context of large-scale production, but on the land that was available to them (Rusenga 2017). Against this backdrop, attempts to civilise black farmers through strategic partnerships and mentorships without any adaptation exhibit the reproduction of an earlier liberal, reformist colonial mentality (of Imperial Britain) which viewed non-Europeans as children that should be educated and assimilated into western modernity (Mantena 2010).

Why are black farmers still treated with suspicion more than two decades after apartheid? Ben Cousins (2007) comments on the stereotypes against small-scale agriculture embraced by the ANC government, but effectively emanating from the lobby by organised commercial agriculture through the farmers' union, AgriSA. Cousins list four stereotypes, but three of those are cited here for their relevance in this discussion:

- Only commercial agriculture is real agriculture, and successful small-scale farming can only be a scaled-down version of technologically sophisticated and profit-maximising commercial farmers.

- Subsistence farmers are inefficient and unproductive.
- Land reform in southern Africa should thus focus primarily on deracialising commercial agriculture.

Cumulatively, such stereotypes are partly behind the current push to reproduce large-scale agriculture in the land reform projects. However, crediting the current state mentality to lobbying by organised agriculture seems to allude that government bureaucrats are only affected from without.

On the contrary, Ngugi wa Thiong'o (1981) would locate the problem in the type of African bourgeoisie that mainstream western education created out of the African. For him, mainstream western education creates people who are Africans in colour but western in everything else. The product is an African who looks down upon the African endogenous forms of knowledge and practices, including the agricultural practices of the African people. This kind of African bureaucrat uncritically adopts western values and models of development for which large-scale forms of production are an example.

This chapter argues that imposing large-scale forms of agriculture on black farmers in land reform projects will not succeed. Although important lessons can be learnt from large-scale commercial agriculture, an African identity should be promoted and/or preserved while incorporating only those aspects of large-scale commercial agriculture that are useful and adaptable for black farmers (Ndhlovu 2017). Most black farmers would do well in the small-scale model which could be supported even with modest investments (Mafeje 2003) such as off-farm income. Those with access to many resources should be allowed to produce on larger scales should they wish, but this should not be a blanket law for anyone who want to participate in land reform.

In fact, promoting small-scale production will even be cheaper for the state to provide post-settlement support. Reconfiguring land reform will enable blacks to be the main beneficiaries of land reform rather than the agribusiness and white commercial farmers currently enjoying the benefits of land reform in the context of strategic partnerships. Thus, the current form and implementation of strategic partners in land reform reincarnate *apartheid* in a democratic dispensation. This is a contradiction and anomaly that should not be allowed to continue.

BIBLIOGRAPHY

Abbey, L. A., Baer, W., and Filizzola, M. (2006). "Growth, efficiency, and equity: The impact of agribusiness and land reform in Brazil." *Latin American Business Review*, Volume 7(2), 93–115.

Amin, S. (1972). "Underdevelopment and dependence in Black Africa-origins and contemporary forms." *The Journal of Modern African Studies*, Volume 10(4), 503–524.

Amin, S. (2012). "Contemporary imperialism and the agrarian question." *Agrarian South: Journal of Political Economy*, Volume 1(1), 11–26.

ANC. (1994). *Reconstruction and Deverlopment Programme*. Johannesburg: Umanyano Publications.

Anseeuw, W., and Mathebula, N. (2008). *Evaluating land reform's contribution to South Africa's pro-poor growth pattern*. Paper presented at the TIPS Annual Forum, Cape Town.

Arrighi, G. (1970). "Labour supplies in historical perspective: A study of the proletarianization of the African peasantry in Rhodesia." *The Journal of Development Studies*, Volume 6(3), 197–234.

Arrighi, G., Aschoff, N., and Scully, B. (2010). "Accumulation by dispossession and its limits: The Southern Africa paradigm revisited." *Studies in Comparative International Development*, Volume 45(4), 410–438.

Binswanger-Mkhize, H. P. (2014). "From failure to success in South African land reform." *African Journal of Agricultural and Resource Economics*, Volume 9(4), 253–269.

Bitzer, V., and Bijman, J. (2014). "Old oranges in new boxes? Strategic partnerships between emerging farmers and agribusinesses in South Africa." *Journal of Southern African Studies*, Volume 40(1), 167–183.

Bundy, C. (1972). "The emergence and decline of a South African peasantry." *African Affairs*, Volume 71(285), 369–388.

Cotula, L., and Vermeulen, S. (2009). "Deal or no deal: The outlook for agricultural land investment in Africa." *International Affairs*, Volume 85(6), 1233–1247.

Cousins, B. (2007). "Agrarian reform and the 'two economies': Transforming South Africa's countryside." In Ntsebeza, L., and Hall, R. (Eds.), *The Land Question in South Africa: The Challenge of Transformation and Redistribution*. Cape Town: HSRC Press.

De Schutter, O. (2011). "How not to think of land-grabbing: Three critiques of large-scale investments in farmland." *The Journal of Peasant Studies*, Volume 38(2), 249–279.

DLA. (1997). *White Paper on South African land Policy*. Pretoria: Government Printers.

DRDLR. (2013c). *State Land Lease and Disposal Policy*. Pretoria: Government Printers.

Ekeh, P. P. (1975). "Colonialism and the two publics in Africa: A theoretical statement." *Comparative Studies in Society and History*, Volume 17(1), 91–112.

Fraser, A. (2007). "Hybridity emergent: Geo-history, learning, and land restitution in South Africa." *Geoforum*, Volume 38(2), 299–311.

Friedman, H. (2019, 24 May). "'Farm flipping': How land reform was broken by the elite." *Mail & Guardian*.

Hall, R. (2004). "A political economy of land reform in South Africa." *Review of African Political Economy*, Volume 31(100), 213–227.

Hall, R. (2011). “Land grabbing in Southern Africa: The many faces of the investor rush.” *Review of African Political Economy*, Volume 38(128), 193–214.

Hall, R., and Kepe, T. (2017). “Elite capture and state neglect: New evidence on South Africa’s land reform.” *Review of African Political Economy*, Volume 44(151), 122–130.

Hall, R., and Ntsebeza, L. (2007). “Introduction to the land question in South Africa.” In Ntsebeza, L., and Hall, R. (Eds.), *The Land Question in South Africa: The Challenge of Transformation and Redistribution*. Cape Town: HRSC Press.

Harvey, D. (2004). The new imperialism: Accummulation by dispossession. *Socialist Register*, 63–87.

Kepe, T., and Hall, R. (2018). “Land redistribution in South Africa: Towards decolonisation or recolonisation?” *Politikon*, Volume 45(1), 128–137.

Lahiff, E., Davis, N., and Manenzhe, T. (2012). *Joint Ventures in Agriculture: Lessons from Land Reform Projects in South Africa*. London: IIED.

Mabandla, N. (2015). “Rethinking Bundy: Land and the black middle class–accumulation beyond the peasantry.” *Development Southern Africa*, Volume 32(1), 76–89.

Mafeje, A. (1988). The agrarian question and food production in Southern Africa. In Prah, K. K. (Ed.), *Food Security Issues in Southern Africa: Selected Proceedings of the Conference on Food Security Issues in Southern Africa, Maseru, 12–14 January 1987*, 92–124. Maseru: Institute of Southern African Studies, National University of Lesotho.

Mafeje, A. (2003). *The Agrarian Question, Access to Land, and Peasant Responses in Sub-Saharan Africa*. Geneva: UNRISD.

Mafeje, A. (2004). *The Land and the Agrarian Question in Southern Africa*. University of Fort Hare.

Mantena, K. (2010). *Alibis of Empire: Henry Maine and the Ends of Liberal Imperialism*. Princeton and Oxford: Princeton University Press.

McMichael, P. (2011). *The Food Regime in the Land Grab: Articulating ‘Global Ecology’ and Political Economy*. Paper presented at the International Conference on Global Land Grabbing. Land Deal Politics Initiative, University of Sussex, Brighton.

Movement of Rural Landless Workers. (2013). *Agrarian Program of the MST: Struggle, Build People’s Agrarian Reform*. Paper presented at the Sixth National MST Congress.

Moyo, S. (2001). “The land occupation movement and democratisation in Zimbabwe: Contradictions of neoliberalism.” *Millennium*, Volume 30(2), 311–330.

Moyo, S. (2004). *African Land Questions, the State and Agrarian Transition: Contradictions of Neoliberal Land Reforms*.

Nabudere, D. W. (1997). “Beyond modernization and development, or why the poor reject development.” *Geografiska Annaler: Series B, Human Geography*, Volume 79(4), 203–215.

Ncapayi, F. (2013). *Land and Changing Social Relations in South Africa’s Former Reserves: The Case of Luphaphasi in Sakhisizwe Local Municipality, Eastern Cape* (PhD dissertation). University of Cape Town, South Africa.

Ncube, S. (2018). *The Role of Social Capital in the Fast Track Land Reform Programme (FTLRP) of Zimbabwe: A Case of Rouxdale (R/E) Farm, Bubi District, Matabeleland North Province* (PhD thesis). University of Cape Town, South Africa.

Ndhlovu, F. (2017). "Southern development discourse for Southern Africa: Linguistic and cultural imperatives." *Journal of Multicultural Discourses*, Volume 12(2), 89–109.

Ostry, J. D., Loungani, P., and Furceri, D. (2016). Neoliberalism: Oversold. *Finance and Development*, 38–41.

Palmer, R. H. (1973). The agricultural history of Rhodesia. In Palmer, R. H., and Parsons, N. (Eds.), *The Roots of Rural Poverty in Central and Southern Africa*. London: Heinemann.

Rusenga, C. (2017). *The Socio-Economic Consequences of the Agribusiness Model on the Land Reform Beneficiaries in Greater Tzaneen Municipality, South Africa: The Case of Elangeni Project* (PhD thesis). University of Cape Town, South Africa.

Santos, B. D. S. (2006). *The Rise of the Global Left: The World Social Forum and Beyond*. London: Zed Books.

Scoones, I., Marongwe, N., Mavedzenge, B., Murimbarimba, F., Mahenehene, J., and Sukume, C. (2011). "Zimbabwe's land reform: Challenging the myths." *Journal of Peasant Studies*, Volume 38(5), 967–993.

Shivji, I. G. (2004). *Good Governance, Bad Governance and the Quest for Democracy in Africa: An Alternative Perspective*. HakiElimu Working Paper 04.8.

Stedile, J. P., and Leon, O. (2014). People's agrarian reform: An alternative to the capitalist model. http://www.mstbrazil.org/content/popular-agrarian-reform-alternative-capitalist-model.2016.

Wa Thiong'o, N. (1981). *Writers in Politics: Essays*. Oxford: James Currey.

Worden, N. (2006). "Coercion and freedom in the Cape Colony, 1652–1856." In Kleijwegt, M. (Ed.), *The Faces of Freedom: The Manumission and Emancipation of Slaves in Old World and New World Slavery* (pp. 185–209). Leiden: Brill.

Chapter 9

Promoting Customary Land Rights in Post-Colonial Namibia

An Overview of Prospects and Challenges with Respect to Communal Land Claims

Tapiwa Victor Warikandwa

INTRODUCTION

Customary law has been in operation in Namibia for over thirty years since this legal system was recognised in the Constitution as an equal part of the legal order collectively with common law. This chapter examines policy and legislative frameworks that have had an impact on the recognition of customary land rights emanating from pre-colonial Namibia and related cases of communal land claims in post-apartheid Namibia, against the background of the protections that the Constitution gives to cultural property rights. The chapter concludes that the cause of incorporation has not been well-served by the legislature which has shied away from protecting the deep values embedded in customary law by deferring too readily to Western notions that have found their way into Namibia's Constitution. The chapter concludes by advocating for a different approach that is more considerate to the values underpinning customary law even where, as sometimes happens, these have been obscured by practices that appear adverse to Namibia's Constitution.

In the greater parts of Namibia, the land question remains a fundamental subject with regards to food security, efforts to reduce poverty and the quest to realise the much sought after yet "elusive" economic development. In principle, the land question is of fundamental significance to Namibian societies and their economies of scale. Land has a significant and direct bearing on the livelihood of over 80 per cent of Namibia's land-based population (Becker 1997; Barnes 1995; Fuller 1999, 111–117; Fuller 2004, 83–86; Horn 2005, 81–94; Kaapama 2007, 29–49; Melber 2005, 135–204; Melber 2007; Mendelsohn et al. 2009). It also impacts the country's gross domestic product (GDP) as well as wealth and employment creation. Regrettably, due to the never-ending scramble for African land, it has become insufficient in many areas (Warikandwa and Nhemachena 2017, 529–549; Warikandwa et al. 2017), including Namibia. Population growth and unrelenting pressure on the land as a resource have led to its inadequacy (Warikandwa and Nhemachena 2017, 529). Incessant pressure on land has been attributed to a sharp increase in competition for land between different multiple land users (Bank of Namibia 2012). Such land users include but are not limited to the following: (1) foreign investors, (2) well-connected political and urban elites, (3) white livestock and crop farmers, (4) an emerging class of black bourgeoisie livestock and crop farmers and (5) the marginalised small scale farmers (Bank of Namibia 2012, 11). The globalisation driven socio-economic transformation has also eroded the rules and institutions of traditional authorities as well as customary norms that were used in administering land rights in most African communities, including Namibia (Von Carlowitz and Mandimika 2015, 2015).

In view of the outlined issues, discourses on land have assumed prominence in Namibia, largely due to perpetual injustices inherited from the colonial past, characterised by substantively unjust added to unequal land distribution patterns. The inequality in land distribution patterns has significant socio-economic and -political ramifications at both national and regional levels. Informing such inequalities are matters related to control over limited resources as well as the distribution of wealth and power in most Namibian, and indeed, African communities (Warikandwa and Nhemachena 2017, 529–549).

To address such challenges, a number of African countries, including Namibia, have adopted legislation and policies aimed at reforming land relations in the post-colonial era. In Namibia, such policy and legislative reforms have taken place within the broader context of restructuring societal relations in the country's communities. It is, therefore, not surprising that Namibia has adopted a Constitution inspired by principles of human rights (Chapter 3 of the Namibian Constitution), freedom (article 21 of the Namibian Constitution), "democratic" culture (article 19 of the Namibian Constitution) and good governance (article 18 of the Namibian Constitution). This Constitution enshrines fundamental principles on land relations which in turn are articulated through relevant legislation (article 16(1) of the Namibian Constitution guarantees all persons the right to acquire, own and dispose of all forms of property in any part of Namibia. Article 16(2) gives the power to parliament to make laws that would allow the state or a lawfully established body or organ to expropriate property in the public interest, on the condition that the state pays what is termed "just compensation" to those affected by such an expropriation. See also the Agricultural (Commercial) Land Reform Act 6 of 1995; and Communal Land Reform Act 5 of 2002).

In Namibia, settler colonialism caused a racially predisposed land distribution pattern (Hinz 2010, 3–12). Most communal areas in the country became over-populated with challenges related to land degradation and tenure insecurity being widespread. Such colonial legacy has led to calls for land redistribution and raised tenure security issues reaching a crescendo. The second Namibia Land Conference held towards the end of the year 2018 provides evidence to this claim (Government of Namibia 2018). It is common cause that discourses on land are politically charged with the independence of Namibia being centred on land, amongst other issues. To that end, land policies and legislation that are succinctly clear and well-articulated are significant to realising development and socio-economic stability in Namibia. The realisation of most basic human rights and carrying out of economic activities are largely dependent on access to and ownership of land hence underscoring its significance thereof (Warikandwa and Nhemachena 2017, 529).

In post-colonial Namibia, disputes around a need to reform the land tenure system resonate with similar practices unfolding in other parts of Africa. This chapter thus undertakes a study of discourses and legislative frameworks on the place of customary law in ascertaining authority over communal land and the nature of communal land rights in Namibia. Particular emphasis will be placed on Namibia's legislation and policies aimed at reforming communal or customary land tenure. Epsen and Cousins pointed out that the use of registered forms of private property entitlements to land, as a legal mechanism to replace customary tenure, is now deemed as being unsuitable by policy analysts and policy-makers (Espen and Cousins 2009, 1–9). The central question in land tenure reform in Namibia, and other parts of Africa is how to identify and protect land rights that are clearly distinct from private property (Espen and Cousins 2009, 1–2). Such land rights are communal in nature, yet cannot be classified as being purely traditional, owing to the significant impact of the swift political and socio-economic transformation that has characterised the post-colonial era in Africa (Espen and Cousins 2009, 1–2).

It has remained a predicament from a policy perspective to determine the type of rights, held by a specific category of claimants, which have to be secured by way of land tenure reform (Goheen and Shipton 1992, 318). Further, the manner in which they are secured has to be established to ensure that the existence of such rights does not just "add to possibilities of manipulation and confusion" (Goheen and Shipton 1992, 318) and result in a broad range of unintended outcomes. The fundamental problem is to describe intricate and dynamic actualities which can guide the policy and legislative formulation as well as the nature of such laws and policies.

A fundamental subject of land tenure reform is the aspect of authority over land issues and the formulation of suitable institutional frameworks for land administration in Namibia (Cotula et al. 2004). If administration of land matters has to be efficient, democratic, transparent and accountable, the recognition of the role of indigenous people as well as implementation of customary law to ensure land tenure is of the essence (Cotula et al. 2004). Lund argued that: "From an analytical perspective, authority and power dynamics are key to understanding how tenure regimes work in practice, since 'struggles over property are as much about the scope and constitution of authority as about access to resources'" (Lund 2002, 11–43).

This chapter will further contend that communal or customary land tenure regimes are not solely confined to tradition and therefore not static, as often argued by scholars theorising from the North, but dynamic and evolving just like customary law. Nevertheless, several significant interconnections can be ascertained over space and time, which emanate from pre-colonial land relations. Such values, embedded in socio-political life, have reinforced and influenced the continuing adaptation of land tenure systems across Africa.

It will be proposed that the most suitable approach to land tenure reform in Namibia is to ensure that valid customary law occupation and land use rights become the point of departure for recognising such rights and for the formulation of institutional frameworks for land governance in the country. In many instances, occupation and use rights are entrenched in land tenure systems which are communal in character. The book chapter thus explores the prospects as well as challenges of such an approach to land tenure reform and governance in Namibia.

COMMUNAL LAND RIGHTS AND CUSTOMARY LAW: A HISTORICAL OVERVIEW

Namibia is characterised by a dual land tenure system. About 43 per cent of Namibia's land area is held under freehold title (generally referred to as the commercial sector), whereas 15 per cent consists of proclaimed state land such as game parks (Werner 2015, 67–87). The remaining 42 per cent consists of non-freehold or communal land (Werner 2015, 67–87). After independence, the new Namibian Government initiated an ambitious Land Reform programme (Werner 2015, 67; Malan and Hinz 1997). It sought to improve access to agricultural land for previously disadvantaged communities as added to securing the tenure of households and individuals who hold land under different customary land tenure regimes (Werner 2015, 67).

A National Conference on Land Reform and the Land Question was hosted by the Namibia Government, in 1991, to discuss how the country's Land Reform programme in the freehold and non-freehold sectors should be conceptualised and implemented (Mendelsohn 2006, 39; Cousins and Claassens 2004, 139–158). The general consensus at the conference was "that the communal areas should be retained, developed and expanded where necessary," as communal lands sustained a majority of the Namibian population, "especially poor farmers" (Werner 2015, 67). To protect the rights of access to communal land for farming households, it was resolved that new applicants for access to communal land "should take account of the rights and customs of the local communities living there" and that "farmers with the potential to become commercial farmers can be encouraged, if necessary through government schemes, to acquire land in the commercial sector" (Werner 2015, 68). Lastly, "farmland now used by large farmers in the communal areas should not be expanded and in future should be reduced to make space for small farmers" (Werner 2015, 68).

"COMMUNAL TENURE" AS A CONCEPT

Developing the appropriate terminology to define Africa's property regimes is challenging due to the historically specific character of legal concepts and language derived from European systems of law, which therefore may not be appropriate in African contexts. This difficulty was acknowledged by colonial administrators and in early anthropological research (Bohannon 1963, 101–115; Okoth-Ogendo 1989, 6–17). According to Biebuyck, "common general formulae like . . . ultimate or sovereign rights, rights of allocation or of control, or rigid oppositions between ownership, possession, use and usufruct . . . have often obscured understanding of the scope and nature of rights and claims relating to land" (Biebuyck 1963, 52).

The term "communal tenure" as used in the African context has been debatable. It appears to imply joint or collective ownership and use of all land and natural resources, yet most African systems, as a matter of fact, include clearly defined individual or family rights to some types of land and land use as well as common property resources (Biebuyck 1963, 52). These systems generally involve the conferral of rights on the basis of accepted group membership, and a degree of group control or supervision of land matters. This approach "relativises" individual rights to a greater degree than in systems of private property (Biebuyck 1963, 52). Bruce argued that "communal tenure" systems are in fact *mixed* tenure regimes, comprising variable bundles of individual, family, sub-group and larger group rights and duties in relation to a variety of natural resources (Bruce 1993; Bruce and Mighot-Adholla 1994).

The term "communal tenure" is preferred in this chapter primarily as a way of distinguishing this tenure system from that of individual, private property ownership. The term "community-based property rights" should be used, since the distinguishing feature of these forms of property rights is that they derive their authority from the community in which they operate, not from the nation-state (Berry 1990). This would also be an acceptable term in the African context, but of course would require clarity as to what constitutes a "community."

The terms "customary," "communal" and "traditional" tend to be used interchangeably; yet do not necessarily have the same meaning. It is possible "to have communal tenure systems that support poor people's livelihood strategies that are not based on customary law or dependent on traditional institutions for their administration" (Bennett 2008).

AN AFRICAN PERSPECTIVE TO COMMUNAL LAND TENURE

This section of the chapter attempts to delineate the key features of contemporary systems of communal tenure in Africa. This sets out the basis for a discussion of tenure reform policy issues.

Customary Land Rights in the Colonial Era

A number of scholars have described the extensive reconfiguration of "custom" that took place in the early colonial period (Chanock 1991, 61–84; Chanock, for example, suggests that: There is a profound connection between the use of the chieftaincy as an institution of colonial government and the development of the customary law of land tenure. The development of the concept of a leading customary role for the chiefs with regard to ownership and allocation of land was fundamental to the evolution of the paradigm of customary tenure . . . the chiefs were seen as the holders of land with rights of administration and allocation. Rights in land were seen as flowing downward). This feudal model fitted well with British ways of thinking about states and societies. It linked British land law and colonial contexts, and served the interests of regimes seeking to acquire land for settlers (Chanock 1991, 61). The Privy Council pronounced in 1926 that the notion of individual ownership is foreign to native ideas (Chanock 1991, 61). Land belongs to the community not to the individual (Chanock 1991, 66). In contrast with these models, there is much evidence in the early colonial period of both the vigorous assertion of individual rights and of land sales, during a period of major changes in settlement and land use, and when new economic opportunities were emerging (Chanock 1991, 66). People spread out from fortified villages and hilltop settlements to cultivate new lands they had been unable to use safely before, and were less dependent on immediate kin for security (Chanock 1991, 66). The colonial state was generally happy to concede to them rights of permanent occupation and use, which accorded well with the promotion of new crops and markets, but the question of whether these rights could be bequeathed, and by whom and to whom was more contentious (Chanock 1991, 69–70). Prohibition of sales of "communal" land became a central feature of colonial land policy (Chanock 1991, 69–70).

In addition, there was "spirited opposition to individuation" from within the African society itself. This was partly because the ambitions of settlers and corporations to increase their land holdings and to limit those of Africans aroused the resentment and anxiety of peoples already displaced and fearing further loss of their land (Chanock 1991, 70; Warikandwa and Nhemachena 2017, 529–549). Given the politics of the colonial situation, land rights had to be discussed in terms of groups. As such, communalism was "a way of certifying African control of occupation, use, and allocation of land, rather than a description of rights exercised . . . Individualism was a code word for sale to Europeans" (Chanock 1991, 66). Under these conditions, what had previously been porous boundaries between villages and chieftaincies were now vigorously enforced (Chanock 1991, 66).

Chanock proposed stepping back from attempts at systematisation and from "ideologies of traditional communalism" (Chanock 1991, 70, 72–73; A cultivator might say "mine" when title was challenged, or if it was advantageous to sell or mortgage, may think in terms of "ours" – in terms of nuclear family – when asserting a right of inheritance against a larger group of kin, or "ours" in terms of a lineage – if the claimant was outside the lineage (as a spouse might be)). Rather, he contended that questions should be asked about specific conflicts of interest over land during the colonial period. Such questions are as follows: (1) just who was pressing for a greater individualisation of rights? (2) What sort of rights did they have in mind? and (3) who was resisting this pressure, and why? Chanock concludes that "an indigenous system of land tenure did not exist under colonial conditions" and that its "shadow" was used to deny the establishment of freehold tenure for Africans in an increasingly capitalist economy (Chanock 1991, 70). This also "distorted the rights recognizable and assertable in the customary land tenure system" (Chanock 1991, 82).

Colson had previously advanced a similar argument as Chanock, noting that customary courts were under the control of colonial officials, whose stereotypes of African land tenure were used to assess the legality of decisions (Colson 1971, 193–215). Systems of communal tenure with "precisely defined rules" came into being, that now inhibited the development of individual rights in unused land because it was deemed that "such rights encroached upon the ancient right of some community, lineage, or 'tribal' polity" (Colson 1971, 197). This was despite the fact that in those parts of the reserves located near railway lines, where commercial farming proved to be profitable, "cultivators improved their fields, passed them on to heirs, and treated them as though they were a form of private property," engaging in both sales and rental (Colson 1971, 209).

Biebuyck's overview of changes in land tenure in the early colonial period pointed out the influence of a growing scarcity of land due to increased population (Warikandwa et al. 2017, 453–493), agricultural development, the development of new markets and growing demand for good quality land; new ideologies of inheritance and economic co-operation; new legislation and interventions by the courts; and large-scale resettlement of people (Biebuyck 1963, 1–64). Biebuyck also observed that:

> in many situations the growth of a feeling of insecurity and of hostility towards outsiders, as the outcome of increased land scarcity and greater demand for land, have resulted in stressing the concepts of inalienability, of group ownership and of ritual sanction in land tenure. (Biebuyck 1963, 60)

Land tenure is thus always historically situated and patterns of change and continuity emerge from the interactions and contestations of heterogeneous interests which are both enabled and constrained by wider political dynamics, unequal economic structures, the operation of markets and cultural discourses and practices (Moore 1998, 33–49). Historically informed ethnographies suggest that land-holders and land authorities have sometimes retained elements of "customary land tenure," sometimes radically reinvented it, and sometimes moved on and effectively abandoned claims to land based on past identities and values (Moore 1998, 33).

TRANSFORMATION AND SUSTAINABILITY IN THE CONTEMPORARY ERA

Competition and conflict over land are increasing in Africa because of a number of intersecting processes: (1) the need of many rural families to produce more from their land even though inputs are declining; (2) civil servants and others in employment seeking to produce food and cash crops from family land; (3) the state and environmental groups trying to extend the area under conservation; (4) and the intensification of the exploitation of resources such as minerals, wildlife, water, and trees (Peters 2004, 269–314; Peters 2002, 45–66; Daley and Hobley 2005; Woodhouse 2003, 1705–1720; Warikandwa and Nhemachena 2017, 529). According to Peters and other scholars, these realities require analysts to go beyond formulations of land being "socially embedded" to raise questions about "the type of social and political relations in which land is situated, particularly with reference to relations of inequality – of class, ethnicity, gender and age" (Peters 2004, 278). Peters saw a key "socio-cultural dynamic of differentiation emerging within social units such as the family, lineage, village, 'tribe' or ethnically defined group, which can be understood as 'a process of narrowing in the definition of belonging', with 'group boundaries (becoming) more exclusively defined'" (Peters 2004, 302).

Cotula and Toulmin assessed evidence from across Africa on the cause, extent and effects of changes in "customary" land tenure regimes, in the context of profound structural transformation (Cotula and Toulmin 2007, 103–111). The impacts of social transformation vary substantially because of the diversity of local contexts, and the assumption that population growth leads inevitably to individualisation does not hold in all cases – in some it is associated with the "rediscovery" of collective dimensions of land tenure (Cotula and Toulmin 2007, 105). They emphasise that the dynamic and adaptive character of customary systems is nothing new – far from being static, such systems have always been reinterpreted to fit changing circumstances. In their view, the "customary" and the "statutory" are now intertwined in "complex mosaics" of resource tenure, and the line between the "formal" and the "informal" is increasingly blurred (Cotula and Toulmin 2007, 109). Given that land access typically involves multiple and overlapping rights over the same resource, and that claims evolve and are continuously renegotiated, determining who has rights to which resources is far from straightforward (Cotula and Toulmin 2007, 109).

Other scholars have drawn attention to the increasing prevalence of land being acquired through a variety of market transactions, including purchase, rental and sharecropping, in defiance of the idea that "customary" land tenure prohibits such alienability (Andre 2003, 153–172; Chimhowu and Woodhouse 2006, 346–371; Woodhouse 2003, 1705–1720; Lund 2002, 11–43; Warikandwa and Nhemachena 2017, 529). This brings with it "an increasing individualisation of control of land and in some instances its alienation from any form of customary authority, amounting to effective privatisation of land" (Chimhowu and Woodhouse 2005, 392).

A picture thus emerges of an evolutionary change towards individual property and the disappearance of "customary" identities and claims to land. Mathieu *et al* suggested that where land becomes scarce and has increasing economic value, "there is a social demand for more individualised, precise and formalised land ownership rights," but that "this change is not so simple, nor is it linear or automatic" (Mathieu Zongo and Pare 2003, 109–128). The process is "totally embedded in social relationships" and hence "contradictory, complex and ambiguous," since past meanings of land "retain their significance in the local social reality" (Chimhowu and Woodhouse 2005, 401). Chimhowu and Woodhouse acknowledged that "the transition from the 'gifts' expected as tokens of acknowledgement of customary authority and of anticipated reciprocity, to payments more closely related to exchange values of the land, is not always easy to define" (Chimhowu and Woodhouse 2005, 401). Lund pointed out that formalisation of individual and private titles, as in Kenya, has not necessarily produced greater certainty and security of land rights because of a lack of social legitimacy, and that processes of "informal formalisation" probably depend on a degree of uncertainty remaining as to the status of such transactions at the "margins of the law as well as of customs" (Lund 2001, 144–162).

More generally, processes of change often generate resistance, contestation and the re-assertion of "customary" claims to land. As Peters (2004, 302) suggested, they are inevitably "uneven and contradictory" in character. "Moreover, boundaries, physical and legal, do not automatically ensure exclusion where (some of) the excluded reject the legitimacy of the exclusion" (Peters 2004, 303). Alongside change is continuity in the nature of land rights, argued for and actively reproduced because of its advantages for many within the rural population, including, in some contexts, women (Peters 2004, 303). Characteristics of flexibility and negotiability, which in many places have given way to "differentiation, displacement and exclusion," are still "an important asset to small-scale producers across the continent" (Peters 2004, 305–306).

DO AFRICAN COMMUNAL TENURE SYSTEMS HAVE "DISTINCTIVE FEATURES?"

Okoth-Ogendo provided a persuasive analysis of the nature of property rights in Africa (Okoth-Ogendo 1989, 6–17). The core of his argument is that a "right" signifies a power that society allocates to its members to execute a range of functions in respect of any given subject matter; where that power amounts to exclusive control one can talk of "ownership" of "private property" (Okoth-Ogendo 1989, 6–17). However, it is not essential that power and exclusivity of control coincide in this manner (Okoth-Ogendo 1989, 6–17). Access to this power (a "right") and its control are distinct, and there are diverse social and cultural rules and vocabularies for defining access and control (Cousins 2008, 109–137; Claassens and Cousins, 3–31; Bennett 2008).

In Africa, land rights tend to be attached to membership of some unit of production; are specific to a resource management or production function or group of functions; and are tied to and maintained through active participation in the processes of production and reproduction at particular levels of social organisation. Control of such access is always attached to "sovereignty" (in its non-proprietary sense) and vested in the political authority of society expressed at different levels of units of production (Okoth-Ogendo 1989, 11). Control, according to Okoth-Ogendo, occurs primarily for the purposes of guaranteeing access to land for production purposes (Okoth-Ogendo 1989, 11).

In African land tenure regimes, there is no coincidence of access and control, and property does not involve the vesting of the full complement of power over land that is possible (private property), and variations in power (rights) derive from social relations, not the market (Okoth-Ogendo 1989, 11; Benjaminsen and Lund 2003). Rights over land are trans-generational and control is exercised through members of the units of production and is not simply the product of "political superordination" (Okoth-Ogendo 1989, 11; Benjaminsen and Lund 2003). Different land uses attract varying degrees of control at different levels of sociopolitical organisation (e.g., allocations of arable are often controlled at the family level, while grazing is the concern of a wider segment of society) (Okoth-Ogendo 1989, 11; Bennett 2008).

Using this conceptual framework, the distinctive features of African tenure regimes can be listed:

- Land rights are embedded in a range of social relationships and units, including households and kinship networks and various levels of "community"; the relevant social identities are often multiple, overlapping and therefore "nested" or layered in character (e.g., individual rights within households, households within kinship networks, and kinship networks within local communities) (Cousins 2009, 8; Chimhowu, 897–903).
- Land rights are inclusive rather than exclusive in character, being shared and relative. They include both strong individual and family rights to residential and arable land and access to common property resources such as grazing, forests and water (Cousins 2009, 8).
- Rights are derived from accepted membership of a social unit, and can be acquired via birth, affiliation or allegiance to a group and its political authority, or transactions of various kinds (including gifts, loans and purchases). They are somewhat similar to citizenship entitlements in modern democracies (Cousins 2009, 8).
- Access to land (through defined rights) is distinct from control of land (through systems of authority and administration) (Cousins 2009, 8).
- Control is concerned with guaranteeing access and enforcing rights, regulating the use of common property resources, overseeing mechanisms for redistributing access (trans-generationally), and resolving disputes over claims to land. It is often located within a hierarchy of nested systems of authority, with many functions located at local or lower levels (Cousins 2009, 8).
- Social, political and resource boundaries while often relatively stable are also flexible and negotiable, given the nested character of social identities, rights and authority structure (Cousins 2009, 8).

THE NATURE OF COMMUNAL AREAS IN NAMIBIA: A LEGAL AND POLICY PERSPECTIVE

The Traditional Authorities Act 17 of 1995 (TAT) defines communal area as that land which is "habitually inhabited by a specific traditional community" (section 1 of the TAT). A traditional community in turn is defined as an "indigenous, homogenous, endogamous social grouping of persons that shares a common language, culture and customs and recognizes a traditional authority" (section 1 of the TAT). The legal definition alludes to a common characteristic of communal tenure systems across the African continent, which includes "a degree of community control over who is allowed into the group, and thus being able to obtain residential and farming rights, which are usually strong and secure" (section 1 of the TAT). The legal definition also alludes to homogenous groups of people, suggesting a high degree of social equity in communal systems (section 1 of the TAT).

The reality in Namibia's communal areas at independence and since then has been much more complex than simple legal definitions suggest. To start with, communal areas were characterised by growing inequalities. It was estimated in the early 1990s that approximately 50 per cent of farming households in the north-central regions, for example, did not own any livestock (Werner 2015, 69; Cox et al. 1998). Farming was no longer restricted to subsistence farming but was becoming commercial in orientation, at least for a small but growing group of farmers (Werner 2015, 69). Increasing inequalities in asset ownership characterised communal areas across the country (Werner 2015, 69). The individualisation of communal grazing areas for private farming supports this assertion.

The growing enclosures of communal grazing areas were also a manifestation of the weakening of customary governance systems in some communal areas. The legitimacy of traditional authorities to administer customary land rights in some areas was called into question (Werner 2015, 69). A socio-economic survey conducted across Namibia in preparation for the First National Land Conference found widespread dissatisfaction with the system of land allocation in the war ravaged north-central regions (Werner 2015, 69). The treatment of women's rights and private enclosures was singled out. By contrast, traditional authorities in Caprivi-now Zambezi-Region, were "highly respected" and their continued role in land governance was widely supported. In the southern communal areas, issues of privatisation of communal land rather than a lack of legitimacy of traditional leaders were more prominent (Werner 2015, 69). This, in turn, pitched the interests of a "rich, politically powerful minority . . . at odds with those of the poor majority" (Werner 2015, 69). Tenure reform in Namibia thus had to address a complex situation, characterised by significant regional differences (Werner 2015, 69).

The only commonality across the country was that under the Namibian Constitution, the state is the legal owner of all communal land (schedules 5(1) and 5(3) of the Namibian Constitution). This, as Adams *et al* have argued, "can be an opportunity or a difficulty, depending on how tenure reform is perceived to affect the interests of those with power and influence" (Martin et al. 2000, 1–15; Fiona and Werner 1990). The state had the power to give effect to the consensus resolutions of the First National Land Conference, which called for the development of communal land in the interests of poorer sections of society, or assert the interests of the new elite by promoting the commercialisation of communal areas through a transformation of customary tenure systems to individual rights (Werner 2015, 70).

NATIVE RESERVES IN SOUTH-WEST AFRICA

The land question in Namibia was shaped by large-scale expropriation of land and livestock from indigenous communities (Werner 2015, 70). This process was uneven, insofar as it affected primarily communities that practised extensive livestock farming in the southern, more arid parts of the country (Werner 2015, 70). Communities that combined livestock farming with cultivation were largely spared. The subsequent establishment of a Police Zone separated those parts that were settled by white settlers as a result of land dispossession, and the mixed farming areas in north-central and north-eastern Namibia (Werner 1993, 135–146).

After 1915, so-called native reserves were created in the Police Zone to provide a wage subsidy particularly to the developing commercial farming sector, which was the preserve of white settlers (Werner 1993, 135; Sikopo et al. 2016). These areas were never intended to "create reserves to which tribes could remove themselves and thus restore their old tribal methods of living under the Chiefs" (Werner 1993, 135; Sikopo et al. 2016). Instead, married women and children should live on the reserves and have the benefit of the milk from their cattle . . . men should go out like the natives of the Transvaal and leave their women at home on the reserves until they return (National Archives Namibia (NAN) 1920).

Between 1923 and 1926, a total of sixteen such native reserves were established. The system of "native administration" – and hence the administration of land – in native reserves in the Police Zone differed from the system pursued in areas outside the Police Zone (Werner 2015, 70). The existence of strong and relatively well-defined traditional leaders outside the Police Zone made it possible for the colonial administration to implement a system of indirect rule (Werner 2015, 70). By contrast, the large-scale process of land dispossession of livestock farming communities in the Police Zone also destroyed their traditional leadership (Werner 2015, 70). This was used as a pretext by the colonial administration to fashion an administrative system that minimised the powers of traditional leaders and gave colonial officials extensive powers to administer native reserve (*Uazengisa & Another v The Executive Committee of the Administration for Herero's and 11 Others*, Judgement, the Supreme Court of South West Africa, 22 September 1989, 57–58 Annexure 'D'; Werner 2018). An "authoritarian local administrative structure" was established in native reserves, "which combined a strict line of command running from central offices in Windhoek via the district magistrate to the reserve Superintendent" (Werner 2015, 70).

In terms of colonial legislation, traditional leaders in the Police Zone were stripped of all their powers relating to the allocation and cancellation of land rights (Werner 2015, 70; Thiem 2014, decade of communal land reform. Review and lessons learnt, with a focus on communal land rights registration). These now became the exclusive preserve of colonial officials and in particular reserve superintendents (Werner 2015, 70). The extent to which these new governance structures effectively replaced customary regimes on the ground has not been established and is likely to have differed across native reserves (Reinhart 2005, 49; Thiem and Muduva 2015). However, the legitimacy of this system was contested as late as the 1980s, when the need to clarify the validity of customary laws and the powers of traditional leaders resulted in several court cases (*Ndisiro v Gemeenskapsowerheid van die Mbanderu Gemeenskap van die Rietfonteinblok in Hereroland en 9 ander: Uitspraak, Hooggeregshof van Suidwes-Afrika*, June 7, 1984; *Uazengisa & Another v The Executive Committee of the Administration for Herero's and 11 Others*, Judgement, 1989).

Colonial policy was focused on limiting class formation in the reserves to ensure the continued supply of labour to the colonial economy (Werner 1998, 193). Opportunities to accumulate limited amounts of capital by a few were thwarted, as this might have led to "instilling a certain greed for money" that would gradually undermine "the co-operation that is so essential for the good management of reserves" (Werner 2015, 71). Capital investments in water supply and other essential infrastructure were kept to a minimum and were tightly controlled by the colonial administration, enabling the latter to control economic development in native reserves and ensuring that sufficient labour was available for settler farming (Werner 2015, 71).

THE ODENDAAL COMMISSION

The Odendaal Commission developed a discourse on communal land development that differed from the previous policies in so far as it no longer regarded native reserves simply as labour reservoirs but as potential sites of capital accumulation (Republic of South Africa, Report of the Commission of Enquiry into South West Africa Affairs 1962/1963 (No. RP 12/1964); Pretoria 1964, 425). It acknowledged that "social stratification according to income and level of occupation" had taken place as "the traditional system of supplying their own needs" had gradually been "supplanted by a money system peculiar to the system of the Whites" (Republic of South Africa, Report of the Commission of Enquiry into South West Africa Affairs 1962/1963 (No. RP 12/1964); Pretoria 1964, 425). It proposed to capitalise on this by providing blacks with "the opportunity, necessary assistance and encouragement to find an outlet for their new experience and capabilities" Republic of South Africa, Report of the Commission of Enquiry into South West Africa Affairs 1962/1963 (No. RP 12/1964), Pretoria 1964, 429).

Although the Odendaal Commission was "much more an intervention into politics than agricultural production per se," its proposals on agriculture were developed in the Five Year Plan for the Development of the Native Areas (Pankhurst 1996, 418). This plan recommended specific interventions for improving agricultural production in the communal areas (Werner 2015, 72. See also NAN OVA, 49, 6/8/4/1 Vergadering van die Onderkomitee oor Dorpsbeplanning en ontwikkeling en Landbouontwikkeling van die Beplannings- en Koordinerende Komitee op Woensdag, September 2, 1970, 2). The underlying assumption guiding its deliberations was that "agricultural planning must . . . pave the way in converting an existing subsistence economy to an exchange economy" (Adams and Werner 1990, 161).

On the basis of detailed assessments of soil types and carrying capacities in existing "native reserves," the Five Year Plan recommended far-reaching measures to transform customary land tenure systems into more individualised land tenure (Werner 2015, 72). It recommended "a large scale fencing programme" for the predominantly Otjiherero speaking reserves, arguing that "proper pasture rotation" was "a prerequisite for optimal utilization of available resources" that could only be achieved through enclosure (Werner 2015, 72).

Such recommendations for large-scale fencing programmes were not made for all communal areas. But the privatisation of communal range lands by way of fencing as a necessary condition for improved animal husbandry and range management became firmly embedded in agricultural planning in communal areas generally (Kerven 1998, 65–90). Native Affairs officials soon promoted the individualisation of customary rangeland tenure through the introduction of fencing in other communal areas. In 1970, a sub-committee of the "Planning and Co-ordinating Committee" in Owamboland submitted that "the present system of land ownership and utilization had a limiting influence on the administration (extension) and production (lack of continuity) as economic asset [*sic*]" (Cliffe 1994, 33. See also South West Africa, A Five Year Plan for the Development of the Native Areas, Windhoek, 1966).

The implementation of the recommendations of the Five Year Plan started in earnest in the Okamatapati area of former Hereroland East in 1970/71 (Werner 2015, 73). Due to the shortage of underground water, a pipeline was constructed from Berg Aukas to Okamatapati with the objective of opening up new pastures for individual livestock farmers (Adams and Werner 1990, 161). Branch lines from the main pipeline supplied water to fifty-six farming units, covering approximately 275,000 ha (Kerven 1998, 65–90). Surveys were carried out for the erection of fences (Kerven 1998, 65). In the Owambo Mangetti, ninety-six farms were similarly surveyed and allocated to individual farmers. (Kerven 1998, 65; Werner 2015, 73).

These official developments set in motion a spate of private enclosures in communal areas. In response to the official surveying of communal land in the Owambo Mangetti, the Ndonga Traditional Authority (TA) authorised the fencing of communal land by people under its jurisdiction (Kerven 1998, 66). These authorisations were recorded by the TA and were found to exist in the mid-1990s (Kerven 1998, 66). Using these authorised enclosures as precedent, many wealthy livestock owners proceeded to fence off communal land at their own expense with the objective of improving livestock husbandry and promoting commercialisation (Werner 2015, 73).

POST-INDEPENDENCE DISCOURSES ON COMMUNAL LAND IN NAMIBIA

During the first ten years of independence, little attention was paid to land administration in the communal areas. The new elite of well-connected, wealthy people exploited the policy and the legal vacuum during the first decade of independence to fence off commonages for their own private use (Werner 2015, 75). Customary governance systems were further eroded in the absence of clear guidelines on the powers and mandates of traditional leaders, leading to what some would call open access regimes (Werner 2015, 75). That the role of traditional leaders in a democratic Namibia was a contested issue is confirmed by the appointment of the Commission of Inquiry into matters relating to Chiefs, Headmen and other Traditional or Tribal Leaders while preparations for the First National Land Conference were underway (Republic of Namibia, Report by the Commission of Inquiry into Matters Relating to Chiefs, Headmen and Other Traditional or Tribal Leaders, Windhoek 1991, 1). It was tasked with investigating the appointment and recognition of traditional leaders as well as their powers, duties and functions and to make recommendations on "the viability or otherwise of traditional or tribal authorities," but left the land issue to be dealt with by government (Republic of Namibia 1997). The delay in passing the Communal Land Reform Act of 2002 was partly caused by contestation about the future powers of traditional leaders in communal land administration (Republic of Namibia 1997).

The first Outline of a National Land Policy and the first Communal Land Bill represented attempts by the state to assert itself in communal land administration by displacing traditional authorities (Republic of Namibia 1997). Underlying the proposed tenure reform was Article 100 of the Constitution (article 100 of the Namibia Constitution titled, "Sovereign Ownership of Natural Resources" provides as follows: "Land, water and natural resources below and above the surface of the land and in the continental shelf and within the territorial waters and the exclusive economic zone of Namibia shall belong to the State if they are not otherwise lawfully owned"), which vests ownership of communal land in the state. As the owner of such land, the state proposed to create regional land boards to take over land administration functions in communal areas (Iyambo 1997, 18; Werner 2015, 75). The Outline of a National Land Policy proposed to transfer "all authority over and rights to communal land which are currently exercised or held by traditional leaders and other customary authorities on behalf of communal area residents to the Regional Land Boards" (Republic of Namibia 1997, 163–166). Traditional authorities duly recognised under the Traditional Authorities Act could be designated to perform such land administration functions as Regional Land Boards might have specified (Werner 2015, 75–76).

These proposals were modelled in part on the practices in Botswana, where communal land is vested in Land Boards (Werner 2015, 75–76). They amounted to stripping traditional leaders of all powers with regard to the administration of customary tenure. Part of the reason for attempting to restrict the powers of traditional leaders in communal land administration must be sought in the particular form of state governance that was established at independence (Werner 2015, 76). At the national level, political leaders were elected to the National Assembly based on party lists (Werner 2000, 2). The number of members of parliament from each party was determined by the percentage of votes the party obtained during national elections.

Crucially, these elected representatives at the national level did not have a constituency to which they were answerable (Malan and Hinz 1997, 69). Regional Councillors, on the other hand, were elected in thirteen regions by constituencies to which they were answerable (Malan and Hinz 1997, 196). Within this newly established political structure, only traditional authorities enjoyed widespread legitimacy and considerable influence in areas under their jurisdiction (Werner 2015, 76). It is conceivable that traditional authorities with their well-established areas of jurisdictions in the rural areas might have been perceived as threats to attempts by the new state to establish itself in rural areas (Werner 2015, 76). During a consultative conference on communal land administration in 1996, the state's proposals to relegate traditional leaders to a subordinate position were rejected out of hand by the traditional leaders in attendance (Malan and Hinz 1997, 69). The general sentiment of traditional leaders from across the country was put very succinctly in a submission by seven traditional authorities from Owambo (*sic*) which stated that "the traditional leaders should not be made to be the back-yard boys of what should be technical and advisory bodies, namely the Regional Land Boards" (Malan and Hinz 1997, 69). The outcome of the conference was that the draft land policy and Communal Land Bill had to be revised to allow the continued participation of traditional authorities in the administration of customary land tenure (section 4(1) of the Communal Land Bill, which proposed to transfer the regulation and control over the occupation and use of communal land to Regional Land Boards, was deleted and the Regional Land Boards were to be composed of persons recommended by traditional authorities). The Conference, which was attended and addressed by senior cabinet ministers, also placed the future of communal land on the agenda. The policy options that faced government at the time were summarised by a senior member of the SWAPO party, who argued that at independence government had three basic options to deal with the existence of first and second class systems of tenure, i.e., freehold and customary tenure (Hamutenya 1997, 32). These were: (1) Nationalising freehold land for redistribution; (2) Completing the process of alienating and privatising all communal land and (3) Continuing with the status quo (Hamutenya 1997, 32).

Each of these options had far-reaching implications. Nationalisation might have resulted in the destabilisation of the agricultural sector with a resultant loss of employment opportunities (Werner 2015, 77). Turning communal areas into private property would have placed most communal land "into the hands of a small elite of white and black landlords," creating large-scale landlessness and destitution (Angula 1997, 51). For these reasons, government opted for the third option, "at least temporarily and then to introduce a process of gradual reform of that system" (Ministry of Lands 1998, 1). The role of the state was to lay "the foundation and framework upon which private economic activities can flourish" (Werner 2015, 77).

The reforms envisaged referred to the gradual transformation of customary tenure systems into private ownership. Arguments presented in favour of this transformation read like a rehash of the recommendations of the Odendaal Commission which reported thirty years earlier. Freehold and customary tenure were now characterised as "first and second class systems of land tenure," a categorisation that was incorporated into the National Land Policy (Ivula-Ithana 1997, 12). What defined second class tenure was that people holding customary land rights were not able to use their land as collateral for credit (Werner 2015, 77). Consequently, they were unable to develop economically. Moreover, because the second class tenure system did not provide for ownership of land, land degradation due to overgrazing and over-cropping ensued (Werner 2015, 77). And finally, little investment was taking place particularly in newly created towns in communal areas because of the absence of private ownership.

Contestation over the future of communal land areas did not only take place in conference halls. While government was procrastinating over where to go with tenure reform in the communal areas, a veritable land reform was taking place on the ground. Reinvigorated by the official privatisation of communal land for private farming and emboldened by the constitutional provisions that the citizens of Namibia had a right to settle wherever they wished, the uncontrolled enclosure of communal grazing areas continued unabated. To this day, the extent of private enclosures on communal land is not known, but is believed to be considerable.

THE COMMUNAL LAND REFORM ACT: AN APPRAISAL OF THE KEY PROVISIONS

The Communal Land Rights Act (CLRA) was promulgated to improve the system of communal land tenure through the creation of Communal Land Boards for specific communal areas. While people initially had rights in respect rights in respect of communal land rights that were not granted under customary law (an illustration of this right is the permission-to-occupy. See section 17(1) and (2) of the CLRA), the CLRA has done away with the current system by converting such rights into rights of land. It is imperative for the purposes of this chapter to outline what communal land is in terms of the CLRA.

THE DEFINITION OF COMMUNAL LAND IN THE CLRA

Section 15 of the CLRA defines communal land in a manner that appears to suggest that the land that was "not otherwise lawfully owned" (Namandje 2018) as contemplated under article 100 of the Namibian Constitution (article 100 of the Namibian Constitution provides that: "Land, water and natural resources below and above the surface of the land and in the continental shelf and within the territorial waters and the exclusive economic zone of Namibia belong to the State if they are not otherwise lawfully owned"). Section 15 of the CLRA provides that:

Extent of communal land

15. (1) Subject to subsection (2), communal land consists of
    (a) the areas described in Schedule 1 to this Act;
    (b) any area which is declared to be communal land under section 16(1)(a);
    (c) any land which is incorporated under section 16(1)(b) into a communal land area referred to in paragraph (a) or (b).
  (2) Where a local authority is situated or established within the boundaries of any communal land area that land comprising such local authority area shall not form part of that communal land area and shall not be communal land.

In principle, section 15 states the areas which constitute communal land in Namibia as described in Schedule 1 of the Act as already pointed out in section 15(1)(a) of the CLRA. In the case of *Ndevahoma v Shimwooshili* (HC-MD-CIV-ACT-OTH-2017/03184) [2019] NAHCMD 32 (January 25, 2019), the courts had to address issues of customary law, communal land, and communal land rights in so far as whether or not the CLRA empowers a leaseholder to cancel a sub-lease and evict a sub-lessee from a communal land area which forms part of communal land as contemplated in section 15. In the *Ndevahoma* case, Ueitele J held that despite the fact that the concept of communal land defies precise definition, it has, in Namibia, generally been understood that communal land includes land owned in trust by the government but administered by traditional authorities who make allocation of parcels of land to members of the community, ordinarily but not exclusively to live thereon, till and or graze thereon and generally to make a living, without acquiring ownership or title to that land (*Ndevahoma v Shimwooshili* (HC-MD-CIV-ACT-OTH-2017/03184) [2019] NAHCMD 32 (January 25, 2019).

ESTABLISHING OF COMMUNAL LANDS

In terms of section 16 of the CLRA, with the approval of the National Assembly, the president may by proclamation declare any defined state land to be communal land, add any state land to an existing communal land area or withdraw a defined area from communal land. Section 16 of the CLRA provides as follows:

Establishment of New Communal Land Areas and Additions to or Subtractions from Communal Land Areas

16. (1) The President, with the approval of the National Assembly, may by proclamation in the Gazette –

(a) declare any defined portion of unalienated State land to be a communal land area;
(b) incorporate as part of any existing communal land area any defined portion of unalienated State land; or
(c) withdraw from any communal land area, subject to the provisions of subsection (2), any defined portion thereof which is required for any purpose in the public,

And in such proclamation make appropriate amendments to schedule 1 to Act so as to include the description of any new communal land area declared under paragraph (a) or to redefine any communal land area affected by any change under paragraph (b) or (c).

(2) Land may be withdrawn from any communal land area under subsection (1)(c), unless all rights held by persons under this Act in respect of such land or any portion thereof have first been acquired by the State and just compensation for the acquisition of such rights is paid to the persons concerned.

In principle section 16 of the CLRA makes provision for the establishment of new communal land areas and additions to or subtractions from communal land areas. When land is withdrawn, it becomes state land and can be disposed of as state-owned land. Compensation is determined either by agreement between the person whose rights are acquired and the minister, or by arbitration under the Arbitration Act (see the Namibia Arbitration Act 42 of 1965). When new communal land is created, added or withdrawn, the changes must be made to Schedule 1 of the CLRA.

IN WHOM IS THE OWNERSHIP OF COMMUNAL LAND VESTED?

In the 1990s, in the post-independence era, there appeared to be an inconsistency between Articles 15, 100 and Schedule 5 of the Constitution of Namibia (Harring 1996, 467). Governmental policy on communal lands emanated from state "ownership" (Geingob 1991). Relying on article 100 of the Namibia Constitution, the then prime minister and now president of the Republic of Namibia, Hage Geingob once stated that, "people in the communal lands (some 65 to 70 percent of the population) have no acknowledged right, independent of the will of the State, to live and farm in Communal Areas" (Geingob 1991). What is thus questioned about this legal position is whether or not the state can just simply disposes 70 per cent of the Namibian population who are settled on communal land. This has left some scholars to argue against the significant blindness in the Namibian Constitution in so far as its failure to recognise or explicitly protect communal lands, which are arguably the most important property rights of a majority of Namibian citizens (Harring 1996, 481). Harring argued that:

> Even if the State "owns" communal land, it should provide for this directly through the political process of constitution-making and not derive its "ownership" indirectly through conscious avoidance, tricks of language, colonial law, or rules of constitutional or statutory construction.

The Constitution of Namibia provides that "all property of which the ownership or control immediately prior to the date of Independence was vested in the Government of South West Africa shall vest in the Government of Namibia" (Schedule 5 of the Constitution of Namibia). However, Muyongo argued that:

> I want to make reference to . . . the fact that very important things . . . were left out (of the Namibia Constitution) and that is the issue of communal land. In this Constitution there is no reference to it, except customary and common law which, to my mind, do not tie in with the very important issue of communal land. We have our people living in these areas, the land belongs to them, but our Constitution has not made reference to it. So, Mr Chairman, I wish to ask that a few of these issues be tackled again . . . so we can allay the fears of our people wherever they may be, that nothing belongs to them is forgotten, that nothing that belongs to them in terms of land is going to be snatched away in a dubious manner. (Namibian Constituent Assembly Debates 1990, 166; Diescho 1994, 30. Diescho argued that, "Since the actual process of drafting the Constitution was done ... and no minority reports and no minutes were kept of the sub-committees that debated and drafted the different sections, nothing is known about the reasons why schedule 5 was not redrafted to deal explicitly with the ownership of communal lands." See further, *Rehoboth Baster Gemeente and Johannes Gerard Adolf Diegaardt v The Government of the Republic of Namibia* A 163/93 1993/10/22)

It is thus argued that the CLRA is recognised state ownership of communal land. Section 17 of the CLRA affirms this position by providing as follows:

> Vesting of communal land
>
> 17. (1) Subject to the provisions of this Act, all communal land areas vest in the State in trust for the benefit of the traditional communities residing in those areas and for the purpose of promoting the economic and

social development of the people of Namibia, in particular the landless and those with insufficient access to land who are not in formal employment or engaged in non-agriculture business activities.

(2) No right conferring freehold ownership is capable of being granted or acquired by any person in respect of any portion of communal land.

Section 17 of the CLRA makes it abundantly clear that all communal land areas belong to the state, which must keep the land in trust for the benefit of the traditional communities living in those areas. The state is enjoined to put systems in place to make sure that communal lands are administered and managed in the interests of those living in those areas. The CLRA also makes it clear that communal land cannot be sold as freehold land to any person. However, in a landmark ruling the Supreme Court of Namibia in *Agnes Kahimbi Kashela v Katima Mulilo Town Council and Others* (SA 15/2017 [2018] NASC 409 16 November 2018). Deputy Chief Justice Damaseb held that rights over communal land that were granted before Namibia's independence are protected by the Constitution and are not terminated when the land becomes the property of a local authority (*Agnes Kahimbi Kashela v Katima Mulilo Town Council and Others* SA 15/2017) [2018] NASC 409 (November 16, 2018); Justice Damaseb held that: "Schedule 5(3) of the Constitution creates a *sui generis* right in favour of the appellant and those similarly situated over communal lands succeeded to by the Government of Namibia and such right continued to exist even when transferred to a local community. He further pointed out that a right created by schedule 5(3) of the Constitution did not necessarily have to be vindicated in terms of article 16(2) of the Constitution because the framers of the Constitution must have intended a remedy to be fashioned by the courts to give effect to the right created by the schedule. In other words where there is a right, there must be a remedy." Most importantly, Damaseb J pointed out that:

> The State as owner of land, in the context of Schedule 5, has social "obligations" which a private owner does not have. It has to use that land for the public good. I do not see what public good is served by a construction of Schedule 5 which has the effect of perpetuating injustices of the past which the Constitution has removed. (*Agnes Kahimbi Kashela v Katima Mulilo Town Council and Others* SA 15/2017) [2018] NASC 409 (November 16, 2018) paragraph 76)

It is thus evident that from the landmark ruling by Damaseb J, the nature and content of a customary land tenure right is a matter either of general knowledge or of historical notoriety (Zeffert and Paizes 2009, 868).

CASE LAW ON COMMUNAL LAND RIGHTS IN NAMIBIA

There are a number of instructive cases that have been decided by Namibian courts in so far as communal land rights are concerned in Namibia. This section will discuss some of the pertinent cases in so far as communal land rights are concerned.

Agnes Kahimbi Kashela v Katima Mulilo Town Council and Others

In *Agnes Kahimbi Kashela v Katima Mulilo Town Council and Others*, Damaseb DCJ commented that the concept (of communal land) defies precise definition (section 33(1)(b)(2) of the CLRA). The Supreme Court further held that the state as the owner of land as prescribed in Schedule 5 of the Constitution of Namibia has an obligation which is not similar to that of a private owner and has the duty to use land for public good. Schedule 5 of the Constitution of Namibia vests all property in the Government of the Republic of Namibia of which the ownership or control immediately prior to the date of Independence was vested in the Government of South-West Africa. The Supreme Court's findings are justified by two arguments that limit the scope of schedule 5 and article 100 of the Constitution of Namibia. Haring pointed out that:

> Schedule 5 and Article 100 provisions in so far as they are applied to communal lands are inconsistent with other provisions of the Constitution, specifically Article 16 and Article 10 fundamental rights to property and equality. The second while it might concede at least "control" of communal lands to the government, would impose on the government a duty to administer the communal lands for the benefit of the native population that lives there. Therefore, even if the government "controls" or even "owns" communal lands, the people who live there have common law or natural law property rights to land that the government must protect. The government has a kind of trust relationship with those lands. In this analysis actual ownership of the land, while never irrelevant, is not of great importance since the government cannot dispose of those lands without carrying out its trust obligation to people who live there. (Harring 1996, 471)

It is common cause that the nature and content of the communal land right does not require proof (*Agnes Kahimbi Kashela* case para 77). As such, the customary land tenure right was regarded as either a matter of general knowledge or historical notoriety (*Agnes Kahimbi Kashela* case para 77).

Ndevahoma v Shimwooshili (HC-MD-CIV-ACT-OTH-2017/03184) [2019] NAHCMD 32 (January 25, 2019)

In the *Ndevahoma* case, it was Namibia has two main land tenure systems: the freehold land tenure system and the customary land tenure system on communal land. As already alluded to in the *Agnes Kahimbi Kashela case* para 77, the concept (of communal land) defies precise definition. Despite the fact that the concept of communal land defies precise definition, it has, in Namibia, generally been understood that communal land includes land owned in trust by the government but administered by traditional authorities who make allocation of parcels of land to members of the community, ordinarily but not exclusively to live thereon, till and or graze thereon and generally to make a living, without acquiring ownership or title to that land (*Ndevahoma* case para 18).

In contradistinction, freehold land tenure system finds application in respect of surveyed pieces of land in urban areas and "commercial farms" (*Ndevahoma* case para 19). The distinguishing characteristic between communal land and freehold land is that under the freehold land tenure system (whether in an urban area or a commercial farm), the land is surveyed and capable of being privately owned (*Ndevahoma* case para 19). Although the state is under the communal land tenure system, the owner of the land, it holds the land in trust on behalf of traditional communities and their members who live there (*Ndevahoma* case para 20).

Shimuadi v Shirungu 1990 (3) SA 347 (SWA)

The case of *Shimuadi* dealt with the aspect of whether a right of leasehold confers on a party the right to initiate eviction any person who occupies any communal land in contravention of section 17(1) of the CLRA. Section 17(1) of the CLRA provides that: "Subject to the provisions of this Act, all communal land areas vest in the State in trust for the benefit of the traditional communities residing in those areas and for the purpose of promoting the economic and social development of the people of Namibia, in particular the landless and those with insufficient access to land who are not in formal employment or engaged in non-agriculture business activities." Levy, J held that:

> It is trite that in order to eject a defendant from immovable property, a plaintiff need only allege that he is the owner and that the defendant is in occupation thereof. Should the defendant deny any one of these elements, namely that the plaintiff is the owner or that the defendant is in occupation, the *onus* is on the plaintiff to prove the truth of the element which is denied. The plaintiff would succeed in discharging the *onus* of proof in respect of ownership by providing

> registered title deeds in his favour. An inference that plaintiff is the owner would then justifiably be drawn. Should the defendant dispute the validity of the title deeds or that ownership, despite the deeds, is of a "nominal character" ("*nominale aard*"), as in the present case, the *onus* is on the defendant to prove this.

In principle, section 43 of the CLRA provides that a Chief or a Traditional Authority or the board concerned may institute legal action for the eviction of any person who occupies any communal land in contravention of section 17(1) (*Shukifeni v Tow-in-Specialist CC* 2012 (1) NR 219 (HC) and *Angula v Mavulu* (I 2690/2010) [2014] NAHCMD 250 an unreported judgement of this court delivered on August 22, 2014). *Mutrifa v Tjombe* (I 1384/2016) [2017] NAHCMD 162 (June 14, 2017).

In the *Mutrifa* case, the court had to determine whether or not the customary land rights allocated to a party married in community of property in terms of the Communal Land Reform Act 5 of 2002 constitute part of the assets of the joint estate. The court held that the customary land rights awarded to the plaintiff do not accrue to the defendant by virtue of their marriage in community of property. The action instituted and the relief claimed in the *Mutrifa* case did not include a claim for compensation or division in respect of "improvements" made to the land, which is not an asset of the joint estate. In *Shingenge v Hamunyela* (2004 NR 1. In this case, it was held that certain fencing materials had acceded to the land by means of inaedificatio, and as a result became part of the land and the owner of the land acquired ownership thereof), it was pointed out that the question of "ownership" in regard to "improvements" made to the land, requires an enquiry into a number of facts including: (1) the nature, extent and value of the "improvements" in question and (2) whether or not such "improvements" have become part of the land by attachment to it, and therefore now owned by the owner of the land. The court in the *Mutrifa* case thus held that a customary land right is a personal right inseparable from its holder and does not constitute part of the assets of the joint estate (*Mutrifa* case para 38). In principle, the customary land rights allocated to the plaintiff are the plaintiff's exclusive property and do not constitute part of the assets of the joint estate (*Mutrifa* case para 38).

Vita Royal House v The Minister of Land Reform and 10 Others (*Vita Royal House v The Minister of Land Reform and 10 Others* Case No. 109/2015 (November 7, 2016) (Unreported) at para [12])

In the *Vita Royal House* case ((See also *Kaishugu v Minister of Land Reform and Others* (HC-MD-CIV-MOT-GEN-2017/00292) NAHCMD 329 (October 18, 2018)), the applicant brought an application seeking orders to evict the respondents form a communal area under its jurisdiction. According to the applicant, between the years 2002 and 2015 the respondents moved and settled permanently into the communal area without permission having been granted to them by the applicant in terms of section 29(4) of the Communal Land Reform Act, 2002. Initially, some of the respondents were granted temporary grazing rights during the drought period. After the expiry of the temporary grazing right, they were requested to leave the area but failed and/or refused to vacate the area. Other respondents simply moved into the area and settled without the necessary permission from the applicant. The respondents opposed the application on varied grounds. Some of the respondents contended that they were granted permission by the Chief, others by the traditional councillors and others by the members of the community and others even by the applicant or by a Traditional Authority adjacent to the applicant's area. The court held that the respondents did not have valid permissions as envisaged by section 29(4) of Communal Land Reform Act, 2002, which entitled them to permanently reside in the communal area under the jurisdiction of the applicants. Accordingly, the respondents were held to be in unlawful occupation of the area under the applicant's jurisdiction. As such, it was held that once a traditional community has established a Traditional Authority, the authorised body to act on behalf of the traditional community is the Traditional Authority, and not the Chief.

ALTERNATIVE APPROACHES TO SECURE COMMUNAL LAND TENURE RIGHTS

Are there ways, then, to secure and rights within communal tenure systems without replicating problematic versions of "custom," and in a manner that promotes democratic decision-making? Can policy both secure rights on the ground, and also allow rights-holders to adapt or alter their tenure system through deliberate choices over time in response to changing circumstances? Relevant here are the tenure reform principles set out in the South African White Paper on Land Policy of 1997. These require that the law be brought in line with *de facto* realities, but that these realities also be transformed to bring them in line with constitutional principles of democracy and equality, and thus to include freedom of choice in relation to both land rights and the institutions that will administer those rights.

Tenure reform thinking in Africa currently emphasises a pragmatic, "adaptationist" approach rather than the radical replacement of existing regimes attempted, mostly unsuccessfully, in the past. Bruce suggested that the core elements of the dominant model are: "explicit recognition of indigenous tenure rules, legal protection for land held under them, strengthening of local institutions which administer those rules and recognition or provision of mechanisms for resolving disputes" (Bruce 1993, 46).

This perspective acknowledges that private title does not necessarily bring security of tenure, and that "unsuccessful attempts to substitute state titles for customary entitlements may reduce security by creating normative confusion, of which the powerful may take advantage" (Bruce and Mighot-Adholla 1994, 260). Titling activities should be directed only towards localities where the need for titles has been expressed, as a result of changing social norms or a need for credit, and in particular to areas where valuable land is subject to competition and dispute (e.g., urban and peri-urban areas) or in resettlement areas where no customary system exists (Bruce and Mighot-Adholla 1994, 262).

Phillipe defined the key policy issue in Francophone West Africa as the "harmonisation of formal law and customary land rights" (Phillipe 1999). The need arises from the uncertainty over rights caused by legal pluralism and the weak legal status of customary rights, as a result of which locally determined rules can be overridden through resort to state law by urban elites and local stakeholders (Phillipe 1999). The major problem, however, is "the multiplication of arbitration authorities," which deliver contradictory findings, as a result of which "outcomes cannot be predicted" and "conflicts escalate" (Phillipe 1999). Three main models have emerged thus far:

a) *Codification,* which attempts to integrate local systems and rules into law by systematising them and giving them legal definition. However, this has run into the obstacle of the diversity, variability, imprecision and flexibility of local rules (Phillipe 1999, 9).
b) *Registration* of local rights. However, uncertainty remains over the legal categories to be created (Phillipe 1999, 10) and the process has run into problems recording overlapping or interlocking rights, as well as secondary rights. In general, registration runs the risk of producing a "most unwieldy system" which loses the flexibility of procedurally-based (as opposed to codified and rights-based) local systems (Phillipe 1999, 13). Additional problems which are anticipated include the costs of the administrative systems for managing and updating registers, the possibility of information becoming obsolete, the resort to informal mechanisms for tenure security, and consequent confusion surrounding rights.
c) *Reforming rules and procedures for land rights management, including arbitration,* rather than formalising land rights themselves. It seeks to "reduce ambiguity about which norms are legitimate," by stakeholders at the local level adopting a "system of shared rules," but within a hierarchy of arbitration bodies located within a framework of national law. This will create a "hybrid form of land administration" (Phillipe 1999,

17–18), combining elements of customary authority and formal law. This approach includes an emphasis on decentralisation and devolution of authority over land management, and once again seeks clarity and greater levels of certainty – here in relation to conflict resolution and authority to make decisions on land rights and land use.

There are problems in all these approaches. First, it may be unrealistic to conceive of local institutions such as village committees as "open (and) neutral" fora for managing tenure reform when this "profoundly alters the nature of local landholding systems" (Phillipe 1999, 19). This is because authority and regulation are profoundly political issues, and thus subject to power plays by a variety of stakeholders (Phillipe 1999, 19). Second, tenure reform necessarily involves clarifying multiple claims to land, and resolving conflicting claims to "prior occupancy" while also balancing these against existing use rights is particularly difficult (Phillipe 1999, 19).

These two problems suggest that a hybrid combination of community and state regulation may be required. However, defining this framework more precisely remains a challenge, because it must both align closely with existing practices and anticipate "how the different players . . . will try to use that framework . . . and attempt to distort it to their own advantage" (Phillipe 1999, 22).

The third difficulty is also political, but at the national level – few countries are ready to go beyond rhetoric and devolve real authority over land to the local level (partly because of resistance by the political and administrative class), and furthermore, few states have the real capacity to carry through reform (Phillipe 1999, 22). These are similar to the constraints on tenure reform policies experienced in the colonial and early post-colonial periods (Phillipe 1999, 22).

Reviewing experience in Anglophone West Africa, Adams and Mortimore also considered the pros and cons of formalisation and codification, and of attempts to transcend the inherited dualism in tenure law (Adams and Mortimore 1997, 150–160). On the one hand, codification implicitly contradicts the necessary fluidity of local systems (Adams and Mortimore 1997, 150–160). Formalisation can also over-ride the complexities of marginalised, common access and multiple rights, and often has an in-built bias towards individual and exclusive rights (Adams and Mortimore 1997, 150–160). But codification, if extended to cover the rights of marginalised groups such as pastoralists, can perhaps help to protect informal rights threatened by change. Confronted by rapid rates of social change added to intensifying land use and production, "codification is the only alternative to oblivion" for vulnerable Africans. Protecting "custom" under the authority of state trusteeship, as under indirect rule, is no longer workable as the state has itself "has all too often become the instrument of interest groups" (Adams and Mortimore 1997, 150–160). Moreover, continuation of legal dualism may be unsustainable in the long run because of the real advantages of statutory tenure to those investing capital in land and able to afford its costs, and thus entrenching dualism is likely to increase ambiguity, instability and violent conflict.

The policy choice is thus between on the one hand, a *laissez-faire* strategy allowing social fluidity in resource access and the continuing "natural evolution" of tenure systems, at minimal administrative cost, and on the other, formalisation or codification programmes which aim to preserve the rights of weaker groups which this evolution will eliminate, and reduce the ambiguities and uncertainties of dualism (which are often exploited by the powerful).

Decentralisation of land administration and management to local community level will be insufficient in itself, since decentralisation does not resolve the issue of authority and representation at local level, conflicts of interest are difficult to resolve locally and the disadvantaged may lack voice, and trans-local problems and outside incursions (by state agricultural projects) cannot be dealt with at village level alone. For these reasons, decentralisation requires central government to take responsibility for providing the broad framework and principles underlying tenure, and for ensuring the transparency and accountability of local structures.

CONCLUSION

Land tenure reform remains a key policy issue in Africa, given the large proportion of the population that relies on land and natural resources for their livelihoods. It is not enough to recognise the socially and politically embedded character of land rights, or the unequal outcomes of contemporary forms of "enclosure." Privatisation and complete individualisation of land are uneven and contested, and in many places the nature and content of land rights remain quite distinct from "Western-legal" forms of property. In these situations, individual titling is not a feasible solution, and adapted and democratised versions of communal tenure should be promoted by law and policy. Viewed from within a "rights without illusions" perspective, legal recognition of these distinctive forms of land rights can form part of a broader strategy to secure rights through political mobilisation and pressure for democratic systems of land governance, and must involve external support for rights holders within local institutional and political processes. Customary norms must be at the centre of this approach.

The Namibian Government through the Ministry of Lands and Resettlement is committed to bring tenure security in the communal areas. The Namibian

Government strongly believes that security of tenure promotes socio-economic development of the people as well as encourages better natural resource management. It is open to informed suggestions, willing to listen and engage its people. If Namibian communities who are earning a livelihood from the communal areas feel that there is need to change the current thinking that is being projected by government through the Communal land Registration project, and if their experiences in the past twenty-two years as articulated in the Resolutions of the 1991 Land Conference have changed or requires adjustment, the MLR should be willing to channel its thinking and realise new informed proposals as long as those suggestions will not impoverish Namibians in communal lands and leave them destitute. Customary law forms a key aspect to realising this objective. Its marginalisation will undermine customary land rights and undermine the land reform agenda in Namibia.

BIBLIOGRAPHY

Agnes Kahimbi Kashela v Katima Mulilo Town Council and Others: Case No: SA 15/2017 delivered on 16 November 2018.

Agricultural (Commercial) Land Reform Act 6 of 1995.

Bank of Namibia. (2012). "Unlocking the Economic Potential of Communal Land." https://www.bon.com.na/CMSTemplates/Bon/Files/bon.com.na/7d/7dafdec3-24a1-4817-902a-c4a686f57489.pdf.

Barnes J. I. (1995). "The value of non-agricultural land use in some Namibian communal areas: A data base for planning." DEA Research Discussion Paper 6 (MET: Windhoek).

Beaman, J. (2016). "Citizenship as cultural: Towards a theory of cultural citizenship." *Sociology Compass*, Volume 10, 849–857.

Becker, H. (1997). "Women and land rights." In Malan, J., and Hinz, M. (Eds.), *Communal Land Administration: Second National Traditional Authority Conference – Proceedings* Konrad Adenauer Stiftung: Windhoek.

Bhe & Others v Khayelitsha Magistrates & Others (CCT 49/03) [2004] ZACC 17; 2005 (1) SA 580 (CC); 2005 (1) BCLR 1 (CC) (15 October 2004).

Chairman Ohangwena Communal Land Board N.O. v Wapulile (SA 81/2013) [2017] NASC 19 (08 June 2017).

Chiari, G. P. (2004). *Draft Report: UNDP Mission on Rural Livelihoods and Poverty in Namibia*. Windhoek: United Nations Development Programme.

Chimhowu, A., and Woodhouse, P. (2005). "Vernacular land markets and the changing face of customary land tenure in Africa, forum for development studies." *Forum for Development Studies*, Volume 32(2), 385–414.

Communal Land Reform Act 5 of 2002.

Constitution for the Republic of Namibia, 21 March 1990.

Cousins, B., and Claassens, A. (2004). "Communal land rights, democracy and traditional leaders in post-apartheid South Africa." In Saruchera, M. (Ed.), *Securing Land and Resource Rights in Africa: Pan- African Perspectives*. Beville: Programme for Land and Agrarian Studies.

Cox, J., Kerven, C., Werner, W., and Behnke, R. (1998). *The Privatisation of Rangeland Resources in Namibia: Enclosure in Eastern Oshikoto*. London: Overseas Development Institute.

Diala, A. C. (2017). "The concept of living customary law: A critique." *The Journal of Legal Pluralism and Unofficial Law*, Volume 49(2), 143–165.

Fiona, A., and Werner, W. (1990). *The Land Issue in Namibia: An Inquiry*. Windhoek: Namibia Institute for Social and Economic Research.

Fuller, B. (1999). "Returning their rights: A case study of Namibia's communal areas." In Oglethorpe, J. (Ed.), *Tenure and Sustainable Use*. Switzerland & Cambridge: IUCN & Gland.

Fuller, B. (2004). "A Namibian path for land reform." In Hunter, J. (Ed.), *Who Should Own the Land?* Windhoek: Konrad Adenauer Stiftung Namibia Institute for Democracy.

Halidulu v The Council for the Town of Ondangwa (I 389/2015) [2019] NAHCMD 460 (7 November 2019)

Hinz, M., and Kauluma, P. (1994). "The laws of Ondonga – Introductory remarks." In Traditional Authority of Ondonga, Ooveta (oompango) dhoshilongo shondonga/The Laws of Ondonga. Oniipa: Evangelical Lutheran Church of Namibia (ELCIN).

Horn, N. (2005). "Eddie Mabo and Namibia: Land reform and pre-colonial land rights." *Sur – International Journal on Human Rights*, Volume 3, 81–94.

Kaapama, P. (2007). "Commercial land reforms in post-colonial Namibia: What happened to liberation struggle rhetoric?" In Melber, H. (Ed.), *Transitions in Namibia: Which Changes for Whom?* Stockholm: Nordiska Afrikainstitutet.

Kapia v Minister of Regional and Local Government Housing and Rural Development (A 333/2012) [2013] NAHCMD 13 (24 January 2014).

Lebert, J. (2005). "Inheritance practices and property rights in Ohangwena Region." In Gender Research and Advocacy Project (Ed.), *The Meanings of Inheritance: Perspectives on Namibian Inheritance Practices*. Windhoek: Legal Assistance Centre.

Malan, J. (1980). *Peoples of SWA/Namibia*. Pretoria and Cape Town: Hollandsche Afrikaanse Uitgeweers Maatschappij (HAUM).

Malan, J., and Hinz, M. O. (Eds.). (1997). *Communal Land Administration Second National Traditional Authority Conference. Proceedings*. Windhoek: Centre for Applied Social Sciences.

Mandimika, P., and Mulofwa, J. (2018). "Securing customary land rights for development in Namibia: Learning from new approaches, opportunities and social settings." Paper prepared for presentation at the 2018 World Bank Conference on Land and Property, The World Bank – Washington DC, March 19–23.

Martin, A., Sibanda, S., and Turner, S. (2000). "Land tenure reform and livelihoods in Southern Africa." In Toulmin, C., and Quan, J. (Eds.), *Evolving Land Rights,*

Policy and Tenure in Africa. London: International Institute for Environment and Development.

Melber, H. (2005). "Land politics in Namibia." *Review of African Political Economy*, Volume 103, 135–204.

Melber, H. (Ed.). (2007). *Transitions in Namibia: Which Changes for Whom?* Stockholm: Nordiska Afrikainstitutet.

Mendelsohn, J. (2006). *Farming Systems in Namibia*. Windhoek: Research and Information Services of Namibia.

Mendelsohn, J. (2008). *Customary and Legislative Aspects of Land Registration and Management on Communal Land in Namibia*. Windhoek: MLR.

Mendelsohn, J. (2009). "Customary and legislative aspects of land registration and management on communal land in Namibia." A Report prepared for the Ministry of Land and Rural Resettlement and the Rural Poverty Reduction Programme of the European Union.

Mendelsohn, J., Jarvis, A., Roberts, C., and Robertson, T. (2009). *Atlas of Namibia: A Portrait of the Land and Its People* (3rd ed.). Cape Town: Sunbird Publishers.

Millennium Challenge Corporation/Orgut COWI, Legal Requirements for Group Land Rights, Windhoek, Millennium Challenge Account Namibia (2014).

Ministry of Land Reform. (2017). *Mid-Term Report Evaluation, Programme for Communal Land Development*. Windhoek.

Mutrifa v Tjombe (I 1384/2016) [2017] NAHCMD 162.

Ndevahoma v Shimwooshili (HC-MD-CIV-ACT-OTH-2017/03184) [2019] NAHCMD 32 (25 January 2019).

OHCHR. Thematic Advice of the Expert Mechanism on the Rights of Indigenous Peoples: A compilation (2009–2013) 26.

Ongwediva Town Council v Jonas (HC-NLD-CIV-MOT-GEN-2018/00001) [2018] NAHCNLD 22(12 March 2018).

Proposed Guidelines for Group Land Rights in Communal Areas, Windhoek, Millennium Challenge Account Namibia (2014).

Proposed Working Policy for Group Land Rights, Windhoek, Millennium Challenge Account Namibia (2014).

Thiem, M. (2014). *A Decade of Communal Land Reform: Review and Lessons Learnt, with a Focus on Communal Land Rights Registration*. Windhoek.

Tjiriange v Kambazembi (A 164/2015) [2017] NAHCMD 59 (24 February 2017).

Traditional Authorities Act 17 of 1995.

Traditional Authorities Act 25 of 2000.

Traditional Authority of Ondonga. (1994). *Ooveta (oompango) dhoshilongo shondonga/The Laws of Ondonga*. Oniipa: Evangelical Lutheran Church in Namibia (ELCIN).

Vita Royal House v The Minister of Land Reform & 10 Others (A 109/2015) [2016] NAHCMD 339 (7 November 2016).

Von Carlowitz, L., and Mandimika, P. (2015). "Promoting dialogue and raising awareness: Land Reform and the arts in Namibia." A paper prepared and presented at the 2015 World Bank Conference on Land and Poverty – The World Bank-Washington DC, March 23–27.

Wapulile v Chairman, Ohangwena Communal Land Board N.O (A 265/2013) [2013] NAHCMD 340 (15 November 2013).

Warikandwa, T. V., and Nhemachena, A. (2017). "Human rights to land or land rights? Charting a new roadmap to land ownership in Africa." In Warikandwa, T. V., Nhemachena, A., and Mtapuri, O. (Eds.), *Transnational Land Grabs and Restitution in an Age of the (De-) Militarised New Scramble for Africa: A Pan African Socio-Legal Perspective*. Mankon, Bameda: Langaa Research & Publishing Common Initiative Group.

Warikandwa, T. V., Nhemachena, A., and Mtapuri, O. (Eds.). (2017). *Transnational Land Grabs and Restitution in an Age of the (De-)Militarised New Scramble for Africa: A Pan African Socio-Legal Perspective*. Mankon, Bameda: Langaa Research & Publishing Common Initiative Group.

Werner, W. (2008). "Protection for women in Namibia's Communal Land Reform Act: Is it working?" A report published by the Land, Environment and Development Project Gender Research and Advocacy Project, Legal Assistance Centre.

Werner, W. (2015). "Tenure reform in Namibia's communal areas." *Journal of Namibian Studies*, Volume 18, 67–87.

Chapter 10

Ownership, Distribution and Access to Mineral Resources in Namibia

Liina Kalili

INTRODUCTION

In general, there are people who are more privileged because they have adequate access to national resources than others. Some people may lack opportunities and become disadvantaged due to large societal conditions, which must be attended to (Goodman 2000, 1067). The theory of distributive justice means that those who have must give to those who have not, to realise a fair society (Arneson 2008, 1). It is possible to decide whether people are treated fairly in the society by examining their access to primary social goods (Arneson 2008, 1). The main question is who owns mineral resources in Namibia? The question will be answered based on available legislations and bearing in mind the current status quo of mass exports of rough diamonds and other mineral resources sold for the purposes of beneficiation.

Mining is a critical sector of the Namibian economy and mineral assets form a major source of national wealth (Lange 2003, 3). As a result, the mining sector, in Namibia, is the key sector and it contributes 16 per cent to the Gross Domestic Product (GDP). In addition, Namibia and Botswana have diamonds as part of their natural resources (Kojima et al. 2010, 33). Therefore, the development of natural resources is regarded as a prerequisite for the economic growth of many countries (Warden-Fernandez 2001, 4).

Mining can positively contribute to poverty reduction if managed properly and if certain essential preconditions are in place (Warden-Fernandez 2001, 385). That relates to technology transfer, building a strong technological system to exploit minerals, indigenously, which may be the best way to facilitate the expansion of a national innovative capacity (Pegg 2006, 380–381). Another precondition is the creation of downstream industries where the profits from mineral resource extraction would be re-invested in industries that would process and add value to the minerals before they are exported (Pegg 2006, 381). Infrastructure development is necessary for mining projects to take place (Pegg 2006, 381). For example, when a road is upgraded to allow heavy equipment to travel from a mine to a port, the benefits of such an initiative extends to other sectors. Farmers, for example, may use the upgraded road to get their crops to the market quicker and that contributes towards increased trade between previously unconnected villages.

OWNERSHIP OF MINERAL RESOURCES IN NAMIBIA

Ownership is an absolute right that the holder can exercise against the whole world (Amoo 2014, 179). Ownership is the most complete real right in the sense that the holder of such a right, in principle, has the widest powers in respect of something but it must be borne in mind that ownership may sometimes be limited by another (limited) real right, such as usufruct held by a person who is not the owner of the thing (Amoo 2014, 42).

If mining wealth remains with the few, it does not really serve to benefit all of society (Amoo 2014, 42). Does it mean the few that have access to mineral wealth represent the whole nation? The answer may be negative. Some experts are of the opinion that previously disadvantaged Namibians have had no trouble owning and accessing mineral resources, but it is the work commitments, access to funding, skills and technology that limit them (Nyaungwa and Abankwah 2014). It is doubtful if the lack of ownership can be blamed on the work commitments, access to funding, skills and technology. Rather, it is submitted that, if access to funding, skills and technology are the contributing factors, then the country may look at intervention programmes such as mineral resources awareness, financial assistance, like in the UK (Colman 2011, 262), in form of community development for successful access and mineral resources ownership by the locals. It is submitted that financial assistance and skills development has achieved plausible results in the UK, and the UK has been viewed as a centre of excellence in the mining industry, with firms that have a wealth of exploration and mining due to diligence and expertise in the mining industry. Even though article 100 of the Namibian Constitution prescribes who owns mineral resources in Namibia, it does not define what constitutes ownership (1 of 1990 as amended). Nonetheless, the content, and nature of ownership is defined by the society in which ownership functions and as society dictates or demands (Mostert and Pope 2010, 91). Therefore, it may be correct to say that what constitutes ownership is also defined by the society to a certain extent (Mostert and Pope 2010, 91). However, according to common law, ownership focuses on the theoretical completeness of the right by describing it as the most complete right a legal subject can have in relation to an object; therefore, only owners have the most complete and absolute entitlements to such property (Mostert and Pope 2010, 91).

Strydom ACJ in the case of *Namibia Grape Growers and Exporters Associations and Others v Ministry of Mines and Energy and others* (*Namibia Grape Growers and Exporters Associations and Others v Ministry of Mines and Energy and others* 2004 NR 194 (SC), para 209), confirmed that article 100 of the Namibian Constitution (1 of 1990 as amended) vests mineral rights in the state, in so far as they are not privately owned. Currently, Namibia's mineral ownership is prescribed in the Mineral (Prospecting and Mining) Act (33 of 1992) but these mineral resources have been vested in the state ever since colonial times (Imperial Mining Ordinance of German South West Africa, August 8, 1905; Proclamation 21 of 1919; Proclamation of 1940; Ordinance 26 of 1964; Ordinance 20 of 1968). Further, the right to exploit mineral resources in Namibia is treated as separate from land ownership and has been reserved for the state. It is translated to say that the owner of the land does not own mineral resources found on it but the state does. It means that the owner of the land owns the land only but not minerals on that specific land. On the other hand, does it mean there is a contradiction between mineral resources held in trust for the Namibian people in the Minerals Policy of 2002 and the Court's decision in the case of *Namibia Grape Growers and Exporters Associations and Others v Ministry of Mines and Energy and others* of the state owning the mineral resources? There is not, because the mineral resources that are in trust for the benefit of the people are the ones that are not privately owned. On the other hand, one may argue that minerals that are held in trust for the benefit of the Namibian people do not belong to the people *per se* but held in trust for the state. On the contrary, one may argue that the state is the people; therefore, what belongs to the state belongs to the people. However, it is doubtful whether the latter is realistically factual in the context of Namibia.

Nevertheless, in the case of *Rostock CC and Another v Van Biljon* 2011 (2) 751 (HC), the applicant instituted action for eviction against the respondent, who continued to mine on the property, despite the fact that the applicant allegedly cancelled the surface agreement in terms of which the respondent originally obtained the right to mine on the property (*Rostock CC and Another v Van Biljon* 2011 (2) 751 (HC)). After pleadings closed, the applicant brought the interlocutory or incidental application to procure the land pending the outcome of the action (*Rostock CC and Another v Van Biljon* 2011 (2) 751 (HC)). Pending the final determination of the action in the High Court of Namibia in case no I 844/2010 "the main action," the respondent was interdicted from removing any stone of whatsoever nature from the farm Rostock North 393, registration division K, district of Windhoek, north of the C26 road and east of the C14 road, personally or through employees or any person on his behalf (*Rostock CC and Another v Van Biljon* 2011 (2) 751 (HC)).

The state does not own natural resources in a private-law sense (*Rostock CC and Another v Van Biljon* 2011 (2) 751 (HC)). Although article 100 of the Namibian Constitution prescribes that natural resources belong to the state, it must be read in conjunction with the rest of the Constitution (*Rostock CC and Another v Van Biljon* 2011 (2) 751 (HC) paras 8–10), in particular article 1(2) of the Constitution. Article 1(2) provides that all power shall vest in the people of Namibia who shall exercise their sovereignty through the democratic institutions of the state.

SURFACE AND SUBSURFACE RIGHTS

Subsurface rights holders possess the ownership of minerals, while surface holders own the rights to the surface of the land (African Mining and Mineral Policy Guide 2016, 8). Consequently, it is established that it is possible for different persons to own the subsurface and the surface. Therefore, the holder of surface rights is not usually entitled to claim any right of ownership whatsoever over the deposits of minerals (African Mining and Mineral Policy Guide 2016, 8).

During the colonial era in Namibia, German law allowed the state to control access to the subsurface whereas in South Africa the ability to give access to the subsurface was in the hands of private parties, landowners and/or mineral right holders (Mostert and Van den Berg 2013, 21). Namibia adopts the Roman-Dutch law principle *cuius est solum eius est usque ad coelum et ad inferos* (Viljoen and Bosman 1979, 7) which means whose is the soil, his it is up to the sky (Abramovitch 1961, 247–248), or in more simple terms: "he who possesses the land possesses also that which is above it" (Black 1968, 453). Other explanations maintain that "he who owns the soil owns everything above and below from heaven to hell (Abramovitch 1961, 247–248), and he who owns the land owns up to the sky" (Abramovitch 1961, 247–248). The above principle confirms the landowner's rights and entitlements to the subsurface (Wessels 1908, 486); however, it is recognised that this right is not absolute.

The state in Namibia has total control of all subsurface mineral rights (Corry 2003, 6). The Roman-Dutch law conception of landownership did not allow horizontal layering of property, meaning one person could not have ownership of the surface, while another had ownership of the subsurface (Hahlo and Kahn 1960, 761–762). The state has always claimed and exercised territorial sovereignty in space above their surface; as a result there is a view that the landowner has no rights, at all, in the air column above his land (Abramovitch 1961, 248). This view is based on the idea that the air is free to all, and that it is incapable of being possessed and owned

(Abramovitch 1961, 248). It is impossible to have own air, so air is a free gift to all.

Nevertheless, article 100 of the Namibian Constitution stipulates that land, water and natural resources below and above the surface of the land and in the continental shelf and within the territorial waters and the exclusive economic zone of Namibia shall belong to the state, if they are not otherwise lawfully owned. Therefore, it is evident from the above constitutional provision that the subsurface right belongs to the state.

ACCESS

Access is defined as the ability to derive benefits from things, broadening from property's classical definition as "the right to benefit from things" (Ribot and Peluso 2003, 153). Therefore, when someone has access to something, such a person must be able to gain significant positive impact from that thing. However, it must be clearly understood that access is different from ownership (Ribot and Peluso 2003, 153). It is submitted that it does not mean that having access to something is equivalent to owning it. Access is about all possible means by which a person is able to benefit from things and rights holders enjoy a certain kind and degree of social power (Ribot and Peluso 2003, 156). By focusing on ability, rather than rights as in property theory, this formulation brings attention to a wider range of social relationships that can constrain or enable people to benefit from resources without focusing on property relations alone (Ribot and Peluso 2003, 154). Access retains an empirical focus on the issues of who does (and who does not) get to use what, in what ways, and when (that is, in what circumstances) as some people or institutions benefit from resources, whether or not they have rights to them (Ribot and Peluso 2003, 156). Therefore, if the Namibian people do not have power over mineral resources, it is unrealistic to claim having access to these resources and it will be difficult to achieve nation's progress and economic development.

It is not a secret that every state has the right to freely dispose, exploit and use their natural resources (Hofbauer 2009, 29). This is done to preserve and regulate the economy, hence it does not matter how states run their affairs in terms of their natural resources from the mining sector (Hofbauer 2009, 29). However, this shall only occur to further their national development and benefit the well-being of their people (Hofbauer 2009, 29). Therefore, it is stressed that access and benefits from the country's mineral resources be promoted and encouraged significantly. Further, the duty for each state to use its natural resources to improve the nation's progress and economic development serves as justification for many of the extensive rights connected to the principle under the duty of a state to exercise permanent sovereignty over natural resources in the interest of national development and the well-being of the people. The states must also ensure that foreign companies do not plunder the territory's mineral resources to the extent that the continent remains poor despite the wealth.

It has been concluded that the mining legislation in Namibia has enabled foreign private mining companies to plunder the territory's mineral resources while the African population remains one of the poorest in Africa (Kawana 1988, xvi). In Namibia, foreign companies are permitted by Section 17 of the Minerals (Prospecting and Mining) Act 33 of 1992 that prescribes that any person may apply for a non-exclusive prospecting licence, to exploit mineral resources. It is evident that this section does not exclude foreign companies from prospecting the country's mineral resources but allow any person to apply provided that a principal place of business of such company in Namibia is provided (section 18 (2) (a) (ii)) of the Minerals (Prospecting and Mining) Act).

The investment of foreign companies in Namibia's mining industry is also encouraged by the Namibian Constitution (article 99) subject to the provisions of an Investment Code adopted by Parliament. As a result, the Investment Protection Act 9 of 2016 has been enacted with the aim to:

> Provide for the promotion of sustainable economic development and growth through the mobilization and attraction of foreign and domestic investment to enhance economic development, reduce unemployment, accelerate growth and diversify the economy; to provide for reservation of certain economic sectors and business activities to certain categories of investors.

Therefore, it is submitted that foreign investments are suitable for substantial economic development and growth; further, a country may not survive economically without foreign investment. It is further opined that lack of foreign investment may impact development of any country. For that reason, the Namibian Government's ability to attract investment to develop natural resources will strongly influence future economic growth and development (Mobbs 2004, 31.3).

Some examples of foreign investors in Namibia include Bafex Exploration (Pty) Ltd. of Namibia which held eight exclusive prospecting licences in north-western Namibia (Mobbs 2004, 31.2). However, in 2004, Bafex was acquired by Helio Capital Corporation of Canada, which was renamed Helio Resources Corporation (Mobbs 2004, 31.2). Bafex initiated exploration on the Leicester and the Zebra licences. Boulder Mining Corporation of Canada, which was earning 100 per cent interest in the copper-gold Teverede prospect from Bafex, continued exploration at Teverede (Mobbs 2004, 31.2).

AngloGold (Pty) Ltd. of Namibia (a subsidiary of AngloGold Ashanti Limited of South Africa) held a 100 per cent interest in the Navachab open pit gold mine near Karibib. The mine accounted for more than 90 per cent of national gold output (Mobbs 2004, 31.2).

Rosh Pinah Zinc Corporate (Pty) Ltd. (a joint venture of Kumba Resources Ltd. of South Africa, 89.5 per cent interest, and PE Minerals Namibia (Pty) Ltd., 10.5 per cent) operated the Rosh Pinah underground zinc mine (Mobbs 2004, 31.2). In 2004, Rosh Pinah increased production of zinc concentrates by 15 per cent to about 124,000 tones and Zinc concentrates were shipped through Walvis Bay to Kumba's Zincor refinery in South Africa for treatment (Mobbs 2004, 31.2).

EXISTING MINERAL RIGHTS

Section 2 of the Minerals (Prospecting and Mining) Act prescribes the rights in relation to minerals in Namibia. It maintains that any right in relation to the exploration or prospecting of mining activities, including the exercise of control thereof notwithstanding any right of ownership of any person, vests in the state. Further, the Minerals (Prospecting and Mining) Act (section 3(1) (a) & (b)) prohibits the carrying on of certain operations without licence, and transfer of certain licences or grant, cession or assignment of interests in such licences, and joinder of persons as joint holders of such licences or interests.

However, the Ministry of Mines and Energy has the responsibility of accessing mineral rights applications and granting minerals licences as prescribed by the law. Any person may apply for a non-exclusive Prospecting licence (section 18(1) of the Minerals (Prospecting and Mining) Act), provided, in the case of a natural person; such person has reached the age of 18 years. There are also mining claims that are available to Namibian citizens only for the development of small-scale mining (section 33(1) of the Minerals (Prospecting and Mining) Act). These mining claims are valid for three years and two-year extension periods are possible provided that the claim is being developed and up to a maximum of ten claims can be held at any one time (Ministry of Mines and Energy 2018).

The other licence is the reconnaissance licence (section 60 of the Minerals (Prospecting and Mining) Act) that is designed for regional exploitation, mainly remotely sensing exploration, to facilitate the identification of exploration targets and is valid for six months on a non-renewable basis (Ministry of Mines and Energy 2018). There is also an exclusive prospecting licence (sections 68 & 72 of the Minerals (Prospecting and Mining) Act), which is a three-year licence that allows systematic prospecting in areas of up to 1,000 km (Ministry of Mines and Energy 2018). Further, it gives exclusive exploration rights to the land and may be extended twice for two-year periods, if demonstrable progress is shown. Renewals beyond seven years require special approval from the Minister (Ministry of Mines and Energy 2018).

The Ministry of Mines and Energy also gives the Mineral Deposit Retention License (section 79 of the Minerals (Prospecting and Mining) Act) that allows an exploration company, in certain circumstances, to retain tenure on a prospecting licence, mining licence or mining claim without mining obligations (Ministry of Mines and Energy 2018). This licence is valid for five years, with two-year renewal periods. However, the licence holder must meet work and expenditure obligations and submit regular project reviews (Ministry of Mines and Energy 2018).

There is also a Mining License (section 91 of the Minerals (Prospecting and Mining) Act) that gives the holder the exclusive mining right in the licence area for a period of twenty-five years or the life of the mine, with renewals valid for fifteen-year periods (Ministry of Mines and Energy 2018). The holder is required to demonstrate the financial and technical ability to develop and operate a mine (Ministry of Mines and Energy 2018). These are some of the existing mineral rights that exist in Namibia at the moment and are granted in terms of the available legislations as stated above.

THE PRIVATE SECTOR'S INVOLVEMENT IN MINING

The Member States of Southern African Devlopment Community (SADC), through the Protocol on Mining, agreed to adopt internationally accepted regional standards within the mining sector. Through the SADC Protocol, member states agree to share information on exploitable mineral resources in the region, as well as promote policies that will encourage and assist small-scale farming. It is indicated that the SADC Protocol on mining requires the member states to permit the private sectors involvement in mining in their respective countries. Despite the SADC Protocol expectation on member states, it is opined that the Namibian mining law system may be regarded still replicate colonial error system as it does not appreciate distribution and equity. It is opined that Namibia needs to close the gap between rich and poor to reach the objective of National Equitable Economic Empowerment Framework (NEEEF).

NEEEF ANALYSED

It has been circulated that under NEEEF, businesses are required to be at least 25 per cent owned by previously disadvantaged persons (black people) while 50 per cent of top management must be previously disadvantaged pillars. It is submitted that NEEEF is not accommodative in the neo-liberal dimension to a certain extend. Critics have said the black-economic empowerment laws in general have failed to redress inequality but instead benefited a small number of wealthy individuals. Equally, it is observed that the NEEEF has also received high critics, it is admitted that it is not the 25 per cent clause requirement of NEEEF that is a problem but the modality around it. Further, it is worrisome to the fact that the 25 per cent clause for previously disadvantaged Namibians is vague; it is not clear how the 25 per cent will be applied in different sectors. Another question is how the 25 per cent will be implemented and how it shall benefits the private sectors? Imagine investing N$ 100 000.00 in the mining sector then get N$ 75 000.00 returns. The 25 percent clause has since been reduced to 15 percent in the proposed National Equitable Economic Empowerment Bill.

Article 16(2) of the Constitution of Namibia gives the power to Parliament to make laws that would allow the state or a lawfully established body or organ to expropriate property in the public interest, condition that the state pays "just compensation" to affected parties. This is called "expropriation" where the state is required to pay what is termed "just compensation," meaning in this context a "fair price."

Article 16 (1) covers the principle of willing seller/willing buyer, which states that all persons have a right to "acquire, own and dispose" of all forms of property. However, Article 16(2) limits the right to own property in Namibia. It is submitted that the right to own the property including mineral resources from the mining sector is not absolute. Thus, the state has the power to expropriate the property in accordance with the procedures laid down by law, and therefore has the right to interfere with an individual's right to own property.

However, it is not clear whether the 25 per cent (now 15 percent) requirement of NEEEF meant for previously disadvantaged people will be applied on expropriation basis through fair and just compensation, or expropriation basis without compensation or by way of willing buyer will seller basis. Therefore, it is suggested that NEEEF should be reviewed to define clear guidelines and procedures for effective implementation.

DISTRIBUTION AND COMMUNITY PARTICIPATION

Distribution is the process of giving things out to people or spreading or supplying something. However, distribution of Namibian's mineral resources should not be interpreted to be equal to free distribution, there may be costs involved. It is considered that, if the distribution of ownership of natural resources is more unequal than the distribution of other forms of wealth, the inequality of the distribution of income, education or land is directly related to the share of natural resources in national income (Gylfason and Zoega 2002, 32).

There must be contributing factors to uneven distribution of mineral resources and lack of community participation in national resources. One of the factors may be corruption, which is described briefly (Bray 1999, 15–17) as a situation where politicians and officials exercise power without accountability. Corruption affects economic development by rewarding the most dishonest rather than the most competent. The fear of competition is the major justification for paying bribes as one may feel that their competitors may be more qualified than they are. Therefore, governments need to step in to protect mining revenue from being misappropriated, improve mineral resources access and distribution among the unequal society by allowing public involvement.

To protect the national resources, government should prioritise local inputs for policy development and management of the sector that has been the prerogative of the government without any input from local communities (Lebert 2016). Thus, sub-Saharan African communities have called for mining revenues to stay in the countries where they are mined; for raw materials to be processed in the countries where they are mined, thereby adding value; and for governments to act to protect people affected by mining rather than protecting the profit margins of corporations exploiting them (Lebert 2016). With a Gini coefficient of 0.59719 (Namibia Statistics Agency 2012), Namibia's income distribution is still among the most unequal in the world, despite improvements since independence (European Union 2014).

POTENTIAL CHALLENGES TO REDISTRIBUTION OF WEALTH

The eradication of poverty and development progression in Namibia requires a purposeful and coherent approach to policy making across sectors and stakeholders, dedicated resources and accountability (Kameeta 2016, 5). It is submitted that the above can be realised through equitable distribution of mineral resources. However, it is also opined that the capital or neo-liberal economic policies, such as the World Banks' ease of doing business that compares economies, may impact negatively on the redistribution of wealth. On the other hand, the government has the role to protect the rights of the people, including the right to engage in voluntary exchange or redistribution of wealth from rich to the poor (Posner 1985, 99). However, it is submitted that the potential challenges to redistribution of wealth may be caused by various factors such as corruption, bad policies, fear of economic downgrade and lack of essential legislations aimed at wealth redistribution.

As a result, many African countries do not have a strong track record of properly managing mineral wealth due to corruption, bad policies. However, there are a few exceptions of countries with decent policies of distributing a proportion of mining rents to local authorities and traditional leaders in mining-affected communities (Standing and Hilson 2013, vi). It is acknowledged that Ghana and Sierra Leone are some of the few countries in Africa to have developed and upheld policies for redistributing a proportion of its mining wealth directly to communities (Standing and Hilson 2013, 2). In Ghana, royalty being the main sources of revenue derived from the mining sector are provided directly to the government quarterly (Standing and Hilson 2013, 2). It is established that to tackle the potential challenges to redistribution of wealth, lawmakers need to come up with policies of distributing wealth. Such policies must target both local and foreign investors to ensure that all citizens share in wealth benefits derived from the mining sector.

Countries such as Mongolia and Iran have what is called "citizen resource dividend" and the essence of a citizen resource dividend is that all or some proportion of resource revenues are transferred in the form of direct cash benefits (Standing and Hilson 2013, 17). This is normally paid on a monthly basis, to every person in the country, irrespective of their wealth or employment status (Standing and Hilson 2013, 17). The implication is that governments will reduce, or entirely forego, dependency on resource royalty payments for funding the state's budget, and instead rely more on direct taxation as their source of government income (Standing and Hilson 2013, 17). It is acknowledged that this may be one of the alternatives to be considered by the Namibian lawmakers. However, there is resistance to such alternatives of cash transfer based on the presumption that giving people cash will induce dependency and laziness, thereby reducing labour supply. Distributing cash will have an inflationary effect (Standing and Hilson 2013, 17). It is further opined that no country would want to produce lazy citizens.

BENEFICIATION STRATEGY

The beneficiation strategy provides a framework that seeks to translate the country's complete comparative advantage inherited from mineral resources endowment to a national competitive advantage (Department of Mineral Resources of South Africa 2011). The strategy is aligned to a national industrialisation programme, which seeks to enhance the quantity and quality of exports, promote creation of decent employment and diversification of the economy, including promotion of the green economy (Department of Mineral Resources of South Africa 2011). If the mineral resources are held in custody for the benefit of all Namibians, evidence should be there, and if not, people will get frustrated and at the end Namibia will become part of the cursed nations due to natural resources.

CORPORATE SOCIAL RESPONSIBILITY

This responsibility, framed in terms of corporate social responsibility (CSR) or corporate citizenship entails maximising the positive and minimising the negative social and environmental impacts of mining, while maintaining profits (Hamann 2003, 238). It is submitted that this responsibility is meant to give back to the society. Further, it is submitted that since Namibia welcome investors, they are required to contribute to sustainable development of Namibia. The CSR calls for a company to respond not only to its shareholders, but also to other stakeholders, including employees, customers, affected communities and the general public, on issues such as human rights, employee welfare and climate change (Hamann 2003, 238). It is opined that government should regulate CSR so that if investors comply with the corporate citizenship principles to ensure that the Namibian people benefit ultimately from the mineral resources of the country while proper solution is being sought for citizen's development and to allow their access, participation and to nationalise mines. It means that to provide maximum development benefit, CSR must be integrated into the core activities and decision-making of a company and be regarded as a key concern by top management (Hamann 2003, 239). It is therefore recommended that mining companies should be more responsible and take up more interactive role in social transformation and sustainable development. Ignoring CSR may risk losing their licence to operate and their international competitiveness (Hamann 2003, 251).

THEORY OF DISTRIBUTIVE JUSTICE

The theory of distributive justice depicts how a society allocates its scarce resources to individual or groups with competing interest or claims (Roemer 1996, 1). In this regard, it focuses exclusively on inequalities (Robeyns 2003, 538–554). This concept requires those who have to give to those who have not. A society where injustice does not exist is regarded as a society guided by the principles of distributive justice.

To know whether people are being fairly treated by society, an examination on their access to primary social goods is required and this is done through the distribution justice theory (Arneson 2008, 1–9). The nature of justice is difficult to define but "Justice" has concepts associated with the definition of justice such as fairness, equality and rights (Colorado University 2017, 2).

These elements are explained in more details as follows:

Fairness: Similar cases must be treated in the same way. For instance, it would be unfair not to refuse one fish to one person and then respond to another person by giving him hundred boxes of fish. In other words, similar situations must be treated in similar ways.
Equality: The treatment of people ought to reflect the fact that all are morally equal. There are no morally relevant differences between human beings which make it permissible to treat them differently. For instance, there is not one race or gender that is better than the others. To act otherwise is to engage in immoral discrimination.
Rights: There are certain moral claims that everyone ought to be able to exercise against others. (Colorado University 2017, 2)

It is submitted that this theory is important as natural resources ought to be distributed and accessed equally and fairly. Further, according to Namibian law, the state owns natural resources (article 100 of the Constitution); including mineral resources from the mining sectors. Article 144 of the Namibian Constitution also provides that "Unless otherwise provided by this Constitution or Act of Parliament, the general rules of public international law and international agreements binding upon Namibia under this Constitution shall form part of the law of Namibia".

Consequently, international law and international agreements that Namibia has acceded to is part of Namibian law. On that basis, the principle of international law that prescribes people, among others, as criteria that determine statehood (Crawford 1977, 93–182), requires fairness and just treatment of the nationals complemented by rights and enjoyment of national wealth. The reason why state should concentrate on the well-being of the people is because it is made up of people and no state can exist without the people. That is the reason why the Ministry of Mines and Energy holds mineral resources in trust for the benefit of the Namibian people (Namibian Government's Minerals Policy of 2002). However, it must be understood that the freedom to have any particular thing can be significantly distinguished from actually having that thing; what an individual is free to have and not just what he actually has is relevant (Sen 2005, 155). In other words, the person's right to have something is not equal to actually having it. There should be a difference between doing something, having something and being free to do that thing.

Despite what the theory of distributive justice depicts, it is assumed that the current economic order may not accommodate the distributive justice theory considering the World Banks' ease of doing business. The ease of doing business ranking compares economies with one another; benchmarking economies according to regulatory best practice and the regulatory environment

(World Bank Annual Report 2018). Further, the ease of doing business looks at whether the regulatory environment is conducive to business operations and the protections of property rights. Therefore, it is doubtful whether the concept of taking from those who have to give to the have not will survive the World Banks' ease of doing business test, without the country gaining low ranking for the economy. It is further opined that the theory of distributive justice may affect the economy of the country negatively because the regulatory environment may not be conducive to business operations. Further, the theory will also be required to pass the protection of property rights test that is viewed to be at risk in the case of redistribution of wealth.

OBJECTIVE OF STATE CONTROL OF MINERALS

The reason why minerals are mostly under state control was to capture rent and to safeguard the national inheritance, which are resources that have been passed down from previous generations to the current generation due to a perception that international mining companies or foreign investors obtained most of the rent, leaving very little for the host country. Most state-owned mining companies have over the years and in particular in developing countries not been able to operate successfully, leading to privatisation. The success of a state-owned mining company is determined by the governance framework/structure, assets and capital base. It is maintained that the mining sector ought to be governed by experience personnel in mining and finance as board of directors, if such capacity is not available locally should be sourced internationally and the day to day administration be trusted in experienced professional managers who understand both the mining industry and the country-specific conditions.

It is warned that sustainable mining demands re-investment in exploration and development to maintain current reserves and to provide for future production, which includes developing at least five to ten (5–10) years of ore reserves, as mining company cannot only be utilised as a revenue generator by the government to cover budgetary deficits or other demands for money, skills or capital elsewhere in the national economy.

UNDERSTANDING INTERNATIONAL NATURE OF MINING

It should be understood that it takes ten to fifteen (10–15) years to develop a mine and that the industry is a high-risk sector; however, not only the mining sector should be understood but the stability and continuity provided by the mining sector as compared to other sectors should also be recognised and understood. The most important aspect of survival of mining is to have adequate skills and expertise and to invest in succession planning and development. To survive an international competitive environment in mining, companies with the best management and resources survive regardless of whether the owner is a state or private investors.

CONCLUSION

According to the Namibian Constitution, Article 100, natural resources including mineral resources belong to the state but the Namibian Court interprets that the natural resources belong to the people of Namibia and is administered by the state on their behalf. The Ministry of Mines and Energy has been tasked to control the mineral resources henceforth has full custodianship of all mineral resources in Namibia on behalf of its citizens.

Mining is a critical sector of the Namibian economy and mineral assets form a major source of national wealth. It is therefore opined that it is important if the people have access to the natural resources of the country and the distribution of these resources is done fairly and equitable. If state-owned enterprises create a mixed capital type of mining company with a set timetable for gradual transfer of ownership from the state to private national entities and investors on a jointly agreed timetable, would be more beneficial to the nation provided that national entities occupy large share of rent. And it is evident that to survive an international competitive environment in mining, companies with the best management and resources survives regardless of whether the owner is a state or private investors.

Mining sector in Namibia contributes 25 per cent to the GDP. However, nationals are not really getting enough shares of their national resources as it was supposed to be. This may be attributed to the governance style and the laws that are in place. Some diamond companies have been undermining the beneficiation efforts of the Namibian Government by processing on 20 per cent of locally produced diamonds while the rest of the rough diamonds are exported.

It is assumed that previously disadvantaged Namibians have had no trouble owning and accessing mineral resources, but it is the work commitments, access to funding, skills and technology could limit them. However, to survive an international competitive environment in mining, companies with the best management and resources survives regardless of whether the owner is a state or private investor. Therefore, Namibia should move away from the perception of not having enough local skills and capacity to run the mining sector successfully.

In Namibia, the state has total control of all subsurface mineral rights. Namibia has also adopted the Roman-Dutch law principle that means "he who possesses the land possesses also that which is above it." This view is based upon the idea that the air is free to all, and that it is incapable of being possessed and owned. Therefore, access and benefits from the country's mineral resources should be promoted and encouraged because each state has a duty to use its natural resources to improve the nation's progress and economic development.

Despite the plea for the local access to mineral resources, that does not mean a call to abolish foreign investors. Investment of foreign companies in Namibia's mining industry is encouraged by the Namibian Constitution. Therefore, the Namibian Government's ability to attract investment to develop natural resources will strongly influence future economic growth and development.

The Ministry of Mines and Energy has the responsibility of accessing mineral rights applications and granting minerals licences as prescribed by the law to various persons. However, it is opined that the Namibian mining law system still replicate colonial error system as it does not appreciate distribution and equity. With the implementation of NEEEF, the situation may change, however, it is submitted that NEEEF may not be accommodative in the neo-liberal dimension to a certain extent due to what World Bank ease of doing business expects. Critics have said the black-economic empowerment laws in general have failed to redress inequality but instead benefited a small number of wealthy individuals. NEEEF is also found to be vague when it comes to the 25 per cent (now 15 percent) requirement meant for previously disadvantaged people.

The Namibian's score of 58 per cent Gini coefficient perceived unhealthy state of affairs that calls for a radical change in approach in so far as the regulation of the mining sector in Namibia is concerned. If the distribution of ownership of natural resources is unequal than the distribution of other forms of wealth, such as the distribution of income, education or land will be unequal. Besides that, corruption is also regarded as one of the contributing factors to uneven distribution of mineral resources and lack of community participation in national resources, as it rewards undeserving individuals.

Government has the role to protect the rights of the people, including the right to engage in voluntary exchange or redistribution of wealth from rich to the poor. However, capital or neo-liberal economic policies may impact negatively on the redistribution of wealth. It is established that to tackle the potential challenges to redistribution of wealth lawmakers need to come up with policies of distributing of wealth. Targeting local and foreign investors to ensure that all citizens share in wealth benefits derived from the mining sectors. Countries such as Mongolia and Iran have what is called "citizen resource dividend," the essence of a citizen resource dividend is that all or some proportion of resource revenues are transferred in the form of direct cash benefits. Although this may be one of the alternatives to be considered by the Namibian lawmakers, there may be resistance to such alternative of cash transfer based on the presumption that giving people cash will induce dependency and laziness. It is submitted that, generally, no country would want to produce a generation of dependent citizens.

Namibia welcomes investors to contribute to sustainable development of Namibia thus investors are expected to respond to the CSR. The CSR calls for companies to respond not only to their shareholders but also to other stakeholders, including employees, customers, affected communities and the general public.

The reason why minerals are mostly under state control was to capture rent and to safeguard the national inheritance, due to a perception that international mining companies or foreign investors obtained most of the rent, leaving very little for the host country.

Lastly, what the theory of distributive justice portrays may not be accommodated by the current economic order considering the World Bank ease of doing business.

BIBLIOGRAPHY

Bray, J. (1999). Corruption in Africa. *Business in Africa*, 15–17.

Crawford, J. (1977). The criteria for statehood in international law. *British Yearbook of International Law*, Volume 48(1), 93–182.

Gylfason, T., and Zoega, G. (2002). *Inequality and economic growth: Do natural resources matter*. CESifo Working Paper No. 712(5).

Hofbauer, J.A. (2009). *The principle of permanent sovereignty over natural resources and its modern implications*. Master of Laws Dissertation, Faculty of Law, University Iceland, August 2009.

Kandjoze, O. M. (2017). Keynote address at minister's engagement session with the diamond industry. *Hilton Hotel*, March 27, 2017.

Kawana, A. B. (1988). The political economy of mining laws and regulations in Namibia from 1884 to 1986. (xvi). http://go.warwick.ac.uk/wrap/34710.

Kisting, D. (2017). Kandjoze lays into diamond industry. *The Namibian Newspaper*, Thursday March 30, 2017.

Kojima, M., Matthews, W., and Sexsmith, F. (2010). *Extractive Industries for Development Series*. Petroleum Market in Sub-Saharan Africa, ESMAP, World Bank, 33.

Lange, G. M. (2003). *The contribution of minerals to sustainable economic development: Mineral resource accounts in Namibia* (No. 54). Directorate of Environmental Affairs, Ministry of Environment and Tourism.

Littlewood, D. (2014). Cursed' communities? Corporate social responsibility (CSR), company towns and the mining industry in Namibia. *Journal of Business Ethics*, Volume 120(1), 39–63.

Mostert, H., and Pope, A. (Eds.). (2010). *The Principles of the Law of Property in South Africa*. Cape Town: Juta.

Namibia Grape Growers and Exporters Associations and Others v Ministry of Mines and Energy and others 2004 NR 194 (SC) at 209.

Namibian Constitution Act 1 of 1990.

Namibian Government's Minerals Policy of 2002.

Pegg, S. (2003). *Mining and Poverty Reduction: Transforming Rhetoric into Reality*. Indianapolis, IN: Department of Political Science, Indiana University Purdue University Indianapolis.

Ribot, J. C., and Peluso, N. L. (2003). A theory of access. *Rural Sociology*, Volume 68(2), 156.

Robeyns, I. (2003). *Is Nancy Fraser's Critique of Theories of Distributive Justice Justified?* Blackwell Publishing.

Roemer, J. E. (1996). *Theories of Distributive Justice*. Cambridge: Harvard University Press.

Rostock CC and Another v Van Biljon 2011 (2) 751 (HC).

Sen, A. (2005). Human rights and capabilities. *Journal of Human Development*, Volume 6(2), 155.

Warden-Fernandez, J. (2001). Indigenous communities and mineral development. *Mining, Minerals, and Sustainable Development*, Volume 59, 4.

Chapter 11

Public Procurement Policy and Administrative Justice in Namibia

A Critical Appraisal of the Remedies Available for Bidders

Ndatega Victoria Asheela-Shikalepo
and Tapiwa Victor Warikandwa

INTRODUCTION

Public procurement processes are regarded as administrative processes and are regulated by constitutional provisions and legislation enacted in terms of it (for an exposition of aspects that fall under the branch of administrative law, see Parker 2009, 115–127). It is only after the tender is awarded will the parties involved conclude a contract and thereafter their relationship governed by the law of obligations. It should be noted that there are no special contractual principles or terms that apply to public procurement contracts in Namibia. Consequently, these contracts are governed by the general principles of the law of contract. Acknowledging that the concept of administrative justice is broad in that it requires scrutinising the fairness, reasonableness and justice of any administrative action, it cannot be denied that any action or decision that an administrative body takes or makes during the procurement process constitutes an administrative action or decision and should therefore comply with the provisions of article 18 of the Namibian Constitution. It must be affirmed that the exercise and control of public power is always a constitutional matter, implying that each improper performance of an administrative function would implicate the Namibian Constitution and entitle the aggrieved party to an appropriate relief.

The aim of this chapter is therefore to provide a critical appraisal of the policy underlying the Public Procurement Act 15 of 2015 (hereinafter, "the Public Procurement Act" or "the Act") in light of the concept of administrative justice in Namibia, more particularly to outline the available remedies to the bidders in the event that there was an improper exercise of administrative power during the public procurement process. The structure of the chapter is as follows: First, the objectives of the Public Procurement Act relevant to the issue under consideration are explored. Second, an overview of the public procurement process is provided. Third, the remedies available for bidders in terms of the Namibian Constitution and the Public Procurement Act are explored. Finally, the concluding remarks follow.

OBJECTIVES OF THE PUBLIC PROCUREMENT ACT

Public procurement in Namibia is regulated by the Public Procurement Act. This Act came into operation on April 1, 2017, and it represents a complete reform and overhaul of the Namibian public procurement system which was previously clouded with a loss of public trust, corruption and mismanagement of state resources under the auspices of the Tender Board Act 16 of 1996 (Institute for Public Policy Research 2017 2; The Public Procurement Act has been said to be a consequence of the United Nations Convention Against Corruption and of the efforts to conform to the redeveloped 2011 United Nations Commission on International Trade Law (UNICTRAL) Model Law on Public Procurement). Section 2 of the Act outlines the objects of the Public Procurement Act. Relevantly, one of the objects of the Act is:

(a) to promote integrity, accountability, transparency, competitive supply, effectiveness, efficiency, fair-dealing, responsiveness, informed decision-making, consistency, legality and integration in the procurement of assets, works and services including, among others, to
   (i) harmonise procurement policies, systems and practices that apply to public entities and maximise economy and efficiency in public procurement to obtain best value for public expenditures;
   (ii) set and review standards and practices for the public procurement system in Namibia;
   (iii) monitor compliance by public entities; and
   (iv) build procurement capacity in Namibia.

Section 6(1) of the Act establishes the Procurement Policy Unit within the Ministry of Finance. This Unit is responsible for advising the Minister of Finance on any procurement policy directive which *inter alia* includes the promotion of fundamental principles of procurement governing the administration of procurement (section 6(1)(d) of the Act). The fundamental principles, as reflected on above, include as a minimum, the principle of transparency (transparency is a very important value in public procurement and it has been defined as "a means of achieving the various goals of the procurement process such as competition and non-discrimination, and has been interpreted as requiring publicised contracts; disclosure of the rules governing procurement in general and governing specific procurements; and rule-based decision-making and opportunities for verification and enforcement" (Williams 2007, 4; Arrowsmith 2005, chap 7.12; Lennerfors 2007, 381–390). Transparency in public procurement therefore makes it difficult to conceal improper and corrupt practices), integrity, competitive supply (competitive supply implies that a sufficient number of suppliers should be invited to participate in the bidding process to ensure that the government does not pay uncompetitive prices), effectiveness, efficiency, fair-dealing, responsiveness, informed decision-making, consistency, legality, integration and accountability *etcetera* (Bolton 2014, 619). In the exercise of the policy directives from the Minister to achieve the objects of the Act, the operations of the Procurement Policy Unit *inter alia* include influencing the development of public procurement policy, the determination of various thresholds relating to public procurement, advising the Minister on policy for the introduction of e-procurement as a means of simplified and transparent procurement as well as advising public entities on all public policies, principles and practices (section 7 of the Act).

Further, section 8 establishes the Central Procurement Board of Namibia with the object of conducting the bidding process on behalf of public entities for the award of procurement contracts that exceed the prescribed threshold for public entities, entering into contracts for procurement on its own behalf or on behalf of public entities awarded by the Board, and to direct and supervise accounting officers in managing the implementation of procurement contracts awarded by the Board (section 8 read with section 9 of the Act).

The Act also provides that an accounting officer is accountable for the full compliance with the provisions of the Act and further mandates that the accounting officer set up in the prescribed manner an internal organisational structure which includes a procurement committee and procurement management unit for the conduct and management of procurement at the public entity (section 25(1)). An accounting officer is also required to (section 25(4):

(a) engage in procurement planning, plan each step of the procurement process and prepare an annual procurement plan;
(b) certify the availability of funds before the commencement of each procurement process; and
(c) ensure that the proceedings of the internal structures are properly recorded and kept in a safe and secure place in the prescribed manner.

For the purposes of evaluation of pre-qualifications or bids for procurements, the Board or accounting officer must establish an ad hoc bid evaluation committee for the evaluation of bids(section 26(1)(a)). A bid evaluation committee is responsible for the evaluation of pre-qualifications, bids, proposals or quotations and the preparation of evaluation reports for submission to the procurement committee (section 26(4)).

AN OVERVIEW OF THE PUBLIC PROCUREMENT PROCESS

The procurement process generally follows a three-staged cycle comprising of the pre-bid stage, the bidding stage and the post bid-stage. These stages are captured in the Act under Part 6, which is entitled "Bidding Process." Part 6 of the Act prescribes the procedures to be followed in the invitation for bids, pre-qualification proceedings, contents of bidding documents, circumstances under two-staged bidding may be held, requirements for bid security or bid securing declarations, the submission of bids, bid validity period, the opening of bids, examination and evaluation of bids, post-qualifications, cancellation of the bidding process, award of procurement contracts and the briefing of unsuccessful bidders (sections 40–57).

The Public Procurement Act has also introduced mandatory methods to be used in the procurement process. It grants procurement entities different methods from which to choose after having made a decision to engage in a procurement process. These are: open advertised bidding, restricted bidding, request for sealed quotations, direct procurement, execution by public entities, emergency procurement, small value procurement, request for proposals and electronic reverse auction (sections 27(1)(a)(i)–(ix)). It must however be noted that a deviation from the open advertising bid is only permissible if the procuring entity has reason to believe that the open advertised bidding does not support empowerment and other policies of the government contemplated in section 2 of the Act, or if it is not efficient or practical for the procurement in question; or if it is too costly to apply, given the value of the procurement (see section 27(4)(a)-(c). For a detailed exposition of when the various methods of procurement may be used, see sections 28–38 of the Act).

REMEDIES FOR BIDDERS IN PUBLIC PROCUREMENT

Notably, the Public Procurement Act has increased legal regulation of public procurement in Namibia. However, the legal mechanisms which might be invoked to protect the rights of the bidders and/or interests that bidders have in the fair conduct of the procurement are not so clear. It is noteworthy that the general rules of constitutional law and administrative law apply to public procurement because the solicitation, evaluation and award of public contracts amount to administration action (Bolton 2008, 783). It is also undisputable that the Anti-Corruption Act 8 of 2003 finds application to public procurement procedures, as it criminalises corrupt activities relating to contracts and to the procurement and withdrawal of procurement contracts (see section 37). Traditionally, there is a reluctance of procurement systems to cancel existing contracts except in cases of fraud and corruption, although this opens the government to legal challenges by the contractor in question (Williams 2007, 22). However, because the procurement contract is tainted with an illegality, claims for payment made by the bidder could be denied on the basis of illegality (*Chipunza v Muzangaza N.O.* [2004] JOL 12880 (ZH)). It must however be noted that no matter what the grounds may be for the interference in the public procurement contract granted to a bidder, there must always be due process in the decision to terminate (Hoexter and Lyster 2002), 167 and 244. A discussion of the remedies available for bidders in terms of the Namibian Constitution and the Public Procurement Act follows.

REMEDIES IN TERMS OF THE NAMIBIAN CONSTITUTION

The Namibian Constitution is the supreme law of the land (article 1(4) of the Namibian Constitution), all laws and acts should therefore be in accordance with its provisions to be valid (article 1(6) of the Namibian Constitution). It is imperative that the interpretation of the Namibian Constitution should reflect its aims, objects, spirits and values as reflected in its preamble. The preamble of the Namibian Constitution *inter alia* expresses recognition of the inherent dignity and of the equal and inalienable rights of all members of the human family which are indispensable for freedom, justice and peace. Further, article 5 of the Namibian Constitution mandates all organs of the state, its agencies, all natural persons and legal persons in Namibia to respect and uphold the fundamental rights and freedoms enshrined in its chapter 3. Moreover, article 18 grants the right to lawful, reasonable and fair administrative procedures by guaranteeing administrative justice. Article 18 makes provision for administrative justice and it reads:

> Administrative bodies and administrative officials shall act fairly and reasonably and comply with the requirements imposed upon such bodies and officials by common law and any relevant legislation, and persons aggrieved by the exercise of such acts and decisions shall have the right to seek redress before a competent Court or Tribunal.

In Namibia, the court of original jurisdiction which has the power to determine administrative law cases is the High Court and appeals therefrom lie to the Supreme Court (Parker 2009, 118). This means that in terms of Namibian administrative law, the aggrieved person would approach the High Court and request it to review and correct, or set aside the decision complained of, which essentially constitutes what is referred to as judicial review (Parker 2009, 118). Section 18 as referred to earlier, tasks administrative bodies and administrative officials to act fairly and reasonably and comply with the requirements imposed upon them by the common law and any relevant legislation. One of the requirements so imposed by the common law is the compliance with the *audi alteram partem* rule which means the right to be heard. By virtue of this article, unsuccessful bidders or aggrieved bidders whose contracts have been withdrawn have the legal standing to challenge procurement decisions by means of an application for judicial review on grounds of lawfulness, reasonableness and procedural fairness (Parker 2009, 118; Bolton 2008, 784).

Because the public procurement process is regulated by constitutional provisions, each improper performance of an administrative function would implicate the Constitution and entitle the aggrieved party to an appropriate relief. In the South African Constitutional Case of *Steenkamp v Provincial Tender Board, Eastern Cape* 2007(3) SA 121 (CC), it was stated that:

> It is nonetheless appropriate to note that ordinarily a breach of administrative justice attracts public law remedies, to pre-empt or correct or reverse an improper administrative function. In some instances, the remedy takes the form of an order to make or not make a particular decision or an order declaring rights or an injunction to furnish reasons for an adverse decision. Ultimately the purpose of a public remedy is to afford the prejudiced party administrative justice, to advance efficient and effective public administration compelled by constitutional precepts and at a broader level, to entrench the rule of law.

In the Namibian context, the concept of administrative justice in public procurement proceedings was considered in the case of *Pamo Trading Enterprises CC and Another v Chairperson of the Tender Board of Namibia and Others* SA 60/2017) [2019] NASC 583 (03 July 2019). The facts of the case were briefly that during March 2014 the first respondent, the Board, advertised a tender for the provision of catering services to government school hostels for the duration commencing on June 1, 2014, to May 31, 2019. In response to the advertisement, the appellants and eighty-seven other bidders submitted their proposals on/before the closing date, April 1, 2014, which proposals were, seemingly, in compliance with all the requirements (para 8 of the judgement).

After completion of the first tender process, the Evaluation Committee made a written recommendation to award the tender to various successful tenderers, including the appellants in June 2014. This recommendation was, however, sent back to the Committee as there were various issues impacting the tender process which needed to be clarified including questions concerning the bidders' warehouses. During September 2014, officials from the Ministry of Education (the Ministry) conducted site visits at the appellants' sites. The appellants stated that the visits made them optimistic that there were prospects of success on being one of the successful bidders (para 9). During one of its meetings, held on October 2, 2014, the Board awarded the tender for the Khomas Region to the first appellant and for the Otjozondjupa Region to the second appellant. It based its award on the recommendation of the Committee. However, the successful bidders including the appellants were not informed of that outcome (para 10).

It transpired that before the appellants and other successful bidders were notified of the outcome as they should have been in terms of section 16 of the Tender Act, serious allegations surfaced and were reported in two separate local newspapers on October 10 and 13, 2014, regarding the tender. The allegations were that the Permanent Secretary, a senior state official in the Ministry, was involved in the allocation of one of the tenders in respect of one of the regions and the allocation made to a company in which the Permanent Secretary's wife had an interest. In light of the above, the Ministry requested the Board to cancel the tender. This request was considered at the Board meeting held on October 13, 2014 (para 12). After seeking legal advice on the implications of the requests on the powers of the Board, in terms of the Tender Act, the entire tender was cancelled and the cancellation decision was communicated via facsimile to all the bidders on October 15, 2014, indicating that the Board had a meeting where it resolved to cancel the decision to award the tenders (para 13).

The appellants launched an application in the High Court seeking an order *inter alia* reviewing and correcting or setting aside the cancellation decision by the Tender Board based on the following grounds:

a) a procedural ground that the appellants were denied a right to be heard (*audi alteram partem*) and were prejudiced;
b) a substantive ground – that the cancellation was irrational and thus unlawful.
c) that the Board and the Ministry were *functus officio* (A legal maxim described as meaning that an administrator/decision-maker/official who has once "discharged his official function" by making a decision is unable to change his mind and revoke, withdraw or revisit the decision. Hoexter C Administrative Law in South Africa (2 ed) (2012) p. 277).

d) that the Board and not the ministry or prime minister was the sole agency that could cancel the tender after affording them the *audi alteram partem*. This contention was based on allegations that the Board was asked to cancel the tender and that the Board simply rubberstamped the already taken decision to cancel.

The High Court held that the reasons advanced for the cancellation of the food tender were reasonable as the involvement of some of the members of the Committee associated with some of the tenderers was unacceptable and disgraceful (para 36). Regarding the substantive challenge, that the cancellation of the tender was unreasonable and irrational, the Court ruled that because the evidence *discloses corruption* and incompetence on the part of the officers in the Ministry, the cancellation of the tender cannot be said to be unreasonable or irrational (paras 40-41). Concerning the challenge that the Board was *functus officio*, the High Court held that the non-communication was occasioned by the fact that the decision was not final since the *functus officio* doctrine applies only to final decisions, so that a decision is revocable before it becomes final (paras 40–41). On the question of the lawfulness of the extension of the agreements allegedly being *ultra vires* the powers of the Board, the High Court held that it was not the case (paras 48–54).

On appeal, the Supreme Court affirmed that procurement steps taken by public officials and agencies like the Board must be lawful and procedurally fair. These administrators, including the Board as the procurement agency, are therefore held to a more stringent standard to ensure, among other things, that rights are not adversely affected (para 29). The government respondents did not deny that the successful bidders, including the appellants, were not heard or at least afforded an opportunity to make written representation before the cancellation of the tender after the award. Rather, they contended that because of the impropriety and allegations of corruption the Board and the Ministry acted responsibly and in line with their constitutional duty by bringing about the cancellation of the tender to obviate any impression that the state condoned or is indifferent to such wrong-doing (paras 35–36). The respondents thus submitted that a rational basis existed for the cancellation of a tender and that the appellants were thus not entitled to be heard. In light of the core notions of administrative justice, the Court found this approach unquestionably untenable as it "touched in an enduring and far-reaching manner on vital human interest that pointed in the direction of violation" (para 37). The Court dismissed the submission of the respondents suggesting that the successful bidders had no right, in law or under the Constitution, to the award of a tender because a tender is an invitation to do business and not a right to be awarded a contract by indicating that such a proposition is, under the circumstances of this case, demonstrably flawed because the issue is not whether the appellants had a right to be awarded a tender contract, but about the fair process rights aimed towards eliminating the proscribed arbitrariness in a way that gives contents to the rule of law (para 39).

It was stated that the duty to act fairly requires a statutory procurement agent to have discharged its obligations under article 18 of the Constitution and the peremptory prescripts in terms of the Act (paras 41). At a minimum, the Court emphasised that the Board should have allowed the appellants to make representations but failed to do so despite the fact that the appellants had alerted the Board of their predicament particularly that they had been materially prejudiced by the cancellation without having been consulted and that but for knowing about the award in the newspapers, they had not been notified of same (para 42).

Regarding the contention that the decision to cancel was that of the Ministry and not the Board, the appellants argued that the Ministry had no authority to direct the Board to cancel the tender. On this, the court remarked that although the respondents deny that the decision to cancel was made by the Ministry, the appellants' argument is not far-fetched as the respondents also argued that the Ministries had a duty to act on the strength of the allegations of corruption because of their constitutional obligations and that it was precisely for that reason that they caused the committee to deal with the allegations. The committee then resolved to recommend cancellation. It is thus not unexpected that the appellants, given the request to cancel the tender and coupled with the information regarding what the Minister wanted, considered that the Board merely rubberstamped the already taken decision (paras 50–53).

Based on the above, the court held that the cancellation of the tender in these circumstances was irrational and unlawful (para 55). As regards the appropriate relief in this case, the Supreme Court stated that ordinarily, a breach of administrative justice attracts public law remedies. However, a determination of what constitutes an appropriate remedy, given the constitutional and statutory breaches on one hand and the effluxion of time of the tender on the other, is somewhat tricky. The determination is a discretionary matter which discretion must be exercised judicially upon consideration of certain factors in the circumstances, including consideration of fairness to all concerned (paras 56–57; See also *Minister of Health and Social Services v Lisse* 2006 (2) NR 739).

In the same vein, the concept of administrative justice in public procurement process was also considered in the High Court case of *the Central Procurement Board v Nangolo NO and Others* [2018] NAHCMD 357 (9 Nov 2018). The Roads Authority, the fourth respondent in this application, advertised a tender for the personalisation of driving licences cards. The process of the said tender commenced in 2016 and an evaluation of the tender had been completed at both the technical and financial levels. Indications at that stage were that the 3rd respondent was the preferred bidder (para 12). The applicant, a body formed in terms of the Act awarded a tender to the 3rd respondent. The applicant's decision to award the tender was taken on review by the unsuccessful bidders in terms of section 59 of the Act. This review application to the review panel was, however, not served on the applicant. The review panel upheld the review application and ordered the applicant to start *de novo,* holding that it was not *functus officio* and to among other things, consult with the Policy Unit in the appointment of the evaluation committee. The applicant then sought the court's determination on whether the applicant is entitled to notice of an application for review to the review panel and whether it is entitled to properly present its case to the review panel (para 14).

It was submitted on behalf of the applicant that because it was not served with the application for review; it was unaware of who the applicants for review were and therefore not privy to the bases advanced for the review. Further that, it was not afforded any proper or adequate opportunity to prepare itself to appear before the review panel and make meaningful representations that would hopefully assist the said Panel in reaching a proper decision (para 17).

The court mentioned that service of relevant documents on a party that has an interest in a matter, particularly one in a position of the applicant, whose decision is sought to be set aside was fundamental to avoid making a decision based on skewed information provided by the complainant (paras 18–19). It was affirmed that the principle of fairness should never be sacrificed on the altar of convenience, particularly where it comes to issues of notice and the right to be heard (para 26). In light of this, two irregularities were emphasised, namely that the applicant was not served with a copy of the review application notwithstanding that the applicant was cited and listed as a respondent in the matter and that the applicant was denied a proper opportunity to know the case against it but more importantly, an opportunity to present its case to the 1st respondent (paras 28–29). This, the court termed as a "grave failure of justice, an abortion of fairness and an abject aversion to the hallowed principle of the *audi alteram partem.*"

Reference was made to the case of *Swaziland Federation of Trade Unions v The President of the Industrial Court* (11/97) [1998] SZSZ 8 (01 Jan 1998), where the concept of the *audi alteram partem* principle was interpreted to mean (para 30):

> [T]hat the other party must be heard before an order can be granted against him, is one of the oldest and most universally applied principles enshrined in our law. That no man was to be judged unheard was a precept known to the Greeks, was inscribed in ancient times upon images in places where justice was administered, is enshrined in the scriptures, was asserted by an 18th century English

> judge to be a principle of divine justice and traced to the events in the Garden of Eden, and has been applied in cases from 1723 to the present time . . . Embraced in the principle is also the rule that an interested party against whom an order may be made must be informed of any possibly prejudicial facts or considerations that may be raised against him in order to afford him the opportunity of responding to them or defending himself against them.

On account of the above, the review hearing before the review panel was stated to amount to no hearing at all (para 31). Accordingly, as regards the decision reached by the review panel following a fatally flawed process, was held to not stand and therefore set aside (para 32. See also *Vaatz v Municipal Council of Windhoek* 2017 (1) NR 21 (SC) at 25 where the Supreme Court stated that two fundamental requirements that need to be satisfied before a hearing can be said to be fair: there must be notice of the contemplated action and a proper opportunity to be heard).

Based on the above exposition of cases, it is common cause that the decision to cancel or terminate a public procurement contract must comply with the precepts of article 18 of the Namibian Constitution. This implies that:

(a) Written reasons for the decision must be provided after affording the bidder an opportunity to make representations before the public procurement body.
(b) The bidder must be afforded remedies where procedural standards have not been met (du Toit and Henning 1999, 27).
(c) In the event of suspicion of the bidder being involved in irregular activities, the bidder ought to be provided with information in relation to the proposed decision.
(d) The bidder should be afforded an opportunity to present arguments and evidence in response to the allegations against it and should be informed that it has the right to approach the High Court for judicial review of the decision (Bolton 2006, 25).

REMEDIES IN TERMS OF THE PUBLIC PROCUREMENT ACT

Any party in the procurement proceedings who is aggrieved by any decision or action of the procurement entity may apply for review in terms of the Act. Section 59(1) of the Act provides that any bidder or supplier may apply to the review panel in the prescribed manner for review of a decision or an action taken by the Procurement Board or by a public entity for the award of a procurement contract. Naturally, such an application addressed to the review panel should also be served on the bidder who was awarded the procurement contract because of the interest they have in the case. The Act also prescribes in section 60 of the Act the powers of the review panel in relation to an application for review contemplated above. Specifically, the review panel may only grant the following orders:

(a) dismiss the application;
(b) direct the Board or the public entity that has acted or proceeded in a manner that is not in compliance with this Act to act or proceed in a manner that is in compliance with this Act;
(c) set aside in whole or in part a decision or an action of the Board or public entity that is not in compliance with this Act, *other than any decision or action bringing the procurement contract or the framework agreement into force* (own emphasis), and refer the matter back to the Board or public entity for reconsideration with specific instructions;
(d) correct a decision or action by the Board or public entity that is not in compliance with this Act;
(e) confirm the decision of the Board or public entity; or
(f) order that the procurement proceedings be terminated and start afresh.

The provisions of section 60(c) and section 60(f) are of particular importance. There are circumstances where the decision made by the review panel is in accordance with the provisions of section 60(f), although the consequences thereof, whether intended or not, are that of the exception spelt out in section 60(c). When regard is had to the provisions of section 60(f), the operative concepts there are: "the procurement proceedings." The Act however does not define a procurement proceeding. However, section 1 of the Act defines procurement to mean the acquisition of goods, works, consultancy services or non-consultancy services by any means, including purchase, rental, lease or hire-purchase whereas a procurement contract to mean a contract between a public entity and a supplier resulting from a procurement process. Based on the above, the procurement proceeding should be taken to include all processes from the first step aimed at initiating any procurement method implied in section 27 to the awarding of a procurement contract.

Considering that the legislature chose to differentiate between the two types of decisions implied in section 60(c) and section 60(f), it goes without saying that their effects cannot for all intents and purposes be the same. Section 60(c) entitles the review panel to set aside any decision made by the Board or Public Entity except that which has the effect of terminating a procurement contract or the framework agreement (*The Central Procurement Board v Nangolo N.O.*(HC-MD-CIV-MOT-REV-2017/00441) [2018] NAHCMD 357 (9 Nov 2018) paras 50-53). Section 60(f) pertains to review powers of the review panel to consider all review applications brought before them prior to the conclusion of the procurement contract is concluded. This means that as soon as the procurement contract is entered into, then there is no longer any procurement proceeding to terminate and/or to start afresh.

When regard is had to the provisions of section 55(5), it becomes clear that a procurement contract is only supposed to be awarded to the successful bidder in the absence of an application for review by any other bidder within seven days of the notice served in terms of section 55(4). This means that once the procurement contract has been awarded, nothing can thereafter be done by the review panel to temper with the rights of the contractor in terms of the procurement contract.

Once a procurement award has been made or a procurement contract entered into, the language of the Act appears to suggest that such can only be terminated by the body that awarded it due to changed circumstances as described in terms of section 63(1). This section empowers the public entity to withdraw an award or a procurement contract if there are changed circumstances, in that the continuation of the contract is not or will not be in the public interest or if any variation in a contract price causes the total contract amount to exceed by more than 15 per cent. Where such is done, section 63(2) provides that the contractor is entitled to reimbursement of expenses incurred in the performance of the contract, but is not entitled to recover anticipated profits on the completion of the contract. The essence of section 63 is that if the procurement awards the bidder after the bidding process and then later decides to withdraw it for any reason other than the ones outlined in that section, it may be tempting to believe that the public entity may be liable to damages because all bidders are entitled to a lawful and fair process according to the provisions of the Act.

It follows therefore that in terms of section 63(1), a procurement contract may only be terminated by the body that awarded it "on the grounds of changed circumstances (a) in that the continuation of the contract is not or will not be in the public interest; or (b) any variation in a contract price causes the total contract amount to exceed by more than 15 percent," and where such is done, section 63(2) provides that the contractor is entitled to reimbursement of expenses incurred in the performance of the contract, but is not entitled to recover anticipated profits on the completion of the contract. In summary, the review panel does not have the powers to set aside a decision or an action that has resulted in the procurement contract by virtue of section 60(c).

Further, part 10 of the Act provides for procurement integrity. In terms of section 66(1), the Act requires staff members of the public entity involved in the planning or conducting procurement processes to *inter alia* undertake to discharge such functions fairly and impartially and without fear, favour or prejudice to anyone so as to ensure fair competitive access to procurement by suppliers, as well as to act in the public interest and in accordance with the Act.

CONCLUDING REMARKS

Public interest demands the protection of aggrieved bidders, particularly where such interest inevitably protects the public interest. For the same reasons which evolved to the growth of administrative, namely, to curb abuse of power, to impose checks and balances to safeguard fair procedures for decision-making, it is imperative that clear remedies are spelt out for the bidders to ensure the rule of law in public procurement. All bidders must therefore be treated fairly, reasonable and lawfully to achieve a transparent and competitive procurement process. Where a decision is made by the administrative body to terminate the offer to award procurement to a bidder, such constitutes an administrative action which had to be exercised in compliance with the provisions of the Namibian Constitution and Act.

At minimum, the administrative body is required to notify the bidder of its decision to withdraw the offer, provide reasons for such withdrawal after having afforded the bidder an opportunity to make representations before it. This is so because withdrawing an offer that has granted benefits to the successful bidders creates a legitimate expectation on the part of the successful bidder, which can be used as a basis to render the subsequent award procedurally unfair. Taking the words of Roos and de la Harpe when they stated that the principle of accountability in good governance in public procurement entails that there must be a system which provides adequate access for the lodging of complaints and challenges by means also of judicial review or appeal (Roos and de la Harpe 2008, 133, 252), it appears that there is good governance in Namibia's public procurement systems. If the principles of natural justice encompassed under article 18 and provisions of the Act are upheld at all stages of the public procurement process, administrative justice will be achieved and at the same time assist in the upholding of the principles of transparency and accountability.

BIBLIOGRAPHY

Arrowsmith, S. (1994). "Protecting the Interests of Bidders for Public Contracts: The Role of the Common Law." *The Cambridge Law Journal*, Volume 53(1), 104–139.

Arrowsmith, S. (2004). "Public Procurement: An Appraisal of the Uncitral Model Law as a Global Standard." *The International and Comparative Law Quarterly*, Volume 53(1), 17–46.

Arrowsmith, S. (2005). *The Law of Public and Utility Procurement*. London: Sweet & Maxwell.

Arrowsmith, S., Linarelli, J., and Wallace, D. (2000). *Regulating Public Procurement: National and International Perspectives*. Boston: Kluwer Law International.

Bolton, P. (2005). *The Legal Regulation of Government Procurement in South Africa*. UWC, LLD Thesis.

Bolton, P. (2008). "The Public Procurement System in South Africa: Main Characteristics." *Public Contract Law Journal*, Volume 37(4), 781–802.

Bolton, P. (2014). "The Use of Government Procurement as an Instrument of Policy." *South African Law Journal*, Volume 121(3), 619–635.

Bovis, C. H. (2012). "Access to Justice and Remedies in Public Procurement." *European Procurement and Public Private Partnership Law Review*, Volume 7(3), 195–202.

Chipunza v Muzangaza N.O. [2004] JOL 12880 (ZH).

Hoexter, C. (2012). *Administrative Law in South Africa* (2nd ed.). Claremont: Juta & Co Ltd.

Hoexter, C., and Lyster, R. (2002). *The New Constitutional and Administrative Law Vol. 2 – Administrative Law*. Cape Town: Juta & Co Ltd.

Institute for Public Policy Research. (August 2017). "Briefing Paper: Promoting Integrity: The New Public Procurement Framework."

Lennerfors, T. T. (2007). "The Transformation of Transparency: On the Act on Public Procurement and the Right to Appeal in the Context of the War on Corruption." *Journal of Business Ethics*, Volume 73(4), 381–390.

Minister of Health and Social Services v Lisse 2006 (2) NR 739.

Pamo Trading Enterprises CC and Another v Chairperson of the Tender Board of Namibia and Others (SA 60/2017) [2019] NASC 583 (03 July 2019).

Parker, C. (2009). "Administrative Law in Namibia, Its Current State, Challenges, and Proposals for Law Reform." *The Comparative and International Law Journal of Southern Africa*, Volume 42(1), 115–127.

Roos, R., and De la Harpe, S. (2008). "Good Governance in Public Procurement: A South African Case Study." *PER/PELJ*, Volume 11(2), 125/252–170/252.

Steenkamp v Provincial Tender Board, Eastern Cape 2007(3) SA 121 (CC).

Swaziland Federation of Trade Unions v The President of the Industrial Court (11/97) [1998] SZSZ 8 (01 Jan 1998).

The Anti-Corruption Act 8 of 2003.

The Central Procurement Board v Nangolo N.O.(HC-MD-CIV-MOT-REV-2017/00441) [2018] NAHCMD 357 (9 Nov 2018).

The Public Procurement Act 15 of 2015.

The Public Procurement Act Regulations of 2015.

The Tender Act 16 of 1996.

United Nations Commission on International Trade Law (UNICTRAL) Model Law on Public Procurement (2011).

United Nations Convention Against Corruption (2003).

Vaatz v Municipal Council of Windhoek 2017 (1) NR 21 (SC).

Williams, S. (2007). "The Use of Exclusions for Corruption in Developing Country Procurement: The Case of South Africa." *Journal of African Law*, Volume 51(1), 1–38.

Chapter 12

Is Amending Section 25 of the South African Constitution an End to the Land Reform Debate?

Lekunze Joseph Nembo and Luvhengo Usapfa

INTRODUCTION

Failures of the land reform programme in South Africa since 1994 have been attributed to perceived "flaws" in section 25 of the 1996 Constitution of the Republic of South Africa due to the fact that expropriation of land without compensation has not yet been approved by the South African government. If section 25 of the Constitution of the Republic of South Africa is amended to allow for expropriation of land without compensation, a "new non-racial minority land owners" group may emerge leading to a future land reform debate on equity in redistribution not solely based along racial lines. In this chapter, we review both pre- and post-colonial legislations, policies including some recent publications on the discourse surrounding the amendment of section 25 of the South African Constitution. Further, we develop a conceptual process based on the social facilitation theory to explore the ideological and equity strands around the amendment of section 25. The study concludes that an amendment of section 25 of the South Africa Constitution is justifiable as long as equity in redistribution of land to all South Africans irrespective of race is realised. If the amendment of section 25 cannot guarantee non-racial equality in the distribution of land for all South Africans, the emergence of a new non-racial minority land owners similar to those of the colonial era may emerge. This may lead to the resurfacing of the land debate in future along intra-racial lines and may delegitimise the current South African government in the eyes of African people.

In South Africa, the formalisation of land rights along racial lines was given basis to in the Native Land Act (NLA) of 1913 (subsequently renamed the Bantu Land Act, 1913 and Black Land Act, 1913; Act 27 of 1913). The NLA allocated 13 per cent of land to indigenous Africans who constituted the majority of the population following a series of wars with European settlers (Makombe and Phago 2018, 280). The NLA also formalised the expropriation of land through a raft of laws passed during the period 1913–1948 and thereafter. Such laws led to a shift in the pattern of land ownership and equity in South Africa. Through the NLA, land expropriation from African owners was adopted by the government despite the perceived illegitimacy of the process as viewed from an African perspective. Land thus was central to the struggle for legitimacy by African indigenes in South Africa, culminating in a 1994 political settlement that led to the finalisation of a new constitution of the Republic of South Africa in 1996. Section 25(2) of the 1996 Constitution of the Republic of South Africa provides for the protection of property rights and states that, "No one maybe deprived of property except in terms of the law of general application, and no law may permit arbitrary deprivation of property." The implementation of the property clause in the Constitution was guided by the outcome of the political settlement policy of willing buyer, or willing seller or market-led forces as argued by Makombe and Phago (2018). As such, the expropriation of land and the right to land ownership as legitimised by the NLA, and subsequent pieces of legislations thereafter, persisted. However, in interrogating the emerging realities informed by a market driven South African economy, prospects and challenges of expropriation without compensation post 1994, prompted Dlamini and Ogunnubi (2018, 339) to contend that debates on "expropriation without compensation" have sparked more issues and concerns regarding land ownership, use and management especially with regard to land under traditional leadership in South Africa.

Dlamini and Ogunnubi (2018) further argued that since 1994, the land reform programme in South Africa has undergone transformation processes aimed at accelerating equity in redistribution. However, the intended acceleration has not been realised as the redistribution pace has remained very slow pace. The slow redistribution pace has left the government of South Africa in a quandary and without ideas and policies to successfully implement land redistribution for equity. Cousin as quoted by Dlamini and Ogunnubi (2018) has thus argued that the political settlement and the protection of private property rights enshrined in the 1996 Constitution of the Republic of South Africa stands as an insurmountable obstacle in the path of land redistribution in South Africa. Dlamini and Ogunnubi (2018) have in turn pointed out that the 1996 Constitution of the Republic of South Africa allows for expropriation with compensation at level that is just and equitable. Furthermore, the state as provided for in the Constitution has the duty to pass rational laws and adopt any other processes within the ambit of available resources to foster conditions that provide citizens with the opportunity to access land on an equitable basis as enshrined in section 25(5) of the Constitution of South Africa.

This chapter departs from the premise that failures of land reform in South Africa from 1994 were solely as a result of ambiguity in the formulation of section 25 of the 1996 Constitution of the Republic of South Africa which aims at protecting private property rights, provides for expropriation of land with compensation and at the same time uses the market-led willing buyer, willing seller approach to expropriation. The chapter advances the argument that if section 25 of the Constitution of the Republic of South Africa (hereinafter the Constitution) is amended to allow for expropriation without compensation, a future land reform debate on equity in redistribution may emerge, not based along racial lines, but along intra-racial lines as equity in redistribution may still not be achieved.

This chapter examines legislation and recent scholarly reviews and discussions on the amendment of section 25 which point to an ideological belief that the amendment of section 25 may address all barriers limiting state implementation of the land reform programme in South Africa. There was a general consensus in literature that, amendment of section 25(2) of the Constitution to expropriate land without compensation may accelerate the land redistribution processes. However, questions still remain as to whether or not the same process will resolve the issue of equity in redistribution. Molope (2018) submits that South Africa is one of the countries in Africa whose minority segment of the population of the same race control approximately over 80 per cent of the land while a substantial portion of the land has never been returned to indigenous people post-independence (Indigenous people constitute 80 per cent of South Africa's population).

Opponents of the land reform programme in South Africa are in agreement that, a prohibiting factor in the implementation of the land reform programme in the country is section 25 of the Constitution. Section 25 of the Constitution protects property rights and prohibits expropriation of land without compensation but allows for expropriation with compensation. On the other hand, some persons argue that section 25 of the Constitution provides for expropriation (section 25(5)) and allows for the state to put in place reasonable legislative and other parameters to foster conditions that provide citizens with access to land on an equitable basis. As a result, Dlamini and Ogunnubi (2018) argue that failure by government to expropriate land twenty-four years after the promulgation into law of the Constitution can be attributed to inefficiency in the implementation of the land reform programme. Since no land has been expropriated twenty-four years into the land reform programme of South Africa, this failure can equally be attributed to state incapabilities and not solely on section 25 of the Constitution. The state has failed to utilise the minimum power accorded to her under the current Constitution in section 25(5)–(6) of the Constitution. Molope (2018) opined that one factor that emerged from discussions around land reform in South Africa from those who were dispossessed pre- and post-1994 and those who currently own land is that, both sides want to use section 25 of the Constitution to benefit them differently. Dlamini and Ogunnubi (2018) argue as quoted by Kirsten that if land reform in South Africa was implemented correctly, it would contribute to increased equity in redistribution, increased gross domestic production (GDP) growth and reduce poverty. Further, Dlamini and Ogunnubi (2018) suggest that there are ideological reasons and empirical evidence to suggest land reform has the ability to provide equity and benefits to all South Africans; although this has not been achieved twenty-four years since the promulgation into law of the Constitution. The Land redistribution in relation to South Africa's land mass can be summarised as follows: (1) land area of South Africa is 122,320,100 hectares; (2) land area of former homelands is 17,112,800 hectares; (3) land area of former "white South Africa" is 105,267,300 hectares; (4) arable land/commercial agricultural land is 86,186,026 hectares; (5) 30 per cent of commercial agricultural land 25,855,808 hectares and (6) total land distribution to date 4,701,542 hectares. The land redistribution calculated as a percentage of commercial agricultural land in South Africa is 5.46 per cent.

Furthermore, advocates for the amendment of section 25(2) of the Constitution believe that, if the section provides for expropriation without compensation, why are some segments of the South African public advocating for section 25(2) to remain unchanged? Proponents for expropriation without compensation further believe that, although section 25 of the Constitution appears to provide for expropriation, the application is implicit, ambiguous and open to numerous interpretations. It is therefore not questionable that political settlement and the protection of private property rights stand as an insurmountable obstacle in the path of land redistribution in South Africa. As a result, attempts by the government to expropriate land without compensation are not protected under section 25 of the Constitution but expropriation with compensation not purely based on market value is permitted. Such an expropriation with compensation not purely based on market value may involve lengthy legal battles, time and costs to the fiscus as a result of legal challenges. These legal challenges may result in wasteful use of tax payers' monies and polarise the nation further along racial lines.

It is therefore plausible to contend that the post-apartheid South African government has failed to expropriate any land without compensation for twenty-four years. As Molope (2018) summarised, "section 25 of the Constitution of South Africa is illogical and certain clauses in the section have become an unmitigated disaster as prices of land which were expropriated from indigenous people are now inflated above market price in order to redistribute to the same indigenous folks."

RESEARCH METHODOLOGY

This chapter is a review of section 25 of the Constitution and related policies and laws guiding the implementation of the land reform programme in South Africa since 1996. The reviewed policies and laws were meant to measure the extent to which the land reform programme has failed to realise an equitable redistribution of land in South Africa. Extensive legislative review in the chapter focused on the laws such as the Natives Land Act 27 of 1913, as well as the Trust and Land Act 18 of 1936 that led to the formalisation of segregation of South African citizens along racial lines. In the formalization of segregation, a segment of the population estimated at 349,837 grabbed 87 per cent of the land with a meagre 13 per cent of land allocated to indigenous African people who constituted 87 per cent of the country's population. Other pieces of legislations reviewed include the Group Areas Act 41 of 1950, the Bantu Authorities Act 68 of 1951 and the Bantu Homelands Citizenship Act 26 of 1970.

Further, the Land and Assistance Act 126 of 1993, the Land Restitution Act 22 of 1994, the Constitution and the White Paper on South African Land Policy of 1997 were also reviewed. Furthermore, the White Paper on South African Land policy; the Extension of Security of Tenure Act (ESTA) 62 of 1997, the Land Reform (Labour Tenants) Act 3 of 1996 and the Interim Protection of Informal Land Rights Act (IPILRA) 31 of 1996 were also reviewed.

The Traditional Leadership Governance and Framework Act 41 of 2003 which regulates the distribution of land located in the rural areas under the custodian of the traditional leadership or the tribal council was also referred to (Take note that article 17 of the Universal Declaration of Human Rights, provides that everyone has a right to own property and that such a right should not be encroached on arbitrarily by anyone). The Extension of Security of Tenure Act which regulates the eviction of people on farms and the Communal Land Rights Act 11 of 2004 were also reviewed.

The researchers examined the social facilitation theory as the theoretical basis to debate whether amendment of section 25(2) of the Constitution can meet the expectations of the landless majority in South Africa. The social facilitation theory examines the influences of organisation factors on the increase or decrease of performance level of any organisation (government). The assumption was that land reform programme driven by the government will accelerate redistribution, access and equity to landless majority while at the same time section 25(2) of the Constitution must protect property rights for capital investments. The double objective for equity in redistribution and protection of property are testament to the dilemma the South African government is encountering to execute land reform.

This dilemma was confirmed by a research done by Malatji (2018) who in a study found, it was a combination of ideological and pragmatic considerations that informed the protection of private property in the Constitution. Furthermore, the Thabo Mbeki Foundation stated that the adoption of a willing seller, willing buyer (market-friendly) approach to the acquisition of land for redistribution was noble for nation building and political stability. However, two fundamental flaws exist– confusion in policy and expediency in practice – that led to the present outcome(s) of the land reform programme in South Africa.

LITERATURE REVIEW ON LAND REFORM IN SOUTH AFRICA

According to Sebopetsa and Bayat (2018), inequalities associated with land ownership in South Africa have threatened post-colonial democracy in South Africa and whether or not the discourse around the amendment of section 25(2) may put an end to the land question in South Africa is debatable. Sebopetsa and Bayat (2018) analysed the views expressed by citizens during public hearings with regards to the possibility of amending section 25 of the Constitution of South Africa and found that section 25 of the Constitution which provides for land and property rights had some weaknesses:

1) Section 25(2) protects private property and section 25(5) provides for the state to take reasonable measures to expropriation with compensation are not explicit, and
2) The willing seller and willing buyer approach used to transfer land for equity in redistribution was an ideological myth within South Africa's budgetary constraints. In line with these weaknesses, the authors argue that:

   The implicit nature of (1) above and the ideological thinking of (2) above led to ambiguity and interpretations of section 25 of the Constitution with regard to the land question; and
3) The state as an implementing agent may appear inefficient in driving the land reform process due to its bureaucratic nature, political patronage and elitism coupled with vested interests from private groupings that may have contributed to the slow pace of land redistribution for equity, leading to the emergence of a hostile debate around land from 2018 in South Africa.

Therefore, the ideological and practical challenge of private property rights and market-led approach in implementing the land reform programme in South Africa may have acted as an insurmountable barrier to the post-apartheid land reform programme implementation. Furthermore, the land reform process is skewed in favour of political and traditional elites to the neglect of the landless majority at the margins of society. The depletion of resources towards the land reform programme as government expenditures on education, health, housing, sanitation and social welfare safety nets are being expanded poses further hindrance. Sebopetsa and Bayat (2018) concluded that the land reform programme in South Africa has let indigenous Africans down as majority of the people continue to experience extreme poverty, as well as high levels of unemployment that may have been resolved through the land reform programme, if not of section 25(2) of the Constitution and the market-led approach.

There exist several studies on land reform in South Africa that have specifically focused on access, ownership, property rights, approaches and the land reform programme as a whole. However, limited studies exist on the amendment of section 25(2) of the Constitution and debates that may follow once the amendment is finalised. The afore argument prompts the researchers to predict a future land reform debate in South Africa not premised along racial lines but along intra-racial lines emerging from political and traditional patronages. The central questions now are; (i) will amendment of section 25 of the Constitution bring an end to the debate on expropriation without compensation, (ii) can expropriation without compensation address equity in redistribution of land and (iii) can the debate on equity in land redistribution be silenced forever if section 25 is amended to expropriate land without compensation for policy certainty on the land question?

Ideological Consideration behind Section 25(2) of the Constitution

Sikwela et al. (2018) have argued that the adoption of the private property clause in section 25(2) of the Constitution perpetuates existing inequities in the redistribution of land in South Africa. If section 25(2) of the Constitution is seen as an impediment to the land reform process, then an alternative to the current section 25 of the Constitution is needed to satisfy the legitimate and urgent demand for equity in redistribution.

Okumbor et al. (2018) argue that legislative protection of private property is one way the landless poor can gain access to formal property rights and move from informal arrangements to formal arrangements in an economy. It is argued that the poor and landless majority can only get access to capital through formal registration of their assets for integration into the formal economy through a four-stage procedure. They argue from de Soto's viewpoint and quote "property reforms lead to investment and economic growth and the government can generate revenue through taxation to finance the reform process" (De Soto 1989, 2001, 2006). However, in South Africa, section 25(2) of the Constitution guarantees private property rights that protect the existing land owners and hinders redistribution to the landless majority, thus preventing the majority from gaining access to capital for investments.

In this chapter, it is argued that the increasing political noises on land expropriation without compensation and clamour for the amendment of section 25(2) of the Constitution in order to conclude the "land reform programme in South Africa no longer enjoys the support it initially received at the start of the programme twenty-four years ago."

Although some studies on land reform in South Africa have focused on the approach and evaluation of the reform programme, these studies have never predicted a future land reform debate which is not based on racial lines. We argue that intra-race conflicts may emerge if the amendments of section 25 of the Constitution do not address the increasing frictions within racial groupings, interrelationships among role players, patronage, elitism and vested interests held by individual players within the communities to the neglect of the majority at the margins of society.

If equity in land redistribution and access to land is fundamental to social cohesion and the political stability of South Africa, then earlier mistakes made by the government to consider both ideological and pragmatic considerations in executing the land reform programme in South Africa must be reconsidered. The government must either choose to protect property rights and allow the markets to determine the price of land through demand and supply. The government may then create a land sovereign fund where each and every citizen at the margins of society is entitled to a certain sum as set out by the state to buy land in the open market. In this regard, those who oppose amendments to section 25(2) of the Constitution may be guaranteed tenure security, policy certainty and re-investment in the land. On the other hand, if the government chooses to take a pragmatic route, then section 25(2) of the Constitution should be amended to remove the current ambiguity and pave the way for direct expropriation without compensation.

However, simplifying the debate on expropriation of land without compensation strictly along racial lines is also not justified as there exist substantial portions of lands under the control of government and traditional authorities in South Africa. Furthermore, attributing the entire failure of the land reform programme strictly on the ambiguity of section 25(2) as preventing land reform in South Africa is postponing the problem rather than completely solving it. The assumption that equity in redistribution along racial is important, placing control and power in the hands of the elite in the indigenous majority groupings and distributing land to the landless majority may never end the land reform debate in South Africa.

The acknowledgement on the part of the state that there were flaws in the implementation of the existing programme support the views of those clamouring for not amending section 25 (2) of the Constitution. However, failures in the land reform programme of South Africa cannot be solely attributed to section 25(2) of the Constitution. While studies exist debating the pros and cons of the different approaches, and or amalgamation of positive aspects of the different approaches to resolve the land question in South Africa, there has been little debate on alternative factors apart from the property right clause that must have led to failures in land reform and whether these variances, rather than section 25, may equally be responsible for land reform failures.

Equity in Redistribution through Amendment of Section 25(2) of Constitution

Section 25(2) of the Constitution, the property clause, the ideological and pragmatic approaches adopted by post-apartheid government to land reform, have failed the landless majority. It is not debatable that the land history of South Africa and the pattern of ownership, followed dispossession of land from indigenous African land owners through legislative processes along racial lines and not through the market forces. Therefore, land reform programmes mostly advocate for (i) equity in distribution and (ii) efficiency regarding the use of land resources to improve productivity, income and the standard of living of majority of a nation's citizens. However, most countries around the world have challenges in achieving appreciable levels of both equity in redistribution and efficiencies in the use of land resources. The current South African government combines an ideological stance with a pragmatic approach in the design and implementation of its land reform programme. The failure of the land reform programme to contextualise the historical patterns and African majority concerns in favour of powerful lobbyists has led to the renewed call for the amendment of section 25 of the Constitution. This, according to the Department of Agriculture, Fisheries and Forestry has resulted in a huge debate around expropriation without compensation. Although there is notable support for the land question to redress injustice of the past, the debate should be contextualised within a larger ideological and political perspective whose steps must be openly accountable to the people.

Bradshaw and Ntsikelelo (2018) have argued that South African Liberation movements were premised on the question of fighting for the rights of the African majority, dispossession of land to the rights of equity in redistribution of land to all South Africans. Peace and reconciliation were central to the political settlement to the neglect of the differences in origin, ethnicity and wealth, hence the rise of the debate on expropriation without compensation.

The debate on land expropriation since 1994 has neglected the complex interrelationships existing within the landless communities and fails to imagine that future debates on land may not be along racial lines once section 25 of the Constitution of South Africa is amended.

The amendment of section 25 of the Constiution may replace the property clause and permit expropriation without compensation. Once the clause is repealed, expropriation of land without compensation may take place without lengthy legal battles. However, the question remains whether or not the expropriated land will be redistributed to all South African citizens along equity lines irrespective of race. Land acquired as a result of the constitutional amendments may be concentrated in the hands of a few African minority elites. This scenario may result in new intra-racial relationships; whilst expropriation without compensation in future may still enjoy limited support from the landless African majority and still fail to address equity in redistribution of land. The consequences maybe a further breakdown in social cohesion, political instability and economic meltdown leading to future intra-racial tension and a new debate on land redistribution for equity.

Section 25's amendment without considering the citizen's origin, ethnicity diversity, race and wealth disparities may result in a new form of a "non-racial minority" who may own a greater proportion of the land and in future may use land as a political tool for control, patronage and oppression within the very same community they purportedly claim to have liberated; the consequence maybe a never-ending debate on land redistribution for equity. The framework on land expropriation without compensation (i.e. *future debate on equity in redistribution of land in South Africa after amendment of section 25*) is outlined as follows: Step 1 – Public hearings on constitutional amendments of section 25 (expropriation of land without compensation and none equity in redistribution of land); Step 2 – Amendment of section 25 (emergence of intra-racial tension) and Step 3 – Changes in property rights clause (new minority land owners not along racial lines). In South Africa as a state, the Constitution is the supreme law of the country. Section 25 of the Constitution deals with land and land rights. The pace of land redistribution is very slow and equity in redistribution has not been realised as envisaged during the political settlement in 1994. In 2018, the debate on land redistribution for equity resurfaced due to failures in the existing programme attributed to section 25 of the Constitution. The state through the National Assembly embarked on public hearings with the intention to amend section 25 of the Constitution to expropriate land without compensation. To expropriate land without compensation, section 25(2) that protects private property rights and section 25(5)–(6) of the Constitution which gives the state powers in putting reasonable legislative and other parameters to foster conditions that provide citizens with access to land on equitable bases need to be amended. Once there is an amendment of section 25 of the Constitution of South Africa, land can be expropriated without compensation by the state. However, whether the expropriated land will benefit the indigenous Africans as a whole or indigenous African elites to the neglect of equity in redistribution remains unknown. The amendment of section 25 of the Constitution and the emergence of a new indigenous African minority land ownership pattern may herald another round of land debate on equity in redistribution that may no longer be along racial lines but along intra-racial lines leading to potential never-ending debate around land and constitutional amendments.

Can Amendment of Section 25 of the Constitution Silence the Land Debate Forever

Mekoa (2018) has argued that land expropriation without compensation poses strategic challenges in South Africa. The government's primary objective to transfer land for equity, social justice and political stability in pursuit of national interest as a result of promise to the African people to use its new-found political power in 1994 has not been realised. The support enjoyed by the current government, pre-democratisation, was a response to colonial domination of Africans and the dispossession of their land. Twenty-four years into democracy, the government has fallen short of the expectations of the African majority, hence, the basis for the land debate and amendment of section 25 of the Constitution. Central to the government ideological and political perspective is the need to build a nation that is non-racial but characterised by unity in diversity.

Antwi and Chagwiza (2019) submit that since the start of land reform, post-apartheid, the efficiency of the use of the land resource as a key priority for the attainment of benefits for all South Africans has been compromised in the quest to achieve political rather than productivity goals which neglected equity in redistribution for social cohesion and political stability. The results are high levels of unemployment, food insecurity, gross under-utilisation of productive agricultural lands and an increasing landless majority. Pheko (2018) opined that in evaluating the impact of land reform on the lives of beneficiaries, systematic identification of positive or negative effects as well as the intended or unintended consequences on individual households, institutions and the environment must be properly researched.

Thus, the theory of change becomes central to this review because the theory articulates how a particular intervention will bring about results that involve actors of change intervention, their core roles and their ability to overcome existing challenges and their influence on determinants to effect expected outcomes. The theory regarding the relationship between asset ownership and growth in conjunction with the theory of change can be used to evaluate land reform in the economic sense for economic growth.

In South Africa, the primary objectives of the land reform programme were to address the injustices of the past, dignity to indigenous people, increase growth in production, guaranteed food security, job creation and graduate small-scale farmers to commercial farmers in the agricultural sector. The land redistribution, tenure reform and land restitution sub-programmes were established to achieve these set objectives. A target of 30 per cent of the total productive land in South Africa was to be redistributed by 2014 as set out in the 1994 settlement. Since then, there have been five programmes in total between 1996 and 2016, which tried to deliver on the land redistribution imperative for equity as argued by proponents of section 25 amendments (These programmes are as follows: (1) Settlement Land Acquisition Grant (SLAG), (2) Land Redistribution for Agricultural Development (LRAD), (3) Comprehensive Agricultural Support Programme (CASP), (4) Proactive Land Acquisition Strategy (PLAS), and (5) Recapitalisation and Development Programme (RADPT)). However, in 2019, less than 15 per cent of the total productive land as agreed from the onset of the political settlement has been redistributed. Therefore, the debate around the amendments of section 25(2) of the Constitution to expropriate land without compensation cannot be completely ignored.

Some scholars of the land reform programme in South Africa are of the view that, government inefficiency in the implementation of the land reform programme is the cause for the recent debate to amend section 25 of the Constitution and expropriate land without compensation. However, Besley (2000) argued that, lack of interference by the state in land reform processes can entrench considerable inequality, intra and inter-group conflict, illegal sales by traditional leaders and appropriation for private use by representatives of the state.

DISCUSSION AND KEY FINDINGS

In practice, the land reform policy in South Africa has failed to an extent to deliver on equity in the redistribution of land. What the land reform programme did was to maintain the pre-democratisation land ownership regime as reflected in section 25 of the Constitution. However, the failure of the land reform process to deliver on equity in redistribution of land cannot be solely attributed to section 25 of the Constitution. The lack of foresight by the implementing agent (government), in formulating the original policies with a focus on market ideologies to the neglect of the complex interrelationships at community levels and the assumption that landless Africans are a homogeneous group, was misguided.

The pragmatic approach of willing seller or willing buyer further led to minority land owners valuating land above market prices and depleting state resources allocated for redistribution of land for equity. The result has been a further consolidation of power in the hands of existing owners and a few African minority elites. The increasing displacement of the landless farm workers (mainly African) from farms continues to perpetuate conflicts over land rights, land ownership and further entrench inequality through jobs loss, increase in gender bias based on race, age, ethnicity, class and patronage due to the present state policies and legislations.

The emerging minority African land owners in South Africa today are not homogeneous in terms of race but are homogeneous in terms of assets, property rights, control and resources to fight legal battles similar to the colonial minority. Therefore, debates on the amendment of section 25 of the Constitution that protect property rights but allow for contested expropriation with compensation do not only enjoy support from the previous racial minority but also from a new African minority land owners and traditional leaders who fear losing power and control if equity in the redistribution of land for all is achieved. Borros (2006) argued that state-led approaches to land reform are limited in the achievement of desirable changes because they fail to attract support from relevant actors. This is the case with South Africa's the land reform programme.

This chapter articulates the complexity involved in the implementation of the land reform programme in South Africa from an ideological and pragmatic viewpoint and the inherent challenges thereafter for the state to constantly adapt to changing tenure and authority relations on the ground. While those who are for or against the amendment of section 25 may have valid arguments as to why the section should be amended or not, the land reform programme in South Africa has not redistributed land to the extent to which it was intended to redistribute for equity.

The continuous neglect of the vertical and horizontal complexity in relationships that exist within a state and the influence of these relationships on land reform outcomes need to be properly researched. The limits of section 25 of the Constitution within the context of dynamic socio-economic and cultural matrices need to be properly understood. The presence of vested interests, cronyism, patronage, elitism and pressure grouping on the opposite side of the divide on whether section 25 of the Constitution should be amended present a new dimension with regard to the contentious land reform and redistribution discourses.

We contend that, whether section 25 of the Constitution is amended or not, the new alternative arrangements for land expropriation without compensation may not provide for equity in redistribution of land to point where the land question is silenced forever. We argue that the persistence of landlessness or near-landlessness among the majority South Africans is a major driver of inequalities. Redistribution of land is thus seen as a way out of extreme poverty in South African as is the case with many other developing countries. Therefore, though section 25 of the Constitution provides for expropriation with compensation, it also acts as an obstacle for fast-tracking redistribution for equity. To that end, section 25's role in the land reform process needs to be reviewed. This is attributed to the fact that the structures and power relations of South Africa's institutions responsible for land reform mirror those of the apartheid state/regime. The new nation-state in 1994 never considered the post-nation building power relations characteristic of the same structures that created inequality in land ownership in South Africa.

On the other hand, Bejaminsen et al. (2018) have argued that property formalisation similar to the protection of property rights enshrined in section 25 of the Constitution is nothing new in land reform literature. Debates in favour of property rights are that fragmented holdings, collective use and transhumance are obstacles to modernisation even when institutions are restructured to enforce the redress agenda. The existant views are that formalisation enforces structured governance, order, civilisation and that the provision of title deeds to landless people is a path to sustainable development. However, formalisations through property rights have shown failures due increased conflicts, increasing income inequality, asset inequality, legal pluralism and the manipulation of the process by elites to their own advantage to the neglect of the landless and near landless.

In South Africa, the challenge embedded in section 25 of the Constitution and inability of the state to exert pressure on groups within the state with vested interests to conform to the new nation-state of 1994/1996 poses danger even if section 25 is amended to expropriate land without compensation. A study conducted by the Department of Land Affairs in South Africa established that the prevailing customary or communal law and tenure system were a joint construct of colonial officials and colonial African leaders. As such, the idea that locally based community institutions in South Africa are alternatives to lead the distribution of land and the land reform process also needs proper contextual local research.

The design of the land reform project in South Africa twenty-four years ago was an ideological assumption that any land redistribution not based on market forces and protection of property rights would create uncertainty and increase panic among investors to the detriment of economic growth and political stability. Though sections 25(5) and (7) of the Constitution laid the foundations for land redistribution and land restitution with redistribution being the main thrust of the land reform programme in 1994, policy uncertainty around section 25 of the Constitution has not guaranteed investors' confidence due to the openness of the section to multiple interpretations – hence the debate on expropriation without compensation in 2018.

Furthermore, property rights establish not only economic relationships among actors but influences who gets what under which conditions. The re-emergence of the debate on the amendment of section 25(2) of the Constitution has contributed towards decreasing investors' confidence, volatility in the markets, declining agricultural productivity and low economic growth in the face of rising unemployment. All these point to the harmful effects of the never-ending land debate in South Africa. The inclusion of certain clauses (property rights, market approach) in the Constitution coupled with the bureaucratic nature of the state, inexperienced executioners, complex interrelationships, corruption, patronage and no appetite to strictly enforce aspects of the Constitutions when need arises has resulted in land reform failure.

Debates on land reform have thus moved up and down the academic and political discourse ladder for over half a century with the older agreements of security of tenure resulting in increased investment and productivity to newer imperatives for poverty reduction, economic growth and property rights (Lahiff 2007, 1417). The emergence of the debate in South Africa with regard to the amendment of section 25 of the Constitution in 2018 is evidence of the never-ending importance of the land reform process in the building of a nation-state. The ideological and pragmatic approaches to the initial land reform programme which envisage a transfer of 25 million hectares of minority farmland to over 800,000 African farmers by 2014 has not been achieved.

But in the construct of the land reform programme, important questions such as "who are the minority (European colonisers) who own the land?" and "who are the majority Africans who do not own land?" and the complex interrelationships that exist within these groupings have not been fully interrogated and/or addressed. In the discourse, "minority land owners" are used as a single entity and a homogenous group of people in terms of land assets, ownerships, linear relationships and equal land sizes. The "majority dispossessed land owners" are also considered as a single homogenous group of people with no access to land, equal income distribution, equal access to assets, equal control and interest on land with no complex interrelationships and equal standing within societies. These type of assumptions may have led to the initial policy formulation and approach to land reform where a misconception and new debates on land were bound to resurface in due time. Lahiff (2007) commented that "when land reform became a development priority, past studies revealed intense competition over land, changing types of land transfers, claims of ingenuity in land conflicts, intersection of competition over land with that of over legitimate authority; and challenges of growing social inequality and commodification of land emerged."

In economics, the so-called property rights school surmises that property rights evolve in response to changes in technological and economic conditions. Property rights are considered to be institutions that adjust to new cost–benefit relations, induced by changes in the costs and benefits of production. By implication, the premise for property rights to land is that they change in reaction to shifts in productive land values. Land reforms influences and are influenced by broader authority relations as they seek to enhance the land rights of disadvantaged groups by way of legal and administrative acts of the state. Besley and Burgess (2000) were of the view that a more pro-poor pattern of growth is inevitable and rapid pace redistribution is needed to address inequalities. Land reform is a controversial subject and developing countries need to accelerate its implementation for rural development.

The state-led model in the implementation of land reform has been criticized for market-distortion and inefficiency. But as Malatji (2018) puts it, such a distortion of normal market relations to unequal ones that takes place during the land reform process happens once the transfer of land is completed. However, vibrant market relations could re-establish on the basis of a more equitable distribution of wealth. State-led land reform in a short-run supresses productivity but can be augmented by increased state investment, extension of substantial credit to beneficiaries and development of skills. In South Africa, the current debate on land expropriation without compensation focusses on the amendments of section 25 of the Constitution believed to be the main cause of delay in equitable redistribution of land in the country. The section, according to critics, is a key contributor to the failure of the state to effectively distribute land among South Africans. The South African state may have adopted de Soto's approach on property formalisation and critics have identified weaknesses in terms of high costs of implementation, land markets to accentuate wealth differentiation, formalisation of existing inequalities, as well as opportunistic land acquisition by the elite to the neglect of the landless and marginalised (De Soto 1989, 2001, 2006).

The approach used by de Soto was based on previous knowledge and experiences with top-down and customary tenure systems approaches. Critics were of the view that his approach has never been tested. However, the current debate on land expropriation without compensation and the emphasis on amending section 25 of the Constitution in 2018 is a practical test to some of the flaws associated with de Soto's approach. Supporters of de Soto's approach argue that there are promising low-cost approaches to formalisation and the emerging land markets in Africa which seem to enhance the access to land for near landless. This view has proven otherwise in the South African context as limited gains of the land reform process in the past twenty-four years have further entrenched inequality, poverty, increased conflicts through the inclusion of the market mechanism as a means to gain access and formalise land rights. It is important to point out that most African people cannot afford land pegged at the current market rates using the contemporary market mechanism. The land policies promoted across Africa post-colonialism were all based on the premise that customary systems did not provide the necessary security to ensure agricultural investment and productive use of land. The lack of security was thought to lie in the absence of clearly defined and enforceable property rights.

FROM LAND REFORM TO PROPERTY RIGHTS

The debate surrounding land reform in South Africa exemplifies a wider approach in Africa as many African governments have chosen a diversity of strategies to distribute authority rather than focussing on the actual people who need land for livelihood. In the development of land reform policies in Africa, there has been a mistaken belief that a community is homogenous, with the word "community" being centrally placed in the resolution of land questions across the continent. Yet, in practice, community is heterogeneous and consists of varied inter-relations both vertical and horizontal. Further, community can be influenced either explicitly or implicitly. How then do we shift our thinking in finding and developing a suitable approach that may deliver equality in land distribution in heterogeneous communities with both vertical and horizontal interrelationships?

The interactions among social actors may produce community in the narrow sense if they attribute significant decision-making powers and benefits to collective actors reproducing, and generating social inequalities along economic, gender and racial lines. Furthermore, there exists rapidly rising numbers of national and international civil society organizations as a community constituting a powerful bloc to bring changes at grass root level because it is an alternative to land reform processes which exclude local people from decision-making and deprive them from benefits that accrue from their resource environment.

Changes in property may occur by way of patterned shifts in property practices, as these make, modify and unmake property relations in a process of constant negotiations and market forces. In defining the concept of abstract property, one should clearly evoke the notion of "abstract" versus "concrete property." While the former focuses on enforcement of legislations through court rulings and scholarly debates, the latter deals with tangible objects such as land. Scholars have revealed that differences in technological and economic factors underlie the observed variation in property rights to land.

However, the close connection between property and the state is not a universal relationship but contingent to particular historical conditions that give rise to the nation-state. If the nature of property rights to land depends on the context, then land reform needs to be responsive to the variety of property arrangements on the ground. If property rights to land are sanctioned by multiple sources of authority, then land reform cannot be the exclusive prerogative of the state but needs to recognize community-based institutions in the execution of land reform. Expropriation without compensation can be contingent on institutions that may take a wide variety of forms, such as village communities, lineages, clans, tribes and indigenous groups. Yet, together they attest to the significance of community in processes of land reform and in the approach become adaptive to local conditions and changes over time rather than the local condition and environment adapting to land reform.

The complex nature of land restitution, land redistribution and land tenure reforms, therefore, raises the questions on whether section 25 of the Constitution and the market-led approach to land reform twenty-four years into democracy have delivered on equity in redistribution of land in South Africa. If section 25 has delivered, then those arguing for amendment of section 25 of the Constitution have no basis to argue. But, if section 25 has not delivered, even though the section provides for expropriation with compensation, then those fighting for the amendment of section 25 of the Constitution are justified to do so. Unless, proponents of none amendments of section 25 of the Constitution provide practical evidence that the section has equitably redistributed land to dispossessed African majority, then a mind-set shift towards allowing for the uncontested amendment of section 25 of the Constitution should be adopted for the benefit of all South Africans, irrespective of race.

CONCLUSION

The chapter concludes that without addressing the issue of equity in so far as land redistribution for all South Africans is concerned, expropriation without compensation is the only plausible recourse. However, the same expropriation without compensation may form the basis for another multifaceted and/or convoluted future land debate. The only difference between the debate now and that of the future may be that section 25 will be amended and no longer ambiguous, land may be expropriated without compensation, private property rights may still be upheld to some extent but equity in redistribution to all dispossessed South Africans may still not have been achieved. What an amended section 25 of the Constitution may create is a “new non-racial minority land owners group in South Africa" not characterised or informed by racial lines but homogenous in asset, wealth and control of land. Therefore, the very problem that led to the amendment of section 25 of the Constitution may remerge in future in a different form and structure. We support the amendment of section 25 of the Constitution to expropriate land without compensation irrespective of race. Second, the focus of the amendments should centre on equity in redistribution and not the creation of a new non-racial minority land owners group that may use land for the control of the landless African people.

The presence of groupings either for and against the amendment of section 25 of the Constitution of South Africa point to the never-ending debate around land ownership both pre- and post-colonial era in South Africa. If the government was seen, in the eyes of African people, to be illegitimate due to the legitimation of disposed land, the democratic government may in future seem as illegitimate if they fail to equitably redistribute land among all South Africans. The pressure that is being exerted on opposite sides of the divide with regard to the amendment of section 25 of the Constitution of South Africa presents a new cycle in what constitutes the complex land debate. However, in amending section 25 of the Constitution, private property rights must still be protected to an extent and care must be taken to create new non-racial minority land owners in the country.

BIBLIOGRAPHY

Antwi, M. A., and Chagwiza, C. (2019). "Factors Influencing Savings Among Land Reform Beneficiaries in South Africa." *International Journal of Social Economics*, Volume 46, 474–484.

Antwi, M. A., and Nkwe, N. (2013). "Beneficiaries' Assessment of CASP on Livelihoods on Ngaka Modiri Molema District of North West Province in South Africa." *Asia Life Sciences Supplementary,* Volume 9, 379–394.

Benjaminsen, T. A., Holden, S., Lund, C., and Sjaastad, E. (2008). "Formalisation of Land Rights: Some Empirical Evidence from Mali, Niger and South Africa." *Land Use Policy*, Volume 26, 28–35.

Besley, T., and Burgess, R. (2000). "Land Reform, Poverty Reduction, and Growth: Evidence from India." *Quarterly Journal of Economics*, Volume 115(2), 389–430.

Borras, S. M., and McKinley, T. (2006). *The Unresolved Land Reform Debate: Beyond State-Led or Market-Led Models*. UNDP Policy Research Brief, No. 2, International Poverty Centre, United Nations Development Programme (UNDP), Canada.

Bradshaw, G., and Breakfast, N. (2018). "Searching for Common Ground: A Proposal for Managing Land Reform-Related Conflict in South Africa." *Journal of Public Administration*, Volume 53, 376–396.

De Soto, H. (1989). *The Other Path: The Invisible Revolution in the Third World*. New York: Harper & Row.

De Soto, H. (2001). *The Mystery of Capital: Why Capitalism Triumphs in the West and Fails Everywhere Else*. London: Bantam Press.

De Soto, H. (2006). Hernando De Soto Interview. *Reason Magazine*. http://reason.com/archives/2006/ 02/22/hernando-de-soto-interview/1.

Department of Agriculture, Forestry and Fisheries. Economic Review of the South African Agriculture. (2014). https://www.daff.gov.za/daffweb3/portals/0/.../economic%20review%202014.pdf.

Department of Constitutional and Provincial Affairs. (1996). *The Constitution Act No. 108 of 1996*. Pretoria: Government Printers.

Department of Land Affairs (DLA). (1997a). *White Paper on South African Land Policy*. Pretoria: DLA.

Department of Land Affairs. (1997b). *Our Land: Green Paper on South African Land Policy*.

Dlamini, S., and Ogunnubi, O. (2018). Land Reform in South Africa: Contending Issues. *Journal of Public Administration*, Volume 53, 339–360.

FAO. (2007). *Good Governance in Land Tenure and Administration*. FAO Land Tenure Studies.

FAO:Rome, Italy, http://www.fao.org/sd/ltdirect/ltstudies_en.htm. 20/11/2010.

Golele, N. S., Mautjana, H., and Makombe, G. (2018). "An Assessment of the Effectiveness of the Mentorship Programme in Land Reform: The Case of Ba Bina Noko Community Property Association, Sekhukhune District, Limpopo Province, South Africa." *Journal of Public Administration*, Volume 53, 430–445.

Gwandure, C., and Mayekiso, T. (2018). "Land Reform, Contract Farming and Sustainable Development in South Africa." *Journal of Public Administration*, Volume 53, 489–501.

Hall, R. (2004). "A Political Economy of Land Reform in South Africa." *Review of African Political Economy*, Volume 31, 213–227.

Hall, R., and Kepe, T. (2017). "Elite Capture and State Neglect: New Evidence on South Africa's Land Reform." *Review of African Political Economy*, Volume 44(151), 122–130.

Kirsten, J. F., and Van Zyl, J. (1998). "Defining Small-Scale Farmers in the South African Context." *Agrekon*, Volume 37(4), 551–562.

Lahiff, E., Borras, S. M., and Kay, C. (2007). "Market-Led Agrarian Reform: Policies, Performance and Prospects." *Third World Quarterly*, Volume 28, 1417–1436.

Makombe, G., and Phago, K. (2018). "Land Reform in South Africa: Looking to the Future." *Journal of Public Administration*, Volume 53, 280–284.

Malatji, T., and Phago, K. (2018). "Land Reform Constituents for whose Benefit? A Discourse Analysis of Proactive Land Acquisition Strategy in South Africa." *Journal of Public Administration*, Volume 53, 397–412.

Mekoa, I. (2018). "Liberation Political Discourses on the Land Question in South Africa and the Challenges of International Capitalist Discourses." *Journal Public Administration*, Volume 53, 361–375.

Molope, M. (2018). "The Decision to Amend Section 25 of the Constitution Shakes Cohesion: Perceptions of Public Hearing Participants in the North West Province." *Journal of Public Administration*, Volume 53, 413–429.

Okumbor, J. C., Sithole, S. L., and Kirk, N. C. (2018). "Sustainable Rural Livelihood and Agri-Food System: Lessons from Manavhela Land Restitution." *Journal Public Administration*, Volume 53, 446–473.

Peters, P. E. (2009). "Challenges in Land Tenure and Land Reform in Africa: Anthropological Contributions." *World Development*, Volume 37, 1307–1316.

Pheko, M. (2018). "The Land Question in South Africa." *Journal of Public Administration*, Volume 53, 310–319.

Sebopetsa, M., and Bayat, M. S. (2018). "Determining an Appropriate Extension Framework for Land Reform Smallholder Farmers: A Case of the Western Cape Province of South Africa." *Journal of Public Administration*, Volume 53, 413–429.

Sikor, T., and Müller, D. (2009). "The Limits of State-Led Land Reform: An Introduction." *World Development*, Volume 37, 1307–1316.

Sikwela, M. M., Tshuma, M. C., and Tshabalala, T. A. (2018). "Critical Review of South Africa's Land Reform Programme as a Tool to Address the Nation's Triple Challenges." *Journal Public Administration*, Volume 53, 474–488.

Vanclay, F. (2015). "Changes in the Impact Assessment Family 2003–2014: Implications for Considering Achievements, Gaps and Future Directions." *Journal of Environmental Policy Management*, Volume 17(1), 1550003.

Zajonc, R. B., and Burnstein, E. (1965). "Structural Balance, Reciprocity, and Positivity as Sources of Cognitive Bias." *Journal of Personality*, Volume 33(4), 570–583.

Chapter 13

The Fight against Corruption in Namibia

An Appraisal of the Institutional Environment and a Consideration of a Model for Civil Society Participation

Job Shipululo Amupanda

INTRODUCTION

To a developing society, corruption is what cancer is to a human body. Billions of dollars that could build hospitals, educate the learners, build public infrastructures and feed the hungry in Africa are diverted to few individuals whose main concern is crass materialism and less on the humanity of the African people. To avoid this scourge, international, continental, regional and national legal and institutional efforts have been put in place to counter the tide of corruption. This chapter locates this debate in the Namibian context. The chapter finds that Namibia has two institutions, by law and practically, dealing with corruption – a situation this chapter finds as unwise. It is brought forward that harmonisation of scattered corruption mandates is necessary and prudent. The chapter provides evidence of a public trust deficit in the ACC and finds that section 21 and section 31 of the Anti-Corruption Act 8 of 2003 is the foundation of current problems at the ACC. This chapter argues that these sections need to be amended and democratised as is the case with Mauritius's Prevention of Corruption Act 5 of 2002. For Namibia, given the current state of affairs, the text argues that an effective strategy of ensuring meaningful participation of the civil society in the fight against corruption is the creation of a buffer zone between whistle-blowers and corruption-fighting body/bodies. This buffer zone will serve as a safe space for whistle-blowers. The work of the affirmative repositioning movement in fighting corruption over the years is presented as a possible model for consideration.

It is argued that corruption is as old as human history for records of ancient societies have noted it (Schenone and Greeg 2003). The term *corruption* originates from a Latin word *corruptus* – a "the past participle of *corrumpere*," meaning "mar, bribe, destroy" (Biswas and Tortajada 2018). On October 31, 2003, the United Nations General Assembly adopted the *United Nations Convention Against Corruption (UNCAC)*, the first legally binding instrument against corruption in the UN. The UN argued, as one of the driving force for the adoption of the UNCAC, the concerns "about the seriousness of problems and threats posed by corruption to the stability and security of societies, undermining the institutions and values of democracy, ethical values and justice and jeopardizing sustainable development and the rule of law" (United Nations 2004, 5). The convention states the following as the objectives:

> (a) to promote and strengthen measures to prevent and combat corruption more efficiently and effectively; (b) To promote, facilitate and support international cooperation and technical assistance in the prevention of and fight against corruption, including in asset recovery; (c) To promote integrity, accountability and proper management of public affairs and public property. (United Nations 2004, 7)

The UNCAC does not define corruption but identifies offences for what constitute a corrupt behaviour. It is for this reason that in 2007, the Organisation for Economic Co-operation and Development (OECD) developed a corruption glossary for international criminal standards. In this glossary, the OECD identified two ways of defining corruption. One is the definition in terms of criminal law – as provided for by regal instruments – while the other is a definition for policy purposes for which various definitions exist (OECD 2007). Of the various definitions of corruption, the definition for policy purposes, which is the 1997 definition by the World Bank, has gained popularity in the literature on corruption. The Bank defines corruption as the use of "public office for personal gain" (World Bank 1997, 9–10). Several scholars researching on corruption in Africa, Europe and Asia such as Coetzee (2016), Holmstrom (2013) and Hellmann (2017) have all adopted this definition. The OECD (2007, 20) highlights the definition of corruption by Transparency International, which provides a broader context as follows:

> Corruption involves behaviour on the part of officials in the public sector, whether politicians or civil servants, in which they improperly and unlawfully enrich themselves, or those close to them, by the misuse of the public power entrusted to them.

It, therefore, follows that although there are various definitions of corruption in the context of definition for policy purposes, there are three elements inherent in understanding of what constitute corruption. These are public office, self-enrichment or gratification and public resources. This text adopts the World Bank and Transparency International in the wider understanding of discussion of corruption.

The African continent was not left behind when the UN and other international bodies were putting in place legal and institutional instruments to fight corruption. On July 1, 2003, several months before the UN adopted the UNCAC, the African Union (AU) adopted the *African Union Convention on Preventing and Combating Corruption* although it would only enter into force 3 years later, in 2006 (African Union 2003). The Southern African Development Community (SADC), a regional body of the AU of which Namibia is a member, was even more proactive, having adopted the *SADC Protocol Against Corruption* on August 14, 2001 (SADC 2003). In this protocol, SADC defined corruption as acts that include:

> Bribery or any other behaviour in relation to persons entrusted with responsibilities in the public and private sectors which violates their duties as public officials, private employees, independent agents or other relationships of that kind and aimed at obtaining undue advantage of any kind for themselves or others. (SADC 2003, 2)

This definition conforms to the earlier definitions insofar as it includes the elements stated earlier, public office, self-enrichment/gratification and public resources. However, this definition broadens the conceptualisation to include the private sector. Corruption in the private sector is as concerning as in the public sector and it takes many forms such as collusion, money laundering, undue influence, and bribery (Coetzee 2018). In July 2003, the same month and year the AU adopted the *African Union Convention on Preventing and Combating Corruption*, Namibia passed and operationalised the Anti-Corruption Act 8 of 2003. This act established the Anti-Corruption Commission (ACC) and outlined its functions and matters related to the fighting and dealing with corruption in Namibia. The act seems to align with the definition of corruption as the abuse of public office for personal gain. Although the act does not explicitly define corruption, it establishes, in chapter 4, several offences constituting corrupt acts. Some of the offences include accepting gratification (section 34), giving gratification (section 35), accepting gratification by or giving gratification to agent (section 36), bribery of public officer (section 39), bribery of foreign public officials (section 41), bribery in relation to actions (section 42), bribery for giving assistance in relation to contracts (section 43) and corruptly using office or position for gratification (section 44). The Act also considers it a corrupt act when one conceals information relating to gratification and deal with other matters such as conspiracies.

Despite these institutional arrangements in place, from the United Nations, the AU, the SADC and at a country level, corruption remains. In some cases, corruption cases even increased despite the establishment of these bodies. As Biswas and Tortajada (2018) observes:

> Corruption has become a way of life in numerous countries. In 2011, Transparency International (TI) reported that two-thirds of Bangladeshis and well over half of Indians had paid a bribe during the preceding 12 months. In 2017, it further reported that globally one in four people had paid bribes in the previous 12 months to access a public service. Nearly 57% of people around the world felt their governments were doing badly to fight corruption. Only 30% thought their governments were doing well. Another TI study in 2017 showed globally around one-third of people consider their presidents, prime ministers, national and local government officials, business executives, elected representatives and police officers corrupt. Police officers are seen to be most corrupt in Sub-Saharan Africa (47%) and Asia Pacific (39%).

Because of the continuing and damaging effects of corruption particularly on much-needed development, the African Union, during its thirtieth Ordinary Session of the Assembly of Heads of State and Government in Addis Ababa from January 28 to 29, 2018, dedicated the year 2018 as the African Year against Corruption choosing the theme "winning the fight against Corruption: A sustainable Path to Africa's Transformation" (Noa 2018). The anti-corruption discourse implores all members of society to join forces in fighting corruption for it affects the national developmental efforts. This text joins these efforts of collective agenda of fighting corruption. It conducts an appraisal of the institutional environment in the fight against corruption in Namibia by assessing the effectiveness of the ACC. It also identifies specific issues for policy reform. It then considers a model for civil society participation by submitting the work done by the youth-led social justice movement, the affirmative repositioning movement.

ISSUES AND INSTITUTIONAL ENVIRONMENT OF FIGHTING CORRUPTION IN NAMIBIA

In analysing the corruption-fighting environment in Namibia, there are two indicators worth understanding. First is the findings related to the institutions fighting corruption, while the second is the effectiveness and trust deficit in the ACC.

Duplicity of Corruption Fighting Institution

The Namibian Constitution, in article 89, establishes the Ombudsman and states, in article 91(f), that the Ombudsman shall have the

> duty to investigate vigorously all instances of alleged or suspected corruption and the misappropriation of public monies by officials and to take appropriate steps, including reports to the Prosecutor-General and the Auditor-General pursuant thereto. (Republic of Namibia 1990)

The Ombudsman Act 7 of 1990 went to further repeat these constitutional provisions, in terms of section 3(1)(e) on the duties and functions of the ombudsman, providing that the ombudsman shall have power to enquire into and investigate and take actions and steps regarding: "all instances or matters of alleged or suspected corruption and the misappropriation of public moneys or other public property by officials." As stated earlier, the Anti-Corruption Act 8 of 2003 also has similar powers in terms chapter four of this act. There are striking similarities between the mandates of the ACC and the Ombudsman. The Ombudsman has the powers to Investigate Corruption allegations. This is provided for by section 3 (1) (e) and 3 (2) (e) of the Ombudsman Act (No 7 of 1990). The ACC also has powers to Investigate Corruption allegations. This is provided for by Chapter 3 and Chapter 4 of the Anti-Corruption Act 8 of 2003. The Ombudsman can also independently submit reports of the investigations to the prosecutor general for prosecution. This is provided for by section 5(1)(a) (ii)(cc) of the Ombudsman Act (No 7 of 1990). Equally, the ACC can independently submit reports of investigations to the prosecutor general for prosecution. This is provided for in terms of section 31 of the Anti-Corruption Act 8 of 2003. Furthermore, the Ombudsman is required to notify the complainants on the outcomes of the investigations. This is provided for by section 5 (1) (a) (i) of the Ombudsman Act (No 7 of 1990). In a similar manner, the ACC is required to notify the complainants on the outcomes of the investigations. This is provided for by section 19 of the Anti-Corruption Act 8 of 2003. Therefore, it is evident that statutory similarities exist between the ACC and Ombudsman relating to corruption.

From the above outline of similarities between the ACC and the Ombudsman, it emerges clear that, as a matter of fact, Namibia has two institutions mandated to deal with corruption in the exact same matter from reporting, investigation, reference to the prosecutor general. This is not only the matter of legal provisions without a practical manifestation. An illustration of two corruption cases that are of similar dispositions that were dealt with by the two institutions and followed the case cause of action is thus provided. First, in a case on fraud and maladministration by the Forest Research Center in Okahandja in the Ministry of Agriculture, Water and Forestry reported in May 2016, the Ombudsman confirmed the allegations of fraud and maladministration. The matter was submitted to the prosecutor general with nine criminal cases comprising of twenty-six counts of fraud and three counts of theft were opened (Case No CR 32-40/7/2016). Second, in another matter, an amount of N$ 2 632 366, 20 was paid to a company for solar panel systems to be installed in schools. The recommendation of the chosen company was made in a letter by the Education Director on June 1, 2011, while the quotation of the company was dated June 3, 2011. These schools wherein a solar system was to be installed were already identified for electrification by the Government's School Electrification Master Plan. The Ombudsman found that these payments were done outside the State Finance Act (No 31 of 1991) and Tender Board Act (No 16 of the 1996) and other Tender Board regulations. The Ombudsman found that this disregarded created an opportunity to commit corruption. The Permanent Secretary in the Ministry of Education, Arts and Culture was directed to instruct an audit to determine the extent of financial irregularities and identify those responsible after which appropriate actions must be taken.

In case number ACC-HQO-10-00228, a Deputy Director and fourteen others in the Ministry of Agriculture, Water and Forestry corruptly submitted false documentation regarding cut lines that were constructed, while the work was never performed. The ACC found that the accused corruptly used a public office or position for gratification (2 charges) and they were further charged with money laundering. The matter was submitted to the prosecutor general for prosecution. In a second case, case number ACC-OTJ-14-001162, a Chief Administrative Officer in the Ministry of Health and Social Services was involved in corruption in respect of a contract for the renovation of the Otjiwarongo State Hospital valued at N$ 1, 3 million. The ACC found that the Chief Administrative Officer committed a corrupt offence of a person or agent using documentation containing falsification to mislead. As in the first case, the matter was referred to the prosecutor general for prosecution (The illustration covers corruption cases investigated by the ACC and Ombudsman (Anti-Corruption Commission 2018; Ombudsman 2017).

From the illustration above, it becomes clear that both the ACC and the Ombudsman have investigated corrupt cases related to tenders/contracts in the Ministry of Agriculture, Water and Forestry and other ministry. They have both submitted their investigations to the prosecutor general as provided by their respective Acts of parliament. These cases erase doubts in anyone disputing the fact that there are two institutions in Namibia dealing with corruption in exactly the same manner. One may argue that a striking difference exists between the ACC and the Ombudsman given that the ACC, in terms of section 28 of the Anti-Corruption Act 8 of 2003, is given the power to arrest while the Ombudsman does not appear to enjoy the same powers. On close inspection, this power does not grant the ACC any meaningful advantage over the Ombudsman. Section 28(3) of the same Act, in any case, states that "a person arrested must be taken forthwith to a police station to be dealt with in accordance with the Criminal Procedure Act 51 of 1977." If this provision is to succeed, to others, as a significant differentiator, then other provisions need to be explored. It has been a practice that in order for the ACC to freeze the assets of suspects under investigations, the commission is required to make an application to the High Court. The Ombudsman, on the other hand, enjoys wide scope as far assets of persons under investigation are concerned, through this provision under section 4 (1) (b) (v):

> the right to seize anything, but subject to the provisions of this paragraph, which he deems necessary in connection with that inquiry or investigation or which is connected with that inquiry or investigation, as the case may be, and to retain any such thing in safe custody for as long as it is necessary for purposes of that inquiry or investigation.

The same way section 28 of the Anti-Corruption Act – the power to arrest – cannot be used to project the ACC as having an advantage over the Ombudsman can be sustained and applied in arguing that section 4(1)(b)(v) above cannot be brought forward as advantageous to the Ombudsman over the ACC. If the Ombudsman wishes to have an individual arrested such request can be made to the Namibian Police as what happened in the case described earlier in this chapter. Similarly, if the ACC wishes to seize any asset such can be made possible through a court application. None of these sections places any of these institutions at an advantage over the other regardless to investigation of corruption. The argument being submitted here is that Namibia effectively has two institutions dealing with corruption. That Namibia continues to waste scarce resources in this manner is concerning. This duplicity is concerning and must be addressed.

The ACC Effectiveness and Public Trust Deficit

There was euphoria during the early years when the ACC was established. Over the past five years, the ACC has attracted a negative perception from a wide spectrum of society. In 2017, Nico Smith, a Member of Parliament for the Official Opposition, the Popular Democratic Movement, accused the ACC targeting the small fish while the politically connected individuals seems to always remain under investigation (NAMPA 2017). Few months after Smith expressed these sentiments, Tom Alweendo, minister of economic planning and director-general of the National Planning Commission alarmed the growing negative perception that the ACC is unable to perform its duties and that the public has lost trust in the anti-graft body (Smith 2017). These sentiments were also captured by the results of the 2014 Afrobarometer survey wherein 64 per cent of Namibians believed that corruption had increased a lot. The survey had also found in 2012 that 43 per cent of Namibians believe that the ACC avoids politically connected suspects (Weylandt 2017). See the results produced by Weylandt (2017, 2) from the Afrobarometer results demonstrating how Namibians have been losing confidence in the government's ability to deal with corruption).

The ACC itself understands that public trust in the body has been decreasing over the years. In 2018, the director-general of the ACC, Paulus Noa, was quoted in the local media blaming lawyers and magistrates for the delays in the prosecution of corrupt suspects and the slow finalisations of cases in courts which has resulted in the ACC being referred to by the public as a "political stooge and toothless dog" (Chiringa 2018). In 2019, Erna van der Merwe, the deputy director-general of the ACC admitted that Namibians are not coming forth to report corruption (NAMPA 2019). There has been a general decline of the number of cases reported to the ACC as demonstrated by ACC (Anti-Corruption Commission 2018). The public trust deficit in the ACC is concerning and will surely dwarf efforts of curbing corruption. Innovative strategies must, therefore, be sought to counter this state of affairs. The section below offers some consideration for policy reform.

CONSIDERATION OF POLICY REFORM

Amendment and Democratisation of Sections 21 and 31 of the Anti-Corruption Act 8 of 2003

The criticism of the ACC is not only at the institutional level. Most of the criticisms have often been directed at Director-General Paulus Noa whom the official opposition in 2017 labelled a puppet of the ruling party following his decision to block an investigation into the N$ 3 billion mass housing programme in which several politically connected individuals were implicated (Immanuel 2017). There have also been numerous similar criticisms against Noa including his decision to close the files involving former mayor of Windhoek Agnes Kafula who was implicated in dubious land deals, Fisheries Minister Bernard Esau and Labour Minister Erkki Nghimtina. The director-general also faced public criticism over his decision to let an army commander off the hook over allegations of unlawfully using military equipment for personal use (Immanuel 2016; Halwoodi 2017). In 2017, Noa and Finance Minister Calle Schlettwein, engaged in a public spat and war of words over the former's decision to drop investigation into exorbitant legal fees paid by government to UK lawyers for Genocide reparations advice (Immanuel 2017). The criticism against Noa did not only originate from outside. As Halwoodi (2017) demonstrates, there have been numerous reports of dissatisfied staff members. In June 2019, the Namibian reported that ACC employees at the workshop held at Swakopmund earlier in the year expressed concern over Noa's powers. The same report stated that Nelius Becker, head of ACC Investigations and Hendrina Shikudule, the ACC chief investigator, resigned as part of what the paper referred to as an "intensive power struggle" (Iikela and Immanuel 2019).

On close inspection, the criticism, as harsh as they are at times, are not directed at Noa personally but as director-general. More specifically, the criticism must be directed at the specific sections from where the director-general is enabled to behave and exercise the powers he is granted that subsequently results in the "unfavourable decisions." Section 21 and Section 31 of the Anti-Corruption Act 8 of 2003 provides discretionary powers to the ACC director-general in dealing with investigations. Section 21(2) states that "Upon initiating or receiving a complaint which in the opinion of the Director warrants investigation on reasonable grounds, the Director must cause the complaint to be investigated as quickly as practicable." This basically means that for investigations be launched, the director-general, and only him/her, must be of the opinion that an investigation is warranted. As such, this section accords the opinion of the director-general an extraordinary importance. This basically means that if the director-general is of an opinion, regardless of the evidence at hand, that there is no need of an investigation then there will be no investigation. The Act does not make provision of appeal should it occur that investigators or colleagues inside the ACC do not agree with the opinion of the director-general. Section 21(2) seems to suggest that the director-general is infallible.

Section 31 (1) of the act provides that

> If, upon completion of an investigation by the Commission, it appears to the Director that a person has committed an offence of corrupt practice under chapter 4 or any other offence discovered during the investigation, the Director must refer the matter and all relevant information and evidence assembled by the Commission in connection with the matter to the Prosecutor-General.

This section, like section 21(2), places the fate of corruption investigations in the hands of one person, director-general. It is to this single individual it must appear that a corrupt practice under Chapter 4 occurred. If, in the opinion of the director-general, it doesn't appear that an offence has been committed therein lies the end of the road, the matter does not go to the prosecutor general. The section does not provide mechanism of an appeal for investigators who may have a different opinion to the director-general or to whom a different "appearance" occurs. Again, the opinion of the director-general is granted extraordinary status and the individual occupying the position of director-general is seen by the Act as infallible.

Section 21(2) and section 31 1) are a direct cause of the many problems stated above particularly the reference to the ACC as a "political stooge and toothless dog" and the director-general as a "puppet" of the ruling party. These sections are not only problematic on the grounds enumerated above, they also stand opposed to democratic ethos such as transparency and accountability. It follows that section 21(2) and 31(1) must be amended and democratised. The decision whether to investigate and to refer the matter to the prosecutor general must be decided by an elaborate body such as a committee as opposed to an individual.

This has happened in several jurisdictions. In Mauritius, the Prevention of Corruption Act 5 of 2002 is highly democratised and does not give too much power to one individual as in the case of Namibia with specific reference to these sections and others. In terms of the appointment of director-general of the Independent Commission Against Corruption, section 19 (4) states that the director-general shall be appointed by the prime minister after consultation with the leader of the Opposition. In Namibia, the director-general is appointed by the National Assembly on the recommendation of the president. It is for this reason that in Namibia the Official Opposition labels the director-general as a puppet of the ruling party. This would be inconceivable in Mauritius given that the Leader of Opposition is consulted before an appointment is carried out. In Mauritius, when the Commission receives a complaint, it is referred to the director of the Corruption Investigation who then investigates reports to the Commission, under section 46(1), (2) and (3), for the commission to direct whether to proceed with further investigations or to discontinue the investigation. In the case whereby the commission directs further investigation, section 47(5) requires the director-general to seek the opinion of the commission after the investigation is completed. It is only after the opinion of the commission is sought, in terms of section 47(6) that the director-general can submit a report to the Director of Public Prosecutions. What Mauritius has done, with the Prevention of Corruption Act 5 of 2002, is to remove the discretional powers from the director-general and place these into a Commission, a body. Amending and democratizing sections 21 and 31 of the Anti-Corruption Act 8 of 2003 would not be unusual given the Mauritius example.

Combining the Corruption Mandates at Ombudsmen and the ACC

As demonstrated earlier, the ACC and Ombudsman office carry the same mandate as far as corruption is concerned. It has been demonstrated in this text, through the provision of relevant examples from the records of the two institutions, that they have carried out similar investigations and forwarded the same to the prosecutor general. It is, therefore, worth considering if it is tenable to have two institutions doing exactly the same work. The corruption mandates at both institutions need to be examined with a view to create a comprehensive and dynamic institution that will mount a significant challenge to corruption in Namibia. This text does not suggest that one mandate must be removed and given to the other. Such a determination must be arrived at after meaningful engagements for both institutions have strengths and weaknesses. In South Africa, the establishment of the Office of the Public Protector and the Human Rights Commission is one model worth considering in dealing with the ACC and Ombudsman dichotomy.

THE CREATION OF THE BUFFER ZONE – A MODEL FOR CIVIL SOCIETY PARTICIPATION

In this text, evidence has been presented that not only is the public losing confidence in the ACC, there is a general reluctance in reporting corruption. Of the many solutions one can proffer, the participation of the civil society in the fight against corruption is imperative. The African Union, in Article12 of the *African Union Convention on Preventing and Combating Corruption*, calls on parties undertake to

> create an enabling environment that will enable Civil Society in and the media to hold governments to the highest levels of transparency and accountability in the management of public affairs … ensure and provide for the participation of Civil Society in the monitoring process and consult Civil Society in the implementation of this Convention. (African Union 2003, 14)

The ACC has not been successful in securing cooperation and collaboration of the Civil Society in line with this convention. When the Affirmative Repositioning (AR) movement announced in 2018 that it is establishing its own anti-graft body given that huge volume of Namibians that report corrupt cases to the movement, ACC director-general retorted claiming that people really have confidence in the ACC and that corrupt cases can only reported to the ACC and the Namibian Police (Iikela 2018). A year later, the ACC released a statement stating that Namibians are reluctant and afraid of reporting corruption to the ACC (Ikela 2019). Given the reluctance of Namibians to report corruption to the ACC either on account of mistrust and fear, organised civil society organisations that assist members of the public in reporting corruption and subsequently submitting such reports to the ACC would assist in fighting corruption. The AR movement has been playing this role since its establishment in 2014. The following are five cases worth considering in relation to an alternative model and the role of the civil society in fighting corruption.

In December 2015, AR wrote to the ACC requesting the anti-graft body to investigate the case in which the Minister of Defence, Penda yaNdakolo, who corruptly incurred a bill of taxpayers' money on his stay and food at a local hotel. The movement gave the ACC until April 2016 to investigate the matter (New Era 2015). Two months before the due date given to the ACC by the AR movement, the minister was reported to have paid back N$ 186 000 following his meeting with the ACC director-general and former attorney general Sackeus Shanghala (Immanuel 2016). In 2015 again, the AR movement, after receiving information from whistle-blowers, raised the matter of Minister of Education, Arts and Culture, Katrina Hanse-Himarwa, who had allocated a farm to her son while serving as chairperson of the Head Regional Resettlement Committee (Joseph 2015). The ACC Investigations on the matter have now been completed and the matter is submitted to the prosecutor general (Anti-Corruption Commission 2018).

In August 2018, AR launched a formal objection to the application of the minister of trade, industrialisation and SME development, Tjekero Tweya, whose application was not only expedited but was also seen as against the spirit of article 42(1) of the Namibian Constitution with prohibit ministers, as members of cabinet, from placing themselves in a position where their personal interest and the exercise of their duties would be in conflict. Tweya's application for land at Oranjemund to build flats was effectively going to turn him into a landlord while he is expected to regulate landlords in terms of the Rent Ordinance 13 of 1997, a law he administers (Chiringa 2018). This objection is still under consideration by the Oranjemund Town Council at the time writing this text. Upon receiving information that the special adviser to the minister of labour, Vicky ya Toivo, a white woman, got a ressetlement farm, the AR movement wrote to the Ombudsman asking him to investigate how Mrs Ya Toivo obtained such a farm arguing that she does not meet the criteria set out by the government resettlement policy (Beukes 2018). The Ombudsman, following the AR request, launched a full investigation in the government resettlement programme (the Patriot 2018; Namibian 2018). This investigation is still ongoing at the time of writing. The AR movement organised an objection and a protest against a High Court Judge Maphios Cheda, a Zimbabwean national, who was about to get a residential plot dubiously that was already allocated to another person, a Namibian national, and seen as operating outside the existing laws (Hilukilwa 2018). The Oshakati Town Council later resolved not to grant this plot to the judge following AR objection (Kambowe 2018).

The AR resoluteness in fighting corruption did not go unnoticed by the political elite. Towards the end of 2017, Sackeus Shanghala, the minister of justice, sued one of the leading activists of the AR movement, Job Shipululo Amupanda, N$ 500 000 for referring to him, among others, as "epitome and symbol of corruption in Namibia" (Shapwanale 2018). Although the matter was later settled out of court, it is clear that the impact of the AR movement in fighting corruption has had a national footprint (Routh 2018). Having learned and observed the onsluaght from the political elites and against its activists involved in fighting for social justice and against corruption, the AR movement formally established a social justice centre that would coordinate its litigation efforts including its fights against corruption. As such, the People's Litigation Center (PLC) was established and officially registered with the Masters of the high court to consolidate and coordinate these efforts. Part of the objectives of the PLC is to fight for transparency and accountability and against corruption (Ikela 2019). The AR model of fighting corruption is a worthwhile consideration for civil society participation in the fight against corruption as captured in article 12 of the *African Union Convention on Preventing and Combating Corruption* discussed earlier. This model allows for the creation of a buffer between whistle-blowers and the ACC. Whereas the whistle-blowers have no trust or are fearful of reporting corruption to the ACC, the corrupt practices do not remain unreported on account of fear and trust deficit but instead channelled to the safe-zones for onward transmissions.

CONCLUSION

Despite the existence of various definitions of corruption, particularly in the definition-for-policy, all definition has elements that render the definition of corruption as the "the use/abuse of public office for personal gain as of general application." This text traced various understanding and conceptualisation of corruption, both definition for criminal law purpose and definition for policy, from the United Nations, African Union, the SADC and subsequently Namibia finding that corruption is understood, at all these registers, as the abuse of public office for personal use.

Like other countries, Namibia is also battling the scourge of corruption. For Namibia, it has been an uphill battle. The challenges have been institutional and also societal. Institutionally, this text has demonstrated that as a matter of law and practice, there are two institutions dealing with corruption. These are the ACC and the Ombudsman. This situation is not only untenable; it is also a waste of public resources. It is duplicity which Namibia, a country struggling economically and with high levels of inequality, should not sustain. This text has demonstrated that the Namibian public has over the years begun losing trust and confidence in the ACC. The ACC has also admitted that it is facing a public backlash. This text did not simply join the bandwagon highlighting the uselessness of the ACC. It identified specific areas against which the loss of public trust in the ACC can be understood.

The chapter suggests two areas of policy and institutional reform. It is brought forward in this paper that sections 21 and section 31 of the Anti-Corruption Act 8 of 2003 must be amended and democratised. The best practice, on the democratization of the content of these sections, is readily available on the African continent, in Mauritius. It is further suggested that the corruption mandate at the ACC and at the Ombudsman must be harmonised to avoid the wastage of resources. Again, a best practice is brought forward in this text. It is again on the African continent, in South Africa.

With regard to the role of the civil society in fighting corruption, this text submits that given the current climate of public trust deficit in the ACC and to widen civil society participation as envisaged by the *African Union Convention on Preventing and Combating Corruption,* the creation of the buffer zone, to serve as a "safe space" for whistle-blowers, between corruption fighting bodies and the citizens is the best intervention. The work of the AR movement has shown that such a buffer zone is not only possible but can be an effective tool in fighting corruption.

BIBLIOGRAPHY

African Union. (2003). *African Union Convention on Preventing and Combating Corruption.*

African Union Convention on Preventing and Combating Corruption (1st July 2003).

Anti-Corruption Act (No 8 of 2003).

Anti-Corruption Commission. (2018). *Anti-Corruption Commission Annual Report 2017–2018.*

Beukes, J. (2018, March 20). *Ya Toivo Widow in Resettlement Storm.* https://www.namibiansun.com/news/ya-toivo-widow-in-resettlement-storm.

Biswas, A., and Tortajada, C. (2018, September 7). From Our Ancestors to Modern Leaders, All Do It: The Story of Corruption. *The Conversation.* http://theconversation.com/from-our-ancestors-to-modern-leaders-all-do-it-the-story-of-corruption-102164.

Chiringa, K. (2018a, August 21). *Amupanda Races to Stop Tweya Acquiring Oranjemund erf.* https://www.thevillager.com.na/articles/13710/amupanda-races-to-stop-tweya-acquiring-oranjemund-erf-/.

Chiringa, K. (2018b, December 11). *Noa Blames Lawyers, Courts for Failing to Purge Corruption ... As He Struggles to Keep Ark Afloat.* https://www.thevillager.com.na/articles/14364/noa-blames-lawyers-courts-for-failing-to-purge-corruption-as-he-struggles-to-keep-ark-afloat-/.

Coetzee, J. (2016). "Comparative best practices to manage corruption." *Journal for Studies in Humanities and Social Sciences*, Volume 5(2), 143–157.

Coetzee, J. (2018). *The Role of the Private Sector in Tackling Corruption.* Windhoek: IPPR.

Criminal Procedure Act, 1977 (Act No. 51 of 1977) (Namibia).

Halwoodi, L. (2017, December 19). *Noa: The Luckiest Survivor of 2017.* https://www.thevillager.com.na/articles/12250/noa-the-luckiest-survivor-of-2017/.

Hellmann, O. (2017). "The historical origins of corruption in the developing world: A comparative analysis of East Asia." *Crime Law Social Change*, Volume 68, 145–165.

Hilukilwa, P. (2018, April 27). *Demo Against Oshakati Judge.* https://www.namibian.com.na/176919/archive-read/Demo-against-Oshakati-judge.

Holmstrom, L. (2013). *Corruption Within the European Union: A Study of the EU and Its Member States Concerning Their Level of and Fight Against Corruption, and Its Relation to Law and Democracy.* Lund: Lund University.

Iikela, S. (2018, May 9). *Job Says AR Creating an Anti-Graft Watchdog.* https://www.namibian.com.na/177220/archive-read/Job-says-AR-creating--an-anti-graft-watchdog.

Ikela, S. (2019, April 12). *Namibians Afraid to Report Corruption: ACC.* https://neweralive.na/posts/namibians-afraid-to-report-corruption-acc.

Ikela, S. (2019, January 28). *AR establishes People's Litigation Centre.* https://neweralive.na/posts/ar-establishes-peoples-litigation-centre.

Iikela, S., and Immanuel, S. (2019, June 27). *Noa's 'Ark' in Stormy Waters.* https://www.namibian.com.na/80103/read/Noas-ark-in-stormy-waters.

Immanuel, S. (2016, February 17). Ya Ndakolo Pays Pack N$186 000. *The Namibian.* https://www.namibian.com.na/index.php?page=archive-read&id=147472.

Immanuel, S. (2016, September 1). *Noa 'Blocks General's Arrest'.* https://www.namibian.com.na/155118/archive-read/Noa-blocks-generals-arrest.

Immanuel, S. (2017a, October 13). *Schlettwein Attacks Noa Over Genocide Probe.* https://www.namibian.com.na/index.php?page=archive-read&id=170326.

Immanuel, S. (2017b, September 4). *DTA Calls Noa a "Puppet."* https://www.namibian.com.na/168815/archive-read/DTA-calls-Noa-a-&ampamp39puppet&ampamp39.

Joseph, G. (2015, April 13). *Katrina Defends Son's Hardap Resettlement Farm.* https://www.namibiansun.com/news/katrina-defends-sons-hardap-resettlement-farm.

Kambowe, K. (2018, September 6). *Cheda Gets New Plot.* https://www.namibiansun.com/news/cheda-gets-new-plot2018-09-06.

Namibian, T. (2018, May 11). *Ombudsman to Look into Ya Toivo Resettlement.* https://www.namibian.com.na/177248/archive-read/Ombudsman-to-look-into-Ya-Toivo-resettlement.

NAMPA. (2017). *DTA Lambasts ACC Focus on 'Small Fish'*. https://www.namibian.com.na/164450/archive-read/DTA-lambasts-ACC-focus-on-small-fish.
NAMPA. (2019, June 13). *Whistle-Blowers Reluctant to Report Corruption*. https://www.namibian.com.na/79530/read/Whistle-blowers-reluctant-to-report-corruption.
New Era. (2015, December 3). *AR Wants ACC to Probe Ya Ndakolo's N$1 Million Hotel Bill*. https://neweralive.na/posts/ar-acc-probe-ya-ndakolos-n1-million-hotel-bill.
Noa, P. (2018). "Foreword 2017/2018." In Anti-Corruption Commission (Ed.), *Anti-Corruption Commission Annual Report 2017–2018*. Windhoek: Anti-Corruption Commission.
OECD. (2007). *Corruption: A Glossary of International Criminal Standards*. Paris: OECD.
Ombudsman. (2017). *Ombudsman Namibia Annual Report 2016*. Windhoek: Ombudsman.
Prevention of Corruption Act (No 5 of 2002) (Mauritius).
Rent Ordinance 13 of 1997 (Namibia).
Republic of Namibia. (1990). *The Constitution of the Republic of Namibia*. Windhoek: Government of the Republic of Namibia.
Routh, R. (2018, September 6). *Shanghala, Amupanda Showdown Off*. https://neweralive.na/posts/shanghala-amupanda-showdown-off.
SADC Protocol Against Corruption on the (14th August 2001).
SADC. (2003). *Protocol Against Corruption*. Gaborone: SADC.
Schenone, O., and Greeg, S. (2003). *A Theory of Corruption: The Theology and Economics of Sin*. Michigan: Acton Institute.
Shapwanale, N. (2018, February 13). *Shanghala Wants N$500 000 from Job*. https://www.namibian.com.na/174415/archive-read/Shanghala-wants-N$500-000-from-Job.
Smith, S. (2017, October 27). *ACC Has Lost Public Trust-Alweendo*. https://www.observer.com.na/index.php/national/item/8949-acc-has-lost-public-trust-alweendo.
State Finance Act (No 31 of 1991) (Namibia).
Tender Board Act (No 16 of the 1996) Namibia).
The Ombudsman Act (No 7 of 1990) (Namibia).
The Patriot. (2018, May 18). *Public Demands for Resettlement Beneficiaries' List*. https://thepatriot.com.na/index.php/2018/05/18/public-demands-for-resettlement-beneficiaries-list/.
United Nations. (2004). *United Nations Convention Against Corruption*. New York: United Nations.
United Nations Convention against Corruption (31 October 2003).
Weylandt, M. (2017). *The Namibian Anti-Corruption Strategy 2016–2019: An Overview and Analysis*. Windhoek: IPPR.
World Bank. (1997). *The Economic and Social Consequences of Corruption in Transition Economies*. Washington, DC: World Bank.

Chapter 14

Global Apartheid, Economic Sanctions and the Re-Colonisation of the Zimbabwean Economy and Financial Markets

Howard Tafara Chitimira

INTRODUCTION

Notwithstanding the fact that the Zimbabwean political and socio-economic affairs have been rapidly declining since the late 1990s, the chapter seeks to, *inter alia*, unpack the direct and indirect negative challenges caused by economic sanctions on the Zimbabwean economy and financial markets (Nyarota et al. 2015, 29–33). Accordingly, the author argues that the economic sanctions imposed on Zimbabwe could be another form of global apartheid. In this regard, the author concurs with Dunaway and Clelland who correctly argue that: "The problem of the 21st century is the problem of global apartheid because the racist logic of the white master race still exists" (Dunaway and Clelland 2016, 17; Marable 2009, 1). While the author does not condone human rights abuses, dictatorship, nepotism, lack of the rule of law, corruption and other poor governance practices that could have attracted such economic sanctions on the part of the Zimbabwean government, he argues that the severe economic challenges experienced in Zimbabwe as early as the 1990s could have been directly and indirectly influenced, in part, by the countries in the Global North, especially, England and its allies (Nyarota et al. 2015, 29–33). For instance, the Zimbabwean economy started to tumble soon after the controversial economic policies from the Global North, such as the Economic and Structural Adjustment Program (ESAP) policy were adopted in 1990 (Moyo 2001, 1–35). These adverse policies could have been deliberately formulated by the powerful countries in the Global North such as the United States of America (USA) and England as a way to re-colonise and control weaker countries in the Global South such as Zimbabwe. Moreover, the introduction of ESAP and related adverse austerity measures in Zimbabwe was probably another form of global apartheid since the Bretton Woods Institutions, namely, the World Bank and the International Monetary Fund (IMF) are largely influenced by the Global North countries, particularly, the USA (World Bank 2017, 14). Global apartheid could entail, *inter alia*, that a few powerful developed countries in the Global North decide and/or are instrumental in international decision-making on both political and socio-economic matters globally to the detriment of weaker developing countries in the Global South (Köhler1995, 403–413). The term "global apartheid" is obviously derived from the term "apartheid," which was a discriminatory system of government that was enforced in South Africa prior to April 27, 1994. Given this background, it was wrong and ill-advised for the Zimbabwean government to adopt ESAP since it was incompatible to the prevailing Zimbabwean political and socio-economic environment at the time of its adoption (Nyarota et al. 2015, 29–33). Thus, despite the dictatorship, human rights abuse, lack of the rule of law, corruption and poor governance on the part of the Zimbabwean government, ESAP was somewhat an indirect way of the re-colonisation of the Zimbabwean economy and financial markets by some of the Global North countries as earlier stated. It was also an indirect form of global apartheid by the Global North countries, especially, the USA, England and their allies, which could have been aimed at the promotion of Euro-American economic policies and companies at the expense of local Zimbabwean companies and/or economic policies (the so-called global corporatocracy). It is further submitted that ESAP, poor micro and macroeconomic policies, human rights abuses, lack of the rule of law, dictatorship, nepotism, corruption and poor governance practices should never have been embraced in Zimbabwe (Harvey 1996, 1–28). A robust approach without these negative factors as well as the enactment of adequate investment and financial markets laws could enhance foreign direct investment (FDI), Gross Domestic Product (GDP) and improve the Zimbabwean economy and increase public investor confidence in its financial markets (Harvey 1996, 1–28). Accordingly, the relevant regulatory approaches, flaws and challenges contained in legislation such as the Securities Act 17 of 2004 [Chapter 24:25] as amended (Securities Act 2004), the Collective Investment Schemes Act 25 of 1997 [Chapter 24:19] as amended (Investment Schemes Act), the Asset Management Act 15 of 2004 [Chapter 24:26] as amended (Asset Management Act), the Zimbabwe Investment Authority Act 4 of 2006 [Chapter 14:30] as amended (Investment Authority Act) and the Indigenisation and Economic Empowerment Act 14 of 2007 [Chapter 14:33] as amended (Indigenisation Act) are discussed.

THE POLITICAL AND SOCIO-ECONOMIC AFFAIRS OF ZIMBABWE FROM THE LATE 1990S TO DATE

Before I tackle the global apartheid debate, it is prudent to provide a brief overview of the socio-economic and political background of Zimbabwe. Zimbabwe got its independence from the Rhodesian government's white supremacy minority colonial rule which was in place since 1888 on April 18, 1980. Prior to this, the black majority people were segregated and oppressed by the Ian Smith regime. Ian Smith regime used curfews and unfair discriminatory rules in relation to education, residential places, health facilities, social security, social protection, food security, land distribution, economic participation and political participation (United Nations 2014, 1–11). Repressive and draconian laws were employed to enforce the colonial and discriminatory rule by the Ian Smith regime till 1980. Consequently, majority of the black people were banned and excluded from taking part in key socio-economic and political affairs of their country. This apartheid-related racial segregation was mainly aimed at eliminating and weakening black people while strengthening white minority rule in Rhodesia. The apartheid-related racial segregation and white supremacy minority rule continued to be viciously enforced against the black people, especially in the 1960s and 1970s. Nonetheless, the United Nations Security Council (UNSC) only imposed economic sanctions against Rhodesia on December 16, 1966 (United Nations 1966). These UNSC mandatory economic sanctions were meant to force Ian Smith regime to end its white supremacist regime in Rhodesia. Accordingly, the UNSC imposed an international trade embargo on about 90 per cent of the exports of Rhodesia (United Nations 1966). While this was commendable, the United Nations (UN) took too long to condemn and take action against apartheid-related racial segregation and white supremacy minority rule in Rhodesia. Moreover, economic sanctions failed to stop Ian Smith regime from enforcing apartheid-related racial segregation and white supremacy minority rule in Rhodesia (George 1968, 8–12).

As a result, the Patriotic Front Zimbabwe African People's Union (PF ZAPU) led by Joshua Nkomo and the Zimbabwe African National Union Patriotic Front (ZANU PF) took arms to fight Ian Smith regime in the first and second liberation war struggles (chimurenga 1 and 2). One of the key aspects that led both the PF ZAPU and ZANU PF to forge war against Ian Smith regime was the unfair and discriminatory distribution of land in Rhodesia. The black people were resettled in less fertile communal land while the white people took all the available fertile land. After independence, land reform was conducted on a willing buyer and willing seller basis in accordance with the 1979 Lancaster House Constitution. This approach was very slow and expensive; hence, a majority of the black people were still denied access to fertile land. The majority of the land remained in the hands of the white commercial farmers (United Nations 2014, 1–11). In a bid to correct this injustice after independence, ZANU PF embarked on the so-called fast track land reform which saw its members and war veterans embark on violence, looting, killings and other barbaric activities to drive away white commercial farmers out of their farms in 2000 (Masaka 2012, 49–62). While the author condemns the aforesaid barbaric activities and gross human rights violations that were perpetuated during the fast track land reform farm invasions, it is interesting to note that targeted sanctions were promptly imposed on the ZANU PF government by the USA, England and the European Union (EU) nations. This clearly exposes double standards of the UN, the USA, England and other Western countries that rushed to impose sanctions on Zimbabwe for its chaotic fast track land reform yet they took unreasonably long to impose economic sanctions against apartheid-related racial segregation and white supremacy minority rule of Ian Smith regime in Rhodesia (Masaka 2012, 49–62).

The land question has remained unresolved since 2000 to date. Likewise, poor governance, segregation of the poor, lack of the rule of law, disputed elections, socio-economic-political challenges and gross human rights abuses on the part of the ZANU PF government have continued to date. Furthermore, there has been constant politically related violence and human rights abuses, especially during and/or soon after harmonised elections in Zimbabwe since 2000 to date (United Nations 2014, 1–11). It is submitted that this political violence is mostly perpetrated by ZANU PF government against the supporters and members of the Movement for Democratic Change (MDC), human rights defenders and other political activists (United Nations 2014, 1–11). This status *quo* has provided the USA, England and other Western countries with a better excuse to impose and maintain economic sanctions against the Zimbabwean government since 2001 to date (Masaka 2012, 49–62). The USA and EU economic sanctions on Zimbabwe are currently contained in the Zimbabwe Democracy and Economic Recovery Act of 2001 (115 STAT. 963; 115 STAT. 965) (ZIDERA) and the Council Common Position (2002/145/CFSP) of 2002 (CCP), respectively (Masaka 2012, 51; Chingono et al. 2013, 307–317).

GLOBAL APARTHEID, ECONOMIC SANCTIONS, FINANCIAL MARKETS AND THE ZIMBABWEAN ECONOMY

It is submitted that Robert Mugabe once argued that: "Zimbabwe would not kneel down to pray to the IMF, to confess its sins as if it were God. For goodness sake, we are a sovereign state and we should not humiliate ourselves to that extent" (Robert Mugabe: AFP April 18, 1999, as quoted in Tungwarara 2011, 109–113). Robert Mugabe allegedly said this after he had written to IMF to access United States Dollars (USD) 53 million in balance of payment (BOP) support but was denied the funding (Robert Mugabe: AFP April 18, 1999, as quoted in Tungwarara 2011, 109–113). The failure of Zimbabwe to access the vitally needed funding from the IMF could be interpreted as global injustice and a form of global apartheid that has to date directly and indirectly affected the financial markets and economy of Zimbabwe negatively (Chingono et al. 2013, 307–317). Global apartheid is oppugnant to global democracy. Global apartheid is an institutionalised international system that empowers countries in the Global North to, *inter alia*, promote inequalities, minority rule and unfair discriminatory access to global wealth, funding institutions, political power and basic human rights in the world today (Mutasa 2004). This has prompted several persons such as Muammar Mohammed Abu Minyar Gaddafi, Robert Mugabe, Thabo Mbeki, Fidel Castro, Ali Mazrui, Richard Falk, Patrick Bond and others to argue that global apartheid is employed by powerful countries in the Global North to perpetuate global human rights abuses, unjust sanctions, economic stagnation and political challenges against countries in the Global South. There are various types of global apartheid such as socio-economic and political apartheid, salary apartheid, technological apartheid, ecological apartheid and gendered global apartheid (Köhler 1995, 404). For the purposes of this sub-heading I shall discuss the economy and financial markets of Zimbabwe in accordance with the socio-economic and political apartheid concept. The author submits that socio-economic and political apartheid is generally a global form of capitalism that empowers Global North countries to have unfair access and control of the global wealth, global funding institutions, global politics and global decision-making to the detriment of Global South countries such as Zimbabwe (Chingono et al. 2013, 307–317).

It is submitted that the economy of Zimbabwe (previously known as Rhodesia) was relatively strong between 1961 and 1980 (Nyarota et al. 2015, 6–7). During this period, the economy was mainly driven by agriculture and mineral resources that were exported to other countries. The Zimbabwean economy was also relatively stable between 1980 and 1990. Thereafter, the economy started to decline between 1990 and 2000, especially, after the adoption of ESAP. The author submit that ESAP was an indirect instrument used by institutions such as the IMF and the World Bank (Bretton Woods Institutions) to re-colonise and influence economic policies of countries in the Global South, including Zimbabwe. This follows the fact that these Bretton Woods Institutions are controlled by powerful Global North countries so as to re-colonise and impose regressive policies on Global South countries such as Zimbabwe.

Moreover, the economy of Zimbabwe continued to sharply decline between 2000 and 2019 owing to, *inter alia*, constant disputed elections, economic sanctions, poor governance, gross human rights abuses, political instability, hyperinflation, poor micro and macroeconomic policies, rampant corruption and other related malpractices on the part of the ZANU PF government. For instance, the looting of Marange diamonds, looting of over 15 billion USD from the treasury, Zimbabwe Manpower Development Fund scandal and the command agriculture scandal involving the looting of over 3 billion USD are some of the recent examples of the ZANU PF government corruption and poor governance practices that contributed to the poor growth of the Zimbabwean economy between 2000 and 2019 (World Bank 2017, 1–47). While the author does not condone the aforesaid negative practices on the part of the ZANU PF government, he argues that external factors such as economic sanctions, isolation in the decision-making, adoption of ESAP and other regressive political and economic policies have played a huge role in the destabilisation of the Zimbabwean economy to date (Masaka 2013, 314–327). The author submits that although the EU and USA could have meant good by imposing economic sanctions on Zimbabwe for its alleged human rights violations, these sanctions could have been also carefully planned and utilised to destabilise the Zimbabwean economy for the political and economic benefit of the Global North countries (Masaka 2013, 314–327). The so-called targeted economic sanctions imposed by the EU and USA on ZANU PF government officials have to date negatively affected foreign aid, FDI and economic development of Zimbabwe. Accordingly, economic sanctions are crippling not only the economy but are also biting upon most ordinary citizens of Zimbabwe who are currently leaving in deplorable, harsh and abject poverty without access to basic socio-economic services such as health, food, education, transport and other fundamental rights (Masaka 2013, 314–327; Bond 2003, 54–91).

Apart from the global apartheid-related economic challenges discussed above, the financial markets were also directly and indirectly affected by the negative dealings of the Global North countries. The Rhodesian financial markets were fairly developed between 1961 and 1980. During this period, a number of foreign-owned commercial banks as well as the central bank were operating in Rhodesia (Harvey 1996, 1–28). The Rhodesian Stock Exchange (RSE) was established between 1946 and 1952 (Karekwaivenani 2003, 9–34). Nonetheless, the growth of the Rhodesian financial markets was impeded by political instability and economic sanctions that were imposed on Ian Smith regime. Thereafter, between 1980 and 1990, the Zimbabwean financial markets were growing relatively well (World Bank

2017, 1–47). Some investors were actively participating on the Zimbabwe Stock Exchange (ZSE). The financial markets continued to grow between 1990 and 2000. However, this growth was marred by the adoption of ESAP and other negative policies from the Global North in the 1990s. Consequently, the ZSE attracted very insignificant FDI between 1993 and 2000 (Chowa et al. 2014, 1–10). Moreover, the Zimbabwean financial markets progressed slowly between 2001 and 2008. The poor growth of the financial markets gave rise to a very low rate of investments to be obtained in the industrial, financial, agricultural, mining and manufacturing sectors of Zimbabwe (Sikwila 2014, 1–9). This was worsened by the farm invasions, political instability, economic sanctions and electoral disputes that continued to occur between 2001 and 2008. Furthermore, the sustained USA and EU economic sanctions against the ZANU PF government negatively affected public investor confidence and the integrity of the Zimbabwean financial markets during the same period (Maja and Nhara 2016, 1–20). Consequently, ZANU PF has often argued that economic sanctions were imposed on Zimbabwe by the USA, the EU and other Global North countries as part of a vindictive strategy to punish sovereign countries that rejected to give up their land and/or to be re-colonised (Hove 2012, 72–78). On the other hand, the USA, the EU and other Global North countries argue that the sanctions were only imposed on certain ZANU PF individuals in a bid to transform their negative conduct and discourage the ZANU PF government from committing human rights violations and tyranny (Hove 2012, 72–82). Obviously, ZANU PF does not agree with this narrative and it argues that economic sanctions were imposed on its government officials as part of a regime change agenda by the Global North countries (Hove 2012, 72–82). While the aforesaid debate rages on, it is not debatable that economic sanctions have to date caused many investors to shun the Zimbabwean financial markets.

The Zimbabwean financial markets and investments on the ZSE continued to decline in 2008. The position improved during the Global Political Agreement government of national unity (GNU) between ZANU PF and the MDC-T and MDC-M formations. This GNU was in force from 2009 to 2013 (Mukuhlani 2014, 169–179). Soon after the GNU, the 2013 disputed elections triggered new political and economic challenges that deterred most investors from investing in the Zimbabwean financial markets. This position has been further exacerbated by the recent disputed elections of 2018. The fall of Robert Mugabe and rise of Emmerson Munangagwa, albeit through a controversial military intervention, has to date failed to enhance public investor confidence and the integrity of the Zimbabwean financial markets.

GLOBAL NORTH ECONOMIC POLICIES AND THE RE-COLONISATION OF THE ZIMBABWEAN ECONOMY AND FINANCIAL MARKETS

It is submitted that: "Southern African countries were pressured into implementing IMF and World Bank programmes with adverse effects on employment and standards of living . . ." (African National Congress 1994, sections 1.4.17 and 6.5.16b; Bond 2003, vi). This statement was allegedly made by the African National Congress political party sometime after the South African government blindly adopted the IMF and World Bank's economic policies which failed to improve their economy. On the other hand, it is important to note that the pre-colonial economic policies that were adopted in Rhodesia between 1000 and 1890 were poorly developed and enforced (Dube 2013, 10–12). Likewise, economic policies adopted in Rhodesia between 1890 and 1980 were mainly aimed at promoting white supremacy and the colonial agenda of the British led by Cecil John Rhodes, especially, in the 1880s. In 1888, Mr Rhodes colonised the native black people that were residing in what is now known as Zimbabwe through his British South Africa Company (BSAC) and entrenched his colonial economic policies for the benefit of the British people (Bond 2003, 1–91). Poor colonial economic policies continued to be enforced in Rhodesia in about 1895 before Rhodesia was renamed to Southern Rhodesia in about 1898. Mr Rhodes fraudulently duped King Lobengula to acquire farmland investments and mining rights which promoted white supremacy and draconian economic policies in Southern Rhodesia. These draconian economic policies were used to control and colonise black people in Southern Rhodesia. Accordingly, Mr Rhodes was granted a royal charter by the British government to colonise Matabeleland and other parts of Southern Rhodesia (Dube 2013, 10–12). Rhodesia became a full colony of the British government in about 1895 and the BSAC colonial rule ended around 1922. Thereafter, the British government appointed its preferred leaders from time to time to rule over Rhodesia and ensure that colonial economic policies are adopted in Rhodesia, particularly between 1922 and 1980. The Rhodesian colonial economic policies were meant to unfairly empower white people with socio-economic and political rights at the expense of the black majority people (Dube 2013, 10–12). These global apartheid-related economic policies gave rise to an invasion of many European and American companies and business investments in Rhodesia between 1922 and 1980. Sadly, these companies and global apartheid-related economic policies promoted socio-economic, colonial and political interests of the white minority people to the detriment of the native black people. Consequently, most investments involving mineral resources, especially, gold and iron were established for the colonial gain and economic profit of the white people at the expense of the black communities (Hollaway 1997, 27; Kaseke et al. 2015, 90–92). This also led to unlawful mining of minerals by the Global North companies that were affiliated to the Rhodesian government. Accordingly, black communities were prejudiced by the Rhodesian government's global apartheid-related economic and investment policies (Kaseke et al. 2015, 90–92). For instance, black people had little or no access to education, health and other socio-economic services under Ian Smith regime. Consequently, majority of black people were relegated to peasant farming and excluded from the investments, financial markets and other socio-economic activities of their country, particularly between 1922 and 1980 (Harvey 1996, 1–28; Dube 2013, 10–12).

Most Zimbabwean economic policies were generally influenced by the British government while commercial banks were largely owned by foreign companies from the Global North countries between 1980 and 1990 (Harvey 1996, 3–4). Soon after independence, the ZANU PF government reintroduced most of the Ian Smith government's global apartheid-related economic policies (Nhavira et al. 2013, 3). Accordingly, most economic and investment policies that were adopted in Zimbabwe favoured foreign companies at the expense of local companies. Consequently, mining, agriculture, manufacturing, finance and other vital sectors of the Zimbabwean economy were colonised and controlled by Global North companies, especially those from the USA, United Kingdom (UK) and the EU. This approach attracted a relatively good FDI to Zimbabwe between 1980 and 2000. Nevertheless, local industries and companies received very little government support compared to foreign industries and companies between 1980 and 2000. It appears the ZANU PF government wanted to please the Global North countries to get FDI. For instance, the ZANU PF government naively adopted colonial economic policies such as ESAP from the Global North countries and institutions in 1991 (Nyarota et al. 2015, 29–33). It is submitted that the Zimbabwean government was misled by the Global North funding institutions into believing that the mere adoption of ESAP was a sound macroeconomic policy that was going to boost the economy. The IMF's ESAP policy was reportedly premised on rapid financial reforms involving trade liberalisation, financial stability and promotion of international best practices (Nhavira et al. 2013, 3–4). This approach was probably meant to encourage local persons to engage in the banking sector and increase FDI to boost the Zimbabwean economy (Nhavira et al. 2013, 3–4). Nonetheless, the World Bank and IMF inspired policies and ESAP reforms failed to improve the Zimbabwean economy, especially, between 1991 and 1998 (Nhavira et al. 2013, 3–4). Most banks collapsed and the economy had stagnant growth between 1991 and 2000 due to ESAP-related policies that were employed in Zimbabwe during this period. ESAP policies continued to cause negative economic growth, poor FDI and less investments to be obtained in Zimbabwe between 2000 and 2010. Moreover, a stringent foreign policy and barbaric currency controls were adopted in a bid to restrict the dominance of foreign banks and foreign investments in Zimbabwe. Accordingly, the Banking Act [Chapter 24:20] (Banking Act) was amended in 2000 to encourage local banking institutions to get commercial banking licences (Nhavira et al. 2013, 3–4). Despite these efforts, not many local persons were able to invest in the Zimbabwean financial sector and financial markets (Nhavira et al. 2013, 3–4). Persistent political and economic challenges ensued and Zimbabwe was reported as one of the least business-friendly countries by the United Nations Conference on Trade and Development (UNCTAD) survey of African investment promotion agencies in 1999 (United Nations Environment Programme 2000, 10; United Nations Conference on Trade and Development 1999, 45–52).

Several disputed elections led to political instability and severe economic challenges which eventually gave rise to the adoption of more global apartheid-related economic policies that were similar to ESAP (Harrison 2002, 52–57). Consequently, most local and foreign investors shunned to invest in the Zimbabwean mining, manufacturing, agricultural and financial sectors between 1991 and 2010 (United Nations Environment Programme 2000, 10; Nyamunda and Mukwambo 2012, 145–166; Gwimbi and Nhamo 2016, 10–21; Murombo 2010, 570–588; Murombo 2013, 33–49; Chindori-Chininga 2012, 7–22). For instance, the ZANU PF government adopted the Zimbabwe Programme of Economic and Social Transformation (ZPEST) in 1997, the Zimbabwe Millennium Economic Recovery Programme (MERP) in 2000 and the National Economic Recovery Plan (NERP) in 2003 in a bid to improve the economy (Nyarota et al. 2015, 3). Nevertheless, these global apartheid-inspired policies failed to turn around the Zimbabwean economy. Subsequently, the ZANU PF government further adopted the Macroeconomic Policy Framework in 2005 and the Short Term Economic Recovery Plan (STERP) in 2009 which also failed to improve FDI and the economy (Nyarota et al. 2015, 3). Put differently, most of the global apartheid-inspired economic policies adopted by the ZANU PF government between 1997 and 2008 such as the ZPEST, the MERP, the NERP and the National Economic Development Priority Programme of 2007 failed to resolve the Zimbabwean economic woes (Kaseke et al. 2015, 91–92). Furthermore, the indigenisation policy that was introduced in 2007 to ensure that at least 51 per cent of the shares of every public company is ceded to indigenous people of Zimbabwe did not improve the economy (section 3(1)(a) of the Indigenisation Act; Mclean et al. 2012, 313–348). Perhaps, this policy was directly and/or indirectly aimed at combating discriminatory and colonial economic policies from the Global North funding institutions such as the World Bank and the IMF, which were being unfairly imposed on Zimbabwe from time to time. The economic challenges continued and ZANU PF government was forced to employ a multicurrency policy in 2009. This policy was also used during the GNU but it failed to promote sustainable economic growth in Zimbabwe between 2009 and 2019 (Harvey 1996, 3–4). Zimbabwe has since dumped the multicurrency policy in favour of its own mono-currency policy with effect from June 24, 2019. Likewise, the STERP and the medium-term plan (MTP) which were adopted between 2009 and 2015 struggled to enhance the economic outlook of Zimbabwe (United Nations 2014, 9–11). Notably, both the STERP and the MTP policies failed to promote macroeconomic stability, economic transformation and curb hyperinflation in Zimbabwe between 2009 and 2015. Economic challenges continued to haunt Zimbabwe amid severe foreign currency shortages and lack of funding from the Global North's Bretton Woods Institutions since 1999 to date (United Nations 2014, 9–11). Similar colonial and retrogressive economic policies such as the Zimbabwe Agenda for Sustainable Socio-economic Transformation (ZIMASSET) were adopted by the ZANU PF government in 2013. Nevertheless, ZIMASSET has to date failed attract meaningful FDI and promote economic stability in Zimbabwe.

As discussed above, political instability and the adoption of poor micro and macroeconomic policies that are directly and indirectly influenced by Bretton Woods Institutions have somewhat marred Zimbabwe's economic recovery efforts. The Global North funding institutions have carefully managed to dictate, colonise and control the economic policies of Zimbabwe at the expense of its own indigenous economic policies. The recent introduction of a Staff-Monitored Program for Zimbabwe by the IMF commencing on May 15, 2019, to March 15, 2020, is a case in point (IMF 2019). Consequently, Zimbabwe continues to face macroeconomic policy challenges, hyperinflation and fiscal deficits owing to, *inter alia*, accumulated external debt arrears and the direct and indirect negative colonial influence of the IMF and other Global North institutions (Bond 2003, 1–91). The aforesaid *status quo* is exacerbated by the isolation of Zimbabwe and its inability to borrow from the Global North funding institutions such as the IMF and the World Bank since 1999 to date. As a result, Zimbabwe has remained in debt and it owes World Bank about 2.2 billion USD and several amounts of money to the African Development Bank and the European Investment Bank. This global capitalism crisis has been worsened by economic sanctions that were imposed on Zimbabwe as stated in the previous sub-headings (United Nations 2014, 1–11; Van Wyk 2018, 497–511). For instance, ZIDERA statutorily empowers the USA to veto all Zimbabwe's funding applications to the Global North funding institutions such as the IMF and the World Bank (Tungwarara 2011, 110; World Bank 2017, 14; Nyarota et al. 2015, 29–33). Thus, the so-called targeted economic sanctions have to date affected Zimbabwe's BOP. The author submits that the targeted economic sanctions and the global supremacy of the USA and the EU have caused the IMF, the World Bank and other funding institutions to shun advancing funding to Zimbabwe (Masaka 2012, 51). In this regard, the author argues that global apartheid is mainly aimed at promoting white supremacy, Pan-Europeanism and transnational capitalism of Global North countries (Dunaway and Clelland 2016, 17). This approach has entrenched white supremacy and empowered the Global North to control politics and economic activities of many countries, especially those in the Global South such as Zimbabwe (Dunaway and Clelland 2016, 17). Accordingly, the negative influence from the powerful Global North countries such as the USA could have caused the ZANU PF government to constantly fail to apply for funding and/or conduct economic investment policy reviews as required by the Organisation for Economic Cooperation and Development, the World Trade Organisation (WTO) and/or the UNCTAD (United States of America 2015, 3).

THE NEED TO DEVELOP AND ADOPT ROBUST ECONOMIC AND INVESTMENT POLICIES IN ZIMBABWE

As indicated in the introduction, various statutes such as the Rhodesia Stock Exchange Act of 1974 (Rhodesia Stock Exchange Act), the Securities Act 2004, the Investment Schemes Act, the Asset Management Act, the Investment Authority Act, the Indigenisation Act and many others were enacted from time to time in a bid to improve the economy of Zimbabwe. However, most of these statutes were premised on the policies and ideals of Global North countries such as the UK and the USA. For instance, the Exchange Control Act [Chapter 22:05] as amended (Exchange Control Act) was initially enacted in 1965 under Ian Smith regime. It prohibited all persons from, *inter alia*, making any statement or producing any document in relation to the export and import exchange rules and trading of goods or services, which is materially false or misleading (s 5 read with ss 4 and 8). This Act further prohibited any person exercising any functions stipulated under its provisions from using any information which he or she obtained while exercising such functions, for his or her personal gain (s 9 of the Exchange Control Act). Nevertheless, the Exchange Control Act was hugely mirrored on the colonial Rhodesian exchange laws which sought to advance and protect the British' colonial economic interests. Additionally, the Exchange Control Act was later amended in line with the recommendations of the Southern African Development Community and the Global North's funding institutions such as the IMF. These amendments and colonial approach did not improve foreign currency conversions, transfers and other relevant transactions in the Zimbabwean financial markets (United States of America 2015, 6). Related amendments and reforms that were introduced in 2009 also failed to combat the Zimbabwean economic and investments challenges. Investment and economic policies adopted under the Exchange Control Act favoured the British and other Global North countries at the expense of the native black people of Zimbabwe.

Likewise, the Companies Act [Chapter 24:03] as amended (Companies Act) of 1951 has its initial colonial roots in Rhodesia. This Act has continued to be employed in Zimbabwe to date. The Companies Act provides for, *inter alia*, the registration of all companies and the issuing of shares and debentures in Zimbabwe (sections 21–123 and sections 199–337). It further prohibits any falsification of books and the making or publication of false statements by company directors and other related persons (sections 341; 343 and 345). In addition, the Companies Act enumerates a number of offences and stipulates that any fraudulent practices in connection with the promotion, formation or management of a company or the winding up or judicial management of a company are prohibited in Zimbabwe (section 344). While this could be commendable, the Companies Act does not have specific provisions that safeguard and protect local companies and industries against unfair domination by foreign multinational companies from the Global North. Furthermore, the Companies Act fails to provide specific provisions that protect local companies and industries against unfair economic policies from the Global North.

The Zimbabwe Stock Exchange Act [Chapter 24: 18] of 1973 as amended (Stock Exchange Act) also continued to be utilised in Zimbabwe after the demise of Ian Smith regime. It repealed the Rhodesia Stock Exchange Act which regulated the RSE. The Stock Exchange Act was later repealed by the Securities Act 2004. The Rhodesia Stock Exchange Act established the first stock exchange (RSE) which begun operating between 1946 and 1952 (Karekwaivenani 2003, 9–34). The Stock Exchange Act regulated stock broking transactions, the listing of securities, financial instruments and related activities that were conducted on the ZSE (sections 22–62). Unregistered stockbrokers, canvassing and/or advertising for business without the approval from the ZSE Committee was prohibited under the Stock Exchange Act (section 70). The making or publishing of misleading circulars, reports, forecasts or statements regarding listed securities, financial instruments or other transactions that were conducted on the ZSE were also prohibited under the Stock Exchange Act (section 71). Stockbrokers were further prohibited from issuing any circular, report, forecast or statement in writing or otherwise regarding listed securities without prior permission from the ZSE Committee (section 72). The making or causing of fraudulent acts and other misleading business activities on the ZSE were further prohibited under the Stock Exchange Act (section 73). Market participants were obliged not to use words such as "stock exchange" and "stockbroker" without prior consent of the Registrar of the Stock Exchange (section 74). Nevertheless, the operations of the ZSE were complicated and largely influenced by market forces and practices from the Global North countries. These rigid and restrictive Global North economic policies have made the Zimbabwean financial markets illiquid and unattractive for investment since the late 1990s to date.

Furthermore, the Zimbabwean banking sector is regulated by the Banking Act. It, *inter alia*, regulates the registration of banking institutions and prohibits any unregistered institutions from offering banking services to the public in Zimbabwe (sections 5–15). The Banking Act also regulates the conduct and activities of banking institutions in Zimbabwe (sections 16–72). It prohibits all persons from making any statement that is materially and objectively false or misleading in relation to the operations or any activities that are carried out in accordance with this Act (section 75(1)). Any person who destroys, falsifies or makes false or misleading information on banking institutions with the intent to defraud or deceive other people shall be guilty of an offence under the Banking Act (section 75(2)). Unlawful use of confidential information relating to banking institutions' services, customers or activities for personal gain by anyone privy to such information is further prohibited under the Banking Act (section 77). Be that as it may, several local banks have struggled to remain profitable. As a result, most local banks have gone bankrupt and closed. This could have been caused by the fact that most local banks of Zimbabwe have to date struggled to comply with the international best practices for banking institutions which are largely influenced by the Global North institutions such as the Basel Committee on Banking Supervision and the Bank for International Settlements. Zimbabwe is yet to fully implement the Basel II recommendations. Moreover, not many investors have confidence in the Zimbabwean banking institutions. This position is worsened by the ongoing economic challenges in Zimbabwe.

Moreover, the Investment Schemes Act was enacted to, *inter alia*, promote FDI and regulate collective investment schemes that are not covered by the Banking Act and the Companies Act. Notably, any unregistered collective investment schemes are outlawed under the Investment Schemes Act (section 5 read with sections 6–27). Nevertheless, poor governance on the part of the ZANU PF government coupled with global apartheid economic-related sanctions have negatively affected Zimbabwe's efforts to attract FDI from the Global North countries. This position is exacerbated by the fact that the Asset Management Act is largely modelled on Eurocentric policies which protects business interests of Global North countries. The Asset Management Act has failed to curb fraudulent investment and business activities in Zimbabwe because it is restricted to certain persons dealing with asset management businesses involving money markets instruments, property investment portfolios and related financial instruments on a regulated stock exchange (sections 2–3). Over and above, the enactment of the Investment Authority Act has also failed to improve the promotion of FDI in Zimbabwe. Thus, although the Investment Authority Act introduced the ZIA and the Zimbabwe Investment Authority Board (ZIAB), minimal progress has been achieved in the promotion of FDI in Zimbabwe to date (sections 3–4). Instead of attracting FDI, the flaws imbedded in the Investment Authority Act have to date enabled bogus Global North mining companies to be awarded mining tenders in Chiadzwa, where over USD 15 billion diamond mining revenue was looted and siphoned out of the country between 2006 and 2017 (Chindori-Chininga 2012, 7–22; Murombo 2016, 230–263; Nyamunda and Mukwambo 2012, 145–166). Likewise, the Special Economic Zones Act [Chapter 14:34] 7 of 2016 (Economic Zones Act) which introduced the Zimbabwe Special Economic Zones Authority (ZSEZA) and the Zimbabwe Special Economic Zones Board have failed to boost FDI in Zimbabwe (sections 3–5). The ZSEZA has to date failed to effectively grant investment licences to investors in designated special economic zones. Corruption and unfair investment policy deals from the Global North have marred the functions of the ZSEZA. Furthermore, the Indigenisation Act failed to encourage local persons to actively invest in the Zimbabwean economy. This Act was received with a huge resistance from the EU, the USA and other Global North countries for its requirement for foreign investors to cede at least 51 per cent of their shares in public companies and related business to the Zimbabwean indigenous people (section 3(1)(a)). Obviously, most foreign investors from Global North countries had to protect their own interests by shunning establishing their businesses in Zimbabwe. The defiance and failure by most Global North countries to comply with the Indigenisation Act policies meant that Zimbabwe had to continue to struggle to attract adequate FDI (Chinamasa 2017, 1–235; section 42 of the Finance Act 1 of 2018 (Finance Act). Consequently, the Finance Minister (Mthuli Ncube) has reportedly abolished the controversial provision that required foreign investors to cede at least 51 per cent of their shares in public companies to indigenous people of Zimbabwe during his 2019 mid-term budget statement to parliament in a bid to revamp FDI.

The Securities Act 2004 repealed the Stock Exchange Act and it, *inter alia*, regulates the trading of securities and financial instruments on the Zimbabwean regulated financial markets. Nevertheless, this Act has not been consistently enforced to enhance public investor confidence and the integrity of the ZSE in Zimbabwe to date (sections 63–86).

As discussed above, there is a need for Zimbabwe to review its laws, policies, strategies and approaches to promote FDI, a viable economy and efficient financial markets (Munyedza 2011, 1–12). The ZANU PF government is guilty of adopting poor micro and macroeconomic policies that were rigidly influenced by the Global North. For instance, the adoption of economic policies such as ESAP, ZPEST, STERP, MTP and ZIMASSET have negatively contributed to a huge debt bondage and severe economic challenges to be constantly experienced in Zimbabwe (World Bank 2017, 1–47). The IMF and the World Bank–inspired policies such as ESAP have culminated into huge unsustainable debts, illiquid financial markets, economic isolation and poor FDI in Zimbabwe (Munyedza 2011, 1–12). The IMF and the World Bank debts have negatively isolated, oppressed and crippled the economy of Zimbabwe. This follows the fact that the IMF and the World Bank's debt policies have made it very difficult for Zimbabwe to repay its debts and/or be eligible to apply for new funding. For instance, the IMF and the World Bank's economic structural adjustment programmes were introduced to the Global South under guise of sustainable economic policies that rescue debtors yet in reality such policies were meant to negatively control and influence the debtor country's economic policies (Mutasa 2004). The author submits that this approach is another form of global apartheid that is viciously enforced by Global North institutions such as the IMF and the World Bank to promote debt bondage, poverty and economic challenges in poor Global South countries such as Zimbabwe. The WTO, the IMF and World Bank are directly and indirectly used by the Global North to police and entrench global apartheid policies that colonise desperate and poor Global South countries.

The Zimbabwean government need to adopt its own robust economic and investment policies that are not negatively influenced by the Global North and/or the Rhodesian laws, policies and enforcement approaches (Nhavira et al. 2013, 3). Zimbabwe should develop its own socio-economic policies and independent micro and macroeconomic policies that are compatible to its economic needs. This could promote the integrity and public investor confidence in the Zimbabwean financial institutions and financial markets (Nhavira et al. 2013, 3). In addition, Zimbabwe must shun aid policies and regressive development programmes that are imposed from donor countries. Donor countries usually prescribe policies and programmes that protect their own interests rather than the interests of the recipient (donee) countries. Consequently, blindly adopting aid policies and programmes from donor countries could give birth to colonial, repressive and/or bad policies for the recipient country.

CONCLUDING REMARKS

As indicated in the chapter, Zimbabwe has made numerous efforts to enhance its financial markets, FDI, GDP and economy. Various legislative and socio-economic policies have been introduced by the policy-makers and ZANU

PF government from time to time since 1980 to date. However, most of the statutes and policies such as ESAP, ZPEST, STERP, MTP and ZIMASSET were largely and wrongly premised on Eurocentric and Global North policies. Furthermore, most statutes and policies that were adopted in Zimbabwe were wrongly influenced by Rhodesian socio-economic policies which were unlawfully employed by Ian Smith regime to promote colonialism and white supremacy. Consequently, Zimbabwe has encountered numerous investment and socio-economic challenges owing to its blind reliance on incompatible Rhodesian, Eurocentric and Global North policies since 1980 to date. These policies and statutory regulatory measures have been inconsistently enforced in Zimbabwe since 1980 to date. Accordingly, it is submitted that Zimbabwe should carefully review its laws and policies to remove provisions and policies that unfairly advance Eurocentric and colonial interests of the Global North. It is further submitted that Zimbabwe should decolonise its legislation, investment and economic policies to introduce indigenous policy measures so as to attract more FDI. This approach could enable more indigenous people to actively participate and invest in the Zimbabwean economy (United Nations 2014, 9–11). Moreover, the Zimbabwean government should carefully utilise the recent abolition of the equity provision that was contained in the Indigenisation Act to empower all Zimbabweans and foreign investors to invest in Zimbabwe without necessarily entrenching Eurocentric colonial interests and global apartheid-related economic policies of the Global North (United States of America 2015, 3–4).

Zimbabwe should also avoid blindly adopting global apartheid-related policy measures from the Global North international bodies such as the IMF, the WTO and the World Bank so as to attract both domestic and foreign investments (Moyo 2001, 1–5). Additionally, Zimbabwe should abandon the financial sector liberalisation and global apartheid-related policies to improve its GDP, FDI and the economy. Accordingly, Zimbabwe should adopt sustainable monetary and fiscal policies to revamp its economy (Moyo 2001, 1–5). Put differently, the Zimbabwean government should develop and adopt sustainable micro and macro finance policies to enhance the economy (Moyo 2001, 28–29). The Zimbabwe government must strongly make efforts to re-engage with the international community by shunning human rights abuses and other barbaric governance practices. In relation to this, the EU, the USA and other Global North countries should abolish targeted economic sanctions against Zimbabwe since they are contributing to the suffering of ordinary persons. The Global North should not impose neoliberal and global apartheid-related policies on Zimbabwe and other Global South countries to combat global corporatocracy and neo-colonialism. Zimbabwe should reject any global apartheid-related policies, aid or donations from the Global North, which are designed to marginalise and colonise Global South countries. Lastly, Zimbabwe should strive to avoid non-performing loans to combat external debts and promote a viable economy (Nhavira et al. 2013, 22; Nyarota et al. 2015, 18; Harvey 1996, 4–5).

BIBLIOGRAPHY

African National Congress. (1994). *The Reconstruction and Development Programme.* Johannesburg, South Africa: Umanyano Publications.

Asset Management Act 15 of 2004 [Chapter 24:26] as amended.

Banking Act [Chapter 24:20].

Bond, P. (2003). *Against Global Apartheid: South Africa Meets the World Bank, IMF and International Finance.* Cape Town, South Africa: University of Cape Town Press.

Chinamasa, P.A. (2017). "Zimbabwe national budget statement for 2018: Towards a new economic order." *Zimbabwe Parliament*, 3–235.

Chindori-Chininga, E. (2012). First report of the portifolio committee on mines and energy on diamond mining (with special reference to Marange diamond fields) 2009–2013 presented to parliament June 2013 (S.C.4, 2012), 1–28.

Chingono, H., Hove, M., and Danda, S. J. (2013). "Sanctions effectiveness in a globalized world." *International Journal of Humanities and Social Science*, Volume 3(21), 307–317.

Chowa, T., Nyanhete, A. I., and Mhlanga, R. (2014). "An event study of the Zimbabwe stock exchange (ZSE): Implications for post-dollarisation market efficiency." *Mediterranean Journal of Social Sciences*, Volume 5(3), 1–12.

Collective Investment Schemes Act 25 of 1997 [Chapter 24:19] as amended.

Companies Act [Chapter 24:03] as amended.

Dube, C. (2013). "Zimbabwe indigenisation programme: The process, the benefits and the challenges." *ICAZ Winter School*, 1–51.

Dunaway, W. A., and Clelland, D. A. (2016). "Challenging the global apartheid model: A world-systems analysis." *Journal of World-Systems Research*, Volume 22(1), 16–22.

Exchange Control Act [Chapter 22:05] as amended.

Export Processing Zones Act [Chapter 14:07].

George, W. S., Jr. (1968). "The failure of the sanctions against Rhodesia and the effect on African states: A growing racial crisis." *Africa Today*, Volume 15(1), 8–12.

Gwimbi, P., and Nhamo, G. (2016). "Translating mitigation measures proposed in environmental impact statements into planning conditions: Promises and practices by multinational platinum mining firms along the Great Dyke of Zimbabwe." *Environmental Science & Policy*, Volume 57, 10–21.

Harrison, F. V. (2002). "Global apartheid, foreign policy and human rights." *Souls*, Volume 4(3), 48–68.

Harvey, C. (1996). "The limited impact of financial sector reforms in Zimbabwe." *Institute of Development Studies*, 1–28.

Hollaway, J. (1997). "Mineral policy in Zimbabwe: Its evolution, achievements and challenges." *Resources Policy*, Volume 23(1), 27–32.

Hove, M. (2012). "The debates and impact of sanctions: The Zimbabwean experience." *International Journal of Business and Social Science*, Volume 3(5), 72–84.

Indigenisation and Economic Empowerment Act 14 of 2007 [Chapter 14:33].

Karekwaivenani, G. (2003). "A history of the Rhodesian stock exchange: The formative years, 1946–1952." *The Journal of Humanities of the University of Zimbabwe*, Volume 30(1), 9–34.

Kaseke, K. E., Chaminuka, L., and Musingafi, M. C. C. (2015). "Mining and minerals revenue distribution in Zimbabwe: Learning from our surroundings and past mistakes." *Journal of Economics and Sustainable Development*, Volume 6(6), 90–96.

Köhler, G. (1995). "The three meanings of global apartheid: Empirical, normative, existential." *Alternatives: Global, Local, Political*, Volume 20(3), 403–413.

Maja, I., and Nhara, Y.S.K. (2016). "The 'principle of non-discrimination' and foreign investor protection: A Zimbabwean perspective." *The Zimbabwe Electronic Law Journal*, Volume 1, 1–20.

Marable, M. (2009). "Globalization and racialization." *Z Communications*, 1. http://zcomm.org/znetarticle/globalization-and-racialization-by-manning-marable/.

Masaka, D. (2012). "Paradoxes in the 'sanctions discourse' in Zimbabwe: A critical reflection." *African Study Monographs*, Volume 33(1), 49–71.

Masaka, D. (2013). "Pitting market economy against planned economy: A false dichotomy in Zimbabwe (1980–2011)." *Journal of Black Studies*, Volume 44(3), 314–329.

Mclean, R. D., Zhang, T., and Zhao, M. (2012). "Why does the law matter? Investor protection and its effects on investment, finance, and growth." *The Journal of Finance*, Volume LXVII(1), 313–349.

Moyo, T. (2001). "Financial sector liberalisation and the poor: A critical appraisal." *The SAPRI – Zimbabwe Initiative Poverty Reduction Forum*, 1–35.

Mukuhlani, T. (2014). "Zimbabwe's government of national unity: Successes and challenges in restoring peace and order." *Journal of Power, Politics & Governance*, Volume 2(2), 169–180.

Munyedza, P. (2011). "The impact of the Indigenous Economic Empowerment Act of Zimbabwe on the financial performance of listed securities." *Business and Economics Journal*, Volume 37(1), 1–14.

Murombo, T. (2010). "Law and the indigenisation of mineral resources in Zimbabwe: Any equity for local communities?" *Southern African Public Law*, 25(2), 568–589.

Murombo, T. (2013). "Regulating mining in South Africa and Zimbabwe: Communities, the environment and perpetual exploitation." *Law, Environment and Development Journal*, Volume 9(1), 33–49.

Murombo, T. (2016). "The effectiveness of initiatives to promote good governance, accountability and transparency in the extractives sector in Zimbabwe." *Journal of African Law*, Volume 60(2), 230–263.

Mutasa, C. (2004). "Global apartheid continues to haunt global democracy." https://www.pambazuka.org/governance/global-apartheid-continues-haunt-global-democracy.

Nhavira, J. D. G., Mudzonga, E., and Mugocha, E. (2013). "Financial regulation and supervision in Zimbabwe: An evaluation of adequacy and options." *Zimbabwe Economic Policy Analysis and Research Unit*, 1–62.

Nyamunda, T., and Mukwambo, P. (2012). "The state and the bloody diamond rush in Chiadzwa: Unpacking the contesting Interests in the development of illicit mining and trading, c.2006–2009." *Journal of Southern African Studies*, Volume 38(1), 145–166.

Nyarota, S., Kavila, W., Mupunga, N., and Ngundu, T. (2015). "An empirical assessment of binding constraints to Zimbabwe's growth dynamics." *Reserve Bank of Zimbabwe Working Paper Series*, No. 2, 3–35.

Rhodesia Stock Exchange Act of 1974.

Securities Act 17 of 2004 [Chapter 24:25] as amended.

Sikwila, M. N. (2014). "Foreign direct investment: Does it matter? A case for Zimbabwe." *Research in Business and Economics Journal*, Volume 10, 1–12.

Special Economic Zones Act [Chapter 14:34] 7 of 2016.

United Nations. (2014). "Zimbabwe country analysis working document." *Working Document Final Draft*, 1–118.

United Nations. (23 December 1966). "United Nations: Sanctions against Rhodesia." *Time*. http://content.time.com/time/subscriber/article/0,33009,840760,00.html.

United Nations Conference on Trade and Development. (1999). "Foreign direct investment and the challenge of development." *World Investment Report*, 3–370.

United Nations Environment Programme. (2000). "Zimbabwe investment and environment outlook." *Division of Technology Industry and Economics Report*, Volume 1, 1–19.

United States of America. (2015). "Zimbabwe investment climate statement." *Department of State Report*, 1–19.

Van Wyk, J. (2018). "Sanctions and summits: Sanctioned African leaders and EU-Africa summits." *South African Journal of International Affairs*, Volume 25(4), 497–515.

World Bank. (2017). "Zimbabwe economic update: The state in the economy." *Country Report*, Issue 2.

Zimbabwe Investment Authority Act 4 of 2006 [Chapter 14:30] as amended. Zimbabwe Stock Exchange Act [Chapter 24: 18] as amended.

Zimbabwe Investment Centre Act [Chapter 24:16].

Chapter 15

Why Poverty Persists in Developing Countries, Especially in Africa

A Case of Institutional Failure or Poor Leadership?

Fritz Nghiishililwa

INTRODUCTION

This chapter examines the problem of poverty and other related political and social challenges in developing countries, particularly in Africa, with a view to determine whether the failure of the continent to effectively address the social and political problems stems from poor leadership or the use of inappropriate political institutions which the former colonial authorities left behind. It could be said that poverty, political instability and the claim of corrupt African leaders are attributed to incompetency of the leadership or are caused by the nonexistence of suitable institutions.

Furthermore, the chapter investigates the root cause of the lack of food needed to feed many starving African populations and how to deal with the issue of corrupt public officials. Recalling the early years after the liberation of Africa from the colonial rulers Bigman points out the continent was promising and the then charismatic leaders, such as Kwame Nkruma in Ghana, Julius Nyerere in Tanzania and Gamal Abdel Nasser in Egypt were optimistic. The new states sailed on the waves of great hopes for the future and rapid economic growth fuelled by the increase in agricultural production and by their abundant natural resources (Bigman 2011, 32–34). However, Bigman argues that things changed when many of Africa's leaders, enchanted by idealistic perceptions of socialism, focused their efforts on land for collective farms and forceful settlement of farmers. Furthermore, the new independence also unravelled old rivalries between tribes and sectarian groups that disintegrated the sense of unity and started a long series of extreme bloody and devastating civil conflicts, tribal wars and sectarian animosities (Bigman 2011, 32–34).

In addition, the political borders of the newly liberated states inherited from the colonial rulers were designed to promote the interests of the colonialists and not the need of the local people. Such an arbitrary division of the continent created barriers between tribes and villages that would become huge stumbling block to African harmony (Bigman 2011, 32–34). However, African leaders have not shown any interest in changing the borders of the continent despite being the potential source of possible future conflicts.

The other problem was that after independence, African leaders took over the political systems and structures which the colonial administration put in place as well as development institutions such as financial and monetary establishment, security institutions, and law enforcement and so on. Adedeji argues that unavoidably, the new institutions were fitted into the only legacy thought to be available: colonial legacy that was authoritarian, invariably centralist, necessarily bureaucratic, and thus concerned above all with top-down forms of governance. These structures produced a disastrous pair of options; either there would be a situation in which clientelism, so-called tribalism, would scramble for power, or else, this scramble becomes intolerable, the power would pass back to some new form of dictatorship (Adedeji 1993, 20). The failure of institutions within the existed and still existing capitalism is referred not to the nature of those institutions, and the context within which they are expected to work, but to the people who have tried to make them work (Adedeji 1993, 21). Contrary to this view, Kaufmann argues that colonial institutions could be useful in solving Africa's post-independence social and economic problems. Regrettably, such institutions were not used for the benefit of the public but instead for personal enrichment of public officials and other private agents (Kaufmann 1997, 1).

Given the low level of education in most of the African countries at independence, it is clear that the institutions of modern states-craft were little understood and regularly misplaced (Adedeji 1993, 34–35). Division among Africans is another problem. The colonial authorities succeeded to divide and rule Africans as a group of individual tribes. Such a system served to divide Africans and discouraged unity among them. For this reason, it was important that after the independence the continent's new leaders had a responsibility of uniting the people who never ruled by an African president but by a King or Chief of a particular tribe. The efforts to bring a bond among different people with varying tribal affiliation proved to be practically impossible mainly because the political institutions which the colonial rulers left behind were not meant for uniting divided people or building a nation. In actual fact, colonial institutions were designed for facilitating the exploitation of the continent's natural resources in the form of raw materials needed for European industries and to enforce law and order among Africans.

ARE EUROPEAN-BASED POLITICAL INSTITUTIONS SUITABLE FOR SOLVING AFRICA'S PROBLEMS?

One former president of an African country was quoted as saying, "Africa does not know political parties, we are tribes and almost closure to people's conference and committees which suits us better than parties. Our people know neither parties nor elections" (Bigman 2011, 246). There have been numerous conflicts and civil wars which have been caused by political differences among Africans because of tribal rivalries. For example, there were a number of mutiny movements such as in the Sudan, Chad, Burundi, Rwanda and Uganda. This illustrates that elections did not solve the outstanding problems. Africa needs stability which shall entail or necessitate firmness in the political leadership (Bigman 2011, 246).

Adedeji argues that there was a disjunction between what he termed the "centuries of pre-dispossession self-development on one side, and, on the other side, Africa of today: a decolonised Africa into which development was to be introduced for the first time in history" (Adedeji 1993, 21). It was partly due to this disjointedness that the Western modelled institutions failed to end Africa's crisis (this refers to lack of sufficient food, clean water, decent housing and dysfunctional democracy. See Bigman 2011, 42–45). Again, it was inconceivable that after Africa's independence, the new leaders were unable to realise that if they fit the new institutions into the only legacy thought to be available: a colonial that was authoritarian, they were bound to fail. It could be possible that the outcome could have been different had the new leadership of Africa considered restructuring or reforming the institutions they have inherited to solve the problems facing the continent. Bigman argues that the conflicts embedded in the boundaries of the African states and the distribution of the population in their territories were, from the outset, major impediments to their development (Bigman 2011, 284–285). He points out that during the colonial times, the African borders did not have any significant political role and served primarily to mark the division of the continent's natural resources between colonial powers. Strangely, however, when the African states became independent, these borders became the political borders that marked the territories of the new states and thus determined the boundaries of their sovereignty and control.

Contrary to the principles of democracy and the rule of law many of the Africa's leaders chose to serve their own interests and were more keen to advance the interest of their supporters, mainly the members of their tribe and as a result openly discriminated against the minority tribes. This has caused conflicts and civil wars. Most African leaders came to power by the support of the dominant tribe and enforced laws by brute force to strengthen their control and weaken opposition to their leadership. The latter combined with profligate public policies, were the main reasons for economic stagnation and high and rising levels of poverty in the African countries. It is worth noting that many of African leaders came to power in military coups, which has been triggered by political exclusion of the minority tribes from benefitting from their country's natural resources and the struggle to hang on to power. This was the case in Sudan, Ghana, Uganda, Burundi, Sierra Leone, Benin and Nigeria from 1956 to 2001 (Bigman 2011, 290–292).

One of the disturbing issues linked to post-independence African leaders is the problem of corruption. Ayittey points out that it is common knowledge that highly placed African government officials extort commissions on foreign loan contracts and deposit them in overseas banks (Ayittey 2000, 104). He provides a detailed analysis of the extent of the problem pointing out that corruption breeds inefficiency and drives away foreign investors (Ayittey 2000, 105–108). However, surprisingly, he remained muted in respect of the European countries which host international banks in which he claimed stolen money from Africa has been deposited. For example, Switzerland has built a reputation as the world's centre for tax evasion, fraud accounting, and money laundering, making it a staunch ally of corrupt third leaders and a great beneficiary of third world corruption.

Corruption in Africa has been on the rise due to the lack of appropriate institutions needed to control and regulate the powers of its leaders. In addition, colonial institutions were designed for addressing the economic and political needs affecting developed nations. Unfortunately, after the colonial governments handed over political power to the new African leaders, the issue concerning whether colonial institutions were able to unite Africans and be used for developing the continent appeared to have been overlooked. In addition, laws which were designed for the conditions pertained in the industrialised world were complex and foreign to both the political and economic conditions in Africa. For example, in the African tradition, jobs are given to the people who were trusted by those in power particularly individuals from the same tribe as the appointing authority. In contrast, under Western democracy a job is applied for and the successful candidate gets it. In African tradition, unquestionable loyalty to the appointing authority has been a "licence" to a decent job. Tribal leaders were above the tribal institutions such as committees and conferences through which the affairs of the tribe were managed. Cohesion among tribal communities was of utmost importance and the latter shared life intensively in common.

In fact, under African traditions, the power of a Chief is unlimited. It did not matter whether it was in relation to appointment of someone into office, relieving a person from certain responsibilities or in terms of the allocation and utilisation of community resources. Under African tradition, there was nothing like accusing the leader or Chief of embezzling the public funds or being corrupt. As Bigman points out that under the tribal system, the leaders had absolute authority to set rules and serve as judges. These rules reflect tribal traditions, however, and were therefore accepted by all. Moreover, by giving authority to make the rules and serve as judges to a group of elders, the tribal system prevented any perception of autocracy that is necessarily divisive, and thus strengthened the acceptance of the rules (Bigman 2011, 244).

It appeared that many African leaders wrongly believed that tribal style of leadership could work for the newly independent states of Africa. Notwithstanding the fact that the existed political and legal institutions were based on Western model of democracy which was more advanced and disregarded Africa's prevailed problems. Emery and Smythe argue that the European-based political system operates through a central government which comprises of a number of departments of state headed by government ministers and staffed by permanent civil servants. The official power of public authorities is determined by a statute whether in the form of the constitution or an Act of Parliament (Emery and Smythe 1986, 4–5). In the context of Africa, the tribe's elders were, and still are, both the governing administration and the judicial authority, and they rule according to a system of laws and codes of ethics deeply embedded in the tribe's heritage and commonly accepted by all members. That system and the leadership to which all the tribe's members are strongly committed kept the tribe together, protected its members, and preserved the widely accepted social rules and standards.

After the independence of the African countries the vast majority of the population still lived in rural areas and maintained their organisation and social structure as tribes, according to their traditions, social rules and norms, and under the authority of the tribe's elders. Bigman argues that these rules were no longer suitable, however, for the much more complex structure of the state, for the many and much more complex interaction between peoples and communities from different tribes that became citizens of the same state and for the relations between the tribe and the central authority of the state (Bigman 2011, 284–287). Even the struggle for independence against the colonial power was conducted primarily by the larger tribe, while the smaller tribes were excluded both from the fighting forces that led the struggle and from the governing authority of the state that was formed when they became independent. Unlike in Europe, in Africa, neither the formation of the independent states nor the establishment of central governments evolved gradually. All these developments were practically imposed upon the African people when the main colonial powers left the continent in the aftermath of World War II. The developed nation's government system inherited by African leaders has been mainly used to facilitate corrupt practices among most Africa's presidents their cronies (Hope and Chikulo 2000, 40–104).

The absence of proper legal framework which aims at regulating and limiting the power of those individuals who held public offices after the independence of African states left a gap and created opportunities for the abuse of power. Bigman argues that the embezzlement of state funds by African leaders brought most of them to the abyss of long stagnation (Bigman 2011, 3–10). The obvious consequence was that the continent was not able to provide the basic services the people needed, for example, food, health services and shelter which forced the leaders of Africa to turn to the Western governments for assistance in the form of aid. The latter has been used as a means to influence policies in the developing countries and as a result developed nations were able to protect their interest in the developing nations. The obvious consequence was that the sovereignty of the developing states has been compromised; particularly the latter's dependence on aid from the developed nations.

In the context of Africa, despite its abundance of natural resources, the continent's majority of the people live under extreme poverty. According to Miller poor people live without fundamental freedoms of action and choice, that the better-off take for granted. They often lack adequate food and shelter, education, and health, deprivation that keep them from leading the kind of life that everyone values. They also face extreme vulnerability to ill-health, economic dislocation and natural disasters (Miller and James 2003, 15). Poverty is the result of economic, political and social processes that interact with each other and frequently reinforce each other in ways that exacerbate the deprivation in which poor people live. Meagre assets, inaccessible markets, and scarce job opportunities lock people in material poverty. To address the problem, it is essential that job opportunity is promoted by stimulating economic growth, making markets work better for poor people, and building up their assets (Miller and James 2003, 15).

While many scholars blame poverty on those who hold political power in developing countries (Bracking 2007, 15–30; Guest 2004, 10–20), Harrison blames the tropical weather affecting most of the third world. Tropical weather that is characterised by too much rain or too little, too much heat, that is not moderate. These brutal physical facts of life in developing countries are not often mentioned as primary causes of poverty (Harrison 1993, 21). Industrialised countries also played their part in depleting developing counties' natural resources, particularly the African continent. In this regard, Beckford blames poverty in developing nations on the West and its allies by owning a considerable share of the resources of the third world. Plantations and mines are important sources of income generation and potential "engines of growth" in many developing counties. But these are, in most instances, owned by metropolitan corporations (Beckford 1983, xvi).

The plantation economies of the world are not chiefly found in Africa but elsewhere (this refers to tropical America and Asia; Beckford 1983, 3). In these areas, the plantation has been the dominant economic, social and political institution in the past continues to be in the present and from all indications will continue to be in the future. It was an instrument of political domination; it brought capital, enterprise, and management to create economic structures which basically remained the same (Beckford 1993, 4). Plantations were a major target in the independence struggle of many colonial peoples. As a result of their hegemony of scarce land in some places and the depressing low level of wages and living conditions everywhere, the pressure which they created on the peoples' plantation economies gave rise to peasant movements and labour unions which mobilised colonised peoples organised themselves in revolutionary movements that led to the independence of their countries (Beckford 1993, 4). However, the challenge common to most of the developing states was that, after the attainment of the political independence, they have failed winning economic independence allowing the former colonial masters continue owning and controlling third world economies.

It is worth noting that, pre-colonial societies of all the three continents (Africa, Asia and Latin America) of what is now known as "third world," were the home of sophisticated civilisations, with many of their cities being centres of fabulous wealth far advance of anything their first European visitors knew back home (Beckford 1993, 4). Harrison points out that, mathematics, astronomy, medicine were all highly developed among the Arabs, the Indians and the Chinese and in an intellectual, moral and spiritual sense, several of them was far in advance of Europe. However, Europe was able to bring them on their knees for one reason only: because she was more developed in purely material respects. She had achieved breakthroughs in the technology of war and of sea travel which were the basis of her military conquest and out greedy evolved industrial capitalism, along with its peculiar contempt for exploitation of human beings and nature (Beckford 1993, 4).

The colonial "discovery" of the varied mineral resources in developing countries led to a retching-up of the influx of Europeans and the destruction of pre-colonial economic systems by entering into mining concession contracts using multinational corporations with local leaders who had little knowledge about the effects of such long lease to the citizens of their countries. As a result, much of the profits from developing world's natural resources exploitation leave the continent entirely in the hands of foreign-owned companies. This means that the natural resources that could have benefited the local people were used to develop other continents, mostly Europe and the United States of America (USA) where major mining corporations originated from. Poverty and underdevelopment in respect of the developing countries appear to have been deliberately created by the former colonial authorities in order for the former to remain dependent on the latter, in terms of the supply of food and other essential commodities. In turn, the former colonial masters shamelessly continue exploiting poor nation's natural resources to develop Europe. In the context of Africa, the continent's natural resources are being extracted frequently without countries and citizens of those countries get their fair share. It amounts to looting not only by multinational companies (MNCs) but also by their countries of origin. The Western countries and the USA continue facilitating the exploitation of the mineral resources from the developing countries through MNCs with the support of the International Monetary Fund (IMF) and the World Bank. The latter two institutions are the agents used to press African governments for transforming their economies from a socialist economy which usually after independence dominated by the state-owned companies into a free market system. A detailed analysis of the role of the IMF and the World Bank in the preservation of poverty in developing countries specifically in Africa will be discussed below.

Africa's mineral resources have been the main attraction of Europeans to have an interest in Africa. Abubakar argues that the origin of the colonial situation was capitalism and the resulting rivalry among European nations. Capitalism needed raw materials, markets and outlets for capital, which were thus required by all those European nations pursuing the capitalist option for organising society. Thus they divided the rest of the world into empires, which then contributed to the growth of capitalism by supplying a labour force, minerals, animals and vegetable products. In addition, this exploitive relationship between the colonialists and the colonised has persisted up to the present in slightly different form. Today, it is called neo-colonialism (Ahmad 1989, 103).

According to Abubakar, most African countries became nominally independent which he described as "flag independence": beyond lowering the colonial flag and replacing it with the national flag, there is no independence and therefore real independence lies somewhere else, beyond flag independence. This somewhere else is the economy. African countries are nowhere near having a firm grip on their economies, which explains Africa's conspicuous weakness and lack of independence, hence the continent remains behind as far as development is concerned when compared with other continents. Furthermore, the problem has been worsened by the practice in Africa where a set of colonial rulers along with a flag was replaced by another set of rulers along with another flag. The new rulers inherited the power and privileges of those they replaced. The colonial rulers were separated from the people by their "wizardry" and colour. It was also a deliberate colonial policy to keep the rulers and the ruled apart to enable the former to exercise relatively easy control over the latter. In this way the ruled were psychologically made to accept their own inferiority along with the corresponding superiority of the rulers (Ahmad 1989, 103). Hence, one of the main challenges African leaders are facing is to move away from advancing the interests of the Western governments and redirect their countries' resources to benefit the people who elect them; however, the danger of cutting the flow of Africa's natural resources to Europe or the USA could be devastating. Although there might be other reasons, the recent overthrow and assassination of the President of Libya, Gaddafi could be linked to the latter's refusal of his country's natural resources channelled to the Western countries and USA.

Another problem that contributes to underdevelopment in Africa is its dependence to a single commodity export as engine of growth. Obasanjo argues that most African countries have mono-crop production structures, particularly export crops, mainly cocoa, coffee, tea, groundnuts, tobacco, cotton, and rubber. Other countries are totally dependent on mineral exports such as copper, iron ore, bauxite, manganese oil, gold and diamonds. Such an economic structure is not conducive to development and limits the ability of the country to eradicate poverty in Africa. In addition, he points out those African leaders have neglected food production which has resulted in an unprecedented food crisis in the continent that eventually resulted in the majority of people die from hunger.

For Obasanjo, the state of underdevelopment in Africa is attributed to the continents weak physical and institutional infrastructures as well as the inadequacy and poor conditions of transport, less developed communication infrastructure coupled with the inefficiency of the related services are a major impediment to the expansion of economic activities within and among African countries. Shortage of skilled manpower, especially, in key areas essential for economic recovery is another obstacle .to development and at the same time, there is a high rate of unemployment, and the phenomenon of brain-drain which, in some countries, has negatively affected the functioning of key development institutions and services. An understanding of the concept of poverty will help those individuals in leadership to formulate appropriate policies needed to address Africa's lack of food and other basic human necessities.

UNDERSTANDING POVERTY

Alcock argues that many people, including academics, campaigners and politicians, talk about the problem of poverty, and underlying the discussion is the assumption that identifying the problem provides the basis for action upon which all will agree. According to him, poverty means going short materially, socially and emotionally. It refers to one's inability to buy basic needs of life, such as food, clothing and the incapability of securing a home

(Alcock 1997, 3). Most people of course claim that their understanding of poverty in the correct one, based on logical argument or scientific research. However, for Alcock there is no one correct, scientific, agreed definition because poverty is inevitably a political concept. Furthermore, the first thing to understand about poverty is that it is not a simple phenomenon that we can learn to define by adopting the correct approach. It is a series of contested definition and complex arguments that overlap and at times contradict each other (Alcock 1997, 4).

It should be noted that poverty exists within a dynamic and changing social order, to some extent; it is created by, or at least recreated by, the social and economic policies that have developed over time to respond to or control it. It is possible to extend the history of poverty as far back as the history of society itself. In his book on the *History of poverty in Britain*, Novak argues that poverty emerged from the period of the gradual replacement of feudalism by capitalism as the modern economy become to develop in the seventeenth and eighteenth century. This was because at that time, the majority of people were separated from the land and became workers, and thus lost control over the means of producing material support and became dependent on wages from paid labour. After that, those who could not work for wages could not support themselves and thus were poor (Novak 1988, 9). Poverty, it is argued from this perspective, is, therefore, a product of capitalism, and it is sustained and recreated by capitalism to provide a discipline through fear of poverty for workers to maintain their commitment to the labour market. For Novak, therefore, poverty is caused by the logic of the capitalist wage labour market and is maintained by capitalism and will thus only be eliminated when capitalism is replaced by some other economic system (Novak 1995, 10). Capitalism flourishes when there is an accumulation of capital using wage-labour as one of its means of production. In his thesis, Godfrey uses world-system analysis to examine continuities between the early history of capitalism and aspects of contemporary capitalism. Quoting the work of Wallerstein, he argues that the world economy is held together by the axial division of labour, rather than a political structure or homogenous culture, and the efficacy of the division of labour "is a function of the constant expanding wealth that a capitalist system provides" (Wallerstein 2004, 24). He further argues that capitalist system requires a particular kind of relationship between economy and polity, with the latter if too strong, then political interest will predominates over the economic interests. Hence, world-systems define capitalism as a social system that "gives priority to the endless accumulation of capital" (Wallerstein 2004, 24).

Referring to the advent of the modern state, Godfrey (2013) points out that, along with the emergence of the capitalist world economy one saw the rise of the modern state which created law to regulate the economy and the market.

Importantly, labour regulation sees the state responding to the interests of the workers as well as to the long-term interests of capital by stabilising labour relations and securing a supply of labour for the future (Godfrey 2013, 37). Essentially, labour regulation is designed to regulate the employment relationship between an employer and an employee in respect of the obligations and duties of the parties. It is vital for an individual to be employed to sustain him or herself and be able to move out from the state of being poor.

Clearly exclusion from paid labour is likely to lead to poverty when there are no or few other sources of material support. At the same time, employers of wage labour will wish to maintain a ready and willing surplus of workers to undertake paid employment at the lowest possible cost. State policies to respond to the problem of poverty have always been directly influenced by such demands, and have created a legacy of policy priorities that have shaped images of the problem of poverty and the needs of the poor (Novak 1995, 11).

Hayter (1990) writing on the *Creation of World Poverty*, discussed the extent to which the Western countries created poverty in developing countries through the long history of exploitation of the mineral resources of the latter arguing that the international inequalities created by such exploitation are of course even more glaring than the inequalities within individual market economies. They have given rise to a whole industry of what is euphemistically called foreign aid. Institutions have been set up whose purpose is said to be to help the rest of the world develop. They never, or seldom, or only partially, recognise that the Western government that they serve, and the economic system whose survival they were in reality set up to secure, are themselves responsible for what they see as the third world's failure to develop (Hayter 1990, 7).

Moreover, Hayter (1990) argues that the condition attached to official aid, especially to the lending of the World Bank and the IMF, are now designed above all to extract resources from the third world's poor to enable their governments to services their debt. The policies demanded have the effect of redistribution income from the poor to the rich and the burden has been borne not by the governments and elites of the developing nations, nor of course by the banks or the tax-payers of the West, but overwhelmingly by the third world's poor. They have been forced to pay for a situation that is not their fault. Although the official publication continues to claim the West is helping by providing aid in fact, even in terms of strictly financial flows, resources are flowing in the opposite direction (for example, in 1988, the net flow was US$ 50 billion (Hayter 1990, 8).

For Hayter (1990), capitalism is the root cause of poverty arguing that it reached its fully fledged form in Britain in the nineteenth century. He points that the main distinguishing feature of capitalism is that it is a form of production in which the tools, materials and the land necessary for producing goods are no longer owned by the people who do the work, but by the capitalists who employ labour for a wage. He continues explaining that the earlier forms of social organisation, each family or group provided for its own needs. Specialisation and a division of labour grew up later, at first in the form of individuals working in their own houses to produce particular goods, then, as in the guild system in mediaeval Europe, in small workshops in which craftsman worked with their own tools and usually sold directly to the public. Hayter argues that the organisation of wage labourers into factories and mills made it possible much greater efficiency in production and it is generally agreed that for capitalist forms of production to develop, two main conditions are necessary: a free labour force and the accumulation of money capital in the hands of potential investors (Hayter 1990, 34).

In Britain, such a labour force became available, from the fifteenth century up to the nineteenth century, mainly as a result of enclosures and evictions of small peasants to increase the size of holdings. Small farmers and tenants were deprived of their means of subsistence when landlords found that it was profitable to enclose what had been previously been common land and to take over small farms, often to use the land for grazing sheep and producing wool. As a result, this has created a situation where large numbers of people who had "nothing to sell but their labour-power" and eventually many of those made landless found jobs in the new industries of the industrial revolution (Hayter 1990, 34).

Much of the capitalist wealth was gained from the gains to be made in overseas trade, a term that included conquest, piracy, and plunder. Summarising how the exploitation of Africa and America's mineral resources started, Hayter quoted from the work of Marx as follows:

> The discovery of gold and silver in America, the extirpation, enslavement, and entombment in mines of the aboriginal population, and the beginning of the conquest and the looting of East Indies, the turning of Africa into a warren for the hunting of black skin signalised the rosy dawn of the era of capitalist production. (Marx 1976, 36)

In Africa, the economics of most of today's poor countries were forged in the colonial era to serve European imperialists. During the "scramble for Africa," African colonies supplied raw materials, but never became the markets manufactured goods that some hoped for (e.g., copper from the Congo and Zambia, gold and coca from Ghana, and palm oil from Nigeria. See Open Door Web Site 2007, 33).

A modern economy was forced upon Africa even more brutally and rapidly than it had been elsewhere, making each colony or protectorate face outwards, towards European and global markets. Such transport, trade and other communications as were developed linked each territory, or parts of it, to the African coats and outside world rather than to neighbouring colonies or even other regions of the same territory (Lines 2008, 33). Africa, found itself in the worst of all the worlds, territorially fragmented, it was ruled by foreign powers directly to facilitate the extraction of wealth wherever possible and as mentioned before, did not meanwhile develop the local markets that existed elsewhere (Lines 2008, 33).

THE IMF AND THE WORLD BANK'S CONTRIBUTION TO POVERTY IN AFRICA

Bond and Dor argue that it is conventional wisdom both that during the past decades, Africa was "marginalised" by globalisation and that the Bretton Wood Institutions' strategies for stabilisation and recovery often produced neither. According to the IMF and the World Bank, for an African country to qualify for donor aid, certain neoliberal conditions and/or policies should first be. These include removal of import/export barriers, financial liberalisation, currency devaluation, lower corporate taxation, export-oriented industrial policy, austere fiscal policy (especially aimed at cutting social spending) and monetarism in central banking (with high real interest rates) (Bond and Dor 2003). In terms of micro-development terms, neoliberalism implies not only three standard microeconomic strategies, that is, deregulation of business, flexibilised labour markets and privatisation of state own enterprises, but also various mandates specifically for social sectors: the elimination of subsidies, promotion of cost-recovery and user fees, disconnecting of services to those who do not pay, and reliance upon market signals as the basis for local development strategies (Bond and Dor 2003).

In terms of the IMF's structural adjustment policies, countries were required to undergo economic stabilisation as a condition of receiving its loans. These were used to support the call to replace the import substitution policies of the biggest debtors. The biggest debtors referred were countries such as Brazil. The programme entails sharp reduction in tariffs and removal of other barriers to free interplay with the world markets as well as the reduction of public spending, especially in unproductive areas such as health and education. Debtor countries were required to accept the IMF's programme before the creditors would revise their loan repayment schedules. Developing countries were trapped by the World Bank's principles that required that countries should cease trying to produce substitutes for imports and instead concentrate on exports to earn foreign currency and balance their trade. Right from the beginning, many commentators argue that doctrine of export orientation was fallible and correctly so, did not work, but rather led to extreme poverty of developing countries (Lines 2008, 42–45). The policies of the IMF and the World Bank regarding structural adjustment not only impoverish the people of Africa but also have weakened its authority in the sense that debt relief programme and aid are used as a means of controlling governments of developing counties, particularly, in Africa. These policies require that for an African government to qualify for the world's financial institutions loans; the former must spend less in the areas of health, education and water supply to its people. In addition, the size of civil servants should be cut in terms of good governance doctrine. It is natural that less spending on state hospitals and medicine implies that let people to get ill and eventually die from untreated illness. Again, spending less is education implies that; let people remain illiterate and as a result unable to get productive and decent jobs. The requirement by the IMF and the World Bank that developing countries should demand fees from the people provided with social services discussed earlier, implies that poor people should not be provided with free services. The obvious conclusion is that poor health, malnutrition and illiteracy among the people of Africa have been partly caused by the implementation of the IMF and the World Bank's structural adjustment policies.

There is little African leaders can do to eradicate poverty among their subjects, particularly the fact that they depend on foreign aid from the West and the USA. Mr Eugene Black, the former president of the World Bank quoted by Hayter regarding the aid programme put it succinctly clear, when he said:

> Our foreign aid programs constitute distinct benefits to American business. The major benefit is that foreign aid provides a substantial and immediate market for the United States goods and services stimulates the development of new overseas markets and orients national economise toward a free enterprise system in which United States firms proper. (Hayter 1990, 82–83)

Another statement supporting the supposition that foreign aid has been used as a tool for control was made by one of the former president of the United States, who said that "Foreign aid is a method by which the United States maintains a position of influence and control around the world and sustains a good many countries which would definitely collapse or pass into the communist bloc" (Hayter 1990, 82–83).

Forced by the policies of the International MF and the World Bank, coupled with the giving corruptive "aid" to developing countries, the latter embarked on policies of withdrawal of state support in the areas of health, education and water supply that has resulted in seeing accelerated poverty among women, children and the rural poor. For example, in Tanzania, where government introduced user fees in the areas of health, education and water supply in compliance with the IMF and the World Bank's policies saw, poverty accelerating among the vulnerable people of that country (Structural Adjustment Program (SAP) alert on IMF and World Bank).

THE "BLAME GAME" AND THE FIGHT AGAINST POVERTY IN AFRICA

Poverty can only be fought in the presence of strong institutions, and equitable distribution of resources. This requires a non-corrupt government. However, programmes designed to fight poverty are not fully implemented because the funds end up in the hands of corrupt individuals who pocket the money at the expense of the majority. Majority if not all corrupt African leaders are proxy of the Western governments whose job is to facilitate the channelling of Africa's mineral resources to the developed world. Many developing countries have signed bad contracts that give disproportionate share of the resources' value to private foreign companies. But such contracts could be renegotiated so that money gained through natural resources should be used to promote development and that the processing of such resources should be done locally.

Despite clear evidence showing that many Western nations, such the UK, France, Canada, the USA as well as the emerging economic powerhouses like China exploits Africa's natural resources until today causing the state of poverty in Africa to persists. Yet, inconceivably the USA and the West are adamant blaming poverty on African governments for pursuing the wrong policies; this is despite the loss of control over policies which came with structural adjustments and IMF loan conditionality that actually forced developing countries into life debt situation.

Lines admits that the failings of African governments of being corrupt and incompetent do exist, just as they do in many other parts of the world, including some countries which are very rich. For example, in the late eighteen and early ninetieth centuries, the United Kingdom's ruling class was actually nicknamed Old Corruption, and the United States hundred years later was scarcely better. (Lines 2008, 50–52). In fact, African leaders have "surrendered" the sovereignty of their states by accepting conditional aids from the West and the USA. Dembele, the Senegalese economist, was quoted as saying:

> Many African States have been stripped of all but a handful of their economic and social functions . . . Sates retrenchment primarily aimed at eliminating subsidies for the poor, removing social protection, and abandoning its role in fighting for social justice through economic retribution and other social transfer to the most disadvantaged. (Dembele 2004, 57)

Dembele's conclusion was that the IMF and the World Bank are instruments of domination and control in the hands of powerful states whose long-standing object is to perpetuate the plumber of the resources of the global south. The USA and its allies have never interested in reducing poverty in developing countries, much less than in fostering development, and for a quarter of a century Africa should have learnt that the road to genuine recovery and development begins with a total break with the failed and discredited policies imposed by the IMF and the World Bank (Dembele 2004, 57).

Hayter argues that the explanation given for poverty in Africa tend to be based on what might tactfully be called Eurocentric view of the world, which in itself is a product of historical circumstances, and of colonial mythology in particular. Europeans who began by being impressed and indeed overawed by what they found in civilisation sometimes more sophisticated than their own, gradually built up theories of racial superiority (Hayter 1990, 19). This was especially from the nineteenth century onwards, they felt the need to justify to themselves their domination of the colonial peoples, and in particular the institution of slavery. In so doing the Europeans conveniently maintained that the natives or the inhabitants of developing nations were lazy, stupid, and barely human. The natives were made to believe that the Europeans were the bearers of order, civilisation and Christianity to the benighted natives. In fact the "original African affluent society," people did not suffer from hunger and that they did work less (Hayter 1990, 19). However, today many people in the developing countries work far longer hours in far worse conditions than people in the West, but yet they are still poor. The reality is, Africa's natural resources benefit those who control global economy through the IMF and the World Bank. Led by the USA, stronger nations determine what they consider as "good or bad governance" and impose European-based democracy on developing nations. The danger could be that a political system that is applicable in developed nations might not suit developing countries for various reasons.

The debilitating human and economic poverty of African nations have been conveniently blamed on bad governance of corrupt African leaders and physical geography of the continent. This is not entirely true. The matter is more complex, in the sense that, external forces indirectly influence the kind of policies African leaders should adopt. Such policies serve as the guiding principles for what is called by the West "good governance." Unfortunately, it appears that African leaders do not know nor understand the meaning of what "good governance" is all about and what is expected from them by their controllers in Europe.

It is, however, confusing as to why the West and the USA give aids to Africa with a view to develop the continent and reduce poverty, when at the same time attach detrimental conditions to the assistance given? Today,

African leaders are competing for IMF loans and donor aid; and hence are quickly cutting the expenditure in the areas identified by the Bretton Wood Institutions that resulted in persistent poverty in their respective countries.

The marginalisation of Africa by the IMF and the World Bank resulted in finding a solution which resulted in the formation of a new initiative known as the New Partnership for Africa's Development (NEPAD which was launched in 2001). Not surprisingly, the World Bank and the IMF are at the same time promoting "Poverty Reduction Strategy Papers" (PRSPs) and with the Highly Indebted Poor Countries (HIPC) initiative (Bond and Dor 2003). Bond *et al.* argue that although NEPAD is advertised as a home-grown mandate, it is notably for strengthening the role of the Bretton Woods Institutions and World Trade Organisation (WTO) in Africa, for it promotes neoliberal economic policies (Bond and Dor 2003).

It is unfortunate that the West and the USA, with their financial agents, the IMF and the World Bank, are under the illusion that Africa's social and economic problems can be solved within the world neoliberal economic model. The problem of poverty, hunger, ill-health and poor education in Africa, require a special but tailor-made approach. Insisting on the implementation and application of West based economic system, simply escalates the already surge level of poverty and unemployment in the continent. Africa needs a different economic system. The celebrated world free market economy does not suit the conditions of Africa. More importantly, cutting social spending and the privatisation of state-owned enterprises in Africa, implies that the poor and the unemployed should not be cared for.

WHAT SHOULD BE DONE TO SOLVE THE PROBLEM OF POVERTY AND UNDERDEVELOPMENT IN AFRICA?

To tackle the problem of poverty and underdevelopment in Africa, a new approach should be found. One of the critical issues Africa considers addressing is its total reliance on the export of raw materials to the developed nations. The continent's leaders need to map out its own strategy for development and must vigorously pursue its implementation of policies that aim at eradicating poverty and hunger among its people. Efforts towards African economic integration should be enhanced to create a continent-wide framework for the much-needed co-operation for development and to ensure full participation of the people in the development process (Abubakar 1989, 2–3).

Africa needs to improve its transport and communication infrastructure to enable the much-needed expansion of economic activities within and among African countries by cutting the transport and communications links directed outside the region for export of primary commodities and import of manufactured goods. It is very important that internal transport and communications infrastructure is improved to promote the movement of goods (especially agricultural commodities), and people, and to the harmonious distribution of industrial production facilities within the countries (Obasanjo and d'Orville 1990, 38–40).

This could only be realised if African leaders demonstrate a political will and ensure that they create viable political and economic structures that can ensure genuine economic recovery, beyond the temporary reliefs resulting from short-term structural adjustments imposed on them by the IMF and World Bank discussed earlier. There is no doubt that the continent's survival depends on its commitment to economic integration among its members, as the first step, and means of pooling resources in a coordinated and efficient manner.

Another important issue African leaders must pay attention to is the lack of insufficient or scarcity of food. The problem of food crisis in Africa is attributed to many factors. Among these factors are inappropriate policies, adverse climatic conditions and population growth, which resulted in a parallel rise in demand for food (Obasanjo and d'Orville 1990, 40). The increase of urban population which is not involved in food production is another problem that calls for a shift from conventional developmental policies which usually target cities, disregarding developing rural areas where majority of the population in Africa live. The sharp reduction of the arable land area in Africa has resulted in the decline in agricultural output, especially food. This has been caused by many factors, such as rapid desertification, land tenure systems that reduce soil fertility, reduced rainfall and water unavailability, just to mention but a few. Traditionally, African farmers depend on the seasonal rainfall that is a major obstacle to increasing agricultural productivity. This calls for new or advanced agricultural techniques to be employed to move away from the present subsistence farming.

There is no doubt that a vigorous growth in food and agricultural production will undoubtedly create more employment and earning opportunities, particularly for the majority of population living in the rural areas which is an essential condition for African economic recovery. For decades, Africa's growth has been largely dependent on the growth of primary commodity production and exports. Such practice impedes development especially that the bulk of Africa's trade has been with developed market economies and thereby directly accelerates development in the latter. Africa needs to seek an alternative growth pattern for economic recovery and ensure long-term growth. Most African countries have mono-crop production structures such as coffee, tea, groundnuts tobacco and rubber. Other countries depend on oil and mineral l exports namely gold, diamonds, copper and iron ore.

It is unfortunate that many educated Africans succumbed to the psychology of inferiority imposed on the populace by the Europeans to the extent that most of their scholarly work concentrates on exposing corrupt African leaders and not aim at solving the continent's poverty and underdevelopment problems (Hope and Chikulo 2000, 1–36; Ayittey 2000, 105–118; Chikulo 2000, 161–180). Similarly, the wrong perception that Europeans were superior to Africans by virtue of the colour of their skin led to the ruling elite internalise such false claim, as a result, most African leaders became "yes boys" of the Western governments and ceased to identify with the people who elected them and their problems. The consequence was that development strategy was never people centred, but rather urban biased (Abubakar 1989, 4). Therefore, African leaders need to re-adjust the existing developmental policies to attempt alleviate poverty among the people they lead and improve the latter's wellbeing.

In doing so, African leaders should make real efforts to build a self-generating and self-sustaining economic base and refrain from relying on imported goods. Import substitution failed for a number of reasons, namely dependence on imported raw materials and capital goods. In addition, most of the goods which the continent imports could not be purchased by the general public but by the few elites. As a consequence, Africa became a beggar crying for aid from the international community which weakens the bargaining power of the continent's leaders when it comes to negotiating important commercial contracts with the donors.

Since attaining its independence, Africa has been faced with cute social and economic challenges and it appears practically impossible for the continent to solve its problems without first achieving economic independence which is likely to be met with hostility by developed nations particularly those benefitting from Africa's natural resources.

To have economic independence, African leaders should strive to have control over the continent's natural resources so that the local people could benefit from the sale and proceeds of such resources. However, one of the obstacles which could impede African governments have control over the continent's wealth is partly attributed to the constitutional entrenchment of a strictly free market-based economy.in their countries (see article 1 of the Namibian Constitution of 1990; section 1 of the South African Constitution of 1996). For example, most of the countries in southern Africa, their constitutions protect the right to property which has been regarded as being a basic human right, meaning that, large tracks of commercial land which is owned by the white people in South Africa and Namibia cannot be expropriated by the state for redistribution among the landless unless fair and just compensation is paid in favour of the owner of such land. Again, the principle of the willing seller/willing buyer entrenched in the constitution could be used to challenge any attempts to address the inequalities in society and it imposes severe limitations on land reform (article 1 the Constitution of Namibia of 1990).

The consequence is that the pace of (land) restitution has been negatively influenced by the "willing buyer/willing seller" principle. In Namibia, the land resettlement programme which aims at addressing the past unequal access to land by the black population is moving very slowly and frustrates the landless. It is not clear whether the patience of the people continues to hold or the country is waiting a Zimbabwe style of land grab. In the context of South Africa, the land issue is politically sensitive and it can turn ugly any time if not addressed soon. This is particularly the case in the context of Namibia and South Africa. In the context of the latter the country's celebrated transformation from apartheid pariah to bastion of non-racial democracy has earned it an international reputation especially its liberal constitution market stability. However, South Africa is arguably the country with the most biased land distribution in the region in favour of the minority white population. A similar situation is found in Namibia. This leads to the question whether the unresolved land issue could be satisfactorily solved under the present economic structure which is based on Western-style democracy.

Bigman quoted Abdullah Wade, president of Senegal when the latter expressed his views on Western-style democracy, saying that multiparty system in Africa proved to be a failure and that elections provide no stability in the continent. He claimed that while multiparty system is formal, it is a mere accession to the orders of the West, World Bank, IMF and the USA. He continued saying that "Africa does not know political parties, we are tribes and almost closer to the people's conferences and committees which suits us better than parties" (Bigman 2011, 246).

Unfortunately, the above statement does not provide any clue how African leaders intend to address the scourge of poverty and unemployment which affect the majority of the people in the continent. This is particularly important because the present world economic set-up is based on free market, meaning that decisions regarding investment, production and distribution are based on principles of supply and demand. It is believed that market forces were capable of bringing about economic growth which eventually benefits all the people including the poor. In the context of the developing countries, particularly in Africa, regrettably, this has not been the case. Despite the rising poverty and high unemployment, African governments continue to pursue economic policies which are dictated by the West, the USA and the international financial institutions, namely the IMF and the World Bank. Such policies discourage governments of the third world to intervene through legislation to alleviate unemployment or help the poor people in their countries. Using aid as a strategy for influencing developmental policies, recipient countries are expected to reduce spending in public health and education to qualify for donor money from the IMF and World Bank. Under the capitalist system, this is commonly known as *laissez faire* economics in which a handful of people profit greatly from the system while the majority of the population get poorer.

Based on the above discussion, surely the problem of poverty and underdevelopment in Africa cannot be resolved under the modern capitalist system which appears to work better in the developed world. This suggests that the third world is yet to find an appropriate system capable of addressing its social and economic problems including corruption.

CORRUPT PRACTICES IN AFRICA IS ENCOURAGED BY THE WEST

Corrupt practices in Africa have links with banks in Europe. Harsh argues that corruption in Africa has been mostly blamed on its leaders with the late former President Mobutu Sese Seko of the Democratic Republic of Congo (formerly Zaire) accused of diverted some US$ 8 billion into foreign European accounts, business and real estate holdings (Harsch 1997, 26–27). Strangely, owners of the foreign banks in which the stolen billion of money was deposited were not regarded as being corrupt neither the leaders of the host country in which recipient banks were located. This is double standard. The effective way of fighting such corrupt practices is to expose and to shame all the parties involved, that is to say, the corrupt leader, the receiving bank and its shareholders and the host country of the latter. The managers and the shareholders of the banks who have accepted to use and administer the stolen money which has been acquired through corrupt practices make themselves guilty of being accomplices under criminal law. In fact, in most cases, if not in all, there are more than one person involved in a corrupt deal, that is, the corruptor and the corrupted. A holistic approach should be found to combat corruption not only for example, expose and punish the corrupt African leader but also those who encourage and benefit from corrupt deals. In Africa, the late Mobutu Sese Seko of Zaire (now Democratic Republic of Congo) was regarded as one of the most corrupt leader in the continent however he was at the same time considered as a reliable, pro-Western ally in Central Africa and the USA regarded him as their man in Kinshasa (Mbaku 2000, 119–126).

Ayittey argues that corruption in Africa is endemic with is leaders particularly head of state and high-ranking ministers embezzle state funds and divert enormous resources from public coffers into private hands (Ayittey 2000, 104–110). However, he conveniently avoided mentioning the link between corrupt leaders in Africa and their corrupt European partners in whose banks the stolen money is kept, making certain individuals in Europe benefits from the stolen money, so their governments too.

Corruption in Africa could be tackled in many ways. Hope argues that transparency and honesty are some of the important aspects that individuals who are holding public offices should maintain and there should be a code of ethical conduct to regulate the conduct of those individuals managing public affairs (Hope 2000, 12). Bigman has generalised the issue of corruption in Africa, arguing that government officials in charge from the top down, were mostly concerned with their own "piece of the pie" and the interests of their tribes. Adding that "the only way to "grease the wheels" of the bureaucratic jumble and obtain permits that would otherwise take weeks and months was through bribes (Bigman 2011, 238–239). This cannot be true with all government officials in Africa. For example, Botswana has earned international reputation for its democratic traditions, good governance and accountability, making it one of Africa's well-managed countries (Hope 2000, 12). It appears that even the government of the USA is impressed by the way the Botswana government adheres to the principles of good governance and rule of law to the extent that the two countries' military special forces have been jointly conducting training in that country under what is called Africa Command (AFRICOM). In addition, the USA has constructed a large airport facility in Botswana of which the purpose is only known by the two governments.

Apart from Botswana, Namibia and South Africa are reportedly to be among the least corrupt countries in Africa. Another country which is rated the least corrupt nation is Senegal being the only country in the north of the continent. It is misleading and unfair to label corruption in Africa as the AIDS of democracy as Hope suggested (Hope 2000, 1). In fact, there is no any corrupt-free country in this world. The only two nations which are judged to be "very clean" of corruption are Denmark and New Zealand. The rest of the countries of the world are corrupt but with different ratings.

FAILURES OF AFRICAN LEADERS CONTRIBUTES TO THE CRISIS

Adedeji points out that the failure of African leaders to discover, acknowledge and act their continent's wealth of collective wisdom largely accounts for the endemic crisis that has confronted the region since independence (Adedeji 1993, 208). Furthermore, he argues that colonialism became neocolonialism; old colonial masters became donors; African countries became recipients and that oppression and corruption have not become more tolerable when practised by one's kin (Adedeji 1993, 209). Africa must develop a culture of not just speaking, but also acting in its own interest, not in the interest of others or in the interest which others perceive for it. It must grapple with the reality of developing itself through primary reliance on its own resources and pursue restitution policies if it is to transcend its protracted dispossession and loss of autonomy. Adedeji advices that Africa should look back to look forward with greater experience and better vision. This specifically applies to African systems of governance and accountability, traditions check and balances of power as well as sanctions on flawed leadership. As a people, Africans must abandon contagious lethargy, distrust for one another, unjustified fatalism and, above all, the dependence syndrome of the continent (Adedeji 1993, 210).

Bigman argues that the failure of African leaders to stop the waves of migrants from rural areas are turning more cities into megalopolis in which the country's security forces have no control and violent gangs establish their own law and order (Bigman 2011, 297–299). Such situation has resulted in the increase of slums in which the majority of the poor people in African cities live. With the income divide between rich and poor rising, the latter has become more threatening to the central regime with rises in food crisis which result in many people die from lack of sufficient food. Most people in the urban centres have little hope to find decent work that will enable them to improve their living conditions and this is the main problem facing Africa. The growing congestion in urban centres increased crime, health problems and pollution. According to Bigman, poverty in Africa historically concentrated in rural areas however with rapid migration to urban areas, majority of the urban population will be unemployed, dismally poor, and forced to live in debilitating shanty towns that do not qualify as human habitat (Bigman 2011, 158).

CONCLUSION

One of the solutions to the problem of poverty in Africa is to adapt its economies by making the transition from an agricultural-based economy to an industrial-based economy as was experienced in many Asian countries. However, it is important that Africa's developmental initiatives should be devised by Africans themselves with a view to end poverty and creates employment for its population (Egendorf 2005, 112). Africa is deeply affected with high rate of unemployment especially among the youth, which is attributed to a defective education system and lack of vocational training facilities and guidance. The continent is rich with abundant labour which is a tool needed to be expanded with intensive skills to meet the global labour market standards, yet Africa is rather placing more emphasis on capital intensive techniques instead of labour intensive. High rate of unemployment leads to increase in poverty and deprives an individual of all sources of income. This has resulted in many Africans unable to satisfy the basic necessity of life due to poverty arising from unemployment which led to many people in the continent live in the streets across the capital cities, because of their inability to afford a decent accommodation. The implication of prolonged unemployment can result in some form of social pathology, as reflected by an increased crime rate and violent agitators. Such situation breeds discontent against the state and any slight provocative issue or incident may trigger violent demonstrations and social unarrest.

To solve unemployment problem in Africa, the continent's leaders should make efforts to improve the education system with a greater focus on vocational skills and training. In addition, African governments should support the struggling industries to try save jobs and at the same time increase resource allocation out of the national budget in respect of employment promotion activities by supporting the informal sector to be able to increase production and income. Furthermore, African governments should facilitate access to the means of production such as land and capital in order for small businesses to be able to compete in the markets.

BIBLIOGRAPHY

Abubakar, A. (1989). *Africa and the Challenge of Development, Acquiescence and Dependency Versus Freedom and Development.* New York: Praeger Publishers.

Adedeji, A. (1993). *Africa within the World: Beyond Dispossession and Dependence.* London: Zed Books.

Akiri, B. (2014). "Is there any corruption free country in this world?" www.quora.com/Is-there-any-corruption-free-country-in-this-world.

Alcock, P. (1997). *Understanding Poverty.* London: Macmillan Press Ltd.

Ayittey, B. N. (2000). "Combating corruption in Africa: Analysis and context." In K. R. Hope (Ed.), *Corruption and Development in Africa: Lessons from Country Case-Studies.* London: Macmillan Press Ltd.

Beckford, G. L. (1983). *Persistent Poverty: Underdevelopment in Plantation Economies of the Third World.* London: Zed Books Ltd.

Bigman, D. (2011). *Poverty, Hunger, and Democracy in Africa: Potential and Limitations of Democracy in Cementing Multiethnic Societies.* London: Palgrave Macmillan.

Bond, P., and Dor, G. (2003). "Neoliberalism and poverty reduction strategies in Africa." *Discussion paper for the Regional Network for Equity in Health in Southern Africa* (EQUINT), March 2003. www.equinetafrica.org/bibl/doc/DIS4trade.pdf.

Bracking, S. (2007). *Corruption and Development: The Anti-Corruption Campaigns.* London: Palgrave Macmillan.

Chikulo, B. C. (2000). "Corruption and accumulation in Zambia." In K. Hope and B. Chikulo (Eds.), *Corruption and Development in Africa: Lessons from Country Case Studies.* London: Palgrave Macmillan.

Dembele, D. M. (2004). "The international monetary fund and world bank in Africa." quoted in Lines, T. (2008). *Making Poverty a History*. London & New York: Zed Books.

Dilek, E. (2014). "Africa is not poor, it is being robbed." www.progress.net/Africa-is-not-poor-it-is-being-robbed-video/.

Egendorf, L. K. (2005). *Africa: Opposing Viewpoints*. New York Greenhaven Press: Thomson Gale.

Ejizu, C. I. (2014). "African traditional religions and the promotion of community-living in Africa." www.africaworld.net/african/community.htm.

Emery, C. T., and Smythe, B. (1986). *Judicial Review*. London: Sweet & Maxwell.

Frimpong, P. (2015). "Unemployment in Africa: What policy makers should know." www.modernghana.com/news/435566/1/unemploymnet-in-africa-what-policy-makers-should.k.htmlon.

Godfrey, S. D. (2013). "A study of changes and continuities in the organization and regulation of work with an empirical examination of the South Africa and Lesotho clothing/retail value chain." Thesis presented for the Degree of Doctor of Philosophy in the Department of Sociology, Faculty of Humanities (University of Cape Town, South Africa).

Government of the Republic of Tanzania. (1999). "Structural Adjustment Program (SAP) alert on IMF and World Bank lending to Tanzania." www.tanzaniagateaway.org/docs/SAP_alert_on_IMF_and_world_Bank_lending_to-Tanzania.pdf.

Guest, R. (2004). *The Shackled Continent: Power, Corruption, and African Lives*. Washington: Smithsonian Books.

Harrison, P. (1993). *Inside the Third World: The Anomy of Poverty*. London: Penguin Books.

Harsch, E. (2004). "Africa taking action on corruption." *UN/Africa Recovery*. http://www.un.org/ecosocdev/geninfo/afrec/vol11no1/corrup.htm.

Hayter, T. (1990). *The Creation of World Poverty*. London: Pluto Press.

Hope, K. R. (2000). *Corruption and Development in Africa: Lessons from Country Case-Study*. London: Macmillan Press Ltd.

Jacobs, G. (n.d). "Botswana, Namibia and South Africa the least corrupt countries in Africa." www.thesouthafrican.com/botswana-namiba-and-south-africa-the-three-least-corrupt-countries-in-afriaca/.

Kagara, A. (n.d). "Poverty in Africa." www.worldissues360.com/index.php/poverty-in-africa-270.

Kaufmann, D. (1997). "Corruption: The facts." Foreign Policy, No. 107(summer), quoted in Hope, K., and Chikulo, B. C. *Corruption and Development in Africa: Lessons from Country Case Studies*. London: Palgrave Macmillan.

King, T. M. (n.d.). "U.S, Botswana special forces train together." www.airlines.net/photo/4924oo/M/.

Lines, T. (2008). *Making Poverty a History*. London & New York: Zed Books.

Lord Adusei, A. (2009). "Switzerland: A parasite feeding on developing world?" wikileaks.org/wiki/Talk:Switzerland:_A_paraiste_feeding_on-developing_world%3F.

Marx, K. (1976). "Capital." Quoted in Hayter, T. (1990). *The Creation of World Poverty*. London: Pluto Press.

Mbaku, J. M. (2000). "Controlling corruption in Africa: A public choice perspective." In K. Hope and B. Chikulo (Eds.), *Corruption and Development in Africa: Lessons from Country Case Studies*. London: Palgrave Macmillan.

Miller, B., and Torr, J. D. (2003). *Developing Nations*. San Diego: Greenhaven Press.

Novak, T. (1988). *Poverty and the State: A Historical Sociology*. Open University Press, Quoted in Alcock, P. (1997). *Understanding Poverty* (2nd ed.). London: Macmillan Press.

Novak, T. (1995). "Rethinking poverty." Critical Social Policy issue 44/45 (Autumn), quoted in Alcock, P. (1997). *Understanding Poverty* (2nd ed.). London: Macmillan Press.

Obasanjo, O., and d'Orville, H. (1990). *Challenges of Leadership in African Development*. New York: Taylor & Francis.

Patrick, S. M. (2012). "Why natural resources are a curse on developing countries and how to fix it." www.heatlantic.com/international/archives/2012/04/why-natural-resources-are-a-curse-on-develoing-countries-and-how-to-fix-it.

Stiglitz, J. (2007). "Africa's natural resources economic curse." www.theguadian.com/businss/economics-blog/.

Wallerstein, I. (2004). *World-Systems Analysis; An Introduction*. Durham: Duke University Press.

Chapter 16

Challenging Global Apartheid through Financial Inclusion in Zimbabwean Agency Banking

Brighton Nyagadza, Itai Kabonga, and Promise Machingo Hlungwani

INTRODUCTION

This chapter examines the importance of financial inclusion based on empirical review of agency banking in Zimbabwe. Morrison and Shapiro (2016) cited in Nyagadza (2019) point out that agency banking is convenience banking that benefits both the customer and the bank. The chapter appreciates the value behind financial inclusivity, as we seek to level the field and allow all value contributions towards reduction of the adverse effects of global apartheid. The research method used was based on the review of literature in the qualitative domain. The main findings indicate that financial inclusion needs to be aligned to the general populace's needs and it has to help deliver services expected by the majority. The argument is that global apartheid is not just a metaphor: it is a reality marked by the operation of undemocratic institutions that systematically generate economic inequality. Therefore, financial inclusion through agency banking can help to counter the related problems. Contribution/value added by the research includes the apprehension of the policies that govern financial inclusion in agency banking through effective use of a wide range of products and services, quality, accessibility, fairness and transparency, formal regulation of entities as well as sustainability. All these aspects challenge the phenomenon of global apartheid.

The phenomenon of global apartheid is defined by Washington-based African advocates Salih Booker and Bill Minter as "an international system of minority rule whose attributes include differential access to basic human rights, wealth and power, and is the outcome of the specific political power associated with late twentieth century capitalist economic crisis, and of the accompanying ideology of neo-liberalism" (Bond 2003, 5). For instance, the financial crisis in the developed countries did not initially affect developing and transition economies as the crisis did not originate within their financial systems (Abreu et al. 2009). It was even hoped that the real economy in the developing countries would escape unscathed and that growth in developing countries would help to buoy the world economy as it did in the recession at the beginning of the twenty-first century (Abreu et al. 2009). The neoliberal approach to state policy, especially during the 1980s and 1990s era of intensifying globalisation, continued to exacerbate the contradictions of capitalism, especially historically unprecedented inequality between countries (Bond 2003, 5). Bond (2003b, vi) cites the ANC RDP (1994) contending that "Southern African countries were pressured into implementing (IMF and World Bank) programmes with adverse effects on employment and standards of living." All this was part of the Washington Consensus that had debilitating effects on the economies of the Third World.

To reduce financial challenges, Zimbabwe joined the SADC Integrated Regional Electronic Settlement System which was launched in 2014 to promote regional cross-border transactions (RBZ Zimbabwe National Financial Inclusion Strategy Report 2016). As on December 31, 2015, fourteen (14) Zimbabwean banks had joined the regional platform (RBZ Zimbabwe National Financial Inclusion Strategy Report 2016). The various retail payment streams including mobile financial services will be incorporated as part of encouraging formal remittances in the region. The main principles that govern financial inclusion are effective use, a wide range of products and services, quality, accessibility, fairness and transparency, formal regulated entities as well as sustainability (RBZ Zimbabwe National Financial Inclusion Strategy Report 2016). In the past decade, financial inclusion has been the epicentre of development strategy. Underlying this consensus is the belief that the access to financial services is a powerful tool for poverty eradication (Donner 2016). The authors believe that the aim behind financial inclusion, through agency banking, is on ensuring that a nation's populace has an inclusive financial system that is responsive to their needs. Financial inclusion therefore facilitates the usage of quality and affordable financial services by the entire populace as well as to minimize financial exclusion, as in agency banking. Financial exclusion is the inability by individuals to access basic financial services as a result of the challenges that have to do with access conditions, prices, marketing as well as self-exclusion in relation to discouraging experiences or perceptions of individuals (Kiriuki and Birner 2016). On the other hand, in line with Beck et al. (2017) argument, agency banking is a latest innovation that banks are using to provide services to the un-banked and under-banked at a cheaper fare. With this concept, the population is taken out of the brick and mortar banking halls, to kiosks and villages, as shown in this chapter. The next section gives an overview of the global financial crisis and global apartheid context.

DEBATING THE CONCEPT OF GLOBAL APARTHEID

Dunaway (2012) contends that one of the problems of the twenty-first century is that of global apartheid because somehow the logic of racist white supremacy still exists. For Bond (2004), global apartheid is one of the intractable problems confronting Africa today. "Global apartheid, like globalisation, is a new buzzword that has evolved to describe a global paradigm" (Mutasa 2005, 1). Put simply, global apartheid is an international system of minority rule that promotes inequalities, disparities and differential access to basic human rights, wealth and power (Harrison 2004). Mutasa (2005, 1), contends that "global apartheid is the anti-thesis of global democracy . . . People like former South African President Thabo Mbeki, Fidel Castro of Cuba and the scholars Ali Mazrui, Richard Falk and Patrick Bond, among many others, have used this concept to describe the global or economic injustice of our time." Thabo Mbeki once framed it as "We have all converged at the Cradle of Humanity to confront the social behaviour that has pity neither for beautiful nature nor for living human beings. This social behaviour has produced and entrenches a global system of apartheid. The suffering of the billions who are the victims of this system calls for the same response that drew the peoples of the world into the struggle for the defeat of apartheid in this country" (Bond 2004, 1). This is the condition of the contemporary world. The contemporary world is embedded in a system of global apartheid when viewed from "interrelated and interpenetrative global issues" (Muroy n.d, 2). Although we are not arguing that the structures of South African apartheid are replicated at global level, our argument is that the similarities are strikingly disturbing.

Political global apartheid is clear in that not only few countries control the world's political and economic affairs but that these states are situated in Europe and the global north. Overall, this mirrors the colonial trends in many ways, no wonder Dunaway's (2012) contention that the logic of racist white supremacy persists. United States, Britain and France are the chief decision-makers on world security affairs whereas Japan, Germany and United States are the chief architects of economic affairs (Huntington 1996, 54). The aforementioned countries control international capital markets, operate international banking systems and always itch for military interventionism across the world. Institutions such as the Bank of International Settlements, the International Monetary Fund (IMF), the World Bank, the United Nations (UN) Security Council and various other global institutions are controlled by Western countries (Huntington 1996). The implications of this control are shown by Maroy. "The consequence of this of course is that the rest of the world, although being the majority, has no political or economic power to reject decisions made by the Western minority. This means that the Western world dictates the rules of the game, which are inherently in favour of the white minority and wealthy states, whose wealth in many instances relies, at least to some degree, on the exploitation of the less developed world." The power of these so-called "International Government Organizations (IGO)" is so paralysing and overwhelming, as they use at times violence and coercion (Bond 2004). The intersection with race is as lucid as ever, as these institutions are controlled by old white men.

Global apartheid can also be understood from an economic perspective particularly the financial and economic disparity that characterises the world today. For instance, 1 per cent of the world population controls the quantum of the world finances and wealth. No wonder the increasing global civic action such as occupy wall protests directed towards the increasing inequalities in patterns of wealth ownership. On this point, inequalities *within states* are in many ways contributing to inequalities *between states*. For instance, in the United States the top 1 per cent owns wealth that equals the bottom 80 per cent combined whereas in the UK, the top 1 per cent owns as much wealth as the bottom 57 per cent combined (Maroy n.d.). Resource wise the inequalities are conspicuous in as much as they are despicable. G7 countries have 12 per cent of the world resources and yet they use 70 per cent of the world resources. The above shows why global apartheid has been viewed as "poverty for many and prosperity for only a few" (Harrison 2004). The effects of wanton use of resources have resulted in exacerbation of climate change that affects poor countries more than anyone else (Harrison 2004).

Large corporations from Western countries will do anything in their pursuit of profits for minorities even at the expense of human life, in most cases Black lives. The "Big Pharma" debacle in South Africa showed that large corporates would rather protect profits instead of allowing the implementation of laws that would have made HIV/AIDS lifesaving drugs available to the majority of Black lives in South Africa (Bond 2004). In the main, there is disturbingly growing patterns of global apartheid resulting in "an ever-growing disparity between people's quality of life, human rights, security, freedoms, access to services, self-determination and so forth, based on the lines of race, geography, gender and class, and entrenched in the neoliberal global system which we have come to accept as the norm, the doxa" (Maroy n.d, 4).

LINKING GLOBAL APARTHEID AND GLOBAL FINANCIAL CRISIS

The origins of the current global financial crisis are now well known (Abreu et al. 2009). They lie in the worldwide financial excesses of the past few years and even decades; the bursting of the housing and oil price bubbles;

excessively low interest rate policies; massive trade surpluses in some countries and trade deficits in others; and savings rates that are too low in some parts of the global economy and too high elsewhere (Abreu et al. 2009). The cumulative effect is a financial and liquidity crisis that threatens to become a global macroeconomic upheaval, with significantly negative world GDP growth, perhaps for two or three years (Abreu et al. 2009). This has sharply increased unemployment, pressures on public revenues and deflation. "Current manifestations of global apartheid are exhibited in the dominance of bilateralism and the hegemonic behaviour of the United States, the unbalanced and undemocratic processes in the World Trade Organisation (WTO), and the disproportionate power of multinational corporations and the Washington based international financial institutions (IFIs)" (Mutasa 2005). The current global apartheid, predominantly, has an economic face as opposed to the political face that characterised the imperial state during colonialism. However, it should be noted that, in this era of globalisation, both faces are sometimes manifested through undemocratic global institutions (Mutasa 2005). The global apartheid phenomenon is rooted in the international relations literature that presents other states as more equal than others. This pervasive and invasive scenario dates as far back as the beginning of the eras of slavery and imperialism. Inherently, the term presupposes that power is being used to determine who gets what, when and how. Thus, over the years, powerful states have sought to expand their physical territories and access as well as control over resources encroaching geographical boundaries. Thus, the rule of the minority over the majority has always been supported by power and not authority. This means it is the capacity to influence decisions and finance those decisions that have defined how the international community operates. Although the institution of the apartheid system is formally trekked to the 1948 South African political as well as socio-economic system, it is apparent that state capability and resources have pre-dated the exercise and control of bigger states (military and economic prowess) over the smaller, poor and under-resourced states.

In the contemporary world, this is epitomised by the integration of smaller states in the global system of trade liberalisation and capital flows under the tag name of globalisation. A striking example is the fact that transferred wealth is higher, in net terms, from Africa to the already industrialised countries of the North. The irony is that policies of independent African states are largely responsible for not only perpetuating "global apartheid," but intensifying it. African governments are themselves captured to work in the interest of "global apartheid." It is imperative that the struggle against the dominance of global finance capital is as salient as the struggle for democratisation. This may sound like a cliché, and indeed it is easy to sloganize anti-imperialist and pro-democracy rhetoric, but the practice of engaging in transformative politics is harder than chewing rocks. As a consequence of global apartheid, poor countries have apparently been frog-marched into accepting unilateral decisions from multi-lateral institutions, donor countries and more specifically international financial institutions. Indeed, governments are forced to be accountable to donors, the IMF and the World Bank rather than to their own people. Zimbabwe has been subjected to a crippling international economic environment that is being worsened by sanctions (Cotright and Lopez 2002). Furthermore, according to Nzaro et al. (2011), these sanctions have already led to the closure of nostro-accounts, failure by banks to access offshore credit lines among other difficulties affecting international money transfers as well as incapacitating financial intermediation by commercial banks. These restrictive measures demonstrate the dominance and hegemony of the Bretton woods institutions as well as their principal funders.

It is important to remember that economic and structural adjustment initiatives were also mooted by these same institutions resulting in economic stagnation in most of the Third World countries. Thus, neoliberal policies have created the same effects in the rest of Africa: deindustrialisation, unemployment, increasing debt and aid dependency. In a bid to reduce the effects of global financial crisis and global apartheid, the Zimbabwean government has taken a bold step towards financial inclusion. This is aimed at promoting fairness, equity and transparency as expressed in the following section of the chapter.

GLOBAL FINANCIAL INCLUSION PERSPECTIVE

The World Bank (WB) (2008) puts forward that financial inclusion is the absence of price or non-price barriers in the use of financial services. It further states that poor individuals and small entrepreneurs have to rely on informal sources to invest in between opportunities because of its timely availability and easy accessibility but at a much greater interest burden. Financial inclusion is the universal access to a wide range of financial services at a reasonable cost. These include not only banking products but also other financial services such as insurance and equity (Beck 2009). According to the UNDP (2010), financial inclusion is the process of ensuring access to financial services and timely and adequate credit where needed by vulnerable groups such as weaker sections and low-income groups. Opening a bank account, though a positive step, does not move one from being excluded to being included. In this manner, Regan and Paxton (2013) state that financial inclusion is not about the access to financial products but also the quality of engagement with whose products and the need for individuals to develop skills and confidence to make informed decisions. Leeladhar (2015) is of the view that there are multiple levels of financial inclusion. At one extreme, there are customers who are actively and persistently courted by the financial services industry and have at their disposal a wide range of services and products. These are super included. On the other extreme, there are financially excluded people who are denied access to even the most basic financial products. In between are the "under-included" who use the banking services for deposits and withdrawal of money. These have only restricted access and may not enjoy the flexibility of access offered to the more affluent customers. Sarma (2009) notes that financial inclusion is measured by the use of three comparable dimensions thus accessibility, availability and the use of banking services.

ESTABLISHING FINANCIAL INCLUSION THROUGH AGENCY BANKING

Chan and Gupta (2007) perceived usefulness as the extent to which an individual believes that using agency banking will be useful. Kim et al. (2009) argued that an individual usually makes an evaluation of the consequences of his/her behaviour, and then decides with basis on desirability of the system usefulness. Perceived usefulness therefore influences one's intention to adopt a system. In the agency banking context, one of the core objectives why people use agency banking is because the system is useful in making the transaction and it saves times. Bhati (2010) goes on to say that the benefits are seen by banks in the manner of a declined number of branches which further minimises the cost per transaction. According to Wang and Sun (2013), usefulness is the most significant factor that influences one's intention to use agency banking. This suggests that agency banking has to be seen as a useful and quicker way of making bank transactions in comparison to the traditional banking system. This would make it attractive and acceptable to users. Luarn et al. (2015) also affirms that perceived usefulness is an important factor that determines the customer usage of agency banking. This is also supported by Wang (2013) who concurs that customers opt for agency banking as a result of the relative advantage it has to offer.

Elsewhere, Suoranta (2003) postulates that the lack of awareness of agency banking's usefulness as well as the realisation of the benefits it has are the main factors that hinder the acceptance of agency banking. Relative advantage has to do with the comparative benefits that an agency banking user may get which could not be accessed from the traditional banking services as pointed out by (Pikkarainen et al. 2004). Furthermore, Pikkarainen et al. (2004) explain that consumers are more likely to make use of a service agency banking when there are more benefits to gain in comparison to brick and mortar means like ATM as well as non-mobile internet banking; this also includes the cost and time. Moreover, another research carried out by Bhoomika (2014) found that 75 per cent of the banking organisations studied pointed out that they had made significant improvements in the areas related to financial viability, financial profitability and competitiveness, all as a result of agency banking. However, according to Littler and Melanthiou (2006), malfunction issues of banking server minimises the willingness to make use of banking services and the same notion is apparent in agency banking. There is a security/privacy risk that is associated with the potential loss incurred by the customers as a result of system hacking or fraudulent activities which compromises the security of the agency banking consumer. In a similar research, Luarn et al. (2015) used perceived credibility, which is the extent to which an individual believes the use of agency banking has no privacy or security threats. The time/convenience risk is associated with loss of time as a result of an inconvenience incurred due to payment delay or navigation difficulty (Lee 2005). Social risk, on the other hand, is associated with the probability that the use of agency banking can be disapproved by family and colleagues (Lee 2005). Financial risk is the potential of monetary loss because of bank account misuse or transaction errors (Lee 2012). Lee (2005), Lee and Kim (2015) gathered that all these risk factors are negative in the adoption of agency banking.

MODELLING FINANCIAL INCLUSION THROUGH AGENCY BANKING

Ben-Kuen (2013) noted that perceived ease of use has significance on the acceptance of agency banking. His findings suggest that customers look for a simple, easier and faster process and environment to conduct banking transactions. The findings also showed that perceived ease of use is a critical factor in determining the difference in attitudes of the agency banking adopter and non-adopter. According to Rogers (1995), this is the extent to which the innovative service can be tried on a limited basis. In Rogers' thinking, there is a quick adoption of innovation when the innovation is tried before it is fully implemented (Puscel and Mazzon 2010). Tan and Teo (2010) assert that when given the chance to make an evaluation of innovation, customers minimise their concern for the unknown service or product which ultimately leads to acceptance. A repetition of an evaluation as well as assistance in the use of agency banking during the trial period will then minimise the risk of negative perception towards agency banking; this then creates a positive customer attitude to the use of agency banking. Rogers (1995) suggests that complexity is the extent to which an innovation is perceived as easy to understand and use. The adoption of an innovation will be minimised if the innovation is said to be complex to use (Ibid). Zmud (2013) proposed that complexity has a strong relationship with ease of use. According to Chen (2008), compatibility is the extent to which a service is said to be consistent with the existing values, habits, beliefs as well as the experiences of users. Rogers (1995) adds on by stating that compatibility is the extent to which an innovation is said to be consistent with the value of customers, their past experiences as well as the needs of the people that will likely adopt the system. An innovation can therefore be compatible with the socio-cultural values as well as beliefs of the customers, as well as that of a previously introduced innovation or with the innovation needs of the customer.

IN PURSUIT OF FINANCIAL INCLUSION IN ZIMBABWEAN BANKS

Although Zimbabwe has made significant strides in promoting a financially inclusive system, gaps still exist in as far as meeting the demands of the population vis-à-vis the products and services on offer. In particular, products and services to the small to medium enterprises, women, youth, rural population and the small scale agricultural sector (RBZ Zimbabwe National Financial Inclusion Strategy Report 2016, 25). The Census 2012 National Report indicates that the country had a total population of 13.06 million, of which 6.28 million (48 per cent) were males, while 6.78 million (52 per cent) were females (RBZ Zimbabwe National Financial Inclusion Strategy Report 2016, 25). Of the total population, 4.28 million, representing 33 per cent of the total population resided in urban areas while 8.77 million, representing 67 per cent of the total population resided in rural areas (RBZ Zimbabwe National Financial Inclusion Strategy Report 2016, 25). The distribution of the population in Zimbabwe is reflected in the Census 2012 National Report (*RBZ* 2016, 30).

In terms of age composition, the Census 2012 National Report indicates that 7.18 million, representing 55 per cent of the total population comprised economically active individuals between the ages of 15–64 years (RBZ Zimbabwe National Financial Inclusion Strategy Report 2016, 25). Finscope Survey (2014) indicates that there were 7 million adults (i.e., eighteen years old and above) in Zimbabwe as at 2014. "The survey also estimates that 67% of the adult population resides in rural areas while 33% resides in urban areas" (RBZ Zimbabwe National Financial Inclusion Strategy Report 2016, 26). The Finscope Survey (2014) estimates that as at 2014, 23 per cent of Zimbabwe's adult population was financially excluded. It is worth noting that the level of financial inclusion is skewed in favour of the urban population (89 per cent) as opposed to the rural population (62 per cent), despite 67 per cent of the Zimbabwe's population residing in rural areas (RBZ Zimbabwe National Financial Inclusion Strategy Report 2016, 26). The level of financial inclusion among the MSME sector was considerably low as indicated in the FinScope MSMEs Survey Zimbabwe 2012 which revealed the following key statistics:

a) Only 14% of MSME owners are banked, i.e. use formal financial products and services offered by a commercial bank;
b) The majority of business owners do not use/have a bank account for business purposes;
c) 50% of business owners (1.4 million) have/use informal mechanisms to manage their business finances; and
d) 18% of business owners (475 000) are formally served, including both bank and other formal non-bank products/services (MSME Survey 2012 cited in RBZ Zimbabwe National Financial Inclusion Strategy Report 2016, 26).

The major barriers to financial inclusion across the financial sector in Zimbabwe can be grouped into three (3) categories, namely demand side, supply side and regulatory (see *RBZ Zimbabwe National Financial Inclusion Strategy Report,* 2016 for a detailed outline of the three categories of barriers to financial inclusion).

Statistics from the Finscope Survey (2014) indicate that there is more reliance in informal savings channels by Zimbabwe's adult population as opposed to formal savings as only 20 per cent of the adult population made use of formal savings channels in 2014, while 23 per cent made use of informal channels. "Out of the adult population who do not save, 74% indicated lack of disposable income after accounting for living expenses as the main reason for their failure to save, while 21% indicated that they have no money to save" (RBZ Zimbabwe National Financial Inclusion Strategy Report 2016, 28). The Finscope Survey revealed a low uptake in formal investment services by Zimbabwe's adult population, with limited disposable incomes and lack of education and/or awareness being cited as the main reasons for the low uptake. According to the Finscope Surveys for 2011 and 2014, "there was a 12% increase in the number of adults with pensions from 623,000 in 2011 to 774,000 in 2014" (RBZ Zimbabwe National Financial Inclusion Strategy Report 2016, 28). According to Finscope Survey (2014), cited in RBZ Zimbabwe National Financial Inclusion Strategy Report (2016, 28), the majority (58 per cent) of adult Zimbabweans do not borrow. "Out of those who do not borrow, 48% cited the fear of debts as their reason for failing to borrow while 45% indicated that they do not have an ability to borrow" (RBZ Zimbabwe National Financial Inclusion Strategy Report 2016, 28).

AGENCY BANKING EFFORTS VALUE IN PROMOTING FAIRNESS, EQUITY AND TRANSPARENCY

Chidoko et al. (2011) cited in Chokuda-Santu (2017) noted that Zimbabwe's fast-growing informal sector is now the country's largest employer as the economy is failing to absorb many job seekers into formal employment. The banking sector has twenty-one operating banks, including the People's Own Savings Bank and 146 microfinance institutions (POSB) (RBZ 2014; Chitokwindo et al. 2014). Contribution to total bank assets are 82.69 per cent by commercial banks, 1.35 per cent by savings bank, 13.65 per cent by building societies and 2.31 per cent by merchant banks (Ibid). The country adopted a multicurrency system in February 2009 and since then banks have been operating with price structures that the RBZ view as not affordable to the poor people. Most banks are represented in urban centres while only POSB, Agribank and CBZ bank have a strong rural presence. There was a call in 2006, by the RBZ, for banks to open branches in rural areas (Ibid). The same is true for the financial inclusion initiatives that the Bank has been pursuing through timely provision of targeted empowerment facilities to interest groups such as women, SMEs, the youth and the disabled. These facilities have had significant impact in supporting broad-based and inclusive growth for both local consumption and export generation. As part of the National Financial Inclusion Strategy, the Women's Microfinance Bank and Empower Bank are now operational (RBZ 2018). The RBZ came up with a framework for financial inclusion in 2007 (RBZ 2006, 56; Chitokwindo et al. 2014), which was premised on the following pillars:

- expanding the outreach of established developmental financial institutions such as People's Own Savings Bank (POSB), ZIMPOST and Agribank;
- expanding the outreach of established commercial banks and building societies;
- enhancing provision of microfinance services through establishment of microfinance banks (MFI Banks) or Financial Inclusion Centres (FICs);
- urging relevant authorities to ensure provision of adequate infrastructure including roads, telecommunication coverage and provision of electricity;
- Provision of appropriate incentives to financial institutions engaged in rural banking; and
- engaging other stakeholders to facilitate the provision of other incentives.

However, agency banking in Zimbabwe dates back to 2013 when it was introduced by the Steward Bank. The innovative bank was migrating from the TN Bank to Steward Bank after agency conflicts arose. After the lessons learnt from TN Bank, Steward Bank wanted to operate on a low cost strategy while tapping the vertical segment of the populace. Moreover, Agent Banking was seen as the best strategy to execute, considering the nation is aiming to ensure that 70 per cent of the under-banked population is included in the financial sector. The everyday banking for everyday people bank cut down from the 32 TN Branches to 7 Steward Bank branches in the Harare after being absorbed by Econet Wireless. The ever dynamic bank wanted to shift focus from the brick and mortar to agent banking. With such a strategy the bank required agencies that would help it fill up the nation with Steward Bank account holders, thus mass banking. The prospective agents had to be Ecocash Agents as well as people that had businesses that were giving them cash on a daily basis. The bank tried to mitigate the risk of giving agents cash, by introducing making Ecocash agency and the existence of a thriving business a prerequisite. Moreover, Steward Bank also engaged corporates like the sister company Econet and has agents in each Econet outlet. Zimpost is another corporation that received fund advancement as well as branding material which was distributed to 227 Zimpost outlets nationwide. The innovative bank made so much noise about the agent banking to a point that everyone wanted to become an agent. Numerous people opened accounts and others became banking agents. To this day Steward Bank boasts more than 3,000 agent banking outlets, though the banking institution had a target of 5,000 agents. When making use of an agent bank retailer customers are able to open an account, transact, deposit and withdraw their funds. The agent bank is not a brick or mortar but just a tablet where all the details are entered and immediately updated in the banking system, through the Steward Bank network. This would enhance customer-based brand equity when the customer has high level of awareness and familiarity with the brand, the customer will hold strong favourable and unique bank's brand association in memory (Nyagadza et al. 2018). Steward Bank continuously improves the product, updates the system as well as trains the agents to ensure that they deliver quality services to the customer thus enhance financial inclusion. Due to the flexibility of agent banking, numerous accounts have been opened in various areas.

In volume terms, more than 99 per cent of payments are being made through electronic and mobile agency banking platforms with mobile banking constituting 84 per cent (RBZ 2018). This has significantly contributed to the increase in financial inclusion through mobile banking which now stands at more than 80 per cent. In terms of regional comparison, it is pleasing to note that Zimbabwe is now among the leading countries in the use of mobile banking products (Ibid). The FinScope (2014) quoted by Chokuda-Santu (2017), the survey on financial inclusion, estimated that the informal sector had as much as $7.4 billion circulating outside the formal financial system. This presents both an opportunity and a challenge for banks, especially considering that the same survey highlighted the extent of financial exclusion in the economy. There is a significant 54 per cent of the adults that are economically active that is un-banked or under-served by the formal financial system (Santu-Chokuda et al. 2017). With this, the suggested model can serve as guideline to commercial bank managers and management executives in understanding depositors' needs, and building strong agency banking in competitive markets. Banks need to position their agency banking in the minds of depositors, so as increase the room for higher acceptance. To achieve desired goals of their financial inclusion strategy through agency banking, commercial banks have to break the clutter by evolving innovative ways to attract the attention of the target audience. The managers or authorities responsible for agency banking need to make enough monitoring and tracking of the desired performance of the agency banking initiatives. The agency banking as a financial inclusion mode enables companies to leverage the commercial banks to new banking products, and chart new growth paths in specific markets.

METHODOLOGY

Overall, the study adopted systematic review of literature in deciphering how financial inclusion can act as a solution to the problem of financial exclusion. In doing that, the reviewed literature such as journal articles, books, book chapters, reports and conference papers shaped the understanding of global apartheid and its application to the phenomena of financial (in)(ex)clusion in Zimbabwe. In the main, only literature that was relevant to the study was included.

PRACTICAL IMPLICATIONS

Using the concept of global apartheid that denotes a scenario where the world is controlled by few marked by prosperity for the few and poverty for many, there are many practical implications to decipher. In Zimbabwe just like elsewhere in Africa there are certain groups that are financially excluded such as the rural folk, women, youths and informal business sector and are suffering as a result. Given the numbers of those financially excluded, financial exclusion in many cases emanates from global apartheid. Agency banking as demonstrated above becomes an instrument to decimate the inherent financial inequality that exist between men and women, rural and urban spaces, formal and informal business and the old and the young. Once the formally marginalised groups are financially included many opportunities are abound offering a chance for the marginalised groups to escape poverty which in many cases has been created by large corporates from the north and neoliberal policies imposed on the poor (Bond 2004). Global apartheid is a rights issue. The sovereign right of poor societies to self-determination has been eroded because of the phenomena of global apartheid. Similarly, financial inclusion is a rights issue, time has come to ensure that neglected segments of society enjoy the benefits of financial inclusion and agent banking seems to be the right way to achieve that.

CONCLUSION

The chapter discussed financial inclusion through agency banking model based on literature reviewed and with a Zimbabwean focus. It posits that agency banking needs to be attractive to potential customers who are being short-changed by the mainstream banking system. It is in the interests of financial inclusion to appeal to the once side-lined communities, especially the rural women and youth. The chapter also espouses the idea that as part of decoloniality and economic empowerment, the banking sector needs to overcome the traditional neoliberal principles and practices. Without breaking the umbilical code with the Washington Consensus framework, it will be difficult to terminate the global apartheid phenomenon which has been siphoning resources from the global south. It is against this background that this chapter advances the view that quality and affordable financial services that are insulated from the onslaught of international capital are prudent.

With the current economic environment where banks have been incapacitated by a combination of targeted economic sanctions undermining economic activities, agency banking is seen as a panacea to the ills associated with the aggravating turbulent economy. It is common cause that sanctions whether declared or undeclared, financial or trade, undermine the day-to-day economic activities of a country. The fact that sanctions create a bad country image suggests that they precipitate financial institutions' failure to access offshore lines of credit due to country's perceived credit risk. Since Zimbabwe is perceived to be a bank-based economy, it then follows that the economy has been greatly affected by ills affecting the banking sector, especially the failure to access offshore credit lines. Indeed, many people have lost faith with the banking sector following the challenges that are associated with failing access.

BIBLIOGRAPHY

Abreu, M., Agarwal, M., Kadochnikov, S., Mikic, M., Whalley, J., and Yongding, Y. (2009). *The Effect of the World Financial Crisis on Developing Countries: An Initial Assessment.* CIGI Task Force on Developing Countries.

African National Congress (ANC) .(1994). *The Reconstruction and Development Programme.* Johannesburg: Umanyano Publications.

Anderloni, P. (2007). From cash to electronic money: Enabling new business model to promote financial inclusion and integrity. In J. Osikena (Ed.), *The Financial Revolution in Africa: Mobile Payment Services in a New Global Age.* Foreign Policy Centre.

Beck, T., Pamuk, H., and Uras, B. R. (2017). Entrepreneurial saving practices and reinvestment: Theory and evidence. *Review of Development Economics.* DOI: 10.1111/rode.12300.

Bhattacherjee, A. (2012). *Social Science Research: Principles, Methods, and Practices.* South Carolina: University of South Florida.

Bhoomika G. (2014). Financial inclusion and rural development. *Research Journal of Commerce,* Volume 2(1), 1–6.

Bond, P. (2003a). *Against Global Apartheid South Africa Meets the World Bank, IMF and International Finance.* London and New York: University of Cape Town Press, Zed Books Ltd.

Bond, P. (2003b). *Against Global Apartheid South Africa Meets the World Bank, IMF and International Finance.*

Bond, P. (2003c). South Africa and global apartheid continental and international policies and politics. Address to the Nordiska Afrikainstitutet Nordic Africa Days, Uppsala, Sweden.

Bond, P. (2003d). South Africa and global apartheid: Continental and international policies and politics. Discussion Paper 25, Sweden Elanders Digitaltryck AB, Göteborg. ISBN 91-7106-523-7.

Bond, P. (2004). South Africa tackles global apartheid. Is the strategy reform working*? South Atlantic Quarterly,* Volume 103(4), 817–839.

Chan, H. C., and Gupta, S. (2007). Value-based adoption of mobile internet: An empirical investigation. *Decision Support Systems,* Volume 43(1), 111–126.

Chen, L. (2008). A model of consumer acceptance of mobile payment. *International Journal of Mobile Communications,* Volume 6(1), 32–52.

Chitokwindo, S., Mago, T., and Hofisi, C. (2014). Financial inclusion in Zimbabwe: A contextual overview. *Mediterranean Journal of Social Sciences,* Volume 5(20).

Chokuda-Santu, T., Mawanza, W., and Muredzi, V. (2017). An evaluation of the agency banking model adopted by Zimbabwean commercial banks.

Cortright, D., and Lopez, G. (2002). *Smart Sanctions: Targeting Economic Statecraft and International Relations.* New York: Cambridge University Press.

Ducey, A. J. (2013). *Predicting Tablet Computer Use: An Extended Technology Acceptance Model.* Graduate Theses and Dissertations.

Dunaway, W. A. (2012). Challenging the global apartheid model: A world systems analysis. *Journal of World Systems Research,* Volume 22(1), 16–22.

Finmark Trust. (2014). *FinScope Zimbabwe Consumer Survey 2014.* Accessed November 25, 2019. http://finmark.org.za/finscope-zimbabwe-consumer-survey-2014/.

Harrison, F. V. (2004). Global apartheid, environment degradation and women's activism for sustainable wellbeing: A conceptual and theoretical overview. *Urban Anthropology,* Volume 33(1), 1–34.

Huntington, S. P. (1996). *The Clash of Civilizations and the Remaking of World Order*. New York: Touchstone.

Kariuki, J., and Birner, R. (2016). Are market-based conservation schemes gender-blind? A qualitative study of three cases from Kenya. *Society & Natural Resources*, Volume 29(4), 432–447.

Kelly, T. (2003). Executive summary. In T. Kelly and M. Minges (Eds.), *Information and Communication for Development 2012*. Washington, D.C.: World Bank.

Kim, W., Lim, S. K., Chung, E. J., and Woo, J. M. (2009). The effect of cognitive behaviour therapy-based psychotherapy applied in a forest environment on physiological changes and remission of major depressive disorder. *Psychiatry Investigation*, Volume 6(4), 245–254.

Kotler, P., and Armstrong, G. (2010). *Principles of Marketing*. Upper Saddle River: Pearson.

Lee, Q. (2005). Partnerships between bank and mobile operators: Making it work. In J. Osikena (Ed.), *The Financial Revolution in Africa: Mobile Payment Services in a New Global Age*. Foreign Policy Centre.

Lee, Q. (2012). Partnerships between bank and mobile operators: Making it work. In J. Osikena (Ed.), *The Financial Revolution in Africa: Mobile Payment Services in a New Global Age* (pp. 21–23). London: Foreign Policy Centre. https://fpc.org.uk/wp-content/uploads/2012/12/1518.pdf.

Littler, D., and Melanthiou, D. (2006). Consumer perceptions of risk and uncertainty and the implications for behaviour towards innovative retail services: The case of internet banking. *Journal of Retailing and Consumer Services*, Volume 13(6), 431–443.

Luarn, P., Lin, Y., and Chiu, Y. (2015). Influence of Facebook brand-page posts on online engagement. *Online Information Review*, Volume 39(4), 505–519.

Lyman, T. (2016). *Use of Agents in Branchless Banking for the Poor: Rewards, Risks and Regulation*. Washington, D.C.: CGAP.

Muroy. (n.d). *Assess the Appropriateness of the Term "Global Apartheid" as a Description of the Contemporary World*.

Mutasa. C. (2005). Global apartheid and African debt crisis. *Life Over Debt*. Discussion Series. Issue 3.

Njaya, T. (2014). *Exclusion of Informal Sector Enterprises from Banking Services in Zimbabwe: Case of Informal Sector Entrepreneurs in Harare*. Mount Pleasant, Harare, Zimbabwe: Zimbabwe Open University.

Nyagadza, B. (2019). Conceptual model for financial inclusion development through agency banking in competitive markets. *Africanus: Journal of Development Studies*, Volume 49(2) 2663–6522.

Nyagadza, B., Chodeva, T., and Vingirayi, I. (2018). Rebranding strategy affect on brand preference: Perspectives from a Zimbabwean corporation. *Journal of Global Economics, Management and Business Research*, Volume 10(3), 124–136.

Nzaro, R., Njanike, K., and Munenerwa, E. (2011). The impact of economic sanctions on financial services: A case of commercial banks in Zimbabwe. *Journal of Contemporary Management*, Volume 1, 104–110.

Pikkarainen, T., Pikkarainen, K., Karjaluoto, H., and Pahnila, S. (2004). Consumer acceptance of online banking: An extension of the technology acceptance model. *Internet Research*, Volume 14(3), 224–235.

Porteous, D. (2011). *The Enabling Environment of Mobile Banking in Africa*. London: Department for International Development (DFID).

Puschel, J., and Mazzon, J. A. (2010). Mobile banking: Proposition of an integrated adoption intention framework. *International Journal of Bank Marketing*, Volume 28(5), 389–409.

RBZ (Reserve Bank of Zimbabwe). (2014). *Bank of Supervision 2014 Annual Report*. Harare: RBZ.

RBZ (Reserve Bank of Zimbabwe). (2016). *Zimbabwe National Financial Inclusion Strategy 2016–2020*. Harare: RBZ.

RBZ (Reserve Bank of Zimbabwe). (2018). *Monetary Policy Statement*. Harare: RZB.

Rogers, E. M. (1995). *Diffusion of Innovations* (4th ed.). New York: Free Press.

Souranta. M. (2003). Adoption of mobile banking in Finland. *Jyväskylä Studies in Business and Economics*. ISSN 1457-1986; 28.

Tan, J., and Teo, G. (2010). A critical assessment of determinants of financial deepening in Nigeria (1970–2010). *Interdisciplinary Journal of Contemporary Research in Business*, Volume 4(10). Nigeria: Institute of Interdisciplinary Business Research.

Teo, T., Ursava, F. O., and Bahcekapili, E. (2011). Efficiency of the technology acceptance model to explain pre-service teachers' intention to use technology. *International Journal of Information and Learning Technology*, Volume 28(2), 93–101.

Wang, B., and Sun, T. (2013). How effective are macroprudential policies in China? *IMF Working Paper Monetary and Capital Markets Department*. International Monetary Fund.

Chapter 17

Rethinking Policing

Practical Strategies to Combat Human Trafficking in Twenty-First-Century Africa

Pilisano Harris Masake and Lizazi Eugene Libebe

INTRODUCTION

Human trafficking dates to time immemorial. It is pervasive and continues to pose significant policing challenges globally – and Africa is not an exception. The tentacles of human trafficking, aided by cyber and advanced digital era, are indiscriminate, and they can exploit vulnerable members of the societies, such as women and children. Theoretically, challenges related to policing human trafficking are construed to be exacerbated by the peculiar elements of human trafficking, inter alia, are the deception that underlay it, global migration which fuels the vulnerability lines of victims, insufficient police resources (budgetary constraints), technological advancement and the trans-boundary mobility nature thereof, to mention but a few.

This chapter examines the effective and practical policing strategies that may be applied to combat human trafficking. By explication, various policing strategies, among others, such as: technology-based, applied artificial intelligence, evidence-based (empirics), community-based, crime mapping and crime data collection – these proactive strategies, are juxtaposed. On this score, the chapter proceeds from a socio-techno and applied policing theoretical framework – therefore, it offers postulations on the responsive and actionable strategies that are compatible with the African policing philosophy.

Construed from the socio-techno and applied policing theoretical framework, the analysis in this chapter is constructed on the assumption that human trafficking is an ever-present phenomenon and that it is prevalent in Africa – thus, necessitating the effective and practical policing strategies to curb it. This assumption resonates against the human trafficking statistics from various agencies, that is, the United Nation Office on Drugs and Crime

(UNODC), the African Union (AU) as well as the domestic policing agencies – which depicts the prevalence of human trafficking in Africa. Grounded on the ever-present and prevalence assumption, the chapter further analyses the impact or value, if any, of the African social philosophies such as Ubuntu in curbing human trafficking.

HUMAN TRAFFICKING AND SLAVERY – HISTORICAL EXCERPTS IN AFRICA

The definition of human trafficking varies from country to country, scholar to scholar and opinion to opinion. The variations are rooted in context, divergent worldviews, historical backgrounds and findings from studies conducted by scholars (Bello and Olutola 2016). Suffice, to note that literature defines human trafficking varyingly. These differences are further observed from various legal instruments and legislations. However, since the enactment of the Protocol to Prevent, Suppress and Punish Trafficking in Persons, Especially Women and Children, Supplementing the United Nations Convention against Transnational Organised Crime in 2000, there seems to be a universal acceptance of the definition offered in these international instruments (Aronowitz 2009, 1). The UNODC basically describes human trafficking as the acquisition of people by improper means such as force, fraud or deception, with the aim of exploiting them.

Human trafficking is not a recent occurrence in Africa (Allais 2013; Bello 2015; Mollema 2013 as cited in Bello 2019) – it is an age-old phenomenon that dates back to bygone days. The history of human trafficking in Africa cannot be explored in isolation from the broader context of slavery. In the distant past, human trafficking took the form of human slavery in Southern Africa (Bello 2019). The dominance of human slavery in the Southern African sub-region between the seventeenth and eighteenth centuries, with similar practices in other regions of Africa, has been reported (Martens et al. 2003 as cited in Bello 2019).

The first pronounced incidence of human trafficking in South Africa occurred in 1810, shortly before the abolition of slavery. This incidence concerned a South African lady named Saartjie Baartman (a twenty-one-year-old servant who, under fraud and deception of greener pastures, travelled to London with Dr William Dunlop). Upon her arrival in London, she was treated in a gruesome and dehumanising manner. In fact, she was exhibited in the nude before crowds in London who paid one shilling a person to "gawk at the Hottentots Venus from Africa" (Bello 2015, 67; Mollema 2013, 382; Martens et al. 2003, 5 as cited in Bello 2019). In her quest for survival in the face of financial constraints and linguistic and cultural barriers, she turned to prostitution. She died six years after leaving the shores of Cape Town. According to Martens, Pieczkowski, and Vuuren-Smyth (2003, 5) "her body was dissected, her skeleton was removed, and her brain and genitals were pickled and displayed as curiosities in the Musee de l'Homme in Paris for the next 160 years." The humiliating experience of this young African woman represents a pseudo-narrative of the horrendous experiences of several African women and children at the hands of traffickers (Bello 2015). Over time, human slavery in Africa has transformed into what is known in modern times as human trafficking. According to Bello (2015, 68) though human trafficking is different from human slavery, it still contains some "structural practices" that are akin to slavery.

Human trafficking also known as modern slavery is not a modern phenomenon though the term may be contemporary. This chapter finds no quarrel on the interchangeability of these concepts – therefore, the interchangeability approach noted above is adopted in this chapter. Otherwise stated, there is no distinction that is drawn between these concepts. As is demonstrated in the section that analyses the historical context of human trafficking above, it is evident that it is a phenomenon that traces its origins to time immemorial and is linked to multifaceted negative attributes such as slavery and slave trade that was championed by colonialism, sexual exploitation, economic exploitation and a new form of slavery and slave trade, to mention a few.

THEORETICAL ASSUMPTIONS ON THE CAUSES OF HUMAN TRAFFICKING

Numerous factors may make people vulnerable to trafficking in persons. Gender, age, education, disability, a lack of legal documentation and language barriers may all create or increase the risk of exploitation by traffickers. Fundamentally, trafficking is the exploitation of vulnerability (Pratt 2012). Various strategies are employed by traffickers to recruit and exploit victims, ranging from the simple false promise of a job to kidnappings. Often, they gain the confidence of victims through a combination of deception and manipulation. At times, unscrupulous employment agencies deceive workers into entering abusive work situations; what first seems to be a legitimate job is in fact exploitative (UNODC 2015). Women and children are particularly vulnerable to trafficking and may be trafficked by their own communities, families and in public places of business and commerce.

According to Zhidkova (2015, 20), the inclusion of all stakeholders in counter-trafficking efforts, while also noting that governments must engage in efforts designed to lower poverty and inequality in sending countries is pivotal. An analysis on different Southern African countries and information available on trafficking in human beings recognise poverty as the most visible cause for trafficking. The socio-economic conditions in, inter alia, Zimbabwe, Zambia, Mozambique, Angola and to a lesser extent South Africa is poor (Swart 2011, 32). Poverty and the lack of social and economic security are major factors that push people into migration and into situations of vulnerability in Southern Africa (Swart 2011). Addressing these major factors is a central long-term strategy to combating human trafficking in Africa and globally. A combination of demand for cheap labour and commercial sex, propelled by extreme poverty, poor education and high levels of unemployment, have made some South African women, children and, to a lesser degree, men susceptible to trafficking (Allais 2013; Mollema 2013).

Furthermore, globalisation and the technological era have increased awareness and mobility, resulting in larger numbers of people either seeking to migrate through regular channels such as employment or marriage, or seeking to do so outside of legal channels, whether they are fleeing persecution, conflict or simply seeking better economic opportunities (Swart 2011). The International Organisation of Migration also clearly states that trafficking of persons in Southern Africa is rooted in poverty, lack of opportunities, gender discrimination, social and political violence and a demand for service.

As globalisation has increased, so too have gaps in wealth, yet, simultaneously, individuals are increasingly aware of better opportunities elsewhere. Zhidkova (2015, 15) firmly advances arguments that "it is globalisation itself, and its accompanying facilitation of international flows of capital, which in turn facilitates transnational organised crime, which has then led to an increase in trafficking: globalization has created new opportunities for organized crime to increase their profits by creating transnational networks." There is, regardless of other differences of opinion, wide agreement that globalisation, and its accompanying increased mobility, has played a role in the increase in trafficking (Jones et al. 2007; Rahman 2011). The fundamental questions of global disparities in wealth and income and the seemingly endless possibilities – and need for labour – in other countries must be addressed.

Swart (2011, 27) also stress that information at hand indicates that the trafficking in women and children is a global phenomenon. Cross-border trafficking is clearly part of the globalising world and trafficking networks span several countries and continents. In addition, Onuoha (2009, 150) argues that human trafficking in Africa is more fundamentally the result of internal than external factors.

> The internal factors are the nature of the socio-political structures in Africa and the contradictions which they spawn. Among the internal factors associated with it are: bad governance, corruption, wars and societal crises, and other forms of conflicts including poverty, diseases, and unemployment (known as "push"

> factors). External factors (known as the "pull" factors) are attributed to the fundamental changes in the international economy, in particular globalization and, in some cases, the attendant demand for cheap labour provided by trafficked persons. (Onuoha 2009, 149)

These theoretical assumptions point us to rethink on African philosophy and policing strategies, the forces of globalisation and the fourth industrial revolution, and how these maybe manifested in the twenty-first century to combat human trafficking and restore the dignities of Africans.

RETHINKING POLICING TO COMBAT HUMAN TRAFFICKING IN AFRICA

Policing can be defined as that form of coercive action, within the structure of formal social control, which is directed at the maintenance of internal order in conformity with the principles of legal jurisdiction and the constitutional rights of the individual (Van Heerden 1982, 18). According to a sociological perspective, the police have the job of identifying and arresting offenders, discovering breaches of the law and maintaining public order (Smith and Natalier 2005, 83).

Accurate knowledge of policing in African states is severely limited, for a number of reasons. For an English-speaking only observer, the writings, such as they are, on policing in former French or Portuguese colonies, have retained the colonial language as their lingua franca (Marenin 2009, 352). Marenin (2009) adds that criminology and criminal justice as an academic discipline has not been emphasised or developed in African universities. Only a few academics working in African universities are interested in systematically studying the police, or other aspects of the criminal justice system. According to Marenin, problems of policing in an African state include but not limited to:

> an occupational culture which still echoes a colonial mentality rather than abides by a commitment to service, the rule of law, protection of rights, and professional norms; organizational failures, specifically a lack of effective and inefficient management, lack of resources, weak organizational identity, persistent corruption, and impunity for abuses of power; abysmal relations with the public which views the police, and rightly so, as corrupt, brutal, inefficient, and abusive in its normal encounters with the public. (2009, 353)

Despite these obstacles, reforms in African policing and law enforcement are possible to combat twenty-first-century wicked problems and align with globalisation challenges. African policing strategies can harness what works for them – the values embedded in Ubuntu, and forces of globalisation such as the digital era provide unique opportunities to improve policing in Africa. Effective policing is one of the key strategies to combat human trafficking in Africa. The future of policing systems in Africa will be fundamentally shaped by globalisation. Globalisation and the forces of the fourth industrial revolutions (technology, digital era or artificial intelligence) as enablers of human trafficking activities necessitate the adjustment of policing strategies to effectively combat human trafficking in Africa and elsewhere.

In Africa, one continues to witness policing as being extremely influenced by both macro and micro factors such as political, institutional, technological, cultural, social, economic, environmental factors and the internal occupational environment (see Govender 2010). African states need to move beyond all these hindrances to effectively subdue complex crimes and criminal syndicates involved in heinous crimes such as human trafficking or modern slavery, and harness the tools of technology and African methodologies to combat this phenomenon. This will keep up with the evolving trends, patterns and strategies of human traffickers.

PRACTICAL STRATEGIES TO COMBAT HUMAN TRAFFICKING

There are several practical strategies that can be used to combat human trafficking and slavery. These strategies, as was identified by Fichtelberg (2008, 244), inter alia, include educating potential victims; curbing demand; citizen activism; and criminalisation of the act of human trafficking and slavery. Apart from the strategies identified by Fichtelberg above, there are other strategies, from a legal perspective, that are applied to combat human trafficking and slavery, such as prosecution and punishment of offenders; victim support and protection; as well as a structural approach to human trafficking.

It is important that different countries may adopt varying strategies for purposes of combating the scourge of human trafficking. Thus, it is needless to argue that a practically viable strategy in one country may be impractical in another country – due to reasons, among others, such as the political and economic stability of a given country. In the discussion below, this chapter articulates on the utilisation of the aforementioned strategies in the quest of combating the social malevolent such as human trafficking and slavery in a practical manner.

EDUCATING POTENTIAL VICTIMS

True to the old age statement that information is power. A person who is ceased with information, makes informed decisions. A person who is aware about the dangers and tactics used by human traffickers stand a good chance to avoid falling victim of human trafficking and slavery. Fichtelberg (2008, 244) posits that raising awareness about the scourge of human trafficking and slavery through various medium or platforms such as campaigns against human trafficking, community social events, schools and so on, may assist would be (potential) victims to realise the dangers associated with human trafficking and slavery.

The potential victims ought to be educated on the scams and methods that may be used by human traffickers. For instance, Fichtelberg (2008, 236) identifies various stages which may be followed during the process of trafficking human beings including the aspect of vulnerability, recruitment, removal, transportation, establishment of control and exploitation. It is argued that if these stages and the contents of the dangers associated with human trafficking and slavery are effectively brought to the attention of the potential victims – such victims would be in a more and or better position to guard against falling prey or been conned or deceived by human traffickers. Further, according to Fichtelberg (2008, 244), educating potential victims would help them to "understand the violence, lack of control and degradation that they will be subject to when they consent to be trafficked." For this strategy to effectively work, countries and all stakeholders involved ought to continuously conduct research on the typologies of human trafficking and slavery. This is necessary because of the dynamic nature of human trafficking and for the fact that criminals often change tactics to circumvent law enforcement strategies.

Awareness of human trafficking and slavery should not be limited to potential victims, rather it should be extended to all relevant stakeholders (covering a broad range of participants – such as civil societies, business entities, public, non-governmental organisations, law enforcement and educational institutions). By adopting this holistic approach would effectuate the impact of educating potential victims and as the result rendering the application of the strategy more practical.

CURBING DEMAND

Curbing demand strategy is premised on the theoretical assumption that lack of demand for a product or service strongly influences the supply or manufacturing of such product or service. Otherwise stated, if a product is not on demand the probability of its production is relatively low or no production at all. The main object of this strategy is to reduce or decrease the demand of human trafficking and slavery by appealing or discouraging potential customers not to participate in activities related to human trafficking and slavery.

In a synoptic manner, Fichtelberg (2008) invokes the economic concept of supply-demand chain to explain how this strategy operates. By implication, Fichtelberg's formulation attempts to commodify the scourge of human trafficking and slavery – in which human beings are construed as a commodity. For this strategy to practically combat human trafficking – it is required, for example to "[m]ake customers of prostitution and labour providers to be aware of the exploitive relations that trafficked persons are subjected to" Fichtelberg (2008, 244). To curb the demand, for instance, in the case of prostitution – may require countries to prosecute and punish any person who may operate a brothel or persons who may be a customer of prostitution services. Whereas in cases of slavery – organised boycotts or demonstrations may effectively discourage corporations (slave owners) from utilising forced labour.

CITIZEN ACTIVISM

Citizen activism strategy as propounded by Fichtelberg (2008, 245) refers to circumstances where "[c]itizens have acted through non-governmental organisations or church organizations to free slaves and help slaves to save sufficient money to buy their own freedom." Citizens in the context of this strategy, among others, include individuals, civil societies, non-governmental organisation, governments, corporations and churches. Some scholars argue that citizen activism is a vital tool in denouncing or combating human trafficking and slavery (Murray et al. 2015, 729). The strategy's legitimacy is grounded in the principle that human trafficking and slavery constitute an infringement on the moral and dignity (human rights) of the victims. Thus, citizens' intervention in the fight against human trafficking and slavery is justified through the lenses of human rights.

Several empirical studies conducted on the impact of citizen activism against human trafficking and slavery indicate that citizen activism as a strategy has practically helped to reduce human trafficking and slavery. For instance, Potrafke (2016) conducted an empirical study that covered a span of 175 countries on the role of citizen activism, particularly, the role of religion (churches) in combating human trafficking. Potrofke (2016) concluded that "[r]eligion convictions shaped the moral sensibilities of the abolitionist movement in the 18th and 19th century" (p. 374). Undeniably, the role of citizen activism has strongly influenced many countries to regulate or criminalise human trafficking and slavery.

CRIMINALISATION

Criminalisation means turning a conduct that was not punishable by law (regarded as not a crime or offence) into a crime or offence. Human trafficking and slavery have existed since time immemorial – however, the art of criminalising these conducts gained popularity in the nineteenth century. Criminalisation is one of the practical strategies that has achieved measurable success in the fight against human trafficking and slavery. Most countries have adopted legislations that proscribe human trafficking and had made available facilities – such as law enforcement, courts and correctional services to ensure that those who contravene are prosecuted and punished.

In South Africa, there is a series of laws (legal framework) that proscribe slavery – among others, such as Section 13 of the 1996 Constitution of the Republic of South Africa and Section 1 of the Children's Act 38 of 2005. In a holistic manner, the South African Prevention and Combating of Trafficking in Persons Act 7 of 2013 is an ultimate manifestation on issues related to criminalisation of human trafficking. This legislation not only codifies human trafficking as a crime, but it creates sanctions for traffickers and their associates (organised crime networks). It elucidates on the victim protection and generally it is designed to combat and prevent human trafficking and slavery. In Zimbabwe, trafficking in persons constitutes a crime too in terms of the Trafficking in Persons Act 4 of 2014. Nigeria also proscribes all acts related to human trafficking. The concept of trafficking in person, from the Nigerian perspective, is defined and dealt with in terms of the Trafficking in Persons [Prohibition] Law Enforcement and Administration Act 2015.

In Namibia, the Prevention of Organised Crime Act 29 of 2004 section 15 proscribe and contemplates to punish human trafficking by stating that:

> Any person who participates in or who aids and abets the trafficking in persons, as contemplated in Annex II of the Convention, in Namibia or across the border to and from foreign countries commits an offence and is liable to a fine not exceeding N$1 000 000 or to imprisonment for a period not exceeding 50 years.

Namibia further promulgated the Combating of Trafficking in Persons Act 1 of 2018 to specifically criminalise and deal with the problem of human trafficking. This legislation is a milestone; however, it is not yet implemented due to certain reasons. National legislations aim to give effect to the United Nations Protocol to Prevent, Suppress and Punish Trafficking in Persons, Especially Women and Children, criminalise trafficking in persons and related offences, protect and assist victims of trafficking in persons, especially women and children. It is clear that criminalising human trafficking and slavery remains one of the key strategies that is viable in the quest of combating and prevention of human trafficking and slavery.

PROSECUTION AND PUNISHMENT OF OFFENDER

Prosecution of traffickers as a strategy compliments the criminalisation strategy. The complementarity relationship between prosecution and criminalisation is so great to an extent that some authors tend to combine these two strategies. Thus, the former strategy is highly relevant. For instance, there may be laws that proscribe human trafficking and slavery – however, if the machinery to prosecute and punish offenders is not available such substantive laws may not be effective. Therefore, to give effect to substantive laws that proscribe human trafficking and slavery it requires the utilisation of prosecution and punishment strategy. Kruger and Oosthuizen (2012, 284) cited several cases of human trafficking that have been successfully prosecuted and offenders duly punished in South Africa, among the cited cases, includes *S v Zweni and Others Case* No. 41/362/2012; *S v Kogilan Mudaly* Case No. CC21/11; the *S v Dos Santos* Judgment delivered on July 19, 2011, by the Pretoria Regional Court; *S v Sayed* Case No. 041/2713/2008 and *S v Sawatkan* Case No. 41/2045/08. These cited cases reflect the effectiveness and desirability of the prosecution and punishment strategy in the fight against human trafficking and slavery. According to Johnson (2016, 13) prosecution and punishment as a strategy against human trafficking in the United States of America, Lowa state, has to a large extent practically contributed to combating human trafficking and related offences. She cites prosecution and conviction of eighty-three offenders during the year 2014. This was an effective reduction from prosecution and conviction of 140 offenders in the year 2013. A key factor that was identified to have significantly contributed to the reduction in convictions experienced in 2014 was the vigorous punishments that were meted in 2013.

Prosecuting and punishing the offenders can effectuate deterrence in twofold, namely, direct and indirect deterrence. Direct deterrence occurs where the punishment is aimed at dissuading the offender from reoffending. Whereas, indirect deterrence occurs where a punishment is given to an offender with the effect to discourage would be offenders from committing similar crimes. Thus, it is without doubt that for this strategy to be effective it requires that competent punishment must be issued against an offender. It also remains imperative to embed African philosophies of policing, prosecution and punishment in these endeavours.

VICTIM SUPPORT AND PROTECTION

Victim support and protection as a strategy include providing shelters, counselling, affording victims appropriate witness protection facilities, capacity building and strengthening cooperation. In relations to providing shelter – one of the challenges in combating human trafficking is often the fact that in most instances victims of trafficking may be from different countries other than the countries where the offenders were caught and prosecuted. Wherefore, the victims may be deported to the country of origin while the matter is pending in courts. The act of deporting these victims diminishes the chances of successfully calling these victims to testify at a later stage as witnesses. To circumvent this challenge, governments should have shelters to accommodate these victims pending the prosecution of the offenders (from the Namibian context see chapter 23 of Criminal Procedure Act 57 of 1977 and the Witness Protection Act 10 of 2017).

Another element of victim support and protection strategy is counselling and capacity building. The crimes of trafficking in persons and that of slavery are so vile and violent. The effect of this violence (psychological scares) endured by victims are often poorly treated or not treated at all. The failure to effectively treat these psychological scares through appropriate counselling programmes may lead to emotional breakdowns. Thus, subjecting these victims to appropriate counselling services have great potential for victim recovery process; enhancement of their capacity to handle the negative effects of these crime; encourage anti-human trafficking and slavery advocacy or movements as well as citizen activism against the commission of these crimes.

THE STRUCTURAL APPROACH TO HUMAN TRAFFICKING

The structural approach as a strategy recognises that the presence of the law alone is not sufficient to effectively combat human trafficking and slavery. Many countries have good legislations that contemplate to combat human trafficking and slavery on shelves, however, the implementation or enforcement of such legislations is often a challenge. From this premise, a structural approach proffers that there must be an identified body or institution that is vested with the powers to enforce these promulgated legislations.

From the Namibian perspective, the Namibia Police Force is empowered in terms of section 13 and 14 of the Namibian Police Act 19 of 1990 and the Prevention of Organised Crime Act, to combat and investigate all matters related to human trafficking and slavery. To effectively utilise the arsenals of these legislations, there is a specific department, namely, the High-Profile

Crime Investigation Division within the Namibian Police Force which is, among others, mandated to lead the fight against human trafficking and slavery. By designating a specific division or unit that is responsible to lead the fight against human trafficking, is one of the practical strategies that many governments have adopted, and it has yielded commendable results. According to the 2018 US Trafficking in Persons Report on Namibia, the government of Namibia does not fully meet the minimum standards for the elimination of trafficking; however, it is making significant efforts to do so. With rapid globalisation, migration and advances in technology necessitate the need for sophisticated and innovative policing and anti-human trafficking strategies in Africa.

International Law and the UNODC's Response to Human Trafficking

The United Nations Protocol to Prevent, Suppress and Punish Trafficking in Persons, Especially Women and Children, supplementing the United Nations Convention against Transnational Organised Crime is considered to be "the principal, legally binding global instrument to combat trafficking in persons" (UNODC 2018a). Article 3 of this Protocol defines trafficking in persons, that it "shall mean the recruitment, transportation, transfer, harbouring or receipt of persons, by means of the threat or use of force or other forms of coercion, of abduction, of fraud, of deception, of the abuse of power or of a position of vulnerability or of the giving or receiving of payments or benefits to achieve the consent of a person having control over another person, for the purpose of exploitation. Exploitation shall include, at a minimum, the exploitation of the prostitution of others or other forms of sexual exploitation, forced labour or services, slavery or practices similar to slavery, servitude or the removal of organs." Under article 3 of the Protocol, trafficking in persons comprises three elements: (i) an "action," being recruitment, transportation, transfer, harbouring or receipt of persons; (ii) a "means" by which that action is achieved (threats or use of force or other forms of coercion, abduction, fraud, deception, abuse of power or a position of vulnerability, and the giving or receiving of payments or benefits to achieve consent of a person having control over another person) and (iii) a "purpose" (of the action/means): namely, exploitation, which includes, at a minimum, "the exploitation of the prostitution of others or other forms of sexual exploitation, forced labour or services, slavery or practices similar to slavery, servitude or the removal of organs" (UNODC 2018a).

All three elements must be present to constitute human trafficking except in relation to trafficking of children for which the means element is not required. The consent of a victim in trafficking is specified as irrelevant when any of the stipulated "means" are used (UNODC 2018a).

The potential breadth and narrowness of the definition has raised several issues that states have taken quite different positions on. "There is a tension between those who support a conservative or even restrictive interpretation of the concept of trafficking, and those who advocate for its expansion: between understandable efforts to expand the concept of trafficking to encompass most, if not all forms of severe exploitation; and the practical challenge of setting priorities and establishing clear boundaries, particularly for criminal justice agencies involved in the investigation and prosecution of trafficking-related crimes" (UNODC 2018a, 2).

These tensions sit within a broader political and advocacy framework that is impatient with complexity and the need for legal nuance. Certainly, there have been strong and consistent efforts to simplify the definition and forms of trafficking in ways that will advance advocacy or public communication efforts. The increasingly common merging of "trafficking" with "modern slavery," a term that is not defined – or indeed recognised – in international law is one manifestation of this trend, as are claims that "all trafficking is slavery" and "all forced labour is trafficking" (UNODC 2018a, 3).

The adoption in 2000 by the United Nations General Assembly of the Protocol to Prevent, Suppress and Punish Trafficking in Persons, especially Women and Children marked a significant milestone in international efforts to stop the trade in people. As the guardian of the Protocol, UNODC addresses human trafficking issues through its Global Programme against Trafficking in Persons (UNODC 2020a). A vast majority of states have now signed and ratified the Protocol but translating it into reality remains problematic. Very few criminals are convicted and most victims are probably never identified or assisted (UNODC 2020a). The role of the UNODC ranges from research and awareness through raising, improving baseline information and monitoring trends, to promotion of international protocols and capacity building (UNODC 2020b).

Through its Comprehensive Strategy to Combat Human Trafficking in Persons and Smuggling of Migrants and the clear mandates derived from the Protocol, the UNODC support efforts to: prevent and combat human trafficking in persons and smuggling of immigrants, protect and assist victims of trafficking with full respect for their human rights, prosecute traffickers and ensuring an effective criminal justice system, and promote cooperation among states and stakeholders to meet those objectives.

PATTERNS OF TRAFFICKING AND EFFORTS TO COMBAT HUMAN TRAFFICKING IN AFRICA

The Global Report on Trafficking in Persons reveals that large parts of Africa and Asia are weak in detecting victims and convicting traffickers (UNODC

2018b). Most of the detected trafficking victims in sub-Saharan Africa continue to be children. More than 50 per cent of the victims detected in 2016 were children, in near equal shares of boys and girls (UNODC 2018b). However, analysing the data by geographical areas shows that child trafficking is far more commonly detected in West Africa than in the rest of sub-Saharan Africa. East African countries detect larger shares of adults, nearly equally split between men and women. On the other hand, countries in Southern Africa tend to detect more women, as well as men and boys in similar numbers. Girls are rarely detected in East and Southern Africa, whereas in West Africa, they are the most frequently detected victim profile. Countries in West Africa tend to detect far more victims than other countries in sub-Saharan Africa (UNODC 2018b). Better research and data can assist greatly in combating human trafficking.

The means and methods by which the AU attempts to address transnational crimes is has often assessed with reference to its approach towards corruption and trafficking in human beings, as well as the proposed International Criminal Law Section of the African Court. Examples of the methods include hard and soft law approaches, the promotion of harmonisation of laws and cooperative efforts with the African Regional Economic Communities and Mechanisms, and non-African organisations and institutions. Yet, despite AU efforts, the initiatives and approaches have gained limited traction.

Africa has no comprehensive legal instrument to address human trafficking, but the following are found: the Ouagadougou Action Plan to Combat Trafficking in Human Beings (2006) which aimed to prevent and combat trafficking between the European Union and the AU, the ECOWAS Plan of Action to Combat Trafficking in Persons, Especially Women and Children (2002), and the SADC Strategic Plan of Action on Combatting Trafficking in Persons, Especially Women and Children (2009).

CHALLENGES IN COMBATING HUMAN TRAFFICKING IN AFRICA

There are several challenges that may hamper the effectuation or successful implementation of the strategies to combat human trafficking or modern slavery. Among others, these challenges include: first, lack of integration between the criminal justice agencies (customs, police and prosecution). The criminal justice operational model within these agencies resembles the conflict model as opposed to the consensus model which requires effective teamwork among the agencies (Schmalleger 2015, 10). Second, the lack of sufficient resources – it is a given fact that an institution can put in place good strategies such as those identified above – however, if there is lack of adequate resources, these strategies may not be implemented and as a result the institution/police may fail to live up to its aspirations contained in the strategies or policies (Haidula 2017, 3). Third, the other significant challenge is lack of training within the agencies which are mandated directly or indirectly to combat human trafficking and slavery. For instance, in Namibia – the police officers are trained in handling human trafficking crimes, however, other sister agencies (custom and immigration officials) who should work as a team with the police, have no requisite knowledge on how to deal with these types of crimes (Barry 2007, 80). Rahman (2011, 63) notes that weak governance, corruption and insufficient legislation all are contributing factors which allow traffickers to "hide under the cover of the law to engage in their nefarious activities." According to Koppenfels (2017, 345), his argument demonstrates the importance of geographical and temporal context, making the case that while one approach – philosophical and practical – may be appropriate in one region or context, it may only be relevant for that region or context. Human trafficking is a complex, clandestine and sensitive matter. It takes different forms and those in the trafficking chain employs different methods to recruit and exploit victims (Swart 2011, 27). It is mostly a hidden crime that is seldom reported and discovered by accident. Human trafficking is a well-organised crime with national and international connections driven by crime syndicates or groups. These syndicates have been able to use well-established routes and methods to traffic women and children worldwide. Not much has been written about human trafficking in Africa and no attention has been given to a robust collaborative approach in combating it (Swart 2011). To create such a collaborative approach, it is necessary to have a clear understanding of the factors that influence and drive human trafficking.

THEORISING THE ROLE OF AFRICAN UBUNTU PHILOSOPHY AND COMMUNITY POLICING IN COMBATING HUMAN TRAFFICKING

In the midst of policy and ideologies misdirection, the Ubuntu philosophy can provide guidance. Due to the diversity and different means of trafficking, different philosophical approaches play a role in the discussion over trying to determine the most effective approaches to combating trafficking (Koppenfels 2017).

Ubuntu is a humanistic ethic which, in its articulation, is aimed at countering a behaviour that was considered as dehumanising. Ubuntu means humanness – and by implication treating other people with kindness, compassion, respect and care. Murove (2012) states that these virtues are usually referred to as the summation of Ubuntu or humanness. Murove (2012, 37) also argues that:

the efficacy of Ubuntu which lays on the primacy that is given to relational rationality – the original understanding of a human being as a relational being does challenge the contemporary individualistic and self-interested understanding of a human being which has tragically dominated our academic understanding of a human being. In support of this claim, he goes on to show that the African ethical concept of Ubuntu has a tremendous contribution to make a new understanding of human beings. Since Ubuntu is based on a worldview of relationality, its main insight is consequently based on the idea that as human beings we depend on other human beings to attain ultimate well-being. It has been often observed by many scholars that it is the reality of our dependence and interdependence with each other that we attain the fullest of our humanness.

The ethic of Ubuntu was denigrated by colonial scholarship as an ethic that was mainly a phenomenon of human primitivity, as an expression of infantile behaviour, and equally a manifestation of an infliction of dependency complex syndrome (Murove 2012, 38). The influence of Charles Darwin's theory of evolution to colonial anthropology led to the trivialisation of African communalism as it was enshrined in the ethic of Ubuntu.

The quest for an African identity through Ubuntu has also influenced the socio-economic policies of many countries in Africa. The main argument that has been put forward by scholars is that capitalistic values remain alien to those of Ubuntu. In this vein, Jenny Maree and Lovemore Mbigi (1995, 52 as cited in Murove 2012, 42) have this to say: "It is our belief that unless the development structures, strategies and processes can harness these Ubuntu values into a dynamic transformative force for reconstruction and development, failure will be almost certain." The principles of Ubuntu are thus expected to influence the public sector and implicitly these principles were to influence the identity of the public sector – a human-centred public sector. This was crucial when one takes into consideration the fact that public servants were previously used as instruments of repression by colonial governments.

Furthermore, it is instructive to note that community policing predates the era of colonial incursion into most African states (Olutola 2011, 119; Bello 2015). According to Oluwaniyi (2011, 69) traditionally, policing was the responsibility of all adults in the community. In medieval society, all adult males were obliged to contribute towards the prevention and control of crime and disorder under the systems of "hue, cry and pursuit" and the "watch and ward" (Alemika and Chukwuma 2003 as cited in Bello and Olutola 2016, 50). In Nigeria, communities formed themselves into what was referred to as *ode adugbo* (street vigilante group), which still exists in most parts of the country today. In the United States and most of the western world, community policing has also emerged over the past ten to fifteen years as a major thrust of police activity (Govender 2010). However, the emergence of the state, vis-à-vis the need to protect the state (political elites) during colonial rule necessitated the establishment of the police force (Bello and Olutola 2016). From the foregoing, there is a necessity to embrace community policing as a viable mechanism for combating human trafficking in an Africa context (Bello and Olutola 2016). Though the initiative is in force on the continent, its current operability does not reflect the true philosophies of community policing and *Ubuntu*. Whereas these philosophies and practices are overlooked, they may provide significant insights and strategies in combating human trafficking in an age of globalisation.

CONCLUSION

Discussing human trafficking in the context of globalisation and human security touches on issues of inequality, poverty, vulnerability, security, policing systems and technological forces, among others. To address the question of human trafficking, this chapter identified and analysed several practical strategies that may be adopted and applied in combating human trafficking or modern slavery. The practical strategies discussed in this chapter are not exhaustive – that is, different countries may adopt certain strategies depending on such country's need and context. Among the strategies that were discussed include education and awareness among the victims and potential victims, curbing demand, allowing citizens to participate in the fight against the scourge, criminalising, prosecution and punishment of offenders, support the victims. In pursuit of these other strategies, there is a need to reconsider and integrate indigenous community policing practices and Ubuntu philosophy in combating human trafficking in Africa.

Based on theoretical assumptions of causes of human trafficking, socio-economic development, with a special emphasis on women and girls, constitutes perhaps the best long-term approach to combating human trafficking (see Jones et al. 2007). Human trafficking is not a one-off criminal enterprise, but a product of certain socio-economic and cultural factors that affect countries today (Bello 2019). Therefore, combating it would require addressing these factors. The expertise and efforts of the components of the criminal justice system are unable to address these factors. Putatively, the solutions to these factors are outside the scope of the police or criminal justice system (Bello 2019). We need to recognise that the complexity of human trafficking extends beyond the legal realm, and a comprehensive understanding of human trafficking is not possible without the convergence of various disciplines, expertise and perspectives, including the historical, economic, social, political and gender prisms. The transnational scope of trafficking also requires a holistic and multidisciplinary approach, involving numerous complementary actors, expertise and strategies. A holistic approach must involve both categories of counter-trafficking activities/strategies: prevention (education, research, legislation, improved peoples' social and economic conditions, etc.), protection (witness, immigration, etc.), provision (shelter, counselling), prosecution (law enforcement, investigations, trials and convictions, extradition) and participation (from all stakeholders like the public, media, NGOs and academic institutions among others). There is no doubt that the waves of globalisation, the fourth industrial revolution, ineffective policing or law enforcement and factors such as money laundering and corruption syndicates further exacerbate human trafficking in poor states, especially in Africa.

BIBLIOGRAPHY

Allais, C. (2013). The profile less considered: The trafficking of men in South Africa. *South African Review of Sociology*, Volume 44(1), 40–54.

Bello, P. O. (2019). Response to human trafficking in South Africa: Beyond the criminal justice system. *Politeia*, Volume 38(1), 1–18.

Bello, P. O., and Olutola, A. A. (2016). Community policing as a mechanism in combating human trafficking in South Africa: Getting the priorities right. *Politeia*, Volume 35(1), 41–60.

Bertone, A. M. (2000). Sexual trafficking in women: International political economy and the politics of sex. *Gender Issues*, Volume 18(1), 4–22.

Burchell, J. (2011). *South African Criminal Law and Procedure* (4th ed.). Cape Town: Juta.

Cindori, S. (2007). The money laundering prevention system. *Financial Theory and Practice*, Volume 31(1), 59–76.

De Klerk, E. (2018, February 9). One conviction from 31 human trafficking cases. *New Era Newspaper*, p. 7.

Fichtelberg, A. (2008). *Crime Without Borders: An Introduction to International Criminal Justice*. New Jersey: Pearson Education.

Financial Action Task Force. (2015). Effective supervision and enforcement by AML/CFT supervisors of financial sector and law enforcement. www.fatf-gafi.org.

Govender, D. (2010). Policing a changing society in South Africa: Challenges for the police officer. *Acta Criminologica: African Journal of Criminology & Victimology*, Volume 2, 69–83.

Haidula, T. (2017, January 18). Police recruitment frozen. *The Namibian Newspaper*, p. 3.

Hardy, P. D. (2017, June 18). Sting money laundering scheme and cooperating client Ensnares attorney. *Ballard Spahr*.

Hartgerink, P. (2007). Youth justice in action research report: The role of public perception in shaping juvenile justice systems. Article Volume, 40(9), (2), 4–6.

Johnson, S. (2016). *An Analysis of Human Trafficking in Iowa.* Iowa Department of Human Rights. https://humanrights.iowa.gov/sites/default/files/media/CJJP_January_2016_Task_Force_Report_%20Human%20Trafficking.pdf.

Jones, L., Engstrom, D. W., Hilliard, T., and Diaz, M. (2007). Globalization and human trafficking. *Journal of Sociology and Social Welfare*, Volume 34(2), 107–122.

Koppenfels, A. K. (2017). Human trafficking. In K. A. Reinert (Ed.), *Handbook of Globalisation and Development.* Cheltenham & Massachussetts: Policy Press.

Kruger, H. B., and Oosthuizen, H. (2012). South Africa – Safe haven for human trafficking? Employing the arsenal of existing law to combat human trafficking. *Potchefstroom Electronic Law Journal*, Volume 15(1), 283–428.

Marenin, O. (2009). The futures of policing African states. *Police Practice and Research: An International Journal*, Volume 10(4), 349–363.

Mollema, N. (2013). *Combating human trafficking in South Africa: A comparative legal study* (Unpublished doctoral thesis). University of South Africa, Pretoria.

Murove, M. F. (2012). Ubuntu. *Diogenes*, Volume 59(3–4), 36–47.

Murray, V., Dingman, S., Porter, J., and Otte, M. (2015). Victim intervention marketing: An application of social activist marketing in opposition to human trafficking. *Journal of Marketing Theory*, Volume 23(3), 272–286.

Myers, J. M. (1998). *International strategies to combat money laundering.* International Symposium on the prevention and control of financial fraud, Beijing, 19–20 October 1998. www.icclr.law.ubc.ca.

Onuoha, B. (2011). The state of human trafficking and human rights issues in Africa. *Contemporary Justice Review*, Volume 14(2), 149–166.

Potafke, N. (2016). Policies against human trafficking: The role of religion and political institutions. *Economic Governance*, Volume 17, 353–386.

Pratt, L. (2012). Hidden in plain sight: A general overview of the human trafficking issue. *Willamette Law Review*, Volume 50(115), 4.

Rahman, M. (2011). Human trafficking in the era of globalization: The case of trafficking in the global economy. *Transcience*, Volume 2(1), 54–71.

Ramaswamy, J. (2013). *Overview of Asset Forfeiture and Money Laundering Program.* United States Attorney's Bulletin. www.heinonline.org.

Schmalleger, F. (2015). *Criminal Justice Today: An Introductory Text for the 21st Century* (13th ed.). New York: Pearson Education Inc.

South African Department of Justice and Constitutional Development. (2016). The annual report 2015/2016 on the implementation of child justice act 2008. www.justice.gov.za.

Sujee, Z. J. (2016). *A study of the anti-money laundering framework in South Africa and the United Kingdom* (Unpublished LLM Dissertation). University of Pretoria, South Africa.

Swanepoel, P., Lotter, S., and Karels, M. (2011). *The influence of the Child Justice Act 75 of 2008 on the application of justice in South Africa: Interpretation quaeparitabsurdam, non estadmittenda?* 2nd International Conference on Humanities, Historical and Social Sciences IPEDR, 17 IACSIT Press, Singapore.

Swart, D. N. (2011). Problems surrounding the combating of women and child trafficking in Southern and South Africa. *Child Abuse Research in South Africa*, Volume 12(1), 26–37.

Terblanche, S. S. (2012). The Child Justice Act: A detailed consideration of section 68 as a point of departure with respect to the sentencing of young offenders. *Potchefstroom Electronic Law Journal*, Volume 15(5), 436–638.

Terrill, R. J. (2016). *World Criminal Justice Systems: A Comparative Survey* (9th ed.). New York: Routledge.

United Nations Convention against Transnational Organized Crime.

United Nations Office on Drugs and Crime (UNODC). (2018a). The international legal definition of trafficking in persons: Consolidations of research findings and reflection on issues raised, Issue Paper. https://www.unodc.org/documents/human-trafficking/2018/Issue_Paper_International_Definition_TIP.pdf.

United Nations Office on Drugs and Crime (UNODC). (2018b). Global report on trafficking in persons, UNODC research. https://www.unodc.org/documents/human-trafficking/2019/GLOTiP_2018_BOOK_web_small.pdf.

United Nations Office on Drugs and Crime (UNODC). (2020a). Human trafficking. https://www.unodc.org/unodc/en/human-trafficking/what-is-human-trafficking.html.

United Nations Office on Drugs and Crime (UNODC). (2020b). Comprehensive strategy to combat trafficking in persons and smuggling of migrants. https://www.unodc.org/documents/human-trafficking/UNODC_Strategy_on_Human_Trafficking_and_Migrant_Smuggling.pdf.

United Nations Protocol to Prevent, Suppress and Punish Trafficking in Persons, especially Women and Children.

Zhidkova, T. (2015). Globalization and the emergence of non-state actors: The case of human trafficking. *New Global Studies*, Volume 9(1), 1–25.

Chapter 18

The Coloniality of COVID-19 in Africa

Nudgers and Nudgees in the Constitution of the New World Order

Artwell Nhemachena, Clifford Kendrick Hlatywayo, and Tapiwa Victor Warikandwa

INTRODUCTION

Building on contemporary discourses on coloniality and decoloniality (Ndlovu-Gatsheni 2013), this chapter examines COVID-19 using the conceptual framework of what we call the *coloniality of nudging*. Noting ways in which colonialists and slave-drivers similarly nudged Africans by limiting their choice architectures, the chapter connects COVID-19 to colonial pandemics and epidemics through which the choice architectures (environments within which choices are made) of the colonised were limited by the colonialists. It is argued that limiting choice architectures is a way of channelling the behaviour of the enslaved and colonised towards directions desired by the slave-drivers and colonisers. In this sense, colonial era pandemics, famines and epidemics - including smallpox epidemics, rinderpest epidemics and of course droughts and famine – were used as apparatuses with which to limit the choice architectures of the colonised peoples (Anderson 2005; Sarkin & Westerman 2008). Sometimes colonialists deliberately infested blankets with smallpox, they poisoned indigenous people's water wells and they perpetrated genocide on indigenous people (Sarkin & Westerman 2008; Anderson 2005). The colonialists then pretended to assist victims of their colonial projects, on condition that such victims "agreed" to become servants to the colonialists. Bearing this background in mind, this chapter situates COVID-19 in the context of the ongoing new scramble for Africa (Warikandwa et al. 2017) and then it examines ways in which COVID-19 is providing the new empire with an apparatus to nudge Africans into the imperial matrix of power. COVID-19 also coincides with the Malthusian Anticipatory Regime for Africa and the attendant calls for the disposal of "surplus" people in the world; it coincides with a global zeitgeist marked by postulations of posthumanism, anti-humanism, transhumanism, ecocentrism, biocentrism, earth-centrism, all of which decentre and deconstruct humanism and human rights (Nhemachena & Mawere 2019; Nhemachena & Mawere 2020).

COVID-19 is also coterminous with the emergence of a world wherein some humans are deemed to be "dispensable" and to constitute "surplus" people. Thus, the chapter argues that COVID-19 effectively constitutes an apparatus with which to nudge the world into the anti-humanist and transhumanist New World Order marked, on one hand, by the disappearance of humanism and human rights (in particular Ubuntu-based human rights in the African context) and, on the other hand, the emergence of posthumanism, cyborgs, post-liberalism, post-freedom, post-politics, post-democracy and post-identitarianism (Nhemachena & Mawere 2019). In this sense, COVID-19 can be understood as constituting a mask for the anti-humanist and transhumanist New World Order. In this sense, COVID-19 does not only require human beings to wear masks but, like other pandemics and epidemics that have historically constituted masks for colonisation, COVID-19 can be seen and experienced as a mask (in principle, a mask behind a mask). Thus, our argument follows Stern (2017, 19) who argues that masks protect some human beings from the thinking of other people, that is, masks protect some people from unwanted truths or from fair challenges to their views and actions. Also, we argue that in so far as masks evidence liminality, the COVID-19 era constitutes a liminal period in which humanity is being pushed into the New World Order.

COVID-19 AND THE EMERGENT NEW WORLD ORDER

The New World Order is one which is marked by anti-humanism, posthumanism and transhumanism entailing the violation, decentring and disposal of humanism, human rights including rights to freedoms of movement, rights to privacy, freedom of assembly and association, freedom of expression and opinion and so on. Besides, the New World Order is one in which democracy is truncated such that human beings are reduced to the order of animals. In a global context marked by the ascendancy of anti-humanism, posthumanism, transhumanism and postanthropocentrism – all of which decentre humanity and human rights – it is only proper for humanity to question the apparent humanitarianism of COVID-19 vaccines. While vaccines may have helped humanity in the past, the context in which COVID-19 vaccines are being offered is one marked by global elites' efforts to usher in transhumanism, posthumanism, anti-humanism and post-anthropocentrism. Human beings lose their jobs with the emergence of the post-industrial society that is being ushered in by the Fourth Industrial Revolution which is being catalysed by COVID-19. In this regard, the New World Order is one that is anti-humanist in the sense of letting some human beings die – in the sense of ushering in of new eugenics wherein human beings that are considered to constitute "useless" classes are disposed of (Harari 2018; Nhemachena & Mawere 2020). Put differently, an anti-humanist and transhumanist New World Order that is being ushered in by and through COVID-19 is as anti-humanist as it is anti-God and Antichrist in the sense of prohibiting the veneration and supplication of God and Christ. An anti-humanist and transhumanist New World Order is one which is also anti-God and Antichrist in the sense of transhumanist projects that are set to remodel human beings and transform them (into cyborgs/technology-biology hybrids) from the image of God or from likeness to God. In the anti-humanist and transhumanist New World Order, human beings are set to be transformed into cyborgs and monsters comprising fusions of biology and technology. This is evident in nanovaccines and nanomedicines which are being injected into human bodies that are subjected to transhumanist experiments (Flores 2018). These experimentations and transformations are well captured by Poxon's (2001) explication of the Body Without Organs (BWO) which is noted as Antichrist and AntiGod, as infusing human beings with a powerful nonorganic vitality in the order of the Antichrist; the BWO is noted as dissolving the self, as refashioning personhood and as decentring humans. The transhumanist and post-humanist New World Order is one where biological bodies are infused or merged with technology, particularly nanotechnology. In short, the transhumanist and anti-humanist New World Order is achieved through massive experimentation with and on human beings – and by forcing human beings to submit to such experimentation including with nanovaccines and nanomedicines. Human beings are nudged through pandemics and epidemics that limit human beings' choice architectures thereby leaving them with no alternative but to submit to transhumanist, anti-humanist and post-humanist experiments that produce cyborgs or biology-technology monsters out of natural human beings.

We argue herein that, beset by a plethora of problems including indigenous people's claims for restitution and reparations for enslavement and colonisation (Nhemachena & Warikandwa 2019), the present empire badly wants to reset the world as a way to evade the challenges that it is facing. Faced with multiple demands for restitution and reparations for enslavement and colonisation, the present empire seeks to evade the claims by changing the identities (and even turning indigenous humans into post-humans, cyborgs and transhumans) of victims of enslavement and colonisation. Because identity is central to successful claims for restitution and reparations, changing the identities of victims of enslavement and colonisation helps empire by pre-empting the indigenous victims' struggles for justice. Transforming victims of enslavement and colonisation into cyborgs and biology-technology hybrids, empire would ensure that once they have lost their indigenous identities, victims of enslavement and colonisation would not be able to asset their indigeneity and to claim restitution and reparations on the basis of indigeneity (Nhemachena et al. 2018). In this regard, transhumanism and posthumanism are meant to transform indigenous people's identities and thus forestall indigenous people's struggles for restitution and reparations. One can only claim indigeneity and victimhood, due to enslavement and colonisation, only if their indigenous identities are not fundamentally transformed. Empire is well aware that at the core of legal suits for restitution, reparations and compensation, is the question of the identities of the victims and perpetrators; thus by transforming these identities, it pre-empts the legal suits and struggles for restitution and reparations. In this sense, scientific projects are generously funded to transform human genes by editing and deleting them; scientific projects are generously funded to transform indigenous memories by editing and deleting them; scientific projects are generously funded to transform human identities via nanotechnological experiments including via nanovaccines and nanomedicines which are set to be implanted and inserted, as nanorobotic vaccines and medicines, into the bloodstreams of indigenous people (Nhemachena et al. 2020). Thus, transforming human bodies and identities via nanotechnology, biotechnology, information technology and genomics technology, the New World Order is meant to become a safe world for the empire. We argue that the greatest threat for empire are the indigenous people who have been historically dispossessed, enslaved, colonised and exploited and are therefore increasingly claiming restitution and reparations from empire.

If indigenous people remain indigenous to their sovereign territories or nations, the risk for empire is that they will continue to claim restitution and reparations on the basis of their indigenous identities. Empire would therefore benefit from deterritorialising, in Deleuze and Guattari's (1987) sense, indigenous people through the creation of a New World Order ruled by global technocrats, scientists and global elites. The current transformations wherein transnational institutions, organisations, corporations and Western states dictate to Africans and other continents provides the contours of the emergent New World Order that tramples on indigenous peoples' identities, sovereignties and autonomy – this is beneficial for an empire that seeks to efface indigeneity, indigenous identities and indigenous claims for restitution and reparations for enslavement and colonisation. Once indigenous identities, sovereignty and autonomy are disappeared, the empire becomes free from the claims for restitution and reparations. Similarly, once the empire resets the world into a post-God world "order," indigenous people would not be able to claim that their land and other resources are God-given because God will have disappeared from the scene as well. In the light of the foregoing, a post-COVID-19 world "order" threatens to be a post-God world disorder; a post-COVID-19 world disorder also threatens to be a post-human world disorder; a post-COVID-19 world disorder also threatens to be a post-identity world disorder, it threatens to be a post-indigenous, post-sovereignty and post-autonomy world disorder. Put differently, a post-COVID-19 world disorder threatens to be a world that professes to be inclusive of both human and nonhuman entities yet it ironically is a world disorder that excludes God and the attendant order based on the judgement of God in Poxon's (2001) sense. A post-COVID-19 world disorder is one in which empire assumes full-spectrum dominance and it even hopes to assume dominance over God whose judgement is supposedly set to be superseded by the judgement of the empire and its battalion of technocrats evangelising technological solutionism, ironically, in a world that otherwise requires multipronged and multi-sited solutions.

Seeking to assume monopoly of judgement in the world, empire dismisses the judgement of God; similarly, seeking to monopolise knowledge in the world, empire dismisses indigenous knowledge systems; further, seeking to monopolise knowledge, empire dismisses every other form of knowledge as irrational, as misinformation, as disinformation, as infodemic, as belief, as conspiracy theories, as helpless, as foolish, as barbaric, as ignorant and so on. The point we are making here is that all these imperial quibbles have precedents during the colonial era wherein victims of enslavement and colonisation were depicted as barbaric, foolish, irrational, ignorant, as steeped in conspiracy theories and as spreading disinformation and misinformation that would otherwise awaken fellow victims about the ongoing colonisation, enslavement, dispossession and exploitation (Nhemachena et al. 2020). Put differently, colonialists would not have tolerated indigenous discourses that challenged the colonial gospel of civilisation or *mission civilisatrice* that served to mask colonisation. Colonial discourses about "civilisation" were meant to nudge victims of colonisation into the colonial imperial project that was in fact marked by dispossession and exploitation rather than by civilisation. Dispossession was in fact one of the means used by colonialists to limit the choice architectures of the colonised who were thereby forced to submit to and become cheap labour on colonial farms, factories and mines. The point is that nudging is more effective when the nudgees are left with no other options but to submit to the nudgers' projects, no matter how nefarious.

NUDGING SOME HUMANS INTO THE ANTI-HUMANIST AND TRANSHUMANIST NEW WORLD DISORDER

The process of nudging involves structuring how choices are made by individuals (Haugh 2017). Individuals are under the illusion that they have power to choose yet the options available to them are a planned design of social norming. In numerous contexts nudging is used by the global institutions and corporations, global elites, the states and some organisations to get desirable behaviours from their subjects. The nudge is legitimised by depicting some people as making inconsistent decisions – as if it is an offence to make such inconsistent decisions. In nudging, humans are influenced by emotions, environment and settings in which the decision is made. Some people are, conveniently, depicted as making decisions that necessarily are not in their best interests (Griffin 2011). The nudger thus justifies nudging by arguing that depriving other humans of decision-making is in the best interest of such humans. The nudger takes away the available options, supposedly so as to produce an outcome that is good for the subjects of nudging (Arneson 2015). Unsurprisingly, Rainford and Tinkler (2011) state that humans have bounded rationality and therefore they supposedly make biased decisions that sometimes run counter to their own best interests. By this assertion, the authors seek to legitimise nudging certain sections of humanity who are deemed to have bounded rationality.

With nudging, human behaviour can be altered at the mercy of the nudger under the guise of rational innovation. The nudger would argue that decision-making is influenced through the use of "gentle" encouragements, such as by slave-drivers and colonialists. The nudgers would appoint themselves as the judges and jury and then erode other people's freedoms, thus, negating freedom of choice by other humans. Human welfare, dignity and autonomy are all at the mercy of the nudgers as other people's sense of choice is steered in a particular direction at the instance of the nudger (Sunstein 2015). Conveniently for nudgers, experimental psychology and behavioural economics have increasingly cast doubt on the quality and reliability of individual decision-making, especially in complicated choice contexts involving risk and time (White 2017).

The nudger's explicit goal is to endorse their own welfare and subconsciously influence other human beings to behave in ways consistent with the nudging (Thaler & Sunstein 2015). Human decision-making happens subconsciously, thus making it easy for the nudgers to influence human behaviour without the knowledge of the individual. This necessitates questions on whether nudging is ethical. This is so because nudging takes away personal autonomy by violating deeply held normative notions by people (Haugh

2017). Nudges were/are used to shape colonial policy, thus it has penetrated behaviour, socially, economically and politically. Thaler and Sunstein (2015) state that the nudger identifies and implements public policies that manipulate people's tendencies to irrational decision-making to their own advantage. Hansen and Jespersen (2013) believe that setting default rules and making decisions on behalf of citizens, constitutes manipulation, manipulation in the sense of intending to change the perception, choices or behaviour of others through underhanded deceptive, or even abusive tactics.

Some scholars argue that nudges are ethical when transparent and beneficial to public interest (Bousquet 2017) but then the problem is that since the colonial era, colonial/imperial interest has been uncritically taken to constitute public interest. In the contemporary world, imperial interests still preponderate over African interests. The interests of transnational corporations, some Western individuals, institutions and organisations are uncritically deemed to constitute public interest in Africa. The challenge of nudging is that it promises no harm to recipients when in fact the removal of human autonomy, itself, poses harm to fellow humans.

HOW HUMANS GET FOOLED TO ACCEPT THE NEW NORM

Kahneman et al. (1982) argue that human beings' decision-making processes are not perfect and that people fall prey to a number of predictable mistakes because of cognitive biases and dysfunctions. For Saghai (2013) nudges often unconsciously alter the way we perceive the options we are offered, making them either more attractive or more repulsive. In the current COVID-19 pandemic, there is use of one-sided information which dismisses alternative views as fake news or "conspiracy theory." Alternative worldviews are, under COVID-19, summarily dismissed as infodemic, misinformation and disinformation. Throughout the world, humanity is subjected to one-dimensional global policy which does not allow for alternative versions of the world and which stipulate conditions for public gatherings, people staying indoors, social distancing and wearing of masks. Alternative herbal medicines are also summarily dismissed as ineffective, dangerous and ill-advised. Thus, humanity is instilled with fear for COVID-19 as well as, ironically, with revulsion for their own indigenous herbal medicines that would otherwise provide them with solutions to the COVID-19 pandemic. The point here is that such nudging, through inducing fear and constraining choices, is meant to channel human behaviour towards the direction that are desirable to the nudgers, in this case the global elites that seek to transform the world into a New World Order marked by anti-humanism, posthumanism, transhumanism and populated by cyborgs rather than by natural human beings.

We conceptualise the coloniality of nudging in terms of the Shona word, *kuitiswa* (to be made to do). In *kuitiswa*, the nudger assumes the role of a god determining or influencing, directly or indirectly, the behaviour of the nudgee who effectively becomes a zombie that is subject to manipulation and mind control. In the coloniality of nudging, Africans are made to believe that their own indigenous medicines which have served them for centuries before colonialism, are dangerous. The coloniality of nudging is broader than the colonisation of the mind in the sense that the coloniality of nudging is as much about mind control as it is about the control of the behaviours of the nudgee or the subject of nudging. In *kuitiswa* or the coloniality of nudging, there are appearances of consent even when genuine or real agreement is absent – people "consent" because someone has limited or taken away their choice architectures. The point is that it is inaccurate to describe someone as having consented when in fact someone else has deliberately tampered with their choice architectures – it would be more accurate to describe such a situation in terms of an appearance of consent. The challenge of *kuitiswa* is that the nudgee (*muitiswi*) will cease to engage their grey matter and submit all cognitive functions to the nudger (*muitisi*). Thinking for oneself becomes terrifying for the nudgee who then experiences and condemns his/her own thoughts as disruptive of world order. From the nudgee's point of view, it is only the nudger who has the legitimacy to think in ways that even disrupt and change the world order. Thus, over time, nudgees outsource their thinking to the nudgers. This underlies the essence of the Shona proverb *kwadzinorohwa matumbu ndiko kwadzinomhanyira* (some people seek refuge in the spaces of their tormentors). The point here is that once they have outsourced their thinking to the nudger, the nudgees begin to seek refuge and solace in the spaces of their nudger tormentors.

The upshot of the above is that the coloniality of nudging pays attention to the coloniality of depriving other human beings of their autonomy, privacy, sovereignty, free will and humanity. Much like during the colonial and enslavement eras, the nudgees are deprived of their wills to sovereignty, and will to autonomously think and make choices. In this regard, some Eurocentric scholars and thinkers conveniently depict Ubuntu as devoid of notions of autonomy and sovereignty. We argue that the intention is to prepare Africans for the New World Order in which their autonomy and sovereignty are decentred, deconstructed and made to vanish. In line with the emergent New World Order, some Eurocentric scholars already conveniently depict African societies, polities and cultures as devoid of expressions of autonomy and sovereignty. We argue that to be described as devoid of autonomy and sovereignty is not a compliment but a condemnation into the hell of nudging where autonomy and sovereignty are supposed not to matter for some categories of human beings. The nudgee or *muitiswi* may overtime even defend the nudger, when the nudging process has sufficiently cognitively prepared the nudgee to succumb to the new norm of being controlled and tortured through limited choice architectures. As the era of nudging is ushered in, humanity and human rights recede and coloniality sets in.

COVID-19, HUMAN RIGHTS VIOLATIONS AND BEING NUDGED INTO AN INTRACTABLE NEW WORLD ORDER: INSIGHTS INTO THE "NEW NORMAL?"

The era of the COVID-19 pandemic has uncharacteristically been underlined by gross human rights violations (United Nations Human Rights Commission on Human Rights (UNHCR) 2020). Such human rights violations have extended to but are not limited to the following: (1) torture (this is contrary to Article 5 of the Universal Declaration of Human Rights (UDHR); (2) censorship of the media and ordinary citizens; (3) arbitrary arrests (this is contrary to the provisions of Article 9 of the UDHR); (4) discrimination as well as unrestrained xenophobic tendencies in selected countries led by, in particular, China and South Africa (this is contrary to Article 7 of the UDHR); (5) violation of privacy (this is a violation of Article 12 of the UDHR) and (6) exercise restriction of movement (this is a violation of Article 13 of the UDHR). At a time when humaneness would have been anticipated, in a true Ubuntu spirit, uncharacteristic tendencies have been adopted by world governments at the behest of the "directives" and/or promptings of the dithering World Health Organisation (WHO) (Peel et al. 2020) and its "associated entities" such as the Bill and Melinda Gates Foundation (Centre for Health Security 2019) as well as controversial individuals like Bill Gates (Cacioli 2020) and the complex American physician, Antony Fauci (Branswell 2020). Any views regarded as being contrary to the COVID-19 narrative, churned out by the WHO, have seen the proponents of such perceptions being shut out of social media platforms (in violation of their right to freedom of expression and opinion as provided for by Article 19 of the UDHR) and any rights of association being prohibited, and thus criminalised, in supposedly open and democratic societies (in violation of the UDHR's Article 20 rights). Such heavy-handedness, in the face of a "global pandemic" whose real nature has been subject to much debate, has prompted questions as to whether or not COVID-19 is a legitimate virus or one cultured in a laboratory to achieve a particular outcome; the so-called "new normal" which will underline the New World Order (Lowe 2020; Gurnani 2020). It is evident that something beyond a supposed "need" to curb a dangerous global pandemic is at play. The nudgers are using COVID-19 as a tool to progressively compel the nudgees to ascribe to the obnoxious "new normal." The human race (Africans in particular), in the midst of engineered socio-economic disruptions, is concurrently being nudged into adapting to newly developing neoliberal, socio-political as well as economic systems and processes through the use of unorthodox, added to, uncouth policing and legal mechanisms.

Amnesty International has raised concerns about the unusual manner in which efforts aimed at curbing the adverse effects of COVID-19 have been characterised by pointing out that, "Human rights violations hinder, rather than facilitate, responses to public health emergencies, and undercut their efficiency" (Amnesty International 2020). It thus is becoming evident that COVID-19, as a "global pandemic," is fast exhibiting traits of an engineered virus whose sole objective is to change the socio-political and economic order of the world in favour of a few global elites. So brazen is the agenda that even results for supposed COVID-19 "infections" are attributed to shameful acts of doctoring scientific data to suit the proposed agenda (Arkansas Democrat-Gazette 2020; Informante 2020). The president of Tanzania, John Magufuli, exposed the sinister agenda driving the COVID-19 pandemic narrative by pointing out that faulty test kits were behind the alleged increases in "COVID-19 infections" in Tanzania (Kondowe 2020) and indeed the rest of the world, after samples of pawpaws and goats tested positive of COVID-19 (Reuters 2020a). The president of Tanzania's reservations with regards to the existent data on COVID-19 infections in his country have been exacerbated by recent claims that hospitals in the United States of America are being paid huge sums of money for labelling a patient's cause of death as "Coronavirus" (Jensen & Dupree 2020). It is thus not in doubt that COVID-19 has been introduced in the world to usher in unprecedented changes (Committee for the Coordination of Statistical Activities (CCSA) 2020) at the expense of people's civil liberties.

The world is being nudged into a new world dispensation driven by a few global elites whose only concern is amassing wealth at the expense of the poor masses, who are simply collateral damage in the prevailing matrix. Credence to this claim can be found in a 2010 Rockefeller Foundation Report which advanced a Lock Step scenario which proposed, "a world of tighter top-down government control and more authoritarian leadership, with limited innovation and growing citizenry" (Rockefeller Foundation 2010, 18). It is noteworthy to observe that the Rockefeller Lock Step scenario made reference to the outbreak of an influenza virus which would lead to world governments imposing lockdown restrictions on their citizens. In the document, it is further stated that "By 2025, people seemed to be growing weary of so much top-down control and letting leaders and authorities make choices for them" (Rockefeller Foundation 2010, 21). It is evident that from the Lock

Step scenario advanced by the Rockefeller Foundation, the central objective of the nudgers is to nudge the nudgees into submission, to the extent of ceding the nudgees' civil liberties to a rogue cabal of global elites/nudgers. The much-talked-about rule of law has been severely undermined by a raft of Emergency Presidential Regulatory Measures which on the whole have the effect of suspending the operation of ordinary laws in any country. The net effect of this approach is to create Order in Chaos (*Ordo ab Chaos*) at the behest of a disobeying cabal that bizarrely seeks to be obeyed (Austin 1832 [1995]). The nudgers who are behind the creation of Order in Chaos have a moral duty to obey the law, but negate such duty while expecting the nudgees to abide by any such laws. To the unruly nudgers, the law simply constitutes the command of a sovereign that is backed by force and is only applicable to the nudgees. This conceptualisation of the nature of the law is premised on the problematic philosophy behind the legal positivism thesis to the effect that the existence and content of law depends on social facts and not on its merits. It is in this regard that Austin (1970-1859) formulated thus: "The existence of law is one thing; its merit and demerit another. Whether it be or be not is one enquiry; whether it be or be not comfortable to an assumed standard, is a different enquiry" (1832 [1995], 157). The conceptualisation of the law by the nudgers thus gives basis to the Latin phrase, *ordo ab chao*. The term is philosophically an esoteric alliteration of "transformation" and is characterised by the light that shines in darkness while the darkness fails to comprehend such light (Pike 2013). Typically, the world's masses (the nudgees) are in darkness and cannot comprehend the supposed light behind the COVID-19 pandemic. That light, in the nefarious nudgers' view, can only be understood to translate to the sinister agenda aimed at reducing the world population to reduce "pressure on the existing global resources." The nudgees are considered as not being illuminated and thus are regarded as the uninitiated cattle. The COVID-19 pandemic thus constitutes an esoteric concept in the perverted view of the nudgers. This section will thus show how the violation of human rights during the COVID-19 pandemic is evidently a process of nudging aimed at ushering the unsuspecting global masses, and in particular Africa, into an authoritarian New World Order characterised by unprecedented levels of misery reaching epic and/or plutonic proportions.

Violation of the Right to Health

The right to health is the economic, social, and cultural right to the universal minimum standard of health which all individuals in the world are entitled to. Many international agreements such as the UDHR, the Convention on the Rights of Persons with Disabilities and the International Covenant on

Economic, Social and Cultural Rights all recognise the right to health. The WHO's Constitution also recognises the right to health. The WHO's Constitution, in particular, defines the right to health as, "the enjoyment of the highest attainable standard of health." Broadly defined, the right entails, "a state of complete physical, mental and social well-being and not merely the absence of disease or infirmity." Regardless of the recognition of the right in international instruments, many patients with COVID-19 have been turned away from hospitals in countries like China due to excessive numbers of ill people (Qin 2020). In Africa, most countries are largely unprepared for this "mystic" pandemic yet the infection rates have remained relatively low with the exception of a country like South Africa. In Italy, due to high levels of patient inflow, health workers collapsed from exhaustion and elderly patients were left to die as they were simply not a priority but a liability to the state. In Libya, medical facilities were attacked by rockets owing to the ongoing war in the country (UN News 2020). It is imperative to observe that Libya's current predicament was induced by a North Atlantic Treaty Organisation orchestrated nudging into war in the name of removing a supposed dictator in the form of the late Libyan president, Muammar Ghadafi. Today, the country is ill-prepared for the COVID-19 onslaught because it is persistently in turmoil. It is evident that the right to health has been significantly compromised by the release of a virus that arguably was cultured in a laboratory somewhere in the world by nudgers whose sole agenda is to control the world. The Rockefeller Lock Step scenario seems to confirm this assertion. The COVID-19 pandemic has thus been created at the expense of the right to health but with a view to nudging people into an authoritarian New World Order. What is interesting for Africa is that, even though COVID-19 infections are not as defined on the continent as is the case in Europe, America and Asia, where the fatalities have been excessive, those developing the vaccine have already targeted Africans as the "deserving" first recipients of the vaccine as "black lives matter." Evidently, the black lives matter movement has been introduced to nudge Africans into accepting a dangerous vaccine which will compromise their health and significantly reduce their numbers as they are regarded as a burden on global resources. What is the sincerity of those developing vaccines in using Africans as Guinea pigs when many people are dying in Europe, America and Asia? If it is not broken, why fix it? Africans do not need vaccines that compromise their immune systems but need their resources back and the control of their economies for socio-economic growth to take place in their impoverished countries. Being nudged into oblivion by a mischievously cultured virus and being injected with an equally dubious vaccine is simply not a priority for Africans.

Violation of the Right to Privacy

The COVID-19 pandemic has also ushered in the violation of the right to privacy protected by Article 12 of the UDHR. Governments the world over have embarked on surreptitious mass surveillances to conduct contact tracing of the disease spread and its supposed carriers (Human Rights Watch 2020). Governments have been documented as setting up surveillance cameras on the doors of citizens to prohibit them from leaving their homes (Kharpal 2020). Other governments have used wrist-bands linked to Smartphone applications to track those who violate quarantine measures while others have used hand stamps to identify those suspected to be COVID-19 positive (Saiidi 2020). The evident outcome of this constant tracking of individuals by the governments is that post-COVID-19 pandemic, citizens will be tracked in the same manner as persons suspected of being infected with COVID-19 were. Society is being nudged into a new normal in which the right to privacy has been significantly violated by the state in a supposed quest to curb the spread of the mystic COVID-19 pandemic. Prisoners' rights have not been spared as social distancing in prisons has largely been impractical. This prompted the Scottish Human Rights Commission to write a letter to the Holyrood's Justice Committee to point out crucial concerns around the conditions of prisons during the COVID-19 pandemic era (the inhumane treatment of inmates violates Article 3 of the European Convention on Human Rights).

Restriction of Movements

Article 13 of the UDHR affords people the world over with the right to freedom of movement and residence within borders of each state. Strangely, the COVID-19 pandemic has been characterised by excessive border control and quarantine of persons (OSCE 2020). All this has been done to justify the imminent vaccination of people, supposedly against COVID-19. At the centre of this agenda is the WHO, Bill Gates and Antony Fauci. Emphasis has been placed on not opening the borders until "everyone" has been vaccinated. Any person that opts not to be vaccinated will have his or her freedoms significantly curtailed and will not be allowed to travel or reintegrate into society because they are regarded as a "threat that poses harm" to others. Several quarantine centres have been set up the world over with individuals being subjected to appalling conditions in feeble attempts to prevent the supposed spread of COVID-19. Such restriction of freedom of movement has negatively impacted lives and businesses, especially in Africa. The idea implicit in this approach is to send the global economy in a meltdown to nudge the world into a new economic order driven by authoritarianism and serving the best interests of a few global elites. The masses will be left to starve, especially in Africa. The approach appears to be informed by a human culling agenda aimed at reducing the supposed pressure on global resources. The global elites behind the restriction of people's right to movement seem intent on eradicating small and medium enterprises which are the source of livelihood for many Africans. The small and medium enterprises can no longer trade in goods and services due to the closed borders which strangely are only open for big corporates to deliver their products to countries in the world.

The Right Not to be Arbitrarily Arrested and Detained

Article 9 of the UDHR prohibits the arbitrary arrest of individuals. However, there has been an upsurge of the arbitrary arrests of citizens during the COVID-19 pandemic period. Governments have exploited the emergency powers and imposed lockdowns in response to the COVID-19 pandemic. The net effect of these lockdowns and emergency powers has been the silencing of political foes, human rights defenders and journalists. Sharing information about COVID-19 has been censored in China and most countries in the world, including Africa. In the United States of America, the Justice Department pushed Congress to permit chief justices to detain people indefinitely without trial during emergencies, including during the COVID-19 pandemic period. Such detentions have instilled fear in any would be dissenting voices hence silencing anyone who may have fair comments to pass with regards to the mystic pandemic. In principle, the arbitrary arrests have been used as a mechanism to silence all who seek to resist any measures imposed with regards to COVID-19, regardless of whether or not such measures make sense or not.

Freedom of Speech and Expression

Article 19 of the UDHR recognises the right to freedom of opinion and expression. However, global citizens have been nudged into accepting that communication and fair comments passed in relation to COVID-19 are not permissible and thus criminal. China imposed restrictions on any form of communication pertaining to COVID-19. The net effect of this censorship was that the country took long to react to the initial phases of the pandemic. Doctors who spoke publicly about COVID-19, such as Li Wenliag, were censored and detained for allegedly spreading false rumours. What was initially regarded as false rumours has turned out to be a reality as many innocent Chinese nationals perished due to the mystic COVID-19 global pandemic. In Poland, medical workers were prohibited from issuing statements with regards to the COVID-19 pandemic regardless of the fact that Articles 2, 51 and 61 of the Polish Constitution guarantee the health workers' freedom of speech and the public's right to know. In Turkey, journalists were detained with regards to how they reported on the COVID-19 pandemic. Social networks also applied for anti-sperm measures for content that was posted pertaining to COVID-19. YouTube demonetised several videos on coronavirus with some of them being classified as tools for fear mongering or spreading conspiracy theories. In principle, the world was nudged into accepting that any video or comment posted on social media with regards to the potential origins of COVID-19 was sensitive content that was not fit for public consumption. Interestingly, many of the demonetised videos were thought provoking and exposed the shenanigans of those behind the COVID-19 pandemic. Related to the suppression of the freedom of speech and expression is the suppression of access to information. Vital information regarding the nature of the virus as alleged to cause COVID-19 has caused delays in affording treatment to needy patients. The net effect of this regrettable approach has been the loss of innocent lives in the pursuit of reducing pressure on the global resources. In essence, the nudgers are covertly nudging the nudgees to their deaths.

It is evident that the COVID-19-induced lockdowns have been characterised by a drastic curtailing and/or suspension of rights. Other rights which have been significantly limited include religious rights (most lockdown restrictions in countries such as Namibia, South Africa, Austria, Poland and France have imposed restrictions on attending church in the early phases of the COVID-19 pandemic), and the right to assembly (restrictions have been imposed on the number of people that can meet at each gathering or banning entirely any gathering). It is thus evident that the COVID-19 pandemic is a test case on how to usurp the civil liberties of the masses and in the process place them in the direct control of world governments which will serve at the behest of a few global elites. What the COVID-19 pandemic is detailing is a nudging into a supposed new normal which will see many losing their lives at the behest of a few global elites. The world as we see it is on a precipice and will never be the same again. Human rights have been violated by governments to the greatest extents possible with little to no reaction from the unsuspecting victims (the nudges).

Brutal Policing and the COVID-19 Pandemic

A central tool that has been used to force masses to comply with the COVID-19 regulations has been brutal policing and the use of military force. It is imperative to observe that coercive tactics have been relied upon with little regard to fundamental rights to life and liberty of persons (Dewan & Baker 2020), the right to be free from arbitrary arrest and detention, the right to human treatment for detainees and the right not to be subjected to torture (For guidelines on policing civil disturbances see Crawshaw et al. 1998). While it is accepted that maintaining social order is a fundamental element of policing, and that social order itself is a central component to realising human rights, it must be understood that the protection of human rights itself is a policing function (Crawshaw et al. 1998, 33). By implication, the process of policing must be characterised by the respect of human rights, obedience to laws protecting human rights and adherence to rules and guidelines designed to secure compliance with those laws. However, it has become evident that governments, in enforcing policing functions, have disregarded the rule of law in the pursuit of maximising the authoritarian leverage emanating from Emergency Presidential Powers regulations. The net effect of this approach has been the documented gross violation of human rights by policing agents whose key duty, ironically, is to uphold the law. It is therefore trite to conclude that the lawlessness synonymous with policing during the COVID-19 period is a reflection of the imminent New World Order to which the contemporary global society is being nudged towards. It is likely to be a rights deficient society in which mass starvation, the gross violation of human rights and excessive deaths will be the order of the day. Nowhere is such a New World Order catastrophic than it would be in Africa, a continent where years of neoliberal plunder are now being capped with imminent forced mass vaccinations for a virus that has been less potent and/or lethal on the continent. The supposed "Black lives matter" chorus that has emerged post the George Floyd murder at the hands of supposed "law enforcement agents" has thus emerged as a hijacked tool to prioritise the vaccination of black people against the mystic COVID-19. This approach will nudge many of the unsuspecting blacks, especially in Africa to their demise. Black lives only appear to matter when black people can be used as guinea pigs for experiments that will reward the nudgers with healthy bank accounts. The truth is, black lives do not matter and capitalism as well as the imminent New World Order matter most to the shameless nudgers.

Unlawful Lockdowns

In the nudging process outlined in this chapter, questions have been raised in selected jurisdictions as regards the constitutionality of the COVID-19 induced lockdowns. Three judgements in the High Courts of South Africa, Namibia and Malawi are instructive to this chapter. In the *De Beer and Others v Minister of Cooperative Governance and Traditional Affairs* (21452/2020) case, the North Gauteng High Court had to determine whether or not the lockdown in South Africa was constitutional. The High Court held that all regulations passed in relation to the COVID-19 pandemic were unconstitutional and invalid due to the fact that they, "in a substantial number of instances are not rationally connected to the objectives of slowing the rate of infection or limiting the spread thereof" and that, in so far as the regulations "do not satisfy the 'rationality test' their encroachment on and limitation of rights guaranteed in the Bill of Rights contained in the Constitution are not justifiable in an open and democratic society based on human dignity, equality and freedom." The ruling of the North Gauteng High Court in South Africa pokes holes into the nudgers' claims that the lockdowns were necessary to save lives. In fact, the lockdowns are simply illegal, irrational and epitomise a brutal intention by the nudgers to control the global masses at all costs.

In Namibia, the High Court, in the case of *NEF & Others v President of the Republic of Namibia & Others* (HC-MD-CIV-MOT-GEN-2020/00136) [2020] NAHCMD 198 (July 23, 2020), the constitutionality of regulations passed in response to the COVID-19 pandemic was also tested. As was the case in South Africa, the Namibia High Court held that the impugned COVID-19 regulations did not deal with the control or curtailing of the spread of the virus. As a matter of fact, by inference, the court implied that there was another purpose served by the regulations either than that which they were drafted to address. To that end, the court further held that the impugned regulations were not reasonably justifiable for the purpose of dealing with the situation which gave rise to the emergency and to that extent the president in passing the regulations breached the principle of legality. To that end, Regulation 12(1)(a); 12(1)(b); 12(2); 12(5); Regulation 14; Regulation 15; Regulation 16; Regulation 19(1)(a); 19(1)(b); 19(1)(c); 19(2); 19(4); 19(6); 19(8); and Regulation 25 were all deemed unconstitutional and therefore invalid.

Assertions to the effect that COVID-19 is being used as a convenient excuse to realise an agenda of controlling people have been given credence to by the passing into law of the Public Health COVID-19 General Regulations No. 233: Public and Environmental Health Act, 2015 Act No. 1 of 2015) in Government Gazette No. 7342 (on Wednesday, September 23, 2020). The regulations seek to enforce the continued restriction of public gatherings in Namibia, make it mandatory to wear masks in public places, and impose severe fines for parties who violate any provisions of the regulations. These regulations have been passed at a time when all COVID-19 related restrictions have been lifted. It thus boggles the mind as to what purpose the regulations seek to serve if COVID-19 is no longer regarded as a present threat to society. It is thus evident that beyond the mask of regulating to supposedly curb the spread of COVID-19 is an underlying and sinister agenda of human control. This agenda has already been outlined in the analysis of the Rockefeller Lockstep Scenario in which, post-COVID-19, authoritarian governments will emerge while civil liberties will wane. There is therefore something evidently sinister about COVID-19-related regulations in Namibia and indeed in the rest of the world.

The Malawi High Court was not to be outdone in ruling against spurious COVID-19 induced lockdowns. In the as yet to be reported *Malawi Human Rights Defenders Coalition* (HRDC) case, the Malawi High Court temporarily barred the government from implementing a 21-day lockdown to curb the spread of COVID-19 following a petition from the HRDC. The HRDC had argued that the lockdown would nudge the poorest and most vulnerable of society into certain death, not on account of the COVID-19 pandemic but poverty and starvation emanating from the lockdown. It is quite evident that the High Courts in the three selected jurisdictions were able to pick out that the COVID-19 induced lockdowns were simply unconstitutional and unreasonable as they did not serve the purpose of curbing the supposed spread of COVID-19 but an as-yet unspecified objective. It is thus our submission that the COVID-19 pandemic and the related regulations have been introduced the world over for purposes of social engineering and nudging the world into a New World Order underlined by authoritarian governance and the gross violation of human rights at the behest of a few uncouth global elites.

CONCLUSION

This chapter has advanced robust claims to the effect that the COVID-19 pandemic, as a cultured virus, was introduced into the world deliberately. The central objective of the pandemic has been identified as that of nudging the world into a new dispensation to be characterised by an authoritarian global government. The realignment of the world order will see many unsuspecting global citizens being nudged to their deaths whereas others will be forced into irrational vaccinations which only serve to fatten the pockets of the nudgers. The Lock Step scenario advanced in the 2010 Rockefeller report gives credence to such assertions. Post-COVID-19, a new global leadership will emerge as was the case post World War I when Woodrow Wilson emerged as leading the international community. The same happened post World War II when Franklin D Roosevelt emerged to lead the world and introduced neoliberal institutions such as the World Bank, International Monetary Fund and the United Nations. None of these institutions have served the best interests of developing states, in particular Africa. It is thus imperative to observe that the New World Order to which the world is being forcibly nudged to will bring more deaths, hunger, extreme poverty and excessive misery to the already impoverished global masses whereas more financial returns will accrue to a few global elites behind the unscrupulous nudging. African countries, and indeed the rest of the world, should resist being nudged into a "new normal" of gross human rights violations by the state, suffering, increased deaths and excessive restrictions at the behest of recalcitrant global elites. COVID-19 must thus be construed in the context of what it is instead of what it is not; it is in principle a well-calculated biological weapon of mass destruction introduced to nudge many unsuspecting global citizens, especially Africans, into oblivion in pursuit of the multilateral 2030 global population reduction agenda, and not a virus that occurred by chance. Such callous, uncivilised, unreasonable and inhumane nudging must be steadfastly resisted with the contempt that it deserves.

BIBLIOGRAPHY

Amnesty International. (2020). "Here are seven ways the coronavirus affects human rights." https://www.amnesty.org/en/latest/news/2020/02/explainer-seven-ways-the-coronavirus-affects-human-rights/.

Anderson, Rachel. (2005). "Redressing colonial genocide under international law: The Hereros' cause of action against Germany." *California Law Review*, Volume 93(4), 1155–1189.

Arkansas Democrat-Gazette. (2020). "Officials say some states doctoring COVID-19 data." https://www.arkansasonline.com/news/2020/may/20/officials-say-some-states-doctoring-cov/?news-national.

Arneson, Richard J. (2015). "Nudge and shove." *Social Theory and Practice*, Volume 41(4), 668–691.

Austin, J. (1832 [1995]). *Austin: The Province of Jurisprudence Determined* (Wilfrid E. Rumble, ed.). Cambridge: Cambridge University Press.

Ballard, C. (1986). "The Repercussions of rinderpest: Cattle plague and peasant decline in colonial Natal." *The International Journal of African Historical Studies*, Volume 19(3), 421–450.

Bousquet, C. (2017, March 31). "When government nudging is ethical." *GT Data*. httpss://www.google.com/amp/www.govtech.com/data/When-Government-Nudging-Is-Ethical.html%3fAM.

Branswell, H. (2020). "Anthony Fauci on COVID-19 re-openings, vaccines, and moving at 'warp speed'." https://www.statnews.com/2020/06/01/anthony-fauci-on-COVID-19-reopenings-vaccines-and-moving-at-warp-speed/.

Cacioli, L. (2020). "Bill Gates planned COVID-19 pandemic via deep-state 'circular cabal', says disgraced Dr. Mikovits." https://blockchain.news/news/bill-gates-planned-COVID-19-pandemic-via-deep-state-circular-cabalsays-disgraced-dr-mikovits.

CCSA. (2020). "How COVID-19 is changing the world: A statistical perspective." https://unstats.un.org/unsd/ccsa/documents/COVID19-report-ccsa.pdf.

Centre for Health Security. (2019). "Event 201: A global pandemic exercise." https://www.centerforhealthsecurity.org/event201/.

Crawshaw, R., Devlin, B., and Williamson, T. (1998). *Human Rights and Policing*. The Hague: Kluwer Law International.

Dewan, S., and Baker, M. (2020). "Facing protests over use of force, police respond with more force." https://www.nytimes.com/2020/05/31/us/police-tactics-floyd-protests.html.

Flores, D. S. (2018). “Transhumanism: The big fraud – Towards digital slavery.” *International Physical and Rehabilitation Journal*, Volume 3(5), 381–392.

Griffin, D. (2011). *Nudging Students’ Creative Problem-Solving Skills*. Cambridge: American Political Science Association.

Gurnani, C. P. (2020). “COVID-19 is writing a new world order.” https://economictimes.indiatimes.com/blogs/et-commentary/COVID-19-is-writing-a-new-world-order/.

Hansen, P. G., and Jespersen, A. M. (2013). “Nudge and the manipulation of choice: A framework for the responsible use of the nudge approach to behaviour change in public policy.” *European Journal of Risk Regulation*, Volume 4(1), 3–28.

Harari, Y. N. (2018). *21 Lessons for the 21st century*. London: Jonathan Cape.

Haugh, T. (2017). “Nudging corporate compliance.” *American Business Law Journal*, Volume 54, 683–741.

Human Rights Watch. (2020). “Governments should respect rights in COVID-19 surveillance.” https://www.hrw.org/news/2020/04/02/governments-should-respect-rights-COVID-19-surveillance.

Informante. (2020). “Integrity of testing process is paramount.” https://informante.web.na/integrity-of-testing-process-is-paramount/.

Jensen, S., and Dupree, W. (2020). “US hospitals getting paid more to label cause of death as ‘Coronavirus’.” https://www.globalresearch.ca/hospitals-getting-paid-more-label-cause-death-coronavirus/5709720.

Kahneman, D, Slovic, P., and Tversky, A. (eds.). (1982). *Judgment Under Uncertainty: Heuristics and Biases*. Cambridge: Cambridge University Press.

Kharpal, A. (2020). “Use of surveillance to fight coronavirus raises concerns about government power after pandemic ends.” https://www.cnbc.com/2020/03/27/coronavirus-surveillance-used-by-governments-to-fight-pandemic-privacy-concerns.html.

Kondowe, R. (2020). “Tanzania’s president is blaming the sharp rise of coronavirus cases on faulty testing kits.” https://qz.com/africa/1850839/tanzania-president-magufuli-blames-COVID-19-rise-on-faulty-tests-goats/.

Lowe, C. (2020). “COVID-19 is ushering in a new world order.” https://www.legacyresearch.com/the-daily-cut/COVID-19-is-ushering-in-a-new-world-order/.

Ndlovu-Gatsheni, S. J. (2013). “The entrapment of Africa within the global colonial matrices of power: Eurocentrism, coloniality and deimperialization in the twenty-first century.” *Journal of Developing Societies*, Volume 29(4), 331–353.

Nhemachena, A., Hlabangane, N., and Kaundjua, M. (2020). “Relationality or hospitality in twenty-first century research? Big data, internet of things, and the resilience of coloniality on Africa.” *Modern Africa Politics, History and Society*, Volume 8(1), 105–139.

Nhemachena, A., Hlabangane, N., and Matowanyika, J. Z. Z. (eds.). (2020). *Decolonising Science, Technology, Engineering and Mathematics (STEM) in an Age of Technocolonialism: Recentring African Indigenous Knowledge and Belief Systems*. Bamenda: Langaa RPCIG.

Nhemachena, A., and Mawere, M. (eds.). (2019). *Necroclimatism in a Spectral World (Dis)order: Rain Petitioning, Climate Change and Weather Engineering in 21st Century Africa*. Bamenda: Langaa RPCIG.

Nhemachena, A., and Mawere, M. (eds.). (2020). *Securitising Monstrous Bottoms in the Age of Posthuman Carnivalesque: Decolonising the Environment, Human Beings and African Heritages*. Bamenda: Langaa RPCIG.

Nhemachena, A., and Warikandwa, T. V. (eds.). (2019). *From African Peer Review Mechanisms to African Queer Review Mechanisms? Robert Gabriel Mugabe, Empire and the Decolonisation of African Orifices*. Bamenda: Langaa RPCIG.

Nhemachena, A., Warikandwa, T. V., and Amoo, S. K. (eds.). (2018). *Social and Legal Theory in the Age of Decoloniality: (Re)envisioning Pan-African Jurisprudence in the 21st Century*. Bamenda: Langaa RPCIG.

OSCE. (2020). "OSCE organizes online medical training on management of border-crossing points in Turkmenistan." https://www.osce.org/centre-in-ashgabat/452773.

Peel, M., Gross, A., and Cookson, C. (2020). "WHO struggles to prove itself in the face of COVID-19." https://www.ft.com/content/c2809c99-594f-4649-968a-0560966c11e0.

Pike, A. (2013). *Morals and Dogma*. Washington: L. H. Jenkins Inc.

Qin, A. (2020). "Coronavirus pummels Wuhan, a City short of supplies and overwhelmed." https://www.nytimes.com/2020/02/02/world/asia/china-coronavirus-wuhan.html.

Rainford, P., and Tinkler, J. (2011). *Think Before You Nudge: The Benefits and Pitfalls of Behavioural Public Policy*. British Politics and Policy at LSE. eprints.lse.ac.uk/33533/1/blogs.lse.ac.uk-Think_before_you_nudge_the_benefits_and_pitfalls_of_behavioural_public_policy.pdf

Rawls, J. (1996). *Political Liberalism*. New York: Columbia University Press.

Reuters. (2020a). "President queries Tanzania coronavirus kits after goat test." https://www.reuters.com/article/us-health-coronavirus-tanzania/president-queries-tanzania-coronavirus-kits-after-goat-test-idUSKBN22F0KF.

Rockefeller Foundation. (2010). "Scenarios for the future of technology and international development." http://www.nommeraadio.ee/meedia/pdf/RRS/Rockefeller%20Foundation.pdf.

Saghai, Y. (2013). "Salvaging the concept of nudge." *Journal of Medical Ethics*, Volume 39(8), 487–493.

Saiidi, U. (2020). "Hong Kong is putting electronic wristbands on arriving passengers to enforce coronavirus quarantine." https://www.cnbc.com/2020/03/18/hong-kong-uses-electronic-wristbands-to-enforce-coronavirus-quarantine.html.

Sarkin, J., and Westerman, C. F. (2008). "Reparations for historical human rights violations: The international and historical dimensions of the Alien Torts Claims Act Genocide Case of the Herero of Namibia." *Human Rights Review*, Volume 9(3), 331–360.

Slipowitz, A. (2020). "How COVID-19 restrictions have deepened existing inequality." https://freedomhouse.org/article/how-COVID-19-restrictions-have-deepened-existing-inequality.

Sunstein, C. R. (2014). "Nudging: A very short guide." *Journal of Consumer Policy*, Volume 37(4), 583–588.

Sunstein, C. R. (2015). "The ethics of nudging." *Yale Journal on Regulation*, Volume 32(2), 413–450.

Thaler, R. H., and Sunstein, C. R. (2009). *Nudge: Improving Decisions About Health, Wealth, and Happiness*. New York: Penguin Group.

United Nations Commission for Human Rights. (2020). "Beware long-term damage to human rights and refugee rights from the coronavirus pandemic: UNHCR." https://www.unhcr.org/news/press/2020/4/5ea035ba4/beware-long-term-damage-human-rights-refugee-rights-coronavirus-pandemic.html.

United Nations General Assembly. (1948, December 10). *Universal Declaration of Human Rights,* 217 A (III). https://www.refworld.org/docid/3ae6b3712c.html. Accessed 22 July 2020.

UN News. (2020). "Course of coronavirus pandemic across Libya, depends on silencing the guns." https://news.un.org/en/story/2020/04/1061272.

Warikandwa, T. V., Nhemachena, A., and Mtapuri, O. (eds.). (2017). *Transnational Land Grabs and Restitution in an Age of the (De)militarised New Scramble for Africa: A Pan-African Social Legal Perspective.* Bamenda: Langaa RPCIG.

Index

About the Contributors

Samuel Kwesi Amoo is an advocate of the High Court for Zambia and an attorney of the High Court of Namibia. He is also an associate professor of Law at the University of Namibia and is the current acting director, of the Justice Training Centre (JTC) in Namibia. Prof Amoo has also published a much-needed book on property law in Namibia, a field that has very little local material available in the country. The name of the book is appropriately titled "Property Law in Namibia." Prof Samuel K. Amoo has sought to publish in the area of property law, amongst many other legal fields, because there is very little comprehensive texts on property law in a Namibian context. The existing publications generally deal with one or another aspect of law in Namibia, but you do not really find comprehensive books, which have an in-depth reference to all aspects of property law in the country and in Africa. Prof Amoo is a distinguished author and continues to excel in that regard.

Job Shipululo Amupanda is a holder of a PhD in political science from the University of Namibia. He is a senior lecturer in Political Science and The Deputy Dean for the Faculty of Management and Economics at the University of Namibia. He is also a political activist in Namibia. He is also the current mayor of the city of Windhoek the capital city of Namibia. He is a radical proponent for transformation in Namibia with a view to ensuring that indigenous Namibians are included into the economic mainstream for purposes of equity. He is also an avid proponent of eradicating corruption in African societies in pursuit of inclusivity and the realisation of Africa's sustainable development agenda.

Oyesola Animashaun holds a doctor of laws degree and is a post-doctoral fellow from the University of North West in South Africa. He commenced his education at St. Augustine Primary School, Oyo and obtained his West African School Certificate and Higher School Certificate at St. Bernadine's Grammar School Oyo and Olivet Heights Oyo, respectively. He attended the University of Ibadan where he bagged a Bachelor's degree in Geography; he thereafter proceeded to Obafemi Awolowo University where he obtained a master's in business administration. Further academic exploits led him to the University of Lagos where he obtained a Master of Science Degree in Industrial Relations and Personnel Management. His unique interest in the enlightenment that knowledge brings led him to acquire his Bachelor of Laws Degree from the Lagos State University, his B.L from the Nigerian Law School, a Master of Laws from the Ogun State University and a Doctor of Philosophy (PhD) (Law) from the University of Ilorin. Oyesola Animashaunis a seasoned professional with his area of competence covering Sales, Business Development, Banking, Business Operations, Training and Consulting in the area of Labour Law. Oyesola's research and consulting interests cuts across Labour Law, Climate Change Law, Constitutional Law, Business, Company and Tax Law.

Anya Kingsley Anya is a professor of Law Department of Public and International Law-Igbinedion University College of Law Okada. He holds a PhD from the School of Postgraduate Studies Igbinedion University, Okada (2012). He was formerly the head of department, Public and International Law between 2007 and 2009. He was a former sub-dean (2013–2015) and Coordinator, Postgraduate studies, College of Law (2008–2013). He specializes in Jurisprudence, Public and International Law.

Ndatega Victoria Asheela-Shikalepo is a doctor of laws degree holder from the University of Pretoria in South Africa and is the head of the Commercial Law Department at the University of Namibia. She is an admitted legal practitioner in Namibia and has specialization in the area of corporate law, and in particular corporate governance. She has presented guest lectures and papers at international conferences on her area of specialization. She has also served as an internal and external examiner for thesis and dissertations written in her area of specialization.

Howard Tafara Chitimira is a full professor of Law. He teaches at the Faculty of Law of North-West University. He is also an advocate of the High Court of South Africa and a National Research Foundation (NRF) rated legal scholar. Prof. Chitimira holds the degrees LLB *cum laude* (UFH), LLM (UFH) and LLD (NMMU). For his doctorate, he specialised in securities and financial markets law. To date, he has published two books and over twenty journal articles in this field. Prof. Chitimira is a reviewer and editorial board member of several law journals in South Africa and elsewhere, as well as an external examiner for LLB, LLM and LLD degrees at several universities. He serves on editorial boards of journals such as the Potchefstroom Electronic Law Journal as well as being a guest editor for the Interdisciplinary Journal of Economics and Business Law and the Namibia Law Journal.

Julius Cosmas is a PhD holder and senior lecturer at Mzumbe University in Tanzania. He joined the faculty as a tutorial assistant on September 1, 2003. Currently, Julius Cosmas lectures in the department of civil and criminal law. Julius Cosmas is also an advocate of the High Court of Tanzania. He also has research interests in corporate law and mining law. He has a key interest in ensuring equality and equity in the distribution and access to natural resources for sustainable development in Africa.

Eric Omo Enakireru is a doctor of laws degree holder and human rights activist from Nigeria. He is a lecturer in the Department of Art and General Studies, Delta State Polytechnic, Otefe-Oghara. He has research interests in Corporate Law and Environmental Law. He has previously served as a managing attorney with Eric's Consults Juris, lecturer of Law with the Delta State Government (specialising in natural resources law, hydrocarbon pollution, sustainable development, and community coexistence) and corporate services specialist with E.O Enakireru and associates, and litigation counsel with Dr. O.K. Edu and Company.

Clifford Kendrick Hlatywayo is a PhD holder and lecturer in the Human Sciences Department, Psychology section at the University of Namibia. He specialises in Psychology of Work and Labour, Organisation Behaviour, Human Resource Development. Personnel Psychology, Career Psychology, Personality theories are also some of his areas of specialization, amongst other disciplines. He has previously lectured at the University of Fort Hare in South Africa. He also has presented numerous papers at national and international conferences and consistently offers training to organisations in Namibia in his area of specialization. He also supervises postgraduate students in his areas of specialization.

Promise Machingo Hlungwani (PhD) is a lecturer in the Department of Development Sciences and Policy at Marondera University of Agricultural Sciences and Technology. Currently, he is the acting chairperson in the same department where he teaches courses in governance, civil society and development. He has published on policy implementation and policy analyses in rural development.

Itai Kabonga is a PhD student at the University of the Witwatersrand, Johannesburg (Wits School of Governance). Itai lectures development studies at Zimbabwe Ezekiel Guti University (ZEGU). Currently, he writes on civil society – state relations, NGOs and development, and sustainable livelihoods. Equally, he has published on monitoring and evaluation, non-profit sector in Zimbabwe and Zimbabwe's development since 1980.

Liina Kalili is a master of laws degree holder from the University of Namibia. She is also the section head for the Property and Administration Department of the City of Windhoek in Namibia. Liina Kalili is a proponent of socio-economic transformation in Namibia. She is also a proponent for equal access to natural resources in Namibia's vast minerals sector as well as oil and gas sector. She actively advocates for beneficiation in the extractive natural resource industry and calls for the exploitation of natural resources in pursuit of the best interests of Namibians.

Lizazi Eugene Libebe is a former magistrate and lectures in the Faculty of Law, Department of Public Law and Jurisprudence, at the University of Namibia. He holds a B. Juris degree, LLB and LMM in International Law. His areas of interest include public international law, economic law, climate change law and policy, African jurisprudence and decolonization, law of evidence, family law, sociology, political philosophy, leadership, communal conservancies and natural resources law.

Clever Mapaure is a holder of B. Juris CCuL (*Cum laude*), LLB (*Cum laude*), LLM (*Cum laude*) and PhD degrees from the University of Namibia. Clever Mapaure is a Free Lance Legal Consultant and a Member of the World Commission on Environmental Law: International Union of Conservation Networks (IUCN). Best Exchange Student at the University of London School of Oriental and African Studies (with Distinction). He was the Former Chief Legal Officer at the Law Reform and Development Commission: Ministry of Justice – Namibia, Part-time Lecturer at the University of Namibia, Faculty of Law and a recipient of the All-Africa PhandulwaziNge-China Post-Doctorate Fellowship.

Pilisano Harris Masake holds an LLD (Stellenbosch University), LLM (Stellenbosch University), Masters in Policing Practice (Southern Business School), LLB and B-Juris (University of Namibia), is a Candidate: LLM in ICT (OUT), a Lecturer and Deputy Head of Department in the Department of

Social Sciences, in the Faculty of Human Sciences at the Namibia University of Science and Technology. He is a former police officer with the rank of Detective Chief Inspector – Namibian Police Force. He is also the co-founder of the *Unam Law Review* and served as the Head Articles Editor till 2013. He is a co-author of various articles and book chapters. Further, he co-authored a book titled "*The Law of Pre-Trial Criminal Procedure in Namibia.*"

Lekunze Joseph Nembo is a research manager in the Faculty of Economics and Management Sciences, North-West University Business School, Mmabatho South Africa. He has conducted studies on food security and made proposals that suggest government subsidies to farmers through cost-cutting technologies and farm worker's skills development on the use of these technologies. He is also a pro-transformation advocate in the twenty-first century for the best interest of South African indigenes.

Fritz Nghiishililwa is a doctor of laws degree holder from the University of Namibia and a former Acting Dean of the Faculty of Law at the University of Namibia. He actively served in the liberation struggle of Namibia and was instrumental to the realisation of independence in the country. He has also served in strategic portfolios in the police force of Namibia and the army, as well as a survey on the welfare of liberation heroes in Namibia. He currently is serving on the Wage Commission in Namibia which has tasked with the responsibility of establishing a minimum wage in Namibia amongst other issues. He has specialization in labour law and customary. He is a proponent of equality and equity in Namibia through the use of affirmative action.

Artwell Nhemachena holds a PhD in Social Anthropology, master of science in Sociology and Social Anthropology, bachelor of science Honours Degree in Sociology. In addition to having a good mix of social science and law courses in his undergraduate studies, he also has a certificate in law. He has lectured in Zimbabwe before pursuing his PhD studies in South Africa. His current areas of research interest are knowledge studies; development studies; environment; resilience; food security and food sovereignty; industrial sociology; sociology and social anthropology of conflict and peace; transformation; sociology and social anthropology of science and technology studies, democracy and governance; relational ontologies; decoloniality and anthropological/sociological jurisprudence. He has published over eighty book chapters and journal articles in accredited and peer-reviewed platforms. Nhemachena has also published over ten authored/co-authored books including the following: *Relationality and Resilience in a Not So Relational World? Knowledge, Chivanhu and (De-)Coloniality in 21st Century Conflict-Torn Zimbabwe* (2017); *Africa at the Crossroads: Theorising Fundamentalism* *and Fetishism in the 21st Century* (2017); *Mining Africa: Law, Environment, Society and Politics in Historical and Multidisciplinary Perspectives* (2017); *Death of a Discipline? Reflections of the History, State and Future of Social Anthropology in Zimbabwe* (2017); *GMOs, Consumerism and the Global Politics of Biotechnology: Rethinking Food, Bodies and Identities in Africa's 21st Century* (2017); *Transnational Land Grabs and Restitution in an Age of the (De-)Militarised New Scramble for Africa: A Pan African Socio-Legal Perspective* (2017); *Decolonisation of Materialities or Materialisation of (Re-)Colonisation? Symbolisms, Languages, Ecocriticism and (Non)Representationalism in 21st Century Africa* (2018); *Social and Legal Theory in the Age of Decoloniality: (Re-)Envisioning Pan-African Jurisprudence in the 21st Century* (2018); *Rethinking Securities in an Emergent Technoscientific New World Order: Retracing the Contours for Africa's Hi-Jacked Futures* (2018); *Theory, Knowledge, Development and Politics: What Role for the Academy in the Sustainability of Africa?* (2016). He is a visiting professor at Kobe University. He is also a research fellow at the University of South Africa

Brighton Nyagadza is a doctor of philosophy (PhD) (Marketing Management) finalist at Midlands State University (MSU), Zimbabwe and a full-time digital marketing lecturer and Acting Chairperson for Supply Chain Management and Marketing Management Department at Marondera University of Agricultural Sciences and Technology (MUAST), Zimbabwe. He is an associate of The Chartered Institute of Marketing (CIM), United Kingdom, Power Member of the Digital Marketing Institute (DMI), Ireland, Dublin and Full Member of the Marketers Association of Zimbabwe (MAZ). His interdisciplinary research expertise revolves on digital marketing, corporate storytelling for branding and marketing metrics.

Clemence Rusenga is a PhD holder from the University of Cape Town and is currently a guest lecturer at the University of Cape Town. He has also served as a postdoctoral fellow at the Centre for African Studies, University of Cape Town, under the National Research Foundation (NRF) Chair on Land Reform and Democracy in South Africa. His research interests include land reform, agricultural models, political economy and livelihoods in Africa. Clemence Rusenga has published articles in peer reviewed journals and presented papers at national (South Africa) and international conferences.

Luvhengo Usapfa is a lecturer in Agricultural Economics and Extension, in the Faculty of Agriculture, Science and Technology at the North-West University in South Africa. Luvhengo Usapfa has worked on research regarding indigenous crops, as regards their high nutritional value and hardy attributes, and how they offer potential trade opportunities for rural farmers. Luvhengo Usapfa points out that there is a niche market that can be explored for these indigenous crops particularly with the growing demand for high nutritional value food in South Africa. He points out that these crops are mostly produced by rural households or gathered from the wild by rural farmers. Luvhengo Usapfa is also a proponent of transformative policies in South Africa.

Tapiwa Victor Warikandwa holds a doctor of laws in International Trade Law. He is a senior lecturer and head of department in the Faculty of Law at the University of Namibia. He specialises in International Trade Law, Labour Law, Indigenisation Laws, Mining Law and Constitutional Law amongst other disciplines. Prior to coming to Namibia, Dr. Warikandwa worked as a legal officer and later legal advisor in the Ministry of Public Service Labour and Social Welfare in Zimbabwe. Key amongst his duties was legal drafting. Dr Warikandwa worked with the law reviser of the Ministry of Justice in Zimbabwe in reviewing laws administered by the Ministry of Public Service Labour and Social Welfare. Dr Warikandwa also completed an ordinary and advanced training in Labour Law Making at the International Labour Organization's International Training Centre in Turin Italy. On numerous occasions, Dr. Warikandwa was actively involved in the activities of the Cabinet Committee on Legislation on behalf of the Ministry of Public Service Labour and Social Welfare. Dr. Warikandwa has since written books on labour law and women's rights in South Africa and Namibia amongst others, as well as publishing articles in accredited peer-reviewed journals such as Law, Development and Democracy, Speculum Juris, Journal for Black Studies, Potchefstroom Electronic Law Journal, Comparative International Law Journal for Southern Africa and the African Journal of International and Comparative Law, Juridical Tribune, amongst others. He was also a Postdoctoral Fellow and has also worked as a senior lecturer at the University of Fort Hare in South Africa. Dr Warikandwa studied for his bachelor of laws, master's degree and doctoral degree at the University of Fort Hare in South Africa. He currently is the chief editor of the Namibian Law Journal.

Dunia Prince Zongwe is an associate professor of law at Walter Sisulu University in South Africa. He has the following qualifications: J.S.D. (Cornell); LL.M. (Cornell); Certificate (University of Montréal); LL.B. (University of Namibia); and B. Juris (University of Namibia). Dunia P Zongwe specializes in finance, human rights, natural resources, and development, with a heavy emphasis on Africa. His work on (international) finance, corporate law and contracts sits at the interface of law and economics. Since 2008, he has presented lectures at more than thirty-five conferences at many universities, including the University of the Witwatersrand (South Africa), Yale University (USA), and Université de Montréal (Canada). He has written extensively in his areas of specialization. As a consultant, he has done work for The World Bank since 2013. He has also carried out consulting projects for such clients as United Nations Educational, Scientific and Cultural Organization; Oxford University Press (International Law in Domestic Courts), and the Law Society of Namibia (LSN). Furthermore, Dunia P Zongwe has received several merit scholarships and awards, notably the Human Sciences Research Council (HSRC, South Africa) Certificate of Excellence for Best Presenter (2nd Runner Up) in 2016, the Cornell Institute for African Development fellowship in 2007, and the LSN Prize for Best LL.B. Student in 2007, and the University of Namibia Vice-Chancellor's Medal (twice).

www.ingramcontent.com/pod-product-compliance
Lightning Source LLC
Chambersburg PA
CBHW051256200926
51612CB00002B/66
9781793643360